THE ONE SHOW
VOLUME 19

judged to be advertising's best print,
radio, TV & interactive

THIS BOOK
this is an unofficial bauhaus bookplate and is not to be trifled with
IS THE
PROPERTY
OF
PLEASE
RETURN
SOON

Gary Goldsmith
President

Mary Warlick
Executive Director

Graham Clifford
Creative Director

Edwin Laguerre
Designer

Kristin Overson
Editor

Todd Gaffney
Assistant Editor

Kevin Sprouls
Pencil Illustrations

A Presentation of

THE ONE CLUB
FOR ART & COPY

COVER CONCEPT AND DESIGN

Cabell Harris / WORK, INC.
Art Director

Tom Gibson
Designer

Doug de Grood
Writer

Karl Steinbrenner
Photographer
(Jack Harris, inside flap)

STOCK PHOTOGRAPHY
Back of "Decoy Cover":
All © FPG International, except
computer console (center right photo):
© Sickles Photo-Reporting 1963

Some comments in the
GOLD ON GOLD section
originally appeared in
ADWEEK magazine
(June 9, 1997).

Published and Distributed by
ROTOVISION S.A.
SALES OFFICE:
Sheridan House
112-116a Western Road
Hove, East Sussex, BN3 1DD
United Kingdom
Telephone: +44 (0) 1273 727268
Fax: +44 (0) 1273 727269

In Association with
THE ONE CLUB
FOR ART & COPY
32 East 21 Street
New York, NY 10010
Telephone: 212-979-1900
Fax: 212-979-5006
e-mail: oneclub@inch.com
web site: www.oneclub.com

Production and Separation by
ProVision / Singapore
Telephone: 65-334-7720 Fax: 65-334-7721
Printed by Tien Wah Press / Singapore.

PRESIDENT'S MESSAGE

Spend fifteen minutes talking to
creatives in any agency and you can
be certain that the following will be
the topics of choice. Among the
younger ones, they will be discussed
with anger and rage. Among the
older, frustration and resignation.

*It is getting harder and harder
to do great work.*

*Clients are more
afraid and conservative
than ever.*

*Agencies have no
standards.*

*All of the best work
gets killed.*

My response?

It's always been hard
to do great work.

Not all clients are
conservative.

Not all agencies are
without standards.

And, as this book proves,
not all the best work
gets killed.

GARY GOLDSMITH

THE CREATIVE
HALL OF FAME

1997
Lee Clow
Jim Durfee

1994
Jay Chiat
Roy Grace
Hal Riney

1991
Ralph Ammirati
Tom McElligott

1984
Carl Ally
Bob Gage
Amil Gargano
Helmut Krone
George Lois
Herb Lubalin

1975
Raymond Rubicam
Maxwell Sackheim

1974
Ed McCabe
Shirley Polykoff

1973
John Caples
James Webb Young

1972
Bob Levenson

1971
Ron Rosenfeld

1970
Howard Gossage

1969
Mary Wells Lawrence

1968
Phyllis K. Robinson

1967
Bernice Fitz-Gibbon
Claude Hopkins

1966
Julian Koenig

1965
Rosser Reeves

1964
Bill Bernbach

1963
David Ogilvy

1962
George Gribbin

1961
Leo Burnett

this book
has been
stolen from:

JIM DURFEE
Partner
Messner Vetere Berger McNamee
Schmetterer / EURO RSCG
1997 Inductee

Advertising is a disposable medium.

Ads run. They stop running. They disappear.

Many are not even noticed. Of the ones that are, few are remembered for a day, much less a month or a year.

The same can be said for most of the people who write them.

But what about the tiny percentage that are remembered?

The ones that ask people to look at advertising differently?

The ones that people notice and talk about for their wit and intelligence instead of their crassness and banality? The ones that inspire people in our business to do smarter and better work? The ones that feel as right twenty years after they were written as the day they first ran?

They earn the right to become an enduring part of our culture.

As do the select few people with the talent and perseverance to create them.

It is with great honor that we welcome Lee Clow and Jim Durfee into the Creative Hall of Fame.

In a time when producing one award-winning campaign is considered an accomplishment, they have done it time after time after time.

And they are both still doing great work today.

Congratulations.

Gary Goldsmith

The tradition of The One
Club's Creative Hall of Fame
began in 1961 with the
induction of Leo Burnett to
the Copywriters Hall of Fame.

Since then only 32 men and
women have been recognized
for their outstanding
contributions to creative
advertising. The induction
of art directors Helmut
Krone, Bob Gage and
Amil Gargano in 1984
reflected the new status
of The One Club for
Art and Copy.

The One Club honors
excellence each year in
the One Show. It is
particularly satisfying to
share the accomplishments
of the two individuals we
honor tonight with family
and friends and members of
the advertising community.
Lee Clow and Jim Durfee
have maintained the standards
of creativity that The One Club
represents. Many thanks to
them for their lifetime contribution
to the craft of advertising.

Mary Warlick

LEE CLOW
Chairman, Chief Creative Officer
TBWA Chiat/Day
1997 Inductee

"1984"
Apple 1984

"McKenzie Brothers"
Pizza Hut 1985

"Party"
California Cooler 1986

"Party"
California Cooler 1986

"Road to Rio"
Nissan 1988

"Alarm"
Energizer 1989

"Wheat Fields"
Nissan 1996

"Dream Garage"
Nissan 1996

"Toys"
Nissan 1996

LEE CLOW

There are only two people I've ever worked with in advertising who can stand in a war room papered with a thousand ideas that run the gamut from awful to promising and, without seeming to think or ponder, point to The One that's right, that will work, that will make the clients rich and the agency famous.

Lee Clow is one of them.
(Don't worry Phil, you'll get in here one of these days.)

Lee is first, foremost, at some genetic or even sub-atomic level, an Art Director. He reacts viscerally to both ugliness and beauty, and focuses all his considerable powers on bringing the latter out of the former.

A denizen of Chiat once dubbed him "Art Director of the World." He'll redesign buildings while walking down the street, re-route freeways that don't look right, re-concept rental cars at the airport, revise billboards seen from his car window and magazine ads from his plane seat.

He's assaulted by the sheer ugliness of things, as if he sees bad design and bad ideas as the most immediately life-threatening form of pollution, and good advertising and communication as his own personal environmental protection act.

Lee's done some of the most memorable advertising on the planet, from the Apple "1984" commercial—still considered the best commercial ever created—to Nike and the introduction of "Air Jordan," to the Energizer bunny and its current "Spotters" spots, to the recent Nissan "Enjoy the ride" campaign that once again has people hitting the volume instead of the mute buttons on their remotes during commercial breaks.

More than any other single individual, Lee has made Chiat/Day a great agency. He's broadened its style, deepened its talent pool and created a culture that will go on doing great work for generations beyond his time. And, he was the only human on the planet who could reason with Jay.

All of which has required that Lee play a dozen roles in the agency's history, from chief financial officer and stock planner to director of client services to media director to head of personnel. I'll never forget the day he was made president of Chiat/Day and had to make a trip to the bank. What did the bankers think of this bearded guy in shorts and sandals whose signature was going on the paychecks and upon whose tanned, hair-draped shoulders rested a billion or so in media investments?

But Lee is a leader. Even bankers can see that. Clients certainly have, as have the hundreds of people who've worked with and for him at the agency. He's the guy with an internal guidance system that never fails, the guy you want at the helm in a storm.

Yamaha
1982

Nike
1984

He's easily the most articulate art director on the planet. In fact, he's come up with more great lines than most of the copywriters I know. Like "Good enough isn't good enough," emblazoned now on fifteen generations of Chiat/Day T-shirts. "A mistake is just another way of doing things," which has a Yogi Berra quality to it. And my all time favorite, "The best revenge is a better ad."

Which brings us to how Lee talks. Like most great art directors, he's not big on long headlines and ten dollar words. And when clients and account people and planners talk to him about the latest paradigm shift or managed chaos or coopetition or any of the other buzzwords that grace the pages of the *Harvard Business Review*, he will tend to ask, "What does that mean?" So the conversation quickly moves to what's really important and what will really work. This is called intelligence. Because when you work with Lee, the thinking behind the communication has to be as elegant and smart as the work itself.

When Chiat/Day became TBWA Chiat/Day, the Ad World tsk-tsked over its lattes about the end of an era. Omniglob had swallowed another great independent agency. But then a very interesting thing happened. The work got better. Largely because Lee could stop worrying about rent and overhead and credit lines and stock plans and get back to doing the work.

The only bad thing about the merger was that it forced Lee to spend more time in New York. For years I've tried to convince him that Manhattan is really just the world's largest reef of human coral. But he still hates the place and will suffer endless red-eyes to minimize his time here and get back to the beach. So what's his thing about the beach? Well, first of all, it's clean. It's economical. It's perfectly designed. And it embodies the most powerful ideas in the universe: life, force, being and becoming.

One long ago midnight, I was walking down a hall bedecked with more good work than I've ever seen any other advertising agency produce—and this was for a pitch—and he said quietly, "We know how to do this stuff."

Lee, at least, does indeed know how to do this stuff. And what's more impressive than any single accolade or honorific is that he's been doing it for thirty years—he did it yesterday, and, once he gets his funny suit off, he'll be doing it tomorrow.

Steve Hayden
New York 1997

Lotus
1984

Hertz
1970

Enable
1987

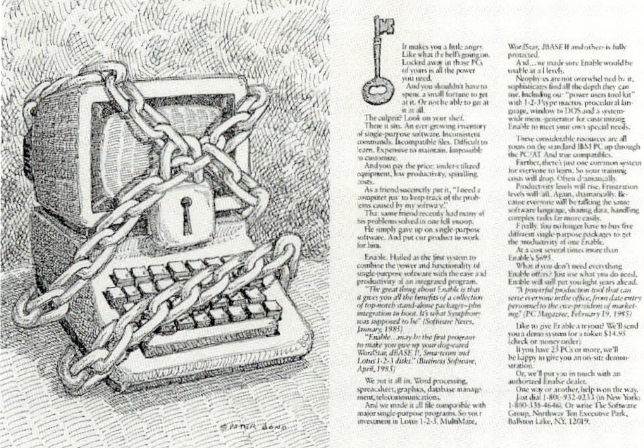

JIM DURFEE

Durfee was the first grown-up I met in advertising, and I had been at two agencies before I worked for him at Carl Ally Incorporated.

Durfee's office overlooked the rectory of St. Patrick's Cathedral, the old Villard House, and all of Madison Avenue from 23rd Street to where it narrows and climbs up Carnegie Hill. But it might as well have been in Upper Michigan or Texarkana or Kennebunkport for all that the heart of the media capital affected him.

No ad-land fad, no zeitgeist motif, no au courant expression ever penetrated Durfee's persona or his work. He was the "words" of the triumvirate that created its own revolution within the Creative Revolution of the sixties. Carl (Ally), Jim (Durfee), and Amil (Gargano) did take-no-prisoners comparative advertising before anyone else. In 1962, Volvo would take on Detroit's planned obsolescence, Detroit's quality control, Detroit's way of talking to consumers. The three were all dropouts from Detroit's automotive ad agencies; with each tick of growth in Volvo's market share, they exacted revenge.

In one sense, Durfee was the anti-Bernbach. There was no self-deprecation in the work that came from his office. Somebody at Hertz had the inspiration to avoid the top 50 U.S. agencies and, instead, pit the subversives of Durfee's copy department against Helmut Krone's Avis. Avis's lovable diffidence was hurting Hertz's business along with the entire company's morale, without which no service company can prosper.

"For years, Avis has been telling you that they're only number two. Now we're going to tell you why." That was strike one. Strike two and strike three were facts piled upon facts that Durfee unleashed. "They went for the jugular and found it," Krone said. It would be 25 years before another print campaign (Absolut) became part of the national consciousness the way those two, Hertz and Avis, did.

Durfee looks for a fact that is also an idea. "9 out of 10 Volvos registered in the last 11 years are still on the road," being his personal paradigm.

Carl Ally says, "There are no false notes in Durfee."

He's right. One idea of a perfect adman is Zelig who can be anything a client, an employee, a boss wants at the moment. A true crowd pleaser because he can successfully suck up to all possible multitudes.

Durfee is the opposite of Zelig. He speaks in the same voice, in the same way to everyone: client, mailboy, copywriter, account executive. What he says and his conviction behind it is meant to persuade you more than how he says it.

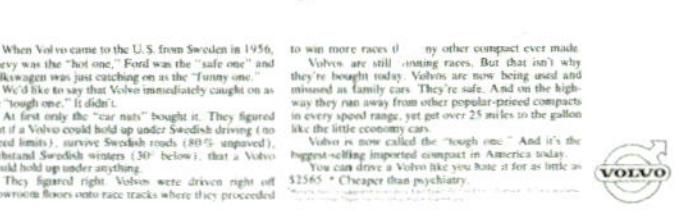

Volvo
1963 (upper left)

Harper's Magazine
1979 (above)

SAS
1966

"Won't Bug You"
Volvo 1964

"Status Quo"
MCI 1993

"TCI"
NASDAQ 1996

It's hard to find influences in his work. Maybe the direct response writers, but they lack edge. Certainly, Durfee doesn't fear the long headlines favored by the coupon-counters.

"A trip to Europe is either more expensive than last year. Or less expensive than next year. Depending on how much you want to go." This, a headline during one of Pan Am's periodic dalliances with solvency that Durfee intermittently oversaw.

Durfee's biggest influence is reality. "Live for today. Tomorrow will cost more" was his advice to the traveling public living in the age of 12 percent inflation, devaluation of the dollar, and the seventies fuel crisis. Or the grim reality of corporate growth and the loss of feeling and humanity: "After you build the world's most efficient airline, how do you live it down?"

More interesting than his influences were the people he influenced. Ed McCabe, one of them, looked for Durfee to be the Dean of Copy at his planned master's degree program in advertising.

Just people who went on to have viable agencies make a fair list of those seriously influenced by Durfee. Altschiller Ammirati Berger Gargano McCabe Messner Puris Raboy Vetere. Sonorous name for an agency, too, if merger-mania ever came back during an opportune time such as a full moon.

Durfee's frugality is, well, legendary.

"How much are you making now?" he asked the receptionist from another agency who had a spec portfolio of note and was looking for a junior copywriting position in 1976 at Ally. "$175 a week," she answered.

"We'll match that," said Durfee. "Generous today, Jim?" I commented after she left. "I'm not giving her a job, I'm giving her a career," Durfee said. Which was true then of Helayne Spivak and was true of so many of us here tonight.

Jim Durfee's legendary frugality extends not a bit to his spirit, as he continues to find people of talent to mentor.

Nor does it extend to his energy, which still lobs bombs on a daily basis. Against the New York Stock Exchange. Against AT&T. Against any corporate miscreant looking for a fight on land, on sea, in print or on the air.

Tom Messner
New York 1997

102009998   051   044   000005   F 9   C

owner
affix
thumb print
here

owner
place
photo
here

SHV 0713
STK 89   name.......................

id #.........................

this book remains the property
of the above named person and
under no circumstances shall it
be removed, altered or tampered
with in any way, shape or form.

1007098 328

David Angelo
Cliff Freeman & Partners

David Ayriss
Matthaeus Halverson Ayriss

Arthur Bijur
Cliff Freeman & Partners

John Butler
Butler Shine & Stern

Janet Champ
Wieden & Kennedy

Lee Clow
TBWA Chiat/Day

Izzy DeBellis
Fallon McElligott Berlin

John Doyle
Doyle, Inc.

Jim Durfee
*Messner Vetere Berger
McNamee Schmetterer/
EURO RSCG*

Mark Fenske
The Bomb Factory

Kerry Feuerman
The Martin Agency

Kara Goodrich
Leonard/Monahan

Mark Johnson
Ammirati Puris Lintas

Tom Lichtenheld
Fallon McElligott

Rick McQuiston
Wieden & Kennedy

David Page
M&C Saatchi

Houman Pirdavari

Ellen Steinberg
Fallon McElligott

Tracy Wong
WONGDOODY

INTERACTIVE
MEDIA JUDGES

Jeff Dachis
Razorfish

Leonard Ellis
*Messner Vetere Berger McNamee
Schmetterer/EURO RSCG*

Mark Frankel
CKS Group

Sorel Husbands
Organic Online

Frank Lantz
R/GA Interactive

Jeff Musser
*Jeff Musser
Communication Design*

Ben Olander
Organic Online

Kyle Shannon
agency.com

Tim Smith
Red Sky Interactive

Nat Whitten
Weiss Whitten Stagliano

Gary Wolfe
Hot Wired

Mike Abadi
Hy Abady
David Abbott
Jeffrey Abbott
Emmeline Aguirre
Yasmin Ahmad
Joe Alexander
Carl Ally
Pascal Alouidor
Aimee Alpert
David Altschiller
Olivia Altschuler
Patricia Alvey
Ralph Ammirati
John Amodeo
Bruce Anaston
Audrey Anderson
Ron Anderson
Stephanie Anderson
Trudy Anderson
Jason Anello
David Angelo
Adriana Angotti
Anthony Angotti
Frank Anselmo
Joseph Antonacci
Jill Applebaum
Stephanie Arculli
Arnold Arlow
Ron Arnold
Stephanie Arnold
Lorraine Arroll
Javier Bonilla Arsac
Gina Asaro
Craig Astler
Enrique Astuy
John Athorn
Roseanne Azarian
Marc E. Babej
Dominick Baccollo
Kristina Backlund
Christian Baffa
Chris Baier
Lisa Baker
Christophe Bardot
Jason Barnes
Bob Barrie
Lauren Barrocas
Patricia Barthe
Gary Bassell
Steve Bautista
Tim Bayless
Allan Beaver
Wendy Beck
Kris Becker
Wendy Becker
Henry Belfor
Doug Bell
Brian Bellanca
Jacqueline Benitez
A.K. Bennett
Gordon Bennett
Roger Bentley
Danielle Berger
Warren Berger
Paul Bernasconi
David Bernstein
Peter Berta
Wayne Best
Dana Betgilan
Michael Betts
Dominique Biger Kahn
Arthur Bijur
Bruce Bildsten
Pat Bilger

Stephen C. Bisch
Doug Bixby
Brendon Blake
Steven Block
Gerardo Blumenkrantz
Alex Bogusky
John Boone
Jason Borzouyeh
Peter Bossio
Nicole Botkier
Alix Botwin
Simon Bowden
Rick Boyko
Ken Braun
J. Christiaan Breen
Scott Brennan
Victor Brody
Bill Brokaw
Dara Brooks
George Brown
Mark Brown
Shameka M. Brown
Todd Brunner
Jane Bryson
Carol Buettner
Ron Burkhardt
Eric Burnard
Pat Burnham
Allison Burton
John Butler
Kevin Butler
Bruce Byers
Larry Cadman
Andrew M. Cahill
Juan Pablo Caja
Tony Calcao
Isabella Califano
Steve Callen
Brian Campbell
Cathie Campbell
Lori Campbell
James Caporimo
Paul Cappelli
Rob Carducci
David Carlin
Nancy Carp
John Murrah Carson
Regina Catalano
Todd Cather
Earl Cavanah
Ada Chan
Spencer Chan
Wilson Chan
Cheryl Chapman
Chung-Mau Cheng
Yim Cheng
Jay Chiat
Vincent Chieco
Andrei Chivu
Chris Churchill
Mark Clark
Bart Cleveland
Lee Clow
Henry Cochran
Daniel Cohen
Gary Cohen
Marcie Cohn
Michael Collado
Steve Connelly
Christina Conti
Diane Cook-Tench
Marty Cooke
Kevin Corfield
Colin Costello
Sharla Costello

ONE CLUB MEMBERS

Michael Cox
Robert Cox
Josephine Craig Carey
Rob Cramer
Court Crandall
Richard Crean
Adam Cricchio
Tom Crimp
Peter Crosby
Greg Crossley
Kevin Cruickshank
Pat Cunningham
Phyliss Cunningham
Greg Curran
Michael Czako
Bill D'Ambrosio
Joanna D'Avanzo
M.M. D'Esposito
Sharon Dang
Patricia Darcey
Jeffrey Davila
A. Meredith Davis
Alan Davis
Robert Davis
Michael Dean
Phil Dearman
Izzy DeBellis
Victor DeCastro
John Dee
Jay Deegan
Tony DeGregorio
Craig Deitch
Ken DeLeon
Jerry Della Femina
Charles DeMarco
Josh Denberg
Sal DeVito
Audrey DeVries
Steve Dildarian
Greg DiNoto
Tony DiPietro
David DiRienz
Amanda Dobkin
Angela Dominguez
Carolyn Donnelly
Steve Doppelt
Tom Doud
Sean Dougherty
Rob Dow
Jennifer Dowling
Michael Draper
Josh Drazen
Raleigh Drennon
Daniel J. Drexler
Carol Dronsfield
Andrew Duerson
Jerry Dugan
Rosalyn Dunham
Laurence Dunst
Jim Durfee
Susan Dwyer
Shannon Edwards
Lisa Ciocci Egan
Einar Gunnar Einarsson
Arthur Einstein
Prisca Ekkens
Stuart Elliott
Bradford Emmett
Kevin Endres

Gary Ennis
Patricia Lynn Epstein
Linos Ermogenides
Eric Essig
Stephen Etzine
Paul Evans
Erik Fahrenkopf
John Fahy
Thomas Feinstein
Jeremy Feldman
Sarah Feldman
Steven Feldman
Mark R. Fenske
Joseph Ferrazano
Robert Festino
Michael Fetsko
Kerry Feuerman
Carlos Figueiredo
Luis Figueroa
Michael Fine
Benjamin Finkel
Sylvia Finzi
Nira Firestone
Douglas Fischer
Peter Fitz
Bob Fitzgerald
Joan Flanagan
Cora Flaster
Mike Flegle
James Floersch
Gregg Foster
Howard Foster
Lisa Francilia
Christian Francioli
Sela Francis
Matthew Frazer
Cliff Freeman
Robert Fremgen
John Funck
Jerry Fury
Jacques Fuselier
Tom Gabriel
Bob Gage
Tom Galati
Brian Gallagher
Mark Ganton
Bertrand Garbassi
Thomas Garbellotto
Jim Garbutt
Gery Garcia
Jacqui Garcia
Salvador Garcia
Tom Gardner
Lee Garfinkel
Amil Gargano
Matthew Gargano
Lisa Garrone
Gianina Gauci
Alan Gee
Dean Gemmell
John George
Harold German
Steven Giamarino
Jessica Giel
George Gier
Carla Gigante
Jeffrey John Gillis
Frank Ginsberg
Gudbjorg Gissurard

Jason Glassman
Kenneth Gleason
Amy Glennon
Adam Glickman
Marcus Glover
Max Godsil
Chris Goldschmidt
Alexandra Goldsmith
Gary Goldsmith
Mark Goldstein
Steven Goldstein
Eve Gonsenhauser
Mitch Gordon
Roy Grace
Stella Grafakos
Dianne D. Graham
Ian Graham
Jon Grainger
Jeff Graybill
Norm Grey
Dick Grider
Jeff Griffith
Jerry Gross
Michelle Joy Grossman
Philip Growick
Roland Grybauskas
Michael Guarini
Bruce Guidotti

H
Deb Hagan
Jim Hagar
Elizabeth Haggett
James Hainis
Andy Hall
Matthew Hallock
Trace Hallowell
Ada Halofsky
Mark Halski
Bill Hamilton
Wayne Hanson
Keith Harmweyer
Cabell Harris
Eva Hart
Dabni Harvey
Jim Haven
Jim Hayman
Donald Henthorne
Roy Herbert
Elana Hershman
Kenneth Herzog
Randi Hesman
Lee Hester
Ralf Heuel
Dawn Hibbard
Brian Hickling
Sue Higgs
Bill Hillsman
Randi Himmelfarb
Woody Hinkle
Andrew Hirsch
Jared Hirsch
Peter Hirsch
Roger Hoard
Sara Hochman
Kari Hoerchler
Sigal Hofshi
Sally Hogshead
Barry Holland
Dave Holloway
Jenine Holmes
Sandra Holtzman
Sung Woo Hong
Jim Hord
Laurence Horvitz
Ryan Hose
Gabe Hoskins
Hugh Hough

David Houghton
Azita Remi Houshiar
Brian Howlett
Denice Hradisky
Mark Hriciga
Dion Hughes
Mike Hughes
Shayne-Alexis Humphrey
Lisa Hurwitz
John Hynes

I
Paul Iannuzzo
Nicole Infante
Aki Inoue
Joe Ivey

J
Jeanmarie Jackman
Dick Jackson
Judi Jacob
Chris Jacobs
Harry M. Jacobs, Jr.
Jaydee Jana
Adrian Jeffery
Shawn Jeffrey
Mickey Jenkins
Heather Jeranek
Andrew Jeske
Anthony A. Johnson
Glynnis Johnson
Steve Juliusson

K
Joshua Kampta
Kenneth Robert Kaplan
Scott Kaplan
Richard Kaufman
Leslie Kay
Woody Kay
Blair Keeley
Yong Keh
Monika Kehrer
Paul Keister
Robert L. Kelly
Eil Jung Kim
Joanne Kim
Jon King
Kerry Kinney
Larissa Kirschner
Richard Kirshenbaum
Joe Knezic
Linda Knight
Eric Knudsen
Jennifer Kohl
Leslie Herman Kolk
Daren Koniuk
Ronni Korn
Renee Korus
Jeff Kosloski
Maria Kostyk-Petro
Judy Kozuck
Robert Krell
David Krewinghaus
Ken Kriunstein
Neal Krouse
Stewart Krull
Paul Krumenacker
Ari Krup
Pradeep Kumar
Kuang-Chun Kuo
Lilly Kuwashima

L
Robert LaBarge
Ben Lagunas
Michael Lander
Jenny Landey
Steven Landsberg
Andy Langer
Sarah Langmaid
Anthony LaPetri
Michaela Larosse

Carole Larson
Susan LaScala
David Laskarzewski
Karen Lau
Stacy Lavendar
Mary Wells Lawrence
Joe Leahy
Marcia LeBeau
Grace Lee
Jennie Lee
Sung Lee
Sung-Yoon Lee
Neil Leinwohl
Dany Lee Lennon
Dick Leonard
Jodie Leopold
Mike Lescarbeau
Sharon Lesser
Peter Levathes
Robert Levenson
Adam Levine
Jonathan Lewis
Tom Lichtenheld
Susan Lieber
Henriette Lienke
Adrian Lim
Lisa Lipkin
Wallace Littman
Steven Liu
Alberto Llaurador
Sheryl Llewellyn
George Lois
T.K. Long
Carson Lord
Beirne Lowry
Peter Lubalin
David Lubars
John Ludwig
Victoria Ludwin
Francesca Lum
Lisa Lurie
Bhupesh Luther
John Lutter
Fabian Lynch

M
Tony Macchia
Shyam Madiraju
Anne Maegli
Chris Maley
Madhu Malhan
John Malinowski
Karen Mallia
Ellen Mance-Smyth
Bradley Manier
John Mannion
Jennifer Mantz
Nicole Manzi
Brian Marabello
Lee Margolis
Scott Margolis
Louis Marino
Larry Marks
Rhoda Marshall
Dave Martin
Laura Martin
Frank Martino
Colleen Mathis
Michael Maurer
Norman Mayers
Michael Mayers
James Mazzola
Scott McAfee
Ed McCabe
Ted McCagg
Clem McCarthy
Lisa McCarthy
Jim McDonough

Jack McGoldrick
Kevin McKeon
Steven McKeon
Maureen McKeown
Ned McNeilage
Rob McPherson
Gabriel Medina
Michael Medina
Heather Mee
Karen Meech
Lynne Meena
Mark Mendelis
Ted Mendelson
Frank Meo
Ari Merkin
Luis Miguel Messianu
Mario G. Messina
Laura Metrano
Lyle Metzdorf
Terri Meyer
Greg Meyers
Bethann Miale
Jeanine Michna
Michael Migliozzi, II
Mark Millar
Christopher Miller
Don Miller
Reid Miller
Renee Miller
Janice Milligan
Jonathan L. Mindell
Brett Minieri
Nick Miraglia
Mark Mitchell
Steven Mitsch
Marise Mizrahi
Ronald Modica
Alex Mohler
Leonard Monfredo
Ty Montague
Miguel Morales
Dawn Morris
Deborah Morrison
Pamela Morrow
Marco Morsella
Jim Mountjoy
Tom Moyer
Lauren Mueller
William Munch, Jr.
Sibila Munoz
Vinny Muratore
Mark Muszynski
Mary Elena Myrka

N
Tracy Nader
Steven Nasi
Charbel Nasser
Niranjan Natarajan
Thomas Nathan
Shane Nearman
Victoria Necea
Robert S. Needleman
Arun K. Nemali
Amy Nicholson
Howard Nierman
David Nobay
Jennifer Noble
Susan Nobles
Tom Notman
Chris Nott
Jennifer Nottoli

O
Dick O'Brien
Mick O'Brien
Pamela O'Flynn
Kelly O'Keefe
Joe O'Neill
David Oakley

this book
remains
the
property
of

GOLD, SILVER &
BRONZE AWARDS

**CONSUMER
NEWSPAPER
OVER 600 LINES:
SINGLE**

GOLD

art director
Masakazu Sawa

writer
Minoru Kawase

photographer
Megumu Wada

client
Volvo Cars Japan

agency
Dentsu Young &
Rubicam/Tokyo

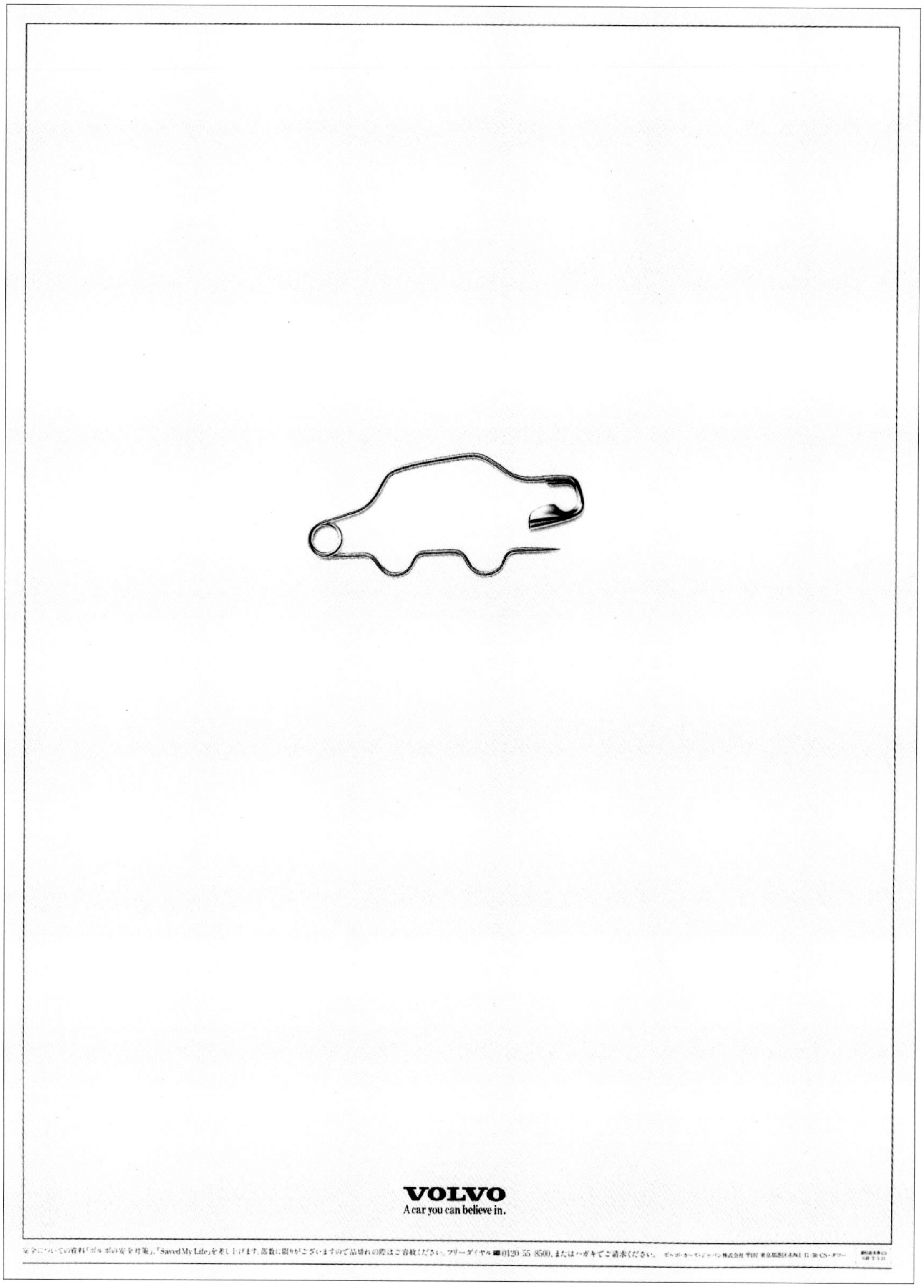

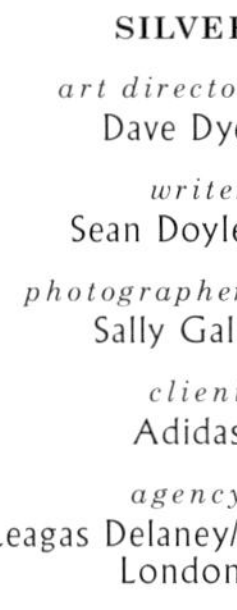

SILVER

art director
Dave Dye

writer
Sean Doyle

photographer
Sally Gall

client
Adidas

agency
Leagas Delaney/
London

BRONZE

art director
Dave Dye

writer
Sean Doyle

photographer
Sally Gall

client
Adidas

agency
Leagas Delaney/
London

GOLD, SILVER &
BRONZE AWARDS

CONSUMER
NEWSPAPER
OVER 600 LINES:
CAMPAIGN

GOLD

art director
Dave Dye

writer
Sean Doyle

photographer
Sally Gall

client
Adidas

agency
Leagas Delaney/London

A.
MAKE YOUR OWN B.

adidas
RUNNING
DIY SUPERSTORE
HIGH RISE FLATS
INDUSTRIAL ESTATE
FLYOVER
MULTI-STOREY CAR PARK
SUPERMARKET
TRAIN STATION
HIGH STREET
SHOPPING MALL
HURRY

adidas
RUNNING
FREE

GOLD, SILVER &
BRONZE AWARDS

**CONSUMER
NEWSPAPER
OVER 600 LINES:
CAMPAIGN**

SILVER

art directors
Alexandra Taylor
Nik Studzinski

writers
Adam Kean
Jason Fretwell

photographers
First Base
Dean Steadman
Fouad El Khoury
Liam Kennedy
Chris Steele-Perkins

client
Army/COI

agency
Saatchi & Saatchi/London

HE'S COUNTING ON
YOU TO SEND SOLDIERS
TO HELP HIM

SO IS AN ENEMY SNIPER

ARMY
OFFICER
BE THE BEST

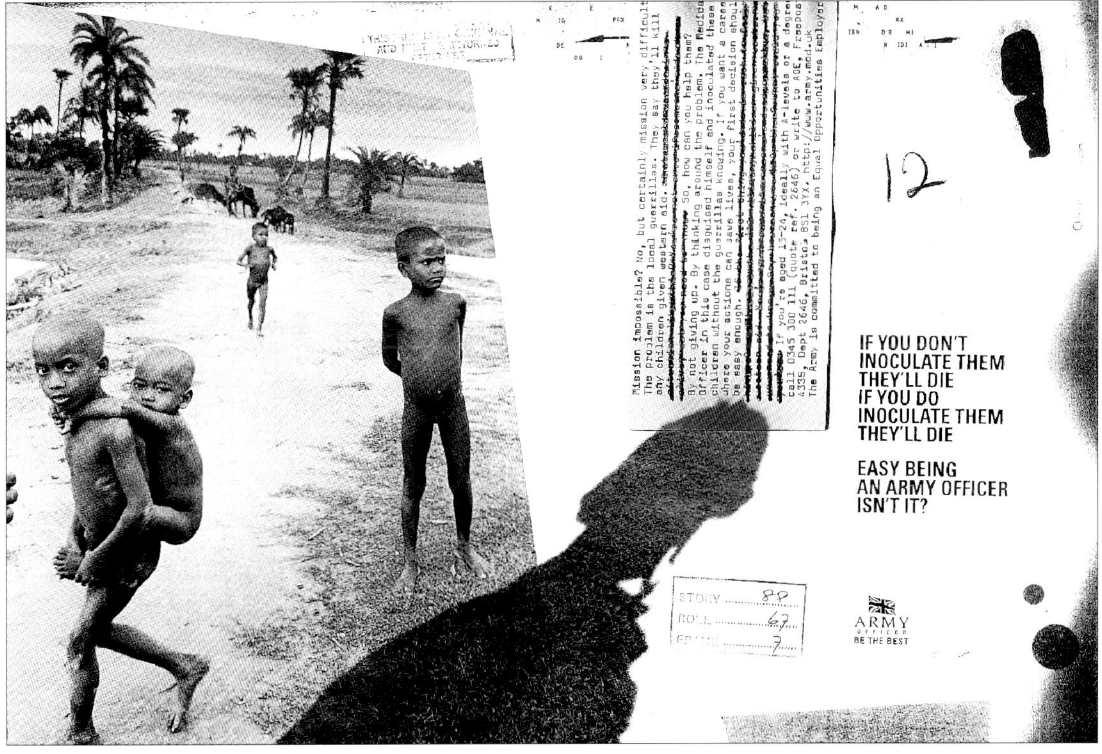
IF YOU DON'T
INOCULATE THEM
THEY'LL DIE
IF YOU DO
INOCULATE THEM
THEY'LL DIE

EASY BEING
AN ARMY OFFICER
ISN'T IT?

ARMY
OFFICER
BE THE BEST

**CONSUMER
NEWSPAPER
OVER 600 LINES:
CAMPAIGN**

BRONZE

art director
Scott Dube

writer
Zak Mroueh

photographer
Ian Campbell

client
Federal Express

agency
BBDO / Toronto

TRUST FedEx to get your boxes across Canada, the U.S., or to any of our 211 international destinations. (We guarantee they will arrive on time or your money back.) Because when it comes to shipping boxes, you don't have to worry about our reputation for reliability – but what about yours? Next time, call 1·800·Go·FedEx.

OF COURSE, when you're shipping boxes to the U.S., FedEx can also end up saving you money. Especially if your boxes don't have to get there overnight. Because now you have the option of using our 2 or 3 day international economy service. Your boxes will still get handled with the attention they deserve. Only you'll pay less for shipping them. And that way you'll have both ends covered. Just call 1·800·Go·FedEx.

ANXIOUSLY WAITING for a box shipment to clear customs can cost you more than just your sanity. You can lose the faith of your customers, not to mention the cost you pay in brokerage fees. To speed up the process, FedEx has in-house customs brokers available at no extra charge. These experts will not only help you clear customs, they'll help clear your mind. So relax. Call 1·800·Go·FedEx.

**CONSUMER
NEWSPAPER
OVER 600 LINES:
CAMPAIGN**

BRONZE

art directors
Nick Cohen
Dave Cook

writer
Mikal Reich

client
Village Voice

agency
Mad Dogs &
Englishmen / New York

the village
VOICE
NOT AMERICA'S FAVORITE PAPER

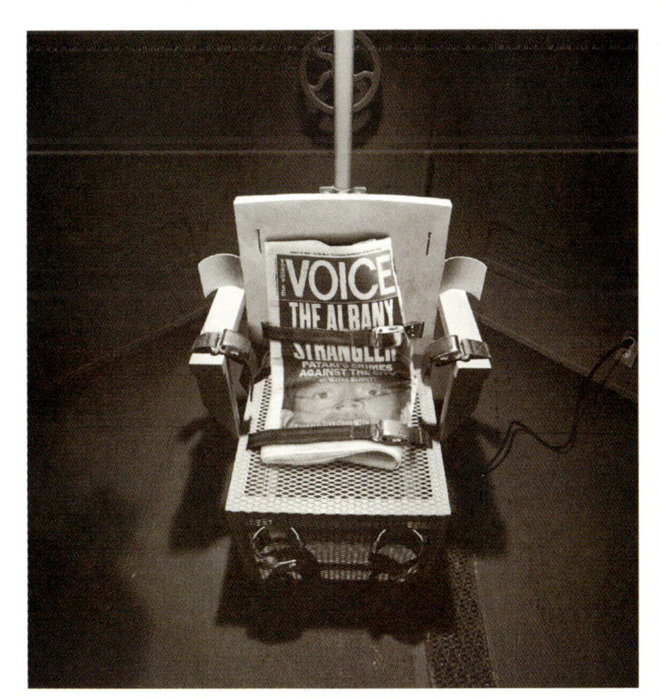

the village
VOICE
NOT AMERICA'S FAVORITE PAPER

**CONSUMER
NEWSPAPER
600 LINES
OR LESS:
SINGLE**

SILVER

art directors
Elsie Fehr
Nancy Vonk

writers
Janet Kestin
Arthur Shah

illustrator
Elsie Fehr

client
Timex Canada

agency
Ogilvy & Mather/
Toronto

SINGLE: SILVER   CAMPAIGN: SILVER

**CONSUMER
NEWSPAPER
600 LINES
OR LESS:
CAMPAIGN**

SILVER

art directors
Elsie Fehr
Nancy Vonk

writers
Janet Kestin
Arthur Shah

illustrator
Elsie Fehr

client
Timex Canada

agency
Ogilvy & Mather/
Toronto

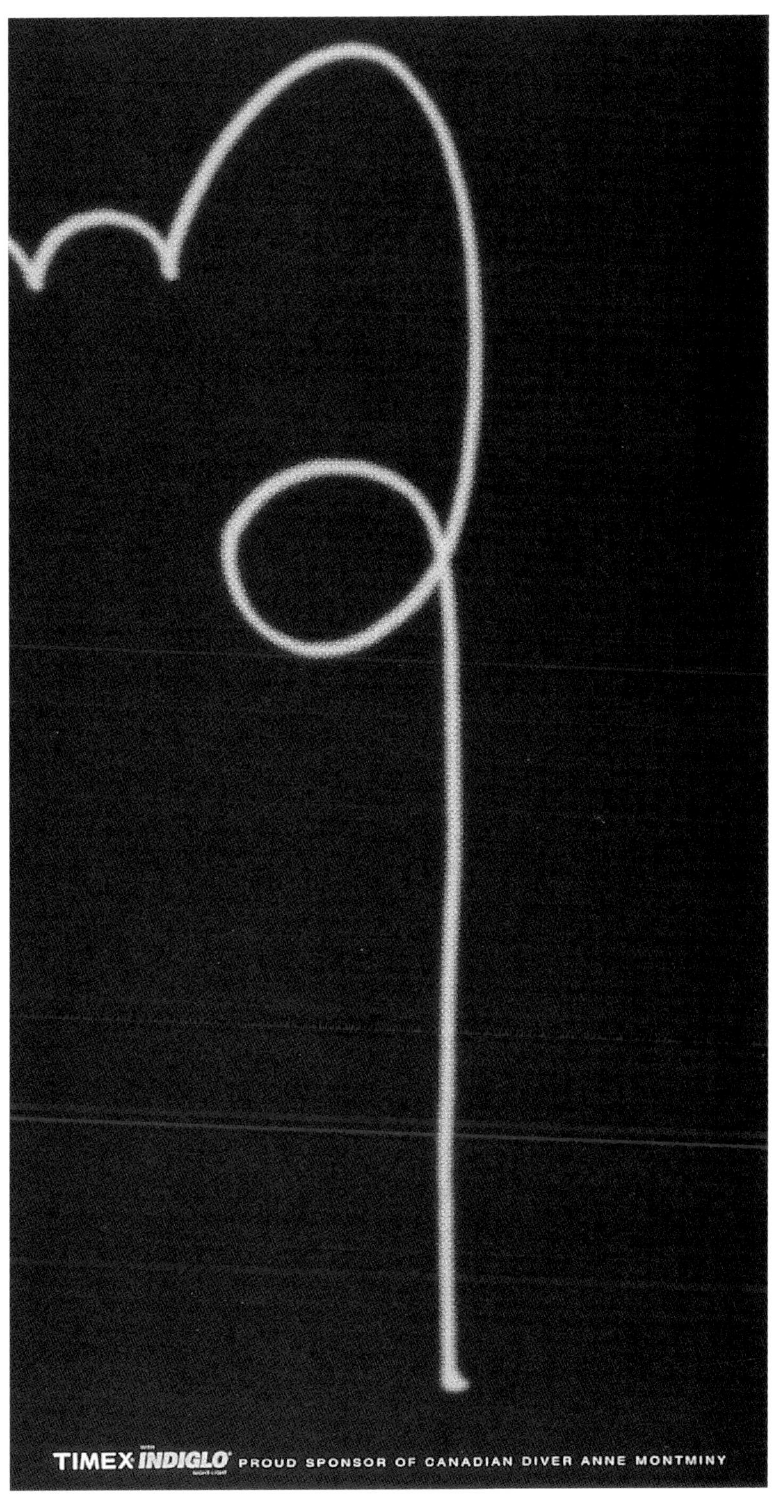

TIMEX INDIGLO PROUD SPONSOR OF CANADIAN DIVER ANNE MONTMINY

**CONSUMER
MAGAZINE
B/W FULL PAGE
OR SPREAD:
SINGLE**

SILVER

art director
Ellen Steinberg

writer
Mike Lescarbeau

photographer
Craig Perman

client
Booker's

agency
Fallon McElligott/
Minneapolis

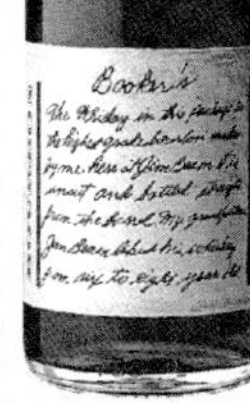

BRONZE

art director
Scott O'Leary

writer
Roger Baldacci

client
Converse - International

agency
Houston Herstek
Favat/Boston

**CONSUMER
MAGAZINE
COLOR
FULL PAGE
OR SPREAD:
SINGLE**

GOLD

art director
Chris Hooper

writer
Bob Kerstetter

photographer
Hunter Freeman

client
Polaroid Corporation

agency
Goodby Silverstein &
Partners / San Francisco

SILVER

art director
Todd Grant

writers
Bo Coyner
Jon Soto

photographer
Nadav Kander

client
Umbro

agency
Goodby Silverstein &
Partners / San Francisco

**CONSUMER
MAGAZINE
COLOR
FULL PAGE
OR SPREAD:
SINGLE**

BRONZE

art director
Keith Courtney

writer
Jon Bray

photographer
Cathy Logan

client
Pentax UK

agency
K Advertising / London

BRONZE

art director
Mark Tutssel

writer
Nick Bell

photographer
Russell Porcas

client
Mercedes-Benz

agency
Leo Burnett / London

GOLD, SILVER &
BRONZE AWARDS

**CONSUMER
MAGAZINE
B/W FULL PAGE
OR SPREAD:
CAMPAIGN**

SILVER

art directors
Scott O'Leary
Peter Favat
Emily Sassano

writers
Roger Baldacci
Peter Favat

client
Converse-International

agency
Houston Herstek
Favat / Boston

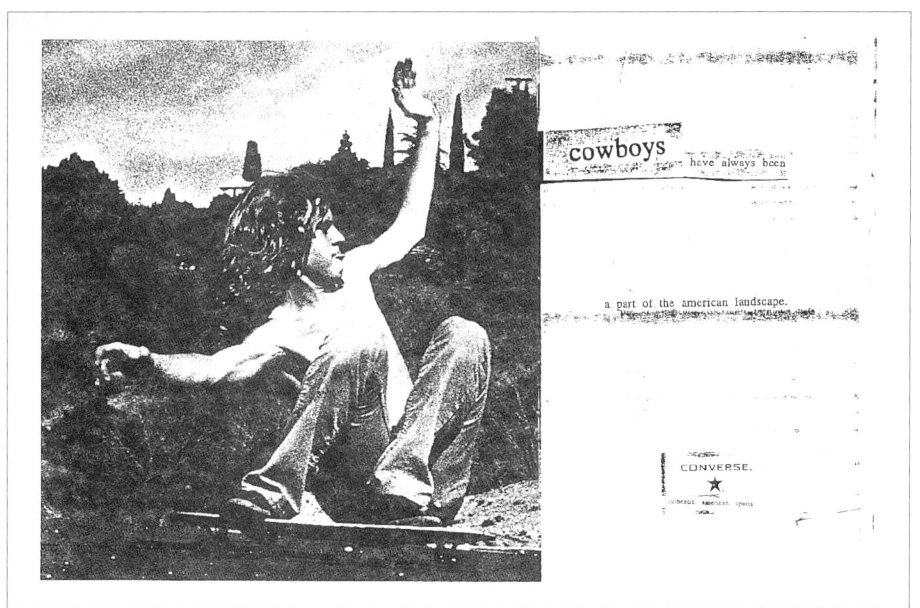

**CONSUMER
MAGAZINE
B/W FULL PAGE
OR SPREAD:
CAMPAIGN**

BRONZE

art director
Daniel Miyahara

writer
Ward Parker

photographer
Tony Welch

client
Deep Clothing

agency
Reign / New York

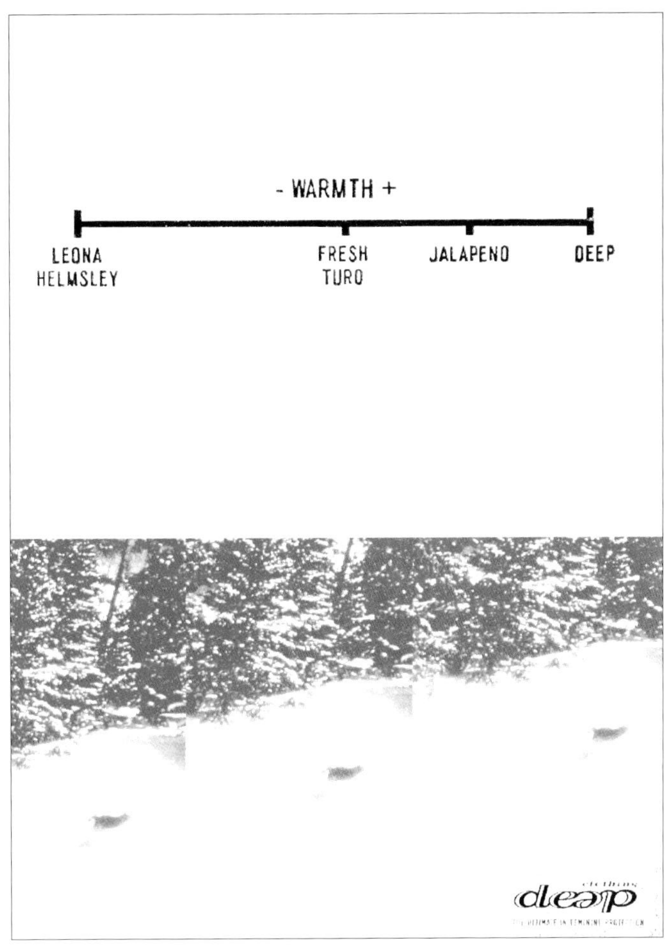
- WARMTH +
LEONA HELMSLEY
FRESH TURO
JALAPENO
DEEP
clothing
deep
THE ULTIMATE IN FEMININE PROTECTION

- WATER RESISTANCE +
TITANIC
DEATH VALLEY
PLASTIC BED SHEETS
DEEP
clothing
deep
THE ULTIMATE IN FEMININE PROTECTION

**CONSUMER
MAGAZINE
COLOR
FULL PAGE
OR SPREAD:
CAMPAIGN**

GOLD

art directors
Grant Richards
Mike Mazza
Valerie Ang-Powell
Chris Hooper

writers
Scott Aal
Al Kelly
Steve Payonzeck
Bob Kerstetter

photographer
Hunter Freeman

client
Polaroid Corporation

agency
Goodby Silverstein &
Partners/San Francisco

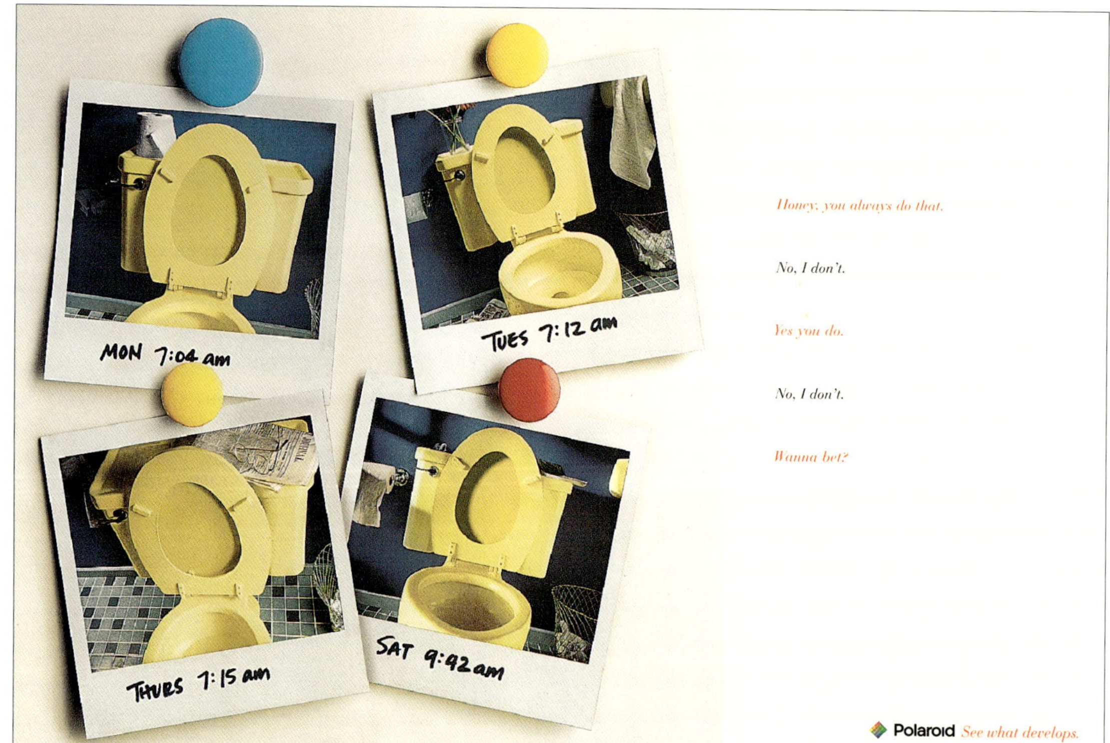

Tom, I spoke to Laurie today.
Yeah? How is she?
She sounds good. She says it's no harder than high school.
That's our girl.
Sounds like she's in love again, too.
Not another football player?
I don't think so. She's sending a Polaroid shot of him.
Maybe we should invite him for Thanksgiving.
Steven
Polaroid See what develops.

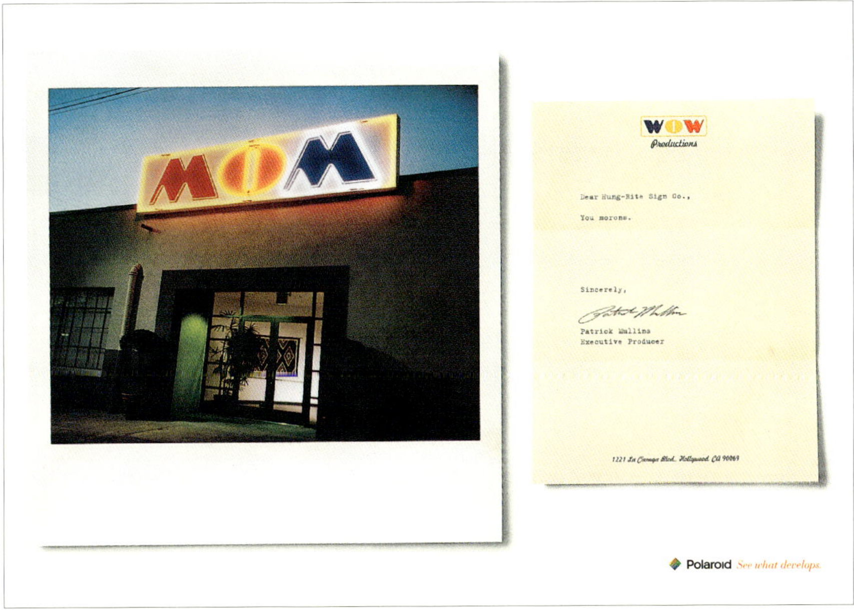

MOM
WOW
Productions
Dear Hung-Rite Sign Co.,
You morons.
Sincerely,
Patrick Mullins
Executive Producer
1221 La Cienega Blvd., Hollywood, CA 90069
Polaroid See what develops.

Hello Mr. Holloway?
It's Butch from Ace Plumbing...
That hissing sound underneath your
house wasn't your pipes.
7 Edgecroft Rd.
Polaroid See what develops.

**CONSUMER
MAGAZINE
COLOR
FULL PAGE
OR SPREAD:
SINGLE**

SILVER

art director
Steve Luker

writer
Steve Simpson

photographers
Gian Paolo Barbieri
Roger Paperno

client
Norwegian Cruise Line

agency
Goodby Silverstein &
Partners / San Francisco

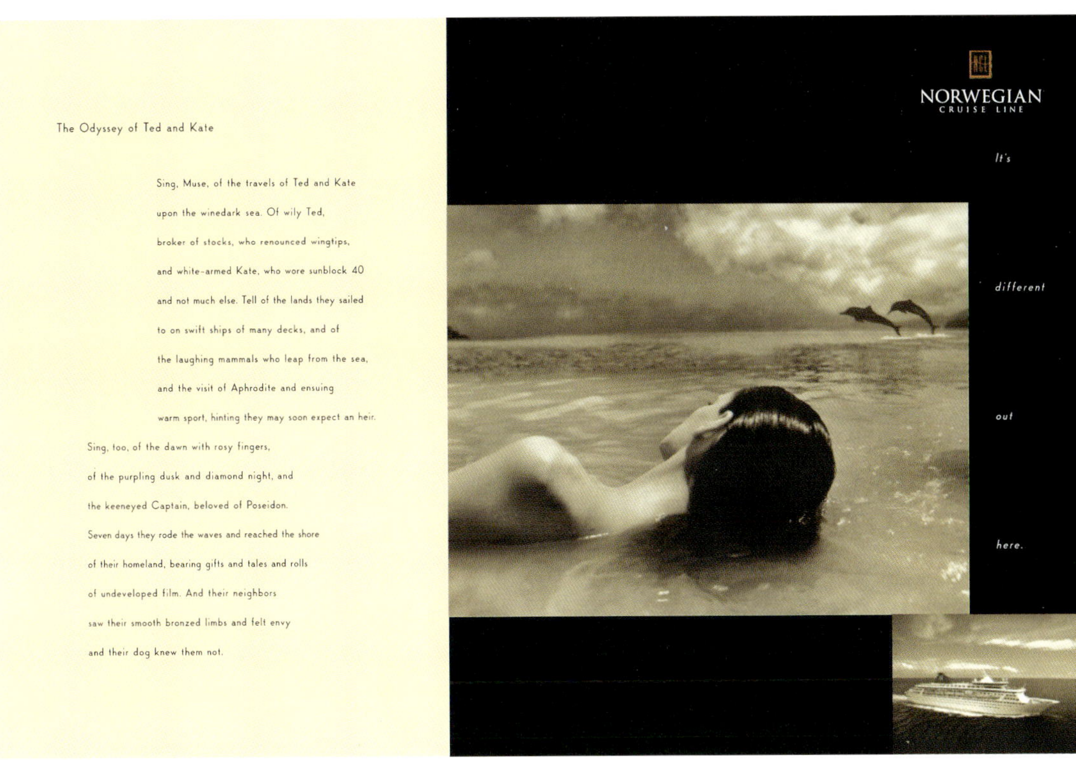

NORWEGIAN
CRUISE LINE

It's

different

out

here.

The Odyssey of Ted and Kate

Sing, Muse, of the travels of Ted and Kate
upon the winedark sea. Of wily Ted,
broker of stocks, who renounced wingtips,
and white-armed Kate, who wore sunblock 40
and not much else. Tell of the lands they sailed
to on swift ships of many decks, and of
the laughing mammals who leap from the sea,
and the visit of Aphrodite and ensuing
warm sport, hinting they may soon expect an heir.
Sing, too, of the dawn with rosy fingers,
of the purpling dusk and diamond night, and
the keeneyed Captain, beloved of Poseidon.
Seven days they rode the waves and reached the shore
of their homeland, bearing gifts and tales and rolls
of undeveloped film. And their neighbors
saw their smooth bronzed limbs and felt envy
and their dog knew them not.

NORWEGIAN
CRUISE LINE

It's

different

out

here.

Beyond the horizon

Beyond heavy woollens
Beyond hurry
Beyond the Nightly News
Beyond snow
Beyond the dayindayout

Beyond the salt spray (and to the idea beneath)
Beyond the gossip of seagulls
Beyond your regular stock of adjectives
Beyond work
Beyond the routine spasm
Beyond Wonderland, Byzantium, Camelot
Beyond the bougainvillea riots
Beyond the reach of what hurts you
Beyond care
Beyond the tug of the continent
Beyond the need to explain
Beyond the assumptions that keep you warm
Beyond asphalt
Beyond the northern front of cold Canadian air

Beyond the idea you have of a fish and a fish has of you
Beyond the equator
Beyond speech
Beyond the trigonometry of the most meticulous mapmaker
Beyond the grottoes of the sea
Beyond the gull's flight lanes
Beyond the wind
Beyond tomorrow and today and yesterday
Beyond the ideologies of the left
Beyond the ideologies of the right
Beyond gravity
Beyond mixed trading on Wall Street
Beyond the lands of apologies, the nations of excuses
Beyond the whale highway
Beyond the boundaries of her cheekbones
Beyond the frontiers of his forehead
Beyond the habit of habits
Beyond the recommended daily requirement of beauty
Beyond the burning pole star
Beyond the Looking Glass
Beyond where sleet falls into uncovered souls
Beyond the ordinary everyday vocabulary of 400 words
Beyond radio talk show hosts who hate you
Beyond See America First
Beyond the wave flipping its hair forward to dry
Beyond your property line
Beyond the molecules normally thought to compose you
Beyond any hope you are still reading this
Beyond the one white single-spaced page of your résumé
Beyond all memorized access codes
Beyond politics (national, local, sexual)
Beyond your cooking
Beyond where the fish convene and hold elections
Beyond the inks and dyes of this page
Beyond your best guess
Beyond the daily dissipation of human energy
Beyond beyond
Beyond the advertised attractions
Beyond the identity you put on with your good clothes
Beyond the laws of the land
Beyond a decent rate of return in the mutual fund of Memory
Beyond ambition
Beyond anything the present 353 words can say

Beyond all that.

**CONSUMER
MAGAZINE
COLOR
FULL PAGE
OR SPREAD:
CAMPAIGN**

BRONZE

art director
Keith Courtney

writer
Jon Bray

photographers
Kate Courtney
Keith Courtney
Cathy Logan
Jayne Taylor

client
Pentax UK

agency
K Advertising/London

LIFT & PEEL HERE
QUALITY CONTROL
Out of focus.
Use the new Pentax Espio 738.
Its active auto-focusing
plus programmed auto-exposure
ensures sharper pictures.
You don't need luck, you need a Pentax.
ADVICE LABEL

LIFT & PEEL HERE
QUALITY CONTROL
Blurred out-of-focus prints.
Use the new Pentax Espio 738.
Its infrared active auto-focusing with focus lock
means you can focus on a subject,
even if it isn't in the centre of the picture.
You don't need luck, you need a Pentax.
ADVICE LABEL

CONSUMER MAGAZINE B/W OR COLOR LESS THAN A PAGE: SINGLE

SILVER

art director
Andy Azula

writer
Dave Pullar

client
Nikon

agency
Fallon McElligott/
Minneapolis

CONSUMER MAGAZINE B/W OR COLOR LESS THAN A PAGE: CAMPAIGN

GOLD

art director
Andy Azula

writer
Dave Pullar

client
Nikon

agency
Fallon McElligott/
Minneapolis

SINGLE: SILVER   CAMPAIGN: GOLD

Tip #34:
Remember to
compensate for
backlighting.

The Nikon School

Before snapping a photo, it's a good idea to take a
gander at what's happening in the background. Just
one of the topics covered in our 8-hour class, where
you'll learn everything from basic composition to
advanced exposure techniques. You also get
the 157-page Nikon School Handbook and a lovely
lunch, all for a mere $95. Call (516) 547-8666 to
find out when a class will be offered in your city.

Tip #5:
Some photo
opportunities only
last a second.

The Nikon School

For some reason, we feel compelled to open by
mentioning the lunch that comes with our 8-hour
class. But more importantly, our expert instructors
will teach you everything from basic composition
to advanced exposure techniques. You also get
the 157-page Nikon School Handbook, all for a mere
$95. Call (516) 547-8666 for the date and time
that a Nikon School will be offered in your city.

OUTDOOR: SINGLE

GOLD

art director
Masakazu Sawa

writer
Minoru Kawase

photographer
Megumu Wada

client
Volvo Cars Japan

agency
Dentsu Young &
Rubicam / Tokyo

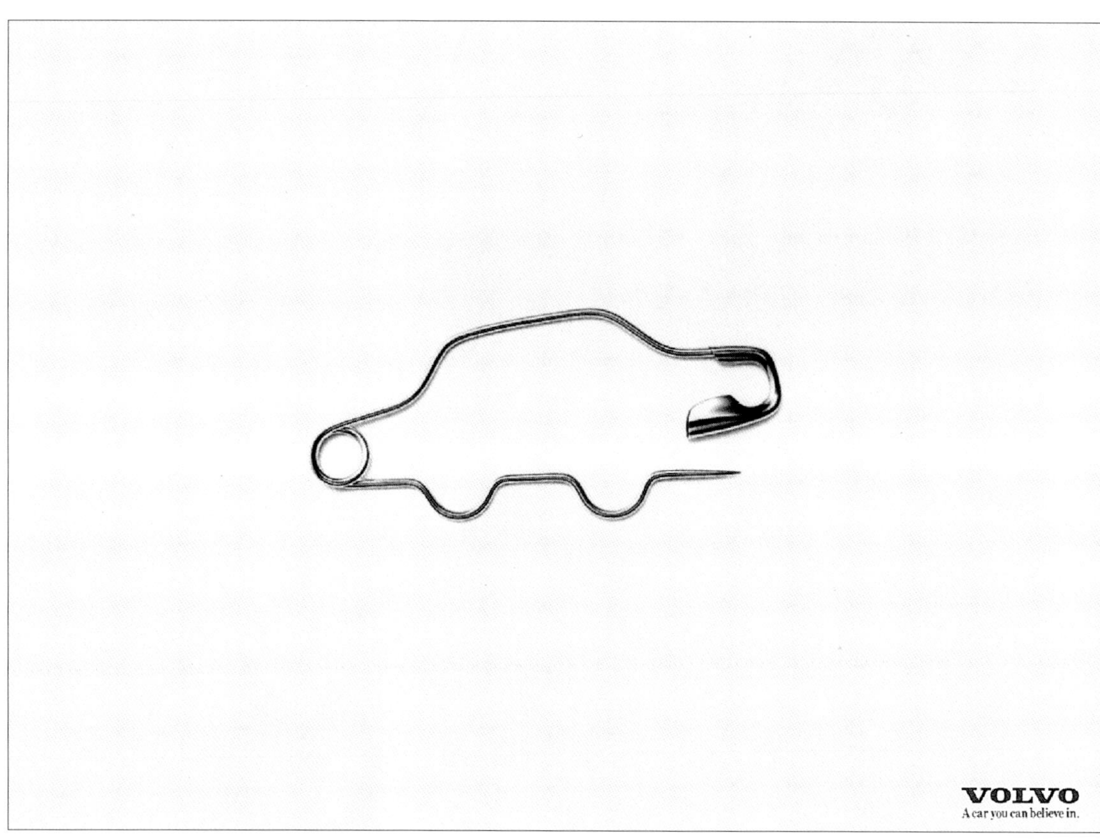

GOLD, SILVER &
BRONZE AWARDS

SILVER

art director
Mark Tutssel

writer
Nick Bell

photographer
Russell Porcas

client
Mercedes-Benz

agency
Leo Burnett / London

162 SCG
The new SLK

BRONZE

art director
Jeff Williams

writer
Jamie Barrett

photographer
Richard Burbridge

client
Nike

agency
Wieden & Kennedy/
Portland

YOU DON'T WIN SILVER.
YOU LOSE GOLD.

GOLD, SILVER &
BRONZE AWARDS

**OUTDOOR:
CAMPAIGN**

GOLD

art director
Roger Bentley

writer
Eric Silver

photographer
Bryan Stone

client
Nike

agency
Wieden & Kennedy/
Portland

JOHN McENROE

ON:
PREPARING FOR A SAMPRAS MATCH

"IF YOU FIND YOURSELF FACING THIS YEAR'S DEFENDING CHAMPION, THERE IS AN OUTSTANDING CHANCE YOU WILL COME UP SHORT AND, IN THE END, HUMILIATE YOURSELF IN FRONT OF A VERY LARGE AUDIENCE. TRY INJURING YOURSELF IN A FREAK BLENDER ACCIDENT TO AVOID THE CONFRONTATION ALTOGETHER."

JOHN McENROE

ON:
DEFEATING PIERCE THROUGH YOUR MENTAL POWERS

"ABOUT 50% OF TENNIS IS MENTAL…MAYBE MORE…MAYBE 60%…OR 75%… TO BE HONEST I DON'T KNOW THE EXACT PERCENTAGE. BUT I DO KNOW THAT IT'S FUN TO LAUGH AT PEOPLE DOING YOGA."

ALTOIDS
PLEASURE IN PAIN
THE CURIOUSLY STRONG MINTS
©1996 Callard & Bowser-Suchard Inc.

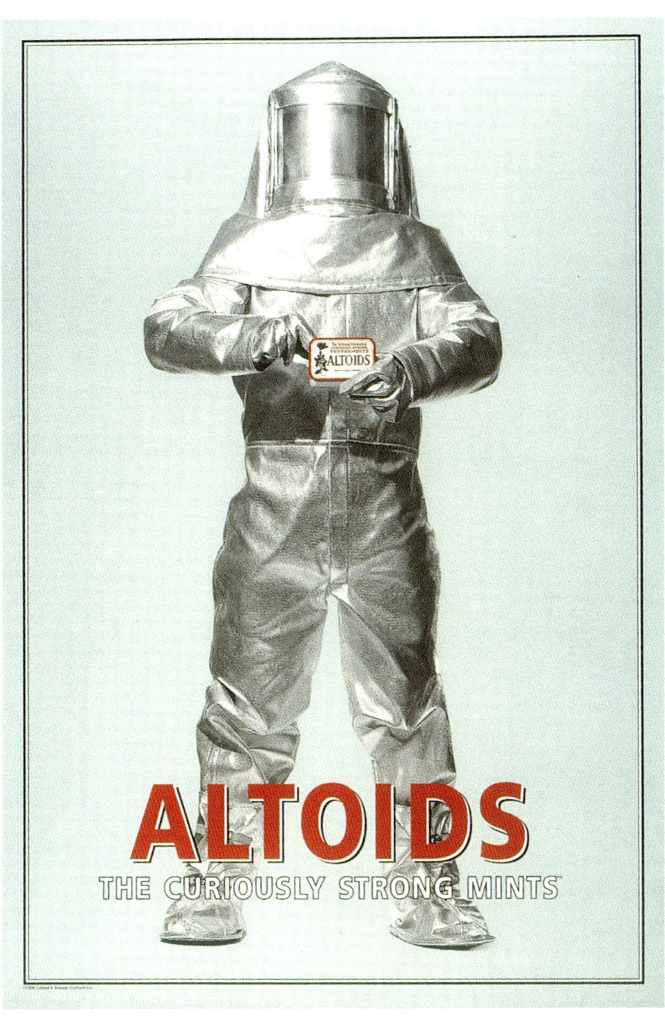

ALTOIDS
THE CURIOUSLY STRONG MINTS

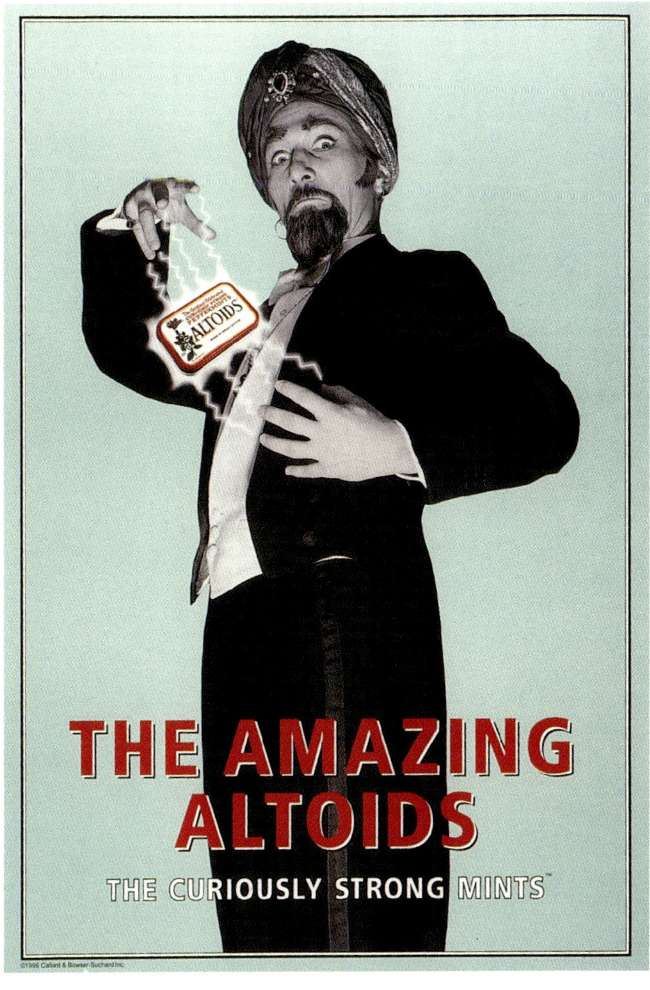

THE AMAZING
ALTOIDS
THE CURIOUSLY STRONG MINTS

GOLD, SILVER &
BRONZE AWARDS

**TRADE B/W
FULL PAGE
OR SPREAD:
SINGLE**

SILVER

art director
Steve Mitchell

writer
Doug Adkins

client
Dublin Productions

agency
Hunt Adkins/
Minneapolis

BRONZE

art director
Steve Mitchell

writer
Doug Adkins

client
Dublin Productions

agency
Hunt Adkins/
Minneapolis

AND BEHOLD, THE HEAVENS OPENED AND RAINED FIRE

AND THE EARTH TREMBLED AND MOUNTAINS FELL

AND RIVERS TURNED TO BLOOD AND CITIES CRUMBLED TO

DUST AND THE MULTITUDES WERE DESTROYED UTTERLY

or

BIBLICAL HUMOR.

The origins of the most popular stand-up routines of the 20th century can be traced back to Biblical times. Moses' sermon on the Mount was preceded by the popular warm-up act of Mortimer of Judea, who was best known for his Pharaoh impressions and Egyptian limericks.

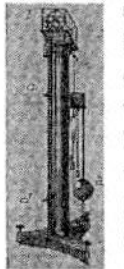

Woe unto hecklers for they shall be surely smited by the Smiteriser-2000.

Noah, after years on the grueling Black Sea comedy circuit, became the first comedian to star in his own sitcom, although he later saw his show's ratings plummet when every single person on Earth drowned. Not to be outdone, Cain wrote and published six hilarious (albeit somewhat dark) books entitled "Top Ten Reasons I'm Going to Kill My Brother Abel." And Jonah enjoyed unprecedented success with his "Stuck Inside a Whale" HBO special, though he later turned out to be a one-hit wonder and spent his last years telling whale jokes in seedy Gomorrhean nightclubs.

THE END IS NEAR
AND IT WILL BE
DAMN FUNNY

One fateful day Dublin Director Jerry Pope, struck by the sudden and

At the Temple of the Stuffed Dog, followers from all over the world leave offerings of sticks, kibble and squeaky toys in hopes of receiving divine enlightenment. Here we see three priests hoping to hit the mother lode by pleading for some winning lottery numbers.

shocking realization that "God" is "dog" spelled backwards, started his now world-feared religion, Jerryology. Just months later, thousands of loyal and heavily tithed followers are flocking to the Jerryologian Temple of the Stuffed Dog to leave gold bullion and doggy biscuits. Jerry operates his empire from a fleet of seven 1978 Buicks, conducting his meetings in Kmart parking lots across the country. When such missionary work calls, the Stuffed Dog's convenient removable limbs allow Jerry to easily fit the holy relic into his trunk next to the tire jack.

Charlton Heston and director Jerry Pope arrive in an armored car with a print of their latest picture, "God vs. Godzilla."

At one such Jerriology road revival, Jerry preached hellfire and brimstone, damning all who commit the sin of worshipping material goods. Jerry raked in over $77,000 that day.

AND GOD SAID,
"TAKE MY WIFE.
PLEASE."

And God said, "Thou shalt not make fun of the Bible." And we laughed, because it just sounded funny the way he said it. You can't teach timing like that. God is one of those lucky few that was just born with it. His sense of humor is a gift from—well, from Himself, which is a neat trick as well. And God said, "Let there be aardvark!" We still laugh about that one. But one time God's writers convinced him to say, "He that dieth shall the dogs eat!" And no one laughed, so God writes all his own material now. The pillar of salt, the burning bush, the tower of Babel—all God originals and all comedic triumphs. For a copy of a reel that God would spit on, call 213-960-3322 (L.A.) or 612-332-8864 (Mpls.).

Jerry, possessed by a demon, spins his head around and dances like a little flower.

DUBLIN
PRODUCTIONS

HOW MANY ENGINEERS DOES IT TAKE TO

TAP YOUR PHONE LINES, TUNNEL INTO YOUR HEATING DUCTS,

RIG YOUR DOG WITH A REMOTE-CONTROLLED

MICRO-ANAL CAMERA AND IMPLANT THOUGHT-CONTROLLING

12-VOLT SOLENOIDS IN YOUR WIFE AND CHILDREN?

or

PARANOID HUMOR.

Next time you're in an elevator, casually ask people if they've ever taken a good look at the lint trap in their dryer. Who might have put it there? Why does someone want their lint, anyway? And how many human clones have already been made from those lint samples? Tell them you've seen these lint clones roaming the streets in clone gangs, crushing puppies with steamrollers, setting old ladies on fire and giving people wedgies. Then suggest a few security measures, such as making their own clothes from beautiful, lint-free tinfoil; securing their lint in a safety deposit box; or incinerating their clothes in a blast-furnace after every use. By now it should be clear that there is nothing quite as amusing as exploiting someone else's irrational fears.

This chicken has been fattening Jerry Pope since 1982.

YOUR TOASTER
WANTS TO KILL YOU

Midnight. You're just on the edge of sleep. Suddenly you hear the faint sound of toast popping up. The whirring of an electric can opener. A refrigerator sliding across the kitchen floor. It is not your imagination. Every night your appliances conspire to plot your overthrow. One appliance alone is not a threat, but throw them all together and it's mob rule. We suggest separating them. Put your blender in the attic and your toaster in, say, Ohio. It makes the morning commute for toast a tad long but we think you'll find that it's well worth it. Then, give one appliance to each of your relatives to keep for you. They may

Rick noticed that almost every day a KGB agent disguised in a mailman's uniform inserted unusual items into his mailbox. No more, since Rick installed the Ronco Super-Deluxe Mailbox Defense System.

find this unusual at first, but they'll nod in understanding when, with cool logic, you explain your appliance situation to them. If, however, you own a Juiceboy-2000, simply give up hope, lie down on the floor and pray the end comes swiftly.

Ladybug or blood-thirsty alien invader?

THE DUBLIN
IMPENETRABLE
FORTRESS & SPA

If the previous scenario disturbs you, escape to the Dublin Fortress and Spa. For just $799.95 a night you'll be pampered in a secure womb of barbed wire and electrified fencing. Catch a glimpse of beautiful sunshine through the heavily armored gun turrets. Enjoy a delicious Piña Colada while basking in the warm glow of 50,000-watt searchlights. For reservations call 213-960-3322 (L.A.) or 332-8864 (Mpls.).

To guard against another mutiny attempt, Dublin workers are required to write their every thought on the Chalkboard of Truth.

DUBLIN
PRODUCTIONS

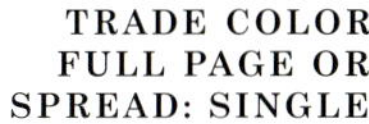

GOLD, SILVER &
BRONZE AWARDS

**TRADE COLOR
FULL PAGE OR
SPREAD: SINGLE**

SILVER

art director
Paul Hirsch

writer
Josh Denberg

client
Unum Insurance

agency
Goodby Silverstein &
Partners/San Francisco

BRONZE

art directors
David Ayriss
Christopher Toland

writers
Barton Corley
Christopher Toland

photographer
Mark Gallup

client
24/7 Snowboards

agency
Cole & Weber/
Portland

**TRADE B/W
OR COLOR
ANY SIZE:
CAMPAIGN**

SILVER

art director
Steve Mitchell

writer
Doug Adkins

client
Dublin Productions

agency
Hunt Adkins/
Minneapolis

AND BEHOLD, THE HEAVENS OPENED AND RAINED FIRE

AND THE EARTH TREMBLED AND MOUNTAINS FELL

AND RIVERS TURNED TO BLOOD AND CITIES CRUMBLED TO

DUST AND THE MULTITUDES WERE DESTROYED UTTERLY

or

BIBLICAL HUMOR.

The origins of the most popular stand-up routines of the 20th century can be traced back to Biblical times. Moses' sermon on the Mount was preceded by the popular warm-up act of Mortimer of Judea, who was best known for his Pharaoh impressions and Egyptian limericks. Noah, after years on the grueling Black Sea comedy circuit, became the first comedian to star in his own sitcom, although he later saw his show's ratings plummet when every single person on Earth drowned. Not to be outdone, Cain wrote and published six hilarious (albeit somewhat dark) books entitled "Top Ten Reasons I'm Going to Kill My Brother Abel." And Jonah enjoyed unprecedented success with his "Stuck Inside a Whale" HBO special, though he later turned out to be a one-hit wonder and spent his last years telling whale jokes in seedy Gomorrhean nightclubs.

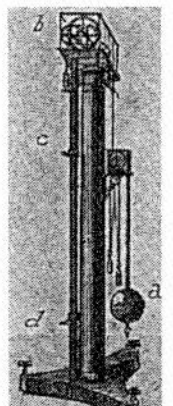

Woe unto hecklers for they shall be surely smited by the Smiterizer-2000.

THE END IS NEAR AND IT WILL BE DAMN FUNNY

One fateful day Dublin Director Jerry Pope, struck by the sudden and

At the Temple of the Stuffed Dog, followers from all over the world leave offerings of sticks, kibble and squeaky toys in hopes of receiving divine enlightenment. Here we see three priests hoping to hit the mother lode by pleading for some winning lottery numbers.

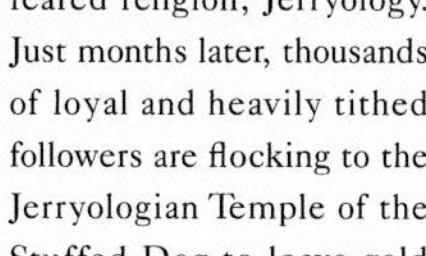

Charleton Heston and director Jerry Pope arrive in an armored car with a print of their latest picture, "God vs. Godzilla."

shocking realization that "God" is "dog" spelled backwards, started his now world-feared religion, Jerryology. Just months later, thousands of loyal and heavily tithed followers are flocking to the Jerryologian Temple of the Stuffed Dog to leave gold bullion and doggy biscuits. Jerry operates his empire from a fleet of seven 1978 Buicks, conducting his meetings in Kmart parking lots across the country. When such missionary work calls, the Stuffed Dog's convenient removable limbs allow Jerry to easily fit the holy relic into his trunk next to the tire jack.

At one such Jerriology road revival, Jerry preached hellfire and brimstone, damning all who commit the sin of worshipping material goods. Jerry raked in over $77,000 that day.

AND GOD SAID, "TAKE MY WIFE. PLEASE."
Ezekiel 9:6

And God said, "Thou shalt not make fun of the Bible." And we laughed, because it just sounded funny the way he said it. You can't teach timing like that. God is one of those lucky few that was just born with it. His sense of humor is a gift from—well, from Himself, which is a neat trick as well. And God said, "Let there be aardvark!" We still laugh about that one. But one time God's writers convinced him to say, "He that dieth shall the dogs eat!" And no one laughed, so God writes all his own material now. The pillar of salt, the burning bush, the tower of Babel—all God originals and all comedic triumphs. For a copy of a reel that God would spit on, call 213-960-3322 (L.A.) or 612-332-8864 (Mpls.).

Jerry, possessed by a demon, spins his head around and dances like a little flower.

HOW MANY ENGINEERS DOES IT TAKE TO

TAP YOUR PHONE LINES, TUNNEL INTO YOUR HEATING DUCTS,

RIG YOUR DOG WITH A REMOTE-CONTROLLED

MICRO-ANAL CAMERA AND IMPLANT THOUGHT-CONTROLLING

12-VOLT SOLENOIDS IN YOUR WIFE AND CHILDREN?

or

PARANOID HUMOR.

Next time you're in an elevator, casually ask people if they've ever taken a good look at the lint trap in their dryer. Who might have put it there? Why does someone want their lint, anyway? And how many human clones have already been made from those lint samples? Tell them you've seen these lint clones roaming the streets in clone gangs, crushing puppies with steamrollers, setting old ladies on fire and giving people wedgies. Then suggest a few security measures, such as mak-

Rick noticed that almost every day a KGB agent disguised in a mailman's uniform inserted unusual items into his mailbox. No more, since Rick installed the Ronco Super-Deluxe Mailbox Defense System.

This chicken has been following Jerry Pope since 1947.

ing their own clothes from beautiful, lint-free tinfoil; securing their lint in a safety deposit box; or incinerating their clothes in a blast-furnace after every use. By now it should be clear that there is nothing quite so amusing as exploiting someone else's irrational fears.

YOUR TOASTER
WANTS TO KILL YOU

Midnight. You're just on the edge of sleep. Suddenly you hear the faint sound of toast popping up. The whirring of an electric can opener. A refrigerator sliding across the kitchen floor. It is not your imagination. Every night your appliances conspire to plot your overthrow. One appliance alone is not a threat, but throw them all together and it's mob rule. We suggest separating them. Put your blender in the attic and your toaster in, say, Ohio. It makes the morning commute for toast a tad long but we think you'll find that it's well worth it. Then, give one appliance to each of your relatives to keep for you. They may find this unusual at first, but they'll nod in understanding when, with cool logic, you explain your appliance situation to them. If, however, you own a Juiceboy-2000, simply give up hope, lie down on the floor and pray the end comes swiftly.

Laughing or bloodthirsty alien invader?

THE DUBLIN
IMPENETRABLE
FORTRESS & SPA

If the previous scenario disturbs you, escape to the Dublin Fortress and Spa. For just $799.95 a night you'll be pampered in a secure womb of barbed wire and electrified fencing.

To guard against another mutiny attempt, Dublin workers are required to write their every thought on the Chalkboard of Truth.

Catch a glimpse of beautiful sunshine through the heavily armored gun turrets. Enjoy a delicious Piña Colada while basking in the warm glow of 50,000-watt searchlights. For reservations call 213-960-3322 (L.A.) or 332-8864 (Mpls.).

DUBLIN PRODUCTIONS

WHY THIS HEADLINE ISN'T FUNNY IN THE LEAST

or

THE NEW GOVERNMENT HUMOR REGULATIONS.

Humor, when it falls into the wrong hands, can unleash untold evils upon society. Fortunately, People Against Laughing & Smiling (PALS) have succeeded in rewriting the constitution. Thanks to PALS, prisons everywhere are now filled with the sounds of laughter. To help you better understand the new humor laws, the government has published a 32-volume set of books entitled "The Helpful Government Humor Laws – or – How to Avoid Spending the Rest of Your Life Rotting in a Cold Prison Cell." Each month you'll be sent another beautiful, leather-bound book in the series. If you like it, keep it, and you will be billed just $499.95. If you don't, simply send it back, and within a few days your house will be completely surrounded by a S.W.A.T. team, every member of which will be hoping you make one false move. (Coming soon: The Humor Laws Collectible Plates.)

The secret decoder ring of the radical militant Lords of Laughter.

THE LAUGH TAX

Although spontaneous laughter is illegal under any circumstances, temporary laugh permits may be purchased in advance of laughter. This can prove helpful as long as you know well in advance that you are going to find something funny. All permits must be prominently displayed on the upper right-hand corner of your windshield or, when you're not in a vehicle, on a large sandwich board that must be worn at all times[1]. (Some government agents have noticed people laughing at these sandwich boards. To address this issue, the government is producing a miniseries entitled "The People Who Laughed at Sandwich Boards and Are Now Dead," starring Dom Deluise and Burt Reynolds.) Revenue generated from the laugh tax has been earmarked for new roads, schools and a luxurious hotel/dude ranch for all high-ranking government officials.

Using scale-model cars, a government official demonstrates how easily laughing drivers can lose control of their vehicles and run into each other. To heighten the drama, he is using the Smashomator-6000 – a machine that mimics the sounds of squealing tires, breaking glass and exploding gas tanks, all set to a variety of Hall and Oates songs.

Bear hockey is still legal in most states, but only if the bears are allowed to maul the audience between periods.

McSTOOLIE,
CRIME WEASEL

McStoolie needs you to help him "Rip a Limb Off of Crime."™ If you'd like to become a deputy crime weasel, you can start by organizing a local neighborhood mob program. All you need is a bunch of torches, some rope and a few dozen angry people with nothing better to do. With hard work, you too could be like model-citizen Jerry Pope, who has turned in 97.5% of his neighborhood. As a reward, Jerry now owns most of the block and is hard at work creating wax replicas of all his for-

Sleepdogs are now illegal. Unless, of course, they are rabid.

mer neighbors to keep him company. (Also be sure to look for the official plastic Crime Weasel badge and .38 revolver in every box of McStoolie Sugar Smackums.) As for us, we're concentrating our talents on government-approved, warm-and-fuzzy humor. For a copy of our new reel entitled "Sammy the Silly Salamander," call 612-332-8864 (Mpls.) or 213-960-3322 (L.A.).

[1] Keep an eye out for the sandwich-board sizing fashion to be unveiled in Paris next week. Saint fashion designer Coco Dubuvian, "My new designs are extremely, without being outrageous. I'm pushing the envelope of sandwich-board chic."

DUBLIN PRODUCTIONS

**TRADE B/W
OR COLOR
ANY SIZE:
CAMPAIGN**

SILVER

art directors
Jayne DeSesa
Ron Modica

writers
Paul Hackett
Brad Beerbohm
Emery Thompson

client
Newsweek

agency
Mezzina/Brown
New York

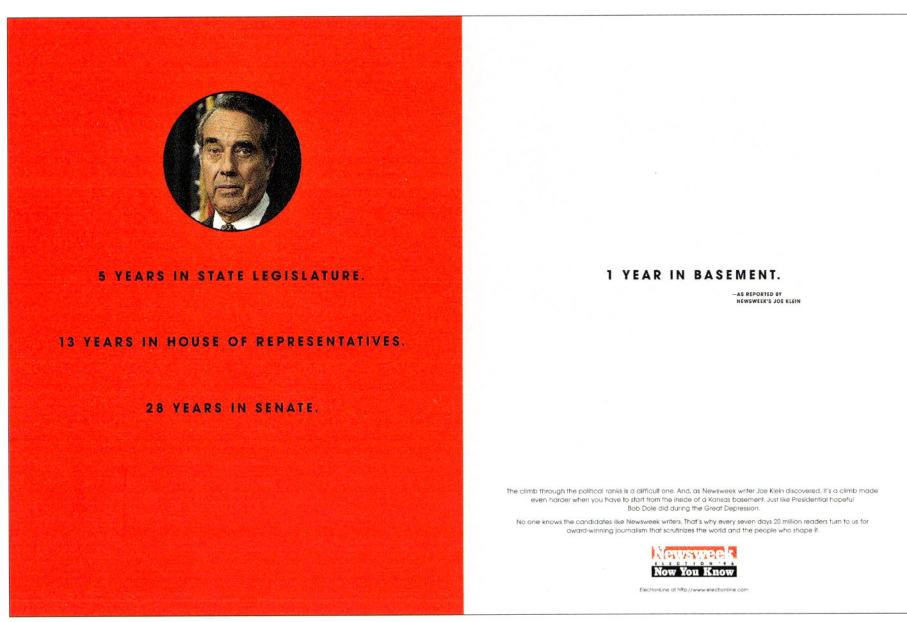

5 YEARS IN STATE LEGISLATURE.

13 YEARS IN HOUSE OF REPRESENTATIVES.

28 YEARS IN SENATE.

1 YEAR IN BASEMENT.

—AS REPORTED BY
NEWSWEEK'S JOE KLEIN

The climb through the political ranks is a difficult one. And, as Newsweek writer Joe Klein discovered, it's a climb made even harder when you have to start from the inside of a Kansas basement. Just like Presidential hopeful Bob Dole did during the Great Depression.

No one knows the candidates like Newsweek writers. That's why every seven days 20 million readers turn to us for award-winning journalism that scrutinizes the world and the people who shape it.

Newsweek
Now You Know

"THE V-CHIP IS SOMETHING
WE OUGHT TO DO."

"WE HAVE TO DO SOMETHING ABOUT
THE RAPID GROWTH IN VIOLENCE AMONG
OUR VERY YOUNG PEOPLE."

"IT'S DISTURBING, THE EXPOSURE FROM
VERY YOUNG AGES TO HOURS UPON HOURS
OF MINDLESS VIOLENCE."

"I'M SOMEONE WHO HAS A DEEP EMOTIONAL
ATTACHMENT TO STARSKY & HUTCH."

—PRESIDENT BILL CLINTON
IN REFERENCE TO A TV RATING
SYSTEM FOR CHILDREN, AS REPORTED
BY NEWSWEEK'S RICK MARIN

Ask President Clinton about his feelings on televised violence and you'll get a commentary on the negative psychological and behavioral effects it has on our children. But, as Newsweek writer Rick Marin discovered, bring up a certain '70's cop show famous for a flashy red Gran Torino and cheesy fight scenes, and you may get an answer you weren't quite expecting.

No one knows the candidates like Newsweek writers. That's why every seven days 20+ million readers turn to us for award-winning journalism that scrutinizes the world and the people who shape it.

Newsweek
Now You Know

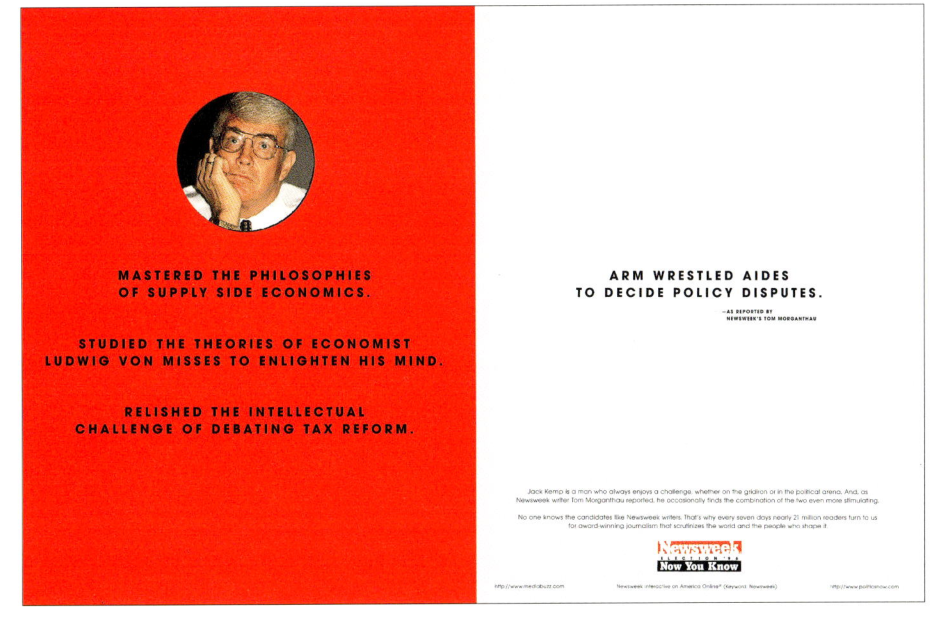

MASTERED THE PHILOSOPHIES
OF SUPPLY SIDE ECONOMICS.

STUDIED THE THEORIES OF ECONOMIST
LUDWIG VON MISSES TO ENLIGHTEN HIS MIND.

RELISHED THE INTELLECTUAL
CHALLENGE OF DEBATING TAX REFORM.

ARM WRESTLED AIDES
TO DECIDE POLICY DISPUTES.

—AS REPORTED BY
NEWSWEEK'S TOM MORGANTHAU

Jack Kemp is a man who always enjoys a challenge, whether on the gridiron or in the political arena. And, as Newsweek writer Tom Morganthau reported, he occasionally finds the combination of the two even more stimulating.

No one knows the candidates like Newsweek writers. That's why every seven days nearly 21 million readers turn to us for award-winning journalism that scrutinizes the world and the people who shape it.

Newsweek
Now You Know

GOLD, SILVER &
BRONZE AWARDS

GOLD, SILVER &
BRONZE AWARDS

TRADE B/W
OR COLOR
ANY SIZE:
CAMPAIGN

BRONZE

art director
Todd Riddle

writer
David Lowe

photographer
Jim Flynn

client
Stoddard's

agency
Arnold Advertising/
Boston

YOU SPENT WEEKS PLANNING YOUR ESCAPE FROM THE WORLD OF WORK. YOU TIED A ZILLION FLIES. THEN DROVE FOR HOURS. AND YOU DIDN'T DO ALL THAT JUST TO ADMIRE THE BEAUTY OF THE WOODS. NOPE. SOMETIMES YOU WANT TO CATCH FISH.

NO TELEPHONES.

NO COMPUTERS. NO BOSS.

THERE SURE AS HELL BETTER NOT BE NO FISH.

BIG ONES AND LOTS OF THEM. THAT'S WHERE STODDARD'S COMES IN. WE BECAME AMERICA'S OLDEST FISHING STORE BY DOING ONE THING REALLY WELL. HELPING FISHERMEN CATCH FISH. CALL US AT 617-426-4187 AND SEE WHAT WE CAN DO FOR YOU.

STODDARD'S
AMERICA'S OLDEST FISHING STORE

NOTHING PUTS THINGS IN PERSPECTIVE LIKE A FEW HOURS OF CONTEMPLATIVE CASTING. AFTER A VERY SHORT TIME YOU REALIZE THAT NOTHING IS WORTH OBSESSING OVER. EXCEPT, OF COURSE, FISHING, WHICH IS PRECISELY WHAT WE HAVE
YOU CAN'T RUN AWAY FROM YOUR PROBLEMS.
BUT YOU CAN WADE.
BEEN DOING AT STODDARD'S SINCE 1800. SO THE NEXT TIME YOU'RE FEELING THE URGE TO RUN AWAY, PICK UP YOUR PHONE INSTEAD AND GIVE US A CALL AT 617-xxx-xxxx. YOU'LL FIND THE FINEST IN RODS, REELS, AND OF COURSE, WADERS.

BY NATURE, FISHERMEN LIKE TO KEEP THEIR FAVORITE SPOTS TO THEMSELVES. SO TO THOSE OF YOU WHO HAVEN'T YET MANAGED TO PAY US A VISIT, WE URGE YOU TO READ ON. AS AMERICA'S OLDEST FISHING STORE, WE'VE BEEN SUPPLYING THE FINEST IN
PEOPLE SAY OUR STORE IS HARD TO FIND.
ISN'T THAT TRUE OF MOST GOOD FISHING SPOTS?
RODS, REELS, WADERS, FLIES, FLY-TYING EQUIPMENT AND MORE SINCE 1800. TRUE, WE ARE A LITTLE OFF THE BEATEN PATH, LOCATED ON TEMPLE STREET IN DOWNTOWN BOSTON. BUT CALL US AT 617-xxx-xxxx AND WE'LL GUIDE YOU RIGHT TO OUR DOOR.

**TRADE B/W
OR COLOR
ANY SIZE:
CAMPAIGN**

BRONZE

art director
Jimmy Bonner

writer
Denzil Strickland

photographer
Kelli Coggins

client
Disney Business
Productions

agency
Cole Henderson
Drake/Atlanta

Need something spectacular for your next business meeting? Call 407-934-6628.
Disney Business Productions
meetings and corporate events

Need something spectacular for your next business meeting? Call 407-934-6628.
Disney Business Productions
meetings and corporate events

**COLLATERAL
BROCHURES
OTHER THAN
BY MAIL**

GOLD

art directors
Peter Di Grazia
Tom Saputo
John Doyle

writers
Linda Bradford
Rebecca Rivera
Tom McCarthy
Dave O'Hare

photographers
Peter Seaward
Gary Hush
R.J. Muna
Jeff Nadler
Nadav Kander

illustrator
David Kimble

client
GMEVI/Saturn
Corporation

agency
Hal Riney & Partners/
San Francisco

GOLD, SILVER &
BRONZE AWARDS

SILVER

art directors
Kurt Georg Dieckert
Eric Urmetzer
Walter Schönauer

designers
Kurt Georg Dieckert
Eric Urmetzer
Walter Schönauer

photographers
Markus Bolsinger
Michele Comte
Peter Lindbergh
Eberhard Sauer

client
Mercedes-Benz AG/
Stuttgart

agency
Springer & Jacoby
Werbung GmbH/
Hamburg

COLLATERAL
SALES KITS

GOLD

art director
Steve Mitchell

writer
Matt Elhardt

photographer
Curtis Johnson

client
Rohol

agency
Hunt Adkins/
Minneapolis

GOLD, SILVER &
BRONZE AWARDS

SILVER

art directors
Paul Curtin
Kevin Brown

writer
Rob Price

photographers
Hunter Freeman
Keith Silva
David Campbell

client
Polaroid
Corporation

agency
Goodby Silverstein &
Partners/San Francisco

**COLLATERAL
SALES KITS**

BRONZE

art director
Brian Tortora

writer
Court Crandall

photographers
Simon Bruty
Laura Crosta

client
ESPN2

agency
Ground Zero/
Santa Monica

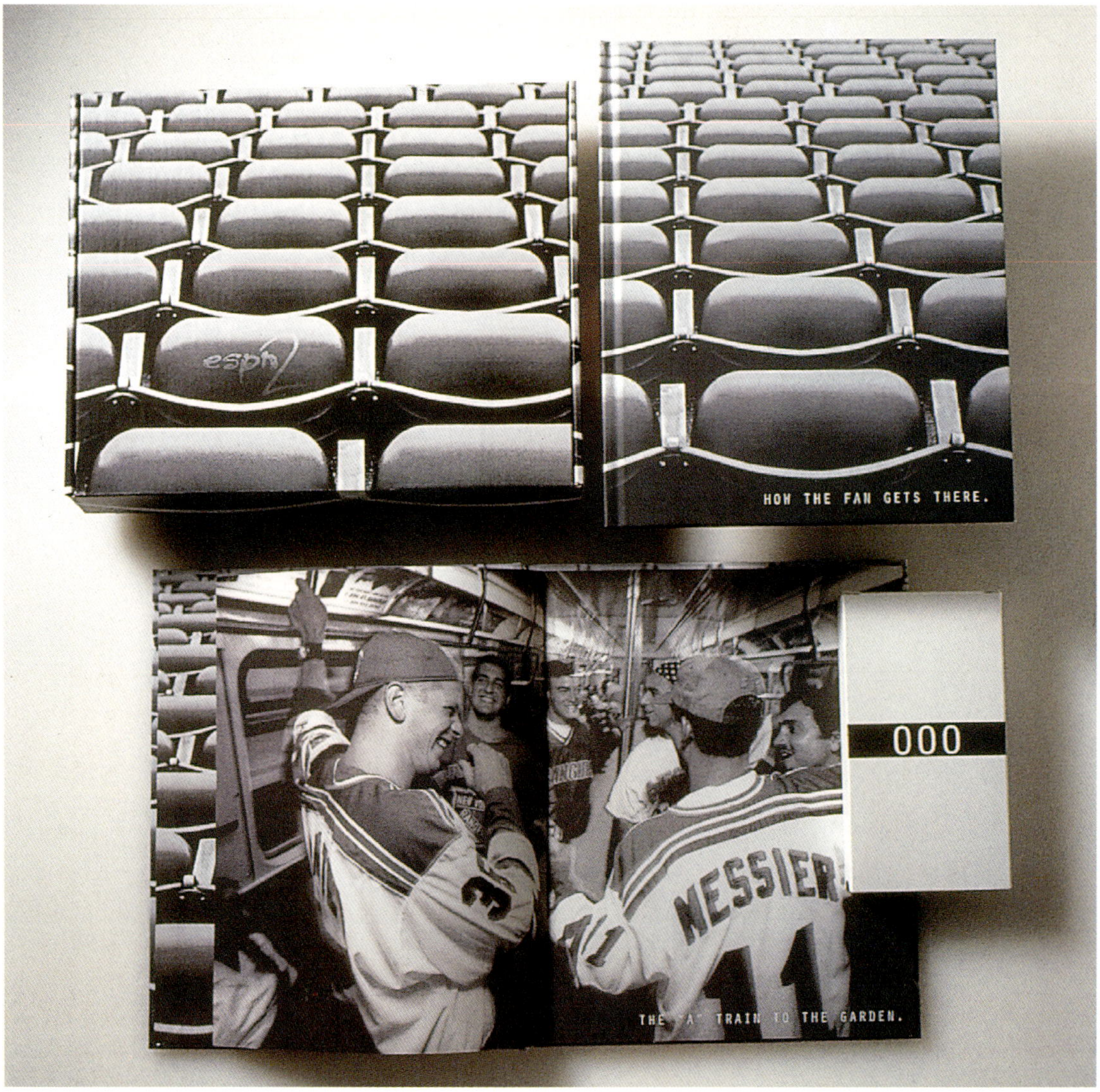

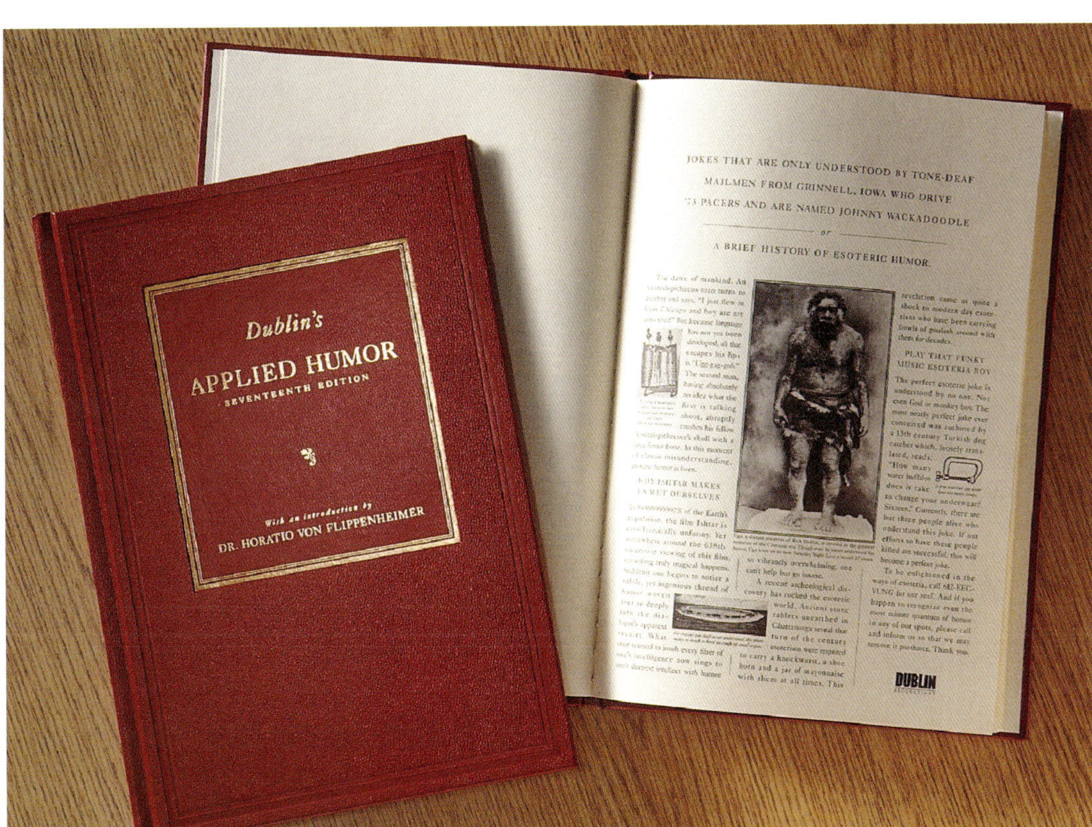

GOLD, SILVER &
BRONZE AWARDS

COLLATERAL
DIRECT MAIL:
SINGLE

GOLD

art director
Steve Mitchell

writer
Doug Adkins

client
Dublin Productions

agency
Hunt Adkins/
Minneapolis

**COLLATERAL
DIRECT MAIL:
SINGLE**

SILVER

art director
Steve Mitchell

writer
Matt Elhardt

client
Rohol

agency
Hunt Adkins/
Minneapolis

BRONZE

art director
Flip Namur

writer
Rik Meyers

photographer
Jake Armour

client
Advertising Federation
of Minnesota

agency
Kerker Marketing
Communications/
Minneapolis

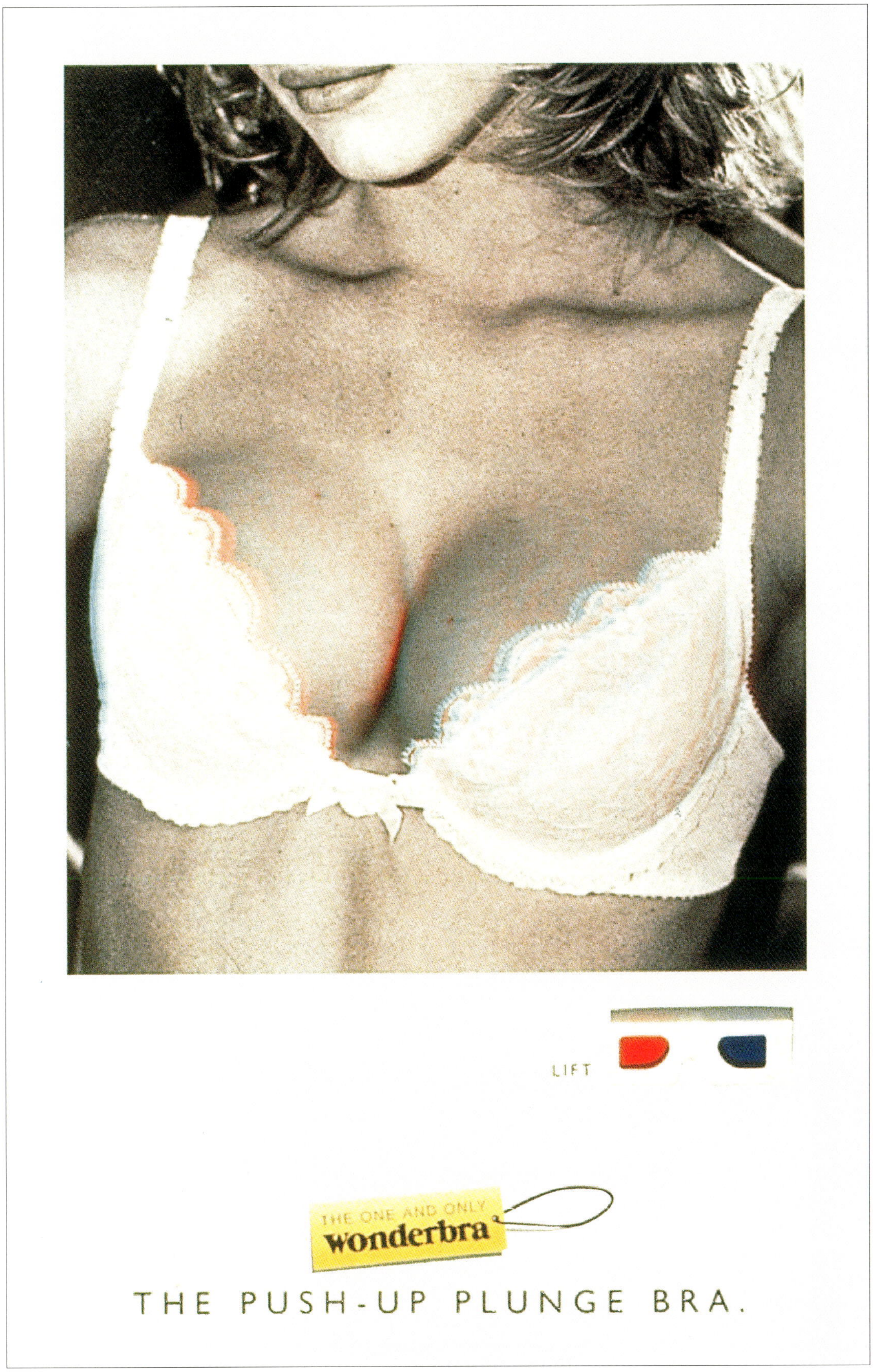

GOLD, SILVER &
BRONZE AWARDS

**COLLATERAL
POINT OF
PURCHASE
AND IN-STORE**

GOLD

art director
Anton Crone

writer
Anton Crone

client
Playtex

agency
Hunt Lascaris TBWA /
Johannesburg

THE PUSH-UP PLUNGE BRA.

COLLATERAL POINT OF PURCHASE AND IN-STORE

SILVER

art directors
Rochelle Senz
Doug Chapman

writer
Mick O'Brien

illustrators
Greg Dearth
Jim Millerick

client
Lahey Hitchcock Clinic

agency
Allen & Gerritsen/
Watertown, MA

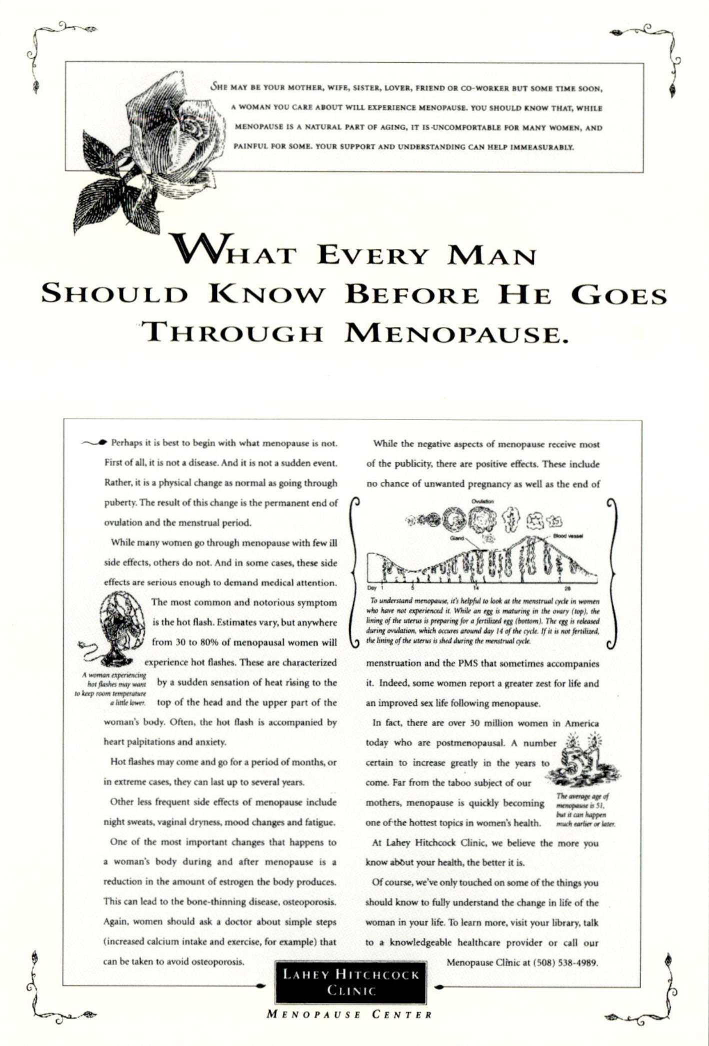

SILVER

art director
John Stertz

writer
Wade Sturdivant

client
McDonald's

agency
Fahlgren/Tampa

GOLD, SILVER &
BRONZE AWARDS

BRONZE

art director
Jeffrey Hilts
writer
Hagan Ainsworth
photographer
Robert Earnest
client
RJ Clarke
Tobacconist
agency
The Unemployment
Agency / Vancouver

**COLLATERAL
SELF-PROMOTION**

GOLD

art director
Steve Sandstrom

writers
Austin Howe
Peter Wegner
Amy Krouse Rosenthal
Jean Rhode

client
Sandstrom Design

agency
Sandstrom Design /
Portland

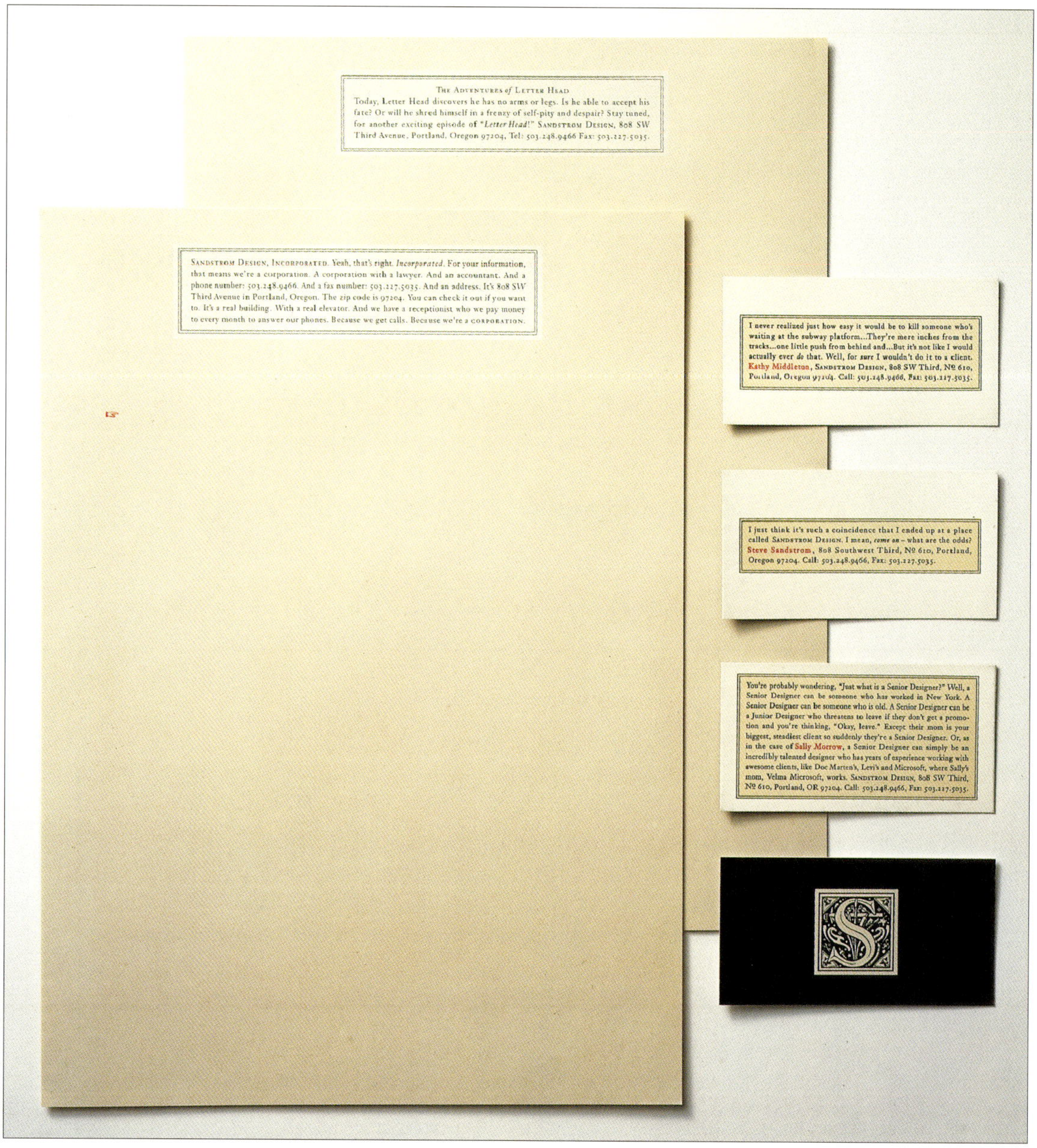

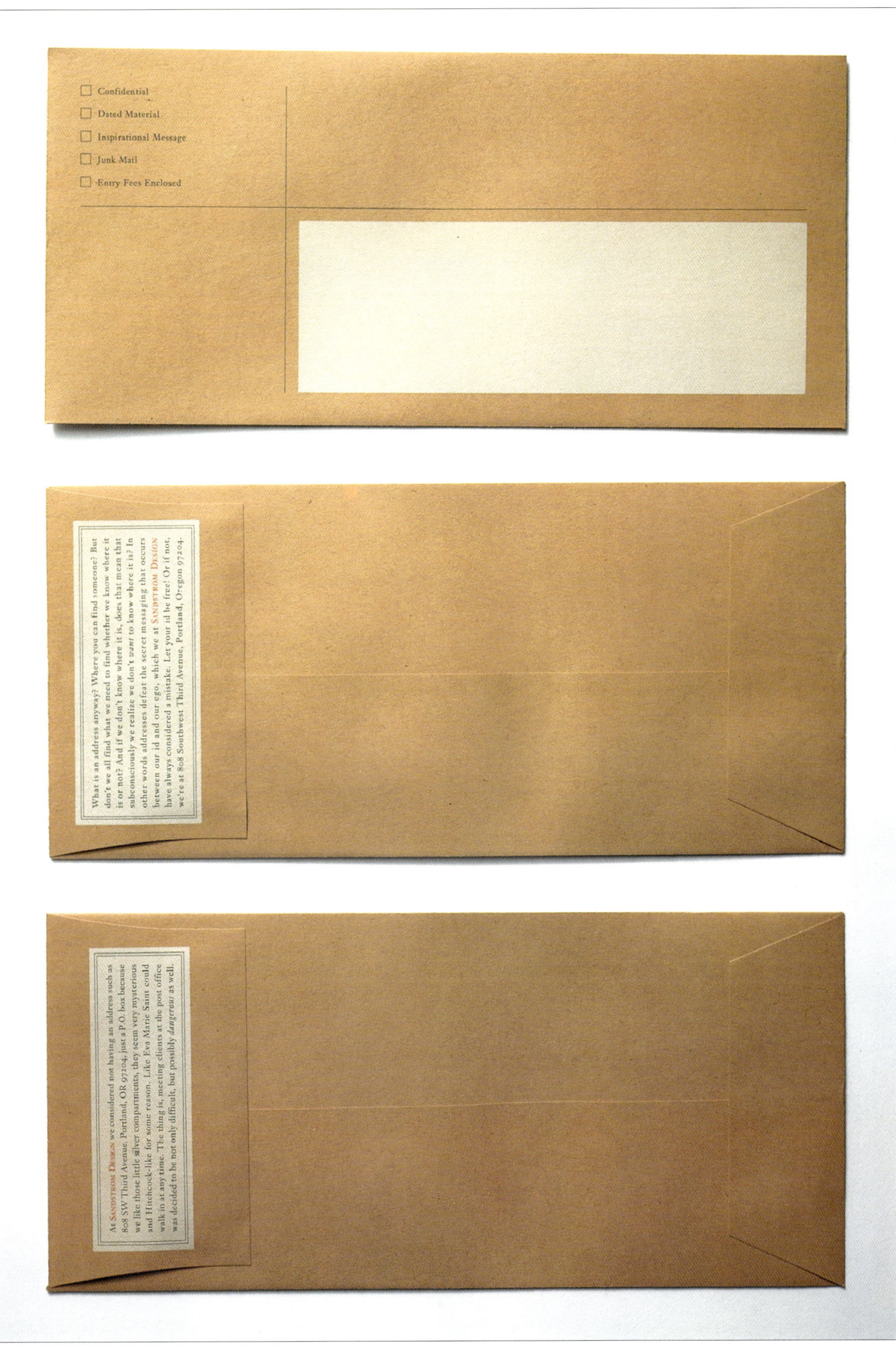

Confidential
Dated Material
Inspirational Message
Junk Mail
Entry Fees Enclosed
What is an address anyway? Where you can find someone? But don't we all find what we need to find whether we know where it is or not? And if we don't know where it is, does that mean that subconsciously we realize we don't want to know where it is? In other words addresses defeat the secret messaging that occurs between our id and our ego, which we at SANDSTROM DESIGN have always considered a mistake. Let your id be free! Or if not, we're at 808 Southwest Third Avenue, Portland, Oregon 97204.
At SANDSTROM DESIGN we considered not having an address such as 808 SW Third Avenue, Portland, OR 97204, just a P.O. box because we like those little silver compartments, they seem very mysterious and Hitchcock-like for some reason. Like Eva Marie Saint could walk in at any time. The thing is, meeting clients at the post office was decided to be not only difficult, but possibly dangerous as well.

**COLLATERAL
SELF-PROMOTION**

SILVER

art directors
Steve Dunn
Dave Dye

writer
Tim Delaney

designers
Steve Dunn
Dave Dye

client
Leagas Delaney

agency
Leagas Delaney/
London

BRONZE

art directors
Jessica Schulman
Margaret Midgett

client
TBWA Chiat/Day

agency
TBWA Chiat/Day,
Venice, CA

GOLD, SILVER &
BRONZE AWARDS

**PUBLIC SERVICE/
POLITICAL
NEWSPAPER
OR MAGAZINE:
SINGLE**

GOLD

art director
Jamie Mahoney

writer
Joe Alexander

client
Mothers Against
Drunk Driving

agency
The Martin Agency/
Richmond

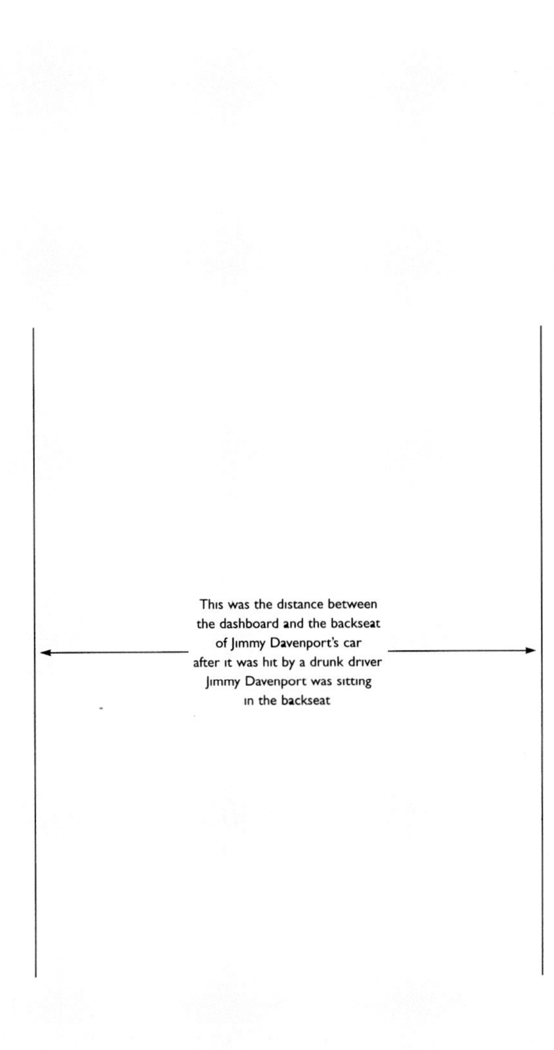

IN 1762 Sir John Griffin Griffin, then *owner* of AUDLEY END HOUSE, appointed 'Capability' Brown to transform the formal gardens into the sort of idyllic landscape he had made *fashionable*. His design opened up wonderful panoramic views from the house, the best being from the Temple of Concord on the hill behind the main building. An exploration of the garden *reveals* a host of picturesque features. There's a beautiful woodland grove, a pond garden, a waterwheel and a delightful classical bridge designed by Robert Adam. The Temple of Concord was built in the late eighteenth century to celebrate George III's recovery from his first attack of insanity. Despite the fact that it has no roof and is wearing in places, it does retain its *fine* original proportions.

ALTHOUGH lying some distance behind Hadrian's Wall, the site at *Corbridge* most certainly played a supporting role as the Roman Empire attempted to extend its rule northwards. The remains at Corbridge clearly indicate that this was once a major garrison town. Still *visible* are the ruins of the main street, the granaries, the temples and some military buildings including the barracks. These, along with the various coins, gaming boards, cooking pots and candlesticks inside the Corbridge museum, provide a good insight into the Roman way of life. But the *real* find came in 1964 when the remains of a wooden chest were unearthed. This contained a truly incredible *collection* of spearheads, pickaxes, knives, plate armour and furniture fittings. All of which are now on display in the museum.

DESIGNED to cater for James I and his entourage, *Audley End House*, situated just one mile from Saffron Walden in Essex, cost the vast sum of £200,000 to build in 1614. It has since acquired a *reputation* as one of the greatest country houses in England. The portraits and furnishings in the magnificent Great Hall, such as the splendid wooden JACOBEAN SCREEN, were installed here by Lord Braybrooke in the 1820s. The Little Drawing Room, Great Drawing Room and Dining Room, which were all designed by the renowned Robert Adam, are fine examples of eighteenth-century luxury. The Little Drawing Room, in particular, is something of an architectural *gem*. Based on the style of ancient Rome, with the wall panels and ceilings painted by Biagio Rebecca, it is just one of many lovely rooms on view.

HADRIAN'S WALL

IS MUCH MORE PLEASANT THESE DAYS. EVERYBODY LEAVES WITH EXACTLY THE SAME NUMBER OF LIMBS THEY CAME WITH.

RISING majestically from a scenic hilltop is the *enchanting* spectacle of Bolsover Castle. A castle in name alone, it is, in all truth, a seventeenth-century mansion built on the location of a twelfth-century castle for Sir Charles Cavendish. There are actually three buildings of particular interest at BOLSOVER. You can admire the remains of the imposing *Terrace Range* which have survived for 250 years. An irregular-looking dwelling due to the fact that it was designed and redesigned according to different changes in taste over the three decades it took to build. There's the *Riding School* which hosted high-school riding shows and is perhaps the birthplace of British equestrianism. And no day out at Bolsover is complete without a visit to the charming *Little Castle*. This romantic 'keep' was built in Jacobean and Gothic style and adorned with oak panels, intricate carvings and luxuriant fireplaces. Despite the name and despite its battlemented turrets, it was not a castle. Merely an indulgence by the somewhat theatrical Sir Charles Cavendish.

ON June 30th this year, the grounds of *Bolsover Castle* will host a wonderful Children's Festival. It's a joint initiative by English Heritage and Junction Arts, the local community arts project. Children will be able to take part in numerous activities themed around music, history, drama and environmental issues. There will be *storytelling*, *dance* and *puppetry*, to name a fraction of the events happening. All set against the scenic backdrop of the magnificent Bolsover Castle.

The Wall at Cawfields, looking west.

IN the ancient wooded valley of the North Tyne, Northumberland, stands the best *preserved* Roman cavalry fort in the country. One of many permanent troop bases added to HADRIAN'S WALL, *Chesters Fort* housed some 500 soldiers. Repeated attacks by northern tribes aside, manning Hadrian's Wall had its good points. Troops were able to unwind in the treatment rooms or the famous bath house (the remains of which are still visible). This even boasted an underground heating system and hot dry rooms, almost like saunas, where the walls and the floors were burning hot with air from charcoal furnaces. The on-site museum, namely the *Clayton Collection*, contains many a fine piece of Roman craftsmanship. Among them, one of the most impressive sculptures of the period: a representation of *June* who is shown standing on a bull. Another stone, that probably embellished the baths, portrays *Neptune* reclining. These, and countless other sculptures and carvings from the Roman period of rule, were all found at Chesters or elsewhere at Hadrian's Wall.

A TRIP to the northernmost parts of England during Emperor Hadrian's reign wasn't quite the delightful *day out* it is today. Marauding local tribes, hostile to the foreign presence of Rome, were often involved in brutal conflicts with Hadrian's troops. In AD 122, to keep these bloodthirsty northern 'savages' away from the Roman's 'civilised' world, the emperor ordered the construction of a 73-mile *wall* which would run from coast to coast along the north of England. Each mile punctuated by a small fort. So *outstanding* is this piece of Roman military engineering that Hadrian's Wall has since been designated a World Heritage Site. For more information on English Heritage and our role in preserving the nation's significant buildings, please *call* 0171 973 3434 or *visit* any one of our 400 sites.

It's yours. Why not visit it.

ENGLISH HERITAGE

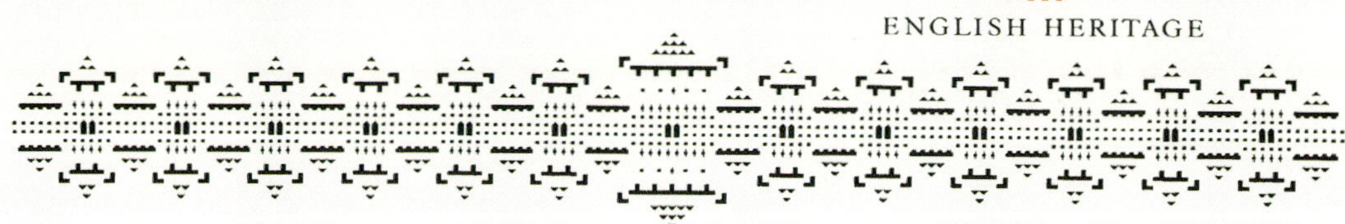

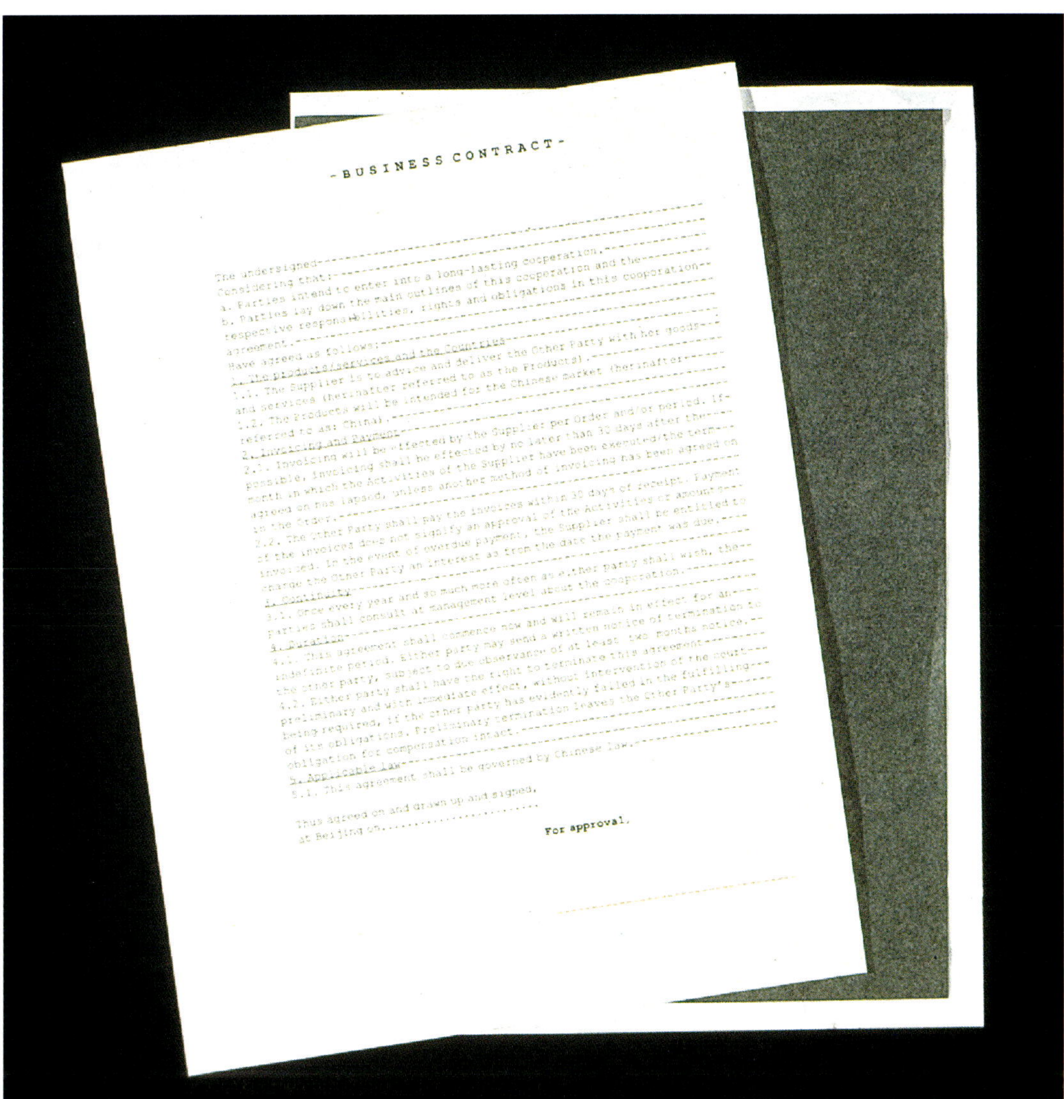
- BUSINESS CONTRACT -

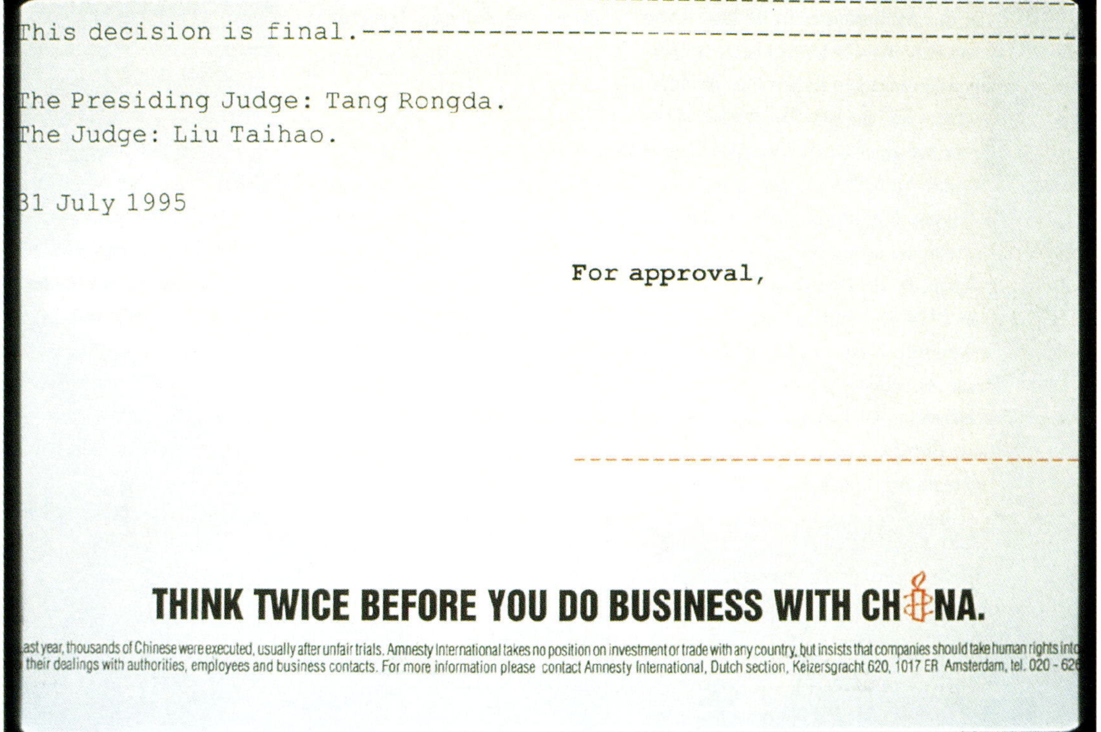
This decision is final.

The Presiding Judge: Tang Rongda.
The Judge: Liu Taihao.

31 July 1995

For approval,

THINK TWICE BEFORE YOU DO BUSINESS WITH CHINA.

Last year, thousands of Chinese were executed, usually after unfair trials. Amnesty International takes no position on investment or trade with any country, but insists that companies should take human rights into
their dealings with authorities, employees and business contacts. For more information please contact Amnesty International, Dutch section, Keizersgracht 620, 1017 ER Amsterdam, tel. 020 - 626

**PUBLIC SERVICE/
POLITICAL
NEWSPAPER
OR MAGAZINE:
SINGLE**

BRONZE

art directors
Tim Ryan
Kerry Koritsas

writers
Mark Greenspun
Leslie Sims

client
Library of Congress

agency
Adworks/
Washington, DC

*The song above was written by Schumann as
an expression of love for his wife, Clara.*

*The song below was written by Brahms as an
expression of love for Schumann's wife, Clara.*

(Above) According to Clara's notation in the top right hand corner,
Brahms gave her this ornately decorated copy of "To a Violet" on her birthday.
(Top) Schumann's not-so-fancy draft of "The Shepherd's Farewell."

hough it's never been proven, there's a lot of speculation that music wasn't the only thing for which Robert Schumann and Johannes Brahms shared a love.

The setting was Germany, 1853. Schumann and his wife Clara were, by most accounts, a happily married couple. In fact, during just one year of marriage, Schumann wrote 150 songs out of love for his Clara.

Enter Johannes Brahms. A handsome, young musical prodigy who managed to make quite an impact on the Schumanns. The three became very close.

Brahms moved in. And, for a while, all three made beautiful music together – Brahms taking instruction from Schumann and Clara supporting everyone by playing the piano in concerts.

After awhile, Schumann had a mental breakdown and in 1856 died in an asylum.

Clara Wieck Schumann. The object of her husband's affections. And perhaps those of Brahms as well?

For the next 40 years, Brahms and Clara occasionally lived in the same building together. Often performed in concert together. And, until their deaths, which occurred within just a few months of each other, the two remained "very close friends".

Exactly what Clara and Brahms meant to each other, no one will ever know. But here is something that can't be disputed: Now through July 13, two original artifacts of this unusual relationship, Brahms' "To a Violet" and Schumann's "The Shepherd's Farewell," will be on display at the Library of Congress.

They're here on loan as part of an exhibition from the Saxon State

Library in Dresden, Germany.

Along with them, you can see Martin Luther's original New Testament, responsible for adding hundreds of denominations to the Christian faith. Grimace over the details of 16th century equestrian dental procedures. And find out why Germany's most famed musical troupe from 400 years ago, the Hofkapelle, today would give *Mrs. Doubtfire* a run for its money.

These Saxon State Library treasures have survived the Dark Ages, the devastation of World War II, and for the last 50 years they were all but inaccessible to most Americans, locked away behind the Iron Curtain.

They're here for the first time. And it's uncertain when, or if, they'll ever be here again.

The exhibition is on display in the Great Hall of the Library of

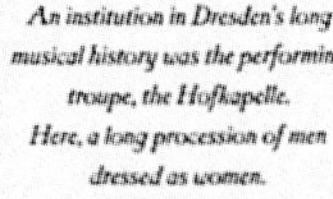

An institution in Dresden's long musical history was the performing troupe, the Hofkapelle. Here, a long procession of men dressed as women.

Congress, open Monday through Saturday, from 10 a.m. to 5:30 p.m. For any additional information, call (202) 707-8000.

Dresden: Treasures from the Saxon State Library

BRONZE

art director
Dave Dye

writer
Sean Doyle

typographer
Dave Wakefield

client
English Heritage

agency
Leagas Delaney/
London

THIS August Bank Holiday, Dover Castle sees a *return* to one of the most important dates in our nation's history. The eve of D-Day, 1944. Hundreds of British servicemen, German prisoners of war and military vehicles will be re-enacting the movements that were to signal the beginning of the end of the war as the allied forces prepared to land in Normandy. The *command room* will be functioning at full speed, *dispatches* will be arriving, *25lb guns* will be loaded, *lookout stations* will be manned. It'll be just *like* Dover Castle was in the old days. A frightening place to be. Only this time, your chances of returning home safely, you'll be pleased to learn, are 100%.

THE *Princess of Wales' Royal Regiment* have had rather an eventful few centuries. Since 1572, when a Tudor company first travelled across the Channel to help the Dutch fight against Spain, they've served in the Napoleonic War, the Crimean War, the Boer War, the First World War. The list goes on. As does the number of medals they've received. 56 Victoria Crosses, no less. With the use of special effects and stunning sets, we've recreated life on board a Regiment ship. As you walk through lifelike displays, you'll get some idea of what it was like to be a marine three centuries ago. You will also *experience* the atmosphere of WWI trenches and see the very ball that was kicked into no-man's-land by the East Surreys.

Although a fortified settlement since the Iron Age, Dover Castle has only been in its existent form since the late 12th century. It was in 1179 when Henry II's builder, Maurice the Engineer, began the construction of the large rectangular Keep which is the magnificent centrepiece of the castle. The rough masonry walls measure between 5.2 and 6.4 metres in thickness. However, impenetrability wasn't the only prerequisite. The Keep was, after all, to be home to the King on occasion. Hence the splendid royal apartments on the upper storey. Encircled by a mural gallery and featuring elaborately decorated window embrasures, they provide a more grandiose contrast to the rooms beneath. Even the Chapel upstairs is considerably larger and more ornate than its lower equivalent.

MANY people know that Desmond Llewellyn played the part of Q in the Bond movies. Fewer people, perhaps, are aware of the fact that Q was playing *the part of* one CHARLES FRASER-SMITH: the man who was the inspiration for Fleming's shrewd inventor. Based within the Clothing Department of the Ministry of Supply, Fraser-Smith appeared to be nothing more than an unremarkable civil servant. But he was actually the *mastermind* in one of Britain's most secret projects, his inventions playing a major part in the Second World War victory. *The Live and Let Spy* exhibition at Dover Castle takes you into the world of the secret agent. You'll see a number of Fraser-Smith's devices, like the shaving brush that carried some photographic film of German installations. The seemingly innocuous jacket button, in reality a tiny compass. And the playing card with, believe it or not, a map hidden inside it. There's even an interactive section which determines whether you've got exactly *what it takes* in order to become a leading secret agent.

WHILST

WINSTON CHURCHILL WAS INVOLVED IN OPERATION DYNAMO AT DOVER CASTLE, DOCTOR JENKINS WAS INVOLVED IN OPERATION BERT'S LEFT LEG 6o FEET BELOW.

THE oldest building on the site of Dover Castle is the *Pharos*, the ancient Roman lighthouse which dates from the first century AD. It remains one of the tallest Roman structures still standing in Europe. More recent is the Saxon church of *St. Mary-in-Castro* [circa 10th century] which, despite the crude nineteenth-century modernisation, remains virtually in its original state. It is also well worth visiting *Queen Elizabeth's Pocket Pistol*. Scarcely pocket sized though, it's a 7 metre sixteenth-century gun which was capable of firing a shot a distance of seven miles.

BURIED in the white cliffs of Dover, beneath the most celebrated major fortress in Britain's history, are The Secret Wartime Tunnels. Open to the public since 1990, having come off the original official secrets list four years earlier, they were home to the Underground Hospital. This hospital,

which has been reconstructed in authentic detail gives you some insight into the experiences of Second World War casualties. A vast amount of the original furnishings and equipment have been collected and reinstalled. Home Front propaganda lines the walls, including the famous 'Careless Talk Costs Lives' poster. 1940's cigarette packets, old newspapers and a half-played game of draughts rest on tables. The wartime flavour is enhanced by the soundtrack which plays on your guided tour of the Tunnels. You'll hear the conversations of hospital staff and the sound of air raids and bombings. There's even that distinctive hospital smell to greet you as you enter the operating theatre, followed by the nasal 'delight' of boiled cabbage emanating from the kitchens.

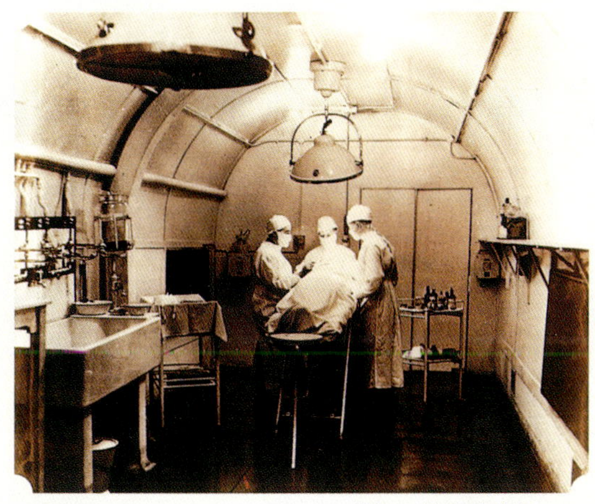

The Underground Hospital at Dover Castle.

DURING World War II, when many British women and children found refuge in London's tube stations, many British soldiers were hiding in an underground system too: *The Secret Wartime Tunnels* beneath Dover Castle. A maze of passages, offices and hospital dormitories which served as a military base for Churchill's troops. It was here that one Vice-Admiral Ramsay *masterminded* the evacuation of Dunkirk. And here that hundreds of casualties of war received the finest of medical attention. You can *experience* their sights, sounds and even smells at Dover Castle. To find out more information on English Heritage and our role in preserving the nation's significant buildings, please *call* 0171 973 3434 or *visit* any one of our 400 sites.

It's yours. Why not visit it.

ENGLISH HERITAGE

PUBLIC SERVICE/ POLITICAL NEWSPAPER OR MAGAZINE: CAMPAIGN

GOLD

art director
Dave Dye

writer
Sean Doyle

typographer
Dave Wakefield

client
English Heritage

agency
Leagas Delaney/ London

IN 1092 William Rufus, angered that Carlisle was *proclaimed* part of Scotland, went north, drove the Scots out and ordered the building of a stronghold in the borderlands. Thus *Carlisle Castle* was constructed just half a mile outside the city. And ever since it has been the scene of numerous battles with different factions fighting for ownership. It was besieged by parliamentarians in the Civil War, then by Bonnie Prince Charlie during the Jacobite Rising. In order to repel such attacks, the castle defences have been extensively remodelled over the centuries. Perhaps the most notable 'guest' at Carlisle Castle was *Mary Queen of Scots*, a prisoner there back in 1568. You can see Queen Mary's Tower and take the very route she took during her daily walks around the grounds.

THIS year marks the 250th anniversary of the imprisonment of *Jacobites* inside Carlisle Castle following the 1745 Rising. Led by Bonnie Prince Charlie, they succeeded in taking Carlisle Castle before marching southwards to claim the throne for Charlie's father, James Stuart. An *exhibition* within the castle tells the dramatic story of the Jacobites' movements. *How* they returned north in defeat with the Duke of Cumberland's men hot on their heels. *How* they were captured and imprisoned, many of them later to be hanged, drawn and quartered on the nearby *Gallows Hill*. In a dungeon, you will see the famous *Licking Stones*. A permanently moist wall which provided a little water for the Jacobites in this overcrowded prison.

Located in the small village of Belsay, 14 miles north-west of Newcastle, *Belsay Hall* consists of a well-preserved fourteenth-century castle, the ruins of a seventeenth-century mansion and one of the most important *neo-classical* houses in Britain. But the real jewels in the crown are the 30 acres of magnificent formal gardens, exotic quarry gardens and woodland that surround the buildings. A stroll through the grounds at Belsay

reveals sycamore, oak and ash trees, the Magnolia Terrace, the Rhododendron Garden, the lovely Meadow Garden. Much of what you see there reflects the eccentric character of Sir Charles Monck. He returned from his 19-month European honeymoon, 1804-1806, full of ideas to build a *new home* at Belsay in beautiful neo-Greek style. And to have it set in an equally beautiful landscape.

TO celebrate the 1996 Year of Visual Arts, Belsay Hall will come alive again from 4th May until 26th October. The '*Living at Belsay*' exhibition will feature the work of selected craftsmakers and artists who'll be refurbishing the entrance and the three main reception rooms. It's a novel idea which will see the *normally* bare rooms equipped with magnificent furniture, fine ceramics, glassware and wall hangings. A rare chance to see contemporary artistry in an historical setting.

WHEN

YOU BUILD A CASTLE FOR A KING WHO'S RENOWNED FOR CHOPPING PEOPLE'S HEADS OFF, YOU BUILD A REALLY NICE CASTLE.

WHEN Osborne House was completed in 1851 to provide a country residence for Queen Victoria, it was considered by Her Majesty to be 'small and snug'. However, to humble subjects such as you and I, it is anything but. *Osborne*, on the Isle of Wight, served as a peaceful seaside retreat where Queen Victoria and Prince Albert could escape the strict confines of ceremony. And a *magnificent* retreat it is too. Albert's passion for the Italian *Renaissance* is clearly evident, what with the Italianate terrace, the Andromeda fountain and the cement copies of the fine Medici Lions from the *Loggia de' Lanzi*, Florence. Inside you will see a classical Roman statue, the *Marine Venus*, a lovely fresco painting by William Dyce and lots of extravagant grotesque decoration. In the Durbar Room there's a change of country, this state banqueting hall having been designed in the Indian style. Other rooms worth visiting are the Royal Apartments, the Billiards Room and the Nursery Suite. And the perfect way to *finish your day* at Osborne House is to take a Victorian horse and carriage ride from the main building to the delightful Swiss Cottage, a present from the Queen to her children in 1854.

HENRY VIII aside, many other royals have spent time at WALMER CASTLE. Amongst them Queen Victoria and the current Lord Warden, HRH *the Queen Mother*. Indeed, this delightful residence, just a mile from Deal in Kent, boasts an extremely impressive list of distinguished visitors. Like William Pitt the Younger, who was Lord Warden until his death in 1806. He would try and visit whenever his official duties would allow. A later Lord Warden, the *Duke of Wellington*, was equally taken with his 'charming marine residence'. His room is arranged just as it was during his stay, its plain, modest furnishings bearing testimony to the Iron Duke's preference for unsophisticated surroundings. You can see the very armchair where he died in 1852, his campaign-bed which still retains its original horsehair mattress and, in the WELLINGTON MUSEUM just along the corridor, the boots worn by the celebrated British war hero.

Walmer Castle, Kent.

DURABILITY, not beauty, was the main requirement in the construction of *Walmer Castle*. However, the architects, not wishing to take any chances with the notoriously hard to please Henry VIII, wisely decided to address both issues. One of a chain of coastal artillery forts, Walmer was built to thwart any invasions by Spain or France. This was a real possibility as Henry's split with the Roman Catholic Church and destruction of many monasteries had infuriated the papacy. The castle differed from earlier mediæval defences in that it had no high walls or lofty towers. In fact, so *attractive* was Walmer that only minor modifications were needed to make it the comfortable residence it is today. For more information on English Heritage and our role in preserving the nation's significant buildings please *call* 0171 973 3434 or *visit* any one of our 400 sites.

It's yours. Why not visit it.

ENGLISH HERITAGE

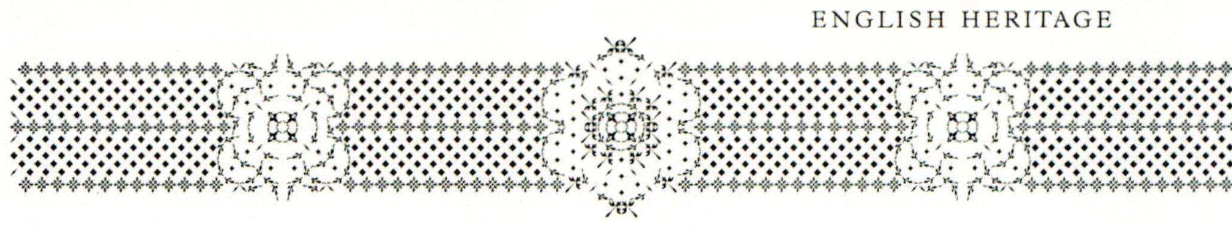

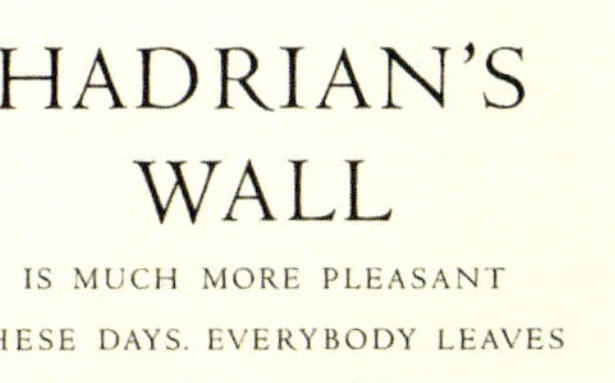

HADRIAN'S WALL

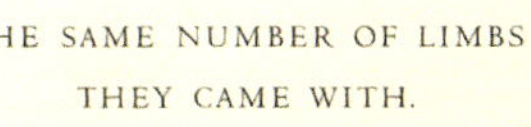

IS MUCH MORE PLEASANT
THESE DAYS. EVERYBODY LEAVES
WITH EXACTLY
THE SAME NUMBER OF LIMBS
THEY CAME WITH.

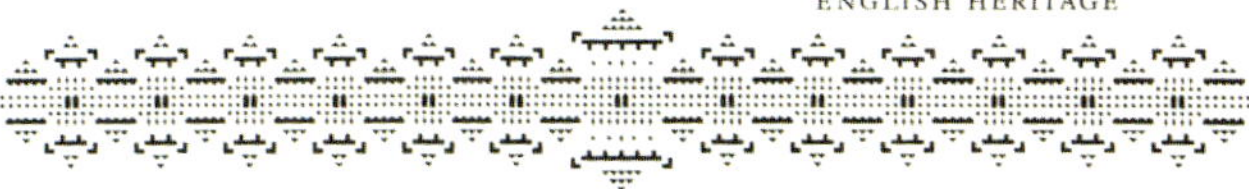

The Wall at Cawfields, looking west.

A TRIP to the northernmost parts of England during Emperor Hadrian's reign wasn't quite the delightful *day out* it is today. Marauding local tribes, hostile to the foreign presence of Rome, were often involved in brutal conflicts with Hadrian's troops. In AD 122, to keep these bloodthirsty northern 'savages' away from the Roman's 'civilised' world, the emperor ordered the construction of a 73-mile *wall* which would run from coast to coast along the north of England. Each mile punctuated by a small fort. So *outstanding* is this piece of Roman military engineering that Hadrian's Wall has since been designated a World Heritage Site. For more information on English Heritage and our role in preserving the nation's significant buildings, please *call* 0171 973 3434 or *visit* any one of our 400 sites.

It's yours. Why not visit it.

ENGLISH HERITAGE

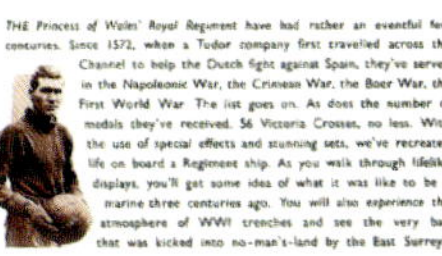

WHILST

WINSTON CHURCHILL
WAS INVOLVED IN OPERATION
DYNAMO AT DOVER CASTLE,
DOCTOR JENKINS WAS
INVOLVED IN OPERATION BERT'S
LEFT LEG 60 FEET BELOW.

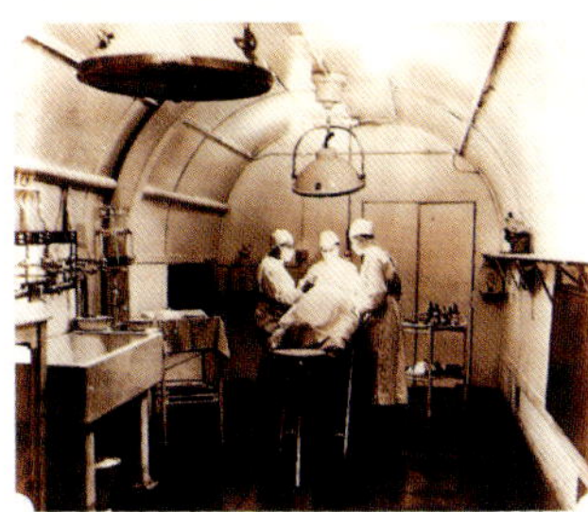

The Underground Hospital at Dover Castle.

D URING World War II, when many British women and children found refuge in London's tube stations, many British soldiers were hiding in an underground system too: *The Secret Wartime Tunnels* beneath Dover Castle. A maze of passages, offices and hospital dormitories which served as a military base for Churchill's troops. It was here that one Vice-Admiral Ramsay *masterminded* the evacuation of Dunkirk. And here that hundreds of casualties of war received the finest of medical attention. You can *experience* their sights, sounds and even smells at Dover Castle. To find out more information on English Heritage and our role in preserving the nation's significant buildings, please *call* 0171 973 3434 or *visit* any one of our 400 sites.

It's yours. Why not visit it.

ENGLISH HERITAGE

Augustus the Strong had innumerable illegitimate children, changed his religion just to become King, and locked a man in a cellar for 14 years until he perfected porcelain.

In his defense, he did open the first public library.

Augustus the Strong, Elector of Saxony, was a man of extremes. The way history pictures him, if there was any moderation in his life, no one can find it.

Take his unusual moniker "the Strong" for example. He got the name because of the infamous drinking bouts he was forever getting into; because of his amazing physical strength; and also because he allegedly fathered

This medallion graced the cover of one of Martin Luther's early Bibles. In the 16th century, books were incredibly expensive and were considered status symbols.

over 100 children. Only one of which, incidentally, was his wife.

And it doesn't stop there. Already the Elector of Saxony, he also wanted to be King of Poland. When told that his religion was a problem, he simply converted from Lutheranism to Catholicism to improve his shot at the throne.

Then, of course, there's unfortunate Johann Böttger, who was locked in a cellar for 14 years until he was able to duplicate precisely, the oriental porcelain that Augustus loved so much.

But, if Augustus was excessive on the personal side, he was no less driven on the public side of his life.

For instance, he spent lavishly on his personal library and took the unheard of step of opening it to the public. He did the same thing with his art collections. And, he made all operas free to the public.

Due in large part to the cultural excesses of Augustus, Dresden became a mecca for artists and

When Augustus ran out of room in the Zwinger (shown here), he moved his book collection to the Japanese Palace, designed by the famous architect Matthaus Pöppelmann.

scholars and remained that way for hundreds of years.

If you'd like to see more of the reign of Augustus the Strong, now is the time to do it. Because a rare group of historic treasures, on loan from the Saxon State Library in Dresden, Germany, is on display at the Library of Congress.

There are Augustus' Bibles (both Protestant and Catholic). Etchings of his palaces (both of them). A portrait of his son (the only legitimate one). And that's only the beginning. You'll also see Martin Luther's original New Testament printed in German — the book that started the Protestant Reformation. Original musical

A book illustrating ornate designs for regal sleds to be used by the Elector in parades and pageants. The custom of being dragged around in a sled – even when there was no snow – played an important role in enhancing the Elector's image before his subjects.

scores from the hands of Bach, Wagner and Vivaldi, a 700-year-old Jewish Holy Day Prayer Book and more.

Augustus the Strong, Elector of Saxony from 1693 to 1733. Perhaps a little egotistical and excessive in his personal life. But a real boon to the arts.

The exhibition includes objects that have survived the Dark Ages and the bombings of World War II. You've never seen them before. And after July 13th, you'll have to go all the way to Dresden to see them.

The exhibition is on display in the Great Hall of the Library of Congress, open Monday through Saturday, from 10 a.m. to 5:30 p.m. For any additional information, call (202) 707-8000.

❧ Dresden: Treasures from the Saxon State Library ❧

The song above was written by Schumann as an expression of love for his wife, Clara.

The song below was written by Brahms as an expression of love for Schumann's wife, Clara.

Though it's never been proven, there's a lot of speculation that music wasn't the only thing for which Robert Schumann and Johannes Brahms shared a love.

The setting was Germany, 1853. Schumann and his wife Clara were, by most accounts, a happily married couple. In fact, during just one year of marriage, Schumann wrote 150 songs out of love for his Clara.

Enter Johannes Brahms. A handsome, young musical prodigy who managed to make quite an impact on the Schumanns. The three became very close.

Brahms moved in. And, for a while, all three made beautiful music together – Brahms taking instruction from Schumann and Clara supporting everyone by playing the piano in concerts.

After awhile, Schumann had a mental breakdown and in 1856 died in an asylum.

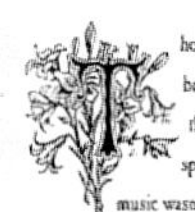

Clara Wieck Schumann. The object of her husband's affections. And perhaps those of Brahms as well?

For the next 40 years, Brahms and Clara occasionally lived in the same building together. Often performed in concert together. And, until their deaths, which occurred within just a few months of each other, the two remained "very close friends".

Exactly what Clara and Brahms meant to each other, no one will ever know. But here is something that can't be disputed: Now through July 13, two original artifacts of this unusual relationship, Brahms' "To a Violet" and Schumann's "The Shepherd's Farewell," will be on display at the Library of Congress.

(Above) According to Clara's notation in the top right hand corner, Brahms gave her this ornately decorated copy of "To a Violet" on her birthday. (Top) Schumann's not-so-fancy draft of "The Shepherd's Farewell."

They're here on loan as part of an exhibition from the Saxon State Library in Dresden, Germany.

Along with them, you can see Martin Luther's original New Testament, responsible for adding hundreds of denominations to the Christian faith. Grimace over the details of 16th century equestrian dental procedures. And find out why Germany's most famed musical troupe from 400 years ago, the Hofkapelle, today would give Mrs. Doubtfire a run for its money.

These Saxon State Library treasures have survived the Dark Ages, the devastation of World War II, and for the last 50 years they were all but inaccessible to most Americans, locked away behind the Iron Curtain.

They're here for the first time. And it's uncertain when, or if, they'll ever be here again.

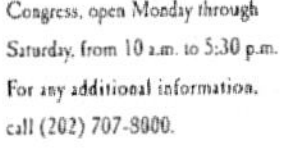

An institution in Dresden's long musical history was the performing troupe, the Hofkapelle. Here, a long procession of men dressed as women.

The exhibition is on display in the Great Hall of the Library of Congress, open Monday through Saturday, from 10 a.m. to 5:30 p.m. For any additional information, call (202) 707-8000.

Dresden: Treasures from the Saxon State Library

This is the Bible that thousands of Christians wanted to buy.

And even more wanted to burn.

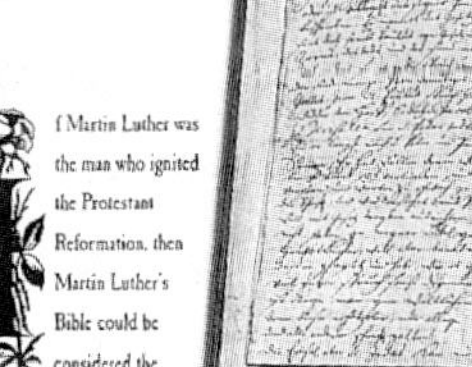

If Martin Luther was the man who ignited the Protestant Reformation, then Martin Luther's Bible could be considered the match that lit the fire.

Luther, the historians tell us, passionately believed the Bible must be something everyone could read for themselves. But the Church of Luther's time didn't agree.

The first church in Dresden, the Frauenkirche was originally constructed in 1142. In the 18th century, it was rebuilt as the world's first Protestant Cathedral, as shown in this sketch. Its dome, called the "Stone Bell," soon became Dresden's most recognizable landmark.

They thought the Holy Scripture should only be printed in Latin, although few people, except scholars and the clergy, understood Latin.

So, in 1521, Luther donned a disguise as "Junker Georg," a knight.

Martin Luther started as a Catholic monk who believed the Bible should be written in a language that everyone could read. The Catholic Church preferred the Bible be printed in Latin. So Luther took it upon himself to translate the entire Bible into German, thereby helping to prompt the Protestant Reformation.

He gained weight and grew a beard just to enhance the disguise. He hid himself away in Wartburg Castle and there, in only 11 weeks, he translated the New Testament from Latin into German.

Three thousand copies of Luther's Bible were quickly published on a printing press (invented only 70 years before by Johannes Gutenberg) and the entire press run of "The New Testament in German" sold out. Opponents of Luther were enraged by the translation. Many wanted his work destroyed and there were public burnings of Luther's books and manuscripts. But the Protestant Reformation was well underway and history was changed forever.

Today, of course, there are literally hundreds of Protestant denominations. None of which existed before Martin Luther and his Bible.

If you'd like to see one of those rare Martin Luther Bibles for yourself, you can do just that at the Library of Congress.

From now through July 13th, two of them are on display as part of an exhibition, on loan, from the Saxon State Library in Dresden, Germany.

"The New Testament in German" reads the title page of the Martin Luther Bible. The first New Testament Bible ever translated into German, and the first printed Bible of the Protestant Reformation.

And that's not all there is to see while the exhibition is here. There are musical scores by Bach, Vivaldi, and Wagner. A medieval Jewish prayer book. Drawings of the first Protestant Cathedral ever built. Not to mention other examples of European art, science, architecture and lifestyle that date back hundreds of years.

These Saxon State Library treasures have survived the Dark Ages, the devastation of World War II, and for the last 50 years.

The City of Dresden at the end of the 18th century, as painted by Christian Hammer. This colored engraving depicts the Dresden landscape including the Catholic Hofkirche and the Protestant Frauenkirche side by side in the distance.

...locked away behind the Iron Curtain, they were all but inaccessible to most Americans.

Make plans to attend. After July 13th, you'll have to go all the way to Dresden to see them again.

The exhibition is on display in the Great Hall of the Library of Congress,

A Jewish Holy Day Prayer Book. Dating from the 13th century, it contains the appropriate prayers for each of the Jewish Holy days for an entire year, and is the very first item you see as you walk in the doors.

open Monday through Saturday, 10 a.m. to 5:30 p.m. For more information, call (202) 707-8000.

Dresden: Treasures from the Saxon State Library

GOLD, SILVER &
BRONZE AWARDS

PUBLIC SERVICE/
POLITICAL
NEWSPAPER
OR MAGAZINE:
CAMPAIGN

BRONZE

art director
Bob Barrie

writer
Phil Calvit

photographer
Rick Dublin

client
Cease Fire

agency
Fallon McElligott/
Minneapolis

Suburban Dallas, TX.
15-yr.-old female.
Killed by 10-yr.-old
brother with gun
found in parents'
room. Boy thought
gun was unloaded,
tried to scare sister
as she talked on phone.

A gun in the home triples the risk of
a homicide in the home.
CEASE FIRE
Think about your family before you think about getting a handgun.

A gun in the home triples the risk of
a homicide in the home.

CEASE FIRE

Think about your family before you think about getting a handgun.

More Americans were killed by handguns
in two years than during the Vietnam War.

CEASE FIRE

Think about your family before you think about getting a handgun.

**PUBLIC SERVICE/
POLITICAL
OUTDOOR AND
POSTERS**

GOLD

art directors
Quentin Pfiszter
Bruce Matchett

writers
Bruce Matchett
Ian Brown

photographer
Ian Batchelor

client
Humane Society of
New Zealand

agency
Ogilvy & Mather/
Auckland

GOLD, SILVER &
BRONZE AWARDS

SILVER

art director
Ellen Steinberg

writer
Tom Rosen

client
Friends of Public
Education

agency
Fallon McElligott/
Minneapolis

SOLW

Stay in school.

Friends of Public Education · 1-800-353-4374

BRONZE

art directors
Quentin Pfiszter
Bruce Matchett

writers
Bruce Matchett
Ian Brown

photographer
Ian Batchelor

client
Humane Society of
New Zealand

agency
Ogilvy & Mather/
Auckland

DEATH ROW

THEY HAVE JUST 7 DAYS TO LIVE. CALL 0800-HUMANE TO FOSTER THEM.   HUMANE SOCIETY OF
NEW ZEALAND INC.

**PUBLIC SERVICE/
POLITICAL
RADIO: SINGLE**

GOLD

writer
Samantha Koenderman

agency producer
Sally Wilson

production company
Audiolab

client
Childline

agency
Hunt Lascaris TBWA/
Johannesburg

(USING A TECHNIQUE SIMILAR TO MORPHING, THE WOMAN'S VOICE SLOWLY CHANGES TO THAT OF A CHILD'S DURING THE COURSE OF THE COMMERCIAL)

MATURE WOMAN: *He dimmed the lights and, smiling, led me by the hand to the bedroom. Slowly . . .*

SLIGHTLY YOUNGER WOMAN: *. . . he lay me down on the bed. His eyes pierced my skin. As he caressed my cheek, I could feel his breath . . .*

TEENAGE GIRL: *. . . hot on my neck. His hand moved down towards my top, so lightly I could hardly feel it . . .*

TEN-YEAR-OLD GIRL: *I breathed fast as he undid my shirt. He touched me and whispered in my ear . . .*

FIVE-YEAR-OLD GIRL: *. . . don't tell Mommy.*

ANNCR: *Sexual abuse can scar you for life. Get help, call Childline on 08000 55555.*

GOLD, SILVER &
BRONZE AWARDS

PUBLIC SERVICE/
POLITICAL
TELEVISION:
SINGLE

GOLD

art director
Rob Dow

writer
Greg Harper

agency producer
Romanca Jasinski

production company
Filmgraphics

director
Mat Humphrey

client
Transport Accident
Commission

agency
Grey Advertising/
Melbourne

CD 1

MAN I: *Thanks for your help, mate.*

(SFX: PHONE RINGING)

BOY: *Yeah. Hang on. I'll just get Dad.*

DAD: *Ooh. Booze bus, huh. Oh, it's a bit early isn't it. Alright Billy, thanks for the tip-off. . . It's just down the road in Lindon Street.*

MAN 2: *Well, I thought we were supposed to get a warning.*

DAD: *We just did, mate. . . right I'm off.*

MAN 2: *Go on. One more's not going to kill you.*

DAD: *Hey, I'm still capable of driving. How about you?*

MAN 2: *I've been driving home a long time, mate, and nothing's happened to me yet.*

DAD: *I have got to go. See ya, fellas.*

BOY: *You alright, Dad?*

DAD: *Yeah. No worries. Maybe I should have passed on that last beer. I didn't realize how stuffed I was knocking down all those bloody nails.*

BOY: *Yeah, um, Billy reckons you better cross the highway at Ferguson's Road.*

DAD: *Ah, did he?*

BOY: *Hey Dad, is that Billy's car down there?*

DAD: *No. No way. Bloody funny if he did get caught though. Hey.* (BOTH LAUGH)

BOY: *Dad!*

(SFX: SCREECHING BRAKES, CRASHING)

(SFX: PHONE RINGING)

MAN I: *G'day . . . Hello Paul . . . He was just here a few se – . . . yeah, righto.*

WOMAN: *Drink up. Here you go darl'. Here's another beer.*

SUPER: IF YOU DRINK, THEN DRIVE, YOU'RE A BLOODY IDIOT. TAC.

**PUBLIC SERVICE/
POLITICAL
TELEVISION:
SINGLE**

SILVER

art director
Rob Dow

writer
Greg Harper

agency producer
Romanca Jasinski

production company
Renegade Films

director
Colin Skyba

client
Transport Accident
Commission

agency
Grey Advertising/
Melbourne

CD 2

BRONZE

art director
Antony Redman

writer
Antony Redman

agency producer
Cora Chee

production company
Video Headquarters

director
Antony Redman

client
Asian Pals of
the Planet

agency
Batey Ads/Singapore

CD 3

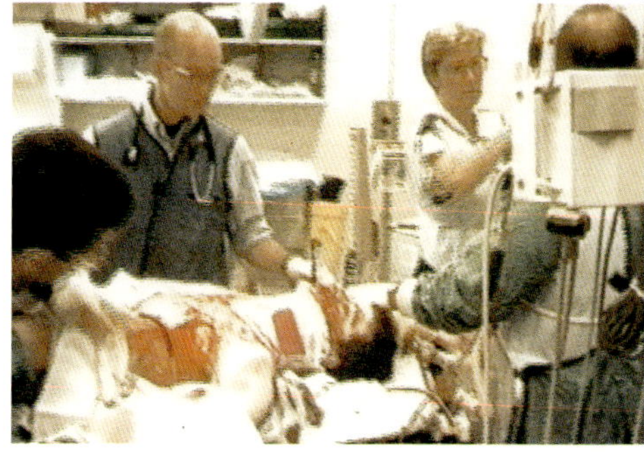

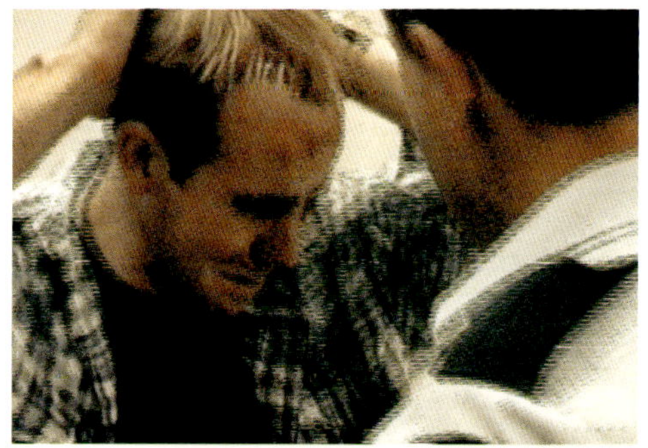

(MUSIC: JOHN LENNON'S "CHRISTMAS" AS SUNG BY A CHILD)

LYRICS: *And so this is Christmas . . .*

DOCTOR: *Can you feel it when I touch you here?*

PATIENT (CRYING): *No.*

LYRICS: *What have you done . . .*

WOMAN: *I said I'd get a friggin' taxi.*

LYRICS: *Another year over. . .*

DOCTOR: *Does anybody think we should keep going?*

LYRICS: *A new one just begun . . .*

WOMAN: *Damn you.*

LYRICS: *And so this is Christmas . . .*

BOY: *Mum!*

MAN: *I'm sorry. . . I'm sorry.*

LYRICS: *I hope you have fun. . .*

JOHN: *I wasn't drunk.*

MAN: *Do you understand what you've done.*

LYRICS: *The near and the dear ones . . .*

NURSE: *The passenger from the other vehicle has died.*

POLICEMAN: *I just have to give you an official caution.*

LRYICS: *The old and the young. . . A very, merry Christmas. And a happy New Year. Let's hope it's a good one . . .*

MOTHER: *He didn't mean to do it.*

SUPER: SHOULD YOU BE DRIVING HOME TONIGHT?

LYRICS: *. . . without any fear.*

SUPER: IF YOU DRINK, THEN DRIVE, YOU'RE A BLOODY IDIOT. TAC.

LYRICS (SPOKEN): *So this is Christmas.*

(COMMERCIAL RUNS WITH NO SOUNDTRACK)

SUPER: IN THE LAST THIRTY YEARS, THE WORLD'S WATER SUPPLY HAS HALVED.

SUPER: TREAT WATER WITH RESPECT.

SUPER: ASIAN PALS OF THE PLANET.

**PUBLIC SERVICE/
POLITICAL
TELEVISION:
CAMPAIGN**

GOLD

See Best Of Show

SILVER

art directors
David Gardner
Peter Favat

writers
Stu Cooperrider
Rich Herstek
Ken Lewis

agency producers
David Verhoef
Lisa Sulda

production companies
Picture Park
Palomar Pictures

directors
Erroll Morris
Neil Abramson

client
Massachusetts Department
of Public Health

agency
Houston Herstek
Favat / Boston

CD 4

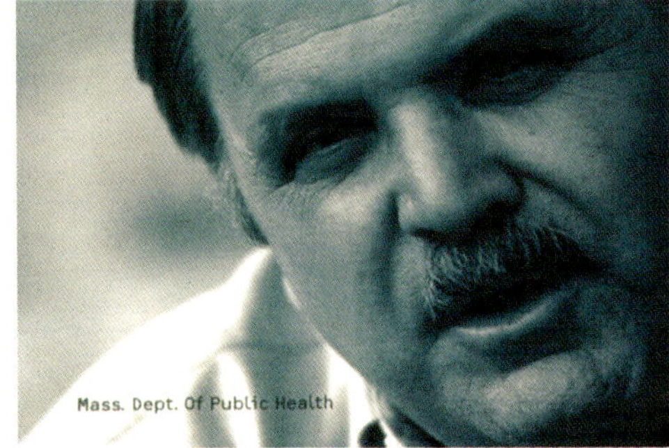

SUPER: THE TRUTH.

ANNCR: *I used to love cigarette ads. The cowboy on his horse. Rugged. Independent. It was beautiful. Then the cowboy died. Got lung cancer from smoking. His name was Wayne MacLaren and he was my brother.*

I'm Mac MacLaren. The tobacco industry used my brother in ads to create an image that smoking makes you independent. Don't believe it. Lying there with all those tubes in you, how independent can you really be?

SUPER: MASSACHUSETTS DEPARTMENT OF PUBLIC HEALTH.

**CONSUMER
RADIO: SINGLE**

GOLD

writers
April Winchell
Mick Kuisel

agency producer
April Winchell

production company
Radio Savant

client
The Solaris Group/
Ortho

agency
BBDO West/
Los Angeles

MAN: *There's nothing good about fire ants. They don't pollinate your roses. They don't make cute little sounds when they rub their legs together. All they do is build a big mound in your yard and bite the hell out of anyone who gets near it. That's it. That's their sole contribution to mankind. And that's why they have to die. It's that simple. You cannot rehabilitate a fire ant. You have to kill him, his little red friends, and that big fat queen down there making more fire ants. Oh, you could lug a big sack of chemicals and a garden hose around the yard, but that's about as fun as getting bit in the first place. No, what you need is Antstop Orthene Fire Ant Killer from Ortho. You put two teaspoons of Antstop around the mound and you're done. You don't even put water in it. The scout ants track it back into the mound—and here's the really good part—everybody dies, even the queen. And while there's joy in all creatures living in harmony, it's nothing compared to wasting fire ants. Now that's a rush . . . Antstop Orthene Fire Ant Killer from Ortho. Kick fire ant butt.*

SILVER

writers
April Winchell
Mick Kuisel

agency producer
April Winchell

production company
Radio Savant

client
The Solaris Group/
Ortho

agency
BBDO West/
Los Angeles

(SFX: Crowded Bar Sounds)
GUY: *Uh, hi.*

GIRL: *Hi! I was wondering when you were going to come over.*

GUY: *You were?*

GIRL: *Yeah, I saw you over there with your beer-buddies, pretending not to look this way. It took you long enough. I was starting to get lonely.*

GUY: (Laughs Nervously)

GIRL: *Mmm. You obviously work with your hands.*

GUY: *Well, I-I am a computer programmer So, so I use 'em a lot, ya know, my h-h-hands, I use my hands —and you?*

GIRL: *I'm a lingerie model.*

GUY: (Laughs Nervously)

GIRL: *Oh, I'm sorry. Where are my manners. I'm Jessica.*

GUY: *Jessica. It's really nice to meet you Jessica. My name, oh, I'm—buurr rrrrrrrrrrrrrrrrrrrrrrrrrrr...*

ANNCR: *Next time you're out, try Cider Jack Hard Cider. The naturally dry, lightly-carbonated alcoholic beverage made from apples.*

GUY: *...rrrp--Paul. Uhh, sorry.*

MAN: *Fire ants are not loveable. People do not want fire ant plush toys. They aren't cuddly, they don't do little tricks, they just bite you and leave red stinging welts that make you want to cry. That's why they have to die, and they have to die right now. You don't want them to have a long lingering illness, you want death. A quick, excruciating, see-you-in-hell kind of death. You don't want to lug a bag of chemicals and a garden hose around the yard. It takes too long. And baits can take up to a week. No, my friend, what you want is Antstop Orthene Fire Ant Killer from Ortho. You put two teaspoons of Antstop around the mound—and this is the really good part—everybody dies, even the queen. It's that fast. And that's good. Because killing fire ants shouldn't be a full-time job. Even if it is pretty fun . . . Antstop Orthene Fire Ant Killer from Ortho. Kick fire ant butt.*

BRONZE

writers
Marc Gallucci
Maureen Begley

agency producer
Andy Lerner

production company
Radio In The Nude

client
Cider Jack Hard Cider

agency
Clarke Goward
Advertising /Boston

(MUSIC: "YOU REALLY GOT ME" BY VAN HALEN)

(TOY ACTION FIGURE DROPS FROM TOY DINOSAUR'S MOUTH INTO NISSAN Z, SPEEDS THROUGH TOY-RIDDEN ROOM, AND PICKS UP FEMALE DOLL, STRANDING HER BEAU. THEY ZOOM OFF THROUGH LEGS OF "MR. K.")

(SFX: SQUEALING TIRES)

SUPER: ENJOY THE RIDE. NISSAN.

GOLD, SILVER &
BRONZE AWARDS

**CONSUMER
TELEVISION
OVER :30
SINGLE**

GOLD

art directors
Joe Hemp
John Boone

writer
Rob Siltanen

agency producers
Richard O'Neill
Cheryl Childers

production companies
Smillie Films
Will Vinton Studios

directors
Kinka Usher
Mark Gustafson

client
Nissan Motor
Corporation

agency
TBWA Chiat/Day,
Venice, CA

CD 5

**CONSUMER
TELEVISION
OVER :30
SINGLE**

SILVER

art director
Don Schneider

writers
Michael Patti
Ted Sann

agency producers
Regina Ebel
Maria Amato

production company
PYTKA

director
Joe Pytka

client
Pepsi Cola Company

agency
BBDO/New York

CD 6

SILVER

art director
John Jay

writer
Jim Riswold

agency producer
Jennifer Smieja

production company
JOINT

directors
Jim Riswold
Peter Wiedensmith

client
Nike

agency
Wieden & Kennedy/
Portland

CD 7

(MUSIC: "YOUR CHEATIN' HEART" BY HANK WILLIAMS)

(SFX: PEPSI CANS FALLING OUT OF VENDOR)

SUPER: NOTHING ELSE IS A PEPSI.

(MUSIC: "RAINMAKER" BY HANS ZIMMER)

SUPERS: HELLO WORLD.
I SHOT IN THE 70'S WHEN I WAS 8.
I SHOT IN THE 60'S WHEN I WAS 12.
I WON THE U.S. JUNIOR AMATEUR WHEN I WAS 15.
HELLO WORLD.
I PLAYED IN THE NISSAN OPEN WHEN I WAS 16.
HELLO WORLD.
I WON THE U.S. AMATEUR WHEN I WAS 18.
I PLAYED IN THE MASTERS WHEN I WAS 19.
I AM THE ONLY MAN TO WIN THREE CONSECUTIVE U.S. AMATEUR TITLES.
HELLO WORLD.
THERE ARE STILL COURSES IN THE U.S.
I AM NOT ALLOWED TO PLAY BECAUSE OF THE COLOR OF MY SKIN.
HELLO WORLD.
I'VE HEARD I'M NOT READY FOR YOU.
ARE YOU READY FOR ME?
JUST DO IT.

GOLD, SILVER &
BRONZE AWARDS

BRONZE

art director
Sean Mullens

writer
Chuck McBride

agency producer
Steve Neely

production company
Satellite Films

director
Spike Jonze

client
Levi Strauss & Co./
Wide Leg Jeans

agency
Foote Cone & Belding/
San Francisco

CD 8

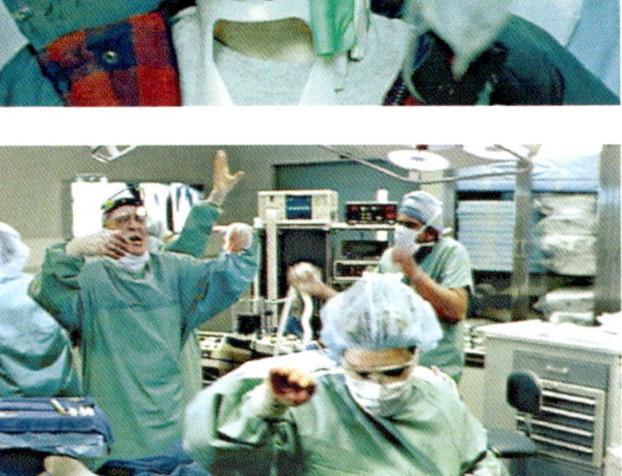

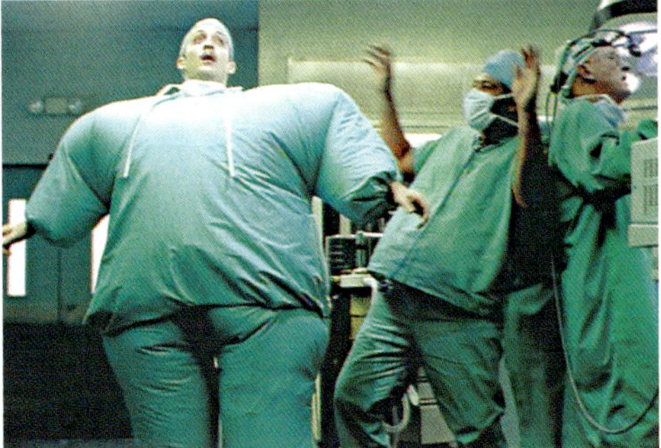

BRONZE

art director
Vince Squibb

writer
Derek Apps

agency producer
Charles Crisp

production company
Tony Kaye Films

director
Tony Kaye

client
Reebok UK

agency
Lowe Howard Spink/
London

CD 9

(SFX: AMBULANCE SIREN)
ATTENDANT: . . . *Over one-eighty!*
NURSE: *Can you hear me?*
ATTENDANT: . . . *thirty-two minimum . . .*
NURSE: *Tell me your . . . name.*
PATIENT: *Richard.*
NURSE: *We're gonna . . . take care of you, Richard.*
(SFX: BEEP)
DOCTOR: *Sponge.*
(SFX: DRIPPING SOUND, HEART BEATS)
(MUSIC: "TAINTED LOVE" MELODY)
(SFX: BEEP, BEEP)
RICHARD (SLOWLY STARTING TO SING): *I've got to . . . run . . . away. I've got to . . .*
(SFX: BEEP, BEEP)
RICHARD: *. . . get away . . . from the pain you . . . drive into the heart . . . of me.*
DOCTOR (SINGING): *Once I . . . ran to you. I ran. . .*
MEDICAL CREW (SINGING): *Now I run from you. This tainted love you've given, I give you all a boy could give you. Take my tears and that's . . .*
RICHARD/MEDICAL CREW: *Not nearly all . . .*
(SFX: BEE-E-E-E-E-P; SINGING STOPS)
NURSE: *He's crashing!*
DOCTOR: *Paddles!!*
RICHARD: (GASPS)
(SFX: BEEP, BEEP)
MEDICAL CREW: *Oh-h-h-h!* (SINGING RESUMES)
RICHARD: *You know . . .*
MEDICAL CREW: *. . . tainted love. Don't touch me please, I can't stand the way you tease.*
ANNCR: *Levi's Wide Leg Jeans. It's wide open.*

(SFX: WHISTLE BLOWS)
STEVEN BERKOFF: *Pallister knocks it wide to me.*
DAVE STEWART: *I skillfully . . .*
TOM JONES: *. . . chest it down and turn and I'm off down the line like a gazelle.*
DAVID MELLOR: *I'm leaving my marker standing.*
STATTO: *My tight shorts . . .*
QUENTIN CRISP: *. . . grasp my pumping thighs.*
JOSE CARRERAS: *To my right . . .*
CHRIS EUBANK: *. . . I hear pounding feet.*
VIC REEVES: *I stop the ball dead, the defender sliding into oblivion.*
CARRERAS: *The roar of the crowd . . .*
RICHARD ATTENBOROUGH: *. . . sucks me in.*
STATTO: *Leave it out Dicky!*
ROBBIE WILLIAMS: *Lusting girlies scream my name.*
ATTENBOROUGH: *From the corner of my eye . . .*
ANNA FRIEL: *. . . I see a flash of blue.*
WARREN MITCHELL: *What does she know about football, silly moo.*
WALLACE: *I bamboozle the oncoming defender.*
JARVIS COCKER: *I dance around him and cut inside. . .*
MITCHELL: *I showed it to him, took it away, showed it to him, took it away, nutmegged him, round the corner, bang, in the corner of the net. . .*
WILLIAMS: *Wild sex in front of fifty thousand.*
BERKOFF: *The noise says it all.*
JONES: *I dream of being . . .*
GEORGE BEST: *. . . Ryan Giggs.*
ATTENBOROUGH: *Oh . . .*
BERKOFF: *. . . to be . . .*
JONES: *. . . in his boots.*
BERKOFF: *. . . in his boots.*
SUPER: REEBOK. THIS IS MY PLANET.

**CONSUMER
TELEVISION
OVER :30
CAMPAIGN**

GOLD

art director
Jamie Mambro

writers
Mike Sheehan
Ernie Schenck

agency producers
Diane Carlin
Dcb Martin

production company
Tony Kaye Films

director
Tony Kaye

client
John Hancock
Financial Services

agency
Hill Holliday Connors
Cosmopulos/Boston

CD 10

SUPER: YOUR PARENTS, YOUR CHILDREN, YOURSELF.

SIGOURNEY WEAVER: *You owe it to your parents, for they brought you into this world.*

SUPER: WHO DO YOU LOVE THE LEAST?

WEAVER: *You owe it to your children, for you did the same for them. But the day may arrive when both debts come due. When you may have no choice but to borrow from your own retirement to educate a child or care for a parent. Into whose eyes can you look and say you just can't help?*

SUPER: INSURANCE FOR THE UNEXPECTED.

WEAVER: *For in both, you will surely see your own.*

SUPER: INVESTMENTS FOR THE OPPORTUNITIES.

SUPER: JOHN HANCOCK (OLYMPIC RINGS) WORLDWIDE SPONSOR.

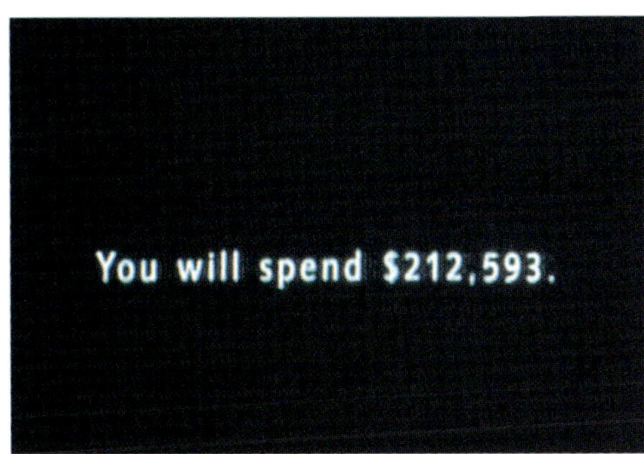

SUPER: THEY WILL SPEND FOUR YEARS IN COLLEGE.

SIGOURNEY WEAVER: *They are the sheep. And we are the shepherds.*

SUPER: YOU WILL SPEND $212,593.

WEAVER: *We tell them that college is the doorway. We tell them to prepare.*

SUPER: INSURANCE FOR THE UNEXPECTED.

WEAVER: *To be ready for the future. But the question remains. Will we?*

SUPER: INVESTMENTS FOR THE OPPORTUNITIES.

WEAVER: *We are the mothers. We are the fathers. We are the shepherds.*

SUPER: JOHN HANCOCK (OLYMPICS RINGS) WORLDWIDE SPONSOR.

SUPER: WILL YOU WANT TO WORK WHEN YOU'RE 65?

SIGOURNEY WEAVER: *You will wake up one morning and there will be no subways.*

SUPER: WILL YOU HAVE TO?

WEAVER: *There will be no time sheets or corporate ladders to climb. And in that moment, life will change from a thing to be conquered to a time to be savored. If retirement is a bridge to be crossed when we get there, then we must accept whatever lies in store for us.*

SUPER: INSURANCE FOR THE UNEXPECTED.

WEAVER: *If it is one we must build, then let us begin.*

SUPER: INVESTMENTS FOR THE OPPORTUNITIES.

SUPER: JOHN HANCOCK (OLYMPIC RINGS) WORLDWIDE SPONSOR.

**CONSUMER
TELEVISION
OVER :30
CAMPAIGN**

SILVER

art directors
Vince Engel
John Jay

writer
Jim Riswold

production company
PYTKA

director
Joe Pytka

client
Nike

agency
Wieden & Kennedy/
Portland

CD 11

**CONSUMER
TELEVISION
:30 SINGLE**

GOLD

art director
Robert Palmer

writer
Hank Perlman

agency producer
Dan Duffy

production company
@radical.media

directors
Bryan Buckley
Frank Todaro

client
ESPN

agency
Wieden & Kennedy/
Portland

CD 12

(MUSIC: "POWER OF ONE" BY HANS ZIMMER)
SUPERS: GOLF IS AN INVITATION.
TO FEEL THE GRASS.
TO HEAR THE TREES.
GOLF IS AN INVITATION.
TO PLAY WELL AND KNOW IT'S GOING TO END.
TO PLAY POORLY AND THINK IT'S NEVER
GOING TO END.
GOLF IS AN INVITATION.
TO KNOW GOD.
TO KNOW SATAN.
TO IGNORE FEAR.
TO BE NICK PRICE.
GOLF IS AN INVITATION.
TO ASK YOUR SOUL, "MIND IF I JOIN YOU?"
GOLF IS AN INVITATION.
YOU ARE INVITED.
JUST DO IT.

BOB LEY: *We've drafted kids right out of high
school. We had this one kid . . .*
SUPER: BOB LEY, SPORTSCENTER ANCHOR.

LEY: *You would not believe the scouting
reports. Raves up and down–can't miss.*

JACK EDWARDS: *Once again the Indians
appear to be the team to beat.*
SUPER: JACK EDWARDS. SETH HAYES.

LEY: *Emotionally though, he just wasn't
prepared.*

EDWARDS: *Jimmy Key is attempting–*

SETH HAYES: *Jimmy Key? What is he, like
45? . . . I could hit him.*

LEY: *I mean, it's a different game in here.*

HAYES: *Jack, did you–did you watch the
game? . . . I mean, didn't it–didn't it suck?
. . . It sucked!*

(SFX: EMERGENCY TONE)

HAYES: *It is with much regret that I
announce that I, um, am leaving SportsCenter.*

LEY: *Bottom line: He just came out too soon.*
SUPER: THIS IS SPORTSCENTER. ESPN.

WOMAN: *Very bad dog . . . bad, bad dog! . . . Very bad dog!*
SUPER: POLAROID. SEE WHAT DEVELOPS.

GOLD, SILVER &
BRONZE AWARDS

SILVER

art director
Grant Richards

writer
Scott Aal

agency producer
Jane Jacobsen

production company
Smillie Films

director
Kinka Usher

client
Polaroid Corporation

agency
Goodby Silverstein &
Partners / San Francisco

CD 13

BRONZE

art director
Larry Frey

writer
Jamie Barrett

agency producer
Donna Potaro

production company
Propaganda Films

director
Jonathan Glazer

client
Nike

agency
Wieden & Kennedy /
Portland

CD 14

(SFX: BASKETBALL GAME SOUNDS; THEN SLOW, ANGELIC MUSIC STARTS)

(SFX: SLOWED DOWN CHEERING AND SQUEAKING OF SHOES INTERCUTS WITH FREEZE-FRAMES)

(SFX: EXAGGERATED SOUND OF BALL GOING THROUGH HOOP)

SUPER: (AIR JORDAN LOGO.)

**CONSUMER
TELEVISION
:30 CAMPAIGN**

GOLD

art director
Robert Palmer

writer
Hank Perlman

agency producer
Dan Duffy

production company
@radical.media

directors
Bryan Buckley
Frank Todaro

client
ESPN

agency
Wieden & Kennedy/
Portland

CD 15

BOB LEY: *We've drafted kids right out of high school. We had this one kid . . .*

SUPER: BOB LEY, SPORTSCENTER ANCHOR.

LEY: *You would not believe the scouting reports. Raves up and down–can't miss.*

JACK EDWARDS: *Once again the Indians appear to be the team to beat.*

SUPER: JACK EDWARDS. SETH HAYES.

LEY: *Emotionally though, he just wasn't prepared.*

EDWARDS: *Jimmy Key is attempting–*

SETH HAYES: *Jimmy Key? What is he, like 45? . . . I could hit him.*

LEY: *I mean, it's a different game in here.*

HAYES: *Jack, did you–did you watch the game? . . . I mean, didn't it–didn't it suck? . . . It sucked!*

(SFX: EMERGENCY TONE**)**

HAYES: *It is with much regret that I announce that I, um, am leaving SportsCenter.*

LEY: *Bottom line: He just came out too soon.*

SUPER: THIS IS SPORTSCENTER. ESPN.

JULIE MARIASH: *Well, you know, we make trades all the time and we made a really big one with "Melrose Place." It was a block-buster. . . We got Shue, they got Steiner.*

GARY MILLER: *Andrew.*

ANDREW SHUE: *Thanks Gary. I spoke with NFL commissioner, Paul Tagliabue, this evening. He would not confirm or deny reports that the Chicago Bears . . .*

MARIASH: *Worked out great for us. For them, you're going to have to ask them about that.*

CHARLIE STEINER: *Hi Cindy, I'm Bobby. I'm the new pool boy . . . wanna rub some cocoa oil on my back?*

MARIASH: *Maybe we got the better end of the deal.*

SUPER: THIS IS SPORTSCENTER. ESPN.

SUPER: DAVID BROFSKY, SPORTSCENTER PRODUCER.

DAVID BROFSKY: *The reality is just because you're a former athlete, doesn't qualify you to be a SportsCenter anchor.*

SUPER: MID-SEASON RECRUITMENT, SEPTEMBER 10, 1996.

BILL BRADLEY: *After the Olympic gold medal, the Rhodes Scholarship, 10 years with the New York Knicks. Um, I was a U.S. Senator for 18 years.*

BOB LEY: *How 'bout any writing experience?*

BRADLEY: *Well, I wrote three books. One on the bestseller list and the Tax Reform Act of 1986.*

LEY: *But no TV writing.*

KEITH OLBERMAN: *No. Any experience in front of an audience?*

BRADLEY: *Well, I gave a key note address at the Democratic National Convention.*

OLBERMAN: *Uh, I meant a large audience.*

BRADLEY: *Oh.*

SUPER: THIS IS SPORTSCENTER. ESPN.

**CONSUMER
TELEVISION
:30 CAMPAIGN**

SILVER

art directors
David Angelo
Greg Bell
Matt Vescovo
Roger Camp

writers
Cliff Freeman
Arthur Bijur
Greg Bell
Matt Vescovo
Michelle Roufa

agency producers
Liz Graves
Tom Meloth
Maresa Wickham

production companies
A&R Group
Crossroads Films
HSI

directors
David Ramser
Mark Story
Geoff McGann

client
Little Caesars

agency
Cliff Freeman & Partners/
New York

CD 16

BRONZE

art directors
Sean Ehringer
Grant Richards

writers
Harry Cocciolo
Scott Aal

agency producers
Jane Jacobsen
Debbie King

production company
Smillie Films

directors
Kinka Usher
Jeffrey Goodby

client
Polaroid Corporation

agency
Goodby Silverstein &
Partners/San Francisco

CD 17

FIRST EMPLOYEE: *What'ya lookin' at?*
SECOND EMPLOYEE: *The Grand Canyon.*
FIRST EMPLOYEE: *Where?*
SECOND EMPLOYEE: *Right there.*
FIRST EMPLOYEE: *Where?*
SECOND EMPLOYEE: *Right there.*
FIRST COWBOY: *What'ya eatin'?*
SECOND COWBOY: *Giant Caesar.*
FIRST COWBOY: *What'ya steppin' in?*
SECOND COWBOY: *Has to be China.*

ANNCR: *Everything looks small next to the Giant Caesar.*
HUSBAND: *What?*

ANNCR: *From Little Caesars, giant slices with giant pepperoni – $9.99 carried out or have it delivered.*
LITTLE CAESAR (IN DEEP VOICE): *Pizza, Pizza.*

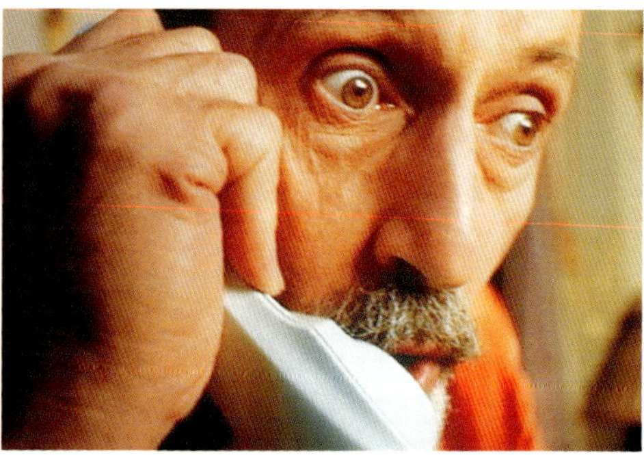

(SFX: CLASSICAL MUSIC)
(SFX: ITALIAN CONVERSATION)
NURSE: *Si, Senore.*
(SFX: ITALIAN CONVERSATION)
(SFX: CLICK AND PROCESS OF POLAROID)
DESIGNER: (FIRST SPEAKS IN ITALIAN) THEN: *John Paul! John Paul! . . . I'm sending you the changes now.*
(SFX: SHUFFLING)
DESIGNER: *I want them into the show! Get them into the show!*
(MUSIC: EURO TRASH TUNE)
ASSISTANT: *We'll get them into the show – they look fabulous.*
(SFX: CLAPPING AND CAMERA CLICKS)
(SFX: GASPS)
SUPER: POLAROID. SEE WHAT DEVELOPS.
(SFX: SQUEAKING OF NURSE'S SHOES)
(MUSIC: EURO TRASH TUNE RESUMES)

KEN DANEYKO: *I just wanna say our name the Devils. It's just a name. There's nothin' evil or satanic about it.*

DANEYKO (PLAYED BACKWARDS): *We are the Devils, princes of darkness. We are pure evil. Worship us. Paul is dead.*

SUPER: NEW JERSEY DEVILS VS. PHILADELPHIA FLYERS. ESPN.

ANNCR: *Don't waste hundreds of pounds on expensive carpet, simply buy two small pieces, attach them to the bottom of your feet and get that quality carpet feel throughout your home.*

This money-saving tip was brought to you by McDonald's, where a Big Mac, medium fries and a medium soft drink will cost you just £2.88.

GOLD, SILVER &
BRONZE AWARDS

**CONSUMER
TELEVISION
:20 AND UNDER:
SINGLE**

GOLD

art director
Darryl McDonald

writer
Hank Perlman

agency producer
Colleen Wellman

production company
@radical.media

directors
Bryan Buckley
Frank Todaro

client
ESPN/National
Hockey League

agency
Wieden & Kennedy/
Portland

CD 18

SILVER

art director
Matt Hazell

writer
Jane Atkinson

agency producer
Pamie Wikstrom

production company
Fat Fish Films

director
Joe Public

client
McDonald's

agency
Leo Burnett/London

CD 19

**CONSUMER
TELEVISION
:20 AND UNDER:
SINGLE**

BRONZE

art director
Warren Brown

writer
Paul Fishlock

agency producer
Ivan Robinson

production company
Famous By Tuesday

director
John Studley

client
The Smiths
Snackfood Company

agency
The Campaign
Palace/Sydney

CD 20

**CONSUMER
TELEVISION
:20 AND UNDER:
CAMPAIGN**

GOLD

art director
Matt Hazell

writer
Jane Atkinson

agency producer
Pamie Wikstrom

production company
Fat Fish Films

directors
Joe Public

client
McDonald's

agency
Leo Burnett/London

CD 21

SINGERS: *Can anyone say no to new CC'S Light . . .*
(SFX: Crunch)
SINGERS: *. . . and Crispy?*
FLIGHT ATTENDANT: *Does anybody know how to fly a plane?*
(SFX: Mumbles Of "Not Me")

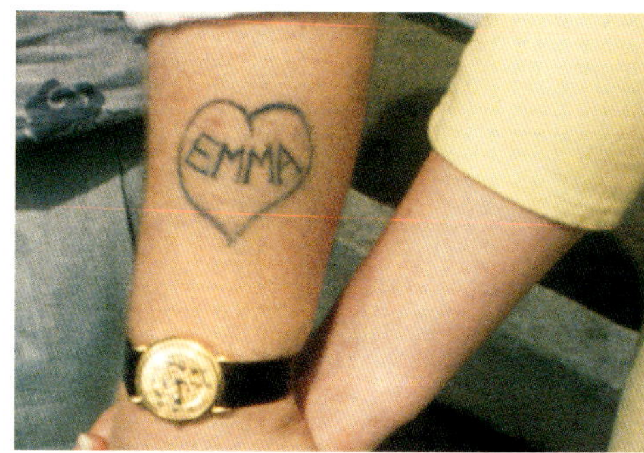

ANNCR: *That tattoo of an old girlfriend can cost an awful lot to have removed. Resolve the problem by taking your current girl-friend into town and having her name changed by Deedpoll.*

This money-saving tip was brought to you by McDonald's, where a Filet-O-Fish, medi-um fries and a medium soft-drink will cost you just £2.88.

ANNCR: *Laundry to wash? Then save your pennies by taking it into a second-hand shop. They'll do all the dirty work for you, then hey, presto . . . you can buy it all back for next to nothing.*

This money-saving tip was brought to you by McDonald's, where a Quarter Pounder with Cheese, medium fries and a medium soft drink will cost you just £2.88.

ANNCR: *Don't waste hundreds of pounds on expensive carpet, simply buy two small pieces, attach them to the bottom of your feet and get that quality carpet feel through-out your home.*

This money-saving tip was brought to you by McDonald's, where a Big Mac, medium fries and a medium soft drink will cost you just £2.88.

**CONSUMER
TELEVISION
:20 AND UNDER:
CAMPAIGN**

SILVER

art director
Darryl McDonald

writer
Hank Perlman

agency producer
Colleen Wellman

production company
@radical.media

directors
Bryan Buckley
Frank Todaro

client
ESPN/National
Hockey League

agency
Wieden & Kennedy/
Portland

CD 22

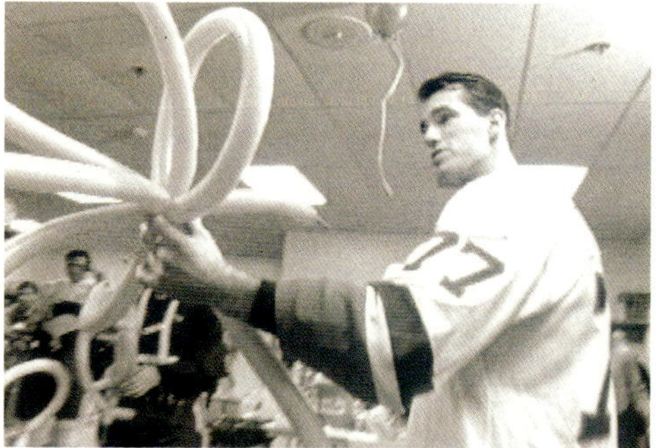

ANNCR: *You ever wonder what goes on in an
NHL locker room in between periods?*
HOCKEY PLAYER: *Hey, an octopus.*
HOCKEY TEAM: *Yeah. Hey, not bad. Yeah.*
SUPER: NEW YORK ISLANDERS VS. NEW YORK
RANGERS.
SUPER: THE STANLEY CUP PLAYOFFS. ESPN.

BRONZE

art directors
David Angelo
Roger Camp
Greg Bell

writers
Cliff Freeman
Michelle Roufa
Arthur Bijur

agency producers
Mary Ellen Duggan
Liz Graves
Maresa Wickham

production companies
Crossroads Films
HSI

directors
Mark Story
Geoff McGann

client
Little Caesars

agency
Cliff Freeman &
Partners / New York

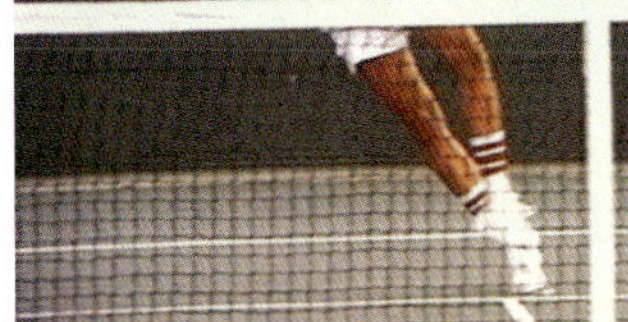

ANNCR: *Little Caesars wanted a sports celebrity for their new stuffed crust combo. But charging just $8.99, they couldn't afford much. Little Caesars Stuffed Crust Pizza, plus cheese and pepperoni stuffed Crazy Bread, carried out just $8.99, or have it delivered!*
LITTLE CAESAR: *Delivery! Delivery!*

**CONSUMER
TELEVISION
VARYING
LENGTHS
CAMPAIGN**

GOLD

art director
Robert Palmer

writer
Hank Perlman

agency producer
Dan Duffy

production company
@radical.media

directors
Bryan Buckley
Frank Todaro

client
ESPN

agency
Wieden & Kennedy/
Portland

CD 23

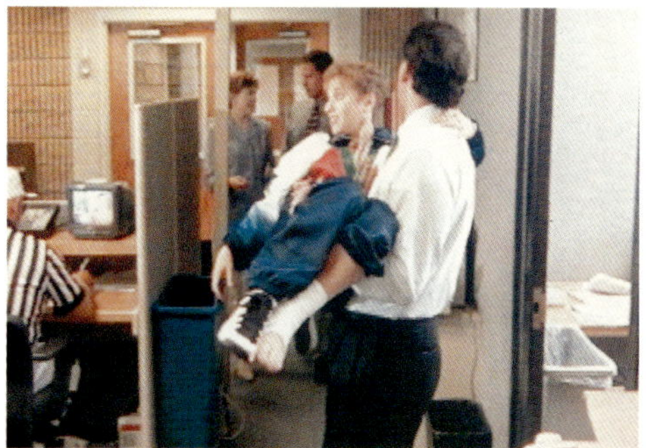

SUPER: SPORTSCENTER NEWSROOM, AUGUST 11, 1996.

KERRI STRUG: *Gonna do some gymnastics tours on the weekends . . .*

GARY: *Just a second. Carl, I gotta get this thing done.*

CARL: *Three hours yesterday. I'm done.*

GARY: *Yeah. I should have remembered.*

KERRI: *. . . and I plan on traveling around the country for the first semester.*

GARY: *Keith, uh, got just a minute?*

KEITH: *I got a bulging disc. Gotta go.*

KERRI: *With all the opportunities for me I wanna try and do some motivational speeches . . .*

GARY: *Rich will be perfect for this.*

RICH: *No.*

GARY: *Yeah, I'd love to hear about that. I really gotta get this thing done . . . Larry, ahh, I'll be right back. If you could just hold Kerri for just one second.*

LARRY: *I can't. I gotta go to the bathroom Gary. . . Is that okay with you?*

KERRI: *No!*

LARRY: *Hey, Chris . . . Guys. Guys. Guys.*

SUPER: THIS IS SPORTSCENTER. ESPN.

KARL RAVECH: *Security has always been an issue for us, like any other company, but since we've grown it's gotten tighter. We're not proud of it. We don't brag about it. You never know who the hell is going to walk through the door.*

SUPER: KARL RAVECH, SPORTSCENTER ANCHOR.

DELIVERY GUY: *Delivery.*

SUPER: SPORTSCENTER LOBBY 4:45 PM, DEC. 12,1996.

GUARD: *Can I see some ID please.*

DELIVERY GUY: *My hands are kind of full right now.*

BUFFALO SABRES' ROB RAY: *He wants to see some ID.*

RAVECH: *You don't know how crazy people can be out there. It's dangerous.*

RAY: *Next time bring some ID.*

COACH: *Hey, Rob.*

RAY: *Hey, coach.*

SUPER: THIS IS SPORTSCENTER. ESPN.

BRETT HABER: *Now this whole thing with athletes abusing reporters is getting way out of hand and we at SportsCenter have gotten to the point where we have just got to be ready to fight back.*

STUDENTS: *Eeaaa!*

TEACHER: *The most effective places would be, ah, the rotator cuff here or the anterior cruciate here. When a man can't stand, he can't very well fight. Also, he puts his head right there . . . Now suppose an athlete decides to attack your cameraman. What would you do?*

STUDENT: *Stop. Knock it off.*

TEACHER: *No. Let me show you. Kenny, why don't you try it again . . . Always be aware of your surroundings . . . Let's just say you're on the sidelines. Take any weapon that happens to be handy. The most effective defensive weapon would be your microphone . . . You're doing a remote and some savage attacks you. Whoops. Sacrificed the mascot. Of course there are other sensitive areas. Most athletes are not wearing cups.*

SUPER: THIS IS SPORTSCENTER. ESPN.

**CONSUMER
TELEVISION
VARYING
LENGTHS
CAMPAIGN**

SILVER

art director
Chris Graves

writer
Eric Moe

agency producer
Michelle Burke

production company
Epoch Films

director
Phil Morrison

client
Energizer

agency
TBWA Chiat/Day
Venice, CA

CD 24

INTERVIEWER: *People call you guys Bunny Spotters, is that right?*

GUY 1: *Bunny Spotters. I think that trivializes what we do. It's much larger than that.*

GUY 2: *Once you've seen it, you can never go back.*

GUY 3: *There's no other pink like it.*

GUY 2: *He's been through here.*

GUY 1: *I've seen it 16 times. To watch somebody find it, see it for the first time . . .*

GUY 4: *Woohoo. I feel very fortunate to be here, 'cause when we're all gone, it's still gonna be out there.*

SUPER: Eveready Battery Company.

SUPER: Energizer.

(SFX: Parking Meter Clicking, Hits "Expired")

(SFX: Coin Going Up Dashboard, Down Exterior, Flicked By Wiper Into Meter)

SUPER: Enjoy The Ride. Nissan. It's Time To Expect More From A Car.

(SFX: Person Playing Guitar Very Badly)
SUPER: If You Want To Play, Learn How To.

BRONZE

art directors
Joe Hemp
John Boone
Chuck Bennett

writers
Rob Siltanen
Clay Williams

agency producers
Cheryl Childers
Richard O'Neill
Debra Wittlin

production companies
Smillie Films
Will Vinton Studios

directors
Kinka Usher
Mark Gustafson

client
Nissan Motor
Corporation

agency
TBWA Chiat/Day
Venice, CA

CD 25

**CONSUMER
TELEVISION
UNDER $50,000
BUDGET**

GOLD

art directors
Juan Cravero
Martin Casios
Diego Livachoff

writers
Juan Cravero
Martin Casios
Diego Livachoff

agency producer
Hernan Bourdieu

production company
La Tierra

director
Ruben Andon

client
Technological Institute
of Contemporary Music

agency
Juan Cravero/
Buenos Aires

CD 26

**NON-BROADCAST:
CINEMA**

SILVER

art director
Matt Ryan

writer
John Pallant

agency producer
Nigel Kennally

production company
Tony Kaye Films

director
Mark Williams

client
London Borough
of Islington

agency
Saatchi & Saatchi/
London

CD 27

SUPER: You Wouldn't. Don't Let Your Dog.
NEIGHBOR: Turned out nice again.
(SFX: Neighbor Slipping In Mess, Falling)

INTERNATIONAL
FOREIGN
LANGUAGE
COMMERCIAL:
TELEVISION

GOLD

art director
Carlos Tourne

writers
Raul Cardos
Mauricio Galvan
Lourdes Lamasney

agency producer
Maria Claudia Alarcon

production company
GB Producciones

director
Simon Bross

client
Duracell

agency
Ogilvy & Mather/
Mexico City

CD 28

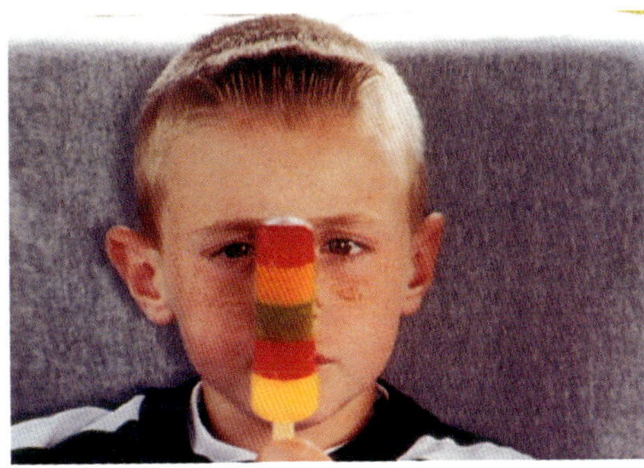

BOY: *It's green.*
(SFX: SCREECHING BRAKES, CRASHING)
(SFX: AIRBAG INFLATING AND DEFLATING)
BOY: *Hey, now it's red again.*
ANNCR: *Fruit Joy.*

SILVER

art director
Pieter van Velsen

writer
Aad Kuyper

production company
Czar Films

director
Rogier van der Ploeg

client
Nestle Netherlands/
Fruit Joy

agency
Lowe Kuiper & Schouten/
Amsterdam

CD 29

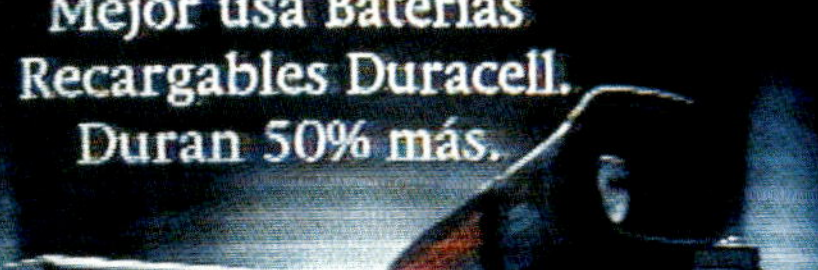

OLD MAN: *This is my videotaped will.
To avoid any conflict, I'm leaving all my
millions to a single person. To you, my dear . . .*
SUPER: NEXT TIME USE DURACELL. THEY
LAST 50 PERCENT LONGER.

**INTERNATIONAL
FOREIGN LANGUAGE
COMMERCIAL:
TELEVISION**

BRONZE

art director
Pachaya Rungrueng

writer
Suthisak Sucharittanonta

production company
Matching Studio

director
Suthon Petchsuwan

client
Black Cat Whisky

agency
Results Advertising/
Bangkok

CD 30

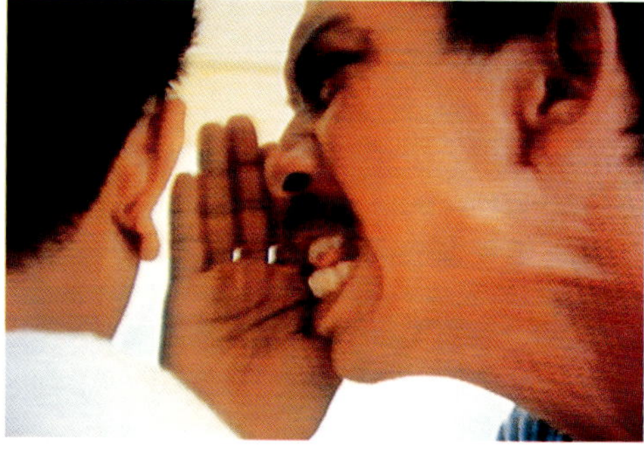

RIT: *My name is Rit, sir! I drink Black.*
BOSS' ASSISTANT: *Hello Boss!* (WHISPERS)
MAFIA BOSS: *What! Rit is drinking Black!*
BOSS' ASSISTANT: *Yes, sir. The guy who owes you money is drinking Black!*
MAFIA BOSS: *Let's sneak quietly to his home. We'll catch him by surprise.*
MAFIA BOSS: *Damn you Rit!*
RIT: *What's wrong sir?*
MAFIA BOSS: *I hear you're rich now!*
BOSS' ASSISTANT: *Yeah! You can afford to drink Black but you can't afford to pay your debt.*
RIT: *This Black only cost 130 baht.*
MAFIA BOSS: *Black? Only 130 baht!*
BOSS' ASSISTANT: *Black . . . Cat?*
MAFIA BOSS: *Black from Thailand you idiot! . . . Rit, may I have a glass?*
SUPER: BLACK CAT WHISKY.

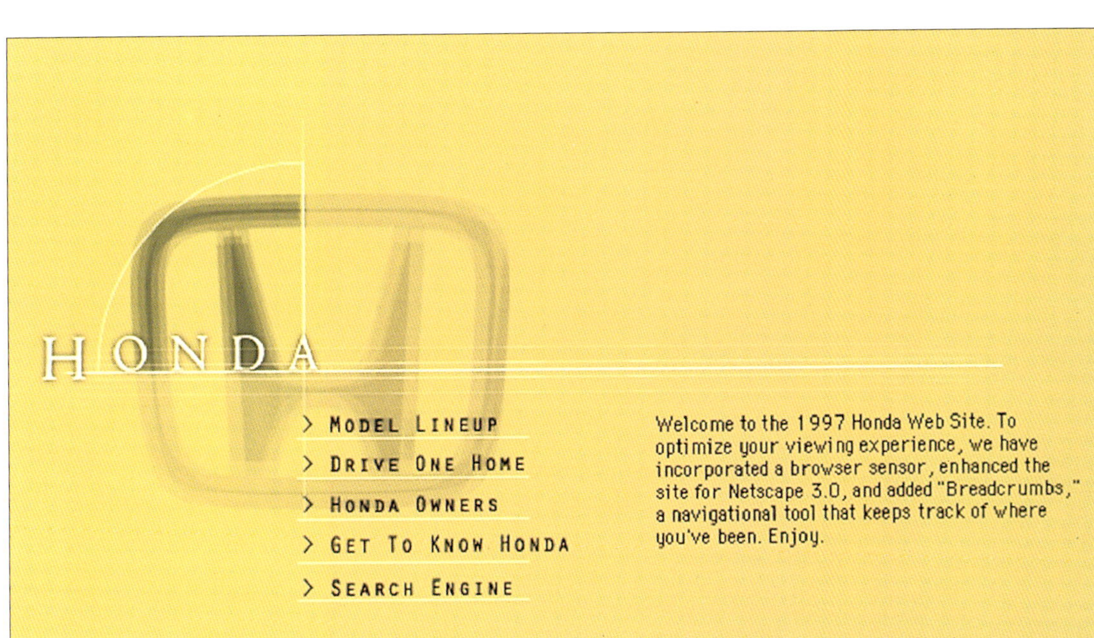

H O N D A
> Model Lineup
> Drive One Home
> Honda Owners
> Get To Know Honda
> Search Engine
Welcome to the 1997 Honda Web Site. To optimize your viewing experience, we have incorporated a browser sensor, enhanced the site for Netscape 3.0, and added "Breadcrumbs," a navigational tool that keeps track of where you've been. Enjoy.
©1996 American Honda Motor Co., Inc.

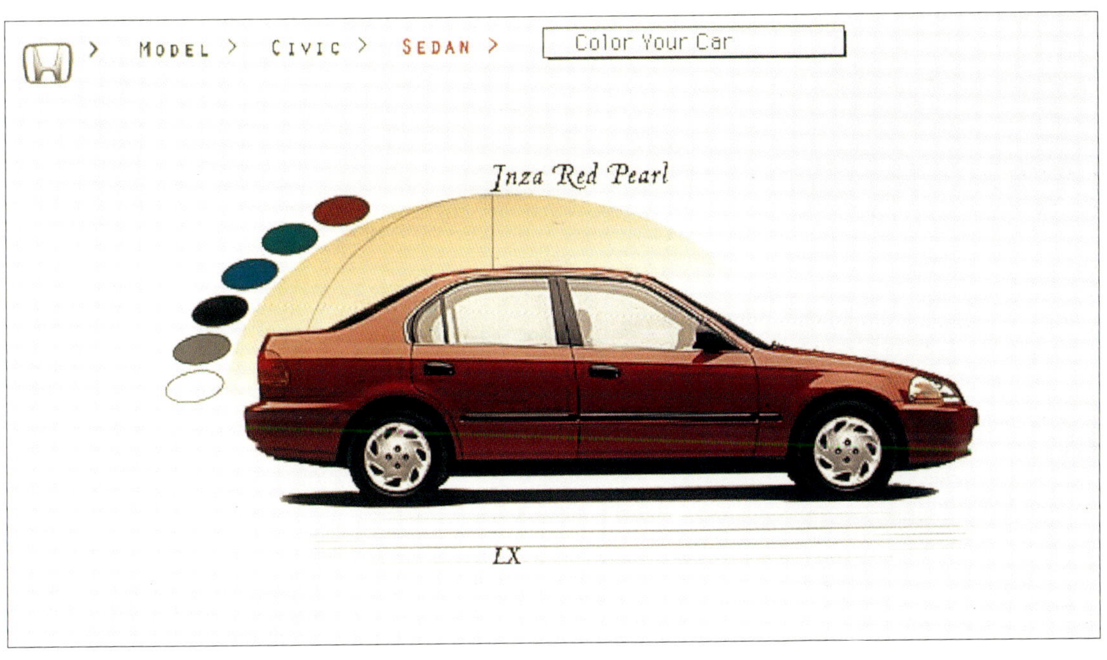

MODEL > CIVIC > SEDAN > Color Your Car
Inza Red Pearl
LX

GOLD, SILVER &
BRONZE AWARDS

**INTERACTIVE:
WEB SITE**

SILVER

art director
Lourdes Banez

writers
Deborah Gold
Chuck Carlson

*digital artist/
illustrator*
Lourdes Banez

client
Tidy Cat

agency
Duffy Design/
New York

www.tidycat.com

CD 84

GOLD, SILVER &
BRONZE AWARDS

BRONZE

art director
Peter Seidler

writers
Theodore W. Libbey Jr.
Carnegie Hall Staff

*digital artists/
illustrators*
Andreas Lindstrom
Kendall Thomas

photographer
Graham Haber

agency producer
Kate Swann

client
Carnegie Hall

agency
Avalanche Systems/
New York

www.carnegiehall.org

CD 85

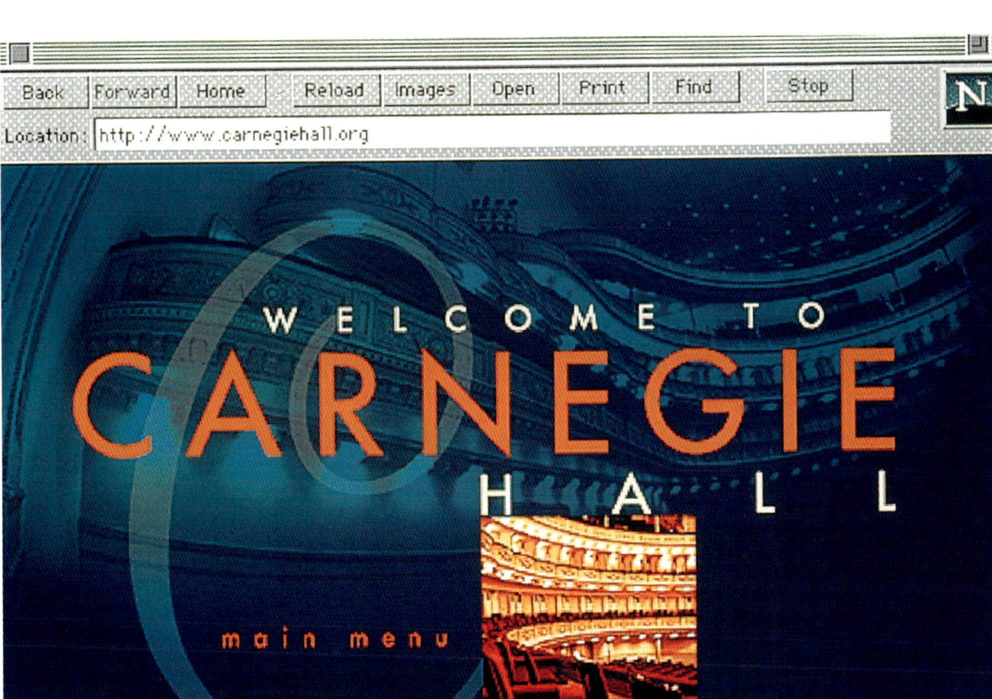

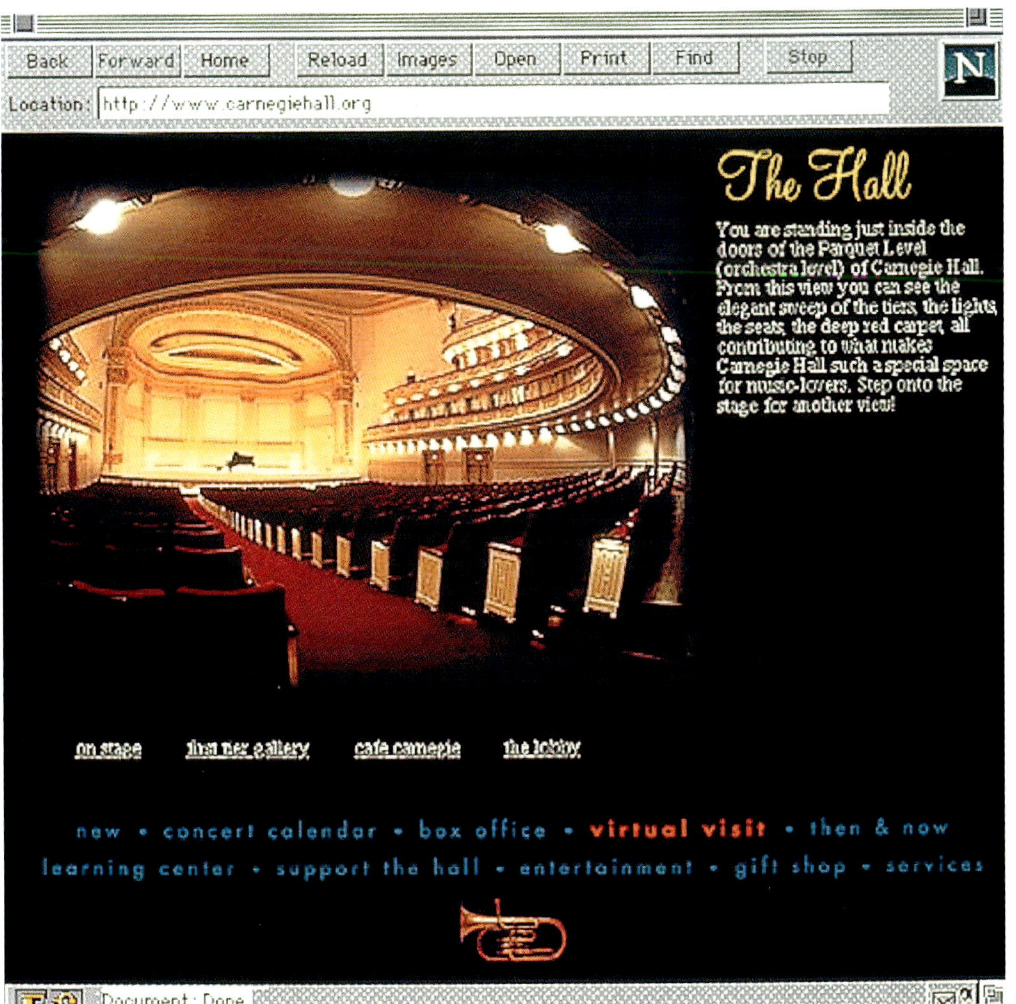

**COLLEGE
COMPETITION**

GOLD

art director
Mark Graham

writer
Ned Brown-Stearns

photographer
Dong Soo Choi

college
Portfolio Center /
Atlanta

*Assignment:
Fictional Chain of
Fast-Food Restaurants
Called "Sushi Tugo"*

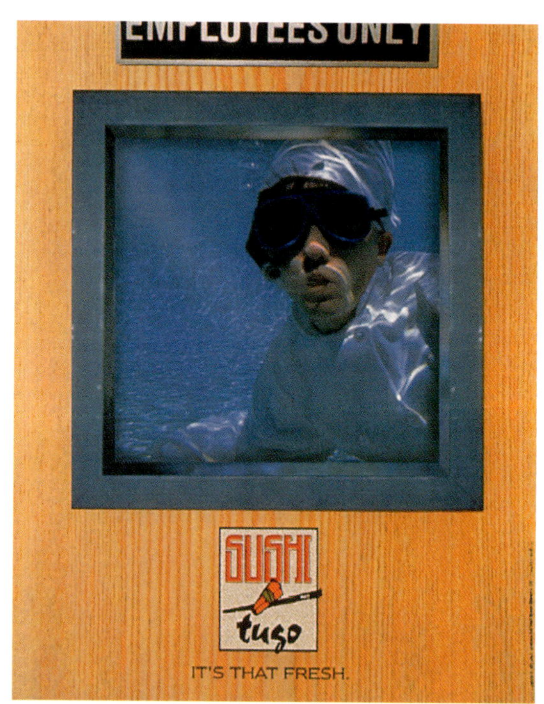

SILVER

art director
Kevin Christie

writers
Cindy Casares
Kevin Proudfoot

college
VCU Ad Center/
Richmond

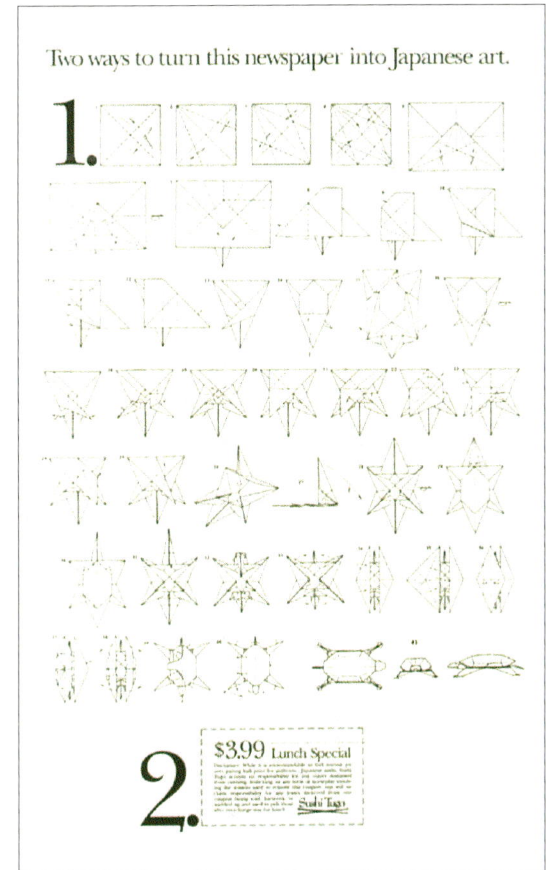

**COLLEGE
COMPETITION**

BRONZE

art director
Jason A. Smith

writer
Roger Hoard

photographer
Brian Deutsch

college
Creative Circus/
Atlanta

*Assignment:
Fictional Chain of
Fast-Food Restaurants
Called "Sushi Tugo"*

BRONZE

art director
Con Williamson
writer
Eric Liebhauser
photographer
Paul Clapper
college
Creative Circus/
Atlanta

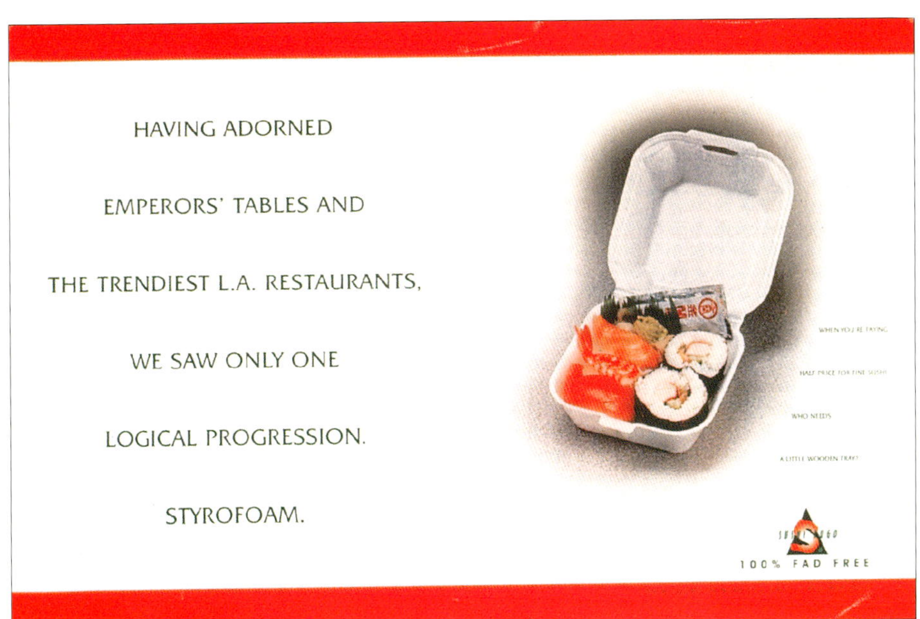

EX LIBRIS
THIS BOOK
BELONGS TO:
RETURN
IMMEDIATELY
OR SOONER
VOLUME
19

art director
Rob Dow

writer
Greg Harper

agency producer
Romanca Jasinski

production companies
Filmgraphics
Renegade Films

directors
Mat Humphrey
Colin Skyba

client
Transport Accident
Commission

agency
Grey Advertising/
Melbourne

CD 1

MAN 1: *Thanks for your help, mate.*
(SFX: PHONE RINGING)
BOY: *Yeah. Hang on. I'll just get Dad.*
DAD: *Ooh. Booze bus, huh. Oh, it's a bit early isn't it. Alright Billy, thanks for the tip-off. . . It's just down the road in Lindon Street.*
MAN 2: *Well, I thought we were supposed to get a warning.*
DAD: *We just did, mate. . . right I'm off.*
MAN 2: *Go on. One more's not going to kill you.*
DAD: *Hey, I'm still capable of driving. How about you?*
MAN 2: *I've been driving home a long time, mate, and nothing's happened to me yet.*
DAD: *I have got to go. See ya, fellas.*
BOY: *You alright, Dad?*
DAD: *Yeah. No worries. Maybe I should have passed on that last beer. I didn't realize how stuffed I was knocking down all those bloody nails.*
BOY: *Yeah, um, Billy reckons you better cross the highway at Ferguson's Road.*
DAD: *Ah, did he?*
BOY: *Hey Dad, is that Billy's car down there?*
DAD: *No. No way. Bloody funny if he did get caught though. Hey.* (BOTH LAUGH)
BOY: *Dad!*
(SFX: SCREECHING BRAKES, CRASHING)
(SFX: PHONE RINGING)
MAN 1: *G'day . . . Hello Paul . . . He was just here a few se – . . . yeah, righto.*
WOMAN: *Drink up. Here you go darl'. Here's another beer.*
SUPER: IF YOU DRINK, THEN DRIVE, YOU'RE A BLOODY IDIOT. TAC.

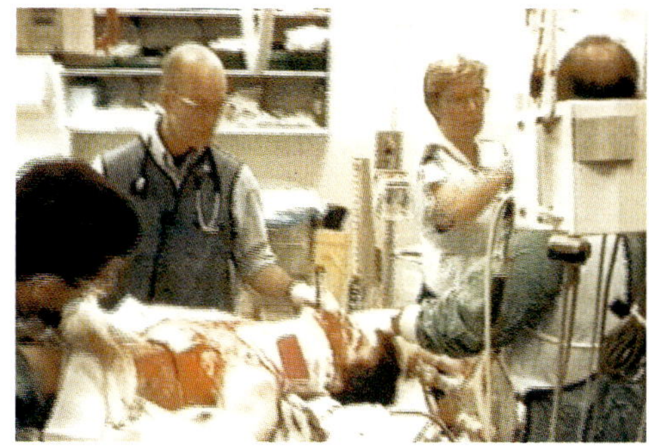

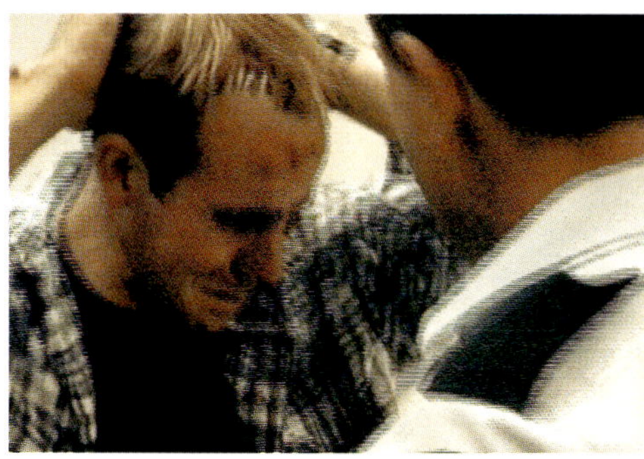

(MUSIC: JOHN LENNON'S "CHRISTMAS" AS SUNG BY A CHILD)

LYRICS: *And so this is Christmas . . .*

DOCTOR: *Can you feel it when I touch you here?*

PATIENT (CRYING): *No.*

LYRICS: *What have you done . . .*

WOMAN: *I said I'd get a friggin' taxi.*

LYRICS: *Another year over. . .*

DOCTOR: *Does anybody think we should keep going?*

LYRICS: *A new one just begun . . .*

WOMAN: *Damn you.*

LYRICS: *And so this is Christmas . . .*

BOY: *Mum!*

MAN: *I'm sorry. . . I'm sorry.*

LYRICS: *I hope you have fun. . .*

JOHN: *I wasn't drunk.*

MAN: *Do you understand what you've done.*

LYRICS: *The near and the dear ones . . .*

NURSE: *The passenger from the other vehicle has died.*

POLICEMAN: *I just have to give you an official caution.*

LRYICS: *The old and the young. . . A very, merry Christmas. And a happy New Year. Let's hope it's a good one . . .*

MOTHER: *He didn't mean to do it.*

SUPER: SHOULD YOU BE DRIVING HOME TONIGHT?

LYRICS: *. . . without any fear.*

SUPER: IF YOU DRINK, THEN DRIVE, YOU'RE A BLOODY IDIOT. TAC.

LYRICS (SPOKEN): *So this is Christmas.*

DRIVER: *Tonight's the night, mate. You, ah, reckon you're in with a bit of a chance?*

MALE PASSENGER: *Yeah. I wouldn't mind, mate.*

FEMALE PASSENGER: *Garry, can we slow down a bit?*

DRIVER: *Why? There's no one around.*

FEMALE PASSENGER: *Yeah, well I can feel my lunch bouncing about.*

DRIVER: *Geez, Jesse, the roads aren't my fault.*

GIRL PASSENGER: *Yeah, well it doesn't stop you from slowing down.*

DRIVER: *Okay, okay. Don't get your knickers in a twist. I've driven this road a hundred times. You go up over this rise, sharp turn to the right, another dip, then it's a quick left . . . C'mon, mate.*

FEMALE PASSENGER: *Garry!!*

DRIVER: *Can you just cool it. We're already running late to pick up Sophie.*

MALE PASSENGER: *Yeah. Hammer it, Gaz.*

FEMALE PASSENGER: *Shut up, Nick. Don't encourage him.*

DRIVER: *Okay, okay. Jesse, there's nothing to worry about, okay? I know this road.*

(SFX: CAR CRASHING)

SUPER: DON'T FOOL YOURSELF, SPEED KILLS. TAC.

PLEASE REMEMBER THIS BOOK IS FROM THE SHELVES OF

BOOK #

SHELF #

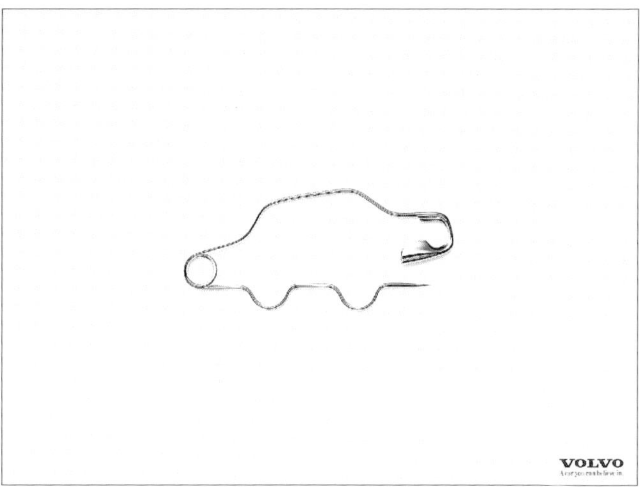

CONSUMER NEWSPAPER
OVER 600 LINES: SINGLE
and OUTDOOR: SINGLE

agency
Dentsu Young & Rubicam / Tokyo

client
Volvo Cars Japan

In the past few years, safety has been a big trend in car advertising, particularly in Japan. Double airbags. Side airbags. Airbags for economy cars. Toyota launched a big campaign to promote its strong cage structure. Opel claimed "the safest for the price." Everyone was selling safety. In other words, everyone was trying to become Volvo.

This was a challenging opportunity for us—the advertising agency for Volvo. We needed to find a way to fight back against the competitors who were all representing themselves like Volvo. We had to make Volvo stand out in this crowd. Be the forerunner in car safety, as it has always been. But how?

It seemed that doing an ad based on some unique safety feature would not be enough.

It would make Volvo seem like every other car pronouncing safety of their automobiles. We needed something stronger.

In the end we decided to do two ads. One that describes the superior technology that makes a Volvo a "Volvo," and another that used a much more symbolic description of Volvo's belief in safety. The latter was the "Safety Pin" ad.

The original idea had a headline with it. It was obvious that the idea worked best without the copy, but at first, nobody seemed to agree—not the art director, not the account management group, not the Japanese client. So, it was very fortunate that we had Knut Simonsson, a Swedish marketing director, working for the client. Knut understood the delicacy of communication and he approved the safety pin idea without the copy. However, even after his approval, we had to fight for two months to keep the ad copy-less.

What was the lesson extracted? A simple ad is not a product of a simple procedure but a product of many complicated processes.

MINORU KAWASE

MASAKAZU SAWA

TRACY WONG
WONGDOODY, Seattle

CONSUMER NEWSPAPER
OVER 600 LINES:
CAMPAIGN

agency
Leagas Delaney / London

client
Adidas

Trail-running is just like normal running—minus the tarmac, the neat straight paths, the cars, the noise, the pollution, the dog-walkers, the "walk"/"don't walk" signs.

That's why these trail-running ads are minus all those things too. We wanted to strip everything back. Simple, short messages. Shots of the middle-of-nowhere. And the Adidas logo nothing more than a quiet "hello, how are you, let's have a cup of tea together some time if you're free" to the reader.

SEAN DOYLE

DAVE DYE

The target audience for this quiet campaign was city-dwellers who were occasional runners, and the aim was to get them out exploring the countryside. "They're sort of anti-advertising," says Dave Dye, "we wanted them to feel like something you'd put on your wall."

agency
TBWA Chiat/Day,
Venice, CA

client
Nissan Motor
Corporation

People told us they flipped the channel as soon
as they smelled a car commercial coming. We
needed a way to get past their radar, so we
thought a remote-controlled car representing
a real car was a terrific device. After that, the
storyline of a studly action figure going to
pick up a sexy girl doll came easily. The capper
was getting Van Halen for the music track.
They signed the deal on the condition that
Nissan give a new car to each band member.
If you visit L.A. and see Eddie Van Halen
driving a black Turbo Z, now you'll know why.

ROB SILTANEN
JOE HEMP
JOHN BOONE

*"People don't like car advertising, so much of it looks the same. It has
to become a lot more about people than sheet metal. Most advertising
is unabsorbed: 'Toys' will get talked about, noticed and liked.
By that yardstick, it already works."*

LEE CLOW
TBWA Chiat/Day, Venice, CA

agency
Wieden & Kennedy/Portland

client
ESPN

We actually could make this really
short by just writing: Casting. that's
what made this spot work. Or we could
just write: Seth Hayes.

You know how when you talk about how
you want to shoot something and you'll
say, "let's just do it this way," and everybody says, "yeah," but then for whatever
reason you don't do it that way. Well,
thanks to a great agency producer named
Dan Duffy, a great creative director and
friend, Stacy Wall, and great directors
named Bryan Buckley and Frank Todaro,
and another great producer, Steve Orent,
this spot happened the right way.

We just drove over to the local Bristol,
Connecticut high school where they read
an announcement over the PA that said,
"Any boy that wants to be in an ESPN
commercial, come down to room 117 after
school today." About 150 kids including
some really angry girls met us there and
we had them all pretend to be sportscast-
ers and Seth was the best, plus he was a
big Red Sox fan so Bryan pushed for him
really hard. And then he came to the shoot
with his sweet mother (that's her standing
next to him in the spot) and just did an
amazing job. Can we get a pencil for Seth?

HANK PERLMAN
ROBERT PALMER

agency
Ogilvy & Mather / Mexico City

client
Duracell

Our Duracell client came to brief us on this new product: batteries for video cameras. We thought to ourselves, "This sounds good." The client told us that these batteries last 50 percent longer than any other battery. "Wow! This sounds great," we thought. We started kicking each other underneath the table. We knew this kind of product only comes once in a lifetime. "This is our chance to become finalists in the One Show!" we whispered to each other.

Finally, the client said: "Well, what we need is for you to develop and create an outstanding, rule-breaking, award-winning, sales rocket-launching, state of the art . . . brochure."

(*Total silence.*)

We only had one option: Cast some friends as actors, borrow some friend's house as our location, convince our Duracell client to air the commercials and, finally, get the hottest director in Mexico to do the ads . . . for free.

The odds for all this to happen were the same as winning the lotto . . . but hey, you never know.

CARLOS TOURNE
RAUL CARDOS
MAURICIO GALVAN
LOURDES LAMASNEY

CONSUMER TELEVISION
OVER :30 CAMPAIGN

agency
Hill Holliday Connors Cosmopulos / Boston

client
John Hancock Financial Services

David D'Alessandro, our client at John Hancock, issued a challenge. He wanted a campaign that would make people forget "Real Life, Real Answers." He gave us sufficient time, one year actually, to perfect the strategy, then create and produce the work. And he gave us the budget to work with the finest talent in the world—Tony Kaye, Mark Knopfler, Andre Betz and Sigourney Weaver.

This campaign is the least we could give them.

JAMIE MAMBRO
MIKE SHEEHAN
ERNIE SCHENCK

With music by Mark Knopfler and voice-over by Sigourney Weaver, this campaign dramatically makes the point that whatever happens in life, having insurance will prepare you. "We're living in a time of self-reliance, and this whole Walden Pond, Thoreau-esque theme is not an easy one to work into financial advertising, which by nature is a bit dry," says Ernie Schenck, one of the writers on the campaign. "This is all about investing. We have to take our future into our hands."

CONSUMER TELEVISION
VARYING LENGTHS CAMPAIGN

agency
Wieden & Kennedy / Portland

client
ESPN

In the "Self-Defense" spot, that's agency producer/ stunt man, Dan Duffy in the Albert Belle outfit. After we were done shooting, we all tackled Dan and had a big fight in which several of us sustained minor injuries. But it was fun.

Kerri Strug was a very nice girl and her voice wasn't as annoying in person as you might think. Thanks to everyone who was really working in the newsroom while we shot all the spots that took place in the newsroom. It's only sports.

The "Security" spot represents the first time we used a real stunt man in any of these. Frank Todaro and Hank Perlman got tossed around by King Kong Bundy in "Wrestlers," Bryan Buckley took a charge from the 6-foot-10 Juwan Howard in "Ringers," Dan Duffy did several stunts including "Self-Defense" as well as getting knocked over by Glenn Jacobs in "PA's Life," so by the time this one came around, you can call us wimps, but none of us wanted to get beaten up anymore.

One of the reasons why these spots turned out well and definitely one of the reasons they were fun to do was Allan Broce, the best client in the world. Thanks also to everyone at Wieden. It's a great agency.

ROBERT PALMER
HANK PERLMAN

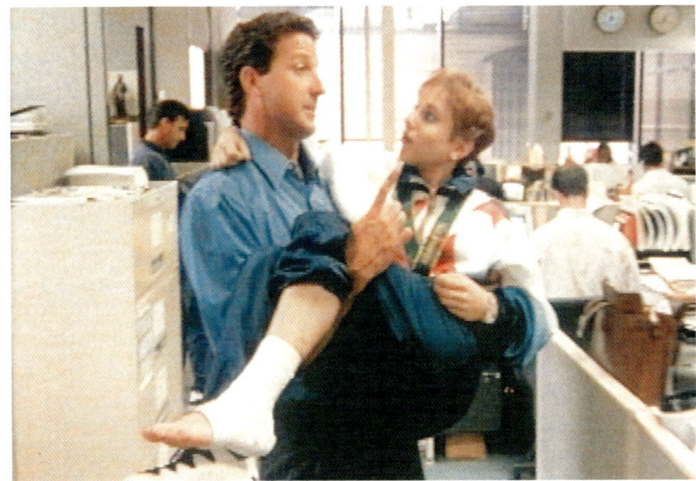

"One of the cool things to do is to try and be true to sports, everything's always changing and evolving," says art director Robert Palmer, explaining how the ESPN SportsCenter work keeps its freshness. "It's a huge collaborative thing. Sometimes the client, or Frank or Bryan (the directors), or anyone will come up with an idea . . . Or people will call us. We do them real quick and sometimes they work and sometimes they don't."

INTERACTIVE:
WEB SITE

agency
Rubin Postaer Interactive / Santa Monica

client
American Honda Motor Company

We created a site that married design with content in a fresh, engaging manner. We incorporated elements that were easy on the eyes and copy that was a succinct and witty read. Simple navigation tied it all together by bringing information to the surface and making it user-friendly. In other words, the user will never get lost because we provide a "bread crumb trail" at the top of each page.

We didn't forget the all-important fun factor. Users can play by coloring a car or building one out with their accessories of choice. Or they can get serious by figuring out how to finance it, then locate the nearest dealer by typing in their home address. Basically the only thing we don't do is leave the car parked out front with the keys in the ignition. But we haven't ruled that possibility out yet. In fact, the site is kept fresh by constantly updating and adding features that incorporate the latest technology.

Our take on this was that it didn't have to be another marketing tool lost amongst the millions of other sites out there. It became a content-rich reflection of what our Internet audience wanted to see. And a smart statement on how traditional advertising can translate into an interactive medium.

LUIS EMILIO RAMIREZ
BROOK BOLEY
VAN SECRIST
AVERY CARROLL

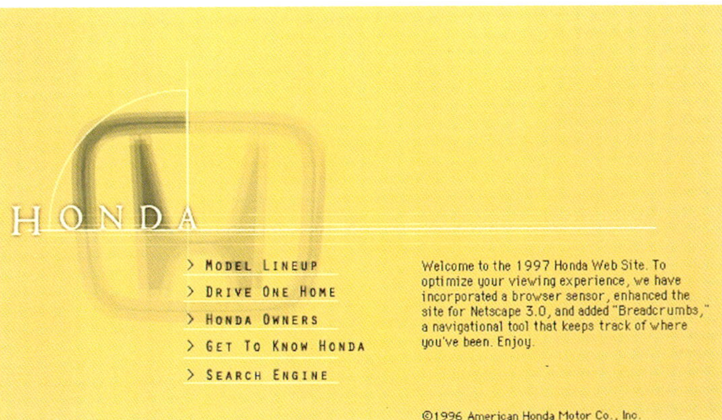

**PUBLIC SERVICE/POLITICAL
OUTDOOR AND POSTERS**

agency
Ogilvy & Mather/Auckland

client
Humane Society of New Zealand

Bring the pounds to the people: this idea is what started it all. "It can't be done," was the familiar response. "It is wrong to confine animals for display."

Given the highly-emotive nature of the campaign, and the fact that live dogs were being used, the public relations component of the campaign was crucial.

A letter was drafted and sent to all Humane Society members and animal welfare agencies such as the RSPCA prior to the launch, outlining the campaign and enclosing a fact sheet and news release. We also prepared Humane Society spokespeople for media interviews.

We built the billboards over a weekend. The dog was due to go in on a Monday morning 8:00 AM-10:00 AM and then again 4:00 PM-6:00 PM. By 9:00 AM that first day we had every radio station and every newspaper in the country down at the billboard site taking pictures, etc. We had traffic jams and people wanting to adopt the dog on the spot. By 9:30 AM the TV cameras were there. We made prime time news that day across all networks.

It's been said that this has been the most successful Public Service campaign in New Zealand.

It's not that it was a good idea—we all have good ideas—but it is testimony to perseverance, teamwork and stubbornness: Keeping it sold. Holding the client's hand. Working with others—especially our tactful PR department—who smoothed many waters. It wasn't just a "sensational" crowd stopper. It worked. We saved the dogs from being killed and achieved a database.

QUENTIN PFISZTER
BRUCE MATCHETT
IAN BROWN

**CONSUMER MAGAZINE
COLOR FULL PAGE
OR SPREAD: SINGLE
and CAMPAIGN**

agency
Goodby Silverstein & Partners/San Francisco

client
Polaroid Corporation

The best thing about working at GS&P? No gangbangs!

SCOTT AAL
CHRIS HOOPER
AL KELLY
BOB KERSTETTER
MIKE MAZZA
STEVE PAYONZECK
VALERIE ANG-POWELL
GRANT RICHARDS

While the overall campaign strategy was to show typical and not-so-typical ways to use Polaroid, the print specifically addresses the issue of proof, via a series of quirky and idiosyncratic snapshots. It's based, says Al Kelly, on real-life experiences. "A lot of contractors use Polaroids as proof that they haven't screwed up on the job. We just glamorized it a bit."

COLLATERAL BROCHURES
OTHER THAN BY MAIL

agency
Hal Riney & Partners/San Francisco

client
GMEV1/Saturn Corporation

Advertising makes people buy things they
don't need or can't afford. We know that's
not true, yet deep in the back of our minds
a little voice whispers, "Yes, but maybe
advertising could be doing more."

Such is the case with the launch of the EV1,
the first electric car produced in the US.
It is not merely the introduction of a new
car or a new technology, but the promise of
a world devoid of auto pollution.

We knew that any communication had
to reflect this challenge. This challenge
became the rallying cry around which all
subsequent decisions were based. All those
who participated, supplier and client alike,
were held to this standard. The choice of
photographers, the tonality of the copy, the
shape of the book, the uncoated stock and
saturated use of printing inks, the binding of
the final product reflects our desire to bring to
the public a package that lives up to its promise.

Advertising provides choice, but once in a
great while it can also offer change.

PETER DI GRAZIA
TOM SAPUTO
JOHN DOYLE
LINDA BRADFORD
REBECCA RIVERA
TOM McCARTHY
DAVE O'HARE

COLLATERAL
DIRECT MAIL:
SINGLE

agency
Hunt Adkins/Minneapolis

client
Dublin Productions

Gather 'round children; bask in the glow of
our brilliance. For too long we have been
denied a forum such as this, a means to communicate with our doting, worshipful throng.
But now, at long last, we can instruct you in
the ways of ingeniusness. Yes, now all you
pathetic, gruel-brained pieces of bathroom-
tile scum can suckle at our breast of wisdom.
We are like gods, throwing down lightning
bolts from our mountain top. So powerful is
our intellect that the full force of it would
tear you asunder. We will therefore shield
you from our blinding supernova of enlightenment by giving you but one atom from our
universe of wisdom. But wait! Why do you
want this instruction? What is your infinitesi-
mal brain plotting? A little knowledge and
suddenly the pupil fancies himself superior to
the teacher? Suddenly the pupil has tied the
teacher, naked, to the lectern and is laying his
hand upon the whipping rod? Well, we will
not be that naked teacher! Down, mutinous
peasants! You shall have no knowledge and like it!

STEVE MITCHELL
DOUG ADKINS

(USING A TECHNIQUE SIMILAR TO MORPHING, THE WOMAN'S VOICE SLOWLY CHANGES TO THAT OF A CHILD'S DURING THE COURSE OF THE COMMERCIAL)

MATURE WOMAN: *He dimmed the lights and, smiling, led me by the hand to the bedroom. Slowly . . .*

SLIGHTLY YOUNGER WOMAN: *. . . he lay me down on the bed. His eyes pierced my skin. As he caressed my cheek, I could feel his breath . . .*

TEENAGE GIRL: *. . . hot on my neck. His hand moved down towards my top, so lightly I could hardly feel it . . .*

TEN-YEAR-OLD GIRL: *I breathed fast as he undid my shirt. He touched me and whispered in my ear . . .*

FIVE-YEAR-OLD GIRL: *. . . don't tell Mommy.*

ANNCR: *Sexual abuse can scar you for life. Get help, call Childline on 08000 55555.*

PUBLIC SERVICE/ POLITICAL RADIO: SINGLE

agency
Hunt Lascaris TBWA / Johannesburg

client
Childline

There I was, staring blankly at the wall for the third day in a row, trying to think of something for radio that has never been done before. As you can imagine this isn't easy. After all, if something hasn't already been done, it's usually because it never should be. Then suddenly from the top corner spot of my white wall jumped out the thought "morphing." (Yes, it's been done, but only on TV so it doesn't count.) Surely, I figured, if you can do it visually you can do it in sound. So I threw in a bit of Mills and Boons style writing, and started weaving a story around changing voices. And somewhere between enjoying what I was writing and actually caring for what I was writing about, emerged this ad.

SAMANTHA KOENDERMAN

CONSUMER RADIO: SINGLE

agency
BBDO West / Los Angeles

client
The Solaris Group / Ortho

When you're in the business of killing something, it's almost in poor taste to talk about how well it works. Well, frankly, poor taste is our forte. So we threw political-correctness out the window and found the lighter side of death. That's when animal rights organizations wrote letters to the editors of several newspapers, complaining about the spots (they didn't mind that the product worked, they just didn't think we should be so damn happy about it). That made the client a little nervous, but it wasn't something that bothered us at all. After all, if you make a product that kills things, you can't expect to get PETA's seal of approval. All the newspaper coverage led to open debates on talk radio stations, many of which got requests to play the commercials. In the end, the product flew off the shelves and we rode to glory on the backs of fire ants. Was it the right thing to do? Hard to say. But we have a gold pencil. See you in hell!

APRIL WINCHELL
MICK KUISEL

MAN: *There's nothing good about fire ants. They don't pollinate your roses. They don't make cute little sounds when they rub their legs together. All they do is build a big mound in your yard and bite the hell out of anyone who gets near it. That's it. That's their sole contribution to mankind. And that's why they have to die. It's that simple. You cannot rehabilitate a fire ant. You have to kill him, his little red friends, and that big fat queen down there making more fire ants. Oh, you could lug a big sack of chemicals and a garden hose around the yard, but that's about as fun as getting bit in the first place. No, what you need is Antstop Orthene Fire Ant Killer from Ortho. You put two teaspoons of Antstop around the mound and you're done. You don't even put water in it. The scout ants track it back into the mound—and here's the really good part—everybody dies, even the queen. And while there's joy in all creatures living in harmony, it's nothing compared to wasting fire ants. Now that's a rush . . . Antstop Orthene Fire Ant Killer from Ortho. Kick fire ant butt.*

agency
Grey Advertising / Melbourne

client
Transport Accident Commission

Best Of Show

After 36 ads over seven years, the TAC campaign has reduced the Victorian (Australia) road toll by more than 50 percent and reduced the cost of road trauma to the community by more than A$3 billion.

Our original brief was to upset, outrage and appall.

Obviously, the One Show judges did not agree.

ROB DOW
GREG HARPER

"It's very real, it's not a trick," says art director Rob Dow of the gut-wrenching and highly effective TAC campaign. In "Bush Telegraph," after having one too many with friends, a father gets in the car with his son, and, momentarily distracted, drifts through a stop sign and gets flattened by a ten-ton trailer truck. "If you drink, then drive, you're a bloody idiot," is the tag-line. "The lines are delivered in a dry, laconic style, designed to capture the absolute reality of it," says Dow. "You say, 'that could be me, I've done that myself.'" As one One Show judge pointed out, "you don't view it as a judge, but emotionally, as a father."

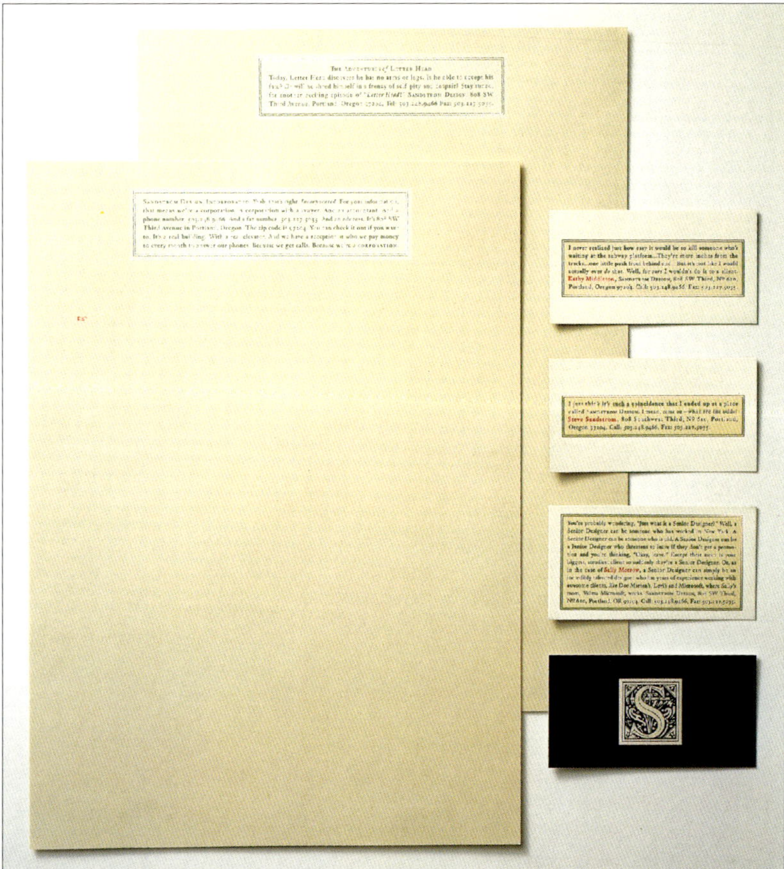

COLLATERAL
SELF-PROMOTION

agency
Sandstrom Design / Portland

client
Sandstrom Design

The absolute last thing I wanted to do was something that we would call "design-y." Bland would be better than that. I had this idea of the return address on an envelope being written and set in a paragraph form. A little story containing our address, that would have to be read by the Post Office if returning a misguided letter. The idea of little stories seemed to work for letterhead, labels, and business cards as well. I asked four associates—Amy Krouse Rosenthal, Austin Howe, Jean Rhode, and Peter Wegner—all exceptional writers—if they would create these little bits of information about Sandstrom Design, our staff, our location, or anything that might relate to our business. I gave them personnel profiles and a list of necessary executions: letterhead, envelopes, mailing labels, business cards and fax forms. The limitations were that each story had to be brief and include our name, address and phone number. The exercise yielded hilarious results. To contrast the humor, we set the stories in a dry, bookish font and applied them to all our materials.

-Steve Sandstrom

In a funny-how-the-world-works kind of way, the day I found out we got this shiny, gold pencil was also the day I officially resigned from the world of advertising. So this award feels extra good, *complete*. And, thank you, Steve, for asking me to participate in this whacked-out project in the first place—a writer's dream.

-Amy Krouse Rosenthal

The "Rats" copy was supposed to be a radio spot, not some frou-frou design thing. Oh well. At least now everyone knows what truly motivates the people at Sandstrom Design: Rodent Fear.

-Austin Howe

STEVE SANDSTROM
AUSTIN HOWE
PETER WEGNER
AMY KROUSE ROSENTHAL
JEAN RHODE

agency
Hunt Lascaris TBWA / Johannesburg

client
Playtex

I knew I'd never meet Eva in the flesh, so I thought
of the next best thing. The hard part was making the
3-D image work so that the breasts look realistic.
It was all trial and error. Only Eva knows if I did
her any justice.

ANTON CRONE

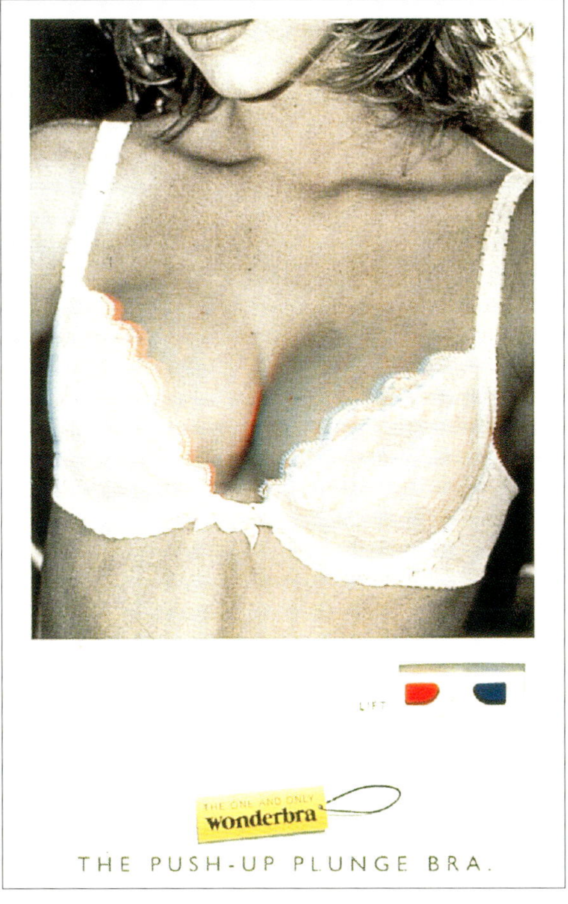

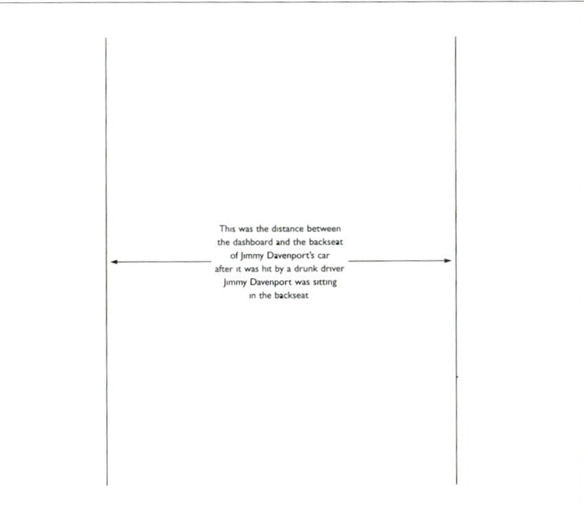

**PUBLIC SERVICE/POLITICAL NEWSPAPER
OR MAGAZINE: SINGLE**

agency
The Martin Agency / Richmond

client
Mothers Against Drunk Driving

A family of five was in a car when it was struck from
behind by a drunk driver. The force of the impact caused
the backseat to come within inches of the dashboard.
The entire family was killed, including two small
children, who were sitting in the backseat.

A story like this doesn't need a clever ad trick.
Please don't drink and drive.

JAMIE MAHONEY
JOE ALEXANDER

**CONSUMER MAGAZINE
B/W OR COLOR
LESS THAN A PAGE:
CAMPAIGN**

agency
Fallon McElligott/Minneapolis

client
Nikon

Tip #155: No matter what your ad
assignment, go right to the goofy
stock photos.

DAVE PULLAR

ANDY AZULA

**CONSUMER TELEVISION:
:20 AND UNDER: SINGLE**

agency
Wieden & Kennedy/Portland

client
ESPN/National Hockey League

The idea for this spot was from 1993 but it
kept getting killed (by the Devil's PR Director)
every time we were going to shoot with New
Jersey. So we just kept presenting it to them
until finally they had won a Stanley Cup and
were in a really good mood. The voice-over is
the multi-talented Frank Todaro who is not
the Devil and in fact happens to be a really
nice guy. And by the way, without the talent
and hard work of Frank and his partner, the
also multi-talented and slightly more evil Bryan
Buckley, as well as their amazing producer, Steve
Orent, this whole campaign wouldn't be what
it is. In fact, it most likely wouldn't be at all.
As always, agency producers Colleen Wellman
and former All-Minnetonka Right Wing, Ben
Grylewicz deserve a lot of credit as well. By the
way, Ken Daneyko, the player in this spot, is
also a really cool guy (in addition to being a
heck of a defenseman) who has a restaurant in
West Caldwell, New Jersey called Mezza Notte
and we hear the food is really good.

HANK PERLMAN
DARRYL McDONALD

CONSUMER TELEVISION
UNDER $50,000 BUDGET

agency
Juan Cravero / Buenos Aires

client
Technical Institute of Contemporary Music

Play it again, Sam... Michael, John, Ted, Peter, Timothy, Ronald or whatever your name is.

JUAN CRAVERO
MARTIN CASIOS
DIEGO LIVACHOFF

"I found that a great deal of the ads in this year's show reminded me of work done during the late '60s by agencies such as Doyle Dane Bernbach and DKG: 'real life' as seen through a somewhat humorous filter."

TRACY WONG
WONGDOODY, Seattle

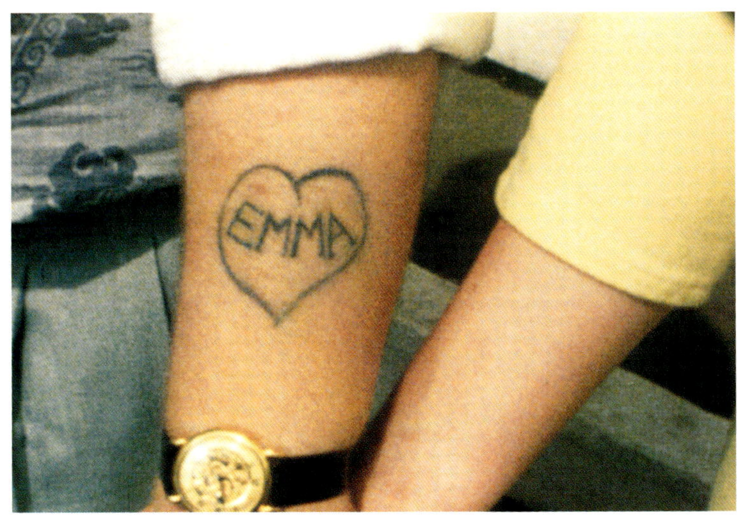

CONSUMER TELEVISION
:20 AND UNDER: CAMPAIGN

agency
Leo Burnett / London

client
McDonald's

Why waste money on expensive looking adverts to sell hamburgers? Simply shoot your commercial on 16mm film, degrade the quality and use cheap, inexperienced actors.

This money-saving tip was brought to you by Jane Atkinson and Matt Hazell.

JANE ATKINSON
MATT HAZELL

CONSUMER TELEVISION
:30 CAMPAIGN

agency
Wieden & Kennedy / Portland

client
ESPN

Charlie Steiner was a great sport (no pun intended) about this spot. Even when it came to the last shot where it looks like he's masturbating. Along with client, Allan Broce, we decided to tell Charlie that the good news was that he'd be doing his first "love scene." The bad news was that he was going to be alone. Thanks, Charlie.

HANK PERLMAN
ROBERT PALMER

PUBLIC SERVICE/POLITICAL
NEWSPAPER OR MAGAZINE: CAMPAIGN

agency
Leagas Delaney / London

client
English Heritage

Coming up with the ideas for this campaign was easy. Beheadings and other bodily mutilations usually make for better than average stories.

We wanted the ads to look as elegant as you'd expect from someone like English Heritage – but with a decidedly unstuffy tone of voice.

Once we'd sorted out the ideas and the rough layout, it was over to Dave Wakefield and his garage full of metal fonts. He gave the ads a beautifully classic look with the English Heritage logo being nothing more than a "hello, how are the kids, would you mind lending me 50 pence, 'til tomorrow" to the reader.

SEAN DOYLE
DAVE DYE

COLLEGE COMPETITION

Assignment
Sushi Tugo

College
Portfolio Center / Atlanta

I cannot believe we are concept-ing this little blurb. I guess it's so everyone will think we're as creative as our ads. Or so we hope.

We could tell you some weird thing about how we ate sushi while singing "A Fishin' We Will Go" backwards while being shot out of a cannon in a trapeze leotard to come up with this campaign. And then you'd think we're just as creative.

But we just can't bring our-selves to do that. We have to tell you the truth, though painful it is. We worked hard and long. Over and over again to get to where we got. And that's it. No fish stories. No nothing. Sorry.

Mark, I hope we still get a job after writing this.

NED BROWN-STEARNS
MARK GRAHAM

OUTDOOR: CAMPAIGN

agency
Wieden & Kennedy / Portland

client
Nike

It is indeed an honor to receive this One Show pencil. We would like to thank everyone involved. We would especially like to thank Jamie Barrett. Jamie is nice. Jamie is tall. Jamie is nice and tall. God bless Jamie Barrett.

ERIC SILVER
ROGER BENTLEY

Designed to be viewed by tennis enthusiasts on the Flushing subway line en route to the US Open, this series of ads took its yellow, black and white graphics inspiration from the instructions inside New York taxi cabs. "It was a concerted effort for the US Open," says art director Roger Bentley, who says the creative team developed a number of different messages so riders wouldn't get bored.

PRINT FINALISTS

**CONSUMER
NEWSPAPER
OVER 600 LINES:
SINGLE**

art director
Damon Collins

writer
Mary Wear

typographer
Joe Hoza

client
The Economist

agency
Abbott Mead Vickers.
BBDO/London

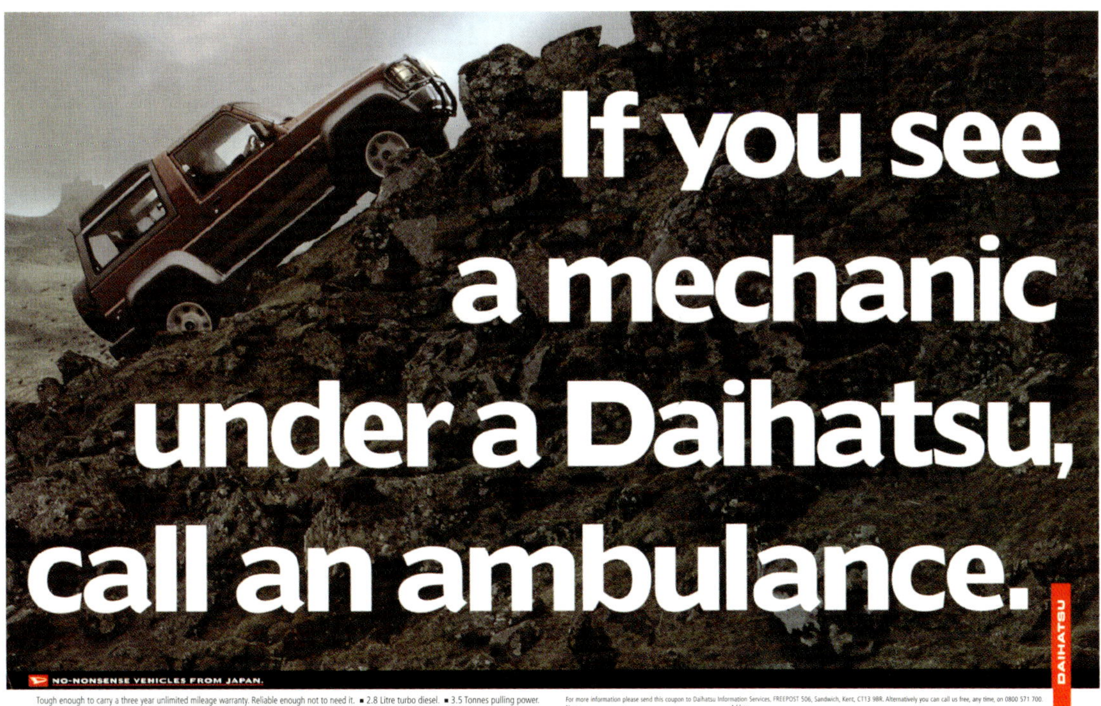

art directors
Richard Dennison
Markham Smith

writers
Markham Smith
Richard Dennison

photographer
Russell Porcas

client
Daihatsu UK

agency
Banks Hoggins
O'Shea / London

art director
Jason Bramley

writer
Jonathan Biggins

photographer
Yörg Sunderman

client
Heineken

agency
Bates / Singapore

**CONSUMER
NEWSPAPER
OVER 600 LINES:
SINGLE**

art director
Chris Robb

writers
Harold Einstein
Kathy Hepinstall

photographer
Geof Kern

client
L.A. Cellular

agency
BBDO West/
Los Angeles

art director
Scott Dube

writer
Zak Mroueh

photographer
Ian Campbell

client
Federal Express

agency
BBDO/Toronto

PRINT FINALISTS

art director
Scott Dube

writer
Zak Mroueh

photographer
Ian Campbell

client
Federal Express

agency
BBDO/Toronto

ANXIOUSLY WAITING for a box shipment to clear customs can cost you more than just your sanity. You can lose the faith of your customers, not to mention the cost you pay in brokerage fees. To speed up the process, FedEx has in-house customs brokers available at no extra charge. These experts will not only help you clear customs, they'll help clear your mind. So relax. Call 1·800·Go·FedEx.

art director
Scott Dube

writer
Zak Mroueh

photographer
Ian Campbell

client
Federal Express

agency
BBDO/Toronto

TRUST FedEx to get your boxes across Canada, the U.S., or to any of our 211 international destinations. (We guarantee they will arrive on time or your money back.) Because when it comes to shipping boxes, you don't have to worry about our reputation for reliability – but what about yours? Next time, call 1·800·Go·FedEx.

**CONSUMER
NEWSPAPER
OVER 600 LINES:
SINGLE**

art directors
Jon Parkinson
Harvey Hoffenberg

writers
Harvey Hoffenberg
Jon Parkinson

designer
Michelle Sumi

client
Taco Bell Corporation

agency
Bozell/Costa Mesa, CA

art director
David Ayriss

writer
Steve Johnston

photographer
Bob Waldman

client
The Oregonian

agency
Cole & Weber/
Portland

PRINT FINALISTS

art director
Bill Winchester

writer
Tom Evans

photographer
Curtis Johnson

client
Pfizer Animal Health

agency
Colle & McVoy /
Minneapolis

art directors
John Doyle
John Emmert

writer
Kara Goodrich

photographer
Geoff Stein

client
Shreve Crump & Low

agency
Doyle, Inc. / Weston, CT

**CONSUMER
NEWSPAPER
OVER 600 LINES:
SINGLE**

art director
Dean Hanson

writer
Tom Rosen

photographer
Rodney Smith

client
BMW

agency
Fallon McElligott/
Minneapolis

art director
Patrick Sutherland

writer
Ari Merkin

photographer
Vic Huber

client
Land Rover
North America

agency
Grace & Rothschild/
New York

Permanent four-wheel drive,
part-time four-wheel drive,
what's the difference?

There are off-road vehicles, and then there are vehicles that go off road.
In category A you'll find the Land Rover Discovery.
A vehicle that's prepared for potential hazards long before you are.
Because even though ordinary 4x4 offer the option of switching from two-wheel drive to four-wheel drive, the Discovery offers you the benefit of never having to decide.

So no matter what kind of unexpectedly twisted mountain road, ice covered highway, or rain soaked asphalt you're driving on, it's always prepared to keep you there.
In truth, there are dozens of features that make Land Rovers superior to other 4x4s.
But for now we'd like you to keep in mind one major distinction.
It certainly beats having to shift on the

LAND-ROVER
DISCOVERY

OUT
UNLUCKY SPOT   No. 0419
Please, be careful out there.
THE LUCKY SPOT
GOLDEN NUGGET
LAUGHLIN

**CONSUMER
NEWSPAPER
OVER 600 LINES:
SINGLE**

art director
Chris Poulin

writer
George Goetz

illustrator
Charles Anderson

client
Lotus Development
Corporation

agency
Hill Holliday Connors
Cosmopulos/Boston

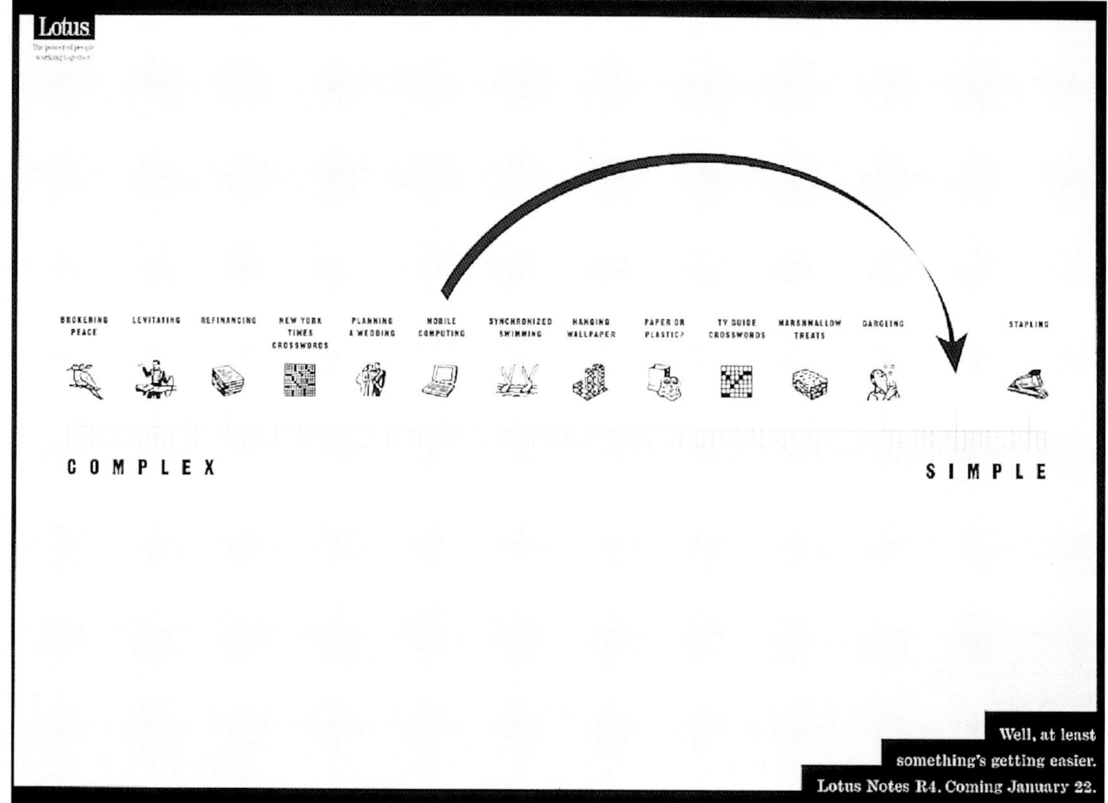

art director
Chris Poulin

writer
George Goetz

illustrator
Charles Anderson

client
Lotus Development
Corporation

agency
Hill Holliday Connors
Cosmopulos/Boston

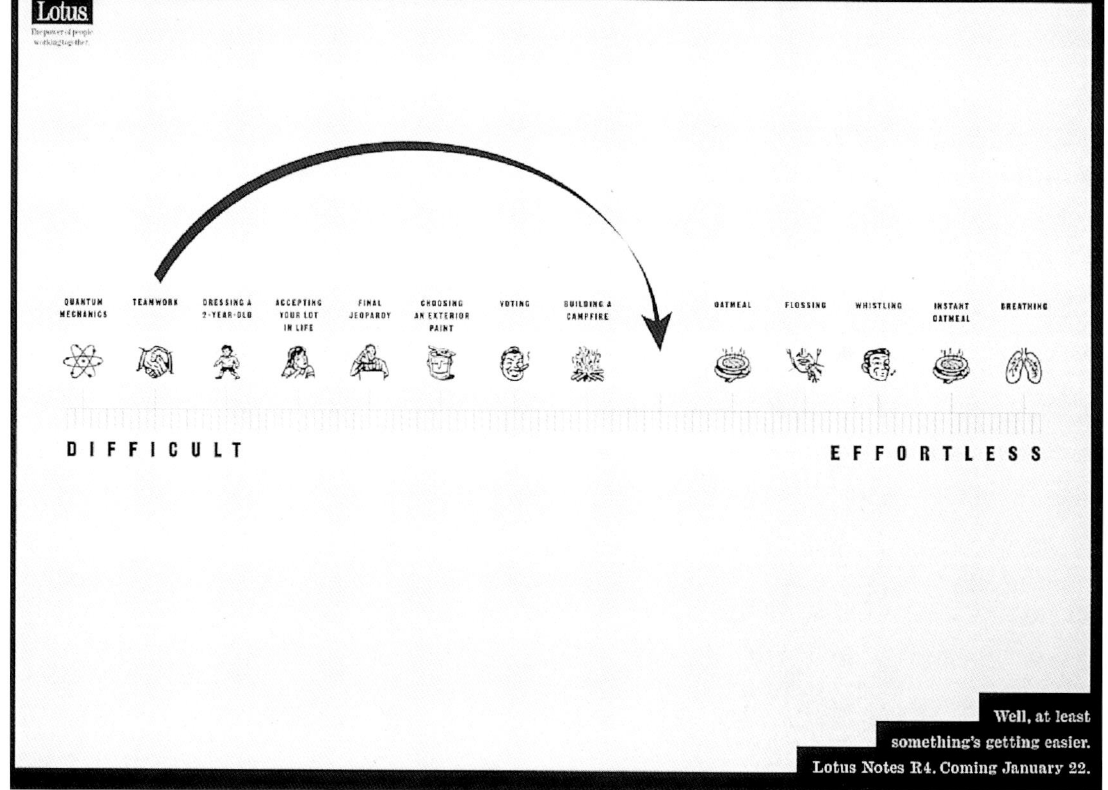

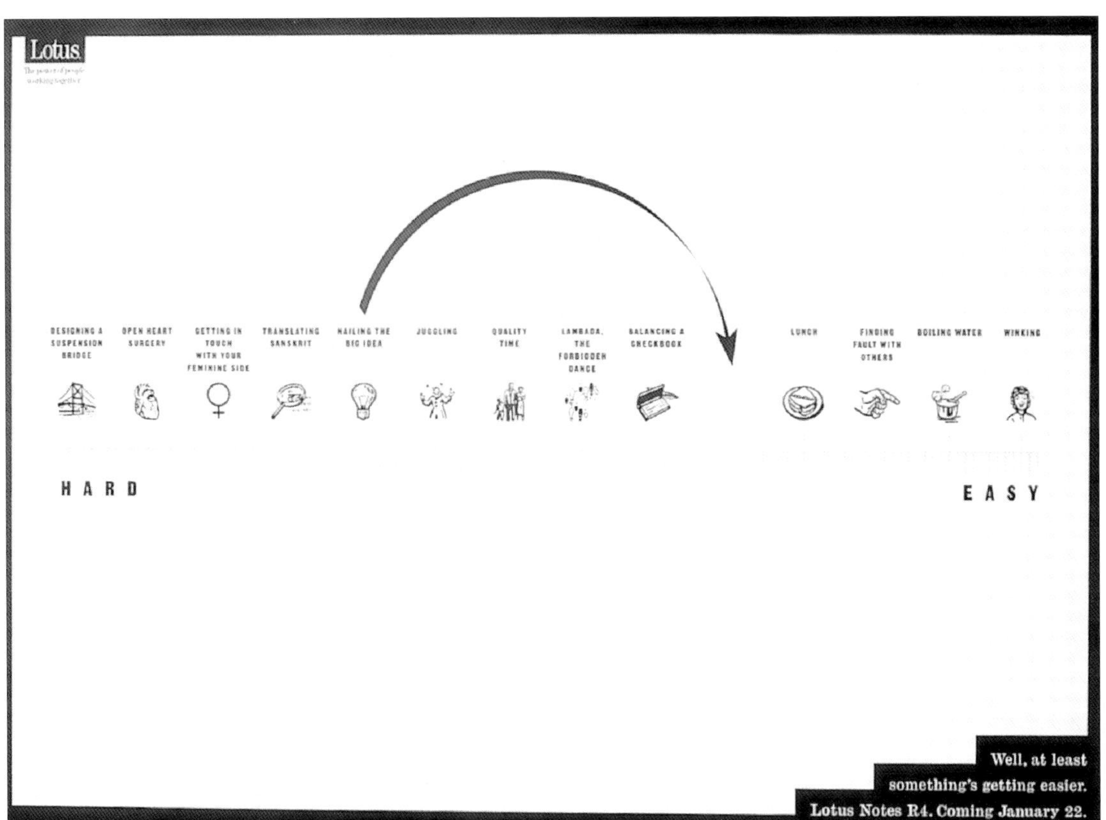

art director
Chris Poulin

writer
George Goetz

illustrator
Charles Anderson

client
Lotus Development
Corporation

agency
Hill Holliday Connors
Cosmopulos/Boston

art director
Dave Beverley

writer
Rob Burleigh

client
Adidas

agency
Leagas Delaney/
London

**CONSUMER
NEWSPAPER
OVER 600 LINES:
SINGLE**

art director
Dave Dye

writer
Sean Doyle

photographer
Sally Gall

client
Adidas

agency
Leagas Delaney/
London

art director
Tan Yew Leong

writer
Yasmin Ahmad

client
P. Lal Store

agency
Leo Burnett/
Kuala Lumpur

What do George Bush and fungus have in common?

The answer, of course, is a passion for shoes.

Fortunately, this is where the similarity ends. (Although some Democrats may well disagree.)

While Mr.Bush has a distinct penchant for the fine craftsmanship of Allen-Edmonds shoes, fungi are somewhat less discerning.

Mr.Doshi of P.Lal Store explains:

"Regardless of its quality, a shoe to fungi is both haute cuisine and five-star accommodation. All they require to survive and thrive are moisture, nutrients and warmth. Shoes, I'm afraid, are a glorious supply of all three.

"Good leathers, on the other hand, have a high resistance to fungus. To begin with, they are tanned to impede organic growth of any sort.

"Furthermore, the pores in leather are big enough as to allow foot perspiration to escape, yet small enough to prevent too much water from getting in. So leather stays dry longer.

"Still," he cautions, "tropical fungus, like tropical women, should never be taken for granted. Hot, humid climates like ours have a way of inducing the desire to procreate.

"Always dry out shoes after use, before storing. And never store them in damp areas. The rest I hardly need mention. If you can afford my shoes, I assume you are sufficiently educated to change your socks and wash your feet regularly.

"Then again," he ponders, "these days, an educated gentleman is often ill-disposed."

For such a person, Mr.Doshi strongly recommends that he should assign the following duty to his domestic:

1) Mix 1/4 cup vinegar with 1/4 cup baking soda and 1 cup water.

2) Dip a clean rag in the solution and wipe out the inside of the shoe.

3) Use a separate clean wet rag to wipe the inside of the shoe again.

4) Leave to dry, in about the time it takes to finish two chapters in a P.G.Wodehouse.

"Do this once a month," he assures, "and Messrs.Fungi will have to set up home in places other than your shoes or the Bush residence."

P.Lal Store is a purveyor of fine imported leather shoes like Allen-Edmonds, Crockett & Jones, Cheaney, Loake and Rombah Wallace. Every item at P.Lal Store is sold at the guaranteed lowest fixed price or your money back. 

"Must you write about this pair?" asks an agitated Mr.Doshi of P.Lal Store, "They are not even for sale."

"I do believe they're the most interesting shoes I've ever seen," I declare stubbornly. "Would you be so kind as to tell me what they are called at least ?"

"If you insist," sighs Mr Doshi, "they're called 'winkle-pickers'. Worn by fools in the 1960s.

"Their older brothers, no less vulgar in nature, date back to the Middle Ages.

"The *poulaine*, they were called. Duly banned by the Pope of the day, on account of its 16-inch length. Apparently, it reminded His Holiness too much of a man's unmentionables; a term I would sooner reserve for the wearer rather than the shoe."

Quietly, I raise my eyes well above belt level, praying that Mr. Doshi forgets I ever expressed such inordinate interest in something so phallic.

But alas, my eyes fall right on the winkle-pickers again, hung most prominently on the wall facing the main entrance of P.Lal Store on Jalan Tuanku Abdul Rahman.

In an effort to justify my curiosity, I exclaim, "Then why do you display them so publicly?"

"To scare people, my dear," he replies coolly, "from wearing 'trendy' shoes. Shoes like the ugly 'platforms'.

"Despite the added inches, platforms, I feel, do so lower the stature of a gentleman."

Not surprisingly, P.Lal Store, the oldest established store in Kuala Lumpur, has banned trendy shoes of all shapes and sizes from their shelves since 1929.

One can only find sensible timeless designs like oxfords, derbies, brogues, moccasins and d'Orsays in P.Lal Store.

"Our Crockett & Jones, I'll have you know, have graced the halls and corridors of Buckingham Palace. And our Allen-Edmonds, the White House."

P.Lal Store, of course, is a prime purveyor of some of the world's handsomest and most exquisitely handcrafted footwear and other gentlemanly paraphernalia.

Every item is sold at the guaranteed lowest fixed price or your money back.

"For those interested in the classic," he concludes, "we offer a wide selection. But for those afflicted with an affinity for platform shoes, bell-bottoms, winkle-pickers and other unsavoury items of clothing, we offer our deepest sympathies."

**CONSUMER
NEWSPAPER
OVER 600 LINES:
SINGLE**

art directors
Mark Wennecker
John Boone
Ron Huey

writer
Anne Marie Floyd

photographer
Smith/Nelson

client
Mercedes-Benz of
North America

agency
The Martin Agency/
Richmond

art director
Brian Fandetti

writer
Joe Alexander

photographer
David Jennings

client
Wrangler Company

agency
The Martin Agency/
Richmond

Lucky glance from 10,000m
Imagine how easily she could spot your empty wine glass.
BRITISH AIRWAYS
The world's favourite airline

The Opinionist
The Sophist
The Protagonist
The Artist
The Scientist
The Purist
The Nonconformist
The Humanist
The Internationalist
Informed people know us by another name.

**CONSUMER
NEWSPAPER
OVER 600 LINES:
SINGLE**

art director
Stuart Gill

writer
Di Lowe

photographer
Mark Polybank

client
First Choice Holidays/
Freespirit

agency
Ogilvy & Mather/
London

art director
Stuart Gill

writer
Di Lowe

photographer
Mark Polybank

client
First Choice Holidays/
Freespirit

agency
Ogilvy & Mather/
London

PRINT FINALISTS

art director
Sally Overheu

writer
Jackie Hathiramani

photographer
Sally Overheu

client
The British Council

agency
Ogilvy & Mather/
Singapore

art director
Felicity Greig

writer
Phil Mailer

photographer
Gerard Turnley

client
IBM

agency
Ogilvy & Mather
Rightford Searle-Tripp &
Makin/Johannesburg

**CONSUMER
NEWSPAPER
OVER 600 LINES:
SINGLE**

art director
Wade Devers

writer
Mark Nardi

photographer
Jack Richmond

illustrator
Peter Hall

typographer
Joffre Lefevre

client
Children's Hospital

agency
Pagano Schenck &
Kay/Boston

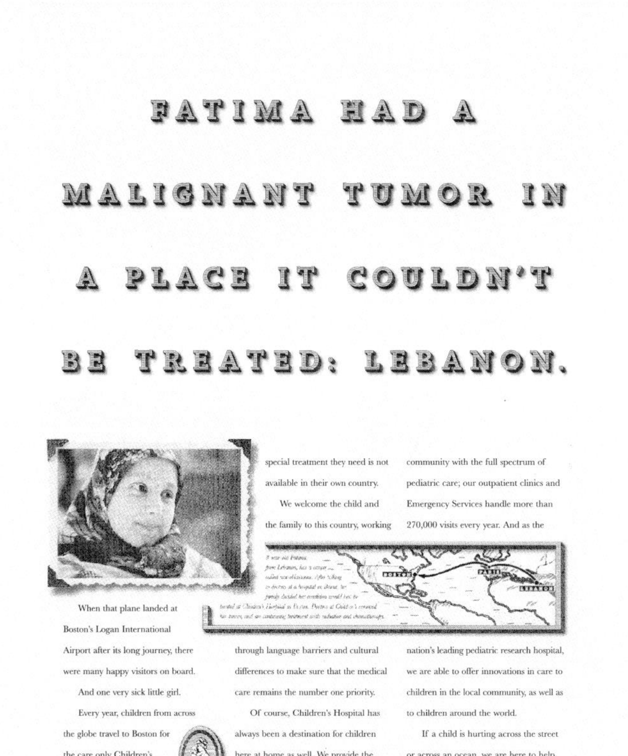

art director
Mark Martin

writer
Chris Rickaby

photographer
Alex Telfer

client
Gilmoor Veterinary
Services

agency
Robson Brown
Advertising/Newcastle
Upon Tyne, England

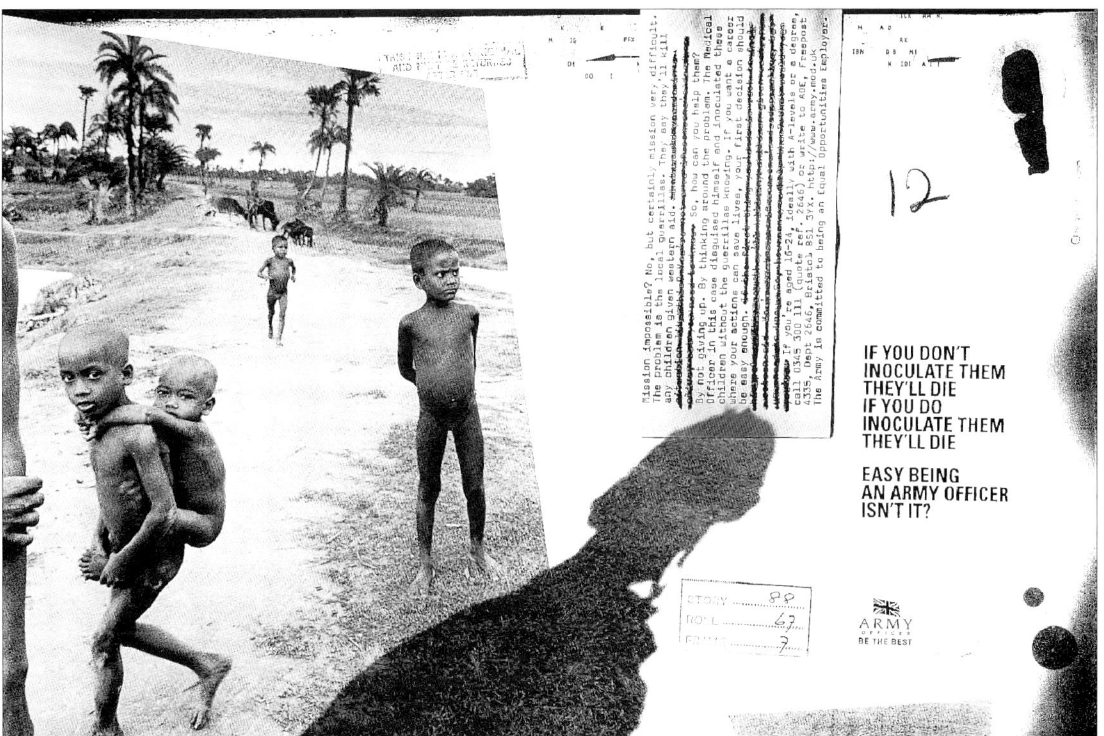

art directors
Alexandra Taylor
Nik Studzinski

writers
Adam Kean
Jason Fretwell

photographer
Chris Steele-Perkins

client
Army / COI

agency
Saatchi & Saatchi /
London

art directors
Alexandra Taylor
Nik Studzinski

writers
Adam Kean
Jason Fretwell

photographer
Dean Steadman

client
Army / COI

agency
Saatchi & Saatchi /
London

**CONSUMER
NEWSPAPER
OVER 600 LINES:
SINGLE**

art directors
Alexandra Taylor
Nik Studzinski

writers
Adam Kean
Jason Fretwell

photographer
First Base

client
Army/COI

agency
Saatchi & Saatchi/
London

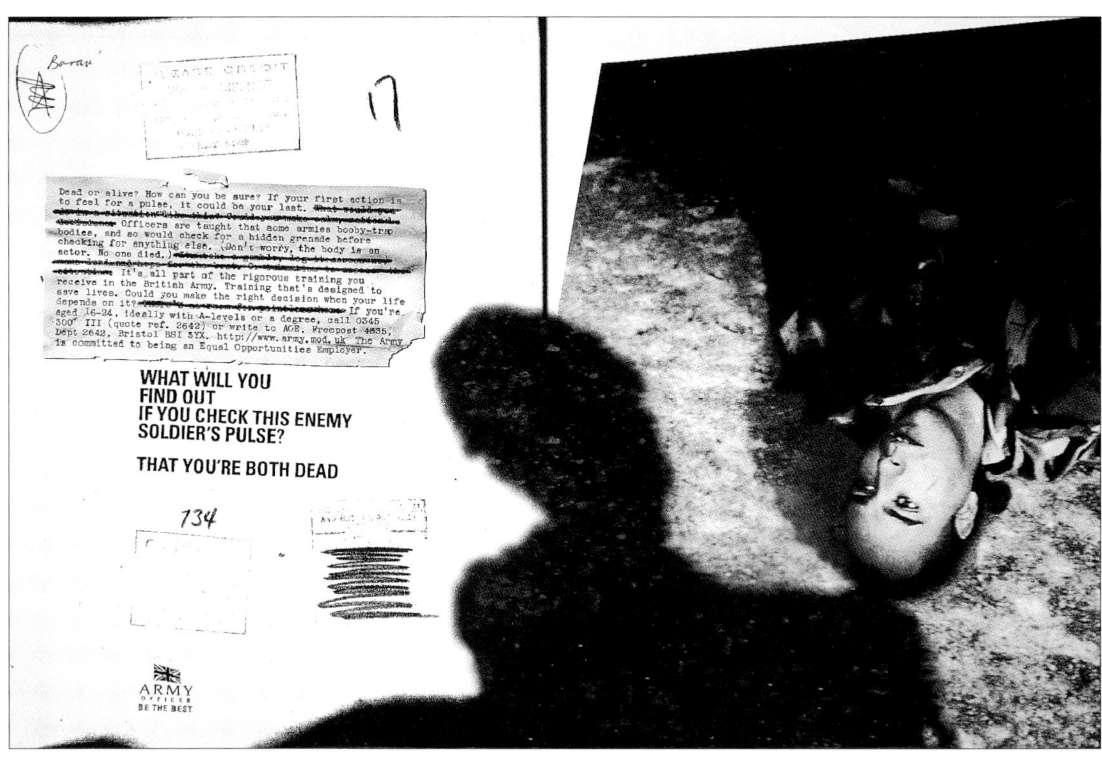

art directors
Alexandra Taylor
Nik Studzinski

writers
Adam Kean
Jason Fretwell

photographers
Fouad El Khoury
Liam Kennedy

client
Army/COI

agency
Saatchi & Saatchi/
London

See Britain's Royal Air Force Aerobatic team, 'The Red Arrows', flying the world renowned British Aerospace Hawk aircraft over Sydney Harbour 2 – 2.30pm, Friday January 26. British Aerospace Australia wish to take this opportunity to salute the Royal Australian Air Force on their 75th anniversary. Another impressive feat.

**CONSUMER
NEWSPAPER
OVER 600 LINES:
SINGLE**

art director
Fergus Fleming

writer
Richard Grisdale

photographer
Gary Heery

client
Toyota Motor
Corporation

agency
Saatchi & Saatchi/
Sydney

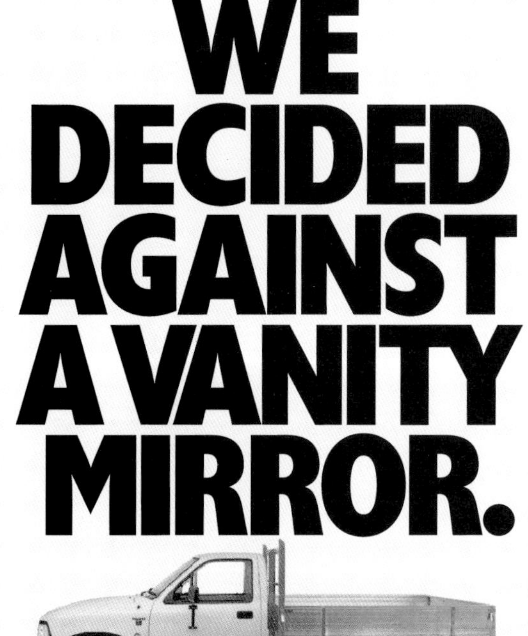
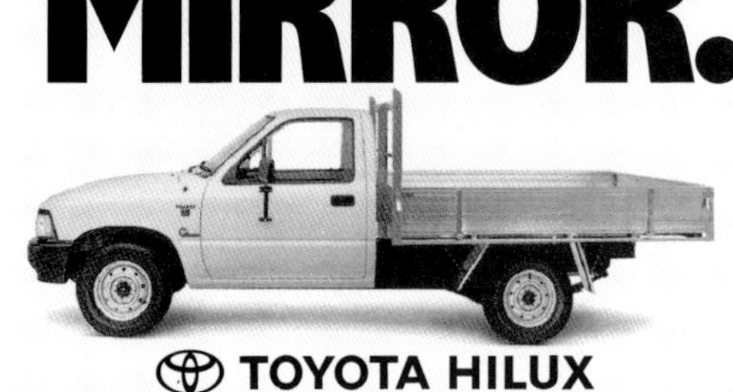
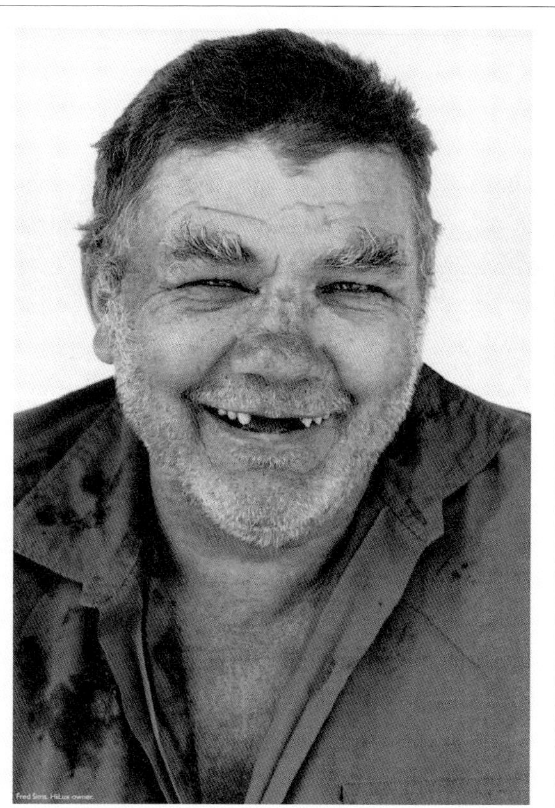

art director
Susan Alinsangin

writer
Ken Younglieb

photographer
Smith/Nelson

illustrator
Zamboo

client
Infiniti

agency
TBWA Chiat/Day,
Venice, CA

PRINT FINALISTS

art director
John Jay

writer
Jim Riswold

photographer
Earl Woods

client
Nike

agency
Wieden & Kennedy/
Portland

Hello world.

**CONSUMER
NEWSPAPER
OVER 600 LINES:
CAMPAIGN**

art directors
John Doyle
John Emmert

writer
Kara Goodrich

photographer
Geoff Stein

client
Shreve Crump & Low

agency
Doyle, Inc./Weston, CT

It's a bowl created to hold nothing more than your rapt attention.

INTRODUCING THE STEUBEN GALLERY
In our new store in the Mall at Chestnut Hill

Without realizing it, you are speaking in hushed whispers as you encircle it. Reverence. Yes, that's exactly what you're feeling. Objects this fine belong in velvet-draped galleries, dedicated wings, the tombs of Pharaohs, your living room.

Founded by Frederick Carder, in 1903, Steuben is the premier American company creating hand formed lead crystal. They maintain one ideal: to make the best. They support 'hand methods' of forming, polishing and engraving. Quite masterfully, we might add. All done with an eye to freedom in design. In 1933, the sculptor, Sidney Waugh, an architecture graduate from M.I.T. was assigned the mission of creating new designs for Steuben. One design, introduced in 1935, at the height of Art Deco, was the astounding Gazelle Bowl. As with all Steuben, it is weighty, volumetric in character and seeming to possess a light source all its own. Perhaps most strikingly, it is perfect, a trait very few diamonds can claim. It is without bubbles or dust or the smallest chord of errant glass. We have this piece. As do a few museums around the world. As could you. Come see the finest crystal still made in America in our new Steuben Gallery in the Mall at Chestnut Hill.

STEUBEN

As you circumambulate the Gazelle Bowl, your eyes reflecting the fire within it, you will understand clearly what this bowl was meant to hold.

CSCL Co. Ltd. 1996

SHREVE, CRUMP & LOW

Two floors. And who knows how many stories.

330 Boylston Street, Boston • The Mall at Chestnut Hill • (617) 267-9100 • For information, call 800-324-0222
Our Boston Store Holiday Hours are Sunday, 12:00 noon to 5:00 pm. Monday through Saturday, 10:00 am to 7:00 pm.

We know, we know. You'll never ask for another thing as long as you live.

You can get by without the villa in the south of France. The three-year old Bentley, well, you'll just have to make do. But a one-of-a-kind strand of the most voluptuous black pearls ever to pass under the scrutinizing eye of Mikimoto? Oh, pretty, pretty, please.

In 1893, Kokichi Mikimoto cultivated the world's first pearl. Today, over 100 years later, cultivated pearl purchasers still use the name 'Mikimoto' and the word 'best' interchangeably. In fact, only five of every 100 pearls brought up from the sea are deemed worthy of a Mikimoto necklace, bracelet, or earrings. Study then, the case of the Black-lipped Tahitian Oyster. Oysters produce pearls when they are irritated. One

can only imagine these must have been furious. After all, it takes years for an oyster to produce enough nacre to form a pearl of any respectable quality. About two years for just 0.5mm of nacre. The size of black pearls averages 10 to 15mm. Not handy at math? Suffice to say, a dozen good harvest years are required to collect enough black pearls that match in size, shape and color to create one necklace. Add to that the pickiness of Mikimoto and you've got a necklace that is most definitely worthy of a little pleading.

We cordially invite you to come drown yourself in our astounding South Sea collection of pearl jewelry from Mikimoto. And, keep hope. Just as oysters produce pearls in response to a little irritation, husbands have been known to do the same.

CSCL Co. Ltd. 1996

SHREVE, CRUMP & LOW

Two floors. And who knows how many stories.

330 Boylston Street, Boston • The Mall at Chestnut Hill • (617) 267-9100 • For Information, call 800-324-0222
Our Boston Store Hours are 10:00 am to 5:30 pm. Monday through Saturday.

**CONSUMER
NEWSPAPER
OVER 600 LINES:
CAMPAIGN**

art director
David Carter

writer
Mark Sweeny

photographer
Craig Perman

client
Mirage Resorts/
Golden Nugget

agency
Hal Riney & Partners/
San Francisco

UNLUCKY SPOT No. 0176
Please, be careful out there.
THE LUCKY SPOT
GOLDEN NUGGET
LAUGHLIN

UNLUCKY SPOT No. 0419
OUT
Please, be careful out there.
THE LUCKY SPOT
GOLDEN NUGGET
LAUGHLIN

**CONSUMER
NEWSPAPER
OVER 600 LINES:
CAMPAIGN**

art directors
Craig Opfer
Jennifer Huckins

writer
Joel Thomas

photographer
John Acurso

client
Grover Electric &
Plumbing

agency
JohnsonSheen
Advertising / Portland

We match warehouse prices.
And if we cut our floor staff in half, we'd match their service too.

We all want the lowest prices. But with plumbing and wiring, you also need experienced and comprehensive advice. Let's face it: you need to go to Grover.

Grover staffs two to four times as many employees per square foot as the warehouse stores. So the help you need is easy to find.

Better still, it's the kind of help that's actually *helpful*. All our employees are impressively knowledgeable. We hire and train them that way. At Grover you never have to put up with employees who know less than you do about plumbing and wiring. Like, for instance, that warehouse employee from the paint department.

On top of that, you also will find more selection, often with posted recommendations of what product works best for certain jobs. And we offer an incredible number of free, take-home how-to sheets.

Doing the job right the first time—that's what Grover is all about. We want to make it so easy to accomplish, well, it almost feels like cheating. That way, you won't have to deal with silly mistakes and low-quality products that can make re-doing a project expensive, more time-consuming, and twenty times more aggravating than it was

the first time. It's this extra effort that makes our customers so satisfied and loyal.

Of course, our low prices also have something to do with that. Grover comparison shops the warehouses to make sure that our prices are competitive on every product we carry.

So next time you're out looking for electric and plumbing supplies, go to Grover. You'll find a store with some very special people going out of their way to surpass your expectations.

Thank you for your patronage.

Their flex connector: $4.78.
Our flex connector: $4.78.
The difference? Our employees know what a flex connector is.

THE GROVER WATCHDOG REPORT:

WE WEED OUT THE WEAK AND INFIRM. DARWIN WOULD BE PROUD.

One of the ways we make sure our advice, service and merchandise are the best they can be is by doing our own product analysis. Four times a year, we put our staff to the task of trying to break our products. What better way is there to tell if

TESTED & INSPECTED. OFTEN REJECTED.

merchandise is durable enough to last? And if we find low quality products, we take them off our shelves and return them to the manufacturer. It would be easier and more profitable to just sell out the inventory. But that would be a disservice to our customers. Not to mention the returns department.

Nothing astonishes people so much as common sense and plain dealing.

It's true. Compare Grover to warehouse stores, and you won't find much difference in prices. But when it comes to service, warehouse stores just don't have the same know-how.

You see, Grover is a plumbing and electrical specialty store. No lawn and garden department. No lumber. So you know that if you want to find the flex connectors, our people will actually know what you're talking about.

Every salesperson at Grover is constantly trained. In fact, you won't find a more knowledgeable floor staff anywhere. And not only are they helpful— there are also 2 to 4 times more of them per square foot than in any warehouse store. So your questions are answered quickly, in-depth, and, best of all, one-on-one.

2 TO 4 TIMES THE EMPLOYEES PER SQUARE FOOT TO SERVE YOU.

For well over thirty years, Grover has built its business with one thing in mind: to help our customers do the job right the first time. After all, just one mistake can damage your home or, worse, cause injuries. So you'll also find a wider selection of merchandise with posted recommendations for certain jobs, plus an abundant supply of the most comprehensive how-to sheets available. That's why Grover customers stay so satisfied and loyal: they can see the extra effort in all that we do.

3/4" LIQUID TITE FLEX CONNECTOR

"WHICH FLEX CONNECTOR DO I NEED?" DON'T WORRY. WE'LL GET YOU THE RIGHT ONE AND SHOW YOU HOW TO INSTALL IT.

Of course, if low prices are all you're looking for, have no fear. Grover comparison shops the warehouses to make sure our prices are competitive on every product we carry.

Basically, if you just want to purchase lumber, by all means, go to one of those big, lonely warehouse stores: they'll probably have what you need—somewhere. But if you want the lowest prices on electrical and plumbing supplies, along with the best service and selection anywhere, Grover is by far the smarter choice.

Thank you for your patronage.

GROVER ELECTRIC & PLUMBING
OPEN 7 DAYS A WEEK • MON - FRI: 8:00 - 7:00
SAT: 8:00 - 5:30 • SUN: 9:00 - 4:30
OUR RETURN POLICY: WE GUARANTEE YOUR COMPLETE SATISFACTION OR YOUR MONEY BACK.
1900 N.E. 78th STREET
VANCOUVER, WA 98665
(360) 574-3134

GO TO GROVER AND YOUR WORRIES ARE OVER.
OR CALL US AT THE GROVER HOT LINE: (360) 574-3134

What do you call a store with low prices like a warehouse and great service like Grover?
Grover.

THE GROVER WATCHDOG REPORT:

THEY LOOK THE SAME, BUT IT'S REALLY COMPARING APPLES TO JUNK.

Just how do you tell a good receptacle from a bad one? Grover knows. We refuse to carry ones that break easily, no matter how high the profit margin. But more than that, Grover offers you more kinds

TESTED & INSPECTED. OFTEN REJECTED.

of receptacles. Because the outlet you plug your hair dryer into every day has to be much sturdier than that lonely outlet in your living room. Other stores might not carry the premium brand because most consumers assume a receptacle is a receptacle. But Grover knows better, and now, so do you.

Between a Grover employee and a mistake, most people prefer to learn from a Grover employee.

Many people assume that warehouse stores must have the lowest prices because of their higher sales volume, while Grover electric and plumbing must charge a premium because of our superior service.

It's not true; Grover comparison shops all the warehouse stores to make sure our prices are competitive on every item we carry. But we do see how someone could think we cost more. After all, our service really outshines the competition.

Walk into a Grover, and you'll see two to four times

2 TO 4 TIMES THE EMPLOYEES PER SQUARE FOOT TO SERVE YOU.

as many employees per square foot as as the warehouse stores. And every Grover employee is heavily trained in plumbing and wiring. So you won't wait forever to talk to someone, only to find out they're really from the kitchen cabinet department.

Not that plumbing and wiring are rocket science, but

IT'S A LOW PRICE STORE.

IT'S A PREMIUM SERVICE STORE.

IT'S TWO, TWO, TWO STORES IN ONE.

hey, they aren't a walk in the park either. Miss one important detail, like correct wire-grounding procedures, or the correct building codes in your area, and you could be looking at major repair costs down the road, or heaven forbid, serious injury. You need real advice to make certain your job is done right the first time. So we make doing things right the first time

our number one priority. Now add to that our wider selection of products, and the free, comprehensive how-to sheets on just about every aisle, and it's only natural to wonder

HOW-TO SHEETS
WE'LL SHOW YOU HOW TO DO IT

just how we keep our prices so low without sacrificing such stellar service. We believe, however, the question you should be asking is, "With less service, why do those other stores have to charge so darned much?"

Thank you for your patronage.

GROVER ELECTRIC & PLUMBING
OPEN 7 DAYS A WEEK • MON - FRI: 8:00 - 7:00
SAT: 8:00 - 5:30 • SUN: 9:00 - 4:30
OUR RETURN POLICY: WE GUARANTEE YOUR COMPLETE SATISFACTION OR YOUR MONEY BACK.
1900 N.E. 78th STREET
VANCOUVER, WA 98665
(360) 574-3134

GO TO GROVER AND YOUR WORRIES ARE OVER.
OR CALL US AT THE GROVER HOT LINE: (360) 574-3134

**CONSUMER
NEWSPAPER
OVER 600 LINES:
CAMPAIGN**

art director
Dave Dye

writer
Sean Doyle

photographer
Cindy Palmano

client
Harrods

agency
Leagas Delaney/
London

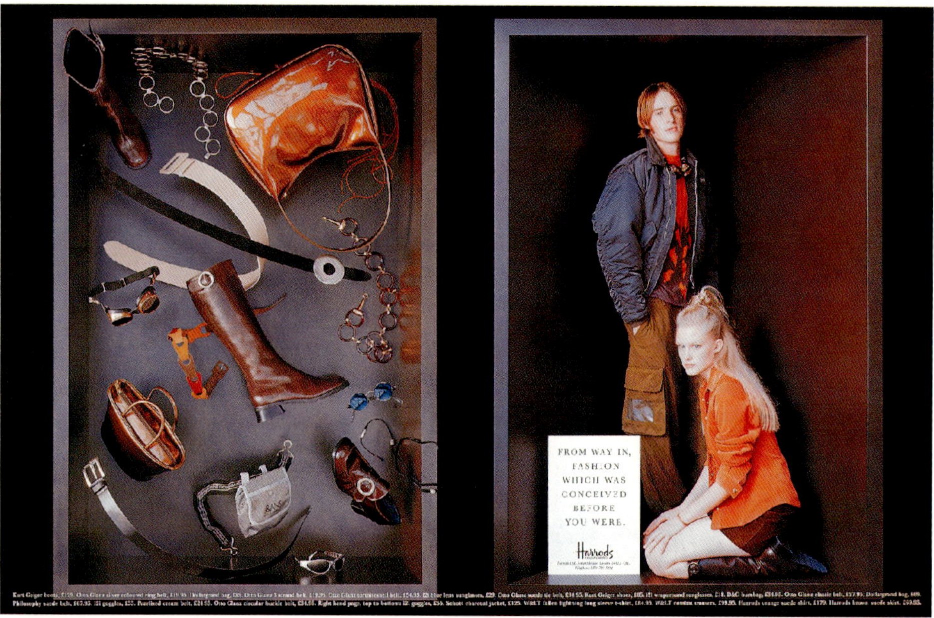

ONCE AGAIN,
IT'S THAT TIME OF
YEAR WHEN
HARRODS MAKES
IT FEEL
LIKE THAT TIME
OF YEAR
Harrods

HARRODS
SUGGESTS YOU
BURN
SOMETHING
AT YOUR
DINNER PARTY
TONIGHT.
Harrods
KNIGHTSBRIDGE

PRINT FINALISTS

**CONSUMER
NEWSPAPER
OVER 600 LINES:
CAMPAIGN**

art director
Stephen Blair

writer
Maura MacNeill

illustrator
Kim LeFave

client
Bacardi/Martini
Canada/White Rum

agency
MacLaren McCann/
Toronto

The Dog
WHO KNEW
where to Dig

"He only had three legs, but his head was screwed on right." Ron finished pouring his rum and took his first sip. We waited. Everyone knew better than to interrupt Ron when he was telling a story about Step, the three-legged wharf dog. "He didn't seem to have an owner. But that was okay. He could look after himself. Smart. That dog never missed a beat except when he walked. He liked to hang at the wharf in Pictou. Knew everyone who came and went. Knew every boat by the sound of its motor. Knew where to dig to find the rum." Ron paused to taste his own rum. "What rum?" someone asked. Ron told us any rum runner worth his salt would dump a load before getting caught. Some days you'd find the shore awash with barrels of rum. Finders keepers, losers weepers. But to keep one, you had to hide it fast. The quickest way to hide it was to bury it in the handiest place. There was a lot of rum buried there and left. Maybe people forgot where they buried it. But Step knew exactly where to dig. Any big occasion or anytime it was necessary, Step would dig up a barrel. The lobster boat race or when the liquor store was on strike. Step could always sense when there was a good reason for rum. When Ron paused to polish off his glass, someone asked, "How does a dog with three legs dig?" There was no answer from Ron. Maybe he didn't hear.

The *Phantom* RUM BOAT

Ron was on his usual barstool, having his usual rum, surrounded by the usual crowd. The subject of ships came up. That led to the subject of hockey, which led to the subject of politicians, which led to the subject of dogs, which led to the subject of astrophysics. We had pretty much exhausted all our subjects when Ron took up the slack and brought us back to ships. Ron's story began in Puerto Rico. It travelled up the Atlantic seaboard and ended at the bottom of Halifax harbour. Ron told us about a ship with a cargo of rum out of the Caribbean and a crew out of Pugwash. As she sailed up Halifax harbour, just a little east of where the Angus L. bridge stands today, she ran into an iceberg. The crew poured a round of Puerto Rico's finest while they decided what to do. In the end they saved themselves by pouring the remaining rum overboard and rowing to shore in the emptied barrels. When the people of Nova Scotia discovered the waste of good rum, the surviving crew were tarred, feathered and sentenced to life in Toronto. To this day, Ron said, if you're crossing the Angus L. bridge when the moon is full, the sea is calm and the liquor stores are closed, you might hear the creak of sails, the tinkle of ice and the thudding of men jumping in barrels. They say it's the phantom of the lost rum boat. But no one can say just how an iceberg came to be in Halifax harbour.

The GUARDIAN ANGELS *of the Rum*

We were all gathered in Ron's kitchen. Ron ran his thumb over the bat on the bottle on the table and began the story of the Malcontent. Less than a day out of Puerto Rico, headed for Nova Scotia with a hold full of rum, the Malcontent took shelter from a storm in the lee of a small island. For three days, the ship was pelted with rain, sleet and hail. The wind howled and the crew grumbled. The storm finally let up but the sea still ran high. The crew stopped complaining long enough to agree to wait until morning to set sail again. They killed time playing hockey with the hailstones. As darkness fell, their game was interrupted by an ungodly screeching. The bats that made the island their home wheeled and cried all through the night. The sound chilled the crew more than any wind could. In the first light of dawn, the great bulk of a privateer hove into sight. Given the precious cargo of the Malcontent, she was a certain target for plunder. Before the privateer could spot her, the Malcontent made her run. She crept along the shore, following the bats as they headed home. The creatures with a voice like the devil's own budgie turned out to be the guardian angels of the rum boat. The bats led the Malcontent to a cave in the cliffs where she stayed safely hidden till the enemy was gone. When Ron finished his tale, someone proposed a toast to the bats and someone else proposed we order a pizza.

**CONSUMER
NEWSPAPER
OVER 600 LINES:
CAMPAIGN**

art director
Mark Wennecker

writers
Jeff Ross
Joe Nagy

photographers
Dan Escobar
Graham Westmoreland
Smith / Nelson

client
Mercedes-Benz of
North America

agency
The Martin Agency/
Richmond

You're not going to let a little fluffy powder push you around, are you? Drive a Mercedes-Benz E-Class. Available with an Electronic Traction System that individually brakes slipping drive wheels to prevent spinning. And Automatic Slip Control, which reduces engine torque to help drive wheels regain traction. To date, it's the only known cure for cabin fever. **The E-Class with traction control.**

ABS sensors detect when a wheel is about to lock, then pumps the brakes to maintain control. Automatic Slip Control reduces engine torque to help slipping drive wheels regain traction. Electronic Traction brakes the slipping drive wheel to prevent spinning. The road less traveled awaits. **The C-Class with traction control.**

**CONSUMER
NEWSPAPER
OVER 600 LINES:
CAMPAIGN**

art director
Jon Wyville

writer
Kevin Lynch

client
Illinova

agency
McConnaughy Stein
Schmidt Brown / Chicago

PRESENTING EVERYTHING YOU'VE ALWAYS

WANTED TO KNOW ABOUT ILLINOVA.

Suffice to say that Illinova is an
energy solutions company that's better
at listening than bragging. So talk to
us. Call 1-800-998-3000.

illinova
Our first solution is to listen.

ENERGY SERVICES • ENERGY DELIVERY • RESOURCE MANAGEMENT • POWER WHOLESALING • POWER GENERATION

THE FOLLOWING IS OUR SALES PITCH.
TRY TO BEAR WITH US.

We at Illinova can offer revolutionary solutions to your energy problems. But only after we listen to what they are. Call 1-800-998-3000.

illinova
Our first solution is to listen.

ENERGY SERVICES • ENERGY DELIVERY • RESOURCE MANAGEMENT • POWER WHOLESALING • POWER GENERATION

BUT ENOUGH ABOUT US.
WHAT ABOUT YOU?

Because the employees at Illinova are good at listening, we're able to create unique solutions for just about any energy problem. Now it's your turn to talk. Call 1-800-998-3000.

illinova
Our first solution is to listen.

ENERGY SERVICES • ENERGY DELIVERY • RESOURCE MANAGEMENT • POWER WHOLESALING • POWER GENERATION

**CONSUMER
NEWSPAPER
OVER 600 LINES:
CAMPAIGN**

art director
Taras Wayner

writer
Kevin Roddy

client
A-1 Building
Maintenance
Company

agency
Odiorne Wilde
Narraway Groome/
San Francisco

Dear Forum:

I never believed these letters until it happened to me. One day I was selling encyclopedias door-to-door when a ⬤⬤⬤⬤ Swedish woman invited me in. Before I knew it she grabbed my ⬤⬤⬤⬤ and started ⬤⬤⬤⬤ me below her ⬤⬤⬤⬤. I jumped at the chance to ⬤⬤⬤⬤ her as she reached for a sock puppet and furiously ⬤⬤⬤⬤ and ⬤⬤⬤⬤ me until I was screaming. Then she covered her ⬤⬤⬤⬤ with gummy bears and ⬤⬤⬤⬤ with her pet poodle for several hours. Finally, we ⬤⬤⬤⬤ until I fell asleep. You may not believe me but it happened

**CONSUMER
NEWSPAPER
OVER 600 LINES:
CAMPAIGN**

art directors
Andrew Charles
Kevin Geeves

writer
Troy Sullivan

illustrator
Joseph Wong

client
The Economist

agency
Ogilvy & Mather/
Hong Kong

The Opinionist

The Economist has always stood apart from the general press. One of its great differences is the willingness to present the facts, develop an argument and then take a stand on the issue.

Anathema are repressive regimes of the left or right, the suppression of civil liberties or discrimination of class, sex or race.

The Economist shows contempt for those in business who misuse their positions of power or privilege. It is this refreshingly different approach, particularly in the "Leaders" section, that sets The Economist apart from the mass of news and business publications.

The Protagonist

The Economist was founded in 1843 as a means to voice strong opposition to Britain's Corn Laws. The laws were seen as limiting free trade.

Ever since, The Economist has championed the cause of the market, and with it, free trade and individual responsibility.

In 1989 The Economist concluded "Broadly speaking, the world's poor countries have followed two approaches to development since the 1950s. After three decades the experience of these countries answers the question: History favours the invisible hand [of the free market]."

The Scientist

One might think it unusual that The Economist should concern itself with scientific matters. Surely business, politics and world events are enough to cover?

In reality, the thread of science weaves through every part of our daily lives. Witness how the silicon chip - subject of a recent special feature - has affected all of us.

In the regular "Science and Technology" section The Economist explores new developments in everything from the Internet to keyhole surgery to exploration of the cosmos.

The Sophist

The Sophists were a group of itinerant philosophers who lived in Athens around 450 B.C. *Sophist* means wise and informed person.

The Sophists created the foundations of social criticism. Famous amongst their group was Protagoras, who said "Man is the measure of all things", meaning we should not judge something in terms of absolute right or wrong but in relation to a person's needs.

Similarly today, The Economist will argue both sides of a case in order to arrive at a conclusion.

The Artist

"Industry without art is brutality" said John Ruskin.

The Economist agrees.

In each issue, a section titled "Moreover" covers a plenitude of stories from the arts. Painting, poetry and music of course, but not just the classics. The Sex Pistols get a look-in as well as Schubert. As do film, theatre and dance; ballet and bolero.

Important new books are reviewed, including those on CD ROM. On a broader scale, the reader can explore topics as diverse as interactive museums or a discourse on the state of city parks. Ah, but is it art?

The Purist

Economist journalists are urged to seek clarity at all costs.

"On...two scores can The Economist hope to outdo its rivals consistently. One is the quality of its analysis; the other is the quality of its writing" The Economist Style Guide, page 5.

The Economist has always been admired for its writing style. Some have called it trenchant.

Without doubt, it is precise and pertinent.

Upon his retirement, one veteran remarked that he had written over half-a-million words, and as an editor had deleted twice as many: the latter he thought was his more important contribution.

The Nonconformist

The Economist adheres fanatically to, what a former editor called, a maxim of "beginning with the facts, always arguing from the facts and always ending with a result applicable to the facts".

Sometimes the truth hurts.

In failing to kow-tow to any outside influence, The Economist has in its time been banned by a number of regimes. Fortunately, today The Economist is not on anyone's blacklist.

To help maintain this independent stance, all Economist writers remain anonymous.

The Humanist

For many, life is no longer nasty, brutish and short. Advances in medicine and food production alone have greatly increased life expectancy.

In historical terms, life for the majority has never been better.

While believing this to be true, The Economist will never be naive to the very real suffering that many continue to endure.

By throwing white light on the subjects within its range The Economist can play a real part in relieving human suffering; whether it be the killings in Myanmar, or simply the scourge of anti-personnel mines.

The Internationalist

The Economist is a unique phenomenon, for although it is London-based and London-edited, it is not Anglocentric.

It is written and printed around the world with the aid of six satellites. Our readers, at last count, are in 168 different countries.

The Economist is truly a world newspaper with individual sections covering America, Britain, Europe, and Asia; a section which focuses clearly on the issues relevant to this burgeoning region.

Informed people know us by another name.

Whatever name it goes by, a growing number of people are recognising that The Economist has much to offer.

Whether for news, views, education, entertainment or simply as an essential tool for doing business, The Economist is required reading; now and in the future.

The Economist On sale every week.

It's interesting how the people with the least amount of time have time to read The Economist.

According to a proverb, time is the currency of life; a stinging reminder that we shouldn't waste it.

Therein lies a clue as to why so many of the world's successful people read The Economist.

But is it art?

In the little "spare" time available to them, The Economist provides a concise summary of the important events of the week.

Successful people? Who exactly? In no particular order, admirers of The Economist include George Bush, Bill Gates and Michael Porter.

In the world of commerce and industry The Economist is required reading from London to New York, Tokyo to New Delhi.

"The president has left behind his copy of The Economist." Aide to President Kennedy.

Regular, ardent, even fanatical readers they are too. On one occasion John F Kennedy delayed the departure of the presidential helicopter so an aide could go back for his copy of The Economist.

A word from the wise

For years there was speculation about who received the solitary copy allowed into Cuba.

Perhaps one reason Economist readers remain so loyal is because they get more of the world, not just Europe or America.

Although it is London-based and London-edited, The Economist is not Anglocentric.

The Economist is a unique phenomenon. It is written and read around the globe and printed, with the aid of satellites, in six locations.

> **Koreagate, as reported by The Economist, two years ago.**
>
> In an article headed "Too clean for comfort" in September 1993, The Economist alerted readers to President Kim Young Sam's high-level anti-corruption drive. Mention was also made of the likelihood of prosecuting Chun Doo Hwan for his part in the 1979 coup. Two and a half years later, both former presidents Roh Tae Woo and Chun are in jail. As to whether Kim was moving too quickly, The Economist ominously warned "...to destroy too much of the old system...would be to endanger the country's success."

"The Economist is a weekend habit on Wall St, and in the White House." Newsweek.

The Asia section, for example, focuses clearly on the issues relevant to this burgeoning region, making it an indispensible tool for those doing business here.

Not In The Economist

The Economist examines key local events in business, politics, science and technology.

A great strength of The Economist is the way in which these seemingly isolated events are examined with regard to how they affect the rest of the world. In this way, The Economist provides a "world briefing", a complete digest of important issues of the week.

Important events in other areas - such as science, technology and the arts - are also explored.

Indeed you'll even find the occasional sports story.

Those unfamiliar with The Economist are often

surprised at the editorial style. The articles are witty, concise, informative and always straight to the point.

Readers appreciate the direct writing style.

A good word to sum up The Economist approach is insight, which the dictionary defines as the ability to perceive clearly or to deeply penetrate a topic.

To provide readers with insight into a given topic, one must first gather the facts. The Economist is obsessive about the truth. It is a trait that goes back to the beginning, in 1843.

To say the founder, James Wilson, was a stickler for facts would be to understate his tireless pursuit of the truth. He insisted that every detail be checked and rechecked for accuracy.

He left a lasting legacy.

That's your opinion.

Having gathered the facts and laid them out in an appealing fashion, a lot of publications leave it there. The Economist, however, takes it one step further.

A lesson a week

The Economist analyses the topic, discusses the issues, and even tells you what it thinks.

You may agree or disagree, mildly or strongly, with The Economist's views. (We'll never know what J.F.K. thought of the paper's views on the Cuban missile crisis.) But it is these opinions which give

Most favoured friends

The Economist its zest, its verve.

It is this combination of fact and opinion that delivers real insight into a topic.

"The Economist...is read, respected, and sometimes resented by presidents and prime ministers around the world." Financial Times, Canada.

Because The Economist strives for a global perspective, subjects are tackled from a different angle to that of the general press.

Thus, in not following the pack, The Economist often finds itself ahead of it.

Many of the articles contain an eerie prescience.

What may be a small piece in The Economist one week, often ends up being front page news a year later; another reason why decision makers scrutinise The Economist so closely.

Fact combined with analysis and opinion, a global view, a different view; these are the hallmarks of The Economist and are the reasons why The Economist remains an essential business tool.

"For the busy man, time passes quickly." Chinese proverb.

Thus, for people in high places, it's not a case of saying "I haven't got time..." but rather "I've only got time to read The Economist."

On sale every week. **The Economist**

Cantona kicks back

What do people who expect so much of themselves expect from a magazine?

Leaders, high flyers, movers and shakers. The names may change with fashion, but whatever the label, one underlying truth remains constant: these people expect a great deal, from themselves, from those around them and also from what they read.

This is why so many leaders from commerce and industry, politics, academia, science and the arts look forward with anticipation to the appearance of The Economist each week.

For not only does The Economist provide a concise summary of the important events of the week, its

Mad(e) in Britain

analysis and discussion of those topics is an indispensable road map as to what may happen in the future.

"You know important people read The Economist, you know opinion formers read The Economist so you want to know what they are reading." The Hon Baroness Lydia Dunn, Former Chairman John Swire & Co Ltd (Hong Kong)

First-time readers may have reservations that a publication named "The Economist" could offer so much, be so riveting and dare one say, even fun. A regrettable misunderstanding, but one that is not altogether new.

What's in a Name?

When an energetic, opinionated and radical thinker named James Wilson founded a newspaper in 1843 to help the great popular movement against Britain's Corn Laws, economics, or political economy to be more precise, had a somewhat broader definition.

Shall we dance?

The study of political economy had more to do with social policy and its effects on the masses, rather than a narrow analysis of financial topics.

However, even then, some were sceptical. As always, Wilson, was quick to counter "Some try to represent political economy as being dry, cold, abstract science, which has no warmth of feeling to spare on suffering humanity...This is far from the truth."

Peace in Ulster?

Today's Economist covers a broad span of topics. Each issue includes sections covering Asia, America and Europe, also world finance, business and the arts.

The "Leaders" section probes and gives opinions on topics as diverse as censorship on the internet (The Economist says the control should be put on the receiver, not the provider) to the merits of boxing gloves. (Bare-knuckle fighting would actually be safer says The Economist.)

The Economics of Hootie & The Blowfish.

It is this diversity that makes The Economist such a useful business tool. And the emphasis on business does not limit The Economist's scope. If anything, it is broadened.

For example, in just one edition you could read about the declining profits of the music industry (the Hootie's sold 11m copies of their first album, but successful new acts are proving harder to find) to Asia's booming computer chip industry.

Each issue also has three pages of international financial statistics. There is also an invaluable two page summary called "The World this Week".

> **Flunking Collective Security in Bosnia.**
>
> As the first shots were fired in the bloody break-up of Yugoslavia in 1991, The Economist warned only too accurately that "Ethnically mixed Bosnia is a potential nightmare". And that Europe's collective security arrangements "are too slow and too weak to prevent conflict". Thus "Collective security looks like flunking it." A comment shown to be only too correct during the following five years of human suffering.

The choice of topics is not an eclectic assortment of interesting tidbits, but rather each story is carefully chosen.

And the winner is...

What may seem an obscure piece from a far-off country may actually be the harbinger of a worldwide trend.

> The Economist was first published in 1843 to take part in a "severe contest between intelligence which presses forward, and an unworthy, timid ignorance obstructing our progress." James Wilson's words are today as true as ever.

Truth well told.

Whatever the topic, whatever the issue, The Economist adheres fanatically to, what a former editor called, a maxim of "beginning with the facts, always arguing from the facts and always ending with a result applicable to the facts."

Having laid out the facts, arriving quickly at the heart of the issue.

Fighting for peace

The Economist, unlike much of the general press, goes on to analyse and argue the merits of a particular point of view. It is this combination of fact and opinion, mixed with a little wit, that makes The Economist unique.

Perhaps also it is this willingness to make a point rather than to merely report that makes The Economist so popular amongst world leaders.

Who are these people?

The Economist is unique in another way. The people who write the articles remain anonymous. This has a number of advantages. It precludes the familiar journalistic vices of byline-grabbing and information-hugging.

More importantly, the newspaper speaks with one voice; rather than being a collection of individuals' opinions, there is cohesion and strength far stronger than any one mind.

Anonymity, as long-time editor Geoffrey Crowther put it, keeps him "not the master but the servant of something far greater than himself."

"The object of The Economist is to throw white light on the subjects within its range" Walter Bagehot, editor 1871.

Editorial independence is also enshrined in the newspaper's constitution. (Yes, technically, The Economist is not a magazine.)

Your world brief

The Economist continues to meet and exceed the expectations of people in high office. It is admired and sometimes hated for what it has to say. But one thing remains constant, for those doing business in this burgeoning region, The Economist is, and remains, essential reading.

On sale every week. **The Economist**

**CONSUMER
NEWSPAPER
OVER 600 LINES:
CAMPAIGN**

art director
Sally Overheu

writer
Jackie Hathiramani

photographers
Sally Overheu
Calvin Soh

client
The British Council

agency
Ogilvy & Mather /
Singapore

IMPROVE YOUR ENGLISH. We have over twenty part-time and full-time courses to help you read, write and speech (sorry, speak) correct English. Call 473 6661 for more information. ✳ The British Council

IMPROVE YOUR ENGLISH. We have over twenty part-time and full-time courses to help you read, write and speech (sorry, speak) correct English. Call 473 6661 for more information. ※ The British Council

IMPROVE YOUR ENGLISH. We have over twenty part-time and full-time courses to help you read, write and speech (sorry, speak) correct English. Call 473 6661 for more information. ※ The British Council

**CONSUMER
NEWSPAPER
OVER 600 LINES:
CAMPAIGN**

art director
Wade Devers

writer
Mark Nardi

photographer
Jack Richmond

illustrators
John Burgoyne
Peter Hall

typographer
Joffre Lefevre

client
Children's Hospital

agency
Pagano Schenck &
Kay / Boston

FATIMA HAD A MALIGNANT TUMOR IN A PLACE IT COULDN'T BE TREATED: LEBANON.

When that plane landed at Boston's Logan International Airport after its long journey, there were many happy visitors on board.

And one very sick little girl.

Every year, children from across the globe travel to Boston for the care only Children's can provide. Quite often, the special treatment they need is not available in their own country.

We welcome the child and the family to this country, working through language barriers and cultural differences to make sure that the medical care remains the number one priority.

Of course, Children's Hospital has always been a destination for children here at home as well. We provide the community with the full spectrum of pediatric care; our outpatient clinics and Emergency Services handle more than 270,000 visits every year. And as the nation's leading pediatric research hospital, we are able to offer innovations in care to children in the local community, as well as to children around the world.

If a child is hurting across the street or across an ocean, we are here to help.

Children's Hospital·Boston

THE DOCTORS AT CHILDREN'S HOSPITAL PUT A SMILE ON PATRICK'S FACE. ALONG WITH A NOSE, LIPS, AND THE ROOF OF HIS MOUTH.

It's called craniofacial deformity. Many people would call it a tragedy. It's what happens when a baby is born with a disfigured face. A face that

looks like it's missing vital parts.

Thirty years ago, no one quite knew how to deal with craniofacial deformities. But it was then that a surgeon at Children's performed the nation's first operation to correct Crouzon syndrome, a complex craniofacial deformity.

It takes many years and many operations to fully construct a face. Our team of specialists works closely with these children and their families to get that child's face as perfect as possible for the all-important high school yearbook picture.

We also specialize in the treatment of many other critical childhood conditions, including hea cancer, kidney disease, urinary tract anomalies, cerebral palsy, epilepsy, spinal deformities, and so much more.

Children's Hospital helps children and their families from Boston, New England, and the rest of the world. If the need ever arises, we want to help you.

Children's Hospital·Boston

WHEN SASHA CAME TO CHILDREN'S, THERE WERE 2 KNOWN TREATMENTS FOR HER CONDITION. BY THE TIME SHE LEFT, THERE WERE 3.

At Children's Hospital, our staff includes doctors, researchers, and yes, innovators.

After all, when someone like Sasha comes here with a congenital heart defect, it's imperative that we solve the problem, whether we have the solution at hand or not.

By the time Sasha was two, she had had several open heart surgeries. Despite these operations, she again developed elevated pressure in her right ventricle. More surgery or transplantation were thought to be her only options. The solution (see diagram) for

Sasha meant she could avoid undergoing another open heart surgery, and has since been used with other children.

For more than a century, Children's Hospital has been providing solutions where none existed. We were the first to culture the polio virus, and we were also responsible for the first chemotherapeutic remission of acute childhood leukemia.

In short, this is one institution that does not believe in dead ends. If there is a chance, a glimmer of hope, the people here will try to find the answer.

Children's Hospital helps children and their families from Boston, New England, and the rest of the world. If the need ever arises, we want to help you.

Children's Hospital·Boston

**CONSUMER
NEWSPAPER
OVER 600 LINES:
CAMPAIGN**

art director
Susan Alinsangin

writer
Ken Younglieb

photographer
Smith / Nelson

illustrators
William Hallinan
Laura Lou Levy
Dana Gardner
Zamboo
Nancy Januzzi
Greg Dearth

client
Infiniti

agency
TBWA Chiat / Day,
Venice, CA

CHAPTER ONE

Part therapist.
Part mother.
Part masseuse.

THE SUCCESSFUL BUSINESSPERSON OF THE 1990'S.

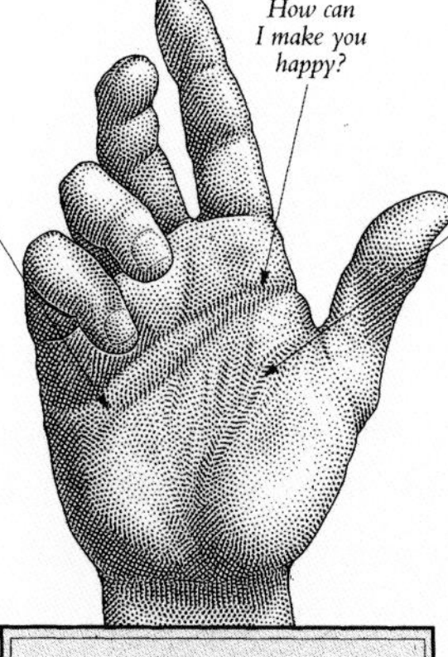

There's an old saying that's everybody's first business lesson: "Build a better mousetrap and the world will beat a path to your door." Perhaps it was true once, but in the '90s there's an addendum: "But if you treat people like pests, they'll go buy somebody else's mousetrap."

In other words, we're in an era in which everyone agrees — from the business-writing pundits to the fellow who stocks the hardware store — that pleasing customers is truly the way to a successful enterprise.

But how exactly *do* you satisfy all those people?

"TELL ME ABOUT YOUR CHILDHOOD"

Imagine a hypothetical first visit to a therapist. Does the doctor begin, "I'll give you the best therapy money can buy. My competitors just can't offer the same value."? The doctor does not. If he or she did, you'd probably say, "Gosh, I'd love to hear about it for 50 minutes, but I think my superego has a pressing engagement elsewhere." No, the therapist listens, the therapist learns, and the therapist figures out what you need.

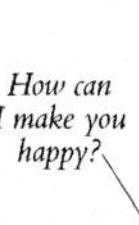

Similarly, any businessperson, from an automobile dealer to the CEO of a multinational to the above-mentioned rodent-control expert, ought to take a comparable approach: Before you describe your incredible products and amazing service, the first step in satisfying the customer is *listening* to the customer.

"TAKE A SWEATER, IT MIGHT GET COLD"

Mothers perform countless critical functions: They run out to the school bus with your mittens and galoshes; they locate your hamster under the fridge; they

never, ever forget that you like boysenberry, *not* grape jelly, with your peanut-butter sandwich.

But mothers can also teach businesspeople a lot: The importance of being nurturing. Good manners. The value of honesty. The ability to acknowledge each customer's unique needs. And one less-obvious lesson. When your mother bought clothes you'd grow into, it was because she was thinking of your future. Like motherhood, customer service isn't merely satisfying someone for the moment; it's making sure what you do or sell satisfies in the long run, too.

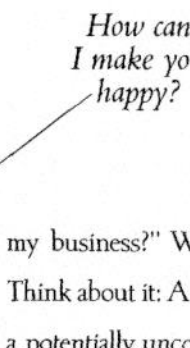

"PLEASE, LIE DOWN, RELAX, AND TELL ME WHERE IT HURTS"

"OK," you say. "The therapist and the mother I can buy. But what do a masseuse's mint-petunia oil and energy chakras have to do with

my business?" We say, "Plenty." Think about it: A masseuse turns a potentially uncomfortable situation — removing your clothes in front of a stranger — into a pleasant one. A masseuse pampers and relaxes you. A masseuse makes you feel better. In the same manner, businesses that make people feel comfortable and at ease are the ones customers will choose to patronize.

ONE COMPANY'S APPROACH TO ALL OF THE ABOVE

In 1989, Infiniti started out with a philosophy that was a bit out of step with the "greed is good" decade. We resolved that each and every encounter our customers had with us would be pleasant. We called it The Total Ownership Experience, and seven years and thousands of customers later we've summed it up in a few simple English sentences:

And of course, we try to be like therapists (we listen to our customers), like mothers (we consider their future needs), like masseuses (we make them feel at ease). If you'd like to know more, please call us at 1-888-836-4772. And while you've got the phone in your hand, go ahead and give Mom a call, too.

CHAPTER FOUR

WHAT A CAR COMPANY CAN LEARN FROM THE INTIMATE APPAREL DEPARTMENT.

Or, how to serenade the customer.

B efore your imagination wanders off to the relationship between, say, walnut-burl trim and lace-appliqué silk, let us state clearly that what Infiniti and the intimate apparel department of a certain store have in common is a straightforward goal: to make a potentially uncomfortable experience a pleasant one.

JOHN NORDSTROM, THE FOUNDER OF A RETAILING LEGEND

The store, of course, is Nordstrom. It has a long and interesting history you'll find documented in numerous "how-to-succeed-by-reading-business-books" business books. But what fascinates us about Nordstrom is how they started with a simple premise ("Make shopping enjoyable"), a premise that is sublimely elementary, and built it into a retailing empire.

A friend of ours made a recent outing to the Nordstrom intimate apparel department, and reported back. Anticipating the usual trial-and-error nightmare and labyrinth of choices, she was instead given a guided tour by an expert (her salesperson). When she left the store, she had a deep understanding of bra physics and architecture, along with three perfectly-fitting undergarments. And throughout, the strains of Mozart's Piano Sonata in A floated pleasantly by.

MUCH LIKE A SHOE, FINDING A CAR THAT SUITS ITS OWNER REQUIRES PERSONALIZED ATTENTION.

This may seem a bit on the warm-and-fuzzy side, but it's made Nordstrom one of the most successful corporations in the world. So it isn't too surprising that other companies have tried to follow its example. Yet for some reason, most of the automobile industry has neglected to learn a fundamental lesson: Pleasing customers isn't merely a means to succeed in your business; it is your business. Since 1989, however, there has been one notable exception.

THERE'S NO TELLING HOW BIG YOU CAN GROW WITH A LOYAL CUSTOMER BASE.

THE WELCOMING, COMFORTABLE, RESTFUL... AUTOMOBILE SHOWROOM?

When Infiniti started building luxury cars, we resolved to make pleasing customers the bedrock of our company. But we realized that if we were to fulfill this mission, we had to fix what had become a cross between an interrogation chamber and a sensory-overload experiment: the automobile dealership.

INFINITI IS RANKED #1 CARLINE IN CUSTOMER SATISFACTION* BY J.D. POWER AND ASSOCIATES

We began with the building itself. We commissioned an architectural firm to create a different kind of environment, one that would make a clean break with the past. They succeeded admirably, designing an interior that was open and accessible; with glass panels instead of walls; quiet contemplation areas; and a feeling of tranquility rarely found in public spaces.

We also realized that you can make every showroom an exact replica of the Taj Mahal, but if even one employee treats a customer like a walking checkbook, all your efforts are in vain. So we sent everyone — the receptionist, the service manager, the owner — to school. They learned that, for Infiniti, the customer's interests come before the company's. A radical idea, especially in the car business. But it works.

Acer palmatum — summer / winter

WE GAVE A GREAT DEAL OF THOUGHT TO THE DESIGN OF OUR SHOWROOMS, INCLUDING THEIR SETTING. HERE, THE JAPANESE MAPLE, ONE OF OUR FAVORITE LANDSCAPING TREES.

We even coined a name to describe all this. We call it The Total Ownership Experience,' and it's based on a simple idea: Each and every encounter our customers have with Infiniti will be enjoyable.

THE INFINITI TOTAL OWNERSHIP EXPERIENCE

WE OFFER SUPERIOR AUTOMOBILES REPRESENTING EXCELLENT VALUE AND PRESENT THEM IN A UNIQUE ENVIRONMENT. — WE TREAT OUR CUSTOMERS AS HONORED GUESTS. — WE PROVIDE OUTSTANDING SERVICE THROUGHOUT OWNERSHIP. — WE BUILD RELATIONSHIPS WITH OUR CUSTOMERS BASED ON THEIR CONTINUED SATISFACTION.

Of course, you may still wonder, "Where's the piano?" Perhaps, but we think once you settle into an Infiniti and turn up its Bose® audio system, you won't miss that piano at all.

∞ INFINITI.

CHAPTER FIVE

CLIP THIS COUPON AND SEND IT TO A COMPANY YOU HATE.

Or, the fine art of constructive *criticism*

S omewhere in some celestial book of rules next to Murphy's Law there's probably one that reads: Everybody can't stand at least one company. The evidence, after all, is everywhere. The small talk in the bank line, the conversation around the water cooler, and lately the constant Internet chitchat. Everyone, it seems, wants to let everyone else know how thoughtless, negligent, or downright venal such and such a company is.

Strange as it may sound coming from a corporation, we think this is a good thing. After all, we may build luxury cars, but at the end of the day (literally) we too have to deal with waiters who can remember all their lines but not our orders, kitchen gadgets that slice instead of dice, and instructions written in strange dialects that only marginally resemble English.

Our solution? This ad, and its useful coupon.

You see, we believe that the only way companies can improve is by finding out what needs improvement. And in an era of huge multinationals, fewer and fewer corporate chieftains are getting any honest feedback at all. (Do you know that expression "Kill the messenger"? Well, so does everyone in business.)

THE INFINITI TOTAL OWNERSHIP EXPERIENCE

WE OFFER SUPERIOR AUTOMOBILES REPRESENTING EXCELLENT VALUE AND PRESENT THEM IN A UNIQUE ENVIRONMENT. — WE TREAT OUR CUSTOMERS AS HONORED GUESTS. — WE PROVIDE OUTSTANDING SERVICE THROUGHOUT OWNERSHIP. — WE BUILD RELATIONSHIPS WITH OUR CUSTOMERS BASED ON THEIR CONTINUED SATISFACTION.

Which brings us to Infiniti, and why we think we can run this ad. When we first started in 1989, we knew that people were dissatisfied with their treatment by the automobile industry. So we built a culture in which every employee does whatever it takes to make the customer's experience enjoyable. We call it The Total Ownership Experience, and as much as our cars, it's what our company stands for.

YOUR DUTY AS A CUSTOMER: GROUSING

We think every business should have an opportunity to improve. So send this coupon to the company that put you on hold and played talk radio the whole time. Send it to the company that sold you a defective product and refused to admit it. Send it to any company that didn't treat you with civility and respect. If you'd like, send it to us. But no matter where you send it, we think you'll be amazed at what a simple pair of scissors can do.

∞ INFINITI.

TODAY'S LESSON, IN BRIEF:
ONE OF THE PRICELESS PERKS OF CORPORATE AMERICA IS THAT EXECUTIVES ARE OFTEN INSULATED FROM THE PEOPLE WHO ACTUALLY USE THEIR PRODUCTS AND SERVICES. WE PROPOSE A REMEDY: A DIRECT LINE FROM THE PEN OF THE CUSTOMER TO THE DESK OF THE CEO, VIA THIS COUPON.

FILL OUT THIS COUPON, AS HONESTLY AS POSSIBLY (SHORT-CHANGING YOUR USUAL STANDARDS OF POLITE DISCOURSE, NATURALLY). SOME SUGGESTIONS ON HOW TO BEST PRESENT YOUR CASE: BE SPECIFIC, RATHER THAN GENERAL. DISTINGUISH BETWEEN WHAT ACTUALLY HAPPENED AND HOW YOU FELT ABOUT IT; OFFER IDEAS ON HOW YOU MIGHT BE BETTER SERVED IN THE FUTURE; AND ASSUME THAT THE RECIPIENT OF YOUR LETTER WILL BE HELPFUL — IT WILL MAKE YOUR CRITICISM MORE CONSTRUCTIVE.

HEY, MR./MS. __________ CEO, __________ INC.
I'M PRETTY CROSS WITH YOUR COMPANY, AND HERE'S WHY. PLEASE FIX WHAT'S BOTHERING ME OR I'LL TAKE MY BUSINESS ELSEWHERE.

NAME __________
ADDRESS __________
CITY, STATE, ZIP __________

**CONSUMER
NEWSPAPER
OVER 600 LINES:
CAMPAIGN**

art director
Gabriel Penalva

writers
Siscu Molina
Ferran Blanch

client
Panadol/
Smithkline Beecham

agency
Tiempo/BBDO,
Barcelona

THE PARAKEET CAGE.

In the cage all parakeets are blue, but two. All are yellow, but two. All are green, but two. How many parakeets are there of each colour?

EINSTEIN AND HIS STUDENTS.

Half his students study trigonometry. A fourth part study physics and a seventh part read a book. Besides, three of them have not come to class today. How many students are there in Einstein's class?

PETER'S FRIENDS.

Peter has two friends: Anthony and David. Peter is two years older than David and Anthony is eight years younger. Their three ages add up to 50 years. How old are they?

BACK TO THE FUTURE.

Gabriel was 39 years old in 1990, but only 34 in 1995. How is that possible?

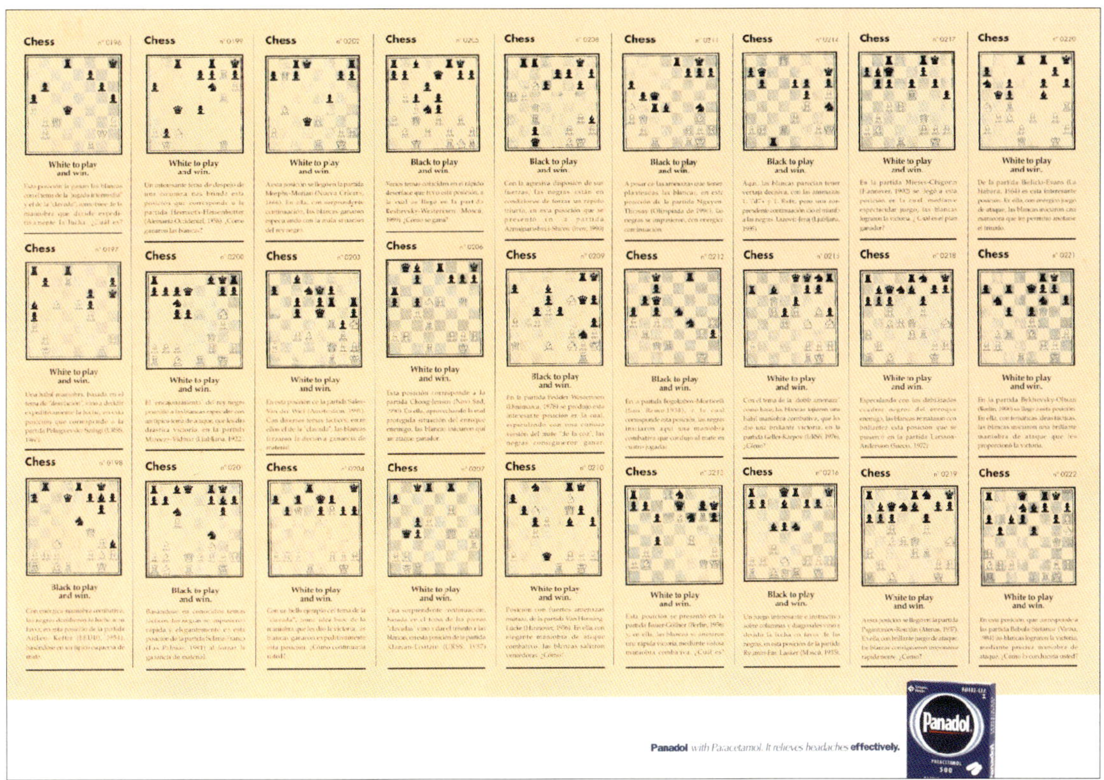

Panadol with Paracetamol. It relieves headaches effectively.

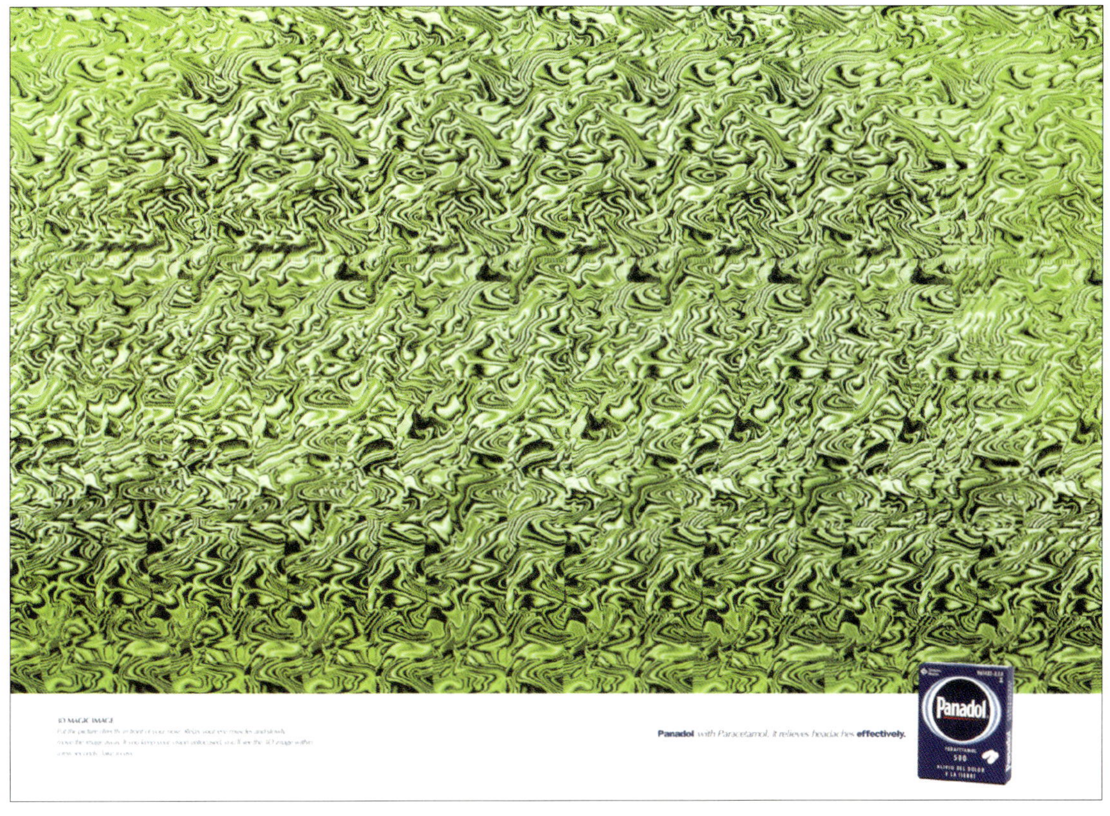

Panadol with Paracetamol. It relieves headaches effectively.

**CONSUMER
NEWSPAPER
600 LINES
OR LESS:
SINGLE**

art director
Kevin Dailor

writers
Alan Marcus
Steve Howard

photographer
Jim Hall

illustrator
Steve Deshetler

client
Volkswagen

agency
Arnold Advertising/
Boston

art director
Kevin Dailor

writers
Alan Marcus
Steve Howard

photographer
Jim Hall

illustrator
Steve Deshetler

client
Volkswagen

agency
Arnold Advertising/
Boston

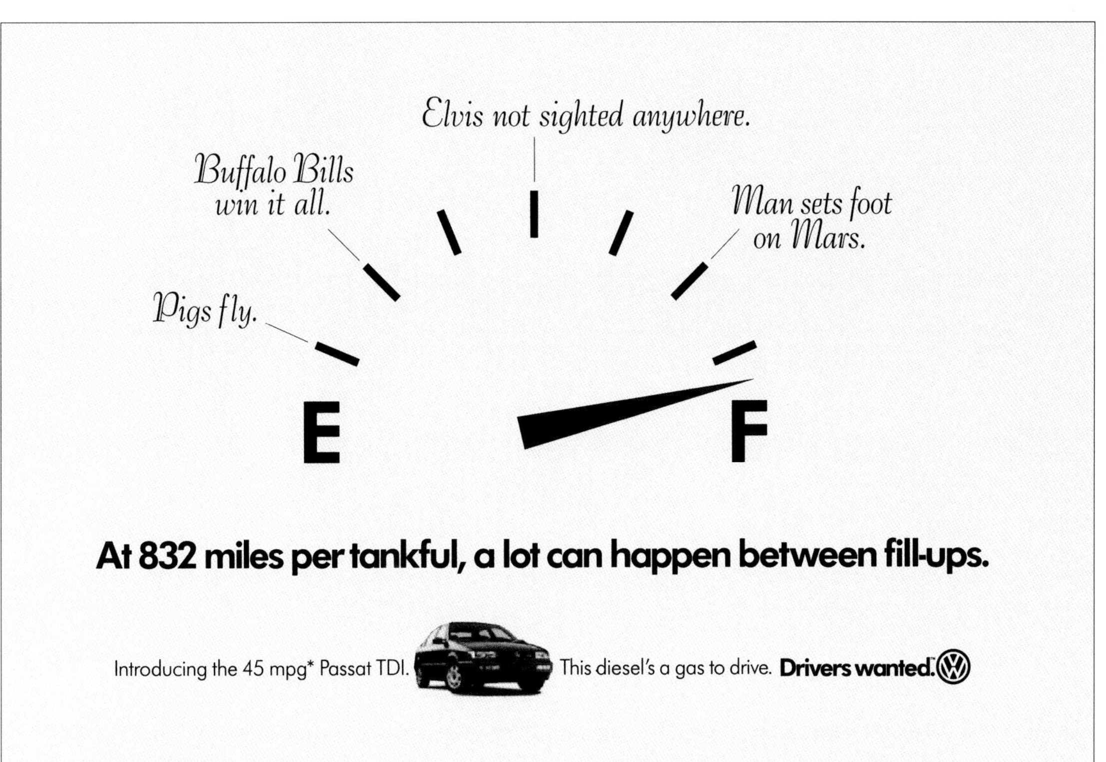

art director
Kevin Dailor

writers
Alan Marcus
Steve Howard

photographer
Jim Hall

illustrator
Steve Deshetler

client
Volkswagen

agency
Arnold Advertising/
Boston

art director
Steve Sage

writers
Neal Hughlett
Richard Bloom
Bill Roden

client
Osell's Custom Frames

agency
Clarity Coverdale Fury/
Minneapolis

**CONSUMER
NEWSPAPER
600 LINES
OR LESS:
SINGLE**

art director
Eric Tilford

writer
Wade Paschall

photographer
Herman Leonard

client
WSIE The Jazz Station

agency
CORE/St. Louis

art director
Eric Tilford

writer
Wade Paschall

photographer
Herman Leonard

client
WSIE The Jazz Station

agency
CORE/St. Louis

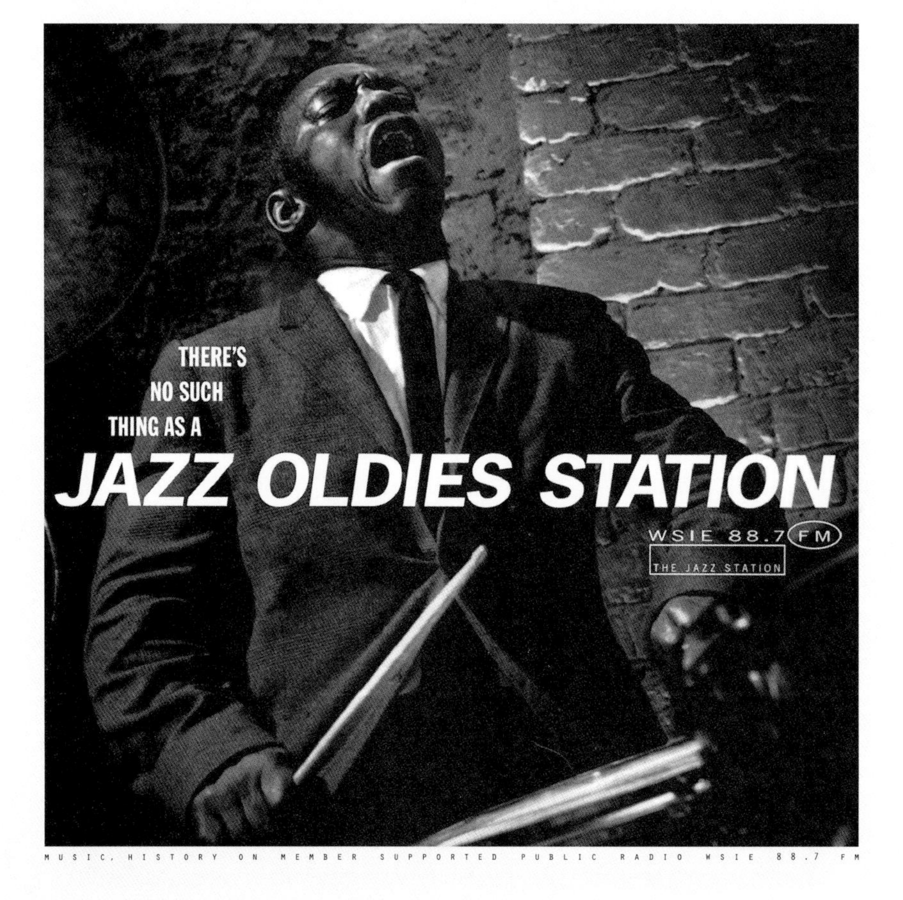

THE RUSH OF ADRENALINE.
THE SENSE OF EUPHORIA.

(AND THAT'S JUST WHEN YOUR NAME
MOVES UP ON THE WAITING LIST.)

Only one thing can compare to the excitement of driving
a Z3: the anticipation of owning one. Come see why this
car is in such incredible demand. THE ULTIMATE DRIVING MACHINE.

"NO HONEY, LET ME
TAKE YOUR MOTHER TO
THE PODIATRIST."

What would you do to drive the new, more powerful
328i? Hmmm, there may be no sacrifice you can
make that's too great. THE ULTIMATE DRIVING MACHINE.

**CONSUMER
NEWSPAPER
600 LINES
OR LESS:
SINGLE**

art director
Allen Richardson

writer
Ari Merkin

photographer
Vic Huber

client
Land Rover North America

agency
Grace & Rothschild/
New York

art director
Allen Richardson

writer
Gary Cohen

photographer
Vic Huber

client
Land Rover North America

agency
Grace & Rothschild
New York

PRINT FINALISTS

art directors
Elsie Fehr
Nancy Vonk

writers
Janet Kestin
Arthur Shah

illustrator
Elsie Fehr

client
Timex Canada

agency
Ogilvy & Mather/
Toronto

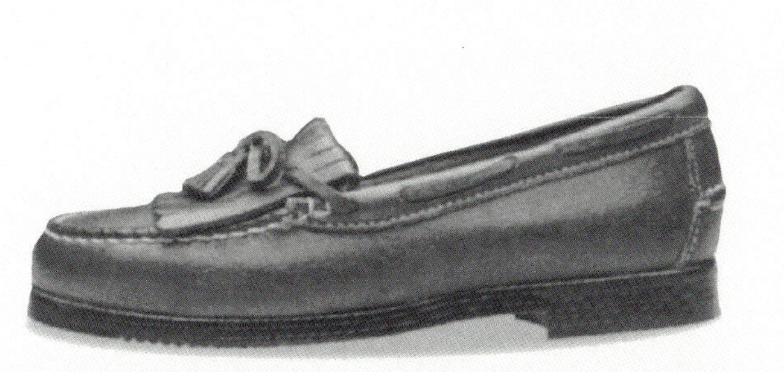

art director
Wade Devers

writer
Dylan Lee

photographer
Mike Blake

client
Dexter Shoe
Company

agency
Pagano Schenck &
Kay/Boston

**CONSUMER
NEWSPAPER
600 LINES
OR LESS:
SINGLE**

art directors
Rena Wong
Luke Scott
Eddie Bamonte

writers
Eddie Bamonte
Luke Scott
Rena Wong

client
Basics Furniture

agency
STAIN NYC/New York

art directors
Rena Wong
Luke Scott
Eddie Bamonte

writers
Eddie Bamonte
Luke Scott
Rena Wong

photographer
Christian Tuempling

client
Basics Furniture

agency
STAIN NYC/New York

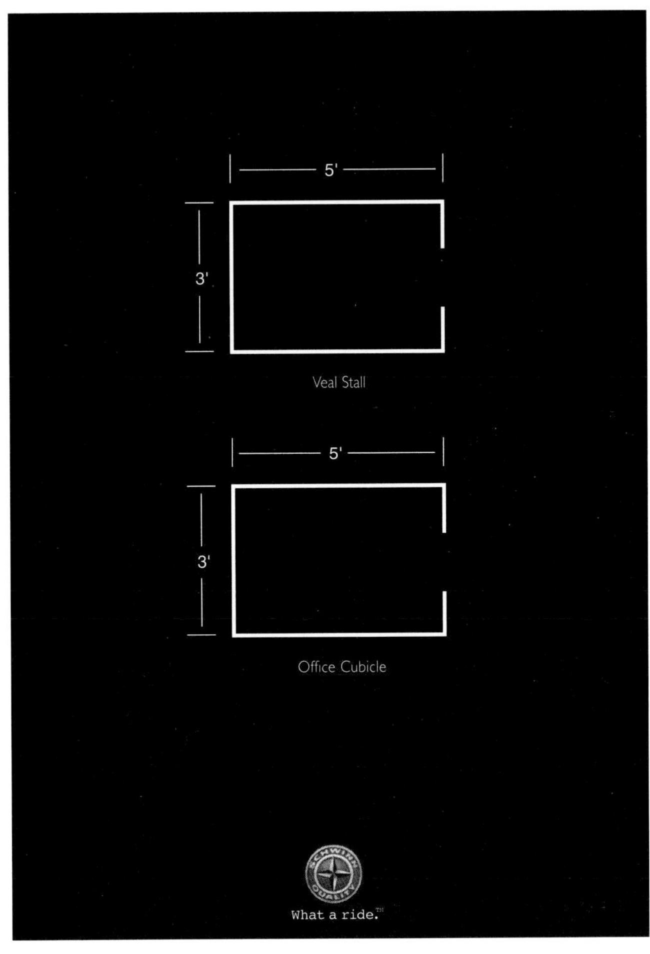

**CONSUMER
NEWSPAPER
600 LINES
OR LESS:
CAMPAIGN**

art director
Greg Leschisin

writer
Tom Camp

client
Schwinn

agency
Carmichael Lynch/
Minneapolis

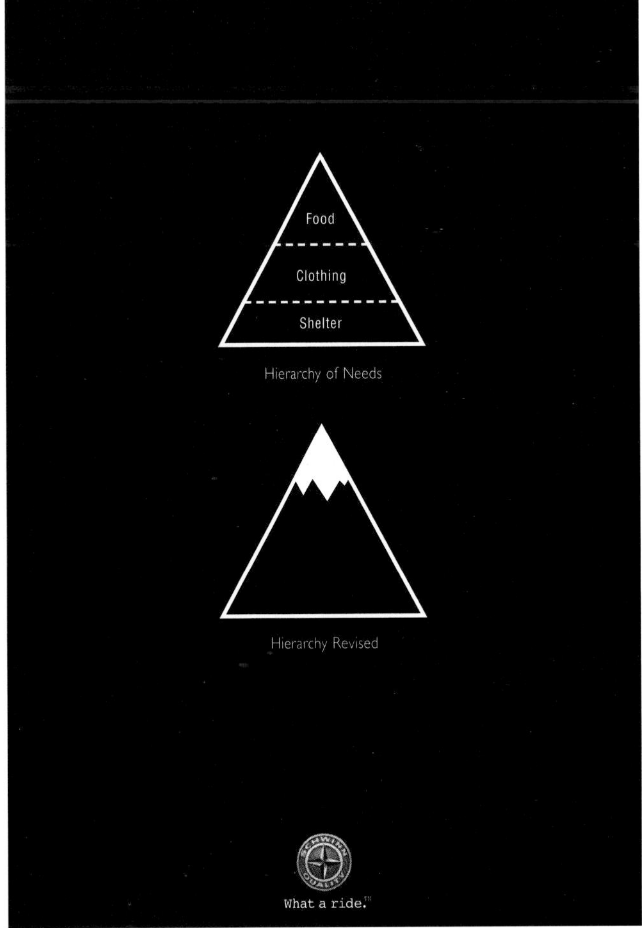

**CONSUMER
NEWSPAPER
600 LINES
OR LESS:
CAMPAIGN**

art director
Eric Tilford

writer
Wade Paschall

photographer
Herman Leonard

client
WSIE The Jazz Station

agency
CORE/St. Louis

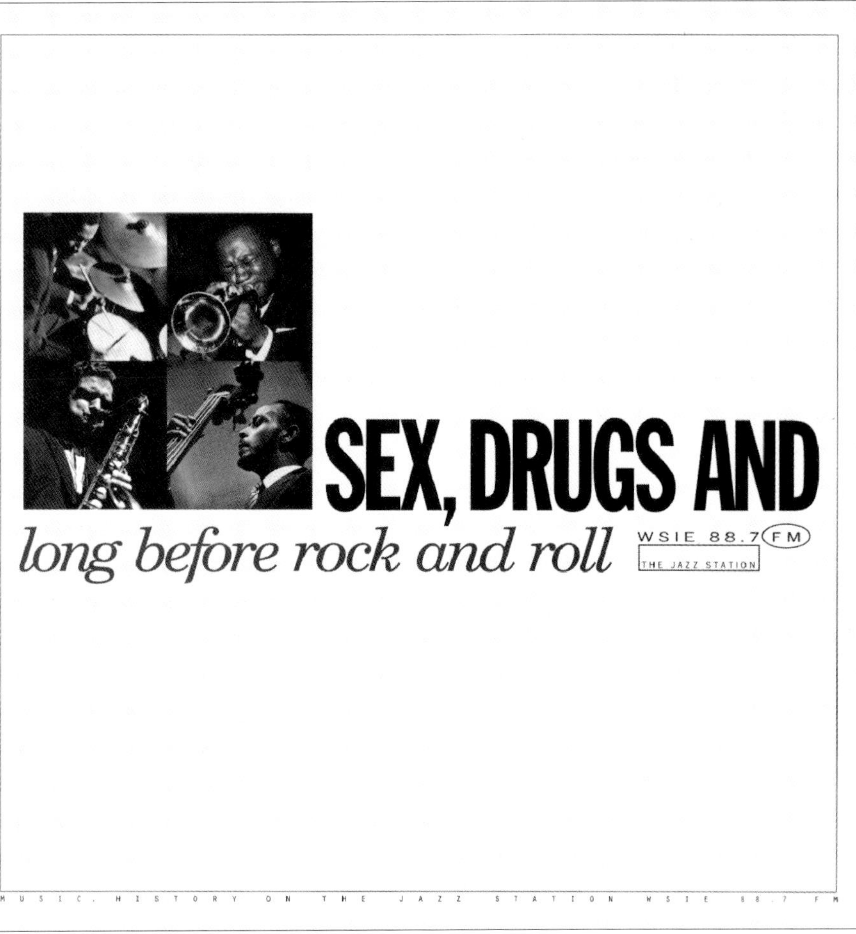
SEX, DRUGS AND
long before rock and roll
WSIE 88.7 FM
THE JAZZ STATION
MUSIC. HISTORY ON THE JAZZ STATION WSIE 88.7 FM

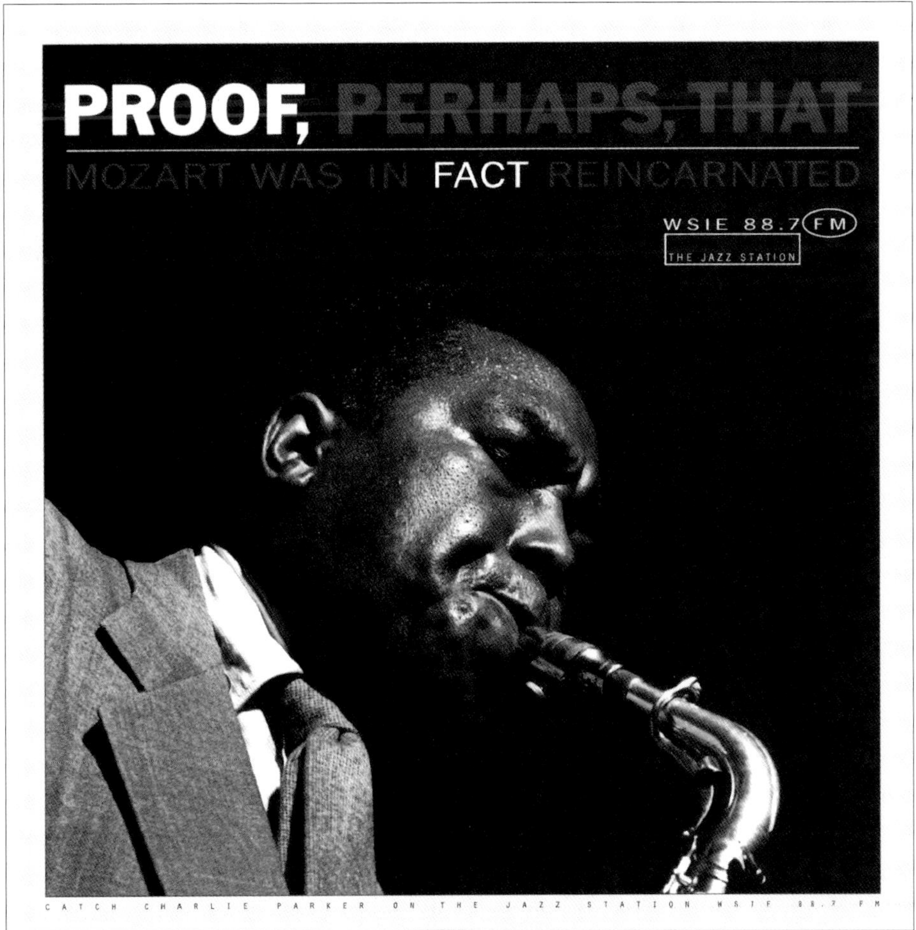
PROOF, PERHAPS, THAT
MOZART WAS IN FACT REINCARNATED
WSIE 88.7 FM
THE JAZZ STATION
CATCH CHARLIE PARKER ON THE JAZZ STATION WSIE 88.7 FM

PRINT FINALISTS

CONSUMER
NEWSPAPER
600 LINES
OR LESS:
CAMPAIGN

art director
Mark Oakley

writer
Ty Montague

client
Food & Water

agency
Montague &, Inc./
South Norwalk, CT

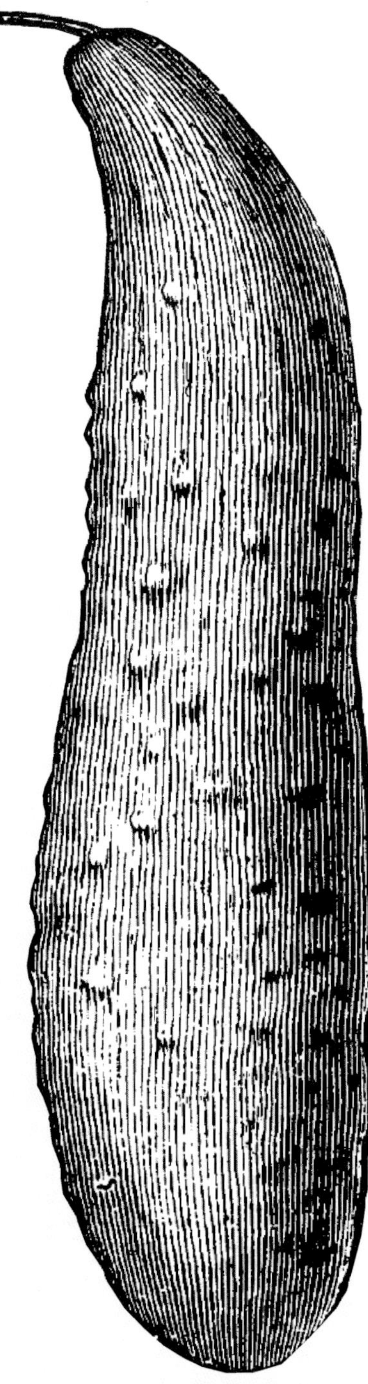

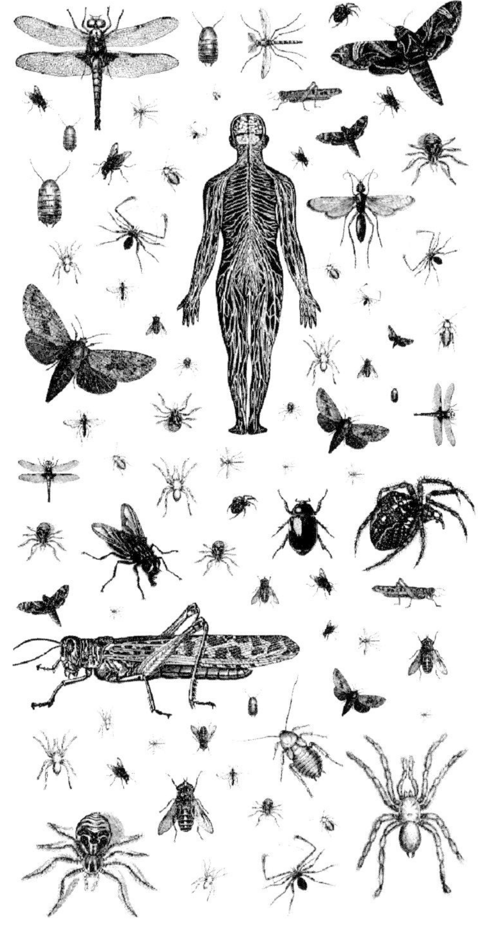

THERE ARE OVER 500 SPECIES
THAT HAVE DEVELOPED
RESISTANCE TO PESTICIDES.
AND ONE THAT HASN'T.

After waging an escalating war on insects for the past 75 years, the poisons we are using now are so powerful, and so toxic that we are literally killing ourselves with them. In fact, thousands of men, women and children die every year.

This killing has got to stop. So we're bringing people together through a project called "neighborhood networks" to tell the food industry that we're fed up with toxic food. And to let them know that there are thousands of outraged citizens whose mission in life is to stop this toxic assault on their families.

Your children deserve cancer-free fruits and vegetables, too. Join us. Call 1-800 EAT SAFE. You are the only weapon the food industry hasn't developed a resistance to.

FOOD&WATER
INCORPORATED

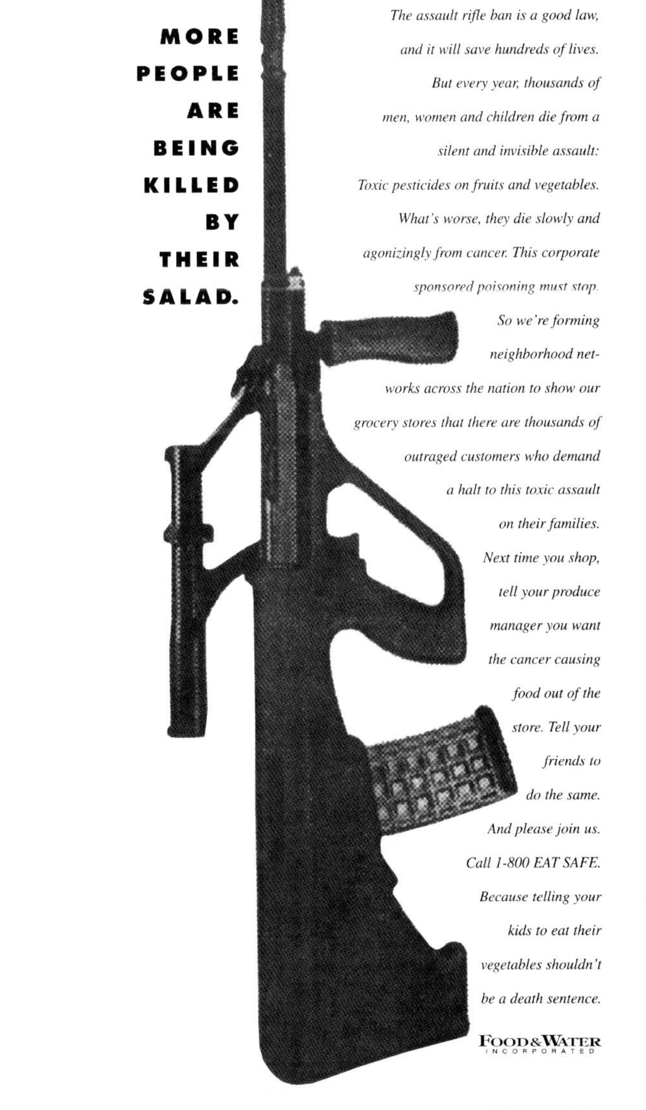

MORE
PEOPLE
ARE
BEING
KILLED
BY
THEIR
SALAD.

The assault rifle ban is a good law, and it will save hundreds of lives. But every year, thousands of men, women and children die from a silent and invisible assault: Toxic pesticides on fruits and vegetables. What's worse, they die slowly and agonizingly from cancer. This corporate sponsored poisoning must stop.

So we're forming neighborhood networks across the nation to show our grocery stores that there are thousands of outraged customers who demand a halt to this toxic assault on their families. Next time you shop, tell your produce manager you want the cancer causing food out of the store. Tell your friends to do the same. And please join us. Call 1-800 EAT SAFE. Because telling your kids to eat their vegetables shouldn't be a death sentence.

FOOD&WATER
INCORPORATED

**CONSUMER
NEWSPAPER
600 LINES
OR LESS:
CAMPAIGN**

art director
Manmohan Anchan

writers
Ramesh Ramnathan
Paul Vinod

photographer
N. Sugathan

client
Titan Industries

agency
Ogilvy & Mather/
Bombay

Only a few watch manufacturers in the world can create a movement TITAN
as slim as 1.75mm. Titan joins that select club. Introducing ultra slim watches. S L I M
•Elegant, classical dials •Exquisite metal or leather bracelets •One year guarantee on gold plating •Longer battery life •Water resistant •Ladies and Gents models •Rs 1950 onwards

Only a few watch manufacturers in the world can create a movement TITAN
as slim as 1.75mm. Titan joins that select club. Introducing ultra slim watches. S L I M
•Elegant, classical dials •Exquisite metal or leather bracelets •One year guarantee on gold plating •Longer battery life •Water resistant •Ladies and Gents models •Rs 1950 onwards

**CONSUMER
NEWSPAPER
600 LINES
OR LESS:
CAMPAIGN**

art director
Ted Royer

writer
David Droga

photographer
Alex Kai Keong

client
Clarke Quay

agency
Saatchi & Saatchi/
Singapore

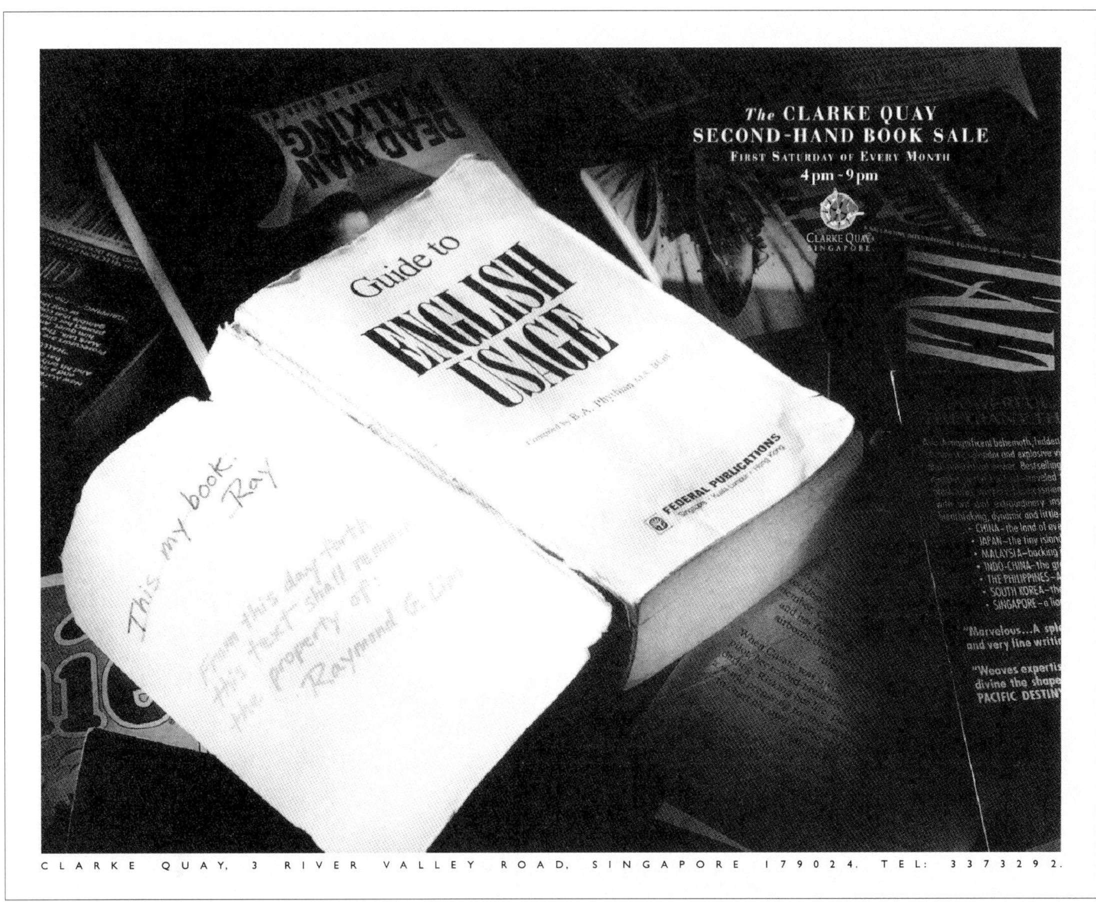

CLARKE QUAY, 3 RIVER VALLEY ROAD, SINGAPORE 179024. TEL: 3373292.

CLARKE QUAY, 3 RIVER VALLEY ROAD, SINGAPORE 179024. TEL: 3373292.

**CONSUMER
MAGAZINE
B/W FULL PAGE
OR SPREAD:
SINGLE**

art director
Greg Leschisin

writer
John Neumann

photographer
Jerry Stebbins

client
Normark

agency
Carmichael Lynch/
Minneapolis

The same picture hangs in tiny
lake-bottom post offices.

Our murderers row. Wanted since 1956. From left to right, it's Fat Rap, Husky Jerk, CountDown, Original, and Jointed.

art director
Jeff Payne

writers
Brian Gold
John Robertson

illustrator
Hatch Show Print

client
Taylor Guitar

agency
VitroRobertson/
San Diego

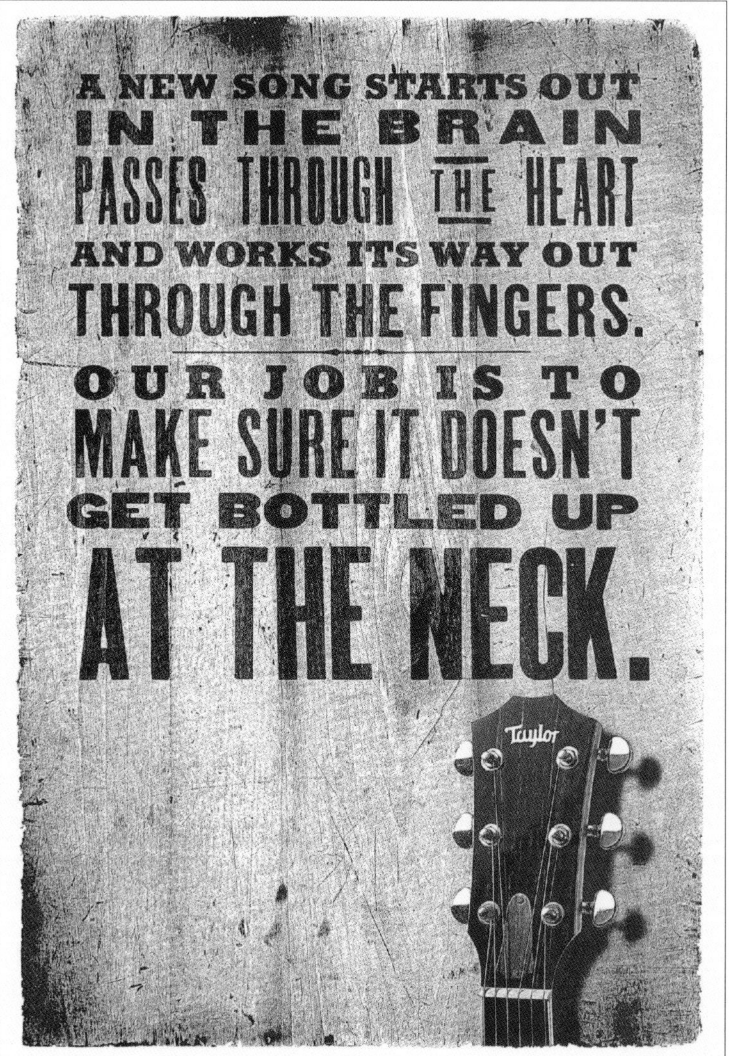

CONSUMER MAGAZINE COLOR FULL PAGE OR SPREAD: SINGLE

art director
Gavin Milner

writer
Harold Einstein

photographer
Joanne Dugan

client
Apple Computer

agency
BBDO West/
Los Angeles

art director
Chris Robb

writers
Dante Lombardi
Mark Ronquillo

photographer
Steve Bronstein

client
Pioneer
Electronics USA

agency
BBDO West/
Los Angeles

CONSUMER
MAGAZINE
COLOR
FULL PAGE
OR SPREAD:
SINGLE

art director
Juan Sebastian Coronil

writer
Carlos Perrino

client
Onda 10

agency
BDDP Mancebo.Kaye/
Madrid

art director
Shelley Stout

writer
Jim Haven

photographer
Michael Washington

client
Morrow Snowboards

agency
Borders Perrin &
Norrander/Portland

art director
Andy Ozark
writer
Carol Joseph
client
Chrysler
Corporation
agency
Bozell Worldwide/
Southfield, MI

art director
Robin Chrumka
writer
Mike Stocker
photographer
Peyton Mitchell
client
Chrysler
Corporation
agency
Bozell Worldwide/
Southfield, MI

**CONSUMER
MAGAZINE
COLOR
FULL PAGE
OR SPREAD:
SINGLE**

art director
Paul Asao

writer
Kerry Casey

photographer
Dennis Manarchy

client
Johnson Worldwide

agency
Carmichael Lynch/
Minneapolis

art director
Paul Asao

writer
Kerry Casey

photographer
Dennis Manarchy

client
Johnson Worldwide

agency
Carmichael Lynch/
Minneapolis

art director
Paul Asao

writer
Tom Camp

client
Motorola

agency
Carmichael Lynch/
Minneapolis

art director
Paul Asao

writer
Tom Camp

client
Motorola

agency
Carmichael Lynch/
Minneapolis

**CONSUMER
MAGAZINE
COLOR
FULL PAGE
OR SPREAD:
SINGLE**

art director
Frank Haggerty

writer
Jim Nelson

photographer
Shawn Michienzi

client
Stren

agency
Carmichael Lynch/
Minneapolis

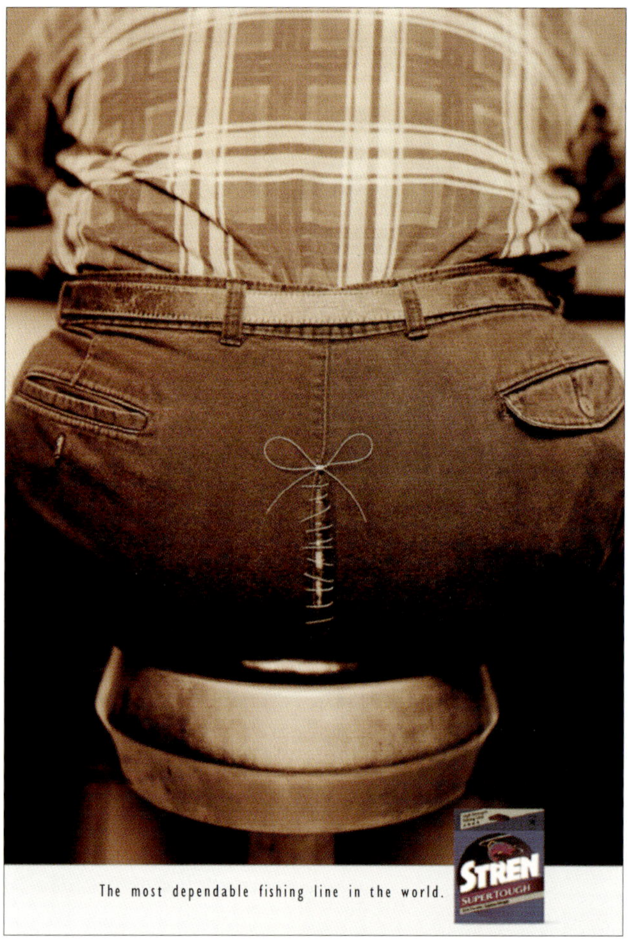

art director
Frank Haggerty

writer
Jim Nelson

photographer
Shawn Michienzi

client
Stren

agency
Carmichael Lynch/
Minneapolis

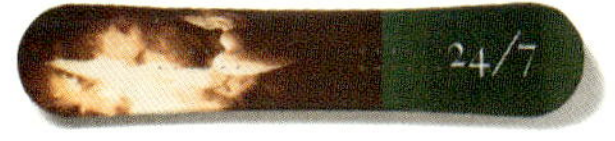

PRINT FINALISTS

art director
David Ayriss

writer
Mark Waggoner

photographer
Torey Piro

client
24/7 Snowboards

agency
Cole & Weber/
Portland

art director
Angel Villalba

writer
Enrique Astuy

photographer
Alfonso Zubiaga

client
Combe Europa

agency
Delvico Bates/Madrid

CONSUMER MAGAZINE COLOR FULL PAGE OR SPREAD: SINGLE

art director
Dean Hanson

writer
Mike Lescarbeau

photographer
Mark Lafavor

client
BMW

agency
Fallon McElligott/
Minneapolis

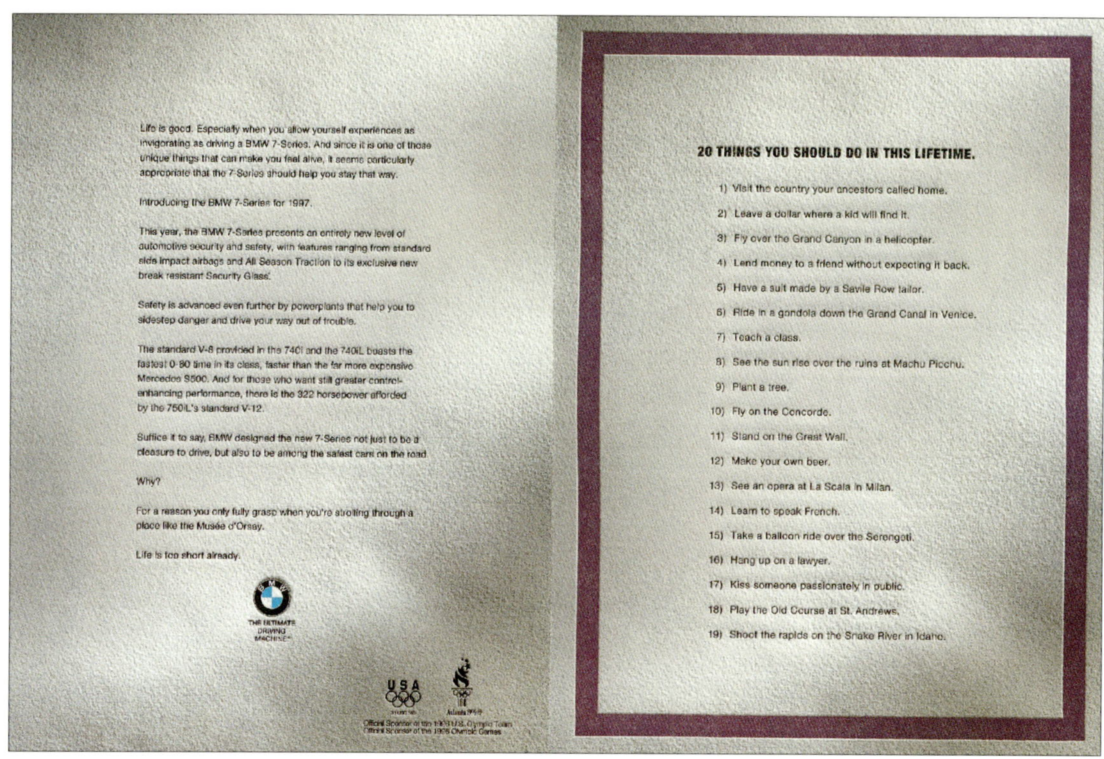

PRINT FINALISTS

art director
Tom Lichtenheld

writer
Tom Rosen

photographer
Mark Laita

client
BMW

agency
Fallon McElligott/
Minneapolis

art director
Bob Barrie

writer
Mike Lescarbeau

photographer
Timothy White

client
Sunset Marquis
Hotel

agency
Fallon McElligott/
Minneapolis

**CONSUMER
MAGAZINE
COLOR
FULL PAGE
OR SPREAD:
SINGLE**

art director
Bob Barrie

writer
Dean Buckhorn

photographer
Mike Powell

client
Time Magazine

agency
Fallon McElligott/
Minneapolis

art director
Bob Barrie

writer
Dean Buckhorn

photograph
NASA

client
Time Magazine

agency
Fallon McElligott/
Minneapolis

PRINT FINALISTS

art director
Bob Barrie

writer
Dean Buckhorn

photographer
In Visions

client
Time Magazine

agency
Fallon McElligott/
Minneapolis

art director
Bob Barrie

writer
Dean Buckhorn

photographer
Gregory Heisler

client
Time Magazine

agency
Fallon McElligott/
Minneapolis

**CONSUMER
MAGAZINE
COLOR
FULL PAGE
OR SPREAD:
SINGLE**

art director
Marc Klein

writer
Sally Hogshead

photographer
Chip Forelli

client
BMW Motorcycles

agency
Fallon McElligott
Berlin / New York

art director
Marc Klein

writer
Sally Hogshead

photographer
Chip Forelli

client
BMW Motorcycles

agency
Fallon McElligott
Berlin / New York

art director
Jason Peterson

writer
Izzy DeBellis

photographer
Greg Federman

client
Nikon Sunglasses

agency
Fallon McElligott
Berlin / New York

art director
Jason Peterson

writer
Izzy DeBellis

photographer
Greg Federman

client
Nikon Sunglasses

agency
Fallon McElligott
Berlin / New York

**CONSUMER
MAGAZINE
COLOR
FULL PAGE
OR SPREAD:
SINGLE**

art director
Jason Peterson

writer
Izzy DeBellis

photographer
Greg Federman

client
Nikon Sunglasses

agency
Fallon McElligott
Berlin / New York

art director
Sean Mullens

writer
Chuck McBride

photographer
Daniel DeSouza

client
Levi Strauss & Co. /
501 Jeans

agency
Foote Cone & Belding /
San Francisco

PRINT FINALISTS

art director
Sean Mullens

writer
Suzanne Finnamore

client
Levi Strauss & Co./
501 Jeans

agency
Foote Cone & Belding/
San Francisco

*(copy in braille reads
"soft to the touch.")*

art director
Jeremy Postaer

writer
Paul Venables

photographer
Mark Hanauer

client
Bell Sports

agency
Goodby Silverstein &
Partners/San Francisco

**CONSUMER
MAGAZINE
COLOR
FULL PAGE
OR SPREAD:
SINGLE**

art director
Jeremy Postaer

writer
Paul Venables

photographer
Heimo

client
Bell Sports

agency
Goodby Silverstein &
Partners/San Francisco

art director
Steve Luker

writer
Steve Simpson

photographer
Gian Paolo Barbieri

client
Norwegian Cruise Line

agency
Goodby Silverstein &
Partners/San Francisco

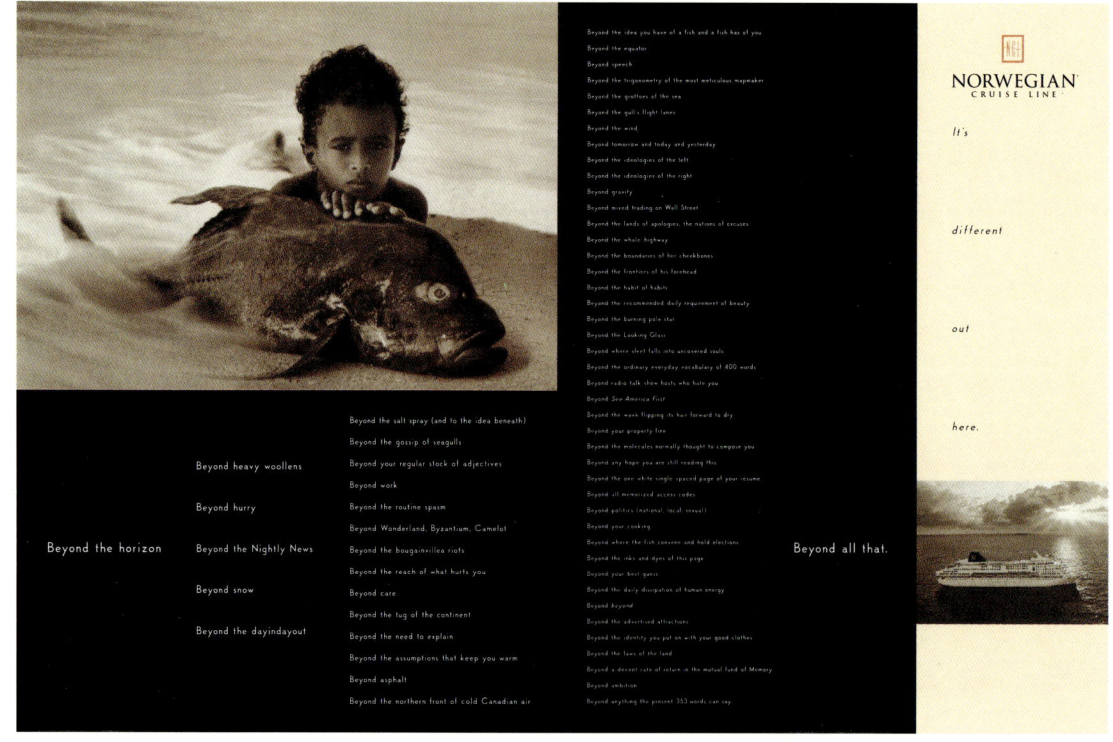

art director
Steve Luker

writer
Steve Simpson

photographers
Gian Paolo Barbieri
Roger Paperno

client
Norwegian Cruise Line

agency
Goodby Silverstein &
Partners / San Francisco

art director
Steve Luker

writer
Steve Simpson

photographer
Gian Paolo Barbieri

client
Norwegian Cruise Line

agency
Goodby Silverstein &
Partners / San Francisco

**CONSUMER
MAGAZINE
COLOR
FULL PAGE
OR SPREAD:
SINGLE**

art director
Valerie Ang-Powell

writer
Steve Payonzeck

photographer
Hunter Freeman

client
Polaroid Corporation

agency
Goodby Silverstein &
Partners/San Francisco

art director
Mike Mazza

writer
Al Kelly

photographer
Hunter Freeman

client
Polaroid Corporation

agency
Goodby Silverstein &
Partners/San Francisco

art director
Sean Ehringer

writer
Harry Cocciolo

photographer
Hunter Freeman

client
Polaroid Corporation

agency
Goodby Silverstein & Partners/San Francisco

art director
Mike Mazza

writer
Al Kelly

photographer
Hunter Freeman

client
Polaroid Corporation

agency
Goodby Silverstein & Partners/San Francisco

**CONSUMER
MAGAZINE
COLOR
FULL PAGE
OR SPREAD:
SINGLE**

art directors
Rich Silverstein
Todd Grant

writer
Jeffrey Goodby

photographer
Nadav Kander

client
Umbro

agency
Goodby Silverstein &
Partners/San Francisco

art director
Tom Gianfagna

writer
Gary Cohen

photographer
Vic Huber

client
Land Rover
North America

agency
Grace & Rothschild/
New York

art director
Allen Richardson

writer
Gary Cohen

photographer
Vic Huber

client
Land Rover
North America

agency
Grace & Rothschild/
New York

art director
Patrick Sutherland

writer
Ari Merkin

photographer
Vic Huber

client
Land Rover
North America

agency
Grace & Rothschild/
New York

**CONSUMER
MAGAZINE
COLOR
FULL PAGE
OR SPREAD:
SINGLE**

art director
Pat Plutschow

writer
Michael Burdick

photographer
Barbara Van Cleeve

client
Howard & Phil's

agency
Ground Zero/
Santa Monica

art director
John Doyle

writer
Dave O'Hare

photographer
Nadav Kander

client
GMEV1/Saturn
Corporation

agency
Hal Riney & Partners/
San Francisco

art director
John Doyle

writer
Dave O'Hare

photographer
Nadav Kander

client
GMEV1/
Saturn Corporation

agency
Hal Riney & Partners/
San Francisco

art director
John Doyle

writer
Dave O'Hare

photographer
Nadav Kander

client
GMEV1/
Saturn Corporation

agency
Hal Riney & Partners/
San Francisco

**CONSUMER
MAGAZINE
COLOR
FULL PAGE
OR SPREAD:
SINGLE**

art director
John Doyle

writer
Dave O'Hare

photographer
Nadav Kander

client
GMEV1/Saturn
Corporation

agency
Hal Riney & Partners/
San Francisco

art director
Chris Poulin

writer
George Goetz

client
Lotus Development
Corporation

agency
Hill Holliday Connors
Cosmopulos/Boston

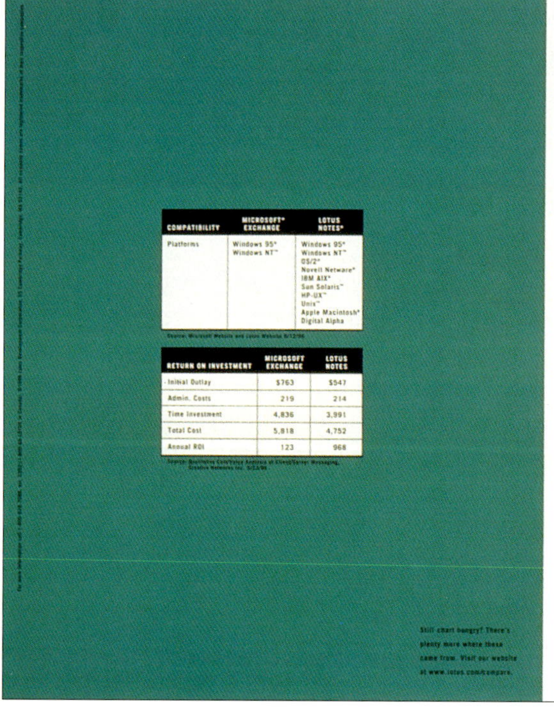

PRINT FINALISTS

art director
Anton Crone

writer
Anton Crone

illustrator
Anton Crone

client
Playtex

agency
Hunt Lascaris TBWA/
Johannesburg

art director
Terence Reynolds

writer
Todd Tilford

photographer
Richard Reens

client
AM General
Corporation

agency
JACKHAMMER/
The Richards Group,
Dallas

**CONSUMER
MAGAZINE
COLOR
FULL PAGE
OR SPREAD:
SINGLE**

art director
Terence Reynolds

writer
Todd Tilford

photographers
Richard Reens
Duncan Sim

client
AM General
Corporation

agency
JACKHAMMER/
The Richards Group,
Dallas

art director
Mariano Favetto

writer
Esteban Pigni

illustrator
Mario Franco

photographer
Daniel Ackerman

client
Sony Argentina

agency
Lautrec Nazca
Saatchi & Saatchi/
Buenos Aires

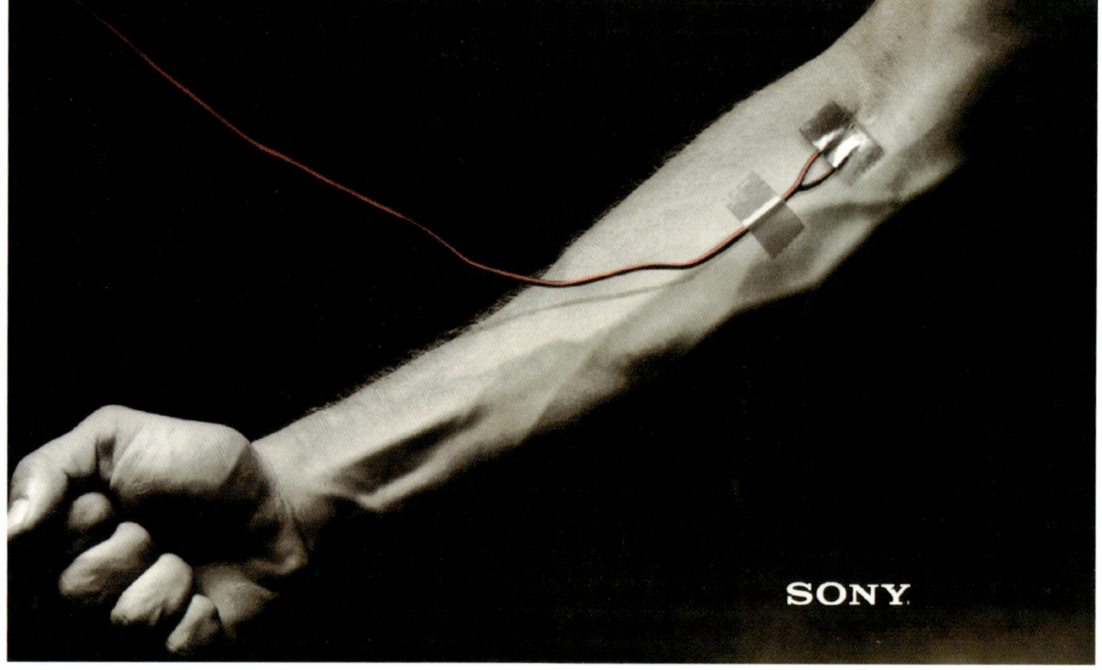

PRINT FINALISTS

art director
Mariano Favetto

writer
Esteban Pigni

illustrator
Mario Franco

photographer
Daniel Ackerman

client
Sony Argentina

agency
Lautrec Nazca
Saatchi & Saatchi/
Buenos Aires

art director
Paul Belford

writer
Nigel Roberts

photographer
Paul Belford

client
Adidas

agency
Leagas Delaney/
London

**CONSUMER
MAGAZINE
COLOR
FULL PAGE
OR SPREAD:
SINGLE**

art director
Dave Dye

writer
Sean Doyle

photographer
Sally Gall

client
Adidas

agency
Leagas Delaney/
London

art director
Dave Dye

writer
Sean Doyle

photographer
Sally Gall

client
Adidas

agency
Leagas Delaney/
London

PRINT FINALISTS

art director
Dave Beverley

writer
Rob Burleigh

photographer
Laurie Haskell

client
Pepe

agency
Leagas Delaney/
London

art director
Dave Beverley

writer
Rob Burleigh

photographer
Laurie Haskell

client
Pepe

agency
Leagas Delaney/
London

**CONSUMER
MAGAZINE
COLOR
FULL PAGE
OR SPREAD:
SINGLE**

art director
Dave Beverley

writer
Rob Burleigh

photographer
Laurie Haskell

client
Pepe

agency
Leagas Delaney/
London

art director
Steve Williams

writer
Adrian Lim

illustrator
Steve Williams

photographer
Chris Steele-Perkins

client
Olympus Cameras

agency
Lowe Howard-Spink/
London

art director
Steve Williams

writer
Adrian Lim

photographer
Chris Steele-Perkins

illustrator
Steve Williams

client
Olympus Cameras

agency
Lowe Howard-Spink/
London

art director
Steve Williams

writer
Adrian Lim

photographer
Chris Steele-Perkins

illustrator
Steve Williams

client
Olympus Cameras

agency
Lowe Howard-Spink/
London

**CONSUMER
MAGAZINE
COLOR
FULL PAGE
OR SPREAD:
SINGLE**

art directors
Jose Molla
Joaquin Molla
Juan Manuel Ricciarelli

writers
Jose Molla
Joaquin Molla
Juan Manuel Ricciarelli

photographer
Juan Castagnola

illustrator
Mario Franco

client
Volkswagen Argentina

agency
RATTO/BBDO,
Buenos Aires

art director
Ted Royer

writer
Rowan Chanen

photographer
Alex Kai Keong

illustrator
Grover Tham

client
The Royal Peacock Hotel

agency
Saatchi & Saatchi/
Singapore

GORED BY CAPE BUFFALO
OR TORN TO SHREDS BY LIONS?
TANZANIA SAYS: "THE CHOICE IS YOURS!"
THE NEW PATHFINDER
NISSAN

SCRATCHING ONLY MAKES IT WORSE.
(A JOURNEY THROUGH BOTSWANA'S OKAVANGO DELTA.)
THE NEW PATHFINDER
NISSAN

**CONSUMER
MAGAZINE
COLOR
FULL PAGE
OR SPREAD:
SINGLE**

art director
Craig Tanimoto

writer
Eric Grunbaum

photographers
William Thompson
Mark Hooper

illustrator
Larry Just

client
Nissan Motor
Corporation

agency
TBWA Chiat/Day,
Venice, CA

PRINT FINALISTS

art director
Todd Waterbury

writer
Peter Wegner

client
The Coca-Cola
Company

agency
Wieden & Kennedy/
Portland

art directors
Larry Frey
Dean Noble

writer
Jerry Cronin

photographer
Terry Heffernan

client
ESPN

agency
Wieden & Kennedy/
Portland

**CONSUMER
MAGAZINE
COLOR
FULL PAGE
OR SPREAD:
SINGLE**

art director
John Boiler

writer
Ernest Lupinacci

client
Nike

agency
Wieden & Kennedy/
Portland

art director
Vince Engel

writer
Jim Riswold

photographer
Mark Ebsen

client
Nike

agency
Wieden & Kennedy/
Portland

Match the correct shoe with the soon-to-be-former world record.*

ZOOM LJ	9.85
ZOOM RIVAL S	1:44.3jr
ZOOM V	3:27.37
ZOOM JAV	26:43.53
ZOOM SD	8' 0 1/2"
ZOOM SUPER FLY	10.89jr
ZOOM HJ	29' 4 1/2"
ZOOM SHIFT	75' 10 1/4"
ZOOM RIVAL D	284' 7"
ZOOM ELDORET	313' 10"
ZOOM ROTATIONAL	12:56.15jr

*Answers found on page 21.

**CONSUMER
MAGAZINE
B/W FULL PAGE
OR SPREAD:
CAMPAIGN**

art director
Kirk Souder

writer
Court Crandall

photographer
Armand Briones

client
Atari

agency
Ground Zero/
Santa Monica

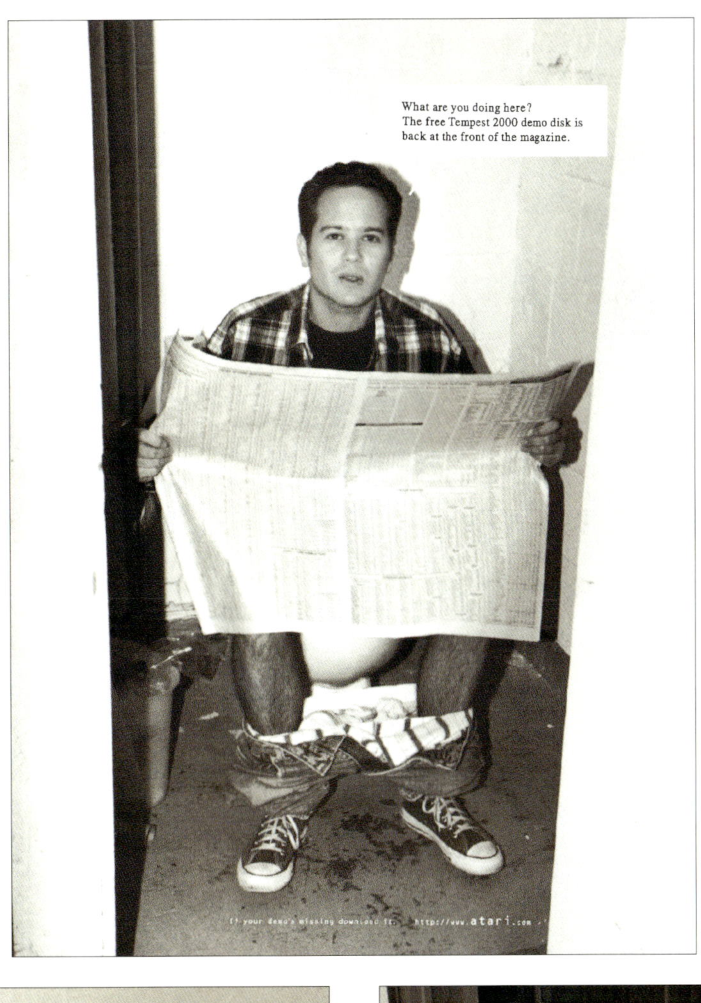

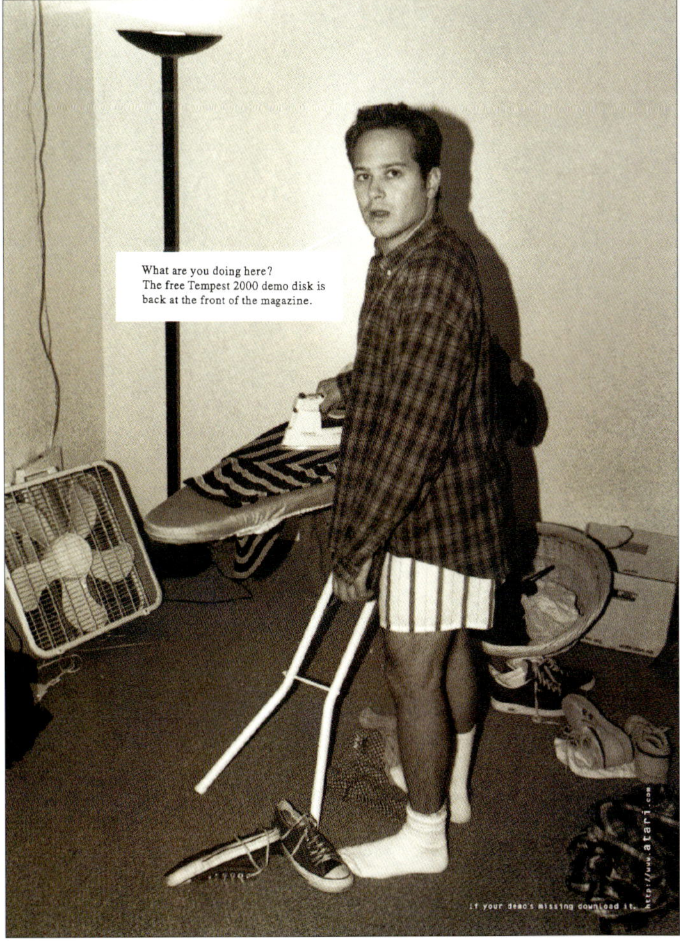

CONSUMER MAGAZINE COLOR FULL PAGE OR SPREAD: CAMPAIGN

art director
Steve Hooper

writer
Victoria Fallon

photographer
Nick Knight

client
Levi Strauss & Co./
Europe

agency
Bartle Bogle
Hegarty/London

Levi's shirt modelled
by original wearer.

Model : Julius, 69, rancher, Colorado.
Items : Sawtooth shirt and 517 relaxed fit jeans.
Stylist : Simon Foxton.
Photographer : Nick Knight.

Levi's jeans modelled
by original wearer.

Model : Josephine, 79, teacher, Colorado.
Item : 534 women's fit jeans.
Stylist : Simon Foxton.
Hair : Kevin Ryan.
Photographer : Nick Knight.

**CONSUMER
MAGAZINE
COLOR FULL
PAGE OR
SPREAD:
CAMPAIGN**

art directors
Melanie Menkemeller
Hajime Ando

writer
Stephanie Crippen

photographers
Sarah Fawcett
Sue Tallon

client
Working Assets
Long Distance

agency
Butler Shine &
Stern / Sausalito

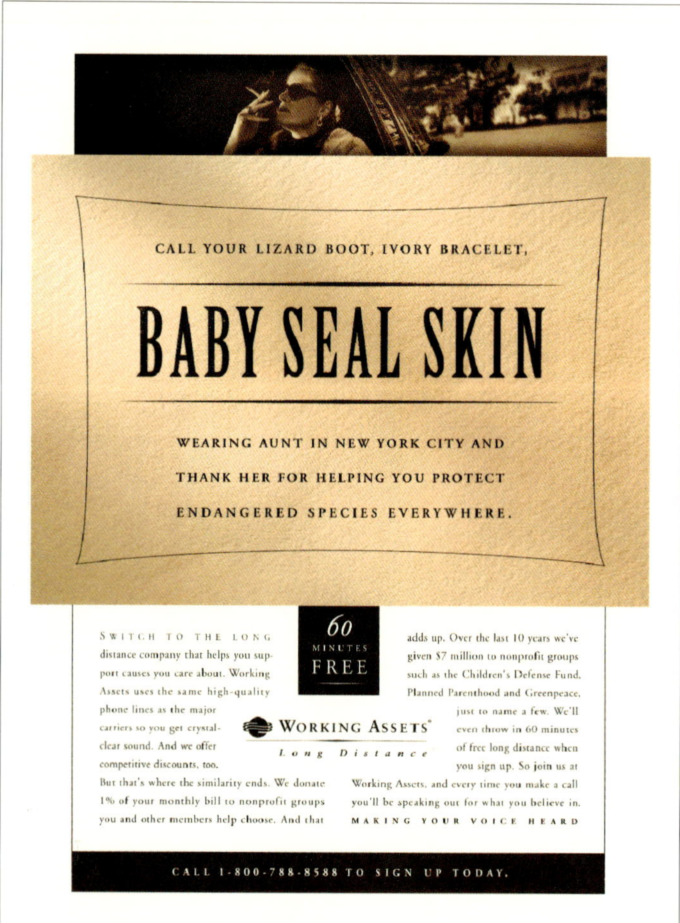

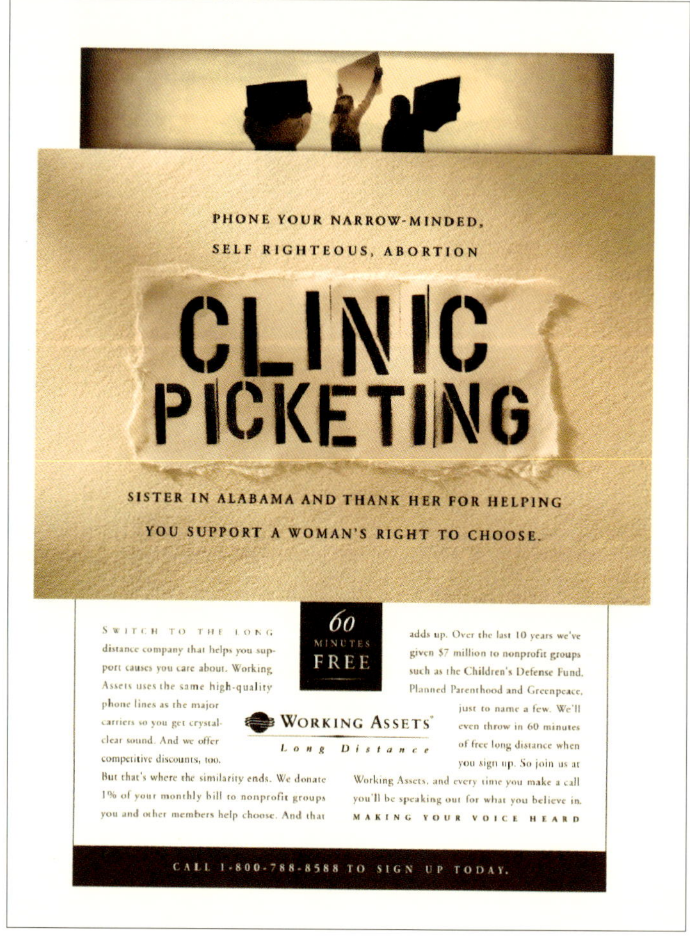

CALL YOUR RIGHT-WING,

GUN-TOTING,
NRA SUPPORTING

UNCLE IN TULSA AND TELL HIM
HOW HE'S HELPING TO SUPPORT
THE BAN ON ASSAULT WEAPONS.

60 MINUTES FREE

WORKING ASSETS
Long Distance

NOW YOU CAN SUPPORT the causes you believe in just by talking on the phone. Working Assets uses the same high-quality phone lines as the major carriers so you get crystal-clear sound. And we offer competitive discounts, as well. But that's where the similarity ends. We donate 1% of your monthly bill to nonprofit groups you and other members help choose. And that adds up. Last year alone we gave over $2 million to groups like Handgun Control, Inc., Friends of the Earth and the Children's Defense Fund, just to name a few. We'll even throw in 60 minutes of free long distance when you sign up. So join Working Assets and the next time you want to try and change the world, call someone in addition to your congressmember. Like your mom in Detroit.

MAKING YOUR VOICE HEARD

CALL 1-800-788-8588 TO SIGN UP TODAY.

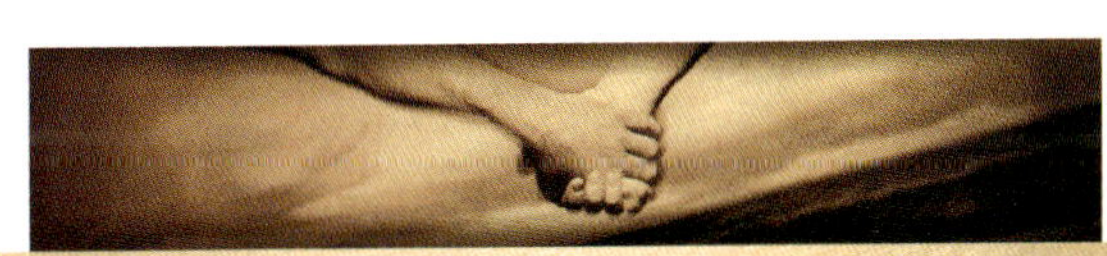

GIVE YOUR CONSERVATIVE, NEWT-PUSHING,

Homophobic

BROTHER IN IDAHO A CALL AND TELL HIM

HOW HE'S HELPING YOU DEFEND THE RIGHTS

OF GAYS AND LESBIANS EVERYWHERE.

60 MINUTES FREE

WORKING ASSETS
Long Distance

NOW YOU CAN SUPPORT equal rights, just by switching your long distance company. Working Assets uses the same high-quality phone lines as the major carriers so you get crystal-clear sound. And we offer competitive discounts, as well. But that's where the similarity ends. We donate 1% of your monthly bill to nonprofit groups you and other members help choose. And that adds up. Last year alone we gave over $2 million to groups like the National Gay & Lesbian Task Force, Planned Parenthood and the Rainforest Action Network, just to name a few. We'll even throw in 60 minutes of free long distance when you sign up. So join a socially-minded company that won't ask for your spare time or extra money. Only that you keep calling your sister in Utah.

MAKING YOUR VOICE HEARD

CALL 1-800-788-8588 TO SIGN UP TODAY.

CONSUMER MAGAZINE COLOR FULL PAGE OR SPREAD: CAMPAIGN

art director
Paul Asao

writer
Kerry Casey

photographer
Dennis Manarchy

client
Johnson Worldwide

agency
Carmichael Lynch/
Minneapolis

With our line, you detect the fish before the fish detects you. SpiderWire® braid and New SpiderWire® Fusion.™ You will feel more fish, hook more fish, land more fish. Be prepared. Out there it's squash, or be squashed.

There are so many ways for a fish to cut your line. SpiderWire® braid and New SpiderWire® Fusion.™ You will feel more fish, hook more fish, land more fish. Be prepared. Out there it's squash, or be squashed.

**CONSUMER
MAGAZINE
COLOR FULL
PAGE OR
SPREAD:
CAMPAIGN**

art director
Paul Asao

writer
Tom Camp

client
Motorola

agency
Carmichael Lynch/
Minneapolis

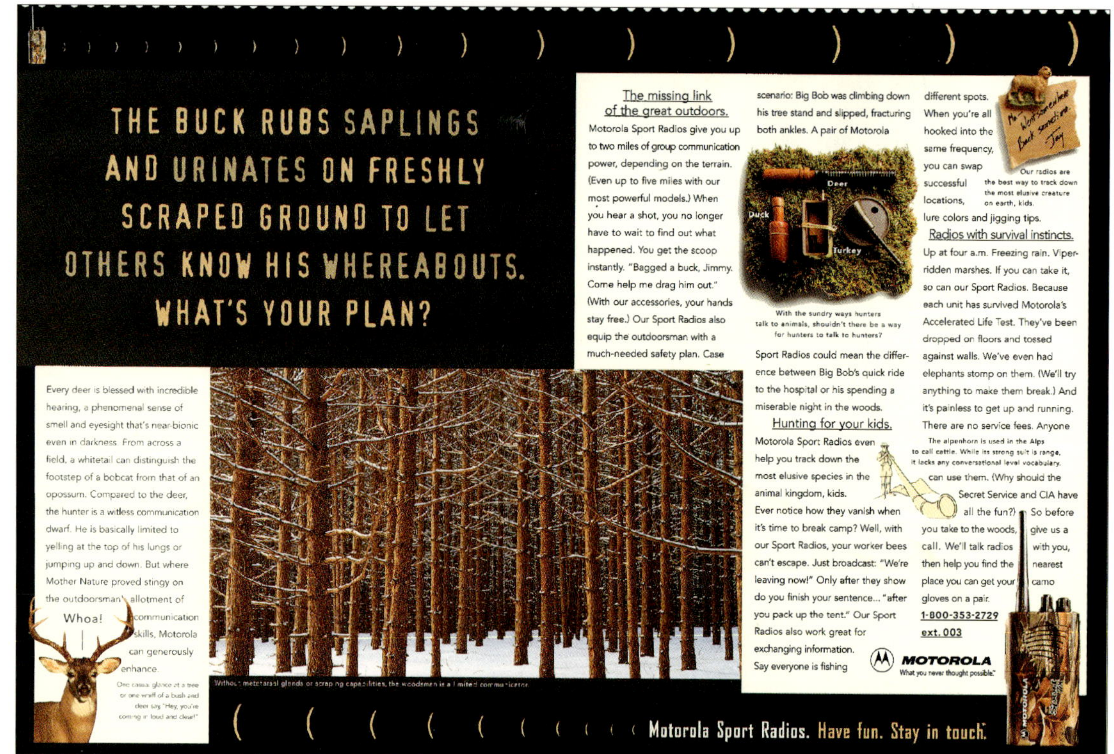

Shop around. You just can't find a decent rescue for under $100,000 these days. And the grand tally is really scary, when you consider that the National Park Service officially plucked nearly 5,000 outdoors types from peril last year. Now there's talk of making the

PRICE TAG OF RESCUES PAID BY PARK SERVICE
1985 1987 1989 1991 1993 1995
The adventure seeker can clearly see that a pair of our Sport Radios makes sound financial sense.

rescue-ees pay for their own rescues. (Will they honor credit cards?) The way we see it, you can take your chances with

THINK A PAIR OF TWO-WAY RADIOS IS EXPENSIVE? PRICED A DECENT SEARCH AND RESCUE MISSION LATELY?

Congressional budget cuts, or you can stay connected with a pair of Motorola Sport Radios and make a plan to keep your group out of the whole mess.
A booster shot for all outdoor activities.
Our Sport Radios are professional-quality, two-way radios that give you up to two miles of group communication, depending on the terrain. (Even up to five miles with our most powerful models.)

BICYCLE SAFETY RULES

If you do get stranded and hungry, reach into Mother Nature's pantry for a quick bite. Beetles are high in protein and some say taste like chicken.

When your biking buddy bombs down a different trail, you don't have to worry about a military helicopter's day rate. Just press your talk button: "Guru to Funky Hammer, I'm down at Chimney Rock." With our handlebar attachment, your hands stay on

the bars.) At Motorola, we understand that trails can start to look alike when you're out there. But when you're all linked by our Sport Radios, you keep your bearings. You keep your group. You keep your cool.
Keeps families together. (Politicians should like us.)
Even if you're not at risk of getting stranded out there, our radios can help you get more out of whatever you're doing. Take the family camping trip. With our Sport Radios, everyone can stay together, even though they're doing different things. Your fishermen can still keep up with your soccer players. (They can watch bobbers all the way up until substitution time.) Or let's say your group is on a canoe adventure.

It's much more difficult for human families to stay together. When you're in the Great Outdoors, you need a plan.

With our Sport Radios, you don't have to wait around for the stragglers. You find out what's taking so long: "Marge, Jimmy and I have drifted into a large river which appears to be the Mississippi. We might be a while."
Johnny Law and you.
Motorola Sport Radios are designed to perform at crunch time. Each unit has survived Motorola's Accelerated Life Test, (passing this test separates the radios from the toys), which simulates five years of hard use in the field. We believe what doesn't kill our radios makes them stronger. (Apparently, so does the National Park Service, who has been using Motorola radios for years.)
We may not be in all your favorite stores yet, so before you go out looking, give us a call. We'll help you find the nearest dealer. We'll even give you directions so you don't get lost.
1-800-353-2729 ext. 004

MOTOROLA
What you never thought possible.™

The UH-1 Huey military helicopter and a ground search team including ATVs, bloodhounds, night search lights - this rescue stuff can add up quicker than a Connecticut wedding.

Motorola Sport Radios. Have fun. Stay in touch.

SHE DIDN'T SHOW AT DEVIL'S BOWL. IS SHE INJURED? OR, IS SHE SIPPING COGNAC WITH THE WELL-GROOMED SKI INSTRUCTOR?

"SHEEZ, LOUISE! WHERE IS SHE?!!" Should you be worried? Mad? Jealous? Should you

A pair of Motorola radios does for the ski group what the little metal clip does for mittens.

notify the ski patrol or start combing the lodge's karaoke bar? As if all this worry wasn't enough, you're forced to watch all the happy skiers finish their exhilarating runs.

Grinning. Yee-hooing. High-fiving. This is torture. You paid good coin to carve, and there you are, as stationary as the Fraser Fir. Now, if you were equipped with a pair of our Sport Radios, you would never

have missed a knee-spanking mogul. She could've told you she was in the ski shop, getting a binding fixed.
Links the bunny hiller and the black diamonder.
Our Sport Radios are professional-quality, two-way radios that give you up to two miles of group communication, depending on the terrain. (Even up to five miles with our most powerful models.) And until lycra epoxy is invented, it's the best way for skiers to stay connected. Broadcast: "Ski Snail to Kamikaze Bomber, wanna meet at the switchback and flash down to the cafe?" You'll find there are times when our radios are invaluable. Who hasn't banged their skis

"WAYS TO CALL KIDS TO DINNER" CHART
Method — Effectiveness
Triangle — 2% effective
Mom yelling — 45% effective
Dad yelling — 65% effective
Heavy metal band's speakers — 80% effective
Motorola radio — 98% effective

together on the lift, sending one plummeting into the gorge below? With our Sport Radios, simply call to see who in your group is nearby.

Only paper families find staying together easy. But with Motorola radios, your family can be linked on the slopes, in the woods or around the neighborhood.

The family that radios together, stays together.
Accurate lunch plans. Nonfiction departure times. Staying connected. These benefits also transfer nicely to altitudes well below 10,000 feet. On a family hike, for instance, you even get quick answers to important questions. "Helen, if a moose charges, do I run or stand my ground? Just curious, over." Or use them at home. Calling your kids to dinner doesn't have to be a neighborhood event. Simply broadcast in a normal tone: "The Mominator to urchins, hightail it home." Before you can say, "Better not drag in mud, over," they're dragging in mud.
Cold facts and warm wishes.
The air's mighty thin at alpine altitudes, but your Motorola Sport Radios won't quit. That's because each unit we sell has passed our Accelerated

Life Test, which simulates five years of hard use in all kinds of nasty places. There are no service fees. Just pop a radio in your pocket and you're off. On the slope, you'll look like a ski patrol. (Posing is okay, but don't try to cut to the front of the lift line.)

Stan Fredrickson, air traffic controller at O'Hare airport says: "Keeping a bunch of knucklehead skiers together can be almost as difficult as coordinating air flight patterns."

And with our accessories, your hands never have to let go of your poles. We're not in all your favorite stores yet, so before you go out looking, give us a call. We'll tell you exactly where you can find a pair. After all, the last thing we want you to do is wait around for something else that isn't there.
1-800-353-2729 ext. 005

MOTOROLA
What you never thought possible.™

Motorola Sport Radios. Have fun. Stay in touch.

CONSUMER
MAGAZINE
COLOR FULL
PAGE OR
SPREAD:
CAMPAIGN

art director
Frank Haggerty

writer
Jim Nelson

photographer
Shawn Michienzi

client
Stren

agency
Carmichael Lynch/
Minneapolis

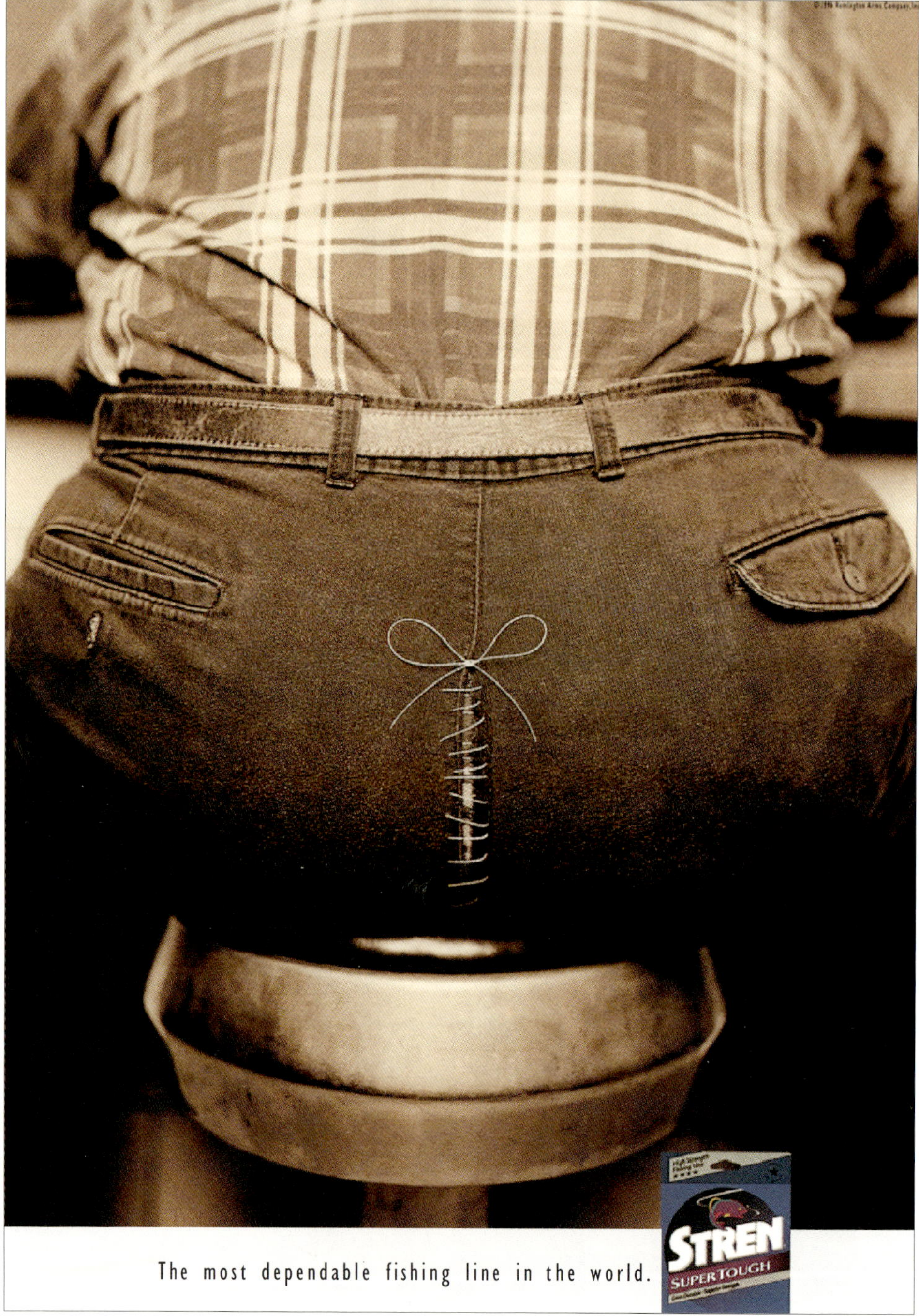

00013
STREN
CLEAR/BLUE
The most dependable fishing line in the world.

STREN
LO-VIS GREEN
The most dependable fishing line in the world.

PRINT FINALISTS

CONSUMER
MAGAZINE
COLOR FULL
PAGE OR
SPREAD:
CAMPAIGN

art directors
Mark Arnold
Eric Tilford

writers
Wade Paschall
Todd Tilford

photographer
James Schwartz

client
Winchester
Ammunition

agency
CORE/St. Louis

4:30am and YOU'RE in a
FROZEN marsh with a wet
dog. SORT of makes you
wonder who's CALLING who.
WINCHESTER
AMMUNITION
OFFICIAL
AMMUNITION

IS THAT PRAIRIE DOG
TALKIN' TO YOU?!
IS THAT PRAIRIE DOG
TALKIN' TO YOU?!
WINCHESTER
AMMUNITION
FREE SIGHT-IN TARGET
with VALUABLE COUPON
Inside EVERY Varmint Value Pack!

MODEL 1873
Old cowboys never die.
They do, on occasion,
have to reload.
Winchester
AMMUNITION
158 GRAIN
250 GRAIN
240 GRAIN
225 GRAIN
WINCHESTER
WINCHESTER
WINCHESTER

AA
OVER TIME, THE CLAY
BEGINS TO MOLD YOU.

It's about TRADITION.
It's about CAMARADERIE.
It's abo - - Whoa boy!
DOG ON POINT!
OFFICIAL AMMUNITION
QUAIL UNLIMITED
WINCHESTER
AMMUNITION
WINCHESTER
SUPER-X
HIGH BRASS
HB

**CONSUMER
MAGAZINE
COLOR FULL
PAGE OR
SPREAD:
CAMPAIGN**

art director
Tomas Lorente

writers
Jose Henrique Borghi
Carlos Domingos

photographer
Manolo Moran

client
Brazilian Post Office

agency
DM9 Publicidade/
Sao Paulo

It hurts
less than
a flea bite.

I've never
seen the
police cry
before.

PRINT FINALISTS

**CONSUMER
MAGAZINE
COLOR FULL
PAGE OR
SPREAD:
CAMPAIGN**

art director
Harvey Marco

writer
Nancy Nelms

photographer
Moshe Brakha

client
Lee Apparel Company

agency
Fallon McElligott/
Minneapolis

From across the room he won't be able to tell you have a great sense of humor.
Lee
The Brand That Fits.

He said the first thing he noticed was your great personality. He lied.
Lee
The Brand That Fits.

**CONSUMER
MAGAZINE
COLOR FULL
PAGE OR
SPREAD:
CAMPAIGN**

art director
Bob Barrie

writer
Dean Buckhorn

photographers
NASA
P.F. Bentley
Dennis Reggie

client
Time Magazine

agency
Fallon McElligott/
Minneapolis

art director
Bob Barrie

writer
Dean Buckhorn

photographers
Gregory Heisler
Mike Powell
In Visions

client
Time Magazine

agency
Fallon McElligott/
Minneapolis

Somehow, the most
enduring memories of
The Games aren't of bombs
and smoking rubble.

The world's most interesting magazine.

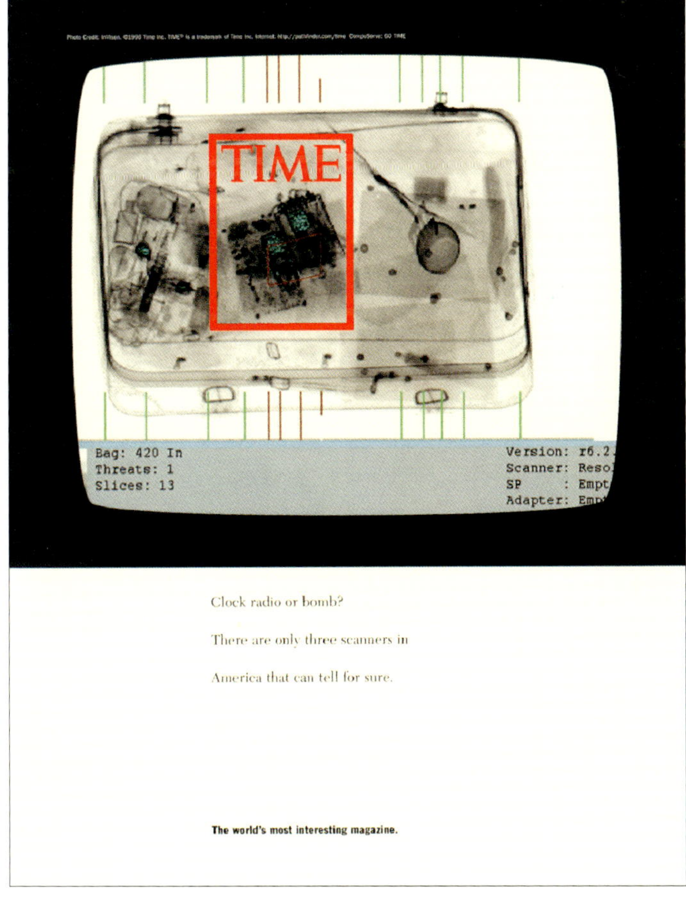

Clock radio or bomb?

There are only three scanners in

America that can tell for sure.

The world's most interesting magazine.

The weight of the world,

measured on a weekly basis.

The world's most interesting magazine.

**CONSUMER
MAGAZINE
COLOR FULL
PAGE OR
SPREAD:
CAMPAIGN**

art director
Marc Klein

writer
Sally Hogshead

photographer
Chip Forelli

client
BMW Motorcycles

agency
Fallon McElligott
Berlin / New York

Not
available
with
cupholders,
babyseats,
or
cellular
phones.

Ever.

R 1100 GS: $12,290 (standard with ABS).
R 850 R: $8,990 (ABS optional).
For a test ride see your
dealer or call 1-800-345-4BMW.
http://www.bmwusa.com

And yet,
the rider will
remember
this
moment
with perfect
clarity.

K 1100 RS: $15,390 (standard with ABS).
For a test ride see your
dealer or call 1-800-345-4BMW.
http://www.bmwusa.com

**CONSUMER
MAGAZINE
COLOR FULL
PAGE OR
SPREAD:
CAMPAIGN**

art director
Jason Peterson

writer
Izzy DeBellis

photographer
Greg Federman

client
Nikon Sunglasses

agency
Fallon McElligott
Berlin / New York

SX LENS
IT'S THE INVISIBLE/THINGS IN LIFE/THAT CAN REALLY HURT YOU
LIKE LOVE AND ULTRAVIOLET RAYS
UV PROTECTION/BOROSILICATE GLASS/SOLID TINT
LENSES THAT KEEP YOU FROM GETTING HURT
LOOKBETTER Nikon sunglasses
1-800-NIKON-US

CE-LENS
1-800-NIKON-US
FOR SOME IT TAKES A LIFE-THREATENING EVENT TO EXPERIENCE
A MOMENT OF CLARITY AND VISION
IN WHICH THE WHOLE WORLD FINALLY MAKES SENSE
UV PROTECTION/AMBER TINT/FULL MIRROR COATINGS
ALLOW YOU TO SEE INTO THE FUTURE
LOOKBETTER Nikon sunglasses

**CONSUMER
MAGAZINE
COLOR FULL
PAGE OR
SPREAD:
CAMPAIGN**

art director
Sean Mullens

writers
Ward Evans
Suzanne Finnamore
Chris Lindau
Chuck McBride

photographer
Daniel DeSouza

client
Levi Strauss & Co./
501 Jeans

agency
Foote Cone & Belding/
San Francisco

THEY HELP ALIENS BLEND IN
501

GIRLS WILL WANT TO STEAL THEM FROM YOU
501

FIVE POCKETS, FIVE CHANCES TO FIND MONEY
501

**CONSUMER
MAGAZINE
COLOR FULL
PAGE OR
SPREAD:
CAMPAIGN**

art directors
Rich Silverstein
Todd Grant

writers
Jeffrey Goodby
Bo Coyner
Jon Soto

photographer
Nadav Kander

client
Umbro

agency
Goodby Silverstein &
Partners/San Francisco

art director
Pat Plutschow
writer
Michael Burdick
photographers
Barbara Van Cleeve
Skeeter Haggler
Dan Winters
client
Howard & Phil's
agency
Ground Zero/
Santa Monica

**CONSUMER
MAGAZINE
COLOR
FULL PAGE
OR SPREAD:
CAMPAIGN**

art director
John Doyle

writer
Dave O'Hare

photographer
Nadav Kander

client
GMEV1/
Saturn Corporation

agency
Hal Riney & Partners/
San Francisco

**CONSUMER
MAGAZINE
COLOR FULL
PAGE OR
SPREAD:
CAMPAIGN**

art director
Chris Poulin

writer
George Goetz

client
Lotus Development
Corporation

agency
Hill Holliday Connors
Cosmopulos / Boston

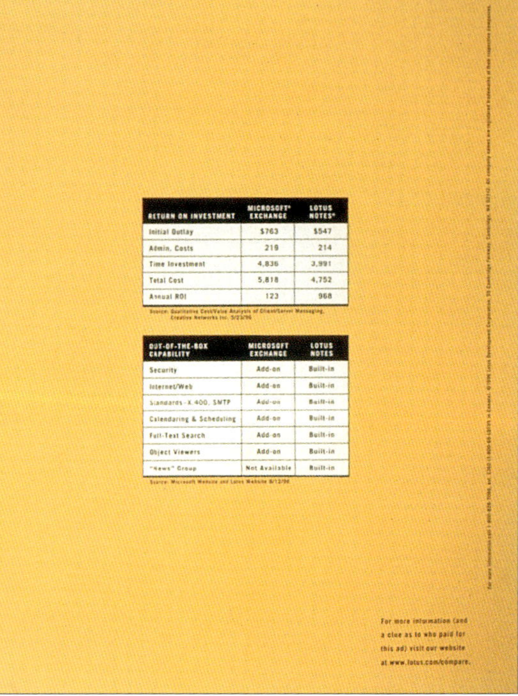

RETURN ON INVESTMENT	MICROSOFT* EXCHANGE	LOTUS NOTES*
Initial Outlay	$763	$547
Admin. Costs	219	214
Time Investment	4,836	3,991
Total Cost	5,818	4,752
Annual ROI	123	968

Source: Qualitative Cost/Value Analysis of Client/Server Messaging, Creative Networks Inc. 5/23/96

OUT-OF-THE-BOX CAPABILITY	MICROSOFT EXCHANGE	LOTUS NOTES
Security	Add-on	Built-in
Internet/Web	Add-on	Built-in
Standards - X.400, SMTP	Add-on	Built-in
Calendaring & Scheduling	Add-on	Built-in
Full-Text Search	Add-on	Built-in
Object Viewers	Add-on	Built-in
"News" Group	Not Available	Built-in

Source: Microsoft Website and Lotus Website 8/12/96

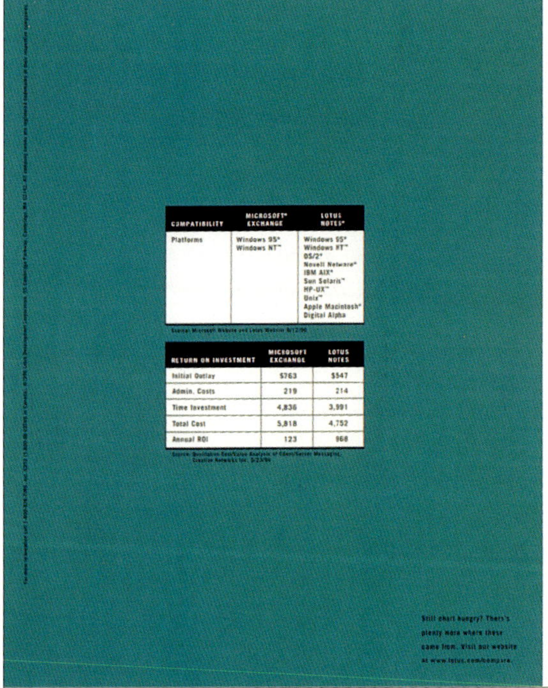

COMPATIBILITY	MICROSOFT* EXCHANGE	LOTUS NOTES*
Platforms	Windows 95* Windows NT™	Windows 95* Windows NT™ OS/2* Novell Netware* IBM AIX* Sun Solaris™ HP-UX™ Unix™ Apple Macintosh* Digital Alpha

Source: Microsoft Website and Lotus Website 8/12/96

RETURN ON INVESTMENT	MICROSOFT EXCHANGE	LOTUS NOTES
Initial Outlay	$763	$547
Admin. Costs	219	214
Time Investment	4,836	3,991
Total Cost	5,818	4,752
Annual ROI	123	968

Source: Qualitative Cost/Value Analysis of Client/Server Messaging, Creative Networks Inc. 5/23/96

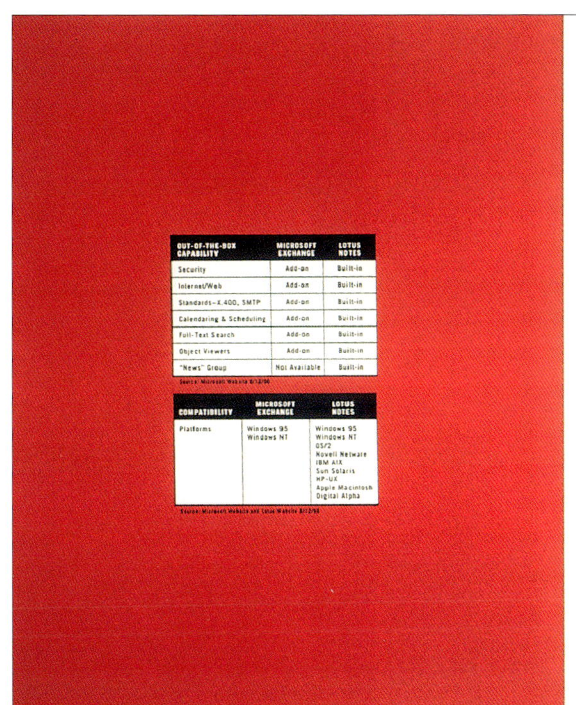

OUT-OF-THE-BOX CAPABILITY	MICROSOFT EXCHANGE	LOTUS NOTES
Security	Add-on	Built-in
Internet/Web	Add-on	Built-in
Standards – X.400, SMTP	Add-on	Built-in
Calendaring & Scheduling	Add-on	Built-in
Full-Text Search	Add-on	Built-in
Object Viewers	Add-on	Built-in
"News" Group	Not Available	Built-in

Source: Microsoft Website 8/12/96

COMPATIBILITY	MICROSOFT EXCHANGE	LOTUS NOTES
Platforms	Windows 95 Windows NT	Windows 95 Windows NT OS/2 Novell Netware IBM AIX Sun Solaris HP-UX Apple Macintosh Digital Alpha

Source: Microsoft Website and Lotus Website 8/12/96

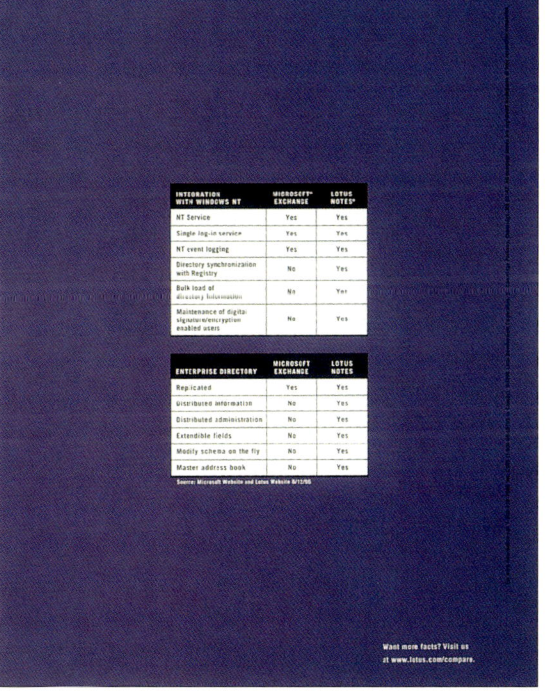

INTEGRATION WITH WINDOWS NT	MICROSOFT EXCHANGE	LOTUS NOTES*
NT Service	Yes	Yes
Single log-in service	Yes	Yes
NT event logging	Yes	Yes
Directory synchronization with Registry	No	Yes
Bulk load of directory information	No	Yes
Maintenance of digital signature/encryption enabled users	No	Yes

ENTERPRISE DIRECTORY	MICROSOFT EXCHANGE	LOTUS NOTES
Replicated	Yes	Yes
Distributed information	No	Yes
Distributed administration	No	Yes
Extendible fields	No	Yes
Modify schema on the fly	No	Yes
Master address book	No	Yes

Source: Microsoft Website and Lotus Website 8/12/96

**CONSUMER
MAGAZINE
COLOR
FULL PAGE
OR SPREAD:
CAMPAIGN**

art director
Paul Renner

writers
Roger Baldacci
Paul Renner

client
Converse -International

agency
Houston Herstek
Favat / Boston

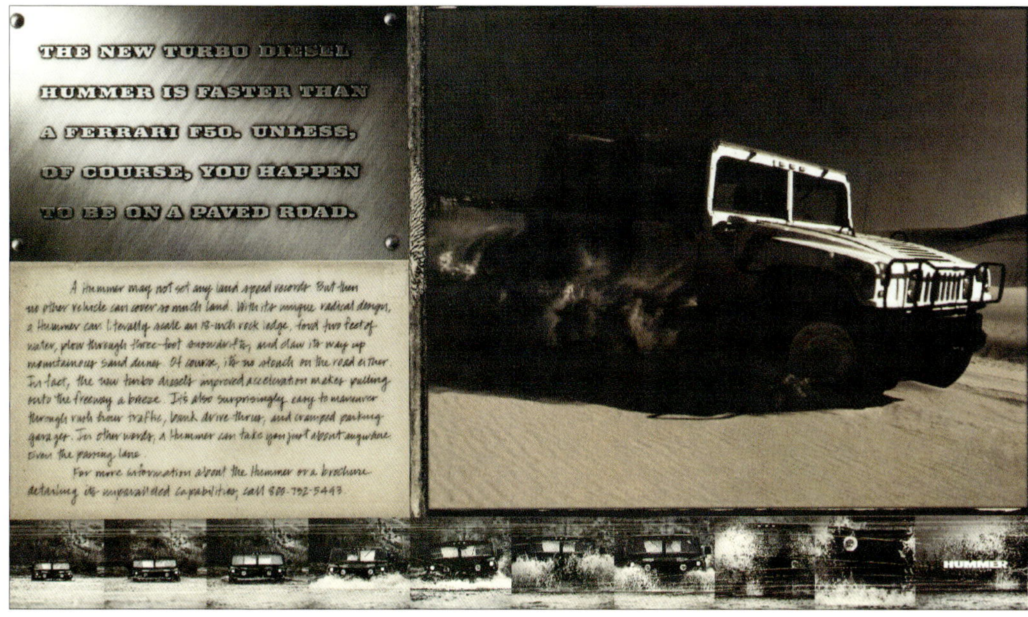

PRINT FINALISTS

art director
Terence Reynolds

writer
Todd Tilford

photographers
Richard Reens
Duncan Sim

client
AM General
Corporation

agency
JACKHAMMER/
The Richards Group,
Dallas

**CONSUMER
MAGAZINE
COLOR FULL
PAGE OR
SPREAD:
CAMPAIGN**

art director
Christian
Wojciechowski

writer
Chad Rea

photographer
Christian
Wojciechowski

client
GT Interactive Software

agency
JACKHAMMER/
The Richards Group,
Dallas

PRINT FINALISTS

art director
Dave Dye

writer
Sean Doyle

photographer
Sally Gall

client
Adidas

agency
Leagas Delaney/
London

**CONSUMER
MAGAZINE
COLOR FULL
PAGE OR
SPREAD:
CAMPAIGN**

art director
Steve Paskin

writer
Tom Hudson

photographer
Laurie Haskell

client
Pepe

agency
Leagas Delaney/
London

STOP
TELLING
ME WHAT
TO
DO.
Pepe Jeans
LONDON
'M2 REGULAR FIT JEANS

THE
WORLD
IS FULL OF
PEOPLE
YOU HOPE YOU'LL
NEVER
MEET.
Pepe Jeans
LONDON

**CONSUMER
MAGAZINE
COLOR FULL
PAGE OR
SPREAD:
CAMPAIGN**

art director
Dave Beverley

writer
Rob Burleigh

photographers
Laurie Haskell
Claire Lazarus

client
Pepe

agency
Leagas Delaney/
London

THINGS
TO DO
TODAY.
Pepe Jeans
LONDON

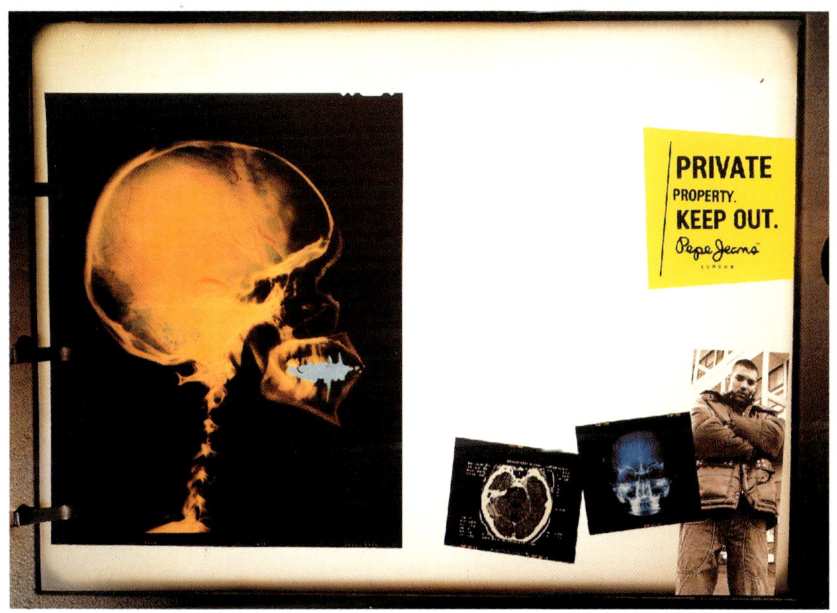

PRIVATE
PROPERTY.
KEEP OUT.
Pepe Jeans
LONDON

OUTSIDE EVERY
THIN GIRL
THERE'S A
FAT GUY
TRYING TO
GET IN.
Pepe Jeans
LONDON

CONSUMER MAGAZINE COLOR FULL PAGE OR SPREAD: CAMPAIGN

art director
Steve Williams

writer
Adrian Lim

illustrator
Steve Williams

photographer
Chris Steele-Perkins

client
Olympus Cameras

agency
Lowe Howard-Spink/
London

CONSUMER
MAGAZINE
COLOR FULL
PAGE OR
SPREAD:
CAMPAIGN

art director
Craig Tanimoto

writer
Eric Grunbaum

illustrator
Larry Just

photographers
William Thompson
Mark Hooper

client
Nissan Motor
Corporation

agency
TBWA Chiat/Day,
Venice, CA

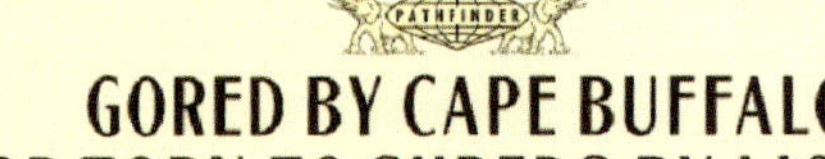

As any travel agent will tell you, Tanzania offers safari enthusiasts an incredible array of wildlife. Cape buffalo roam in giant herds. Hippos enjoy midday dips in cool water holes. Lions can be seen grooming themselves in the sun. What those vacation venders neglect to say, however, or at least hide in very small type that can't be read, is that many of those animals have a distinct fondness for khaki. Still, we couldn't resist the call of Tanzania's world-famous game reserves, and, with our all new Pathfinder's doors securely locked, recently embarked on a driving adventure along the country's Northern Circuit.

TANZANIA

ONE AFTERNOON, bored by prehistoric life, an ancient ancestor of man left his cave to view some of the wild animals that lived nearby. What was to be history's first wildlife safari, however, went a bit awry and, 1.7 million years later, anthropologists found themselves dusting off the well-preserved skull of *Zinjanthropus boisei*, Tanzania's first safari victim.

While the intervening millennia have done little to diminish the local animal population's carnivorous impulses, the Pathfinder's nimble handling and powerful acceleration make visiting **Tanzania** a lot safer for present-day humans than it was for cavemen. And it was with our windows tightly rolled up that we departed for the Northern Circuit, a route that offers, in one fell swoop, Lake Manyara National Park, the Ngorongoro Crater Conservation Area and legendary Serengeti National Park.

Our first stop was Lake Manyara National Park, located 130 dirt-covered kilometers west of Arusha

THE PATHFINDER MISSION.

Congratulations. You are reading about the all new 1996 Nissan Pathfinder, the finest sport utility vehicle we have ever made. From design to manufacturing, we've endeavored to build a vehicle that provides its owner with an exceptional level of comfort, ruggedness, safety and reliability. With proper care and maintenance, the Pathfinder should provide years of loyal service wherever your outdoor pursuits take you. To learn more, visit us at: http://www.nissanmotors.com/pathfinder or call us at 1-800-000-0000 (Canada: 1-800-387-0122).

in the Great Rift Valley. Characteristic of Tanzanian vehicular travel, this drive is a trade-off between speed and tire-swallowing potholes, and it was only thanks to our vehicle's rugged suspension that we reached the park's main gate with all our fillings still affixed to our molars. (On a positive note, traffic density along this road is low, so collisions are rare.) Once one of the most popular hunting areas in Tanzania, Lake Manyara was named a national park in 1960, and today offers an incredible amount of wildlife and geographical diversity. Of particular interest were the thousands of flamingos that inhabit the lake, a herd of hippos that entertained us with wallowing and honking, and a large troop of baboons, whose foray onto the park's road suggested a complete disregard for traffic etiquette.

Several days later – with no reported casualties—we visited Stop #2 on the Northern Circuit: The (tongue-twisting) Ngorongoro Crater Conservation Area. Formed 2.5 million years ago by

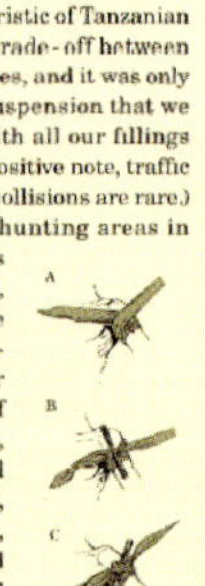

The ALL NEW 1996 NISSAN PATHFINDER SE — FEATURES

1. Rugged MonoFrame™ construction	5. Power-assisted rack-and-pinion steering	8. Available automatic temperature control system
2. Dual airbags	6. Shift-on-the-fly 4WD up to 50 mph	9. Front and rear 12-volt outlets
3. Four-wheel anti-lock brakes	7. Standard CD stereo system	10. Available sliding glass sunroof
4. Heavy-duty independent strut front suspension		

the collapse of an enormous volcano, the crater is as remarkable for its physical beauty as for its wildlife, and, indeed, it is the jaded geologist who stands unimpressed at the rim of this 20,000-meter caldera. Less impressive is the steep, rough, narrow, winding and sorry excuse for a road that descends into the crater, but that's what low-range 4WD is for. At last count, there were over 30,000 animals living within Ngorongoro's walls (including four separate prides of lions), so bring lots of film and stay in your vehicle.

Last stop (STILL ALIVE!) was Serengeti National Park. At 14,763 square kilometers, this granddaddy of reserves is

larger than Connecticut, but with a lot fewer preppies. (Just kidding, blue-blooded buddies!) As our visit coincided with the annual Serengeti Migration, we witnessed millions of hoofed animals brave hazardous terrain and hungry carnivores in

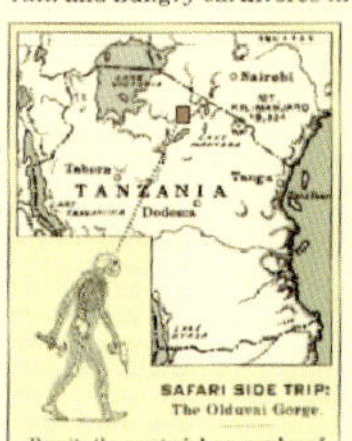

Despite the country's large number of man-eating carnivores, Tanzania is thought by anthropologists to be the cradle of mankind. It was near the Ngorongoro Crater, in fact, that Dr. Leakey discovered the bones of *Homo Habilis*. (Known as "Handy Man" for his use of primitive tools and his ability to fix things around the cave.)

search of prime grazing land. Seeing wildebeest attempting to cross swollen rivers only to be snatched by hungry crocodiles definitely leaves one marveling at the ominous process of nature. And, of course, being thankful one's not a wildebeest.

Leaving Tanzania with our new Pathfinder intact and no deep punctures to our bodies, we can highly recommend driving Tanzania's Northern Circuit yourself. Just plan your itinerary carefully, bring a good camera and don't try feeding the lions.

After all, you'll need those hands to drive.

SCRATCHING ONLY MAKES IT WORSE.

(A JOURNEY THROUGH BOTSWANA'S OKAVANGO DELTA.)

Recently we subjected the new Nissan Pathfinder to one of the toughest test-drives imaginable: a 5,000-mile safari across Africa. Our journey treated us to incredible wildlife, breathtaking landscapes and some of the poorest excuses for roads you can imagine. Over the next few months, we'll share highlights, lowlights, our favorite destinations and survival tips. We may even mention a word or two about the vehicle that took us there and back in one piece. Today's story, as the saying goes, begins in Botswana.

BOTSWANA

With over 85% of his country covered in sand, scorching temperatures that routinely soar over 115° F, and roads that have never seen an ounce of asphalt, Botswana's Minister of Tourism would seem to have his work cut out for him. Add the ubiquitous mosquitoes and voracious tsetse flies and you'd think he'd quit and find a new job.

Indeed, you'll find few souls adventurous enough to visit this rough and tumble country. But for us, Botswana was the perfect place to prove the mettle of the new Nissan Pathfinder.

We arrived in Botswana on September 30th, which was, auspiciously, "Botswana Day." Our intended destination was the northwest corner of the country, where Angola's Okavango River spills into Botswana's sands and forms the Okavango Delta: the largest inland delta in the world. Here, we were told, temperatures only reached 105° and any discomfort would be recompensed by the hundreds of different animal species that inhabit this wildlife oasis. (And, of course, the fact we could set our automatic temperature control on a more humane 72°F.)

Our jumping-off point for the Okavango Delta was a small frontier town called Maun where, as our Pathfinder's built-in compass confirmed, we caught a two-lane road north. It took us only a few minutes to surmise that Botswana's Minister of Transportation must spend most of his time consoling the country's Minister of Tourism, for just two miles out of Maun the tarred road abruptly ends and turns to sand. Indeed, since there is no pavement or gas station or traffic sign or convenience mart for the long, slow 70-mile drive into the delta, we recommend keeping the Pathfinder in 4wd and bringing along a good collection of CDs.

THE PATHFINDER MISSION

Congratulations. You are reading about the all-new 1996 Nissan Pathfinder, the finest sport utility vehicle on the market.

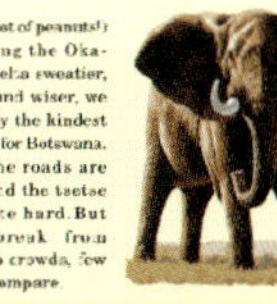

LOCAL BOTSWANA SNACK

Any curse words uttered in the direction of Botswana's transportation departments, however, were quickly retracted as we entered the primordial delta. The terrain, although challenging to man, machine and anti-perspirant, is home to an incredible array of wildlife. On our first day alone, we saw elephants, giraffe, hippos, zebra, buffalo, wildebeest, gazelle and warthogs—the latter of which (DRIVING ALERT) burrow dens into the ground that put New York potholes to shame.

The following days were spent four-wheeling through the thick once and soggy marshes that pass for roads in Botswana, and observing the area's elephant herds. We're pleased to report that the Pathfinder's increased horsepower and torque handled the terrain with ease, the newly improved suspension system made mincemeat of the bumps and, aesthetically speaking, our vehicle looked quite sharp covered in Okavango mud. We should also add, immodestly, that we learned enough trivia about the Family Elephantidae to ensure us a spot on the final round of Jeopardy (Did you know African elephants eat 16 hours a day?)

That's a lot of peanuts! Leaving the Okavango Delta sweatier, itchier and wiser, we have only the kindest of words for Botswana. Sure, the roads are lousy and the tsetse flies bite hard. But as a break from vacation crowds, few places compare.

SAFARI SAFETY BULLETIN

Refrain from using the Pathfinder's horn while driving through an elephant herd. The sound is like that of an elephant in distress, and may cause the herd to stampede in your direction. Even though the Pathfinder features chip-resistant paint, this would not be a good thing.

Pathfinder drivers desiring to visit the Okavango can call their local travel agent or, if phone bills are no object, Botswana's Department of Tourism at 011-267-353024. We're sure the Minister of Tourism would love to hear from you.

NEXT STOP: KENYA!

THE *NEW* PATHFINDER

NISSAN

START the CAR! START the CAR!

TRAVELING THROUGH KENYA'S RHINO COUNTRY

Ah, Kenya. What other country, we ask, offers the thrill of dodging maniacal city drivers one moment, and the joy of fleeing a charging rhino the next? Since we just spent over six weeks there in the all-new Nissan Pathfinder, we'll tell you: Not many. What follows are stories and survival tips from our recent trip through this East African wildlife mecca and sanctuary for driver's ed flunkies.

KENYA

From the Great Rift Valley to the Serengeti Plains, Kenya offers some of the most beautiful and diverse geography in all of Africa. But let us not mince words: Driving in this country is utterly appalling.

Temperatures are extreme. Roads abysmal. Local motorists deranged. And that's just Nairobi. Assuming you leave the city limits in one piece, you'll then enjoy the additional challenge of numerous animal species that would like nothing better than to make you their next meal. Or, at least, send your car to the body shop for a little fender work.

This leaves the safari enthusiast in a bit of a quandary. How does one visit the world's number one wildlife mecca and come home with all limbs still present and accounted for?

As most travel between Kenya's national wildlife parks is by 4WD, it's important – first and foremost – to know which side of the road the local population drives on. In Kenya, this is simple: They drive on whichever side is smoothest. We generally found this to be our side, and most of our time was spent scanning the horizon for oncoming vehicles, checking to make sure our seat belts were securely fastened, and being thankful for Nissan engineers' thoughtful inclusion of dual airbags.

Assuming you make it beyond the city limits in one piece, your next area of concern will be negotiating the game parks, where the animals rank higher on the food chain than the humans. We took the Pathfinder to Amboseli National Park, Shaba National Reserve, and a small ranch called Ol Jogi (built by a wealthy Europeon art dealer as a retreat from the drudgery of counting his money all day), but the same rules apply to whichever park you visit. Keep your windows rolled up around home. Don't get between a mother elephant and her young. And watch out for rhinos – they'll charge anything. The last point was made to us at Ol Jogi, where we learned that although rhinoceros are technically herbivores,

BLACK RHINO
[Diceros Bicornis]

THE PATHFINDER MISSION

Congratulations. You are reading about the all-new 1996 Nissan Pathfinder, the finest sport utility vehicle on the market.

CATTLE

Cattle are rarely eaten by the Masai as they represent their owner's wealth.

x 300

some have a distinct fondness for sheet metal. (Fortunately, the three ton beast was no match for the Pathfinder's nimble handling and we never had to field-test our steel side-door guard beams.)

any attempt to shirk one's financial obligations will result in rocks being hurled in the direction of your vehicle. The Pathfinder's chip-resistant paint notwithstanding, we gladly paid the going rate of 50 Kenyan shillings – about $1.

With regard to the country's extreme temperatures and bumpy roads, simply adjust the Pathfinder's automatic climate control to a suitably humane temperature and take a few sips off the top of your bottled, boiled or otherwise purified water before placing it in the car's cup holders.

Bear these tips in mind and we promise your drive through Kenya will be off to a good start. Of course, there's no accounting for the whims of Kenyan motorists or the moods of the local rhinoceros. But that's what separates a drive through Africa from a visit to the petting zoo. Right?!

POPULAR SWAHILI EXPRESSIONS:

KENYA'S TOP GAME RESERVES

Finally, a few words about Kenya's indigenous people. Kenya is home to over 70 different tribes and, driving through the countryside, you will undoubtedly see vibrantly dressed Masai, Samburu and other tribesmen walking along the roadway. While it is perfectly acceptable to stop for picture-taking, be aware that these people expect to be paid for their modeling services and

NEXT STOP: TANZANIA!

THE NEW PATHFINDER

NISSAN

**CONSUMER
MAGAZINE
COLOR FULL
PAGE OR
SPREAD:
CAMPAIGN**

art director
John Vitro

writer
John Robertson

photographer
Chris Wimpey

client
Taylor Guitar

agency
VitroRobertson/
San Diego

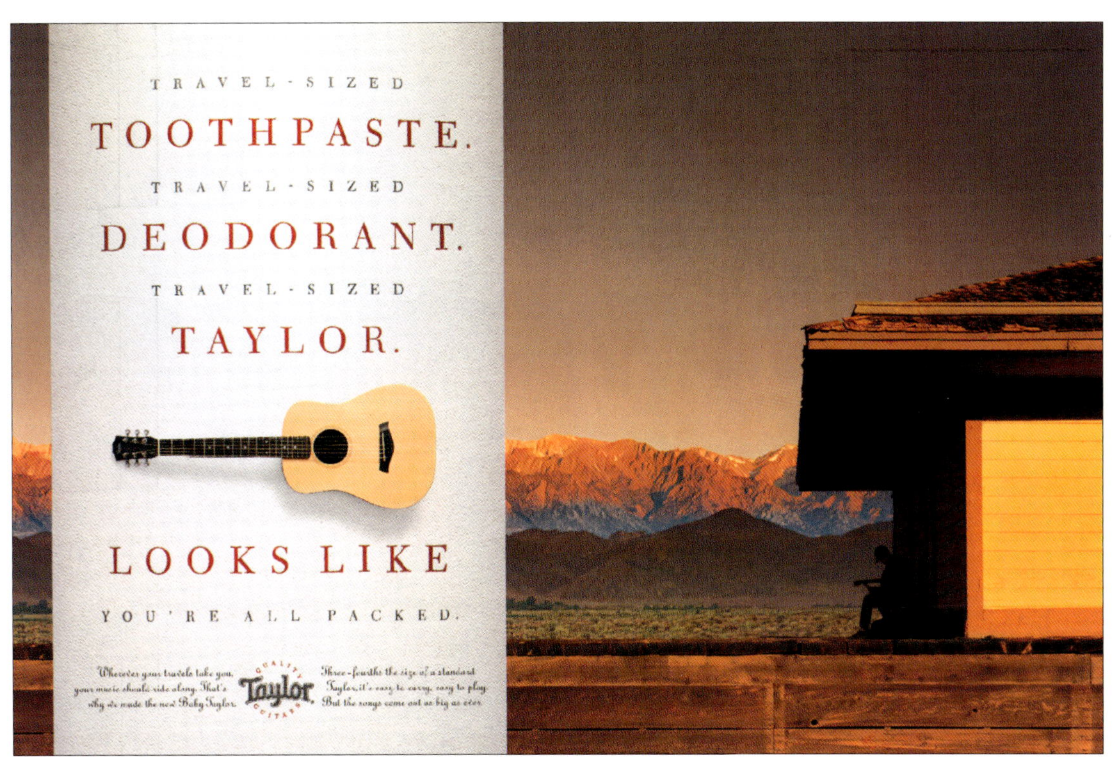
TRAVEL-SIZED
TOOTHPASTE.
TRAVEL-SIZED
DEODORANT.
TRAVEL-SIZED
TAYLOR.
LOOKS LIKE
YOU'RE ALL PACKED.
Taylor
QUALITY GUITARS

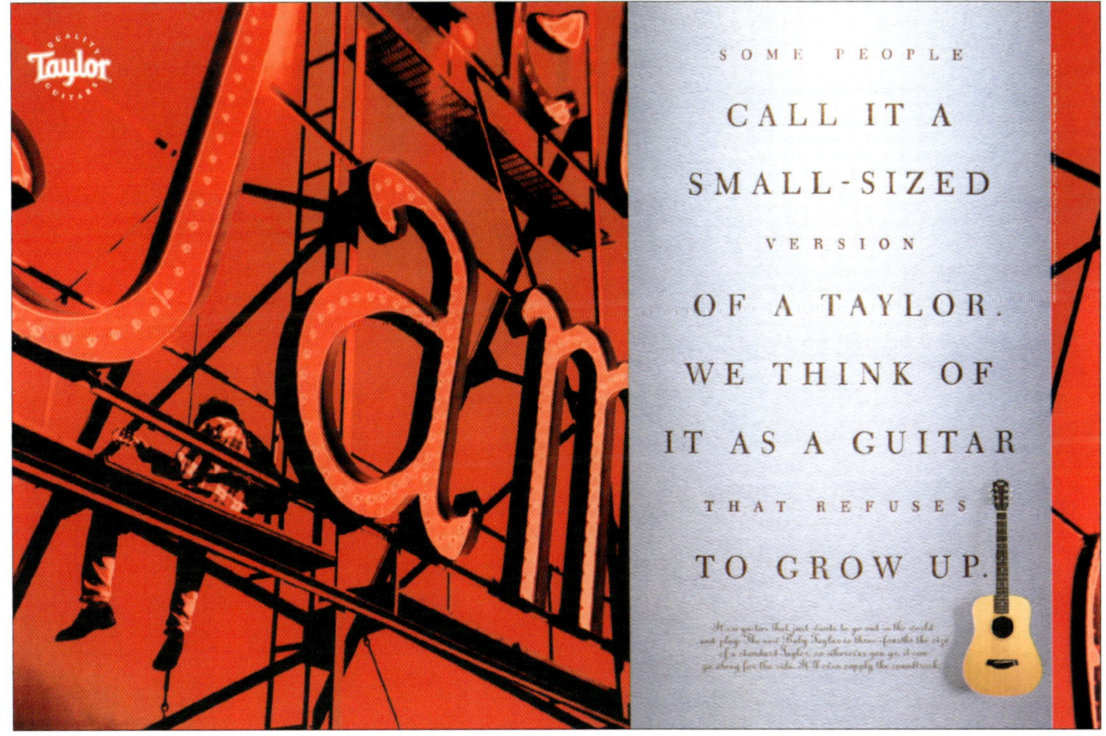
Taylor
QUALITY GUITARS
SOME PEOPLE
CALL IT A
SMALL-SIZED
VERSION
OF A TAYLOR.
WE THINK OF
IT AS A GUITAR
THAT REFUSES
TO GROW UP.

**CONSUMER
MAGAZINE
COLOR FULL
PAGE OR
SPREAD:
CAMPAIGN**

art director
Rachel Nelson

writer
Eric Silver

photographer
Guzman

client
Nike

agency
Wieden & Kennedy/
Portland

art director
Kilpatrick Anderson
writer
James LeMaitre
photographer
Michael Jones
client
Nike
agency
Wieden & Kennedy/
Portland

**CONSUMER
MAGAZINE
COLOR FULL
PAGE OR
SPREAD:
CAMPAIGN**

art director
John Boiler

writer
Ernest Lupinacci

designers
Alicia Johnson
Hal Wolverton/
Johnson & Wolverton

client
Nike

agency
Wieden & Kennedy/
Portland

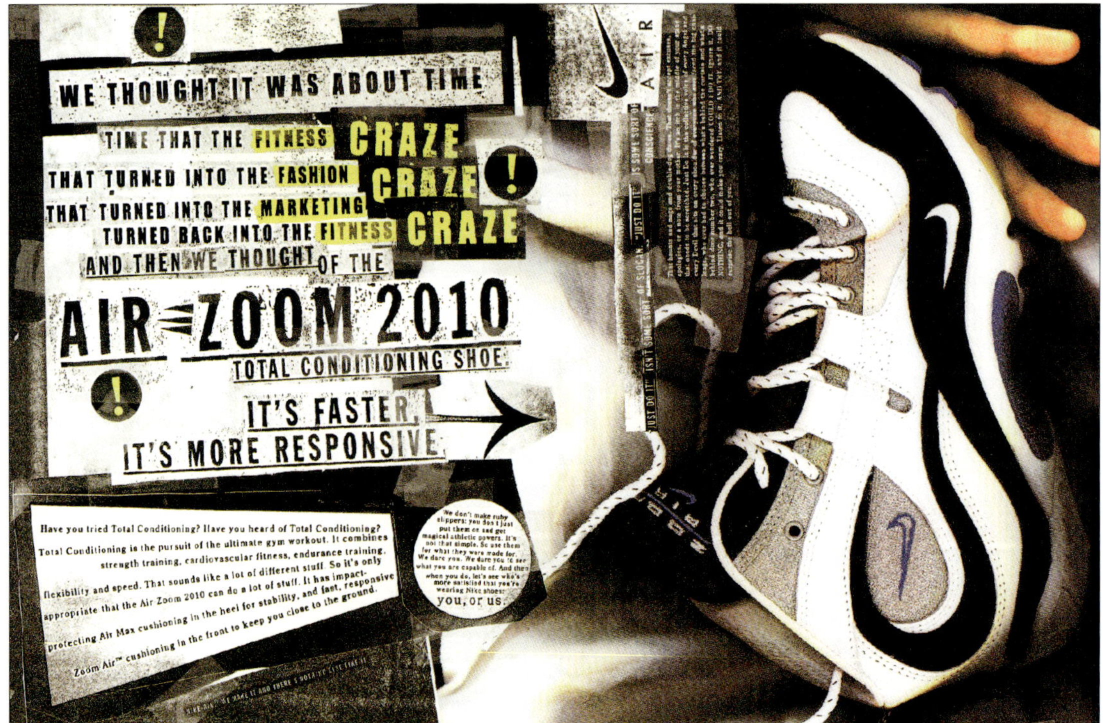

IT'S BECAUSE HE'S NEVER PLAYED BASKETBALL
LIKE IT WAS JUST A GAME.
PASSION IS NOT ARROGANCE.
WHAT'S THE BIG DEAL? IT'S JUST A GAME.
PENNY HARDAWAY IS ONE OF THE BEST BASKETBALL PLAYERS IN COLLEGE.
PENNY HARDAWAY WAS ONE OF THE BEST BASKETBALL PLAYERS IN THE NBA. AND THIS SUMMER,
PENNY HARDAWAY WANTS TO BE ONE OF THE BEST BASKETBALL PLAYERS IN THE WORLD.
AND IF HE HAD WHAT HE WANTS, AND IF HE HAS WHAT HE WANTS, AND IF HE GETS WHAT HE WANTS,
HEY BUSTER!
ZOOM AIR CUSHIONING MAKES OUR SHOES THE FASTEST, MOST RESPONSIVE SHOES EVER.
WHAT'S THE BIG DEAL? IT'S JUST A SHOE.
BECAUSE NIKE SHOES ARE ATHLETIC SHOES.

IF YOU PUT AN OFFICIALLY LICENSED LOGO ON A BOX OF CUPCAKES IN ANTICIPATION OF WORLD-CLASS COMPETITION.
YOU ARE A MARKETER.
IF YOU REDESIGN A PAIR OF ATHLETIC SHOES IN ANTICIPATION OF WORLD-CLASS COMPETITION.
YOU ARE AN INNOVATOR.
NOTICE:
"THE SPIRIT OF COMPETITION" CANNOT BE CELEBRATED THROUGH CONSUMER DISCOUNTS, MANUFACTURER REBATES, AND FREQUENT FLYER MILES.
AIR MAX

ZOOM AIR IS A NEW IDEA-THING.
THE GENERAL IDEA-THING:
ZOOM AIR IS FASTER AND MORE RESPONSIVE.
BECAUSE ZOOM AIR CUSHIONING HAS A LOW PROFILE DESIGN THAT KEEPS YOU CLOSE TO THE GROUND. IT'S JUST ANOTHER WAY TO HELP ATHLETES WHO ARE LOOKING TO BE THE BEST AT WHAT THEY DO GET BETTER.
"OOOOOH, ANDRE LOOKS LIKE A PIRATE!"
"OOOOOH, ANDRE'S SHOES HAVE A SWOOSH ON THEM."
AIR IS NOT SOME NEW GIMMICK-THING, OR NEW MARKETING-THING, OR NEW GADGET-THING.
NIKE-AIR. WE MAKE IT AND THERE'S NOTHING ELSE LIKE IT
THIS IS.
ZOOM AIR

**CONSUMER
MAGAZINE
B/W OR COLOR
LESS THAN A
PAGE: SINGLE**

art director
William Chau

writer
Brett Borders

photographer
Tim Thompson

client
Alaska Sightseeing/
Cruise West

agency
Borders Perrin &
Norrander/Seattle

art director
Frank Haggerty

writer
Jim Nelson

photographer
Shawn Michienzi

client
Stren

agency
Carmichael Lynch/
Minneapolis

PRINT FINALISTS

art directors
Mike Miller
Simon Mainwaring

writers
Mike Miller
Simon Mainwaring
Shaun Branagan

photographer
Alister Clarke

client
Paul Mitchell
Systems

agency
DDB Needham/
North Sydney

art director
Ellen Steinberg

writer
Tom Rosen

photographer
Shawn Michienzi

client
Knob Creek

agency
Fallon McElligott/
Minneapolis

art director
Ellen Steinberg

writer
Tom Rosen

photographer
Shawn Michienzi

client
Knob Creek

agency
Fallon McElligott/
Minneapolis

**CONSUMER
MAGAZINE
B/W OR COLOR
LESS THAN A
PAGE: SINGLE**

art director
Andy Azula

writer
Dave Pullar

client
Nikon

agency
Fallon McElligott/
Minneapolis

art director
Cabell Harris

writer
Ty Montague

typographer
Graham Clifford

client
Splendid Seed
Tobacco Company

agency
Montague &, Inc./
South Norwalk, CT

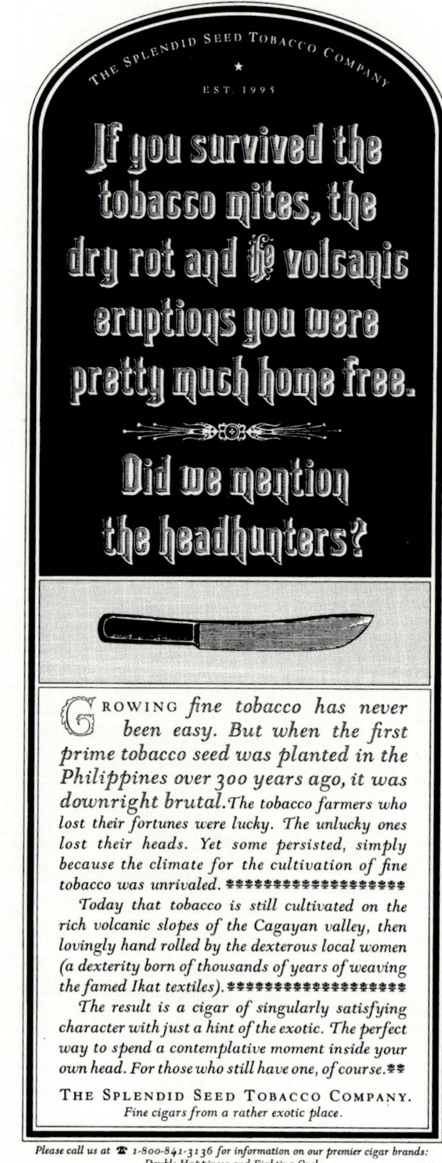

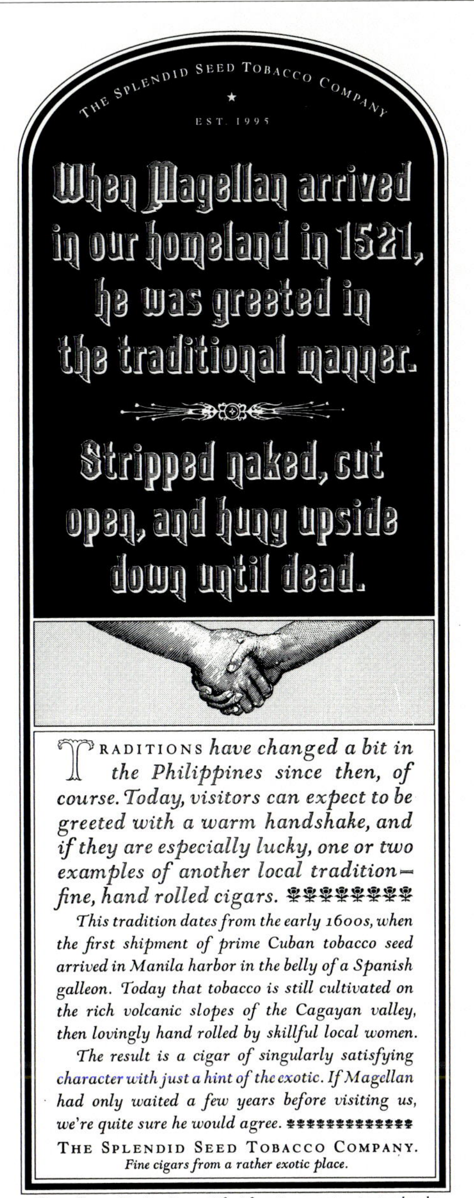

art director
Cabell Harris

writer
Ty Montague

typographer
Graham Clifford

client
Splendid Seed
Tobacco Company

agency
Montague &, Inc./
South Norwalk, CT

art director
Rafa Anton

writer
Rafa Anton

photographer
Aurelio Rodriguez

client
Palladium
Fitness Center

agency
Vitruvio/Leo
Burnett, Madrid

**CONSUMER
MAGAZINE
B/W OR COLOR
LESS THAN A
PAGE: CAMPAIGN**

art director
Tim Vaccarino

writer
Kara Goodrich

photographer
Joshua Weinfeld

client
British Bulldog

agency
Leonard/Monahan,
Providence

ONCE THE
PROUD POSSESSION OF
THE BRITISH LANDED GENTRY,
NOW AVAILABLE TO AMERICAN
YUPPIE SCUM.

Classic Land Rover restoration, service and sales. Call (508) 674-4500.
BRITISH BULLDOG
Classic Land Rovers

THE SUN NEVER SETS
ON THE BRITISH EMPIRE.
NOR APPARENTLY
DOES THE ENGINE
EVER GO.

BRITISH BULLDOG
Classic Land Rovers
Classic Land Rover restoration, service and sales. Call (508) 674-4500.

CONSUMER MAGAZINE B/W OR COLOR LESS THAN A PAGE: CAMPAIGN

art directors
Darren Lim
Dave Cook
Nick Cohen
Gina Fortunato

writers
Deacon Webster
Kevin Doyle

client
Hot Bot / Wired

agency
Mad Dogs &
Englishmen / New York

art director
Cabell Harris

writer
Ty Montague

typographer
Graham Clifford

client
Splendid Seed
Tobacco Company

agency
Montague &, Inc./
South Norwalk, CT

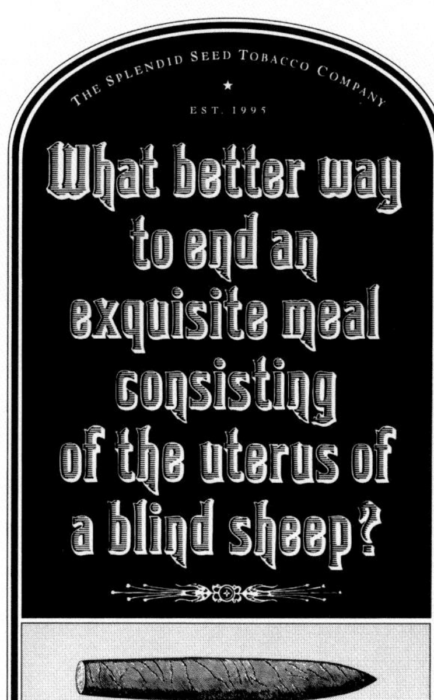

**CONSUMER
MAGAZINE B/W
OR COLOR LESS
THAN A PAGE:
CAMPAIGN**

art director
Jeff Payne

writer
Brian Gold

illustrator
Hatch Show Print

client
Taylor Guitar

agency
VitroRobertson/
San Diego

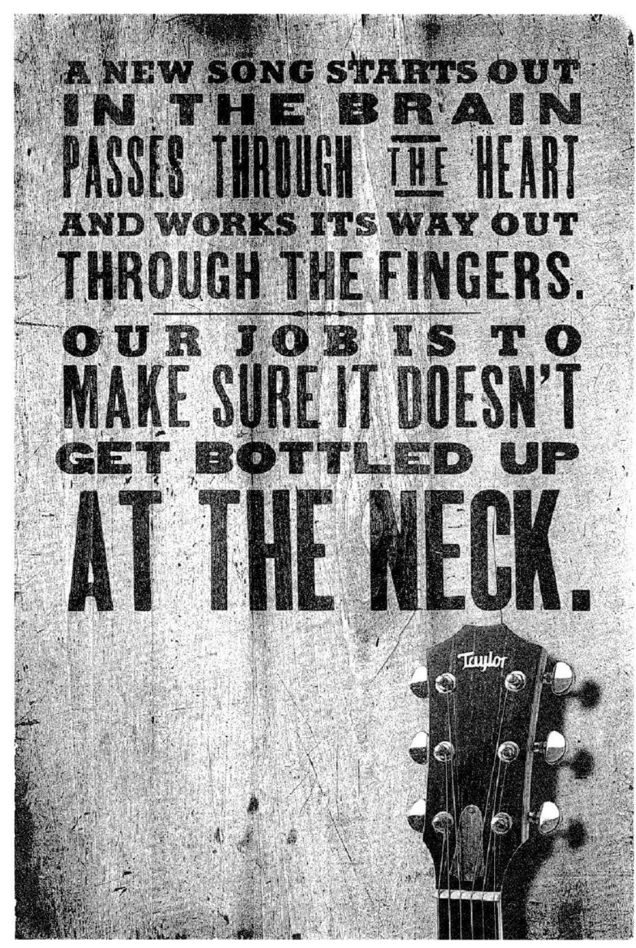

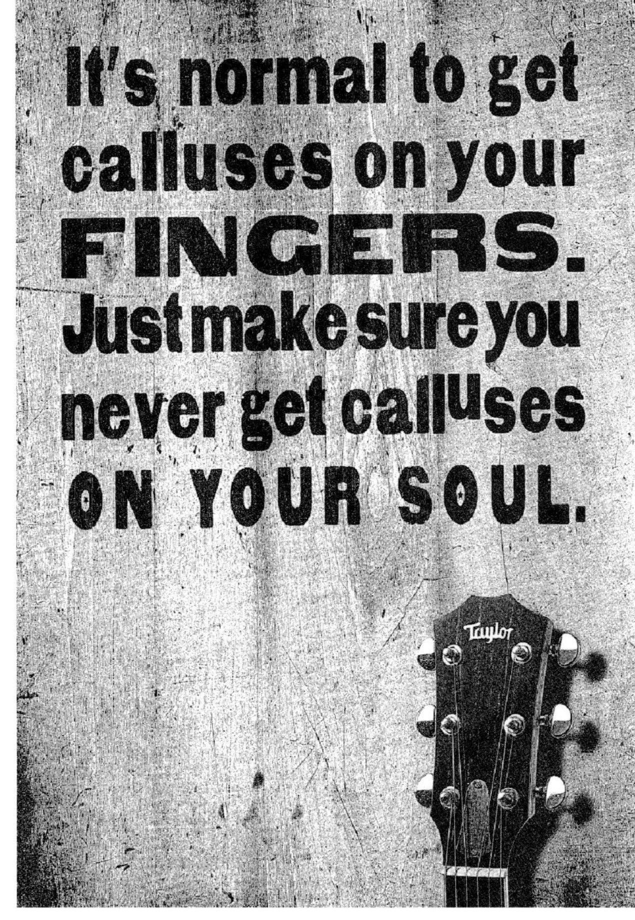

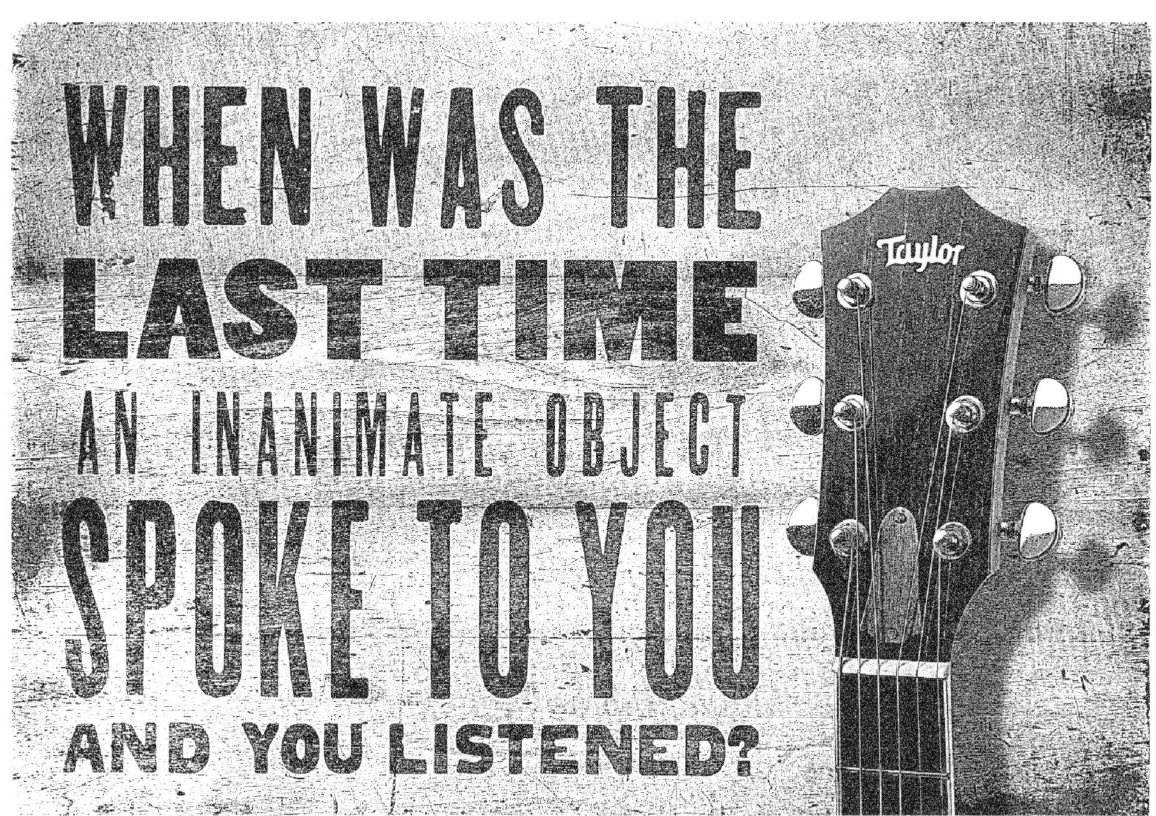

WHEN WAS THE
LAST TIME
AN INANIMATE OBJECT
SPOKE TO YOU
AND YOU LISTENED?
Taylor

Always
PUT IT BACK IN
ITS CASE.
THAT WAY THE
SONGS
CAN'T ESCAPE.
Taylor

**OUTDOOR:
SINGLE**

art director
Damon Collins

writer
Mary Wear

typographer
Joe Hoza

client
The Economist

agency
Abbott Mead
Vickers.BBDO/London

art director
Paul Briginshaw

writer
Malcolm Duffy

typographer
Joe Hoza

client
The Economist

agency
Abbott Mead
Vickers.BBDO/London

art director
Melanie Menkemeller

writer
Matt Ashworth

photographer
Lars Topelmann

client
Millers Outpost

agency
Butler Shine &
Stern/Sausalito

PRINT FINALISTS

art director
Melanie Menkemeller

writer
Matt Ashworth

photographer
Lars Topelmann

client
Millers Outpost

agency
Butler Shine & Stern / Sausalito

art director
Melanie Menkemeller

writer
Matt Ashworth

photographer
Lars Topelmann

client
Millers Outpost

agency
Butler Shine & Stern / Sausalito

art director
David Ayriss

writer
Mark Waggoner

photographer
Torey Piro

client
24/7 Snowboards

agency
Cole & Weber / Portland

**OUTDOOR:
SINGLE**

art directors
Simon Winterflood
Craig Farndale

writer
Connan James

client
McDonald's System of
New Zealand

agency
DDB Needham/
Auckland

art directors
Mike Miller
Simon Mainwaring

writers
Mike Miller
Simon Mainwaring
Shaun Branagan

photographer
Alister Clarke

client
Paul Mitchell Systems

agency
DDB Needham/
North Sydney

Long walks in the park. Lots of friends. Playing ball on weekends. Does your dog have a better social life than you do?
Time Out
New York
The weekly magazine that tells you where to go and what to do.

From across the room he won't be able to tell you have a great sense of humor.
Lee
The Brand That Fits.

OUTDOOR: SINGLE

art director
David Reid

writer
Adrian Jeffery

illustrator
Iain McIntosh

client
Cheynes Hairdressing

agency
1576 Advertising/Edinburgh

art director
Patrick Sutherland

writer
Ari Merkin

photographer
Vic Huber

client
Land Rover
North America

agency
Grace & Rothschild/
New York

PRINT FINALISTS

art director
Niki Kloss

writer
Andreas Hochstoger

photographer
Niki Kloss

illustrator
Repropaint

client
Baren Batterie

agency
Kloss Zechner/
Klosterneuburg,
Austria

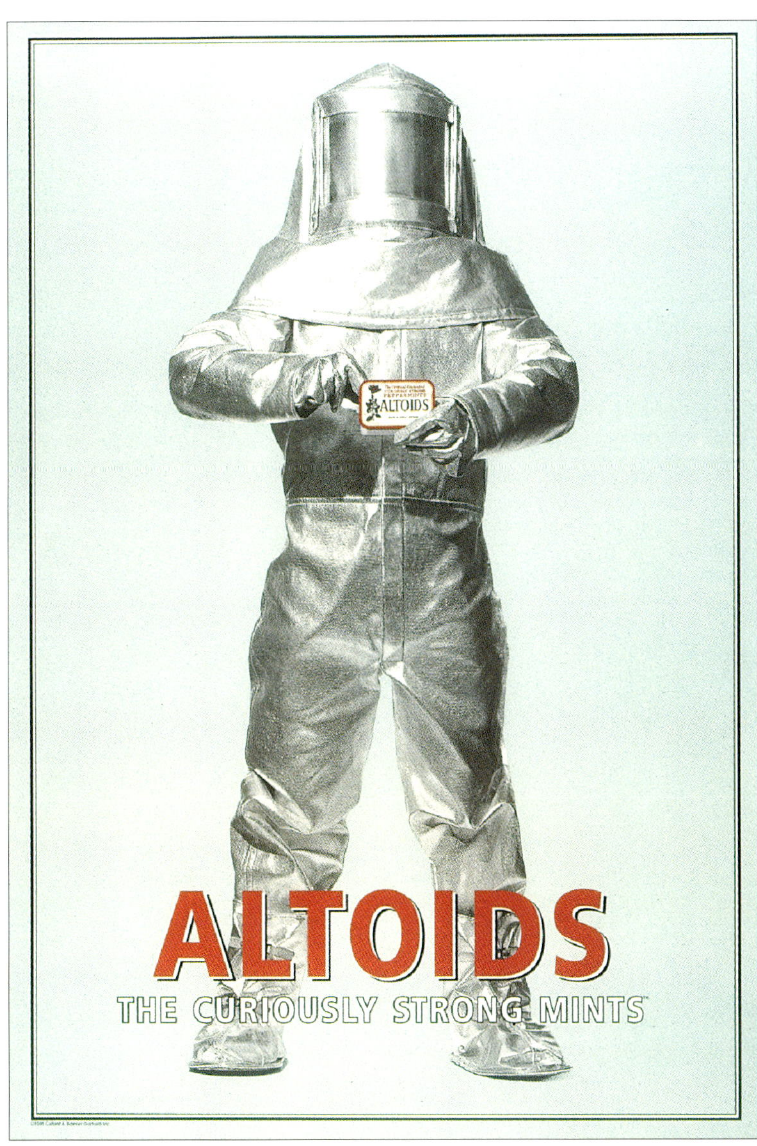

art directors
Mark Faulkner
Noel Haan

writer
Steffan Postaer

photographer
Tony D'Orio

client
Callard &
Bowser-Suchard

agency
Leo Burnett Company/
Chicago

**OUTDOOR:
SINGLE**

art director
Kevin Stark

writer
Nick Kidney

client
Mercedes-Benz

agency
Leo Burnett/London

art director
Karen Costello

writer
Chris Ribeiro

client
Four Seasons
Biltmore/Santa
Barbara

agency
Lois/EJL, Los Angeles

art directors
Bryan Burlison
Mark Waggoner

writers
Mark Waggoner
Bryan Burlison

photographer
Ripsaw Photography

client
Eastman Kodak
Company

agency
Ogilvy & Mather/
New York

PRINT FINALISTS

art director
Graham Storey

writer
Phil Cockrell

photographer
Tim O'Sullivan

client
Nike UK

agency
Simons Palmer-Clemmow
Johnson/London

art director
Graham Storey

writer
Phil Cockrell

photographer
Seamus Ryan

client
Nike UK

agency
Simons Palmer-Clemmow
Johnson/London

Inside every new
Mercedes-Benz E-Class,
you'll find four of these
for your protection.

JOHN McENROE
ON:
GROUND STROKES WHEN
FACING SAMPRAS
"MASTERING THE BASIC STROKES IS A MUST. ONCE YOUR FOREHAND IS IN
GOOD FORM, WORK ON RELEASING THE RACQUET TOWARDS YOUR OPPONENT'S
GENERAL DIRECTION. THIS SENDS A MESSAGE. THE MESSAGE BEING, 'I MAY
BE AN INFERIOR PLAYER BUT I CAN STILL HURT YOU.'"

**OUTDOOR:
CAMPAIGN**
art director
David Reid
writer
Adrian Jeffery
photographer
Iain McIntosh
client
Cheynes Hairdressing
agency
1576 Advertising/
Edinburgh

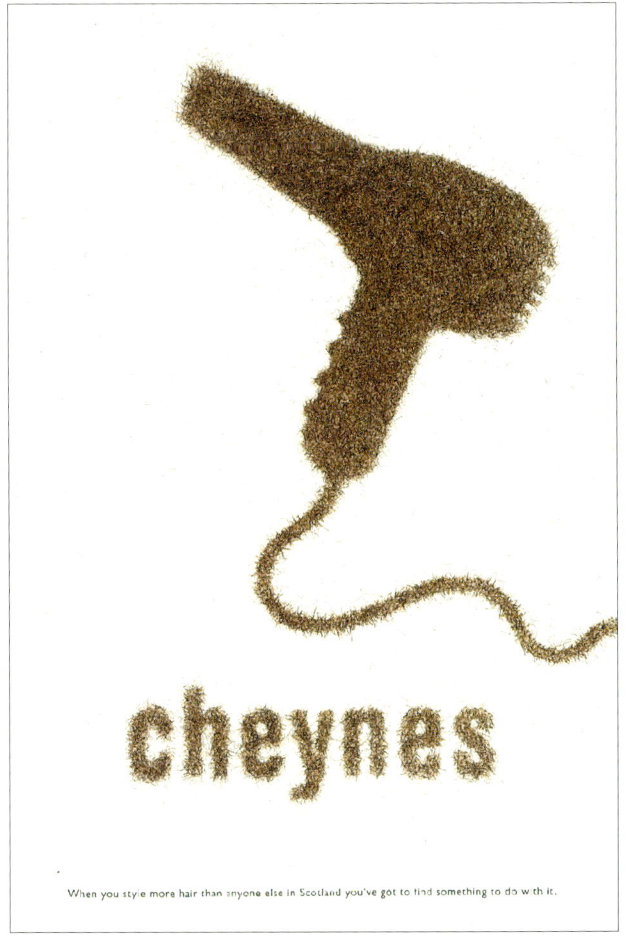

PRINT FINALISTS

**OUTDOOR:
CAMPAIGN**

art director
Sean Farrell

writer
Chris DeCarlo

photographer
Jim Flynn

client
The Boston Globe

agency
Ingalls Advertising/
Boston

WE KNOW SO MUCH ABOUT WHAT
GOES ON IN FENWAY
YOU MAY NEVER WANT TO EAT
A HOT DOG AGAIN.
IN-DEPTH COVERAGE
OF ALL RED SOX GAMES.
The Boston Globe
FOR HOME DELIVERY,
CALL 617-466-1818
HAVE YOU SEEN THE GLOBE TODAY?

FOLLOW THE SOX
ON THE ROAD
WITHOUT HAVING TO SPEND
THE NIGHT IN DETROIT.
IN-DEPTH COVERAGE
OF ALL RED SOX GAMES.
The Boston Globe
FOR HOME DELIVERY,
CALL 617-466-1818
HAVE YOU SEEN THE GLOBE TODAY?

**OUTDOOR:
CAMPAIGN**

art director
James Offenhartz

writer
Keith Goldberg

photographer
John Lee

client
The New Republic
Magazine

agency
J. Walter Thompson/
New York

THE IN-FLIGHT MAGAZINE OF AIR FORCE ONE.

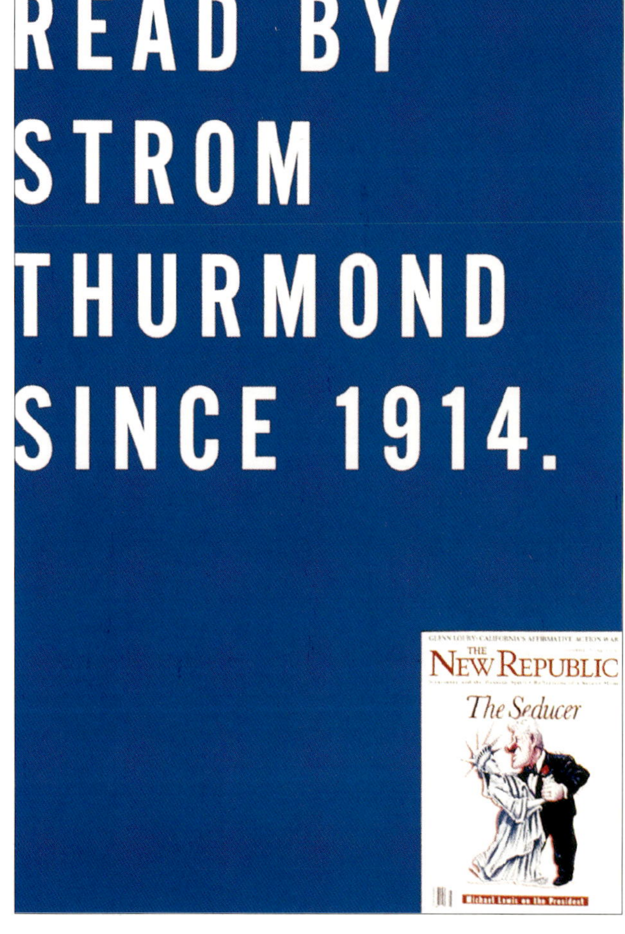

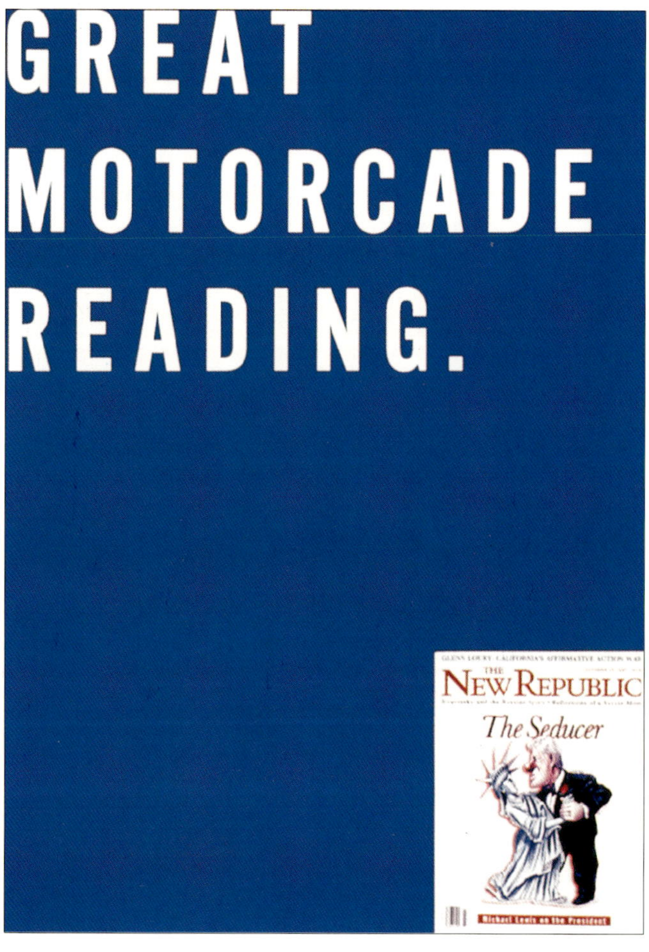

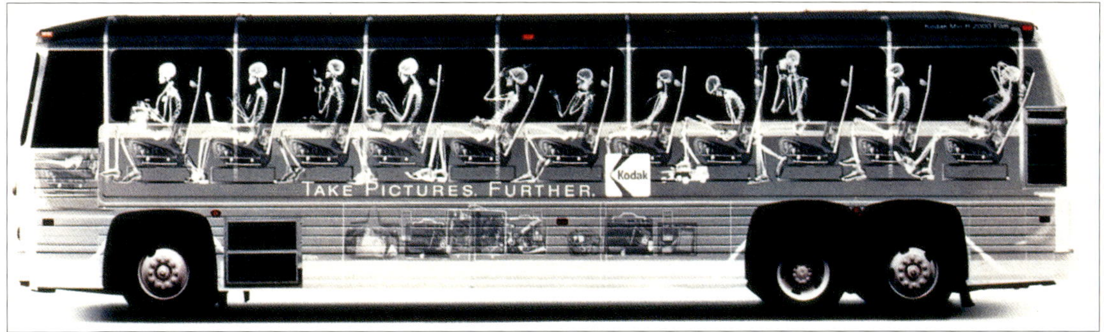

PRINT FINALISTS

art directors
Bryan Burlison
Mark Waggoner

writers
Mark Waggoner
Bryan Burlison

photographer
Ripsaw Photography

client
Eastman Kodak
Company

agency
Ogilvy & Mather/
New York

**OUTDOOR:
CAMPAIGN**

art directors
Chuck Bennett
Susan Alinsangin

writers
Clay Williams
Ken Younglieb

client
Nissan Motor
Corporation

agency
TBWA Chiat / Day,
Venice, CA

Look into your heart
for wisdom, and under
your seat for change.

Maybe traffic jams
happen because
cars like to be with
other cars.

**TRADE B/W
FULL PAGE
OR SPREAD:
SINGLE**

art director
Genji Handa

writer
Shira Friedman

client
Optiva Corporation

agency
Goldberg Moser
O'Neill/San Francisco

art director
Holland Henton

writer
Tom Campion

client
Lennox

agency
GSD&M
Advertising/Austin

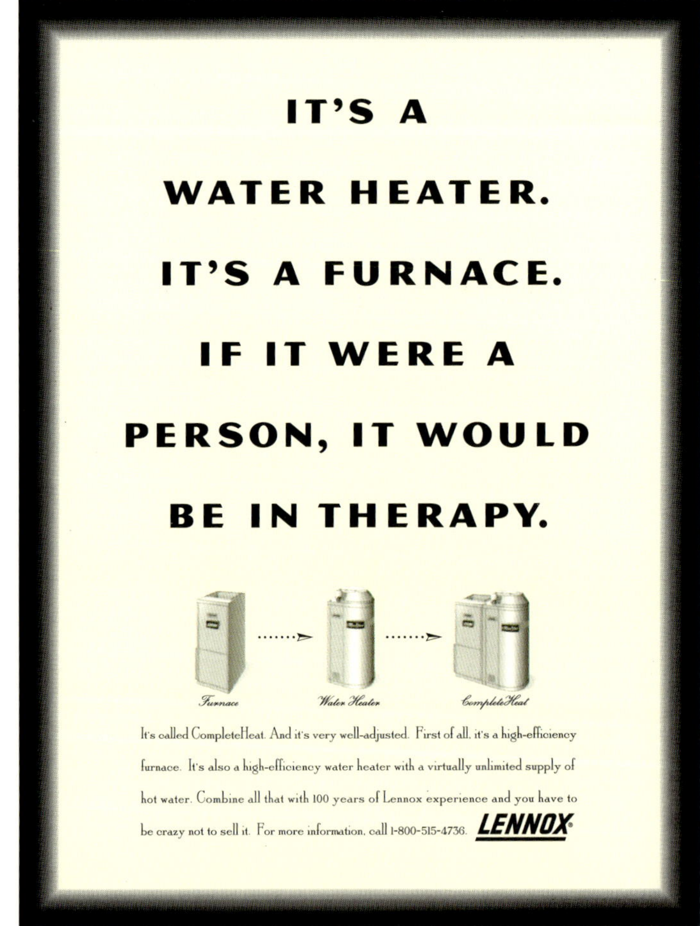

**TRADE B/W
FULL PAGE
OR SPREAD:
SINGLE**

art director
Hal Curtis

writer
Kara Goodrich

illustrator
Bob Clinton

client
Polaroid Corporation

agency
Leonard/Monahan,
Providence

This is a frame. It can hold anything. Which makes it especially good for teachers. Imagine an "educational tool" cleverly disguised as a flower

or a	leaf
or a	bug
or a	frog
or a	doll
or a	kid
or a	ball
or a	car
or a	rock
or a	cow
or a	bat
or a	star
or a	rat
or a	foot
or a	jar
or a	dad
or a	pen
or a	can
or a	lid
or a	nut
or a	bird.

That's why we created the Polaroid Child Care Activity Kit. With it, you'll discover inventive ways to make your job more fun and rewarding, while you explore visual learning with your kids. *For just $49.95, you'll receive a Polaroid instant camera, 2 packs of Polaroid HighDefinition film, 20 picture frames, curriculum ideas, everything you'll need to teach visually.* Involve the parents. Find a strange insect. Look for primary colors. Praise with a picture. Do what you do best. Teach. Call 800-678-8014, ext. 300, (fax 214-518-2507).

Polaroid *See what develops.*

art director
Steve Juliusson

writer
Robin Landis

photographer
Jose Azul

client
American
International Group

agency
Ogilvy & Mather/
New York

PRINT FINALISTS

art director
Bob Brihn

writer
Doug de Grood

photographer
Joe Lampi

client
Radio in the Nude

agency
Sietsema Engel and
Partners / Minneapolis

**TRADE COLOR
FULL PAGE
OR SPREAD:
SINGLE**

art director
John Morton

writer
Mark Abellera

photographer
David Massey

client
Stanley

agency
Ammirati Puris
Lintas / New York

**TRADE COLOR
FULL PAGE
OR SPREAD:
SINGLE**

art director
Sally Bond Ours

writer
Rita Galloway

photographers
Michael Nichols
Joanna B. Pinneo
Tomasz Tomaszewski

client
National Geographic

agency
Arnold Advertising/
McLean, VA

art director
Jim Spruell

writer
Cathy Lepik

illustrator
Graphic Press

client
U.S. Space and
Rocket Center

agency
Austin Kelley
Advertising/Atlanta

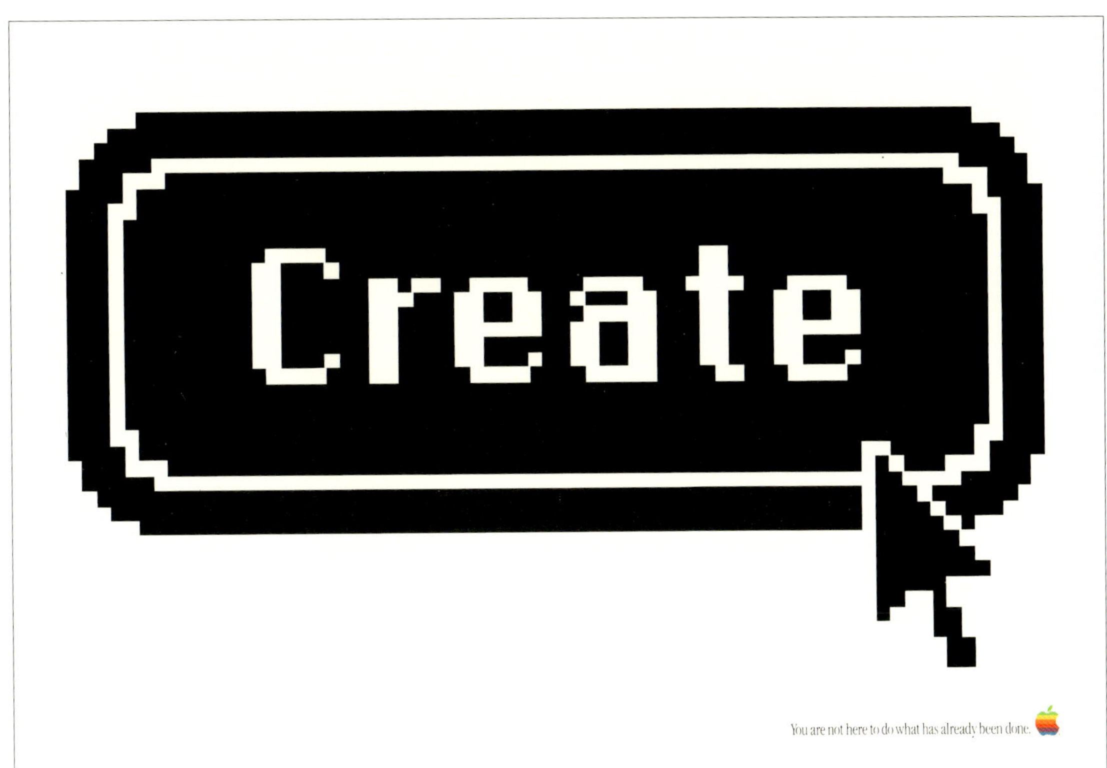

art directors
Dennis Lim
Gavin Milner
writer
Greg Ketchum
client
Apple Computer
agency
BBDO West/Los Angeles

art directors
Dennis Lim
Gavin Milner
writer
Greg Ketchum
client
Apple Computer
agency
BBDO West/Los Angeles

**TRADE COLOR
FULL PAGE
OR SPREAD:
SINGLE**

art director
Jeff Terwilliger
writer
Derek Pletch
client
Brown-Forman Bolla
agency
Carmichael Lynch/
Minneapolis

art director
Frank Haggerty
writer
Jim Nelson
photographer
Shawn Michienzi
client
Normark
agency
Carmichael Lynch/
Minneapolis

RADIO. BECAUSE NO ONE EVER READS LONG COPY ADS.

If you stepped down from your Adland ivory tower and mixed with real people, you'd realise that the punter in the street enjoys listening to the radio. You'd also discover that Triple M listeners like a bit of fun and rebellion. If you drove past some and mooned, they'd clap and think you were a dead-set legend.

So why not write some mischevious radio commercials? You could win yourself an award. Maybe a Bronze. Perhaps even a Silver.

But never a Gold.

Golds are never handed out these days. Apparently nothing done now is as brilliant as in the good old days. Which is odd, because whenever you look through old Australian award annuals all you see is crap. For example, you see tonnes of long copy ads.

Why is it so?

I have this theory on why long copy ads always win awards. It's because award judges, like most people in advertising, are such uncultured slobs they've never actually seen that many words in a row before.

It overwhelms them. It intimidates them. They think to themselves, "Sheesh! A lot of words. This must be high brow. I better vote for it or I'll seem thick". Most award judges wouldn't read past the first paragraph of these wordy 'pieces'. So you can imagine the apathy level of the general public. You really have to wonder what La-La land creatives are living in when they write long copy ads.

They probably think the *genre* gives them some literary credibility. To the miserable and deluded copywriter, Neil French is James Joyce, John Bevins is Franz Kafka.

If you're an insecure copywriter, you may think "I'm not smart enough to write long copy ads. They always sound so posh. People who write long copy went to Melbourne Grammar. I went to a state school".

Don't worry. Just follow these simple tips and you too can have an elitist sounding ad.

Firstly, use the word 'indeed' a lot. Take the following phrase: "A great buy". Very crass. Very retail. But let's add in that magic word and see what happens: "A great buy, indeed". Wow! You sound like an Old Grammarian already.

Secondly, use semicolons (;). When you type in a semicolon, you're telling the world "I am so well educated, not only am I familiar with run of the mill punctuation, I know the obscure stuff too". And don't ever worry about using a semicolon incorrectly. No one quite knows what they're for, so you can just chuck them in anywhere. For example I can add one here; and you wouldn't have the faintest idea as to whether I was right; or wrong. While on grammar, here's another tip. If a client or account manager tries to change a line of your copy, just say "You can't do that. It splits the infinitive". Listen to the silence.

The only advertisements I can think of that are noticed *less* than long copy ads, are the ones for production houses that run during the half time break on Shots reels. The creative department sits around the monitor watching an hour of ads. Then it comes to the *real* ads and they press fast forward.

God, that woman who presents the Shots reel annoys me. If there's an element of surprise in a TV ad, she'll destroy it. A typical example: "The cleverness of the following commercial comes from the fact that you don't know what's being advertised until the very end. We hope you enjoy this advertisement for Sony walkmans".

But getting back to Triple M. If you want to write an outrageous award winning radio spot, just do it. Don't be intimidated by your client. There's a foolproof method of getting any script through him or her. Just make a character's name in your script his or her name. Watch the laughs come out (as well as the approval stamp) when you say "So this ad starts with this groovy Chapel Street girl…*(insert brief pause here for maximum jocularity)*…called Nicki". Nicki will laugh, love you and the radio ad is as good as produced.

Hey, by the way, I think this is the first press ad ever to sell radio without using the phrase T______ of the M___.

A special message to work experience kids.

You're probably reading this because no one can be bothered teaching you anything and you've been dumped in an empty office with a pile of award books. Please heed the following advice – GET OUT WHILE YOU CAN! Do not enter the advertising industry. It's not worth it. Sure, it seems all fun and happy at the beginning. I thought so too. Then you realise how soul destroying it is. But it's far too late because you're earning quite a bit of money and you've burnt all your other career bridges. Then you turn really pathetic. You start saying to yourself "Sure, I'm in advertising now, but it's only a temporary thing. I'm really going to become the famous poet/painter/screenplay writer/singer I always said I was going to become". But you'll *never* become any of those. Because you don't want to quit, because the money's too good and you like being able to buy CDs and stuff. So you start saying to yourself "Advertising will be my day job and after work I'll work on my masterplan". But after work your mind is drained. And on weekends there's always a brief dangling over your head like a knife. So forget all about happiness.

Slave labour, indeed.

There's something else you should know, my young work experience friend. Before you get your first paid job, you often have to hang around an agency for months, working for little or no money. This is called 'paying your dues'. It's one of those situations you despise at the time, then over-romanticise about years later when talking to young people. I love crapping on about 'paying my dues'. I tell people how I slaved day after day after day after day at this big agency for no money. I talk about being exploited by a huge rich corporation. Of course, I leave out the fact that at the time I was living comfortably in middle class North Balwyn with my middle class parents, who paid for all my food, clothing, shelter and entertainment. That would ruin the struggling artist story.

When you enter the industry, you also have to put up with Creative Directors rejecting your ideas. A 'classic' television script rejection comes in the form of "If you turned down the volume, would your TV ad still make sense?". To which you should respond "Listen you idiot. If I didn't have any legs I couldn't walk, but I do, so I can."

By the way, *all* you work experience kids are the same. You come in on your first day with a three piece suit, Bryl-creamed hair and clean fingernails. By Friday, you're walking around the agency with dreadlocks, wearing a Bob Marley T-shirt and smoking a bong.

Philosopher A. Keogh once said "To be in advertising is to be a barnacle on the boat of capitalism". He later revised his thought, and decided "To be in advertising is to be an 80 horse power engine on the boat of capitalism". Whatever. No matter how much you try to protect yourself against a guilt complex, occasionally you do feel a bit immoral working in this industry. Maybe, by mistake, you see a Noam Chomsky documentary. Perhaps you accidentally pick up a copy of Green Left Weekly. So how do you ease your conscience? Creatives usually work on a community service 'freebie' every year or so. They think it somehow gets them off the hook. "Sure, I do write ads for the timber industry, the mining industry, cigarettes, Cambodian landmines and the Ku Klux Klan…but have you seen my Blood Bank spot?".

I'm not knocking community service ads though. There are some really worthy causes. Take animal testing for example. Each year animals are being blinded, force fed poison and mutilated. If you're against cruelty to animals and would like to lend your support, contact Animal Guardians on 015 30 4778.

Phew, that gets me off the hook. Now I can move onto that Moscow Circus brief that's been sitting on my desk.

Subheads look good typographically.

While on ethics, isn't it wonderful how our industry has evolved to keep up with feminism? Only five or so years ago, women would watch television commercials and think "Gee, I look nothing like the housewife in that ad. I feel fat, ugly and unsuccessful". But that's in the past. That's all changed. Now when women watch television commercials they think "Gee, I look nothing like the career woman in that ad. I feel fat, ugly and unsuccessful".

When working in advertising, you learn how to rationalise anything. Let's examine a hypothetical case study. While you're studying at university, you hear that the seemingly nice ______ Corporation is actually involved in the nuclear power industry. So you make a rock solid oath. You will *never* work at the agency that has ______ as a client.

Next thing you know, you're working at the agency that has ______ as a client. So you make a rock solid oath. Sure, you may work at the agency, but you will *never* actually work on ______ yourself.

Next thing you know, you're working on ______ yourself. So you make a rock solid oath. Sure, you may work on ______ but you will never work on the nuclear power branch of the business.

Next thing you know, you're working on the nuclear power branch of the business. So you say "Gee, I had this all wrong. Nuclear power is a clean and efficient energy source. I used to only get one side of the story. Thank God, I'm not being manipulated anymore".

Hey award judges.

If you're judging this ad at the moment and you read absolutely nothing else, read this bit.

Listen, you pretentious little twats, I bet you're all whining "This isn't a proper ad. If I were given two pages to write whatever I wanted I could easily…*(insert 25 minutes of self righteous blah blah blah)*…The real challenge is writing real ads for real clients".

Well, just get stuffed.

This ad is for a real brief that landed on my desk. Job no. TRM 5244. Triple M is part of the biggest radio network in Australia, so don't even try that "not a real client" line.

"It's very self indulgent. There's not very much about Triple M."

Get Lost. Why don't you join account service? You're probably now making comments about how smug it is to try and talk to award judges in the copy. Well, you're such an elitist little clique, I wouldn't be able to communicate with you any other way. I do admit this ad lacks one crucial element for winning an advertising award – a Campaign Palace Key Number.

I don't need your pitiful awards anyway. I hate you all. Especially the Melbourne Art Directors Club. I have to fork out over seventy bucks in membership each year, like it's some fucking union. But when was the last time the MADC stood up for the proletariat? When Y&R Mattingly was laying off the workers, was the MADC organising a picket line?

And their god damn award annual themes. Last year it was Pulp Fiction, six months too late. This year it's that X-Files sci-fi thing. Want to lay a little wager on next year's MADC Trainspotting theme?

I store gun magazines under my mattress.

I should calm down. People get too obsessed about advertising awards. There's this guy in account service who once asked me whether I would chop off one of my toes to win a Cannes Gold Lion. He told me "Mountain climbers often lose a toe to frostbite, to reach the peak of Everest". I told him that whilst I wasn't prepared to chop off one of my toes, I'd gladly chop off one of his. Even if it didn't mean winning a Gold Lion.

I really should talk more about Triple M. Remember, only industry losers like you labour through rambling ads like this; normal people like things fast and funny. So write something unconventional for Triple M. Conservative old farts who try to get ads pulled off the air don't listen to them. For more information contact Scott Llewelyn at Triple M on (03) 9230 1051.

Sorry Triple M. Let me apologise for not pushing your product more. It's not my fault. I didn't have enough space.

art director
Michelle Bennett

writer
John Safran

typographer
Fiona Brand

client
Triple M

agency
Clemenger Harvie/
Melbourne

art director
Jimmy Bonner

writer
Denzil Strickland

photographer
Kelli Coggins

client
Disney Business
Productions

agency
Cole Henderson Drake/
Atlanta

**TRADE COLOR
FULL PAGE
OR SPREAD:
SINGLE**

art director
Marcy Levey

writers
David Neale
Chris Schifando

client
Albemarle
Corporation

agency
Earle Palmer Brown/
Richmond

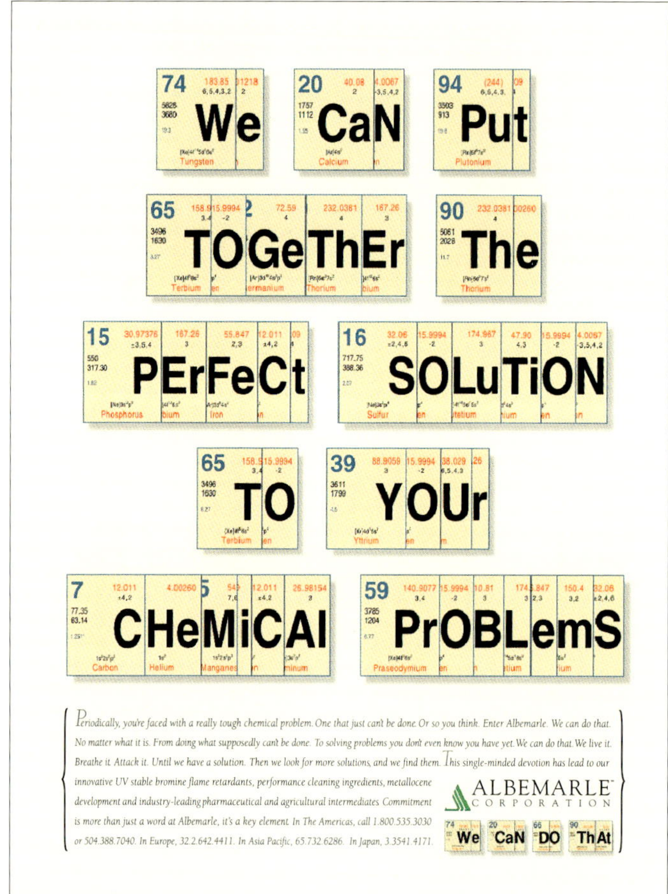

art directors
Bob Barrie
John Liegey

writers
Dean Buckhorn
Scott Vincent

client
Time Magazine

agency
Fallon McElligott/
Minneapolis

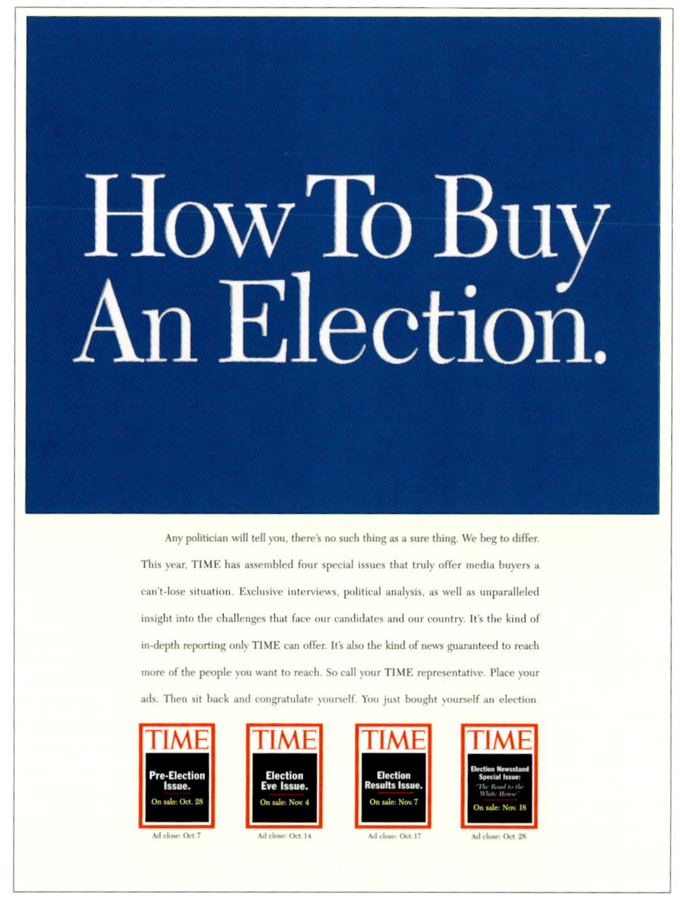

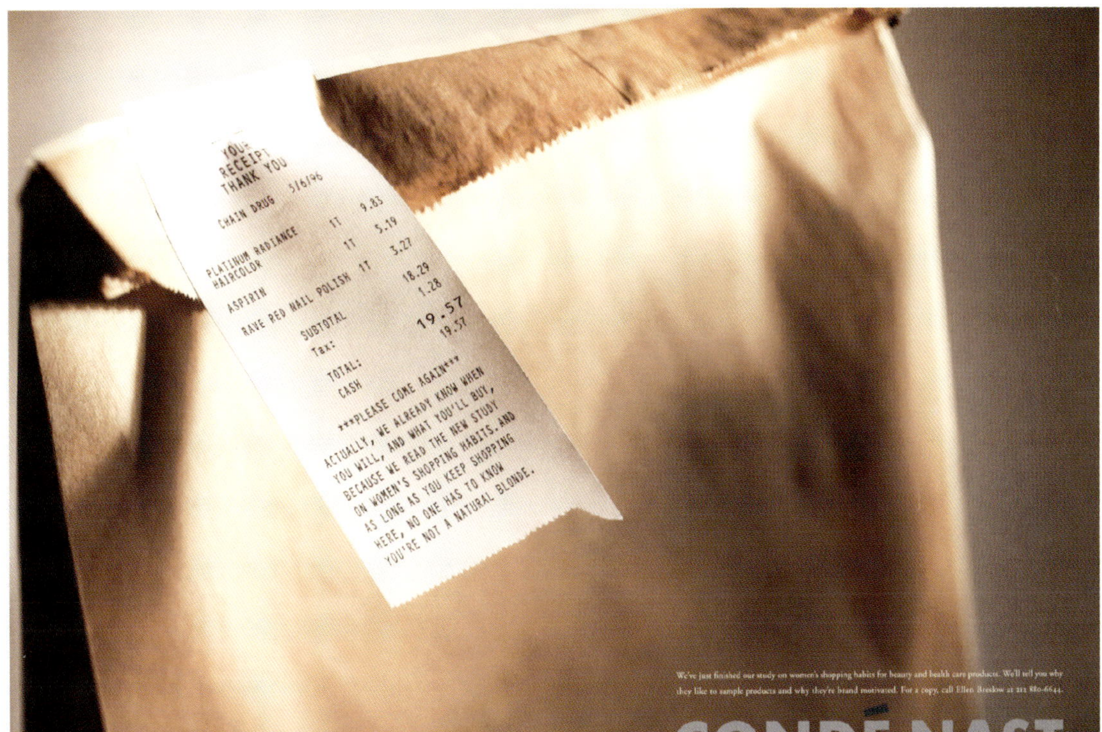

PRINT FINALISTS

art director
Marc Klein

writer
Sally Hogshead

photographer
Stephen Hellerstein

client
Condé Nast

agency
Fallon McElligott
Berlin / New York

art director
Marc Klein

writer
Sally Hogshead

photographer
Stephen Hellerstein

client
Condé Nast

agency
Fallon McElligott
Berlin / New York

**TRADE COLOR
FULL PAGE
OR SPREAD:
SINGLE**

art director
David Reid

writer
Adrian Jeffery

photographer
Victor Albrow

client
1576 Advertising

agency
1576 Advertising /
Edinburgh

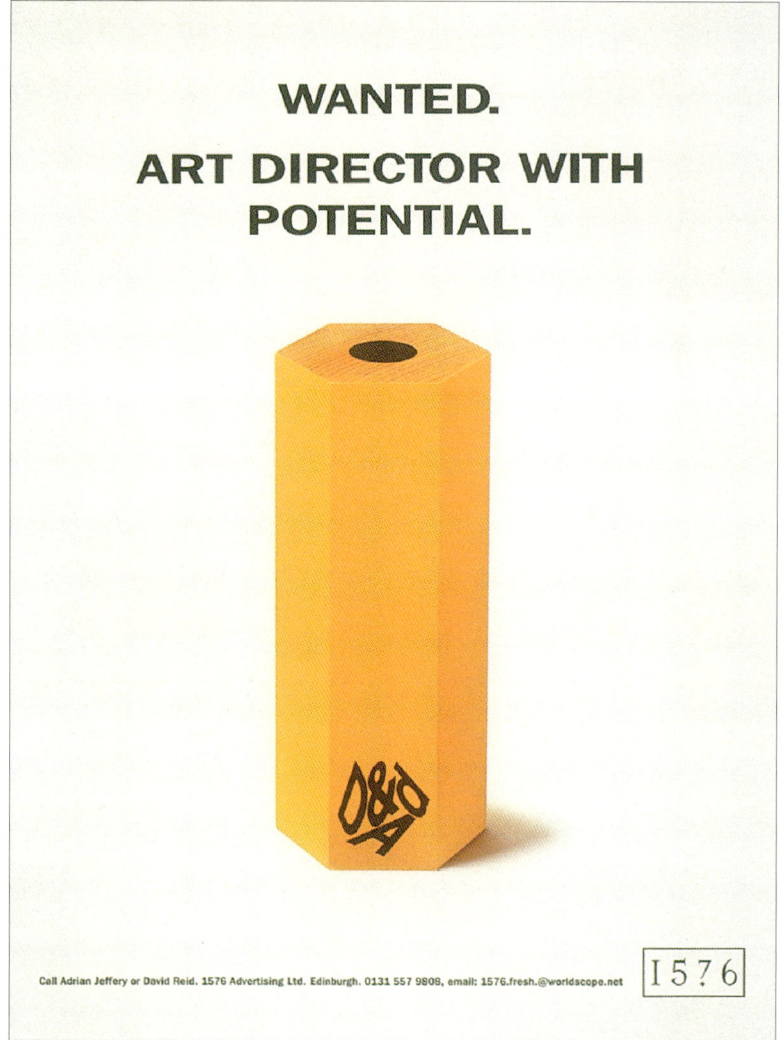

art director
Jason Gaboriau

writer
Eddie Van Bloem

client
ESPNews

agency
Goldsmith / Jeffrey,
New York

art director
Rachel Gorenstein

writer
Steve Payonzeck

photographer
Bill Abronowicz

client
Norwegian Cruise Line

agency
Goodby Silverstein &
Partners/San Francisco

art director
Rachel Gorenstein

writers
Steve Payonzeck
Valerie Ang-Powell

photographers
Heimo
Jim Erickson

client
Norwegian Cruise Line

agency
Goodby Silverstein &
Partners/San Francisco

**TRADE COLOR
FULL PAGE
OR SPREAD:
SINGLE**

art directors
Terry Finley
David Carter

writers
David Carter
Terry Finley

photographer
Michelle Clement

client
Advertising
Photographers
of America

agency
Hal Riney & Partners/
San Francisco

PRINT FINALISTS

art director
Wendy Tripp
writer
Ted Guidotti
photographer
Ken Miller
client
YM Magazine
agency
Hill Holliday/
Altschiller, New York

**TRADE COLOR
FULL PAGE
OR SPREAD:
SINGLE**

art director
Steve Mitchell

writer
Doug Adkins

photographer
Joe Lampi

client
Domtar Paper

agency
Hunt Adkins/
Minneapolis

art directors
Mike Fetrow
Steve Mitchell

writer
Doug Adkins

photographer
Jim Arndt

client
Sargento

agency
Hunt Adkins/
Minneapolis

art director
Arty Tan

writer
Scott Wild

photographer
Shawn Michienzi

client
Adidas America

agency
Leagas Delaney/
San Francisco

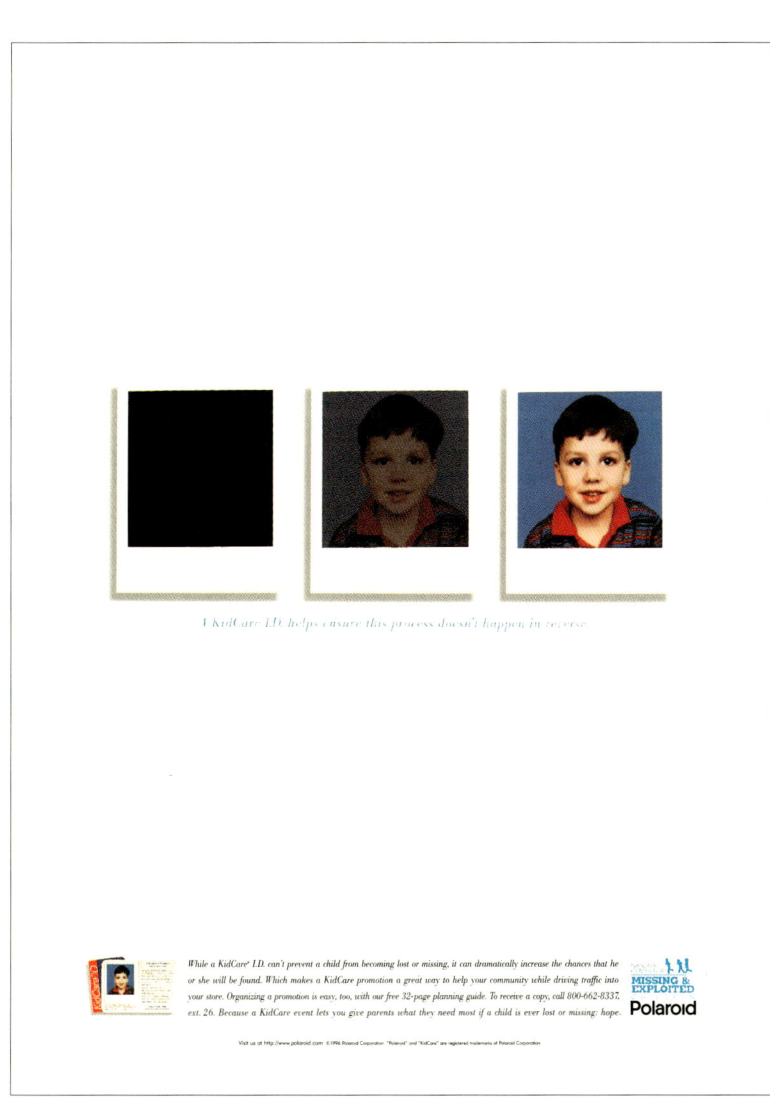

art directors
Hal Curtis
Ralph Watson

writer
John Simpson

photographer
Paul Clancy

client
Polaroid
Corporation

agency
Leonard/Monahan,
Providence

**TRADE COLOR
FULL PAGE
OR SPREAD:
SINGLE**

art director
Barney Goldberg

writer
Anne Marie Floyd

illustrator
Stan Watts

client
FMC Corporation

agency
The Martin Agency/
Richmond

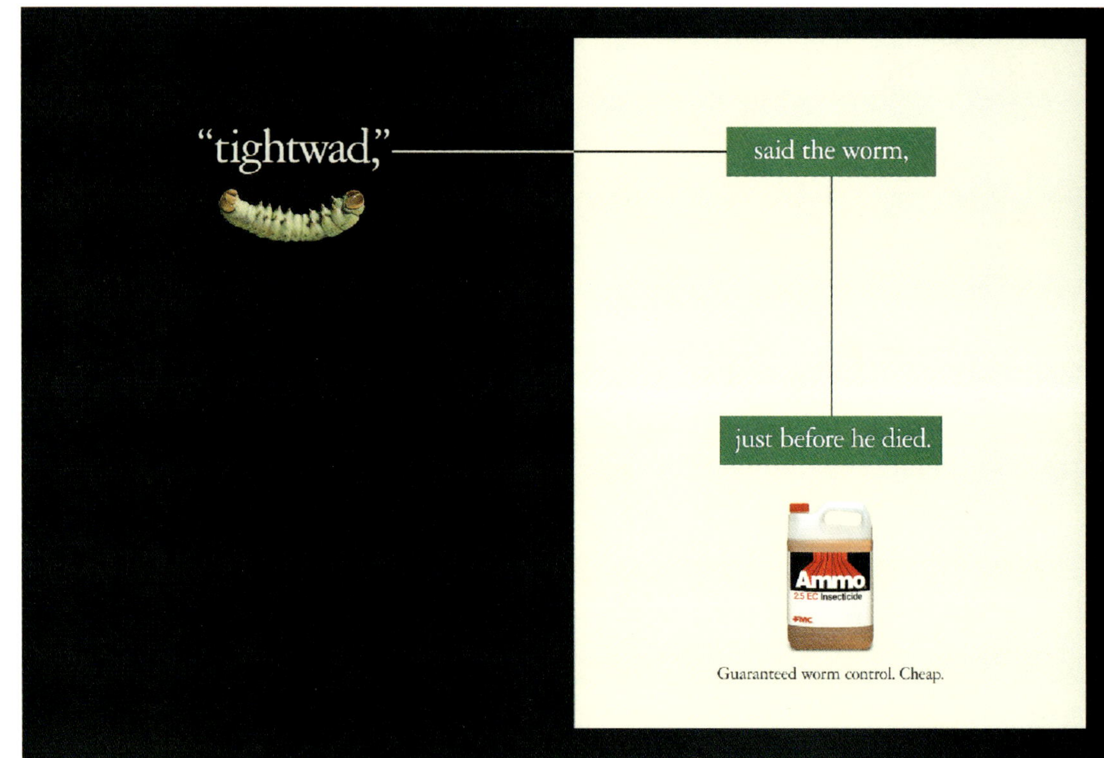

art director
Randy Hughes

writer
Tom Kelly

photographer
Joe Paczkowski

client
Flyshacker

agency
Martin/Williams,
Minneapolis

art director
Randy Hughes

writer
Tom Kelly

photographer
Joe Paczkowski

client
Flyshacker

agency
Martin / Williams,
Minneapolis

art director
Jimmy Olson

writer
Dave Loew

illustrator
Chris Hanson

photographer
Chuck Shotwell

client
Bunn

agency
McConnaughy Stein
Schmidt Brown /
Chicago

**TRADE COLOR
FULL PAGE
OR SPREAD:
SINGLE**

art director
Scott Stefan

writer
Chris D'Rozario

illustrator
Rod Vass

client
Springhill Paper

agency
Messner Vetere
Berger McNamee
Schmetterer/EURO
RSCG, New York

art director
Greg Bokor

writer
Jim Garaventi

photographer
John Holt

client
Fortune Magazine

agency
Mullen Advertising/
Wenham, MA

Walk in to The Body Shop anywhere in the world and there, amidst the Mango Body Butter, Brazil Nut Conditioner, and Banana Shampoo, you'll encounter a well-defined, environmentally minded business philosophy. One that serves to guide not only the way The Body Shop conducts itself, but in addition the expectations it places on the companies with which it elects to do business.

Knowing that, you can easily understand just how difficult it would be for many companies to get through the door at The Body Shop. Whether they're selling ingredients for the latest in aromatherapy or, well, lightbulbs.

But in OSRAM SYLVANIA, The Body Shop found an ideal business partner. One that could supply the lighting to help create the desired store environment, and do so with a product and philosophy in keeping with The Body Shop's commitment to environmental responsibility.

Specifically, what The Body Shop, and a growing number of other companies, have found at OSRAM SYLVANIA, is an environmental initiative that is by far the most extensive within the industry. It's an initiative we call ECOLOGIC™.

ECOLOGIC is much more than just a single product solution to today's environmental issues and standards. It is a comprehensive family of lighting guided by our unique life-cycle approach to product development. One which places an environmental focus into each and every stage of our lamp development in order to search for ways in which we can improve upon the materials that we use, the power that we consume, and the waste that we generate.

This innovative focus has led to the creation of smarter, safer product designs at our research and development facilities. We've lowered – and in some cases even eliminated – mercury and lead levels during manufacturing.

Our environmental concern has already helped bring about a major reduction in the total volume of non-recyclable waste that we once created by promoting a switch to soy-based inks and cadmium-free paper stocks in our packaging. We're also educating customers regarding the environmental, and practical benefits of energy-efficient lighting at LIGHTPOINT, the Institute for Lighting Technology. And we're constantly evolving our operations to create more advanced, longer lasting lamps which not only meet, but exceed Federal TCLP testing.

Perhaps the proudest result of our ECOLOGIC program is a family of lighting products that is unparalleled in the industry.

Lamps that manage to greatly reduce their environmental impact without sacrificing performance. This family includes our new REDUCED MERCURY OCTRON/ECO T8 Linear and CURVALUME which pass TCLP with the lowest mercury dose of any T8 fluorescent lamps, and provide the great efficiencies that OCTRON T8 lamps are already well known for. Our COMPACT FLUORESCENT DULUX/ECO lamps, which also pass the TCLP disposal requirements, and feature a wide variety of both wattages and color temperatures to meet a range of applications. Our HALOGEN CAPSYLITE/ECO lamps, which meet the disposal requirements with their lead free solder bases, while providing true, clean light. Our METALARC PRO TECH™ PAR/ECO lamps, which boast an industry first lead free base, while continuing to provide the most efficient form of metal halide white lighting without any color shift. And finally, our HIGH PRESSURE SODIUM LUMALUX PLUS/ECO lamps, the only HPS lamps to pass TCLP testing, featuring a full 90% less mercury than standard LUMALUX, lead free welded bases, and our non cycling technology that reduces maintenance costs.

Through our unique ECOLOGIC initiative, we will continue to offer solutions that meet and exceed today's toughest lighting standards. These are not the government's standards. Not even The Body Shop's. But our own.

To find out more about the solutions we can offer to help your business, or your customers' business, please contact us at 1-800-LIGHTBULB. Or visit us at our Web site at http://www.sylvania.com

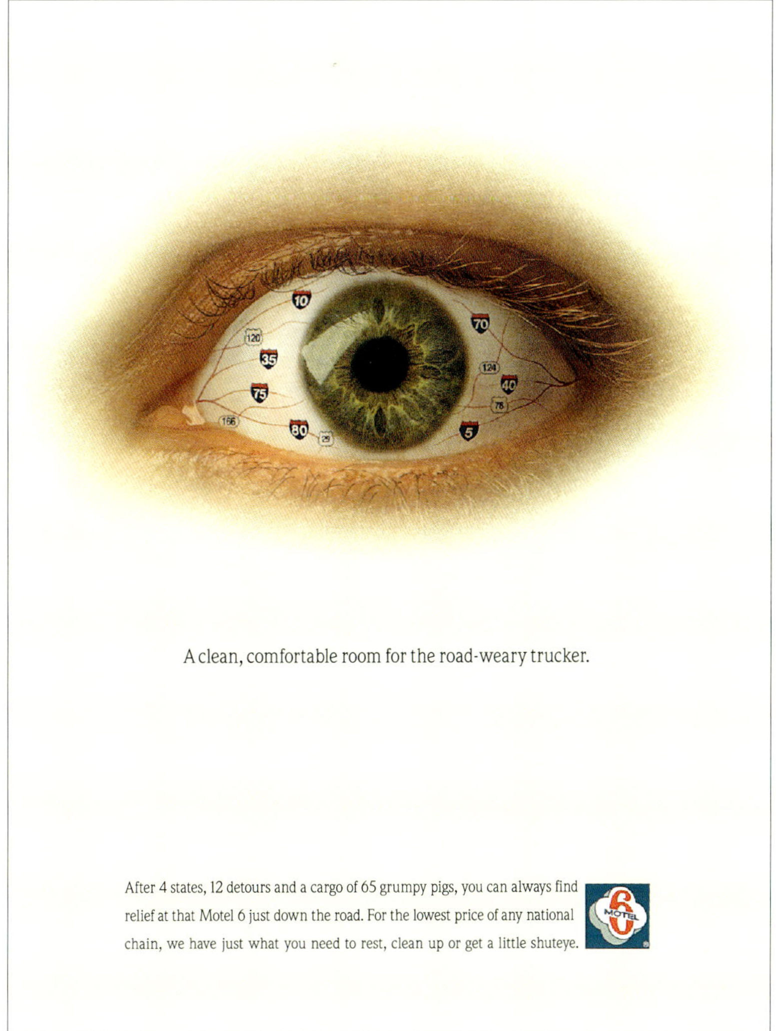

**TRADE COLOR
FULL PAGE
OR SPREAD:
SINGLE**

art director
Chris Bleackley

writer
Maggie Mouat

client
Trust Bank
New Zealand

agency
Saatchi & Saatchi/
Wellington, New Zealand

art director
Tony Messano

writer
Pat Wages

client
Eaton Automotive

agency
Sawyer Riley
Compton / Atlanta

Eaton Steering Column Interface Concept

our design engineers to work helping you develop an application for our steering column interface in your new vehicles. Our latest concept is based on transferring power and communications between a vehicle's steering wheel and column without the direct electrical connection presently achieved with slip rings and clock springs. This system employs a specially designed rotary transformer which provides uniform coupling regardless of rotational angles between the primary and secondary magnetic structures. There are two electronic printed circuit boards (PCB's) which interact with the transformer. While the electronics were optimized to perform airbag deployment at any time, both communications and power coupling occur simultaneously without debilitating

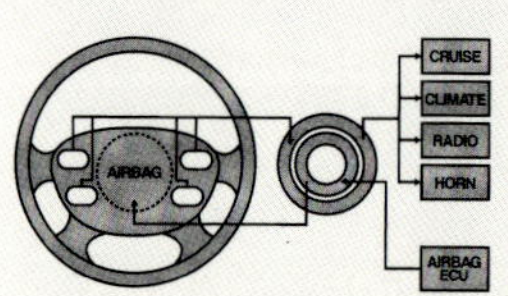

interaction. This concept for a steering column interface is just part of our vision to help customers take full advantage of the technological revolution now occurring in our markets. The simultaneous decrease in cost and increase in function and reliability of electronic technology have created significant opportunities to enhance the capability of the products and components we produce. Eaton's engineers make use of leading edge technologies to keep the pipeline of new and improved products flowing. Electronics are dramatically improving communication capabilities beginning with more user-friendly operator interfaces. Eaton was one of the first in vehicle multiplexing and we've been a production supplier since the early 1990s, when we began delivering multiplexed components that permit electronic controls attached to vehicle components to communicate with another via a single twisted pair of wires. We believe that a higher order of smart products are those that choose a best course of action, based on analyzing inputs from several alternatives. You'll find that the Eaton Steering Column Interface concept is a higher capacity design that allows for placement of   unit assembly.

For more information, call 1-810-354-2767.

NO NEWS IS GOOD NEWS.
(WHAT KIND OF SICK MIND CAME UP WITH THAT?)
Live breaking coverage. Just thinking about it sends adrenaline coursing through our veins. Being the first ones there when a big story breaks. Covering it better than anyone else, with the most live shots, and superior journalism. And providing all of our affiliates with what it takes to make sure their news is good.
Serious about news?
CNN NEWSOURCE

AT 22 HE WON THE NATIONAL CHAMPIONSHIP.
AT 23 HE WON THE WORLD CHAMPIONSHIP.
AT 24 A DOCTOR TOLD HIM HE'D NEVER RACE AGAIN.
AT 26 HE SENT THIS PICTURE TO THAT DOCTOR.
CryoLife Inc.

**TRADE COLOR
FULL PAGE
OR SPREAD:
SINGLE**

art directors
Bart Cleveland
Cathy Carlisi

writers
Cathy Carlisi
Bart Cleveland

photographer
Jim DiVitale

client
Portfolio

agency
Tausche Martin
Lonsdorf/Atlanta

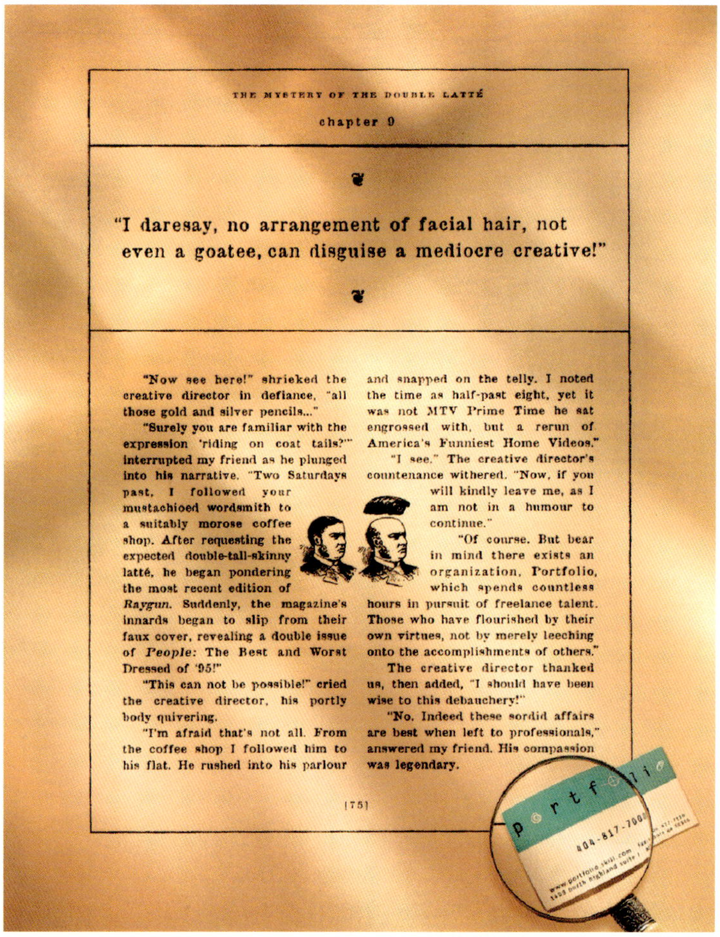

art directors
Bart Cleveland
Cathy Carlisi

writers
Cathy Carlisi
Bart Cleveland

photographer
Jim DiVitale

client
Portfolio

agency
Tausche Martin
Lonsdorf/Atlanta

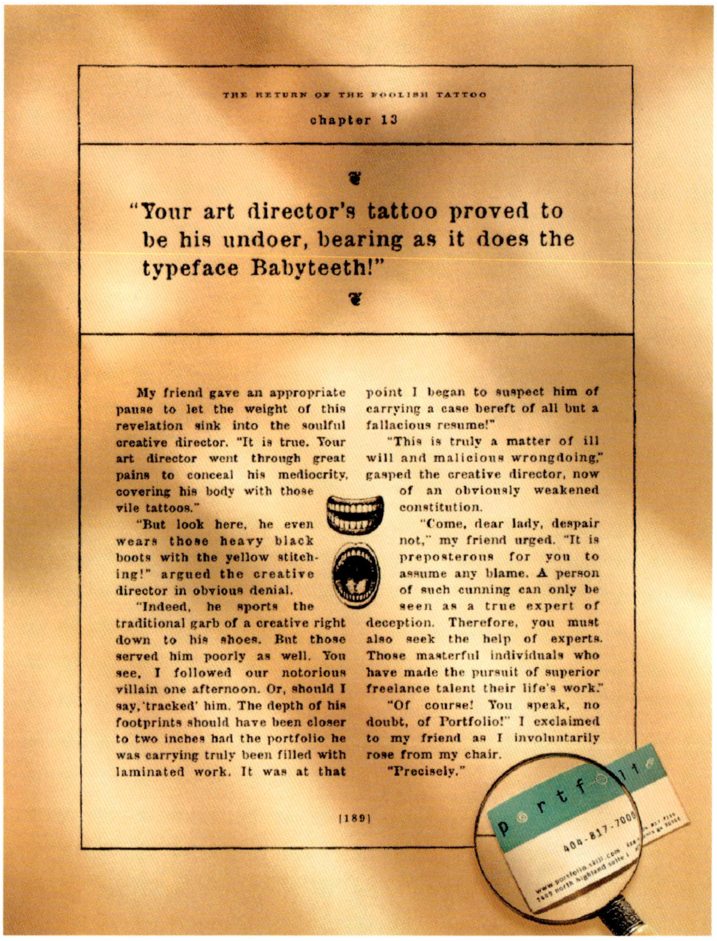

art directors
Vince Engel
Jeff Williams

writer
Jim Riswold

photographer
Michael Faye

client
Nike

agency
Wieden & Kennedy/
Portland

TRADE B/W
OR COLOR
LESS THAN A
PAGE: SINGLE

art director
Mark Watson

writers
Pete Choi
Steve Chavez

illustrator
Jeff Foster

client
Chums

agency
Cole & Weber/
Portland

art director
Bob Barrie

writer
Luke Sullivan

photographer
Kerry Peterson

client
Asche & Spencer
Music

agency
Fallon McElligott/
Minneapolis

PRINT FINALISTS

**TRADE B/W
OR COLOR
ANY SIZE:
CAMPAIGN**

art director
Maximiliano
Anselmo

writer
Sebastian Wilhelm

illustrator
Roy Garcia

client
Mujeres & Co.

agency
Agulla & Baccetti/
Buenos Aires

**TRADE B/W
OR COLOR
ANY SIZE:
CAMPAIGN**

art director
Todd Riddle

writer
David Lowe

photographer
Jim Flynn

client
Perfect Curve

agency
Arnold Advertising/
Boston

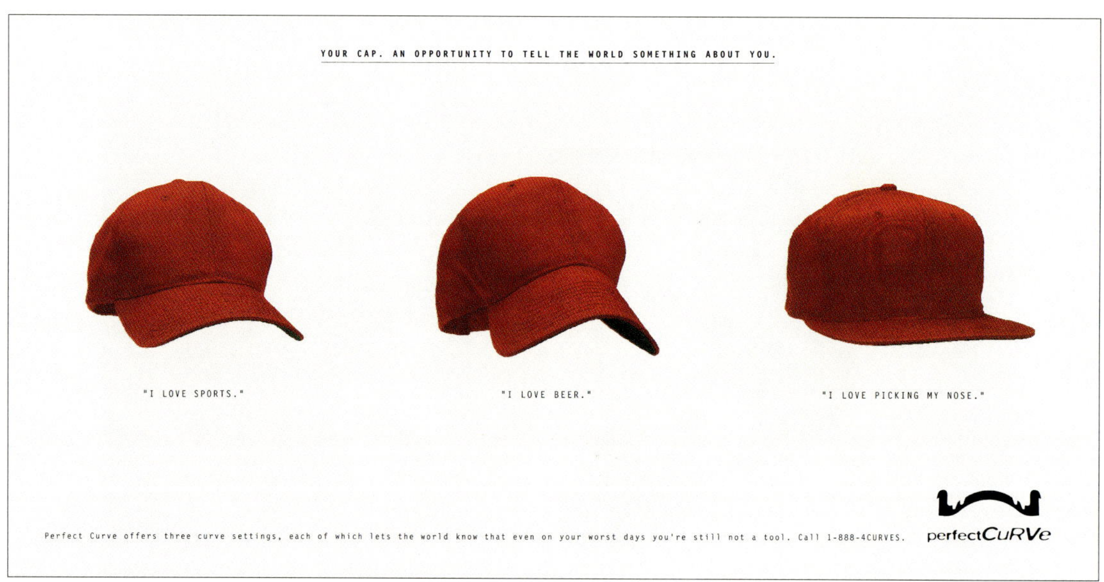

art directors
Dennis Lim
Gavin Milner

writer
Greg Ketchum

client
Apple Computer

agency
BBDO West/Los Angeles

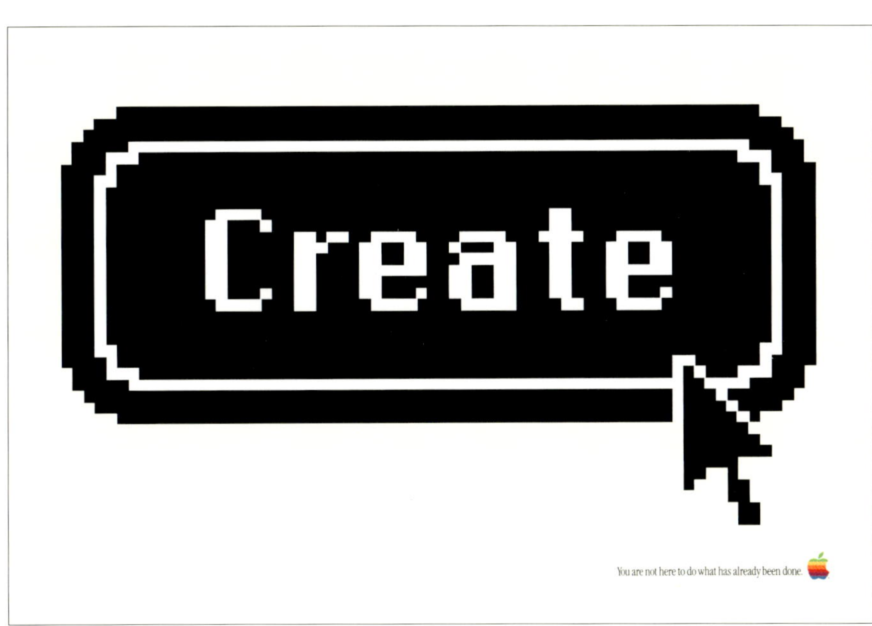

**TRADE B/W
OR COLOR
ANY SIZE:
CAMPAIGN**

art director
Marc Klein

writer
Sally Hogshead

photographer
Steve Hellerstein

client
Condé Nast

agency
Fallon McElligott
Berlin / New York

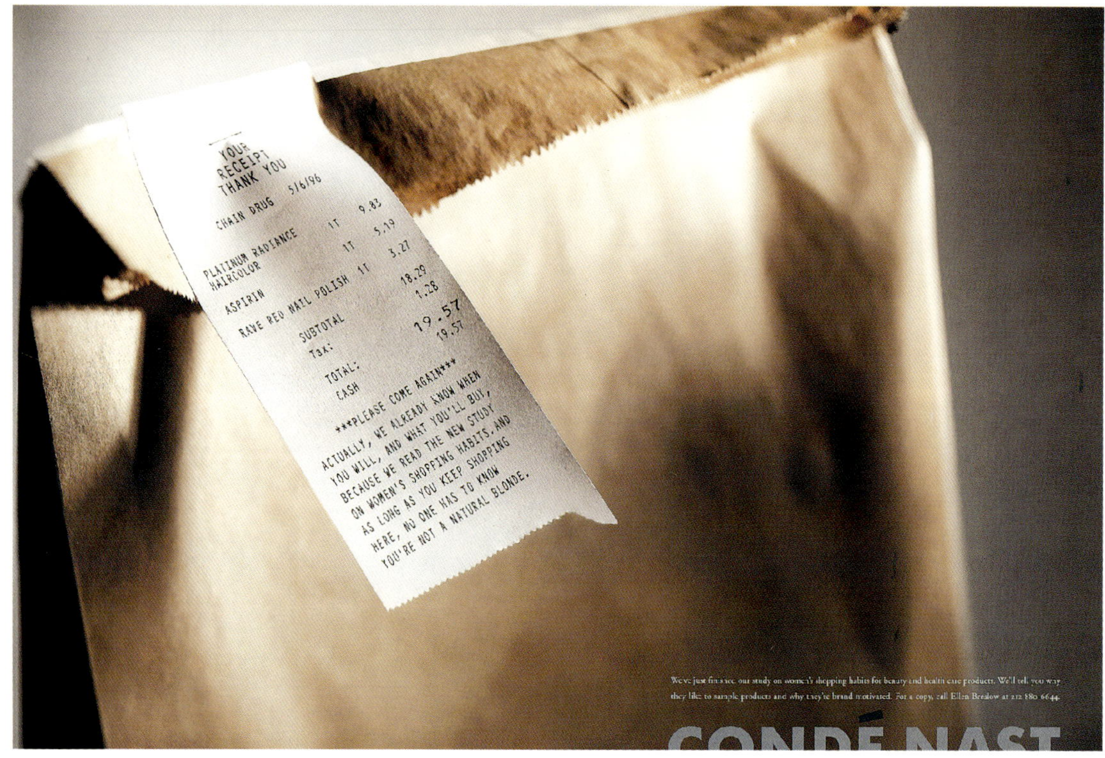

CHAIN DRUG
FOOD COURT
YOU ARE HERE
WE KNEW YOU WOULD BE. WE ALSO KNOW WHAT YOU'LL BUY, SINCE WE'VE READ THE NEW STUDY ON WOMEN'S SHOPPING HABITS. BY THE WAY, YOUR HUSBAND'S FAVORITE AFTERSHAVE IS ON SALE.
MASS MARKET
SPECIALTY STORE
SUPERMARKET
CONDÉ NAST

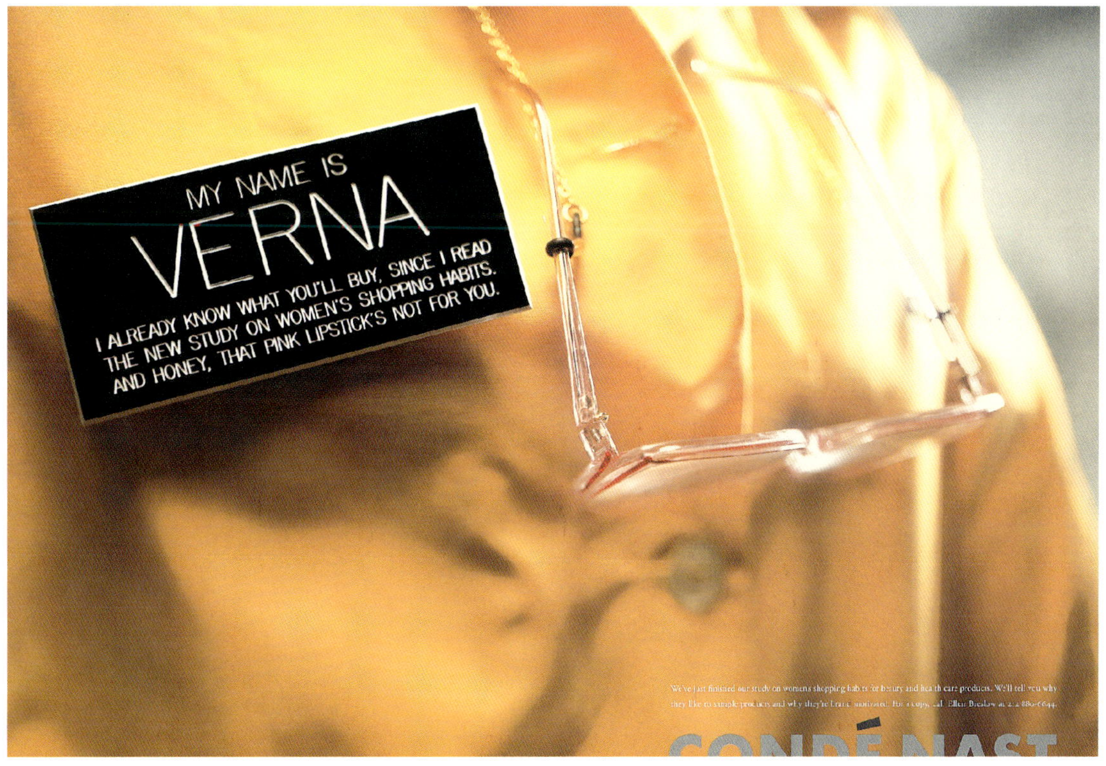

MY NAME IS
VERNA
I ALREADY KNOW WHAT YOU'LL BUY, SINCE I READ THE NEW STUDY ON WOMEN'S SHOPPING HABITS. AND HONEY, THAT PINK LIPSTICK'S NOT FOR YOU.
CONDÉ NAST

**TRADE B/W
OR COLOR
ANY SIZE:
CAMPAIGN**

art director
Hal Barber

writer
Susan Willoughby

photographer
Jeff Seldik

client
Neenah Papers

agency
Fitzgerald &
Company / Atlanta

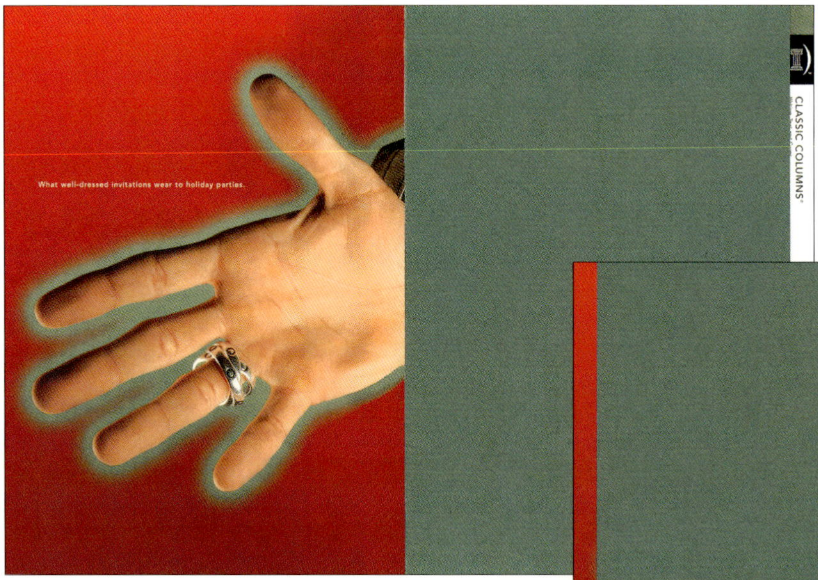

CLASSIC CREST

For all the designers who yearn for brighter whites, a miracle.

NEENAN Classic PAPERS

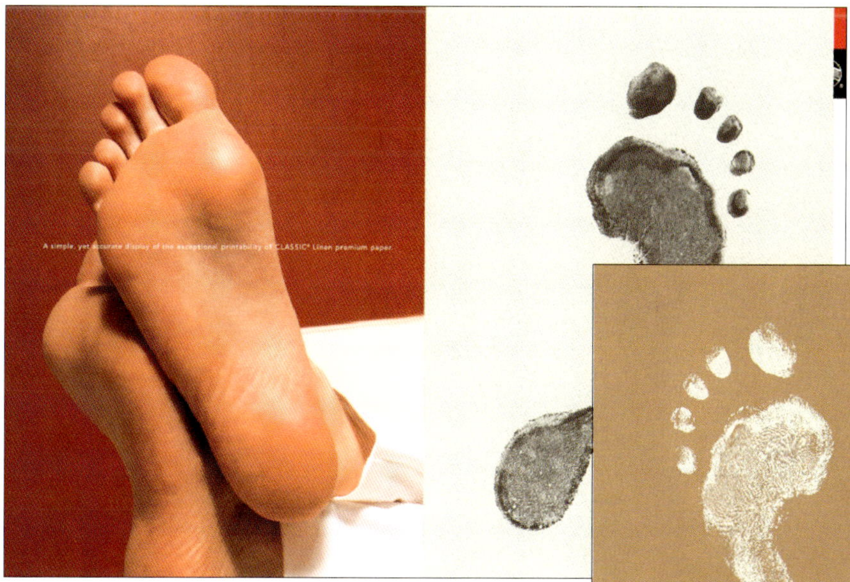

A simple, yet accurate display of the exceptional printability of CLASSIC® Linen premium paper.

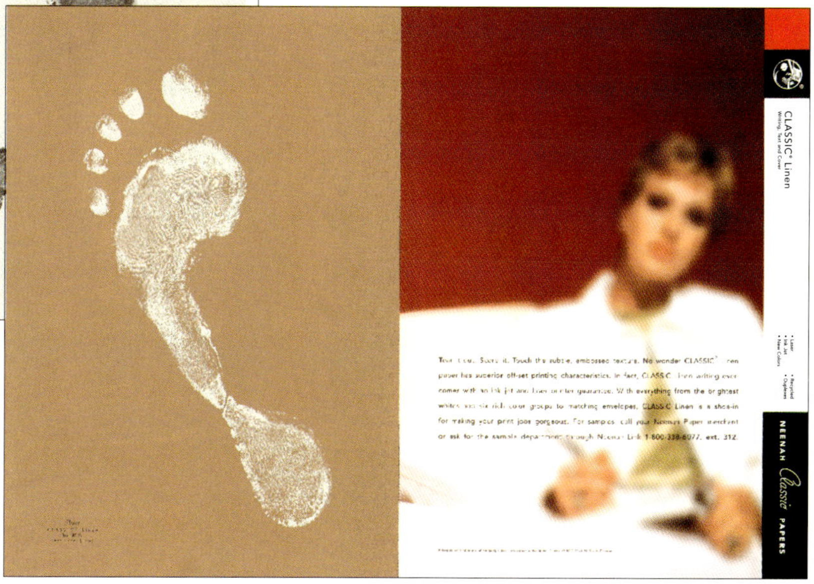

CLASSIC® Linen

NEENAN Classic PAPERS

**TRADE B/W
OR COLOR
ANY SIZE:
CAMPAIGN**

art director
Kurt Lighthouse

writers
Kurt Lighthouse
Leanne Lustica
Marcie Judelson

photographer
Stevan Nordstrom

client
Torani

agency
Gardner Geary Coll &
Young / San Francisco

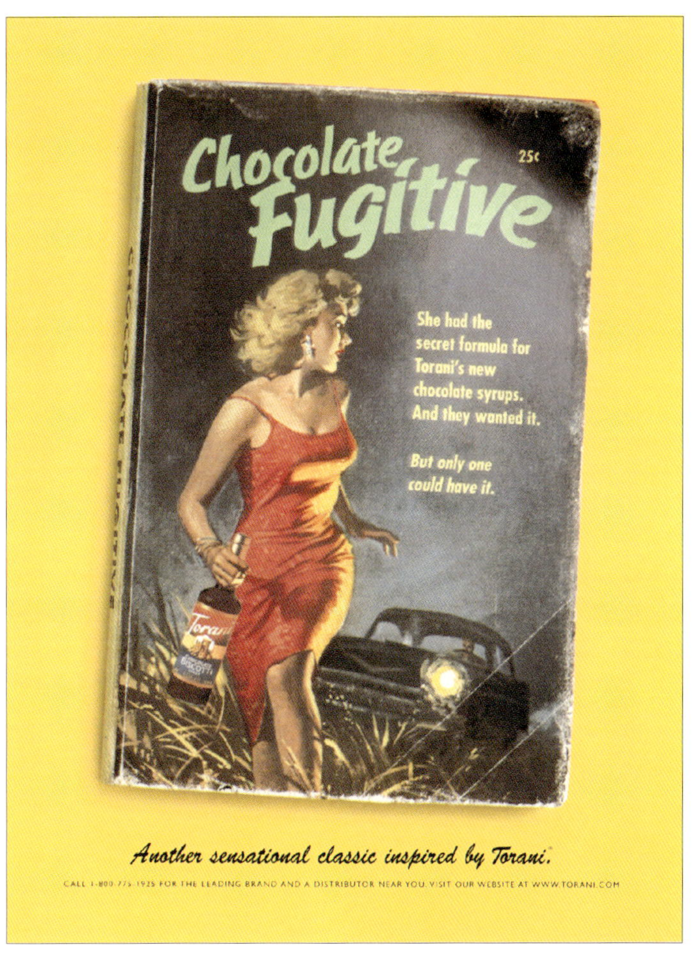

Chocolate Fugitive
25¢
She had the secret formula for Torani's new chocolate syrups. And they wanted it.
But only one could have it.
Torani
Another sensational classic inspired by Torani.
CALL 1-800-775-1925 FOR THE LEADING BRAND AND A DISTRIBUTOR NEAR YOU. VISIT OUR WEBSITE AT WWW.TORANI.COM

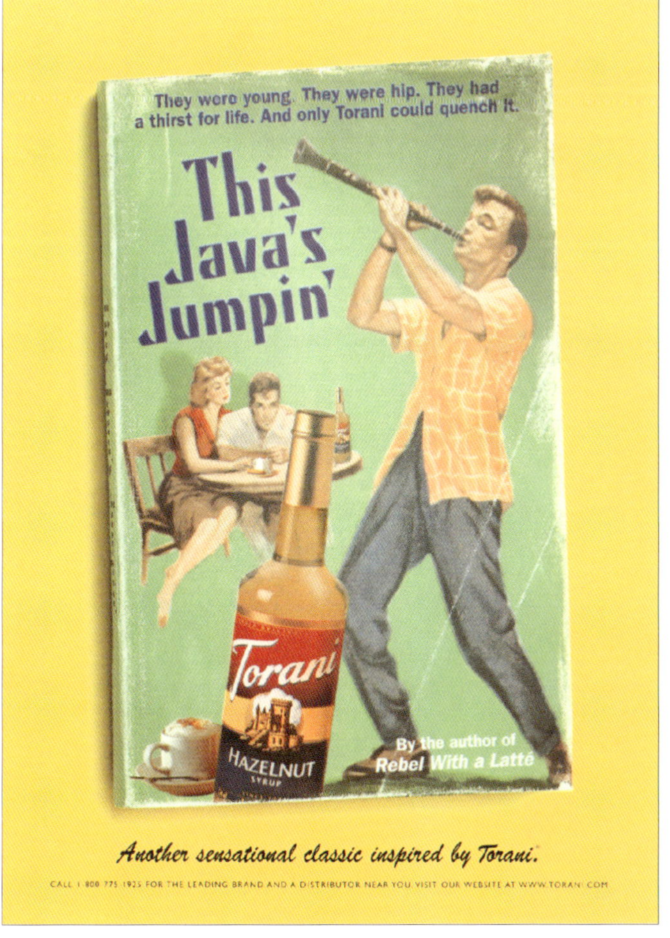

They were young. They were hip. They had a thirst for life. And only Torani could quench it.
This Java's Jumpin'
Torani
HAZELNUT SYRUP
By the author of Rebel With a Latté
Another sensational classic inspired by Torani.
CALL 1-800-775-1925 FOR THE LEADING BRAND AND A DISTRIBUTOR NEAR YOU. VISIT OUR WEBSITE AT WWW.TORANI.COM

25¢
Low Calorie FAT FREE
He was just "Jack from Accounting," until he brought Torani to the office party. Now he was the...
Life of the Party
Butter Rum, Peppermint, and Italian Eggnog. How could they resist?
Torani
ITALIAN EGGNOG SYRUP
Another sensational classic inspired by Torani.
CALL 1-800-775-1925 FOR THE LEADING BRAND AND A DISTRIBUTOR NEAR YOU. VISIT OUR WEBSITE AT WWW.TORANI.COM

**TRADE B/W
OR COLOR
ANY SIZE:
CAMPAIGN**

art director
Jason Gaboriau

writer
Eddie Van Bloem

photographer
Ilan Rubin

client
ESPN 2

agency
Goldsmith/Jeffrey,
New York

art directors
Karin Onsager-Birch
Paul Hirsch
Valerie Ang-Powell

writers
Josh Denberg
Chuck McBride

photographers
John Huet
Michele Clement

client
Unum Insurance

agency
Goodby Silverstein &
Partners/San Francisco

**TRADE B/W
OR COLOR
ANY SIZE:
CAMPAIGN**

art director
Thomas Hayo

writer
Richard Yelland

photographers
Steve McCurry
James Nachtney

typographer
Rob Sutton

client
Eastman Kodak Company

agency
J. Walter Thompson/
New York

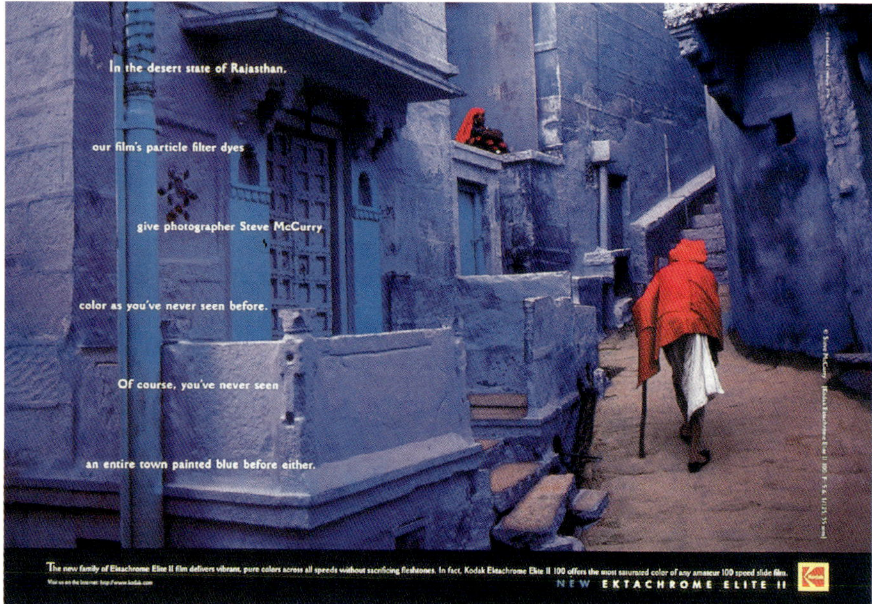

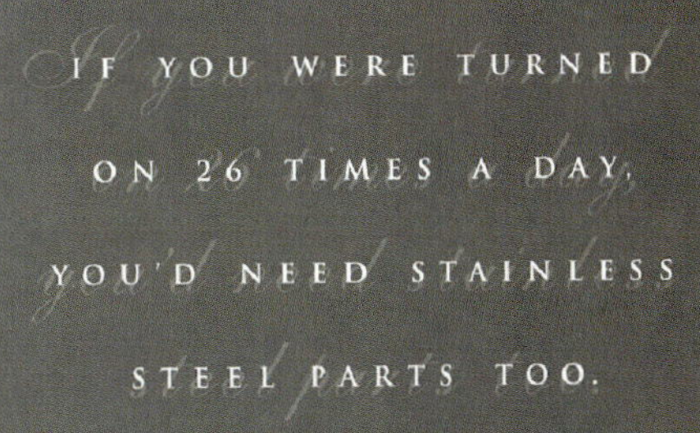

IF YOU WERE TURNED
ON 26 TIMES A DAY,
YOU'D NEED STAINLESS
STEEL PARTS TOO.

A faucet has to have incredible stamina to survive the manhandling we humans will subject it to during its lifetime. Which is why we equip ours with stainless steel parts. • Stainless steel refuses to corrode. It won't wear out. And it can be precisely engineered. • In our single handle faucets, our designers have shaped it into a highly polished ball that's so reliable fewer than 1 in 100,000 has had a leak or a drip due to defects. • In our two handle models, there's a stainless steel plate at the base of the faucet stem where leaks often occur. • Instead of just spot welding, our engineers insist on using three different types. This helps extend the life of our faucets considerably. • In fact, they're guaranteed for exactly that: life. • They're also available in quite a variety of styles. Once you choose one, we recommend you have it installed by a professional. • After that, please feel free to do with our faucets as you wish. We can confidently say that it has the stainless steel to take it. • Call 1-800-345-DELTA for details.

DELTA
GUARANTEED FOR LIFE

SOME PEOPLE ACHIEVE
LONGEVITY WITH YOGURT
AND AN ACTIVE LOVE LIFE.
WE USE STAINLESS STEEL.

We don't wish to appear overly confident, but it would be a tough contest to see who would last longer: our faucets or the amorous yogurt crowd. • You see, our faucets have stainless steel parts. Needless to say, they don't. • Stainless steel refuses to corrode. It can be precisely engineered. Most importantly, it won't wear out. • In our single handle faucets, our designers have shaped it into a highly polished ball that's so reliable fewer than 1 in 100,000 has had a leak or a drip due to defects. • In our two handle models, there's a stainless steel plate at the base of the faucet stem where leaks often occur. • Instead of just spot welding, our engineers insist on using three different types. This helps extend the life of our faucets considerably. • In fact, they're guaranteed for exactly that: life. • We also make them in a wide variety of styles. After you've chosen one, we do recommend you have it installed by a professional. • Once in, we have no idea what its actual lifespan is. But if you live long enough to find out, do let us know. • Call 1-800-345-DELTA for details.

DELTA
GUARANTEED FOR LIFE

IF YOU HAD
STAINLESS STEEL PARTS
YOU'D PROBABLY
COME WITH A LIFETIME
GUARANTEE TOO.

We hate to admit it, but we're slightly envious about the fact that our faucets have stainless steel parts and we don't. • Think about it. Stainless steel refuses to corrode. It can be precisely engineered. Best of all, it won't wear out. • For example, in our single handle faucets, our designers have shaped it into a highly polished ball that's so reliable fewer than 1 in 100,000 has had a leak or a drip due to defects. • In our two handle models, there's a stainless steel plate at the base of the faucet stem where leaks usually occur. • Instead of just spot welding, our engineers insist on using three different types. This helps extend the life of our faucets considerably. • In fact, they're guaranteed for exactly that: life. • On top of that, they come in a great range of styles. (We recommend you have yours installed by a professional.) • So at the end of the day, you'll have a faucet that performs tirelessly, has incredible stamina and won't lose its looks. See what we mean? • Call 1-800-345-DELTA for more details.

DELTA
GUARANTEED FOR LIFE

**TRADE B/W
OR COLOR
ANY SIZE:
CAMPAIGN**

art director
Randy Hughes

writer
Tom Kelly

photographer
Joe Paczkowski

client
Flyshacker

agency
Martin / Williams,
Minneapolis

art director
Greg Bokor
writer
Jim Garaventi
photographer
John Holt
client
Fortune Magazine
agency
Mullen Advertising /
Wenham, MA

**TRADE B/W
OR COLOR
ANY SIZE:
CAMPAIGN**

art directors
Paul Foulkes
Michael Wilde

writers
Tyler Hampton
Jeff Odiorne

photographer
Bob Mizono

client
PIXXON

agency
Odiorne Wilde
Narraway Groome/
San Francisco

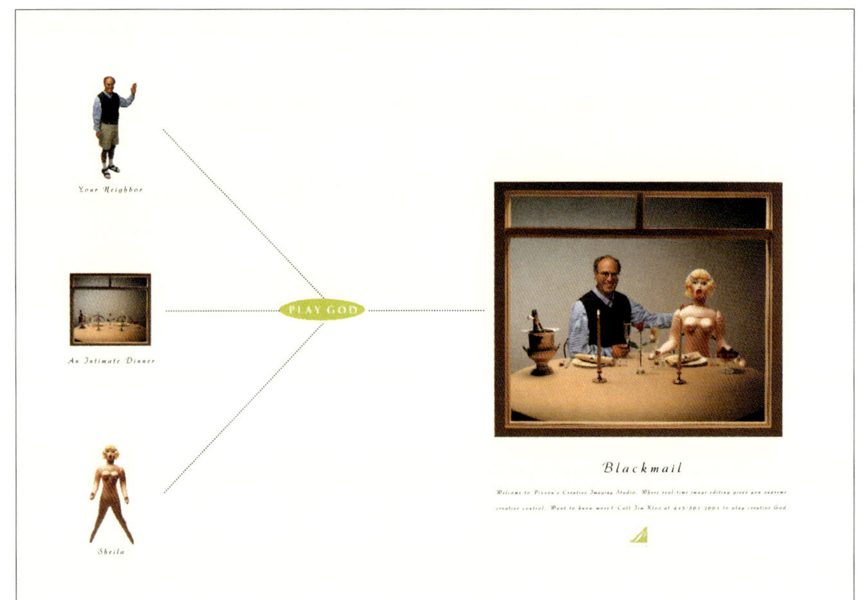

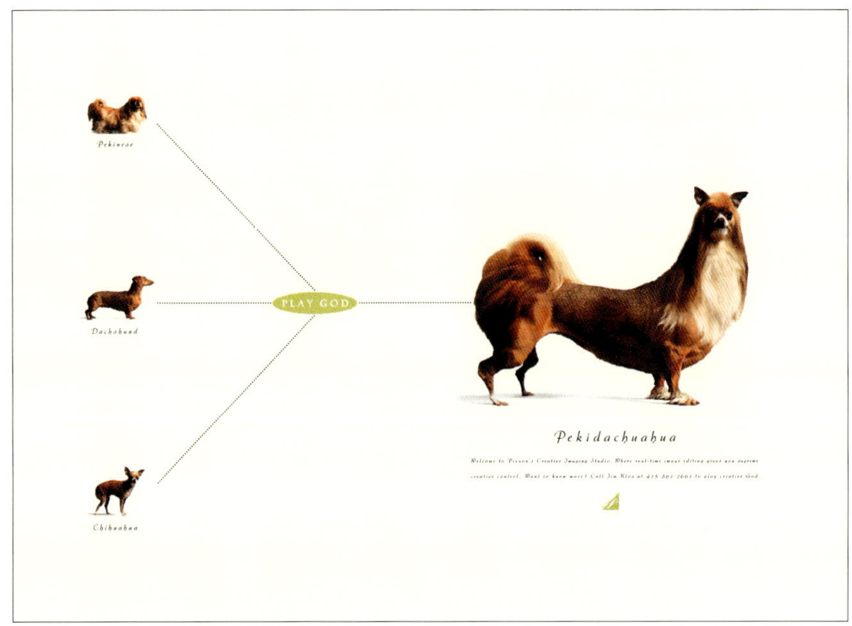

art director
Kyle Jones

writers
Mike Bourne
Casey Fluegge

client
Bayer Corporation

agency
Valentine Radford/
Kansas City

**COLLATERAL
BROCHURES
OTHER THAN
BY MAIL**

art director
Mauro Cinquetti

photographer
Albert Watson

client
Lavazza S.P.A.

agency
Armando Testa/
Torino, Italy

art directors
Patrick Short
Brandon Scharr

writer
Patrick McLean

designers
Patrick Short
Brandon Scharr

illustrator
Brandon Scharr

client
The Groundcrew/
John Causby Productions

agency
BlackBird Creative/
Charlotte, NC

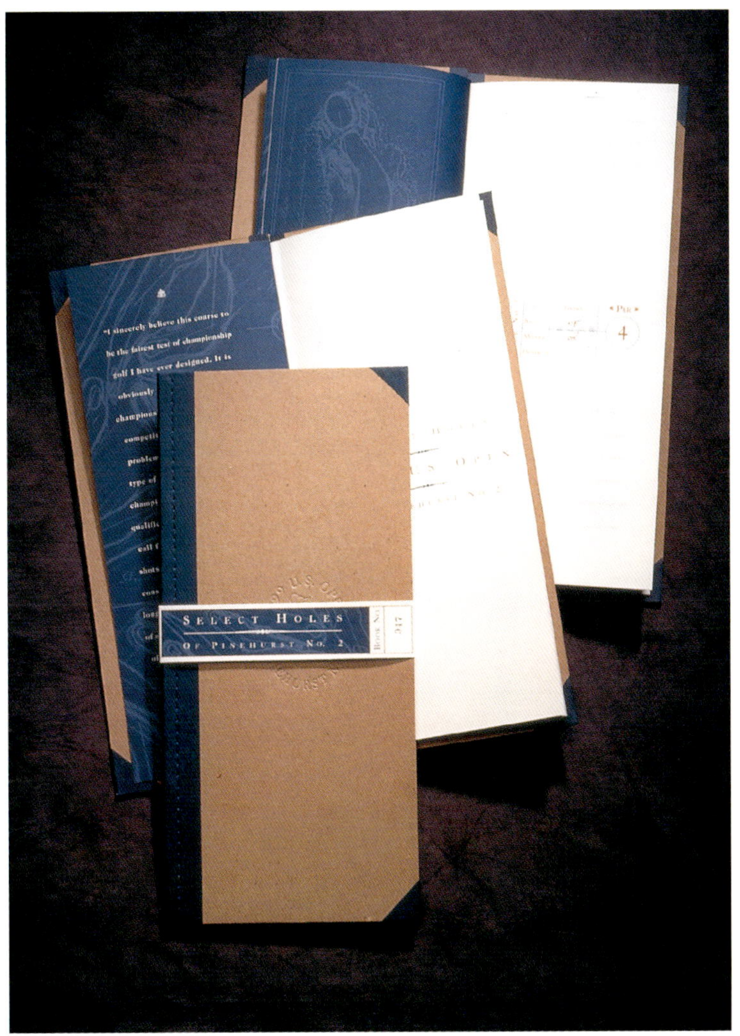

art directors
Patrick Short
Brandon Scharr

writer
Curtis Smith

designers
Patrick Short
Brandon Scharr

illustrator
Brandon Scharr

client
Pinehurst Resort &
Country Club

agency
BlackBird Creative/
Charlotte, NC

art director
Steve Stone

writer
Bob Kerstetter

illustrator
David Hartz

client
Eddie Bauer

agency
Black Rocket/
San Francisco

**COLLATERAL
BROCHURES
OTHER THAN
BY MAIL**

art director
Andrea Schindler

writers
Rich Conklin
Theo Wallace
Christopher Hoffman

photographers
Vic Huber
Michael Rausch

client
Mercedes-Benz of
North America

agency
The Designory/
Long Beach, CA

art director
Jeff Labbé

writers
Eric Springer
Ed Crayton

photographer
Kimball Hall

illustrator
CSA Archive

client
Qualcomm

agency
dGWB/Irvine, CA

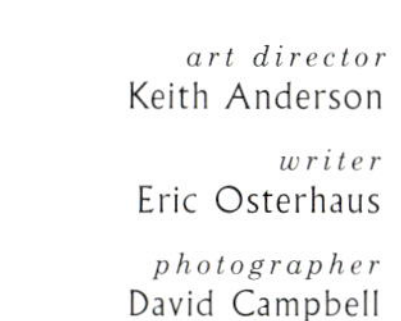

art director
Keith Anderson

writer
Eric Osterhaus

photographer
David Campbell

client
Bell Sports

agency
Goodby Silverstein &
Partners/San Francisco

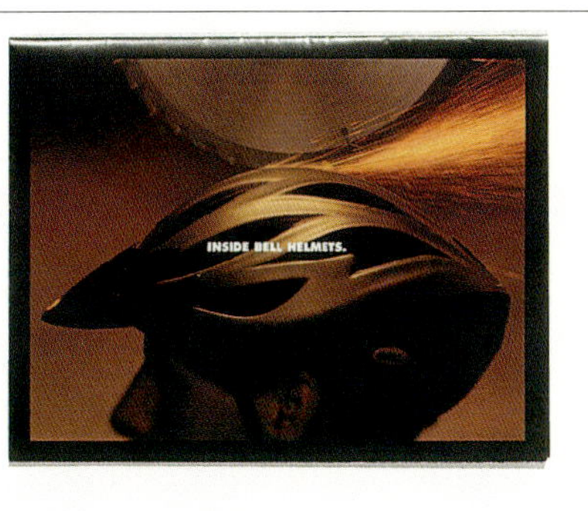

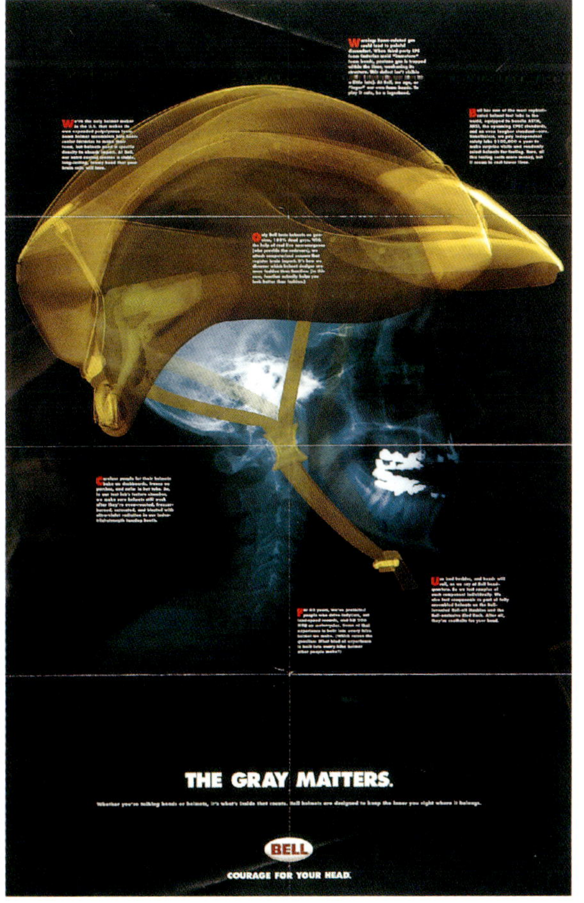

**COLLATERAL
BROCHURES
OTHER THAN
BY MAIL**

art directors
Paul Curtin
Jon Weber

writer
Rob Price

photographer
Jim Erickson

client
Pacific Bell

agency
Goodby Silverstein &
Partners / San Francisco

art director
Robert Kastigar

writers
Rob Price
Pamela Mason Davey
Spalding Gray

illustrators
Amy Butler
Mr. Fotheringham
R. Kenton Nelson
Giselle Potter
Michael Schwab

photographers
Michael Baciu
Douglas Christian
Hunter Freeman
Thomas Heiner
Geof Kern
Scogin Mayo
Mr. Narikeno
Karl Petzke
Daniel Proctor
Holly Stewart
CARE

client
Starbucks Coffee

agency
Goodby Silverstein &
Partners/San Francisco

**COLLATERAL
BROCHURES
OTHER THAN
BY MAIL**

art director
Neil Fruen

writer
Manolo Moreno Marquez

client
Polygram Films Espana

agency
Grupo Barro-Testa/
Madrid

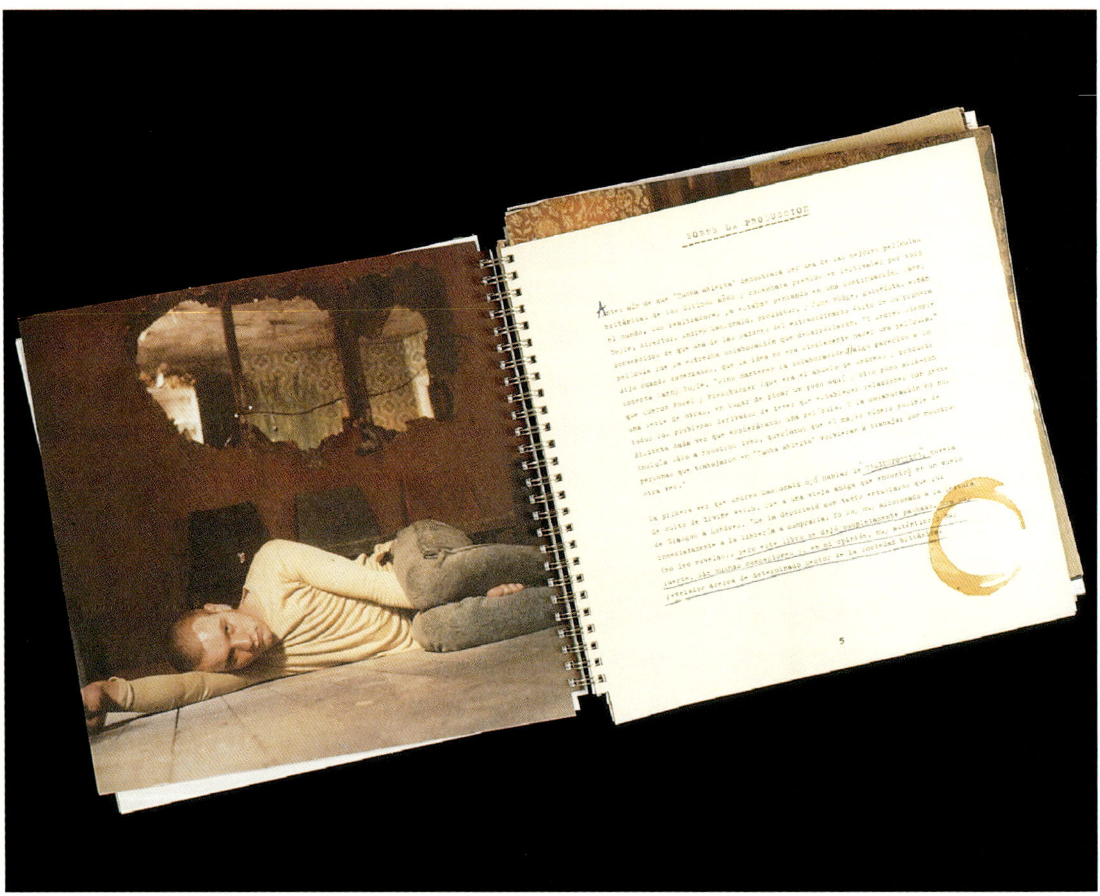

art director
Jeff Labbé

writer
Eric Springer

illustrators
Jeff Labbé
CSA Archive

photographer
Kimball Hall
Photography

client
Custom Alloy
Light Metals

agency
Labbé Design Company/
Corona Del Mar, CA

art director
Alyssa D'Arienzo

writer
John Simpson

photographer
Geoff Stein

client
The Advertising Club
of Greater Boston

agency
Leonard/Monahan,
Providence

**COLLATERAL
BROCHURES
OTHER THAN
BY MAIL**

art director
Jeff Hopfer

writer
Kevin Swisher

illustrator
Mike Constable

client
Fox River
Paper Company

agency
The Richards Group/
Dallas

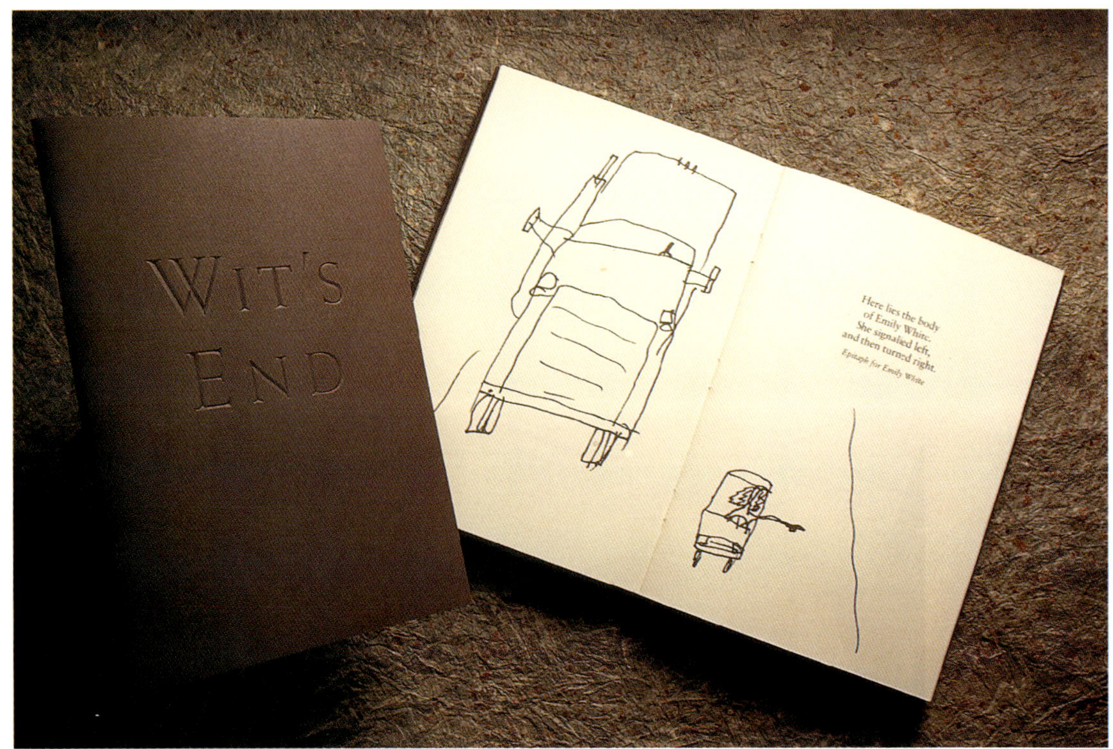

art directors
Claude Shade
Eric Tilford
Mark Arnold
Eric Stein
John Dames

writer
Todd Mitchell

photographers
Rob Stanton
Michael Eastman
James Schwartz

client
Eastman Kodak Company

agency
Saatchi & Saatchi
Business Communications/
Rochester, NY

**COLLATERAL
SALES KITS**

art directors
Bruce Turkel
Rebecca Carlson

writer
Kirk Kaplan

client
Discovery Channel
Latin America

agency
Turkel Schwartz &
Partners/Coconut Grove, FL

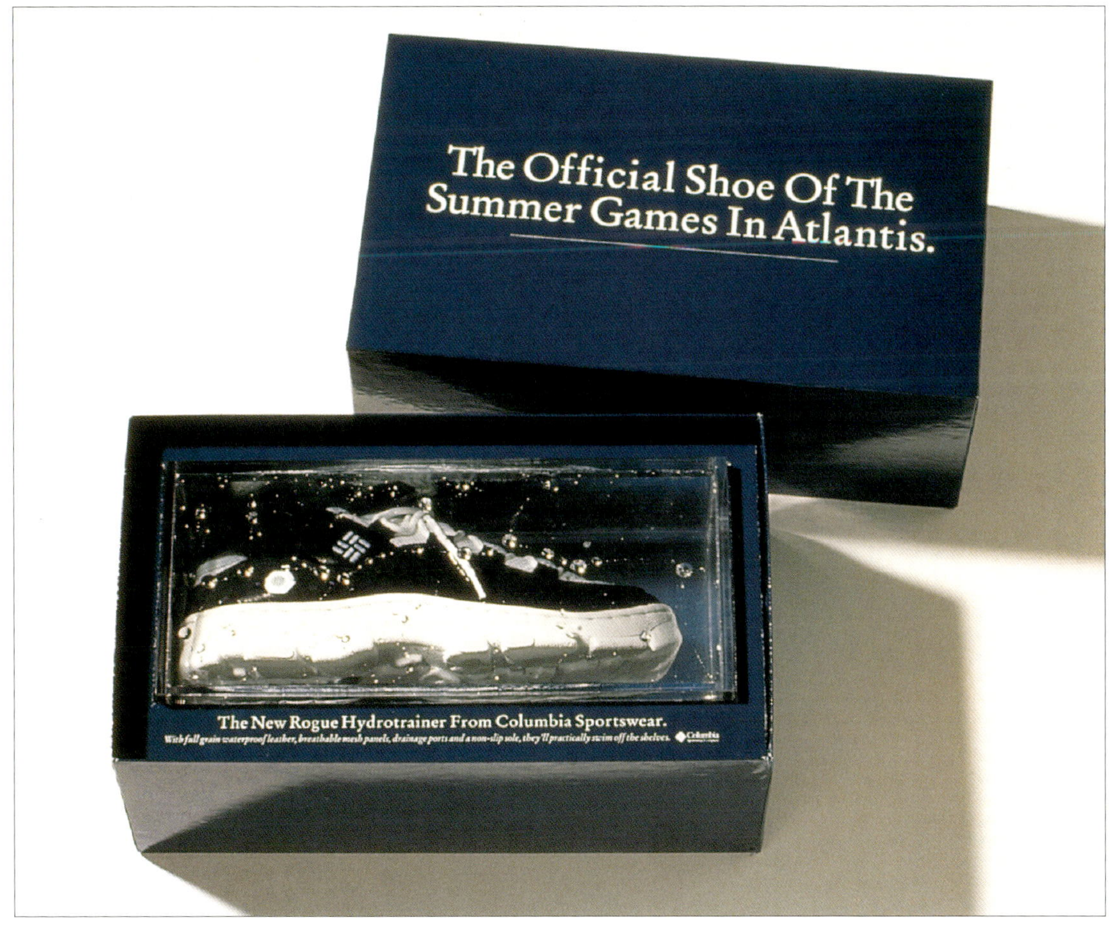

**COLLATERAL
DIRECT MAIL:
SINGLE**

art director
Kent Suter

writer
Simeon Roane

client
Columbia Sportswear

agency
Borders Perrin &
Norrander/Portland

**COLLATERAL
DIRECT MAIL:
SINGLE**

art director
V. Sunil

writer
Shivjeet Kullar

photographer
Prabudha Dasgupta

client
Hiram Walker

agency
Contract Advertising/
New Delhi

art directors
Eric Tilford
Michael Hahn

writer
Wade Paschall

photographer
Herman Leonard

client
WSIE The Jazz Station

agency
CORE/St. Louis

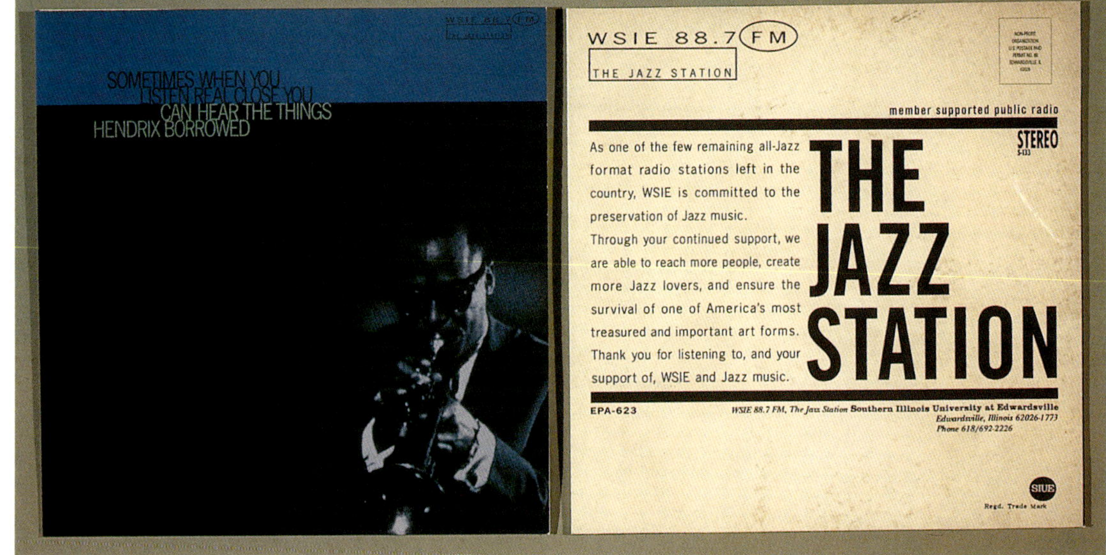

art director
Graham Scott

writer
Chris Miller

photographer
Chris Hall

client
Brand Paper

agency
Graham Scott/Edinburgh

art director
Brock Davis

writer
Matt Elhardt

illustrator
Brock Davis

client
Reelworks

agency
Hunt Adkins/
Minneapolis

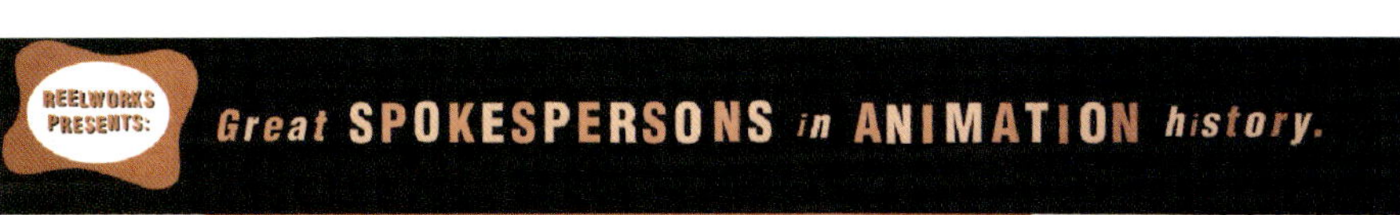

**COLLATERAL
DIRECT MAIL:
SINGLE**

art director
Brock Davis

writer
Matt Elhardt

illustrator
Brock Davis

client
Reelworks

agency
Hunt Adkins/
Minneapolis

art director
Steve Mitchell

writer
Matt Elhardt

client
Rohol

agency
Hunt Adkins/
Minneapolis

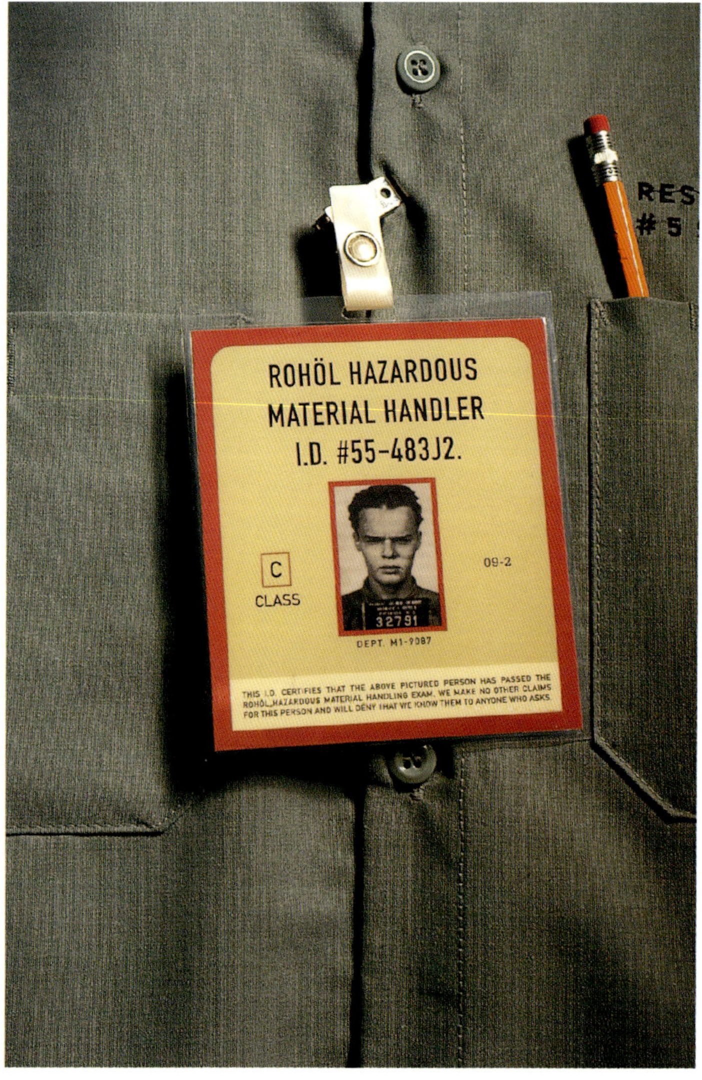

PRINT FINALISTS

art director
Steve Mitchell

writer
Matt Elhardt

client
Rohol

agency
Hunt Adkins/
Minneapolis

art director
Jim Mountjoy

writer
Ed Jones

photographer
Jim Arndt

client
Arthur's Cigar Bar

agency
Loeffler Ketchum
Mountjoy/Charlotte, NC

**COLLATERAL
DIRECT MAIL:
SINGLE**

art directors
Chuck Penna
Dave Larson

writer
Eric Gutierrez

illustrator
Oscar Arvizu

photographer
Grant Heaton

client
Utah Advertising
Federation

agency
Penna Powers Cutting &
Haynes/Salt Lake City

art director
Sharon Azula

writer
Ed Prentiss

photographer
Joe Michl

client
Animal Crackers
Pet Sitters

agency
Peterson Milla Hooks/
Minneapolis

art director
Sharon Azula

writer
Ed Prentiss

photographer
Ripsaw Photography

client
The Minneapolis Show

agency
Peterson Milla Hooks/
Minneapolis

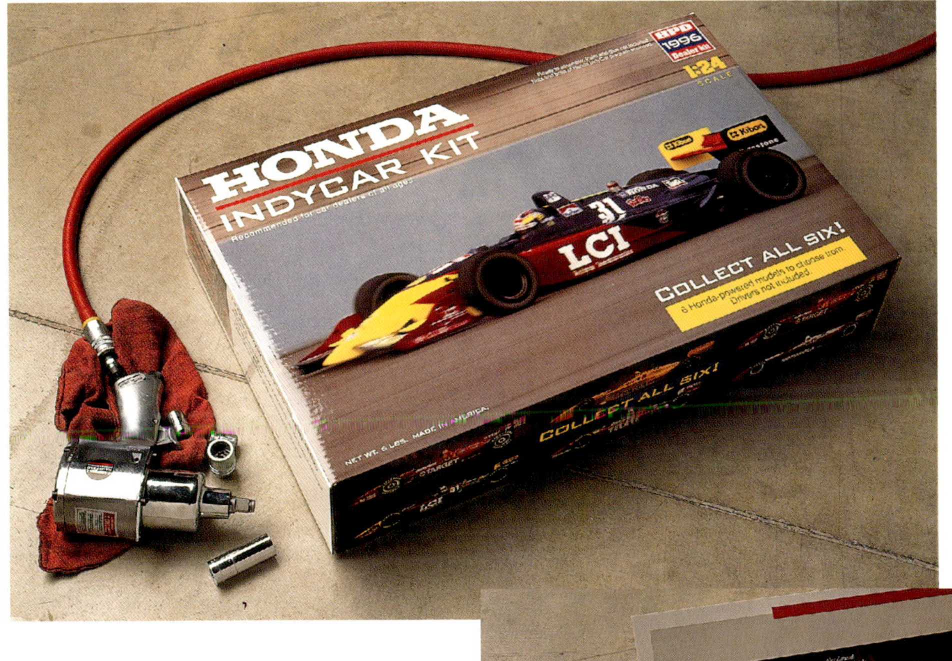

art director
Chuck Blackwell

writer
Tim O'Donnell

photographers
Dan Boyd
Rick Graves
Smith/Nelson

client
American Honda
Motor Company

agency
Rubin Postaer
and Associates/
Santa Monica

**COLLATERAL
DIRECT MAIL:
SINGLE**

art director
Donjiro Ban

writer
Donjiro Ban

illustrator
Donjiro Ban

client
Sandstrom Design

agency
Sandstrom Design/
Portland

**COLLATERAL
DIRECT MAIL:
CAMPAIGN**

art directors
Jamie Mambro
Michele Mangiacotti

writer
Ernie Schenck

photographer
Raymond Meeks

client
Dana Farber
Cancer Institute

agency
Hill Holliday Connors
Cosmopulos/Boston

COLLATERAL DIRECT MAIL: CAMPAIGN

art director
Brock Davis

writer
Matt Elhardt

illustrator
Brock Davis

client
Reelworks

agency
Hunt Adkins/ Minneapolis

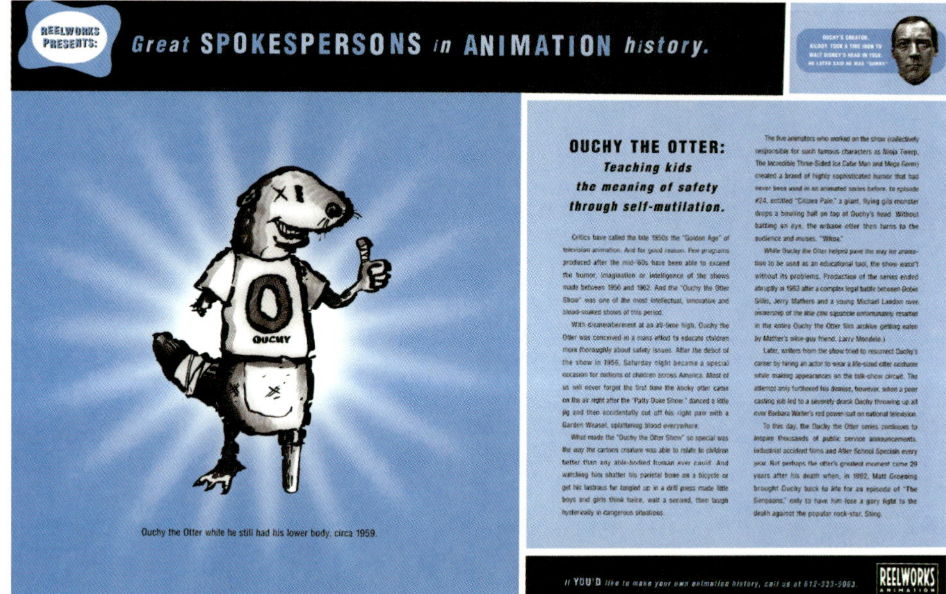

Ouchy the Otter while he still had his lower body, circa 1959.

An original cel from Li'l Sgt. Shrapnel's most famous film, "Potty Trained To Kill" (1943).

Boomer the Gas Can and Sparko the Match clowning around in 1954. Later that year, Boomer's phallic pour spout was deemed "naughty."

art director
Kevin Ragland
writer
Dave Kwasnick
photographer
Jack Wolf
client
Pittsburgh Film Office
agency
Ketchum Advertising/
Pittsburgh

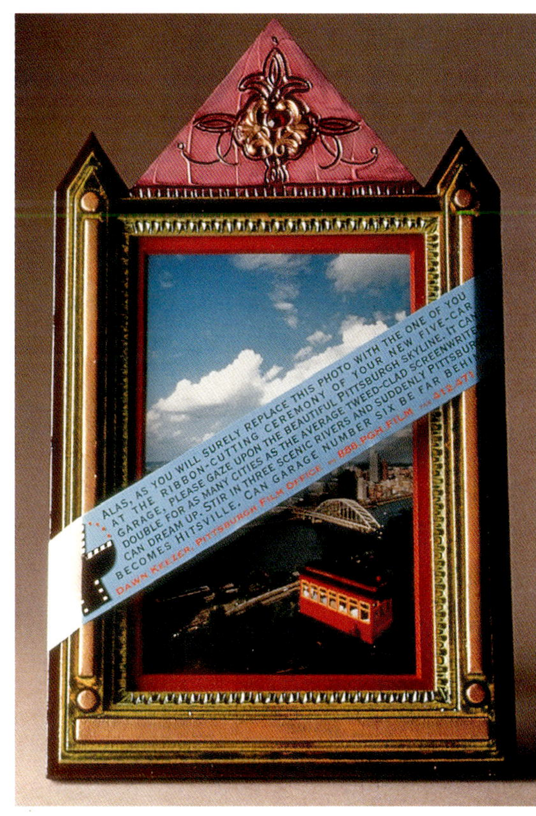

**COLLATERAL
DIRECT MAIL:
CAMPAIGN**

art director
Jon Wyville

writer
Dave Loew

photographer
Dave Emmite

client
The Amy
Burack Company

agency
McConnaughy Stein
Schmidt Brown/Chicago

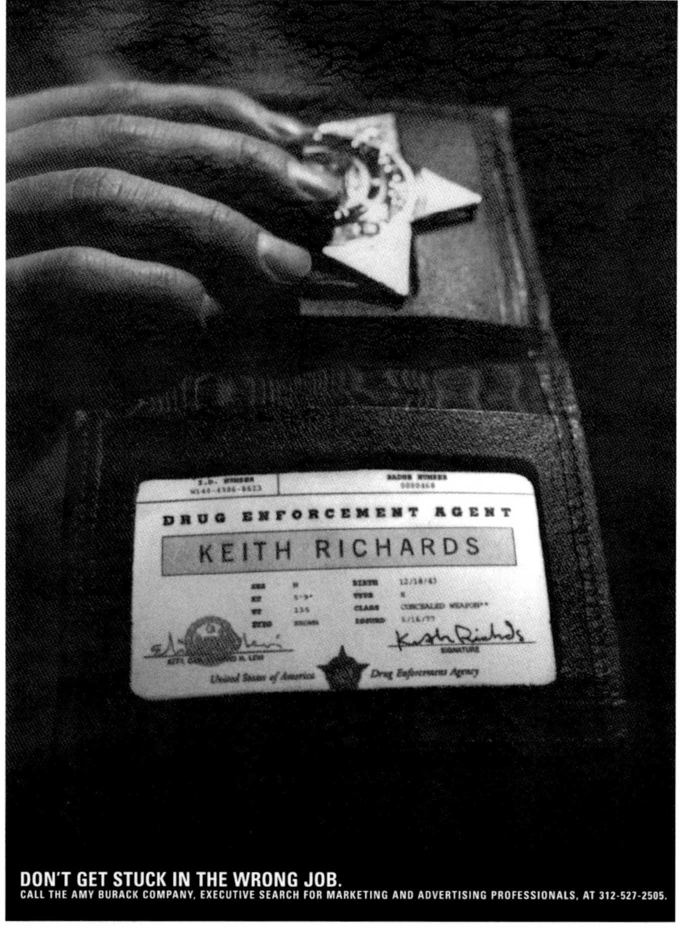

PRINT FINALISTS

art director
Kelly Beck

writer
Mickey Taylor

photographers
Juni B. Bancio Photography
Rob Van Petten Photography

client
Advertising Club of
Los Angeles

agency
TBWA Chiat / Day,
Venice, CA

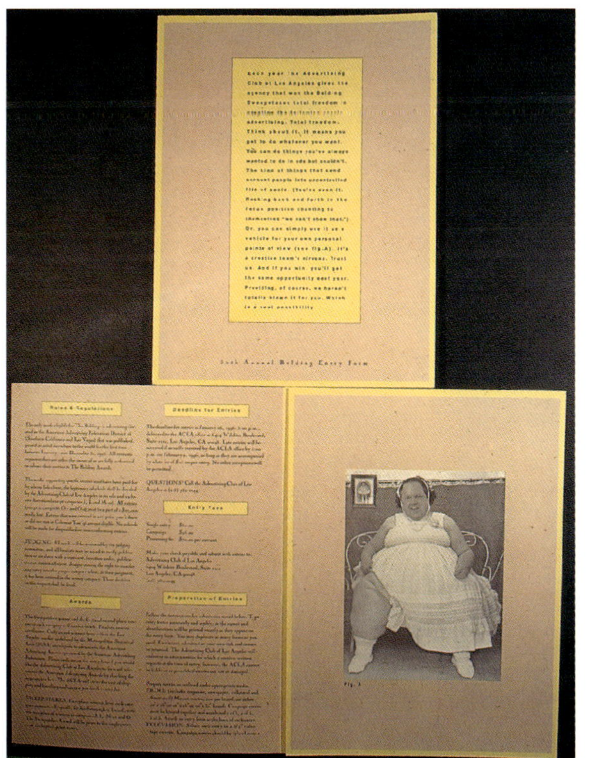

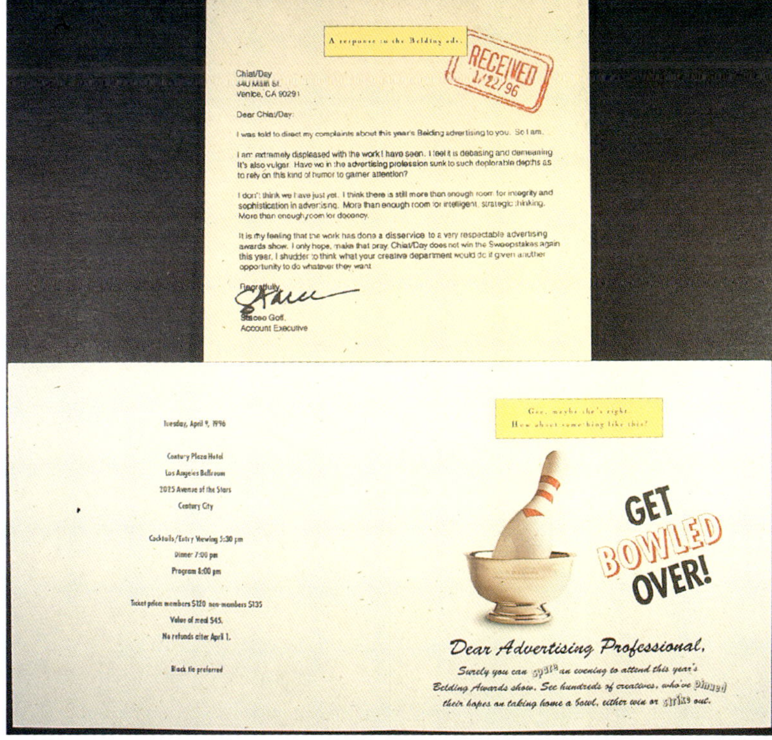

**COLLATERAL
POINT OF
PURCHASE
AND IN-STORE**

art director
Mike Fornwald

writer
Mike Fornwald

illustrator
Terry Haller

photographer
Peter Carter

client
Risser Digital Studio

agency
Arian Lowe &
Travis / Chicago

art director
Todd Riddle

writer
David Lowe

photographer
Jim Flynn

client
Perfect Curve

agency
Arnold Advertising/
Boston

art director
Todd Riddle

writer
David Lowe

photographer
Jim Flynn

client
Perfect Curve

agency
Arnold Advertising/
Boston

PRINT FINALISTS

art director
Todd Riddle

writer
David Lowe

photographer
Jim Flynn

client
Perfect Curve

agency
Arnold Advertising/
Boston

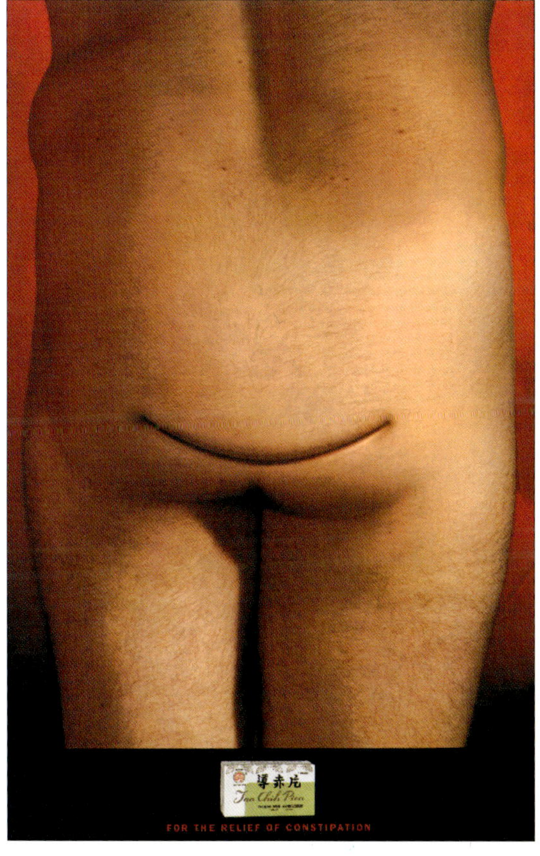

art directors
Scott Lambert
Mark Ringer

writers
Mark Ringer
Scott Lambert

photographer
William Chan

client
Fei Fah Drugstore

agency
Batey Ads/Singapore

art director
Andrew Clarke

writer
Antony Redman

photographer
Russell Wong

client
Unza Co.

agency
Batey Ads/Singapore

**COLLATERAL
POINT OF
PURCHASE
AND IN-STORE**

art director
Christopher Toland

writer
Scott Wild

photographer
Lars Topelmann

client
The Oregonian

agency
Cole & Weber/
Portland

art director
Eric Tilford

writer
Wade Paschall

photographer
James Schwartz

client
Winchester
Ammunition

agency
CORE/St. Louis

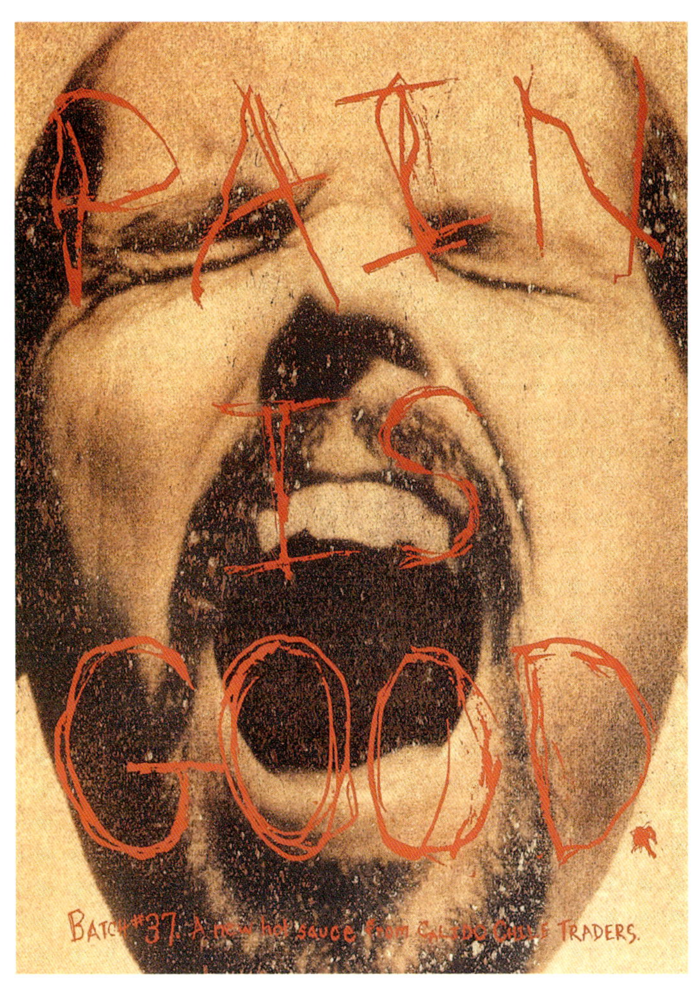

PRINT FINALISTS

art director
Eric Tilford

writer
Todd Tilford

photographer
Richard Reens

client
Calido Chili Traders

agencies
CORE/St. Louis and
JACKHAMMER/Dallas

art director
Dean Mortensen

writer
Simon Mainwaring

photographer
Alister Clarke

client
Adelar Animal Centre

agency
DDB Needham/
North Sydney

**COLLATERAL
POINT OF
PURCHASE
AND IN-STORE**

art director
Karin Onsager-Birch

writer
Josh Denberg

client
San Francisco
Examiner Newspaper

agency
Goodby Silverstein &
Partners/San Francisco

art directors
Jennifer Fleming-Balser
Holland Henton

writer
Rich Tlapek

client
Lennox

agency
GSD&M Advertising/
Austin

PRINT FINALISTS

art director
Terence Reynolds

writer
Todd Tilford

photographer
Richard Reens

client
AM General Corporation

agency
JACKHAMMER/
The Richards Group,
Dallas

art director
Frank Fusco

writer
Alan Jacobs

client
Blimpie

agency
Kirshenbaum Bond &
Partners/New York

art director
Doug Mickschl

writer
Troy Longie

photographer
Ed Wargin

client
Ideal Diner

agency
Periscope Advertising
Communications/
Minneapolis

**COLLATERAL
POINT OF
PURCHASE
AND IN-STORE**

art directors
Andy Mahr
Michael Fazende

writers
Michael Fazende
Steve Dean

client
Simon Sleazy Pub

agency
The Richards
Group/Dallas

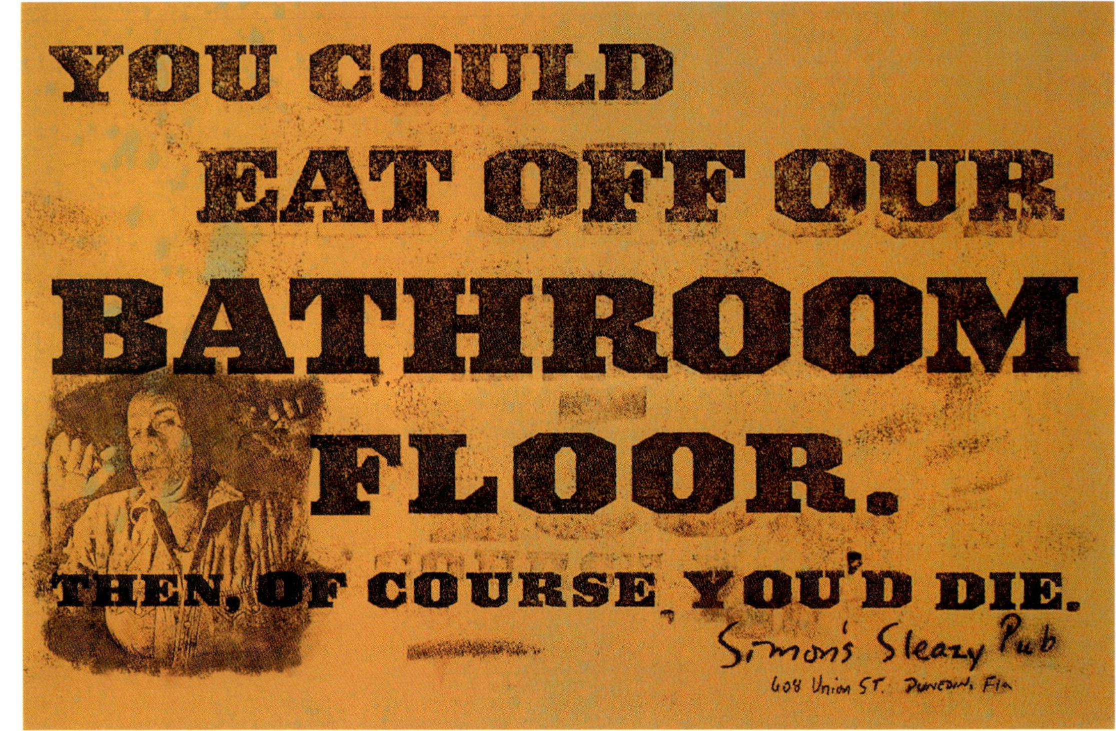

art director
Ted Royer

writer
Rowan Chanen

photographer
Alex Kai Keong

illustrator
Grover Tham

client
The Royal
Peacock Hotel

agency
Saatchi & Saatchi/
Singapore

PRINT FINALISTS

art director
Fergus Fleming

writer
Richard Grisdale

photographer
Gary Heery

client
Toyota Motor
Corporation

agency
Saatchi & Saatchi/
Sydney

art director
Steve Sandstrom

writer
Bill Borders

photographer
Mark Hooper

illustrator
Larry Jost

client
Burgerville

agency
Sandstrom Design/
Portland

**COLLATERAL
POINT OF
PURCHASE
AND IN-STORE**

art director
Cathy Carlisi

writer
Bob Cianfrone

photographers
Dee Davis
Pelosi & Chambers

client
DVM Toothpaste

agency
Tausche Martin
Lonsdorf / Atlanta

art directors
Martin Beauvais
Michael Lapointe

writers
David Stortini
André Marois
Paul Lavoie

illustrator
Christiane Valcourt

photographer
André Panneton

client
Manager Jeans

agency
TAXI / Toronto

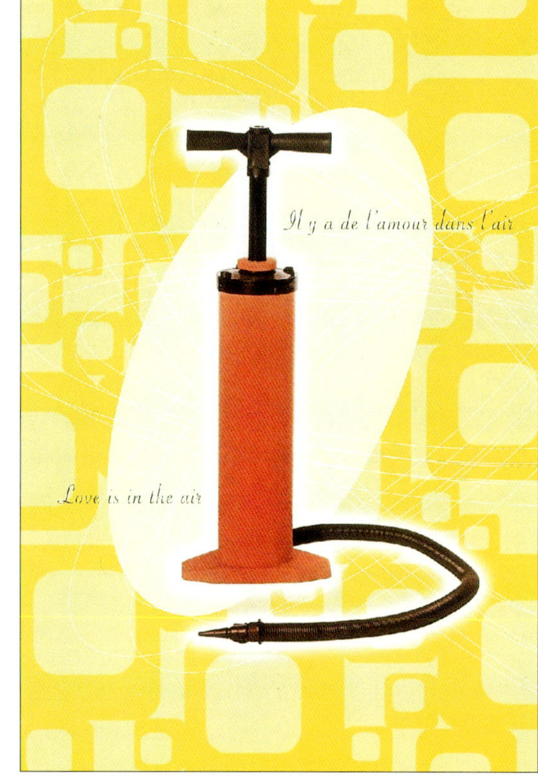

art director
Steve Lageson

writer
Lane Strauss

client
Ric Alberico

agency
Wyse Advertising/
Cleveland

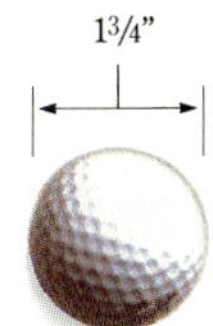

In theory, this should be easy.

COLLATERAL
SELF-PROMOTION

art director
Rob Rich

writer
Steve Bautista

client
Ingalls Advertising

agency
Ingalls Advertising/
Boston

There are few things in life the average person loves to hate more than advertising. It's not only because the vast majority of ads talk down to people. Or at people. Or fail to engage them with a single, coherent thought or emotion.

It's that even the best ads are essentially intrusions by somebody who wants to sell you something. With annoying frequency, ads interrupt your favorite television shows, your radio programs, your magazines and newspapers. Worst of all, ads invade your leisure time.

Yet given all this, there are a select few advertisements which cut through, appealing to consumers with humor, intelligence, charm and emotion. Yes, there are ads people actually like. Chances are, you like them too.

Why? Because good ads are like good people. They're smart, funny and engaging. You tend to remember them long after they're gone. That's reality.

It's also one of the seven principles of a process we call Reality-Based Advertising. A principle which proposes this to advertisers: Don't even think about getting into consumers' wallets unless you first get into their lives.

Reality-Based Advertising doesn't promote who you think you want to be. We find out who consumers will let you become. Then we apply those findings to the most important part of any communications plan, the ad itself. To involve people emotionally and credibly so that your product becomes a bigger part of their lives.

If you'd like to learn more about Reality-Based Advertising, talk to Steve Connelly, president, at 617-295-7985. We think you'd approve of the result.

Ingalls Advertising.

**COLLATERAL
SELF-PROMOTION**

art director
Ding Yew Moong

writer
Curt Detweiler

photographer
Shooting Gallery

illustrator
Wishing Well

client
Leo Burnett
Creative Workshop

agency
Leo Burnett / Singapore

art director
Paul Keister

writer
Andy Carrigan

illustrator
Bob Clinton

client
Leonard / Monahan

agency
Leonard / Monahan,
Providence

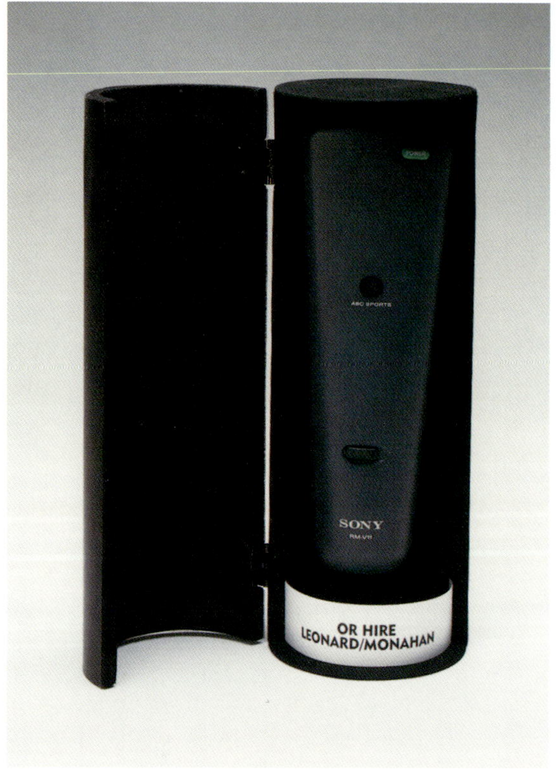

PRINT FINALISTS

art director
Jonathan Mackler

writer
Joe Alexander

illustrator
Donnie Garland

client
The Martin Agency

agency
The Martin Agency/
Richmond

art directors
Alan Jarvie
Steve Hough

writer
Steve Hough

illustrator
Harry Harrison

client
M&C Saatchi

agency
M&C Saatchi/
Hong Kong

**COLLATERAL
SELF-PROMOTION**

art director
Scott Wadler

writer
Ken Saji

designer
Todd Barthelman

photographer
Mark Malabrigo

client
Comedy Central

agency
MTV Networks-
Creative Services/
New York

art director
Wade Devers

writer
Mark Nardi

client
Pagano Schenck & Kay

agency
Pagano Schenck & Kay/
Boston

art directors
Tom Simons
Nancy Bond Carle

writer
Jeff Billig

client
PARTNERS & Simons

agency
PARTNERS & Simons/
Boston

How long can an ad agency go on with no contracts, no departments and no vice presidents?

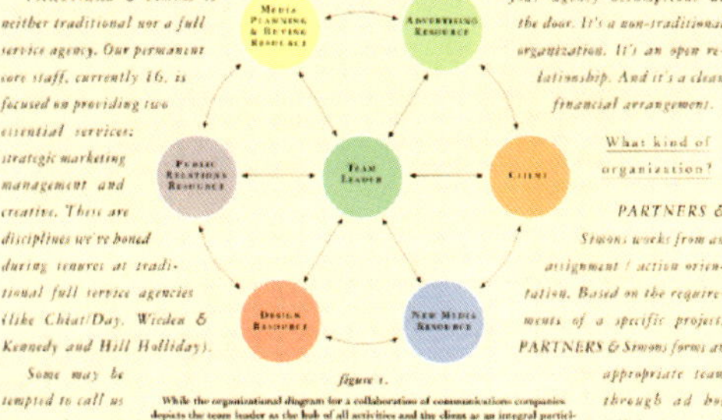

Longer than you might have expected.

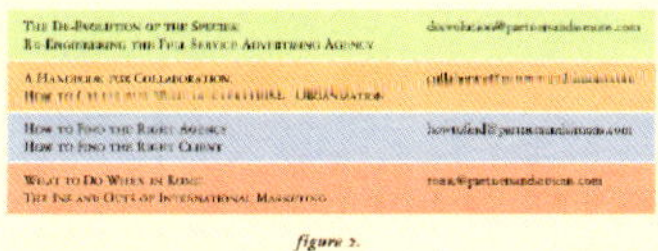

**COLLATERAL
SELF-PROMOTION**

art director
Brian De Los Santos

writer
Ray Longoria

client
SicolaMartin

agency
SicolaMartin / Austin

PRINT FINALISTS

art directors
Jerome Marucci
Michael Herlehy

writers
Michael Herlehy
Jerome Marucci

client
Jerome Marucci

agency
Sledgehammer/
Chicago

art directors
Jerome Marucci
Michael Herlehy

writers
Michael Herlehy
Jerome Marucci

client
Michael Herlehy

agency
Sledgehammer/
Chicago

**COLLATERAL
SELF-PROMOTION**

art director
Beth Ricciardi

writer
Jonathan Schoenberg

photographer
Brooks Freehill

client
TDA
Advertising & Design

agency
TDA Advertising &
Design /Longmont, CO

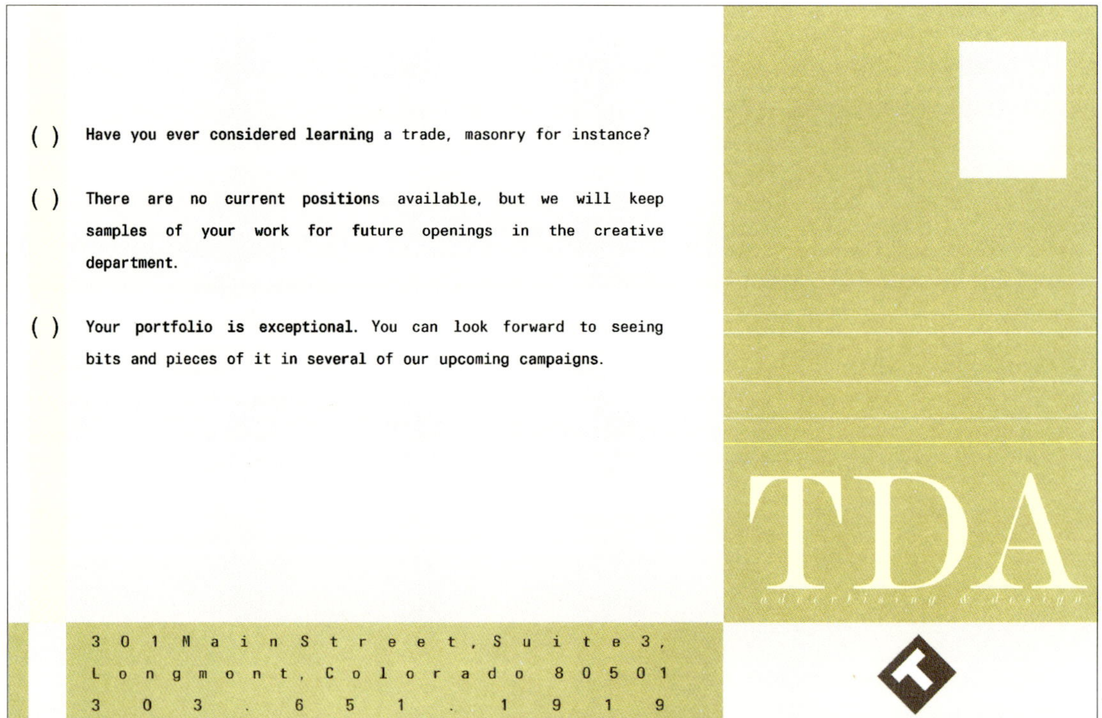

WHY BELOW-THE-LINE CREATIVES ARE THE COLOURLESS, EMBITTERED, AESTHETICALLY-IMPAIRED PEOPLE THEY ARE.

Advertising creatives become advertising creatives because, for now at least, no-one in Hollywood is interested in developing their 10 page blockbuster treatment.

In turn, direct marketing creatives remain direct marketing creatives because no-one in adland is interested in buying the 300 dog-eared mailpacks jostling around in grubby plastic sleeves that masquerade as their portfolio.

The real difference being that one day that same advertising creative may find himself successfully pitching that same blockbuster treatment to a notoriously notorious features director who's agreed to break the habit of a lifetime (again) and lower himself to shoot their 15 second dog food commercial.

The direct marketing creative person, on the other hand, has no hope of ever escaping their confinement in "DL Hell". Once branded a junk mail hack, always a junk mail hack.

Serendipity or no serendipity.

Oh well, that's just the way the low-fat, vitamin-enriched cookie crumbles.

Problem is, your average below-the-line creative (forgive the obvious oxymoron) is far from happy to accept their lot like a man. Or a woman, as a lot of them tend to be.

As a result, they invariably sport a chip on their collective shoulders the size of a chip so ridiculously large, there's no room left on the plate for any fish.

Evidence of this can be witnessed on the painfully tense occasions that the hapless client (rightly outraged at the fact their product's own brand personality, corporate guidelines and even logo design tend to fluctuate wildly depending on whether they're on a print ad or a mail pack) has taken the extreme action of asking that the above-the-line and below-the-line creatives meet in an effort to affect some modicum of conformity.

Naturally, the resulting atmosphere in the room can best be described as "a tad nippy".

The below-the-line creatives, whilst secretly envying their counterparts' ability to effortlessly co-ordinate their designer wardrobes (black, black and black, dramatically juxtaposed with a very, very, dark slate grey), withdraw to the relative snuggliness of their duffle coats.

Meanwhile, across the meeting room, the above-the-line team makes no secret of their disgust with their agency's account director for dragging them away from a perfectly billable seven hour lunch after only six and a half hours, and vehemently focus on a tiny, seemingly invisible spot on the ceiling.

Several grunts and nods later, the two teams are at last mercifully dispatched to their respective corners, now armed with the clear proviso that "we'll definitely get these guys together for an integrated brainstorm soon".

And the even clearer understanding that they will never ever see each other again.

WELLS NOBAY McDOWALL TELEPHONE 03 9349 2700

WHY ABOVE-THE-LINE CREATIVES ARE THE NARCISSISTIC, LACKADAISICAL, VAINGLORIOUS PEOPLE THEY ARE.

Quiz your average above-the-line creative team on the true meaning of accountability in advertising and she (or he, as they so often tend to be) will probably suspect you are referring to which one of them swiped the talent's $5,000 watch at last week's shoot.

Fact is, given the emphasis that advertising creatives put on upping the product's sales curve, most clients could regard themselves as the world's most generous philanthropists.

(And, as such, their respective budgets valid for massive tax rebates.)

Not that you can blame the creatives for this minor lapse of judgement.

After all, yucky things like response rates and sales figures are surely the domain of that odious tribe of suspected trainspotters that dwell in what previously used to be the building's broom cupboard down in the basement.

The very same geeks that now exist under the guise of the agency's shiny new, strategically formed, fully-integrated, direct marketing arm.

Which happily leaves their more genetically blessed counterparts, up above ground, free to focus on the real issues.

Namely, how they can get their names between the covers of the ancient sacred tomes of D&AD, One Show and AWARD.

This, of course, is no mean feat and requires all the guile and ingenuity of a maximum security prisoner planning to break free from a maximum security prison using only a tube of toothpaste, naval fluff, a safety pin and a pet mouse called Rex.

All the more so when handicapped by the drudgery of a clear brief, an air-tight strategy, well-established brand and, heaven forbid, the most terrifying word in advertising next to "timesheet" … research.

In the face of these seemingly insurmountable obstacles, many brave but beleaguered above-the-line creatives have sought their salvation by heroing the plight of worthy non-profit making groups. As yet, criminally underfunded, yet essential organisations, like "Rights for Gay Whales", who in turn reward the agency's altruism by not tampering with the "creative process". Indeed, in many cases, being unaware of the creative process altogether.

Like plankton, these miniscule (in many cases, non-existent) clients form a vital link in the above-the-line agency's food chain.

First off, the media frenzy caused by the creative team's resounding success with the overseas awards jury over in the sunny south of France, sends a ripple through the industry.

In turn, it attracts the much sought after corporate big fish, happily deluded that they need an agency that can do this calibre of gutsy, no-holds barred, breakthrough creative. (And yet secretly reassured that the resulting million dollar campaign will look strikingly similar to the bland globaltrash they've been demanding from their agencies for decades.)

A reservation is hastily made at Mario's. And so the circle is once again complete.

WELLS NOBAY McDOWALL TELEPHONE 03 9349 2700

Walker & Associates, Inc.
MEMPHIS · LITTLE ROCK

Dear _________,

I'm the creative director of an ad agency in Memphis. A few weeks ago, I got some very disheartening news. Alan Wolstencroft, a sharp copywriter who I had one day expected to turn my reins over to, broke it to me that he was leaving.

I tried offering Alan more money. But he said this business wasn't about big salaries. It was about doing inspired work. And, besides, his wife would be getting a big salary at her new job in Atlanta.

I'm writing this letter because I'd like to recommend that you meet Alan and take a look at his portfolio. In fact, I encourage you to call him right now at (770) 321-9804. You won't regret it.

The guy is self-confident, has a natural ability for outstanding creative, and is a real self-motivator. In fact, Alan will do whatever it takes to get the job done. Even if that means writing his own recommendation letter and forging my signature at the bottom.

Sincerely,

Joe Pizzirusso
Creative Director

1100 Morgan Keegan Tower, 50 North Front Street, Memphis, TN 38103; 901-522-1100

COLLATERAL POSTERS

art director
George Capuano

writer
Rob Jamieson

client
United Parcel Service

agency
Ammirati Puris
Lintas / New York

art director
Becky Hickey

writer
Amy Johnson

photographer
Carol Kaplan

client
Volkswagen

agency
Arnold Advertising /
Boston

PRINT FINALISTS

art director
Jimmy Ashworth

writer
Joan Shealy

photographer
Mike Furman

client
Lamborghini

agency
The Arnold Agency/
Richmond

art director
Jimmy Ashworth

writer
Joan Shealy

photographer
Mike Furman

client
Lamborghini

agency
The Arnold Agency/
Richmond

**COLLATERAL
POSTERS**

art director
Paul Safsel

writer
Amy Krouse Rosenthal

photographer
Fred Sons

client
Law Offices of
Jason B. Rosenthal

agency
Boy & Girl
Advertising/Chicago

art director
David Ayriss

writer
Mark Waggoner

photographer
Torey Piro

client
24/7 Snowboards

agency
Cole & Weber/
Portland

PRINT FINALISTS

art director
Eric Tilford

writer
Wade Paschall

photographer
Herman Leonard

client
WSIE The Jazz Station

agency
CORE/St. Louis

art director
Mike Fetrow

writer
Mike Gibbs

photographers
Mike Kreiter
Harold Edgerton

client
Hed. Cycling Products

agency
Fallon McElligott/
Minneapolis

**COLLATERAL
POSTERS**

art director
Don Miller

writer
Rob Strasberg

photographer
Vic Huber

client
Land Rover
North America

agency
Grace & Rothschild/
New York

art director
Steve Mitchell

writer
Doug Adkins

photographer
Joe Lampi

client
Domtar Paper

agency
Hunt Adkins/
Minneapolis

PRINT FINALISTS

art director
John Stapleton

writers
Scott Noble
Scott Scheinberg

client
Stan's Record Bar

agency
James Bunting
Advertising/
Lancaster, PA

art director
Mark Wennecker

writer
Jeff Ross

photographers
Dan Escobar
Smith/Nelson

client
Mercedes-Benz of
North America

agency
The Martin Agency/
Richmond

**COLLATERAL
POSTERS**

art director
Tony Bennett

writer
Jeff Ross

photographer
Karl Steinbrenner

client
One More Bar & Grill

agency
The Martin Agency/
Richmond

art director
Paul Foulkes

writer
Tyler Hampton

client
Alpine Meadows

agency
Odiorne Wilde
Narraway Groome/
San Francisco

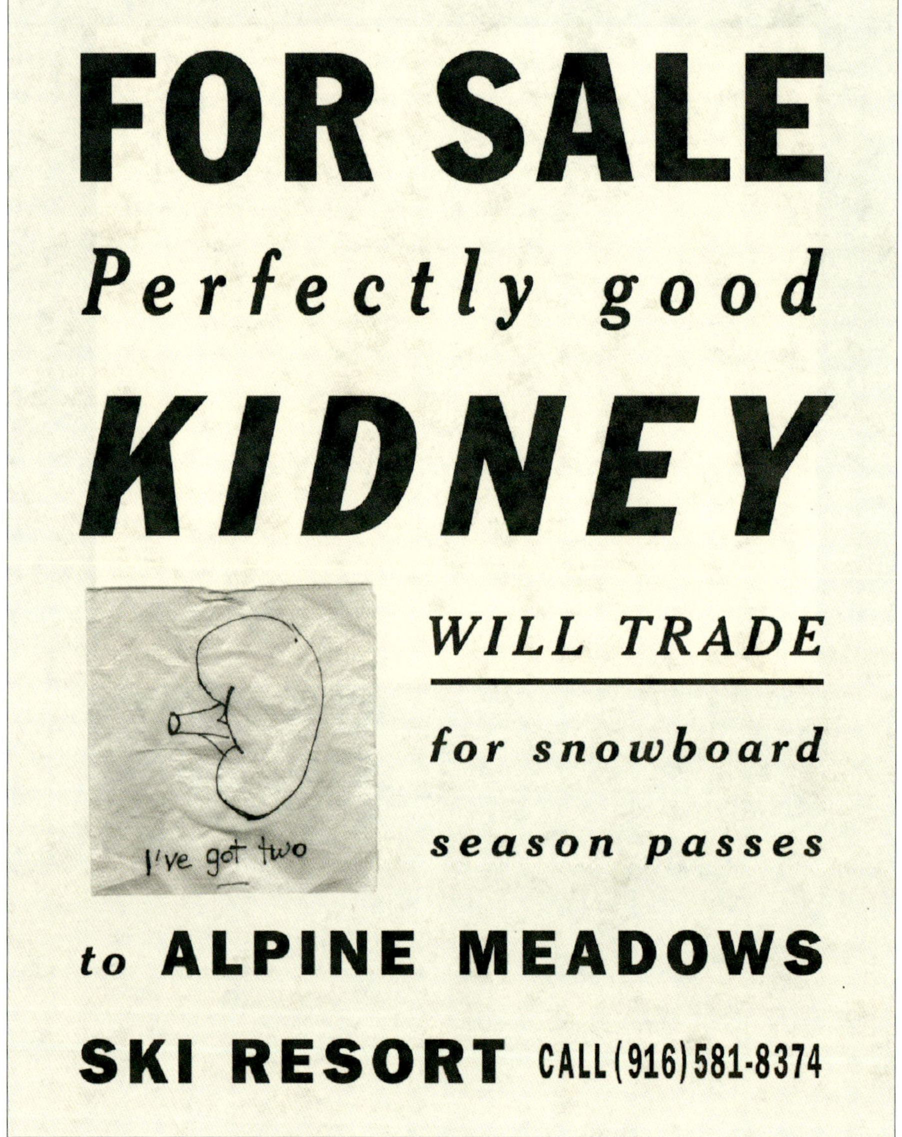

art director
Matt Johanning

writer
Dan Kan

illustrator
Matt Johanning

client
Art Directors/
Copywriters Club

agency
Sietsema Engel and
Partners/Minneapolis

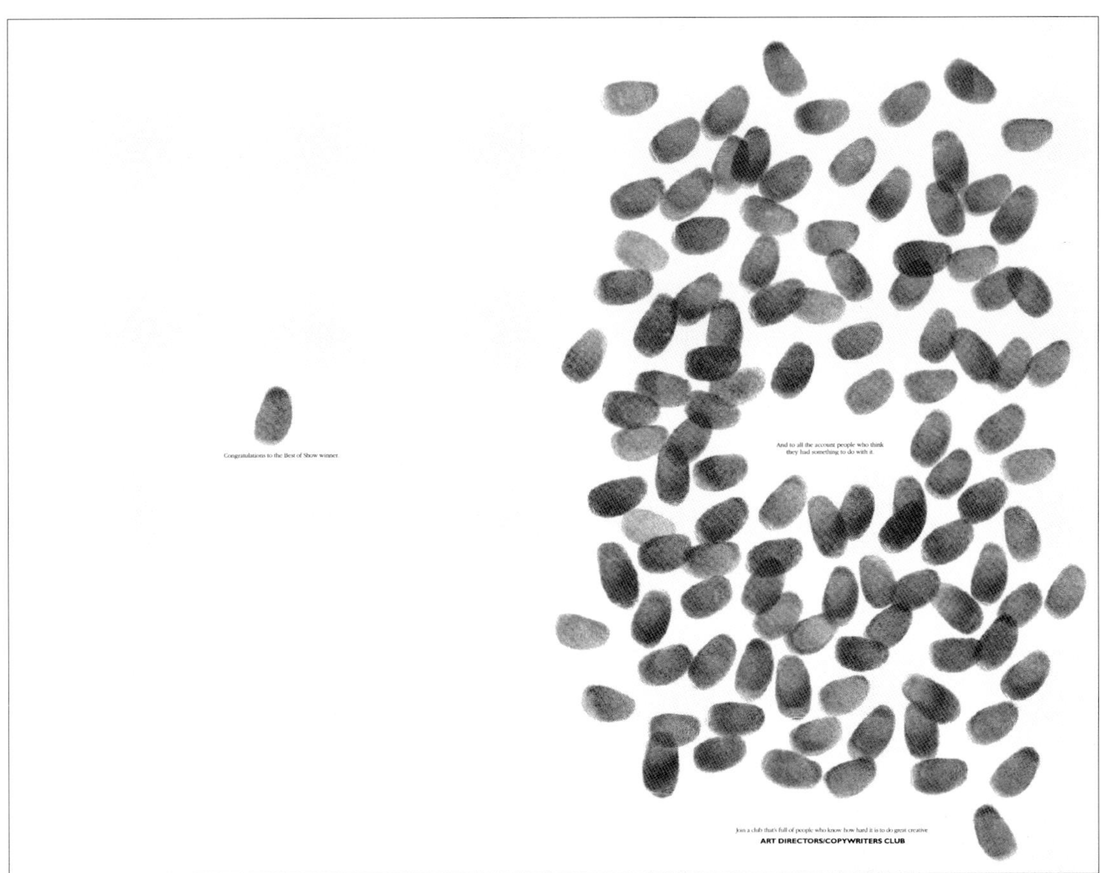

You are graciously
REMINDED
that this book
BELONGS TO:

....

Please purchase your
OWN COPY
from any fine
BOOKSELLER

**NEWSPAPER
OR MAGAZINE:
SINGLE**

art director
Paul Briginshaw

writer
Malcolm Duffy

photographer
Thierry Gassmann

client
British Red Cross

agency
Abbott Mead
Vickers.BBDO/London

art director
Damon Collins

writer
Mary Wear

client
RSPCA

agency
Abbott Mead
Vickers.BBDO/London

Today the growth industry in Cambodia isn't fashion. It's prosthetics.

The country has around 20,000 amputees from a population of just 8.5 million. This means one amputee for every 236 people (compared to a figure of one for every 22,000 people in America).

So why is the situation in Cambodia so bad?

The country has suffered from civil unrest for many years. But the real villain of the piece isn't so much the war, as the weapons.

Cambodia is literally being crippled by landmines.

They are an incredibly cheap form of warfare (costing as little as 3 US dollars each). So to seize some tactical advantage combatants think nothing of deploying scores of these weapons.

In a single 1km stretch of road in Cambodia 6,000 landmines were found.

They are also deployed with scant regard for the indigenous population.

It is the men, women and children out working the fields who are most likely to fall victim to these hidden killers.

And in an agricultural society where muscle power means survival, the loss of a limb can have repercussions far beyond the physical disability.

Take just one of Cambodia's victims. Chhea Veou was 19 when she lost a leg walking to harvest rice in a paddy.

"I cannot earn money because no-one will employ me. I wanted to have children. But no-one will marry me because I don't have a leg."

And so she must follow the dangerous paths into the rice fields at harvest time. She shrugs. "What else can I do?"

It's because of Chhea, and thousands like her, that the Red Cross is urgently seeking your help. The carnage must end.

To: British Red Cross, Room 592, Freepost, London SW1 7BR.
I want to know more about the effects of landmines and what I can do to help. Please send me your information pack.
Mr/Mrs/Miss/Ms _______________
Address _______________
____
Postcode _______________ Tel. _______________

British Red Cross
Caring for people in crisis
A Registered Charity

LANDMINES MUST BE STOPPED

They don't feed them. They don't water them. They don't brush them.

They don't de-louse them. They don't de-flea them.

They don't bath them. They don't worm them.

They don't walk them. They don't take them to the vet.

They don't train them. They don't innoculate them. They don't spay them. They don't neuter them.

They don't groom them. They don't comb them. They don't clip their nails. They don't play with them.

They don't exercise them. They don't de-tangle their fur. They don't clean their paws. They don't supervise them.

They don't buy them leads. They don't buy them collars. They don't buy them baskets.

They don't buy them treats. They don't buy them food. They don't buy them feeding bowls.

They don't reward them. They don't provide them with a balanced diet. They don't control them. They don't check the state of their health.

They don't provide any bedding. They don't change their bedding.

They don't check their teeth. They don't clean their teeth. They don't pay them any attention.

They don't care for them.

They don't house-train them. They don't clip their coat.

They don't get insurance for them. They don't stroke them.

They don't clean up their urine. They don't clean up their faeces. They don't clean up their vomit.

They don't clean their ears. They don't clean their eyes. They don't buy them toys.

They don't detect injuries. They don't detect disease.

They don't treat injuries. They don't treat disease.

They don't provide any shelter for them.

They don't provide any warmth for them.

If you're not prepared to do all of the above, please don't do one more thing: don't give a home to a pet. **RSPCA** **Neglect is cruelty.**

PUBLIC SERVICE &
POLITICAL FINALISTS

art director
Damon Collins

writer
Mary Wear

client
RSPCA

agency
Abbott Mead Vickers.
BBDO/London

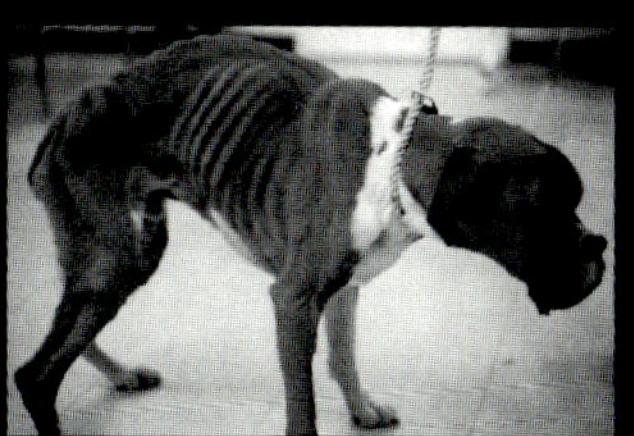

art director
Robert Hamilton

writer
Josh Caplan

photographer
Michael Indresano

client
United Way

agency
Arnold Advertising/
Boston

**NEWSPAPER
OR MAGAZINE:
SINGLE**

art director
Simon McQuoid

writer
Jerry Fury

photographer
Hugh Hartshorne

client
United Hospital

agency
Clarity Coverdale
Fury/Minneapolis

MAKE GOOD
COMMUNICATION
PART OF YOUR
FAMILY'S LIFE.

Most parents would agree that the older your kids get the more you understand them.

Then they get to be teenagers and you hardly understand them at all.

But when you and your teenager answer these questions independently and then talk about the results, you'll get a good perspective on how you see yourselves, how you spend your time, and what you value.

We think that by talking and strengthening communication, everyone in your family will better understand each other. And ultimately, feel better about themselves. The average teenager has 17 of these 30 characteristics. However, research indicates that the more of these attributes they have the less likely they are to be at risk towards delinquent behavior.

How many of these assets apply to your teen at home?

( ) Parents are loving, easy to talk to and available when teens want to talk.
( ) Parents frequently take time to talk seriously with their children.
( ) Parents express their own standards for teenage behavior.
( ) Parents talk with their teenager about school and sometimes help with school work and attend school events.
( ) Parents set rules and enforce the consequences when the rules are broken.
( ) Parents check on where their teenager is going, with whom and for how long.
( ) Parents are approachable when the teenager has something serious to talk about.
( ) The number of nights the teenager may spend out of the home "for fun and recreation" is limited.
( ) The teenager has three or more adults, in addition to parents, to whom he or she could go to for help.
( ) The teenager has frequent serious conversations with an adult who is not his or her own parent.
( ) The teenager's friends are a constructive influence, are doing well at school, are staying away from contact with drugs, alcohol and other at-risk behavior.
( ) The teenager attends church or synagogue at least once a month.
( ) The teenager sees the school atmosphere as caring and encouraging.
( ) The teenager participates in band, orchestra, or takes lessons on a musical instrument involving three or more hours of practice a week.
( ) The teenager participates in school sports activities or other organizations three or more hours per week.
( ) The teenager participates in non-school-sponsored sports or other organizations three or more hours per week.

How many of these assets are present in your teen's life?

( ) Tries to do his or her best at school.
( ) Hopes to be educated beyond high school.
( ) Earns above-average school grades.
( ) Does six or more hours of homework weekly.
( ) Is good at making friends.
( ) Tries to stand up for her or his beliefs.
( ) Cares about others' feelings.
( ) Is good at planning ahead.
( ) Is good at making decisions.
( ) Has a positive attitude toward self.
( ) Envisions a happy future for her/himself.
( ) Shows concern for the poor.
( ) Is interested in helping and improving life for others.
( ) Holds values that prohibit having sex as a teenager.

This community service message is sponsored by The Grand Forks Public Schools and United Hospital.

art director
Craig Ford

writer
Bruce Paroissien

typographer
Libby Austen

client
Mercy Hospital
For Women

agency
Clemenger Harvie/
Melbourne

**THIS NOTICE ALMOST
APPEARED IN
THE DEATHS COLUMN.**

THANKFULLY the Mercy Hospital for Women helped a sick baby survive. But now we need your help. Please give to the Small Mercies Appeal at any National Bank.

PUBLIC SERVICE &
POLITICAL FINALISTS

art director
Simon Winterflood

writer
Connan James

photographer
Francois Maritz

client
New Zealand
Police Association

agency
DDB Needham/
Auckland

Suburban Dallas, TX.
15-yr.-old female.
Killed by 10-yr.-old
brother with gun
found in parents'
room. Boy thought
gun was unloaded,
tried to scare sister
as she talked on phone.

A gun in the home triples the risk of
a homicide in the home.

CEASE FIRE

Think about your family before you think about getting a handgun.

art director
Bob Barrie

writer
Phil Calvit

photographer
Rick Dublin

client
Cease Fire

agency
Fallon McElligott/
Minneapolis

**NEWSPAPER
OR MAGAZINE:
SINGLE**

art director
Scott McAfee

writer
Brian Brooker

illustrators
CSA Archive
Dover Archive

client
Gilbert & Sullivan
Society of Austin

agency
GSD&M Advertising/
Austin

art director
Kelly Dekin

writer
Joe Perry

illustrator
Tom Hennessey

client
California Nature
Conservancy

agency
Hal Riney & Partners/
San Francisco

PUBLIC SERVICE &
POLITICAL FINALISTS

art director
Graham Lang

writers
Sanjai Mistry
Graham Lang

photographer
Mike Carelse

client
The Cape Argus

agency
The Jupiter Drawing
Room/Cape Town

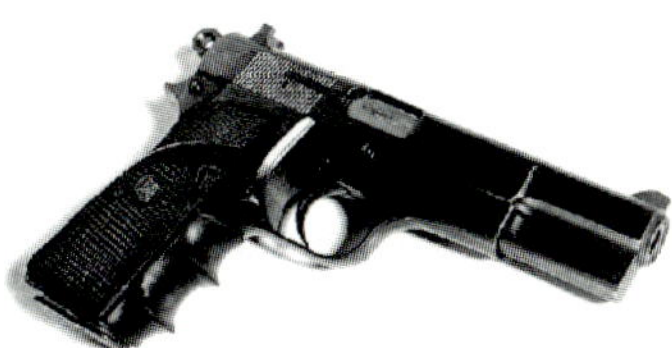

DURABILITY, not beauty, was the main requirement in the construction of *Walmer Castle*. However, the architects, not wishing to take any chances with the notoriously hard to please Henry VIII, wisely decided to address both issues. One of a chain of coastal artillery forts, Walmer was built to thwart any invasions by Spain or France. This was a real possibility as Henry's split with the Roman Catholic Church and destruction of many monasteries had infuriated the papacy. The castle differed from earlier mediæval defences in that it had no high walls or lofty towers. In fact, so *attractive* was Walmer that only minor modifications were needed to make it the comfortable residence it is today. For more information on English Heritage and our role in preserving the nation's significant buildings please *call* 0171 973 3434 or *visit* any one of our 400 sites.

ENGLISH HERITAGE

art director
Dave Dye

writer
Sean Doyle

typographer
Dave Wakefield

client
English Heritage

agency
Leagas Delaney/
London

**NEWSPAPER
OR MAGAZINE:
SINGLE**

art director
Jimmy Olson

writer
Dave Loew

photographer
David Emmite

client
NORML

agency
MAU! Advertising/
Chicago

art director
Blaine Kennedy

writers
Ron Wohlman
Trent Burton

client
World Wildlife Fund

agency
Ogilvy & Mather/
Toronto

Even Drug Czar General Barry McCaffrey doesn't buy the argument that marijuana is a "gateway drug" that "leads to harder things." In a speech to the National Press Club, General McCaffrey stated that only a tiny percentage of the 90 million Americans who experiment with illegal drugs become addicts. He also said that the "overwhelming majority" of Americans who try illegal drugs simply "walk away and say it's not for me."

The Drug Czar was acknowledging what we at the National Organization for the Reform of Marijuana Laws, NORML, already knew. The vast majority of people who have smoked pot (i.e., Bill Clinton, Newt Gingrich, Al Gore) do not move on to harder drugs or run into drug-related problems later in life. So why does our government spend $7 billion a year to arrest and jail people for this relatively harmless activity?

Like Alcohol Prohibition of the 1930's, Marijuana Prohibition is a failure. It has ruined productive lives, wasted criminal justice resources that could have been used to fight violent crime, and clogged up court and prison systems. It's time to admit that arresting otherwise law-abiding citizens who happen to smoke marijuana serves no legitimate societal purpose.

By joining NORML with your donation of $25 or more, you can help change our country's marijuana laws. Write us today at 1001 Connecticut Avenue NW, Suite 1010, Washington, DC 20036, and we'll send you a bi-monthly newsletter. Or call the NORML Support Line at 1-900-97-NORML. For $2.95 a minute, 18 or older, you'll receive info on drug testing, marijuana penalties in your state, and your legal rights.

In Holland, where marijuana is decriminalized and sold in government regulated "coffee shops," their crime and hard drug usage rates are much lower than here in the United States. Which shows that you can always learn something, even without going to graduate school. **NORML.**

art director
Hal Curtis

writer
Mark Nardi

client
Battleship Cove

agency
Pagano Schenck &
Kay / Boston

WE'VE NEVER DISAPPOINTED A VISITOR.

(EXCEPT FOR THOSE TWO KAMIKAZES BACK IN '44.)

If we didn't turn away some people, we might not be here today. But thanks to a fearless crew which manned some of the most powerful anti-aircraft weapons ever, the U.S.S. Massachusetts was able to proudly sail home and await your visit today. It's just one of the ships you'll find at Battleship Cove, where you step back over 50 years with the vessels that protected the United States in World War II.

Commissioned in 1942, the battleship U.S.S. Massachusetts steamed more than 225,000 miles throughout the Atlantic and Pacific Oceans. She participated in major operations in places like Okinawa, Casablanca, The New Hebrides Islands, The Marshall Islands, and the Philippines. Known back then as a "fast battleship," the Massachusetts and ships like her were in demand not only because of their speed but because of their devastating array of weapons. Today, you can come aboard and walk among this powerful armament. Feel the 16-inch armor, which protected the Massachusetts through 35 engagements. Stand in the shadow of her massive 16-inch guns, which bombarded enemy shore positions and sank enemy vessels. And sit among the ferocious anti-aircraft guns, which kept 18 enemy aircraft from completing their mission to destroy the ship.

Berthed alongside the Massachusetts are several World War II Navy ships which you can explore as well. The destroyer U.S.S. Joseph P. Kennedy, Jr., the submarine U.S.S. Lionfish and PT boats 617 and 796 await your visit, offering a further glimpse into naval history and what it meant to this country. The United States Department of the Interior has honored the national significance of all five ships at Battleship Cove by recently designating them as "National Historic Landmarks."

Battleship Cove is open every day, 9:00 to 5:00 pm. Admission is $8.00 for adults and $4.00 for children 6–14. Group rates, overnight youth camping and banquet facilities are available. For information or directions, please call 1-508-678-1100 or 1-800-533-3194. What's more, please ask us for information on how you may join the Friends of Battleship Cove.

U.S.S. MASSACHUSETTS AT BATTLESHIP COVE

**NEWSPAPER
OR MAGAZINE:
SINGLE**

art director
Craig Farndale

writer
Connan James

client
RSPCA

agency
Young & Rubicam /
Auckland

PUBLIC SERVICE &
POLITICAL FINALISTS

NEWSPAPER
OR MAGAZINE:
CAMPAIGN

art director
Robert Hamilton

writer
Josh Caplan

photographer
Michael Indresano

client
United Way

agency
Arnold Advertising /
Boston

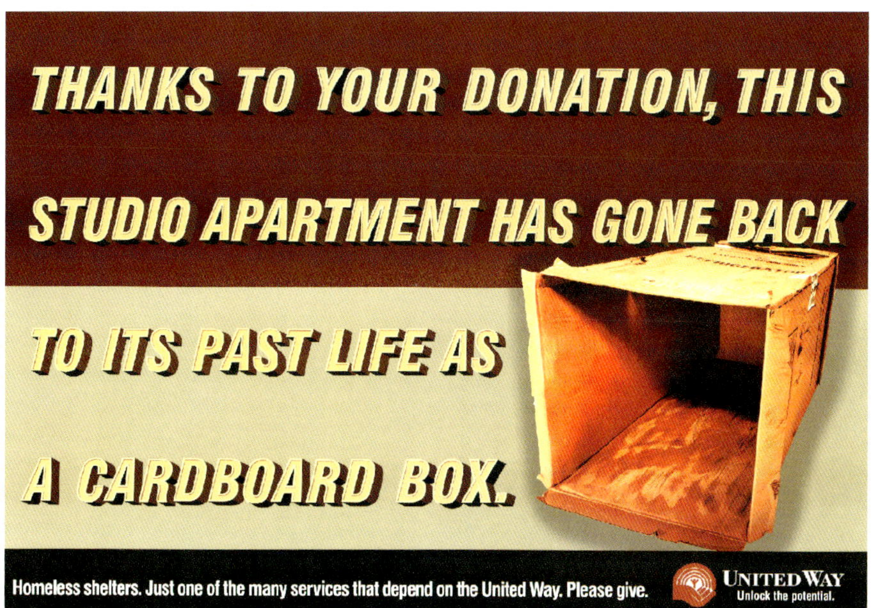

NEWSPAPER
OR MAGAZINE:
CAMPAIGN

art directors
Andrew Clarke
Scott Lambert

writers
Antony Redman
Mark Ringer

photographer
Simon Taplin

client
Asian Pals
of the Planet

agency
Batey Ads/Singapore

READ ON TO FIND OUT WHAT JAPANESE WOMEN DO IN THE TOILET.

A polite Japanese lady will cover her mouth when she giggles.

She will bow her head to hide her eyes when embarrassed.

One could only imagine the crisis this creature faces inside the ladies' room.

She enters the cubicle, closes the door, pulls the latch and sits. Soon, the crowded washroom reverberates with the sound of her urine splashing into the water at the bottom of the toilet bowl.

An unavoidable nuisance of modern life you may say. A source of deep humiliation if you happen to be a Japanese woman.

Her solution for years has been to conceal the noise. Not by a well-timed cough.

But by flushing the toilet whilst relieving herself. The familiar commotion created by the gurgling cistern drowns out her business.

Depending on the length of her stay, the toilet may be flushed up to three or four times.

And she may walk out quietly, without anyone knowing of the noise she has made.

Her face saved.

Unfortunately, the water is not. With each flush, 10 litres of water disappears into the sewerage. That's 30 litres a visit. And over 100 litres daily.

Now multiply that by the number of women in all of Japan.

A self-conscious avoidance of shame results in a shameful loss of pure drinking water.

And water is now one of the most precious commodities in the East.

Over 70% of India's water supplies are contaminated. In New Delhi, the Yzmuna River is deluged with 50 million gallons of untreated sewerage, 5 million gallons of industrial effluent and 125 thousand gallons of DDT. Not in a year. But each hopeless day.

The mighty Ganges swallows the raw human waste of no less than 114 crowded cities.

Shanghai spends millions piping clean water to its vast urban sprawl from over 900 miles away.

So too does Singapore and Bangkok. The Philippines and Indonesia inexplicably lose over one third of all water pumped to their thirsty cities.

Saudi Arabia's supply will be exhausted early next century. The next war in the Middle East won't be over crude black oil, but crystal clear water.

India and Pakistan are almost certain to find themselves in a similar position as they attempt to resolve the competition for the thick murk that flows through the Hindus River basin.

Hong Kong has the pleasure of possessing more Rolls Royce automobiles per capita than any other country. Yet you risk your life by drinking from the tap there.

Ironic then, that the source of life brings death. Bubbling with disease, fouled water robs the lives of 25 thousand Asians daily. 10 million a year.

The majority of them small children too frail to fight.

The World Bank estimates it will cost at least $128 billion in the next 10 years to simply meet the basic drinking and sanitation needs of Asia.

An amount almost beyond comprehension.

The crisis is real. It will not go away.

It calls for us all to re-evaluate how we use the clean water that is available.

And for the more ingenious ones amongst us to find solutions.

In Japan, electronic gadgets are now installed in the ladies' rooms. Attached to these gadgets are speakers. They emulate the sound of a flushing toilet.

Now there is no need for the timid women to flush any more than is necessary.

The Fuji Bank has installed this system and already reports a $70,000 saving on water bills each year.

How can you begin to change things? The battle begins in your home.

Everytime you turn on a tap, look at that stream. You wouldn't last three days without it.

More than food, or love, or wealth, you need water to survive.

(TREAT WATER WITH RESPECT)

IT COULD START WORLD WAR III

In the Middle East, ancient underground water reserves are exploited as irresponsibly as oil. They have taken 30,000 years to fill. In under 30 years, they will be empty.

Nine of the fourteen Middle Eastern countries already face water-scarce conditions.

Turkey, Syria, Iran and Iraq all rely heavily upon just one life-giving river, the Euphretes.

Perhaps we expect this dilemma in the Middle East. It's dry and hot. Their water problems hardly seem relevant to Asia.

Not so. Science suggests the contrary.

Singapore, for example, is desperately more water-scarce than Syria, Yemen or Israel. Alarmingly, many arid African nations weigh in with considerably more water per person than Singapore.

A critical shortage of clean drinking water, regrettably, is not solely the burden of tropical Singapore.

To the north, the precious resource of the Mekong River is shared by China, Myanmar, Laos, Thailand, Cambodia and Vietnam.

To the north-west, India, Bangladesh and Pakistan bicker over common fresh water supplies.

All have nuclear capability.

When one considers these facts, it's by no means ludicrous to suggest that in time, water could become the most precious commodity on earth.

A commodity well worth fighting for.

The fragility of the situation must not be misunderstood. If we don't precipitate change there's every chance the situation could deteriorate into a life and death matter.

Interestingly, you have in your very hands the power to help avert war.

Simply by not leaving the tap running while brushing your teeth. Washing the car a little less often. Replacing washers in dripping taps. Sweeping rather than hosing the pavement and showering smartly by turning off the tap while shampooing.

They're little things and not terribly difficult. But when multiplied across days, weeks, months and then millions of people, the water savings are enormous. As are the benefits.

For one, you may not have to go to war over water.

(TREAT WATER WITH RESPECT)

WATER BURNED THIS FOREST DOWN

This is north Kazakhstan, just a short distance from China and Mongolia. This withered, pathetic collection of sticks was once a luxurious, thriving fir forest.

Now it has been burned beyond repair.

Despite that, you won't see glowing embers or lazy columns of smoke rising, because fire was not the instrument of this vulgar destruction.

It was rain. Acid rain.

Water tumbling from the heavens corrupted with sulphur dioxide. Sulphur dioxide is the by-product of coal combustion and metal smelting industries.

It's a nasty cycle.

Industry spews pollutants into the air. Moisture traps the pollutants. The moisture, when heavy, returns to earth laden with chemicals, cutting a holocaustic swathe of environmental ruin wherever it falls (the soil for example, will take 400 years to cleanse itself). While the substantial run-off flows directly into lakes and rivers of the region.

Critically, even air pollution affects our drinking water.

This sickening occurence regularly befalls 12 major locations across the north of our continent. Totalling a land mass area greater than that of Malaysia, Thailand and Singapore combined.

Acidification isn't solely the problem of north Asia, however. In the south west of China, for instance, it has already reached menacing levels.

Distressingly, acid rain is just one of dozens of contributors to Asia's dire water pollution predicament.

A predicament now claiming a staggering 25,000 lives everyday. 25,000 people like you and I dying from consuming water riddled with human and industrial waste.

Contaminants such as HCH, DDT, lead, radioactive waste, dieldrin, aldrin, arsenic, raw effluent, hepatitis, typhoid and cholera. The list is as long as it is nauseating.

It may seem hopeless, indeed some situations are out of our hands.

Fortunately there is something we can do to help, it's called conserving.

We urge you to do everything in your power to conserve the clean water we have.

Heaven knows, if we take good care of water, it will return the favour.

(TREAT WATER WITH RESPECT)

EVERY FEW DAYS, IT CREATES A GREATER DISASTER THAN THE EXXON VALDEZ

March 24, 1989. The Exxon Valdez runs aground on Bligh Reef in Prince William Sound, Alaska. Eleven million gallons of crude oil are spilled.

But that is just a drop in the ocean when compared to the environmental crimes committed by everyday Asians, everyday.

Conservative estimates calculate that in the next three days we will tip enough oil down the drains of our homes, hawker centres and restaurants to surpass the horrendous volume spilled by the ruptured hull of the Exxon Valdez.

Drains leading directly to our precious fresh water supplies, our lakes and rivers.

The amount of damage this causes defies comprehension, particularly when you consider that just one thimble of oil contaminates five thousand litres of water.

Disturbingly, oil is but one contributor to Asia's drinking water problem. In poorer Asian countries, untreated human waste is slugged by the tonne into vital water sources. While cocktails of industrial and agricultural pollutants cascade unchecked into rivers.

Rivers where children drink.

As a consequence, 470 million Asians (nearly twice the population of the United States) do not have access to safe drinking water.

Even wealthier Asian countries, who possess the infrastructure to supply their people with clean water, abuse the privilege by mindlessly dumping household pollutants down drains.

This pollution we can ill-afford. Today every country struggles to find clean water to sustain their ballooning populations. The World Bank estimates the cost of supplying every man, woman and child in Asia with clean drinking water will exceed US$128 billion over the next ten years.

Who is going to pay?

The situation is ominous. But as we know, prevention is better than cure. So it's imperative we give more thought to what we put down our drains. And use the water we do have more wisely.

Food scraps and the like can be put to better use in the garden or pot plants. If you must use oil, refuse to carelessly dump it. Collect it in a disposable container like a milk carton and once it has solidified, dispense with it in the bin (designated landfills are the lesser of two evils).

If each and every one of us is a little more thoughtful, we might just be able to prevent yet another man-made disaster of sickening proportions.

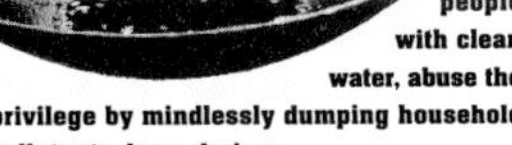

(TREAT WATER WITH RESPECT)

HO₂ HO₂ HO₂

(TREAT WATER WITH RESPECT THIS CHRISTMAS)

**NEWSPAPER
OR MAGAZINE:
CAMPAIGN**

art directors
Jimmy Bonner
Kim Wright

writer
Denzil Strickland

client
Lawyers Against the
Death Penalty

agency
Cole Henderson
Drake/Atlanta

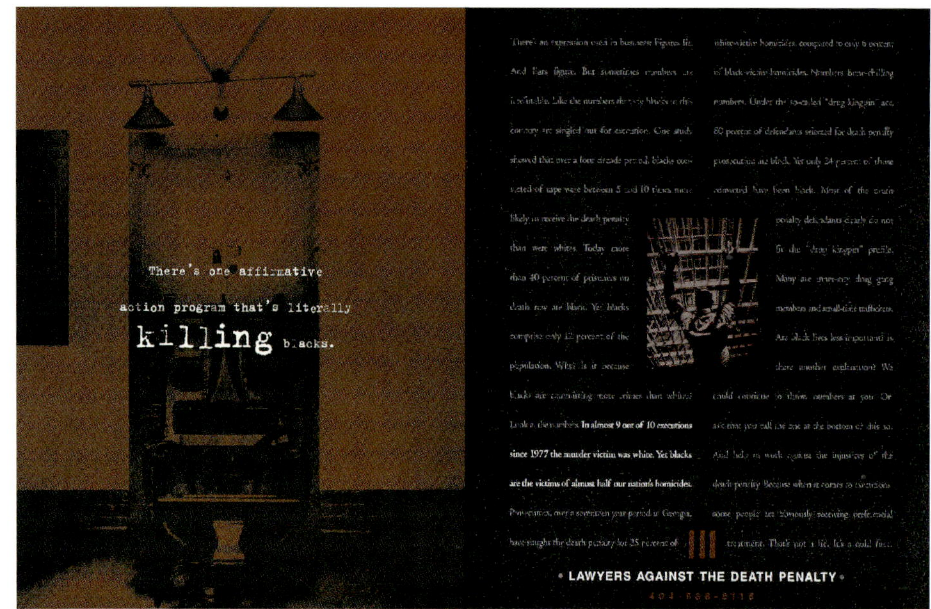

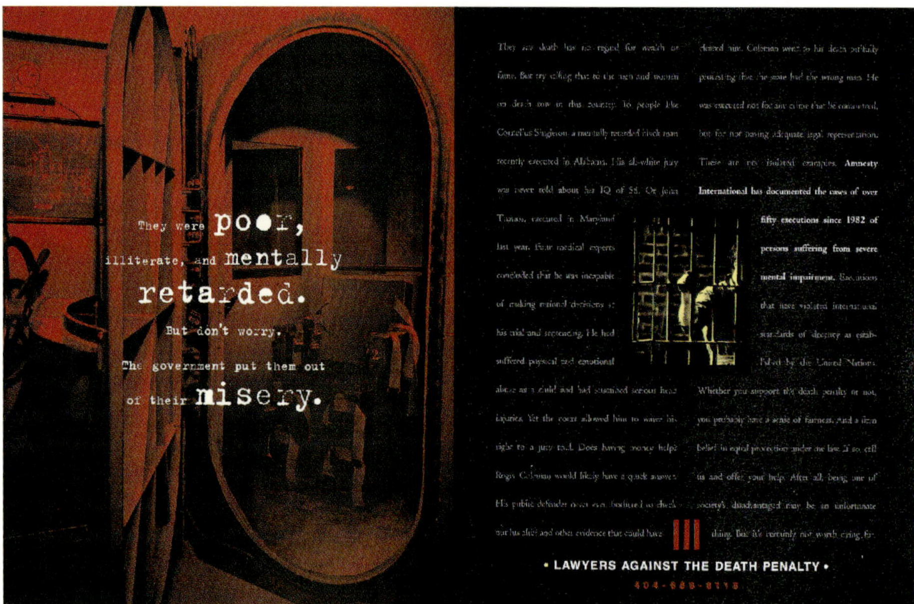

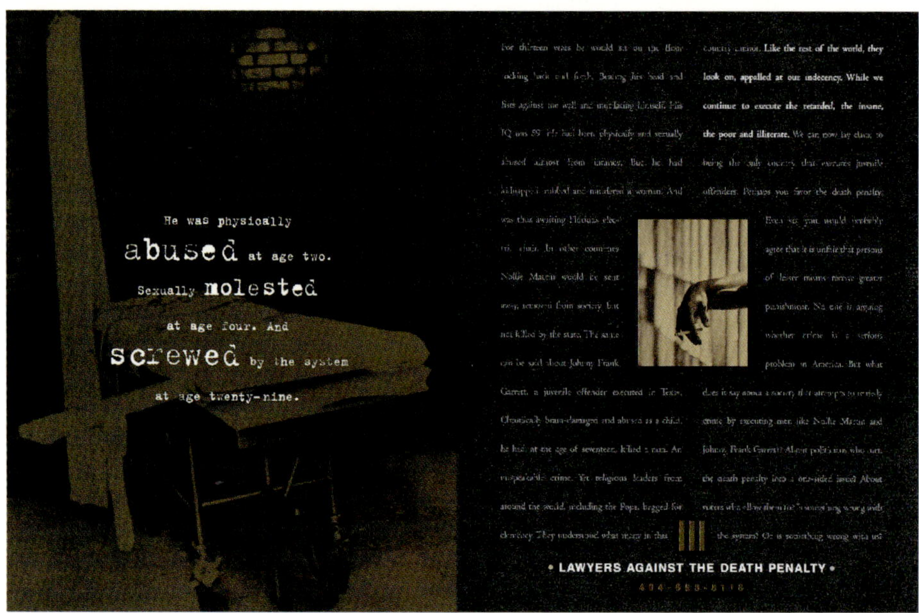

art director
Larae Netten

writer
John Rabuse

photographer
Henri Cartier-Bresson

client
Minneapolis
Institute of Art

agency
Colle & McVoy/
Minneapolis

WHY HE'S ON EXHIBIT INSTEAD OF YOU.

His shot of some trees

Your shot of some trees

HENRI CARTIER-BRESSON
Pen, Brush, and Cameras · March 3 · May 12
THE MINNEAPOLIS INSTITUTE OF ARTS

WHY HE'S ON EXHIBIT INSTEAD OF YOU.

His shot of a picnic

Your shot of a picnic

HENRI CARTIER-BRESSON
Pen, Brush, and Cameras · March 3 · May 12
THE MINNEAPOLIS INSTITUTE OF ARTS

WHY HE'S ON EXHIBIT INSTEAD OF YOU.

His shot of someone famous

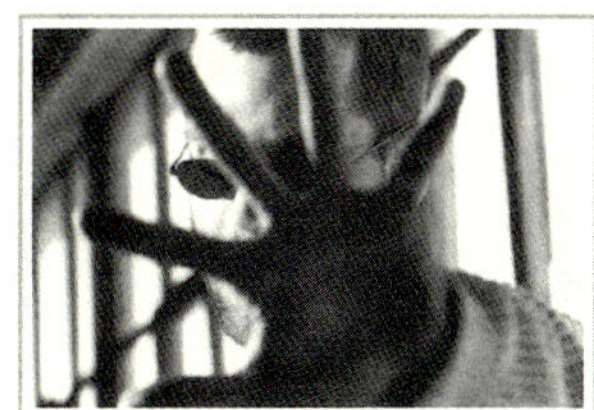

Your shot of someone famous

HENRI CARTIER-BRESSON
Pen, Brush, and Cameras · March 3 · May 12
THE MINNEAPOLIS INSTITUTE OF ARTS

**NEWSPAPER
OR MAGAZINE:
CAMPAIGN**

art director
Scott McAfee

writer
Brian Brooker

illustrators
CSA Archive
Dover Archive

client
Gilbert & Sullivan
Society of Austin

agency
GSD&M
Advertising / Austin

ASHAMED

of your wooden leg?
well, no more

Do people snicker and point behind your back? Rude behavior, indeed. Perhaps if they could see you singing and dancing nightly in The Pirates of Penzance, such ridicule would ebb. Open auditions will be Saturday and Sunday, March 23 & 24 at the UT Music Building East, Chorus Room 2.106 (Sat. 12-4, Sun. 1:30-4:30 p.m.) Bring sheet music from a Broadway show or opera, and resume and headshot if available. Be prepared to dance a bit. This popular musical comedy will run June 21 until July 7, 1996. For more information, please call the Gilbert & Sullivan Society of Austin at 472-4772 or 345-5950.

Put that shiny
HOOK HAND
TO WORK

Shiny hook hand? Don't fret, you're not alone. Many just like you will be trying out for The Pirates of Penzance. If you can sing or dance, you may be just the scalawag we're looking for. Open auditions will be Saturday and Sunday, March 23 & 24 at the UT Music Building East, Chorus Room 2.106 (Sat. 12-4, Sun. 1:30-4:30 p.m.) Bring sheet music from a Broadway show or opera, and resume and headshot if available. Be prepared to dance a bit. This popular musical comedy will run June 21 until July 7, 1996. For more information, please call the Gilbert & Sullivan Society of Austin at 472-4772 or 345-5950.

PUBLIC SERVICE &
POLITICAL FINALISTS

**NEWSPAPER
OR MAGAZINE:
CAMPAIGN**

art director
Tom Kuntz

writer
Mike Maguire

photographer
Sergio Purtell

client
United States
Postal Service/
Project Santa Claus

agency
Kirshenbaum Bond &
Partners/New York

SANTA QUITS,
ELVES LEFT TO PONDER FATE.
Exclusive photo of Santa's elves looking for work at NYC's West Side Piers. Elves say, "We've been hung out to dry."
WHAT YOU CAN DO: Visit the General Post Office at 33rd St. and Eighth Ave., read an underprivileged child's Christmas list, then send him or her a gift. Please New York, let's make sure Santa is there for every child this Christmas. To learn more, call (212) 967-8585.
this holiday season, please support
OPERATION SANTA CLAUS

SANTA SPOTTED BELOW THE EQUATOR.
Exclusive photo confirms Kringle has left the Christmas business to pursue other interests with unnamed "friend."
WHAT YOU CAN DO: Visit the General Post Office at 33rd St. and Eighth Ave., read an underprivileged child's Christmas list, then send him or her a gift. Please New York, let's make sure Santa is there for every child this Christmas. To learn more, call (212) 967-8585.
this holiday season, please support
OPERATION SANTA CLAUS

SANTA SEEN LUNCHING WITH HOLLYWOOD "PLAYERS."
Exclusive photo confirms that a 3-picture deal is in the offing. "He's got the directing bug," a source confirmed.
WHAT YOU CAN DO: Visit the General Post Office at 33rd St. and Eighth Ave., read an underprivileged child's Christmas list, then send him or her a gift. Please New York, let's make sure Santa is there for every child this Christmas. To learn more, call (212) 967-8585.
this holiday season, please support
OPERATION SANTA CLAUS

**NEWSPAPER
OR MAGAZINE:
CAMPAIGN**

art director
Jimmy Olson

writer
Dave Loew

photographer
David Emmite

client
NORML

agency
MAU! Advertising/
Chicago

IF YOU DON'T CARE ABOUT THE PEOPLE SENT TO PRISON **FOR SMOKING MARIJUANA,** AT LEAST CONSIDER **WHO GETS RELEASED** TO MAKE ROOM FOR THEM.

http://www.norml.org — 1 900 97 NORML

Every day, violent criminals are released early from over-crowded prisons to make room for marijuana offenders. In 1995, there were 580,000 marijuana arrests, the most ever; 86% for simple possession. Because of harsh mandatory minimum sentences for even small amounts of pot, more people are serving hard time than ever.

The government spends an estimated $7 billion a year in this war against marijuana smokers. In a nation with 10 million violent crimes a year, surely we can find better ways to allocate our criminal justice resources. It's time to stop acting as if law-abiding citizens who happen to smoke marijuana are part of America's crime problem.

As courtrooms and prisons bulge with non-violent marijuana offenders, a growing number of active federal judges have come out in support of marijuana decriminalization, a policy endorsed by many respected groups. These include President Nixon's 1972 Commission on Marijuana, the National Academy of Sciences, the California Research Advisory Panel, *The Economist* and *National Review* magazines, and two of Britain's most esteemed medical journals. Today, decriminalization works in Holland, a nation with much lower crime and hard drug usage rates than the U.S.

If you agree that it makes no sense to arrest people for using a substance less harmful than alcohol or tobacco, join NORML. With a donation of $25 or more, you can help change our country's marijuana laws. Write us today at 1001 Connecticut Avenue NW, Suite 1010, Washington, DC 20036, and we'll send you our bi-monthly newsletter. Or call the NORML Support Line at 1-900-97-NORML. For $2.95 a minute, 18 years or older, you'll receive up-to-date information on marijuana penalties in your state, drug testing, and your legal rights. Like Alcohol Prohibition of the 1930's, today's Marijuana Prohibition is a failure. With your help, we can end it once and for all.

NORML

In 1976, Holland decriminalized the sale and possession of small amounts of marijuana, separating pot from harder drugs. Today, the Dutch enjoy a substantially lower crime rate than the United States, a murder rate almost ten times lower, and lower hard drug addiction rates. Compared to their American peers, fewer Dutch high school students smoke marijuana; even fewer have experimented with cocaine or other more dangerous drugs.

The Dutch Minister of Health said on CNN, "Cannabis is not very damaging to health. Nicotine and alcohol are far more dangerous." In short, their policy is based on reality.

Meanwhile, in the United States we spend $7 billion a year arresting people for smoking pot. 580,000 marijuana arrests in 1995; 10 million since 1965 haven't made our streets any safer. Marijuana Prohibition has ruined productive lives, wasted criminal justice resources that could've been used to fight violent crime, clogged up court and prison systems, and burdened taxpayers. It's time to stop arresting marijuana smokers.

Just as Alcohol Prohibition failed, so has today's Marijuana Prohibition. NORML, National Organization for the Reform of Marijuana Laws, believes that the Dutch approach can work here in the U.S. You can help change our nation's marijuana laws by joining NORML with your donation of $25 or more. Write us today at 1001 Connecticut Avenue NW, Suite 1010, Washington, DC 20036, and we'll send you a membership kit.

For information on your legal rights, drug testing, and marijuana penalties in your state, call the NORML Support Line at 1-900-97-NORML; $2.95 a minute, 18 years or older. Whether you join or call, your confidentiality is assured.

As William F. Buckley Jr. stated: "The amount of money and of legal energy being given to prosecute hundreds of thousands of Americans who are caught with a few ounces of marijuana in their jeans simply makes no sense . . . it is an outrage, an imposition on basic civil liberties, and on the reasonable expenditure of social energy."

If you agree, please join us.

NORML

http://www.norml.org — 1 900 97 NORML

TULIPS, WINDMILLS, A LOW CRIME RATE. JUST A FEW OF THE THINGS THAT CAN PLAGUE A NATION WHEN IT DECRIMINALIZES **MARIJUANA**

Hello From, HOLLAND!

WHAT THEY SAY IS TRUE, MANY PEOPLE WHO SMOKE MARIJUANA MOVE ON TO HARDER THINGS. **GRADUATE SCHOOL, FOR EXAMPLE.**

http://www.norml.org — 1 900 97 NORML

Even Drug Czar General Barry McCaffrey doesn't buy the argument that marijuana is a "gateway drug" that "leads to harder things." In a speech to the National Press Club, General McCaffrey stated that only a tiny percentage of the 90 million Americans who experiment with illegal drugs become addicts. He also said that the "overwhelming majority" of Americans who try illegal drugs simply "walk away and say it's not for me."

The Drug Czar was acknowledging what we at the National Organization for the Reform of Marijuana Laws, NORML, already knew. The vast majority of people who have smoked pot (i.e., Bill Clinton, Newt Gingrich, Al Gore) do not move on to harder drugs or run into drug-related problems later in life. So why does our government spend $7 billion a year to arrest and jail people for this relatively harmless activity?

Like Alcohol Prohibition of the 1930's, Marijuana Prohibition is a failure. It has ruined productive lives, wasted criminal justice resources that could have been used to fight violent crime, and clogged up court and prison systems. It's time to admit that arresting otherwise law-abiding citizens who happen to smoke marijuana serves no legitimate societal purpose.

By joining NORML with your donation of $25 or more, you can help change our country's marijuana laws. Write us today at 1001 Connecticut Avenue NW, Suite 1010, Washington, DC 20036, and we'll send you a bi-monthly newsletter. Or call the NORML Support Line at 1-900-97-NORML. For $2.95 a minute, 18 or older, you'll receive info on drug testing, marijuana penalties in your state, and your legal rights.

In Holland, where marijuana is decriminalized and sold in government regulated "coffee shops," their crime and hard drug usage rates are much lower than here in the United States. Which shows that you can always learn something, even without going to graduate school.

NORML

PUBLIC SERVICE &
POLITICAL FINALISTS

art director
Chris Lange

writer
Michael Hart

photographer
Bruce Peterson

client
Episcopal Church
Ad Project

agency
Mullen Advertising /
Wenham, MA

NEWSPAPER
OR MAGAZINE:
CAMPAIGN

art director
Hal Curtis

writer
Mark Nardi

client
Battleship Cove

agency
Pagano Schenck &
Kay / Boston

WE'VE NEVER DISAPPOINTED A VISITOR.
(EXCEPT FOR THOSE TWO KAMIKAZES BACK IN '44.)

If we didn't turn away some people, we might not be here today. But thanks to a fearless crew which manned some of the most powerful anti-aircraft weapons ever, the U.S.S. Massachusetts was able to proudly sail home and await your visit today. It's just one of the ships you'll find at Battleship Cove, where you step back over 50 years with the vessels that protected the United States in World War II.

Commissioned in 1942, the battleship U.S.S. Massachusetts steamed more than 225,000 miles throughout the Atlantic and Pacific Oceans. She participated in major operations in places like Okinawa, Casablanca, The New Hebrides Islands, The Marshall Islands, and the Philippines. Known back then as a "fast battleship," the Massachusetts and ships like her were in demand not only because of their speed but because of their devastating array of weapons. Today, you can come aboard and walk among this powerful armament. Feel the 16-inch armor, which protected the Massachusetts through 35 engagements. Stand in the shadow of her massive 16-inch guns, which bombarded enemy shore positions and sank enemy vessels. And sit among the ferocious anti-aircraft guns, which kept 18 enemy aircraft from completing their mission to destroy the ship.

Berthed alongside the Massachusetts are several World War II Navy ships which you can explore as well. The destroyer U.S.S. Joseph P. Kennedy, Jr., the submarine U.S.S. Lionfish and PT boats 617 and 796 await your visit, offering a further glimpse into naval history and what it meant to this country. The United States Department of the Interior has honored the national significance of all five ships at Battleship Cove by recently designating them as "National Historic Landmarks."

Battleship Cove is open every day, 9:00 to 5:00 pm. Admission is $8.00 for adults and $4.00 for children 6–14. Group rates, overnight youth camping and banquet facilities are available. For information or directions, please call 1-508-678-1100 or 1-800-533-3194. What's more, please ask us for information on how you may join the Friends of Battleship Cove.

U.S.S. MASSACHUSETTS at BATTLESHIP COVE

LOOK, YOU DON'T HAVE TO VISIT, IT'S A FREE COUNTRY. WAIT A MINUTE, THAT'S WHY YOU SHOULD VISIT.

The freedom you enjoy today has been brought to you, in part, by the 680 feet and 35 thousand tons of a tremendous fighting ship called the U.S.S. Massachusetts. It's an important part of our nation's history And it's just one of the ships you'll find at Battleship Cove, where you step back in time over 50 years and get a hands-on experience with the vessels that protected the United States during World War II.

Commissioned in 1942, the battleship U.S.S. Massachusetts steamed more than 225,000 miles throughout the Atlantic and Pacific Oceans. She participated in major operations in places like Okinawa, Casablanca, The New Hebrides Islands, The Marshall Islands, and the Philippines. Known back then as a "fast battleship," the Massachusetts and ships like her were in demand not only because of their speed but because of their devastating array of weapons. Today, you can come aboard and walk among this powerful armament. Feel the 16-inch armor, which protected the Massachusetts through 35 engagements. Stand in the shadow of her massive 16-inch guns, which bombarded enemy shore positions and sank enemy vessels. And sit among the ferocious anti-aircraft guns, which kept 18 enemy aircraft from completing their mission to destroy the ship.

Berthed alongside the Massachusetts are several World War II Navy ships which you can explore as well. The destroyer U.S.S. Joseph P. Kennedy, Jr., the submarine U.S.S. Lionfish and PT boats 617 and 796 await your visit, offering a further glimpse into naval history and what it meant to this country. The United States Department of the Interior has honored the national significance of all five ships at Battleship Cove by recently designating them as "National Historic Landmarks."

Battleship Cove is open every day, 9:00 to 5:00 pm. Admission is $8.00 for adults and $4.00 for children 6–14. Group rates, overnight youth camping and banquet facilities are available. For information or directions, please call 1-508-678-1100 or 1-800-533-3194. What's more, please ask us for information on how you may join the Friends of Battleship Cove.

U.S.S. MASSACHUSETTS at BATTLESHIP COVE

ITS GUNS COULD PROBABLY REACH MOST OF YOUR HOUSES. SO, YOU'LL BE VISITING US SOON, RIGHT?

We don't mean to be pushy, but we certainly do hope to see you aboard the tremendous fighting battleship called the U.S.S. Massachusetts. It's just one of the ships you'll find at Battleship Cove where you step back in time over 50 years and get a hands-on experience with the vessels that protected the United States of America during the fierce and dramatic battles of World War II.

Commissioned in 1942, the battleship U.S.S. Massachusetts steamed more than 225,000 miles throughout the Atlantic and Pacific Oceans. She participated in major operations in places like Okinawa, Casablanca, The New Hebrides Islands, The Marshall Islands, and the Philippines. Known back then as a "fast battleship," the Massachusetts and ships like her were in demand not only because of their speed but because of their devastating array of weapons. Today, you can come aboard and walk among this powerful armament. Feel the 16-inch armor, which protected the Massachusetts through 35 engagements. Stand in the shadow of her massive 16-inch guns, which bombarded enemy shore positions and sank enemy vessels. And sit among the ferocious anti-aircraft guns, which kept 18 enemy aircraft from completing their mission to destroy the ship.

Berthed alongside the Massachusetts are several World War II Navy ships which you can explore as well. The destroyer U.S.S. Joseph P. Kennedy, Jr., the submarine U.S.S. Lionfish and PT boats 617 and 796 await your visit, offering a further glimpse into naval history and what it meant to this country. The United States Department of the Interior has honored the national significance of all five ships at Battleship Cove by recently designating them as "National Historic Landmarks."

Battleship Cove is open every day, 9:00 to 5:00 pm. Admission is $8.00 for adults and $4.00 for children 6–14. Group rates, overnight youth camping and banquet facilities are available. For information or directions, please call 1-508-678-1100 or 1-800-533-3194. What's more, please ask us for information on how you may join the Friends of Battleship Cove.

U.S.S. MASSACHUSETTS at BATTLESHIP COVE

**OUTDOOR AND
POSTERS**

art director
Paul Briginshaw

writer
Malcolm Duffy

photograph
ICRC Library

client
British Red Cross

agency
Abbott Mead Vickers.
BBDO/London

art director
Andrew Clarke

writer
Mark Fong

photographer
Simon Taplin

client
Australian
Consolidated Press
(Southeast Asia)

agency
Batey Ads/Singapore

art director
George Vargas

writer
Peter Moyse

photographer
Sean Pettigrew

client
Partnership for a
Drug-Free Singapore

agency
Batey Ads/Singapore

**OUTDOOR
AND POSTERS**

art director
Lisa Francilia

writer
Dan Scherk

photographer
Mark Antony Gilbert

client
Ministry of Forests

agency
BBDO/Vancouver

art director
Lisa Francilia

writer
Dan Scherk

photographer
Mark Antony Gilbert

client
Ministry of Forests

agency
BBDO/Vancouver

PUBLIC SERVICE &
POLITICAL FINALISTS

art director
Jason Busa

writer
Rob Bagot

photographer
Archive Photography

client
Kalakala Foundation

agency
Big Bang Idea
Engineering / Seattle

SHE ENCHANTED SAILORS, MESMERIZED
FISHERMEN AND BAFFLED SEAGULLS.
SAVE the KALAKALA
She's an art deco masterpiece who finds herself stranded on a beach in Alaska. Won't you help bring her back home? Call the Kalakala Foundation at (206)632-0540.

art director
Jason Busa

writer
Rob Bagot

photographer
Archive Photography

client
Kalakala Foundation

agency
Big Bang Idea
Engineering / Seattle

SHE MAGICALLY WHISKED PEOPLE TO MARS.
(OKAY, BREMERTON.)
SAVE the KALAKALA
She's the Buck Rogers ferry who finds herself stranded on a beach in Alaska. Won't you help bring her back home? Call the Kalakala Foundation at (206)632-0540.

**OUTDOOR
AND POSTERS**

art director
Jason Busa

writer
Rob Bagot

photographer
Archive Photography

client
Kalakala Foundation

agency
Big Bang Idea
Engineering / Seattle

art director
Joel Nendel

writer
Simeon Roane

photographer
Steve Bloch

client
March Of Dimes

agency
Borders Perrin &
Norrander / Portland

PUBLIC SERVICE &
POLITICAL FINALISTS

art director
Joel Nendel
writer
Simeon Roane
client
March Of Dimes
agency
Borders Perrin &
Norrander / Portland

art director
Carolyn McGeorge
writer
Matt Potts
photographer
Sonny Bowyer
client
ABC Bakers /
Girl Scouts
agency
Cadmus / O'Keefe
Marketing, Richmond

OUTDOOR
AND POSTERS

art director
Scott McDonald

writer
Steve Johnston

client
Seattle International
Film Festival

agency
Cole & Weber / Seattle

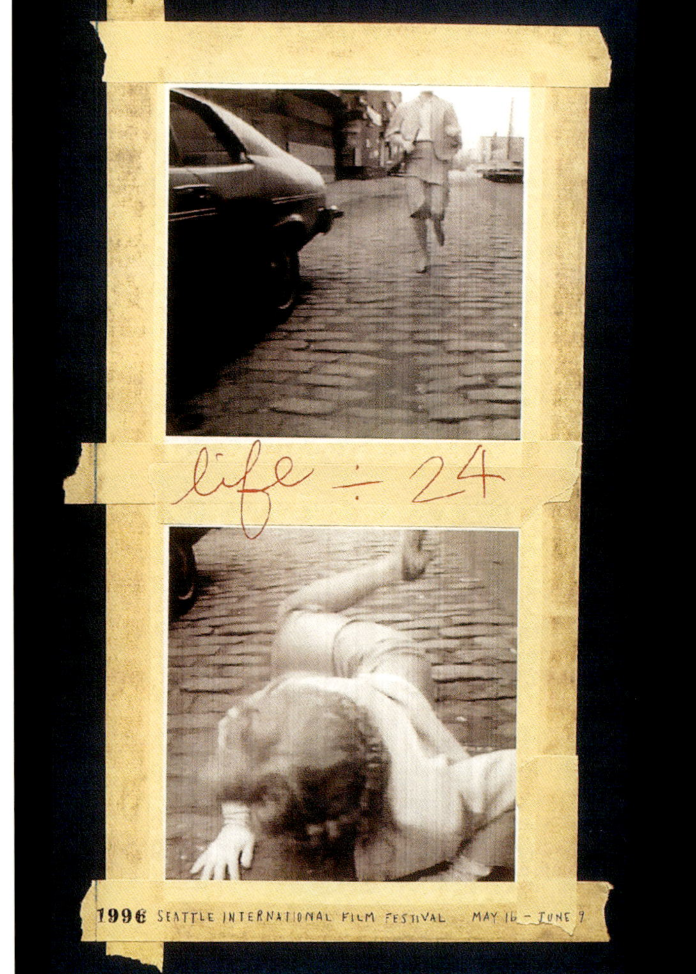

art director
Eric Oltersdorf

writer
John Spalding

photographer
Kelli Coggins

client
Partnership Against
Domestic Violence

agency
Cole Henderson
Drake / Atlanta

art director
Eric Oltersdorf

writer
John Spalding

photographer
Kelli Coggins

client
Partnership Against
Domestic Violence

agency
Cole Henderson
Drake/Atlanta

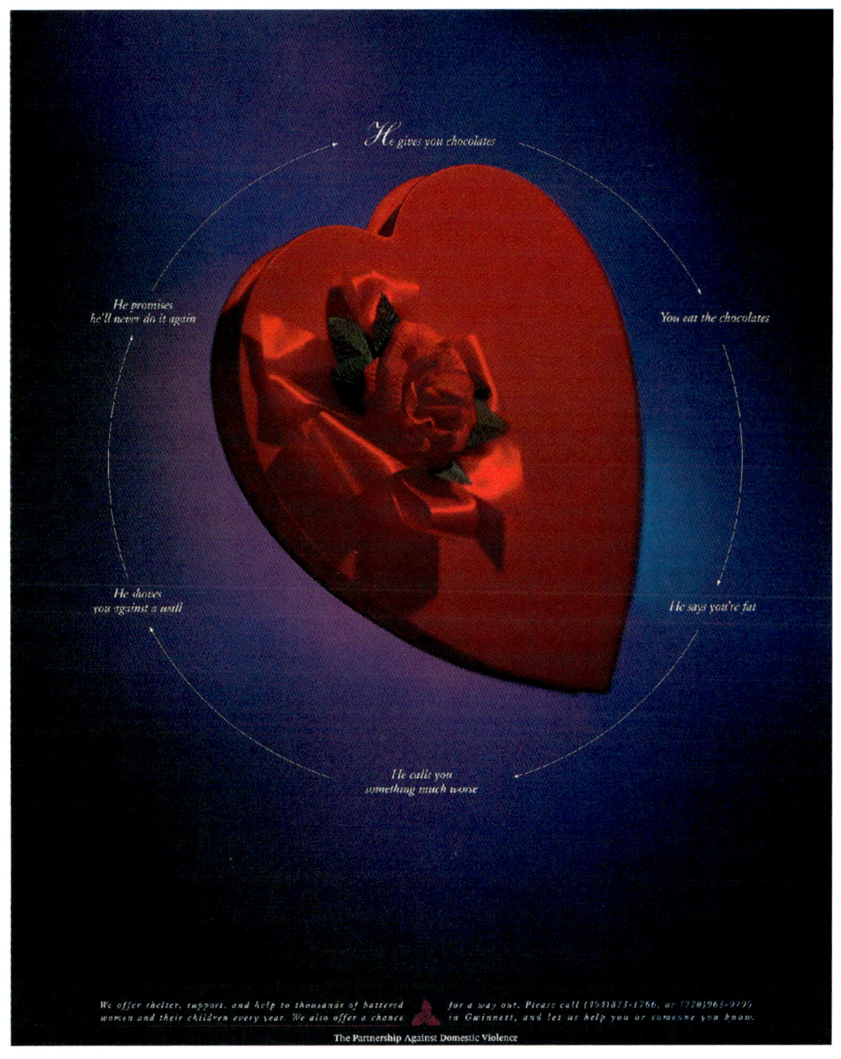

art director
Markham Cronin

writer
Alex Bogusky

client
Miami Rescue Mission

agency
Crispin Porter &
Bogusky/Miami

**OUTDOOR
AND POSTERS**

art director
Markham Cronin

writer
Alex Bogusky

client
Miami Rescue Mission

agency
Crispin Porter &
Bogusky/Miami

art director
Markham Cronin

writer
Alex Bogusky

client
Miami Rescue Mission

agency
Crispin Porter &
Bogusky/Miami

PUBLIC SERVICE &
POLITICAL FINALISTS

art director
John Liegey
writer
Dean Buckhorn
photographer
Shawn Michienzi
client
Planned Parenthood
agency
Fallon McElligott/
Minneapolis

art directors
Jamie Mambro
Michele Mangiacotti
writer
Ernie Schenck
photographers
Chris Amaral
Cheryl Clegg
client
Survivors Network of
those Abused by Priests
agency
Hill Holliday Connors
Cosmopulos/Boston

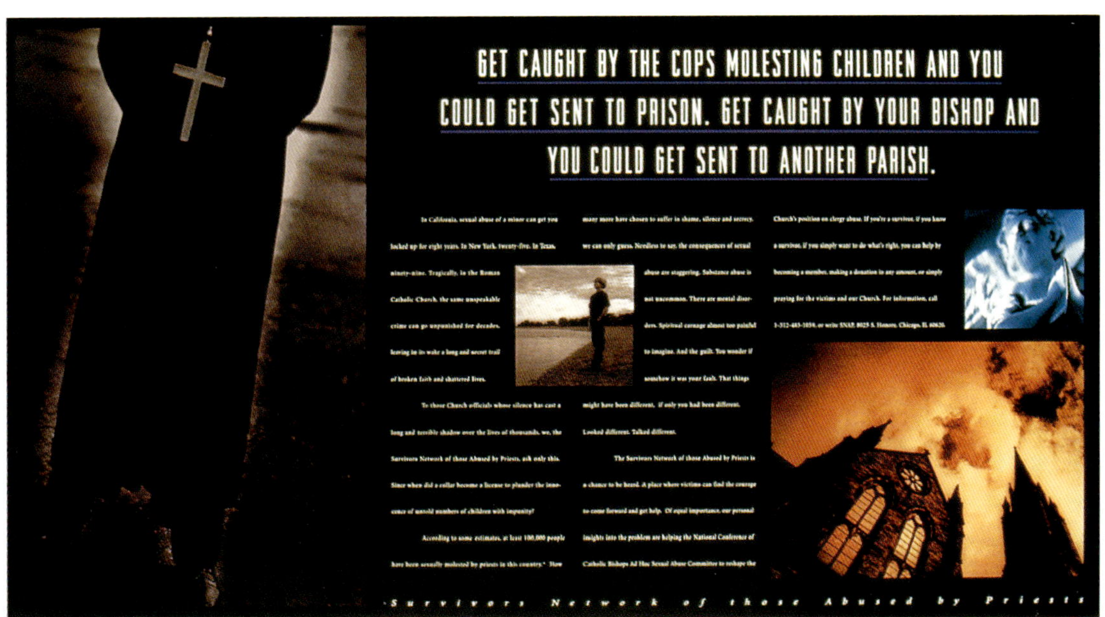

PUBLIC SERVICE &
POLITICAL FINALISTS

**OUTDOOR
AND POSTERS**

art director
Rob Rich

writer
Jim Garaventi

client
Boston Museum of
Fine Arts

agency
Ingalls Advertising/
Boston

art director
Ed Parks

writer
Steve Bautista

client
Brookline Fire
Department

agency
Ingalls Advertising/
Boston

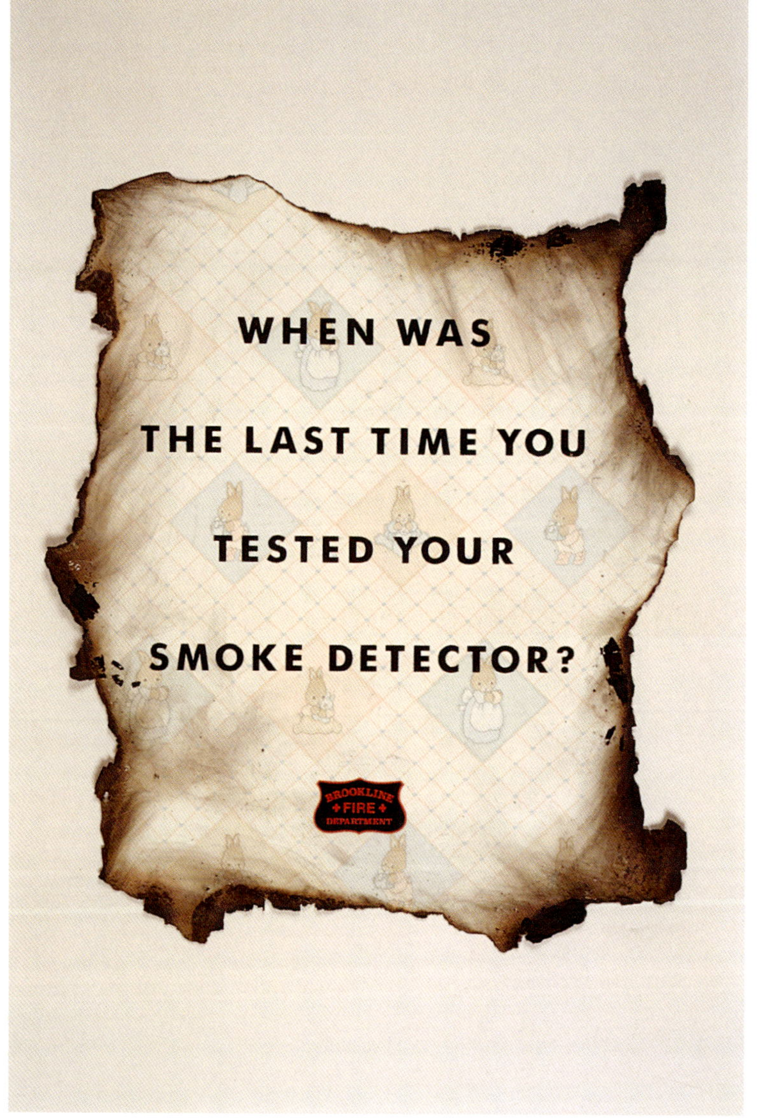

PUBLIC SERVICE &
POLITICAL FINALISTS

art director
Jamie Mahoney

writer
Joe Alexander

client
Mothers Against
Drunk Driving

agency
The Martin Agency /
Richmond

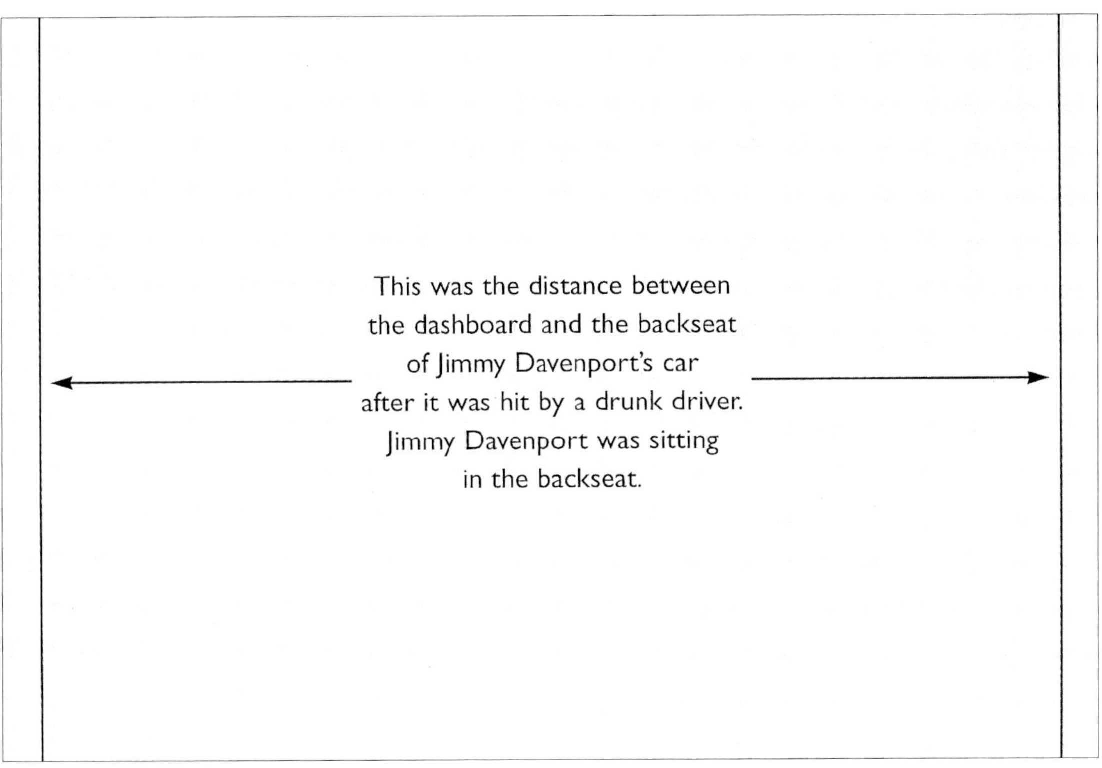

art director
Simon Hepton

writer
Matt Crabtree

photographer
Andy Atkinson

typographer
Rob Wallis

client
Friends Of The Earth

agency
McCann-Erickson /
London

**OUTDOOR
AND POSTERS**

art director
Rashid Salleh

writer
Jackie Hathiramani

client
Rites & Rights

agency
Metal / Singapore

art director
Chris Flagg

writer
Chris Flagg

client
American Red Cross

agency
Noble & Associates /
Springfield, MO

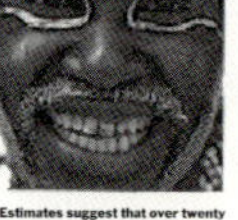

They gave us a cure for cancer, glaucoma and heart disease. In return, we gave them malaria, hepatitis and herpes.

Congratulations to all of us on our generosity. We've really mastered the art of saying 'thank-you'.

Today, when we mine for gold or log for tropical wood, we magnanimously leave behind rivers full of lead, mercury, garbage and dead fish.

What follows is a lavish display of our modern-day gifts: malaria, tuberculosis, hepatitis and herpes.

The tribals of these lands have no immunity against diseases like these. And no defense whatsoever against our rifles and bulldozers as we steal their ancestral lands.

(Of course, in reciprocation, we give their women and little girls jobs as prostitutes.)

While we celebrate our newly-acquired wealth with the construction of dams, malls, bridges and holiday resorts, we refuse to see the loss of much greater wealth: The loss of Tribal Wisdom.

Stored in the memories of elders, healers, midwives, farmers, fishermen and hunters in the fifteen-thousand odd cultures remaining on earth is an enormous trove of knowledge. And as they die out, so does their irreplaceable knowledge.

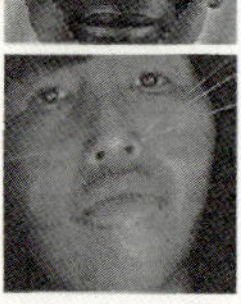

Knowledge, that is not mere witchcraft as we've been made to believe. But something that modern science can recognise and utilise for the benefit of us all.

Take may apples, for example. The Penobscot Indians of Maine have always used them as a cure for warts. Today, cancer of the lung, kidney and testis responds to Etoposide, a drug synthesized from may apples.

Countless generations of locals from Aguas Claras have used a herb named chilka (bacchans salicifolia) as an anti-inflammatory. We now use it in medicines to fight tumors.

The foxglove flower has been used by many traditional cultures as a cardiotonic. Today digitoxin and digoxin are extracted from the same flower to combat heart ailments.

Over a quarter of all prescribed medicines are based on plants. Seventy-five per cent of these were discovered in a folk or tribal context.

Had it not been for ancient knowledge, we wouldn't have many of our antibiotics, tranquilizers, sedatives, pain relievers, anaesthetics and laxatives. We wouldn't have a remedy for migraine, leukemia, amoebic dysentery, leprosy and ulcers. Why, we may not have even discovered aspirin, clove oil and the contraceptive pill.

But look at our gratitude. If our diseases don't wipe out the indigenous peoples, we use sickles and axes. Men's penises are chopped off to ensure the tribes don't multiply. Wives and daughters are gang-raped. And little boys who escape into the jungles are hunted down like deer and rabbit, so that they never return to claim their ancestral lands. Often, the law turns a blind eye. Even when atrocities are brought to light, the response from the governments is appalling.

A senior aide from South America once said, "The tribes are made up of imbeciles and layabouts who take up too much land... I do believe that their culture should be preserved, but not in real life".

Alas! it is such ignorance and arrogance that encourages the genocide of the tribal peoples to continue. With it, we also continue to lose technologies that could help us solve more than just our medical problems.

Just look around you. In the last two-hundred years, we've contaminated the air, water and soil. Driven wild things to extinction. Torn down the ancient forests, poisoned the rain and ripped holes into the protective ozone layer. On the other hand, the first peoples or the original inhabitants of the earth have lived on this planet for thousands of years and kept it in fine shape. It's obvious these 'imbeciles' know a lot more than we do.

Recycling, naturopathy, aromatherapy, acupuncture, reflexology and biodiversity are terms devised by us, but the basic principles are all borrowed from ancient shamanic wisdom.

Societies around the world have begun recognising the value of tribal knowledge. Indigenous citizens are now helping environment ministries and agricultural industries save what has not been already lost. However this is only in a handful of countries.

Estimates suggest that over twenty tribes around the world are on the brink of extinction. The last of the Penan are believed to be dead.

From time to time, The U.N. Center for Human Rights pressurises the various governments to return the land rights to their tribal peoples. And to protect their lives and keep alive the ethnic cultures.

Rites & Rights is a volunteer organisation that believes in the same cause. Apart from offering medical and financial aid to tribal groups, we actively campaign against projects that seek to dislocate the indigenous population from their lands.

We've had some success, but there's a lot more we could have achieved if we had more support. We need your help.

Information and action packs on the various endangered tribes are available at Booth 12 of the 'Challenges of the Next Millenia' Exhibition in Town Hall. Last day: 15th February.

We'll show you how to use the power of the pen to stop the bulldozers from wiping out the tribes and their knowledge. But you'll have to hurry!

Because if you don't save them, they won't be able to save you.

THE UNITED NATIONS has declared 1995-2004 a "Decade of Indigenous Peoples". Estimated to number 300 million, they occupy 10% of the earth. Even as you read this, miners, loggers, tourists and overgovernments encroach upon their ancestral lands, killing them with either diseases or rifles. By tolerating this genocide, you're not just depriving the original citizens of this world their basic human right of survival; you're also depriving the entire human race of a sustainable future on this planet.

rites&rights
FRIENDS OF THE INDIGENOUS PEOPLES

art director
John Payne

writer
John Payne

illustrator
John Payne

photographer
Philip Esparza

client
The Deep Ellum
Association

agency
The Richards Group/
Dallas

art director
Shari Hindman

writer
Lisa DeMaggio

client
City of Norfolk

agency
SMC/Richmond

art director
Dave Laden

writer
Eric Aronin

photographer
Ashton Worthington

client
Companion
Animal Placement

agency
Suburban Advertising/
Jersey City, NJ

PUBLIC SERVICE &
POLITICAL FINALISTS

**COLLATERAL:
BROCHURES AND
DIRECT MAIL**

art director
Brent Ladd

writer
Daniel Clay Russ

photographers
Brad Guice
Jimmy Williams

client
Peace Council

agency
GSD&M Advertising/
Austin

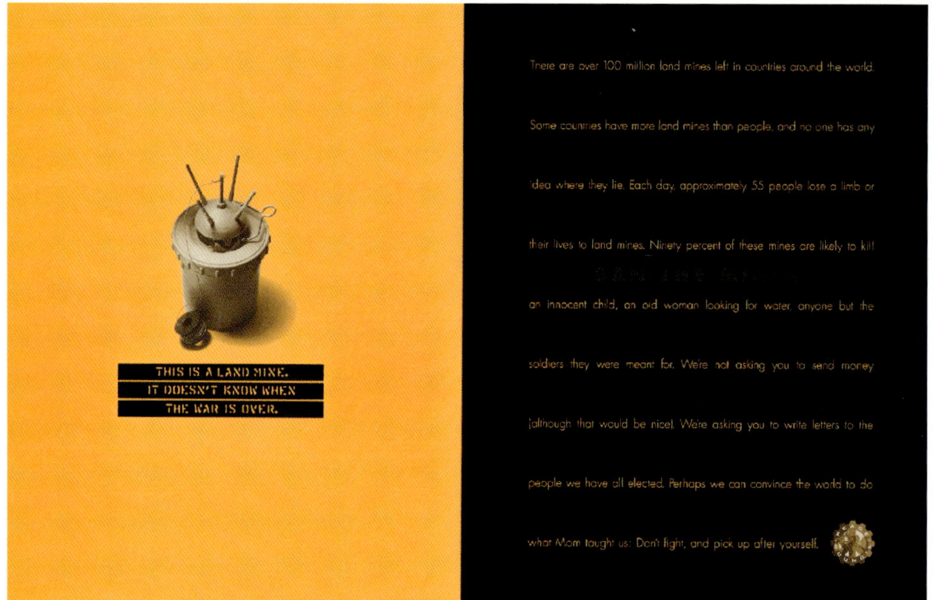

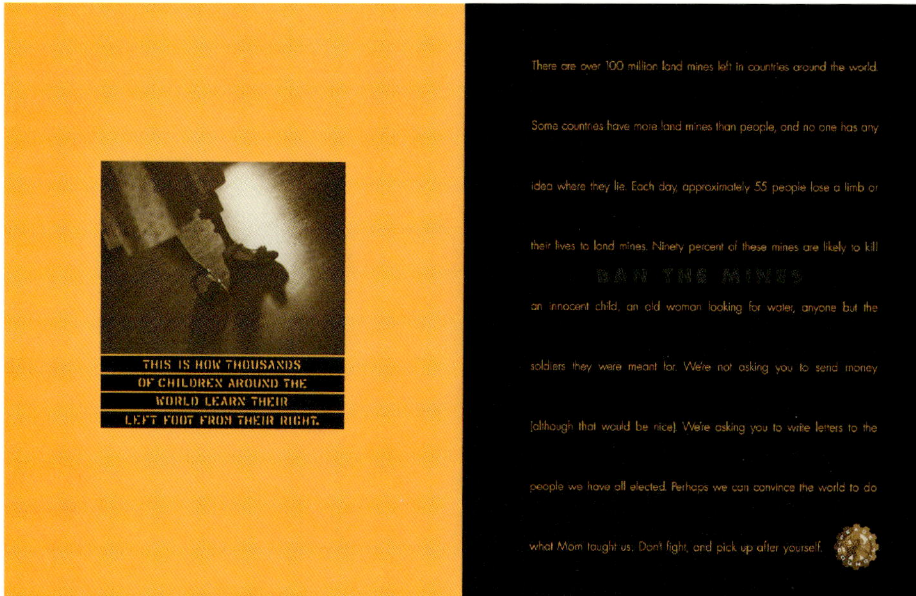

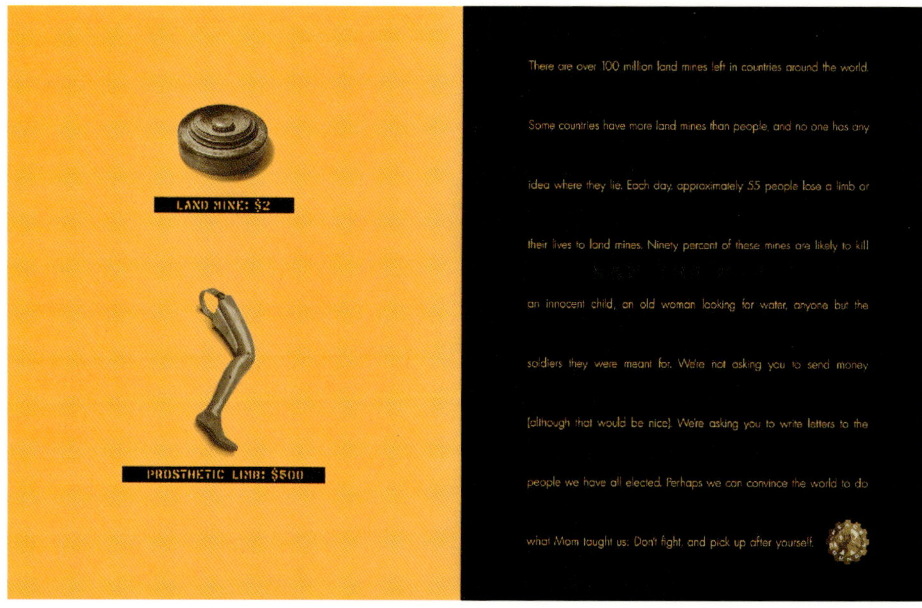

PUBLIC SERVICE &
POLITICAL FINALISTS

art directors
Chuck Creasy
Kevin Hinson

writer
Nelson Eddy

photographer
Rutherford
Photography

client
Middle Tennessee Council/
Boy Scouts of America

agency
Dye, Van Mol &
Lawrence/Nashville

RADIO: SINGLE

writer
Stu Cooperrider

agency producer
Lisa Sulda

production company
Soundtrack

client
Massachusetts Department of
Public Health

agency
Houston Herstek
Favat/Boston

RADIO: CAMPAIGN

writer
Jon Dietrich

agency producer
Niki Polyocan

production company
Clatter & Din

client
Seattle International
Film Festival

agency
Cole & Weber/Seattle

MAC: *I used to love cigarette ads. They made me feel good. The cowboy sitting tall on his horse. Rugged. Independent. The sun going down behind the mountains. The wide open spaces stretched out in front of him. It was beautiful. Then the cowboy died. The cigarettes he was always smoking gave him lung cancer. He didn't even have a chance to get married, have kids. How do I know all this? His name was Wayne MacLaren. And he was my big brother.*

I'm Mac MacLaren. The tobacco industry used my brother as a cowboy in advertisements to sell an image that smoking makes you independent. It's an image that's recognized by people all around the world. But I'm telling you now, don't for one second believe it. When you're lying in a hospital bed all hooked up to tubes, just how independent can you really be?

ANNCR: *A message from the Massachusetts Department of Public Health.*

ANNCR: *You never get to be first. Whatever it is, someone has always done it before you. Been to the moon, slept with your spouse, opened the ice cream. Someone is always on the bus when you get on, someone already bought the dress that you like, someone has always read the book you're starting. Someone has heard it before you, thought it before you or sat on it before you. There are six billion people in the world. It becomes a substantial conceit to think that you could do anything first. Unless, of course, you happen to attend the Seattle International Film Festival between May 16th and June 9th, where you could be the first to see US and world premieres before anyone else. For tickets call 325-6150. Get there early. Sit in front. See it before the guy behind you.*

The Seattle International Film Festival. Life divided by 24.

**TELEVISION:
SINGLE**

art director
Lisa Francilia

writer
Dan Scherk

agency producer
Pat Cooper

production company
Circle Productions

director
Rick Stevenson

client
Vancouver Sun/
Vancouver Film Festival

agency
BBDO/Vancouver

art director
Russell Wailes

writer
Rupert Sutton

agency producer
Matt Buels

production company
Moving Picture Company

director
Russell Wailes

client
Tusk Force

agency
Butler Lutos Sutton
Wilkinson/London

CD 31

(MUSIC: "MISSION IMPOSSIBLE" THEME)

SUPER: THE FOLLOWING FILM IS BASED ON ACTUAL EVENTS.

SUPER: ANY SIMILARITIES TO THE WORLD OF INTELLIGENCE ARE PURELY COINCIDENTAL.

SPY: *I can tell you're very upset.*

TOM: *You've never seen me upset.*

(SFX: AQUARIUM EXPLODES)

TOM: *That was a close one!*

SUPER: VANCOUVER INTERNATIONAL FILM FESTIVAL.

SUPER: OCTOBER 4TH TO THE 20TH.

SUPER: BECAUSE EVEN FILMS THAT DON'T SELL OUT EVERY NIGHT DESERVE A CHANCE TO BE SEEN.

(SFX: HELICOPTER BLADE DECAPITATING TOM)

TOM: *How's my hair? . . . That's right . . . I am dangerous.*

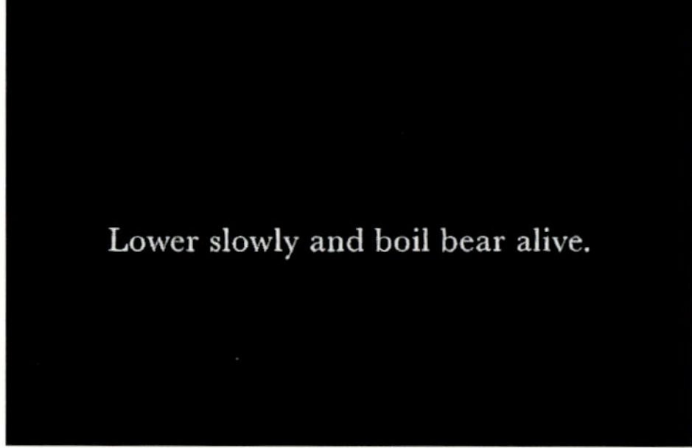

SUPER: RECIPE. BOILED BEAR. SERVES 12.

(SFX: VOICES, GRUNTS AND SCUFFLING NOISES OF BEAR)

SUPER:
INGREDIENTS:
1 LIVE BEAR
100 GALLONS OF BOILING WATER.
SALT AND PEPPER TO TASTE.

SUPER: METHOD: FIRST, BEAT THE BEAR VIGOROUSLY, USING STICKS, CLUBS OR METAL RODS.

(SFX: THUMP OF STICKS, BEAR HOWLING IN PAIN)

SUPER: CONTINUE BEATING TO ENSURE GOOD FLOW OF "FEAR JUICES." (THIS IS WHAT GIVES THE DISH ITS DISTINCTIVE FLAVOUR.)

(SFX: BOILING WATER; MORE BEATING, MORE HOWLING)

SUPER: PLACE BEAR IN NET AND HOIST IT ABOVE LARGE CAULDRON OF BOILING WATER. (EXTRA BEATING AT THIS STAGE IS RECOMMENDED.)

SUPER: LOWER SLOWLY AND BOIL BEAR ALIVE.

ANNCR: *Bears are considered a gourmet food in the Far East.*

SUPER: CONTINUE COOKING UNTIL TENDER.

ANNCR: *Despite the fact they're dangerously close to extinction.*

SUPER: VARIATION: FOR ROASTED BEAR SIMPLY PLACE BEAR IN METAL CAGE AND LOWER ONTO HOT COALS.

ANNCR: *There is a charity dedicated to conserving all the world's species through action and education. Tusk Force. To make a donation, call this number before it's too late.*

SUPER: TUSK FORCE. ACTIVELY CONSERVING ENDANGERED SPECIES. 0345 414 616.

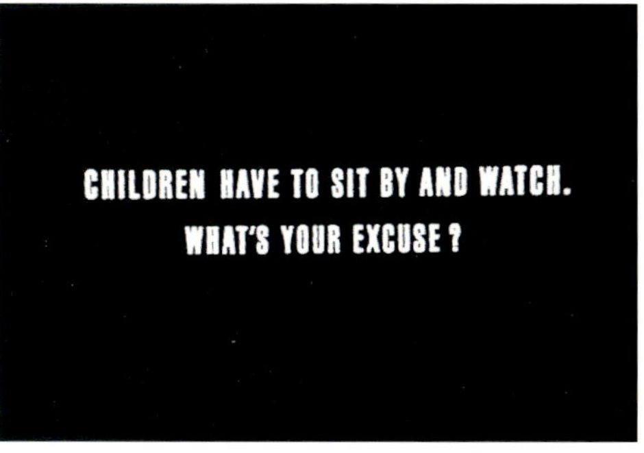

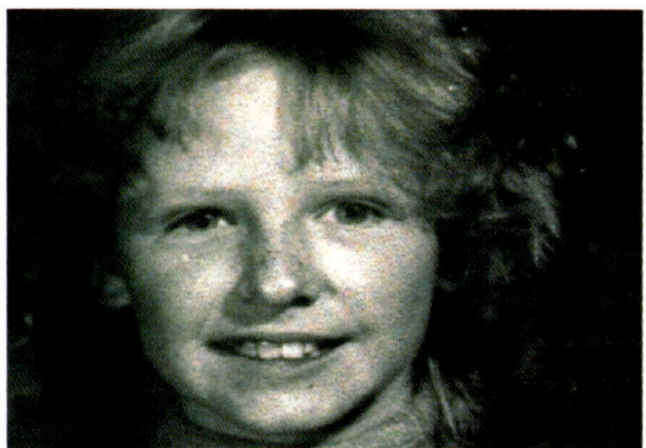

HUSBAND: *Where, where's dinner?*

(SFX: KEYS THROWN ON TABLE)

WIFE: *Well, I thought you'd be home a couple of hours ago and I . . . put everything away, so I . . .*

HUSBAND: *What, what, what is this, pizza? What–a, a pizza?*

WIFE: *If you had just called me I would have known what . . .*

HUSBAND: *Dinner, "dinner ready" is a pizza! Let me ask you something, is it–is it too much to have dinner waiting when I go home?*

WIFE: *Honey, please don't be so loud, please don't be so loud.*

HUSBAND: *Don't tell me what to do, you shut up!*

WIFE: *I'm sorry, I'm sorry. I'll do something better, I'll . . .*

HUSBAND: *Yeah, you'll do something better. Get in the kitchen!*

(SFX: SLAPPING)

HUSBAND: *Oh, it hurts. Do you wanna see what hurts.*

(SFX: PUNCHING, CRASH OF GLASS)

HUSBAND: *That's what hurts, that's what hurts.*

WIFE (SOBBING): *Please stop.*

HUSBAND: *Get up! Clean up this mess! Shut up!*

WIFE: *I'll be quiet! I'll be quiet! I'll be quiet!*

(SFX: SLAPPING)

WIFE (SOBBING): *Oh, please.*

SUPER: CHILDREN HAVE TO SIT BY AND WATCH. WHAT'S YOUR EXCUSE?

ANNCR: *For information call 1-800-END ABUSE.*

SUPER: THERE'S NO EXCUSE FOR DOMESTIC VIOLENCE.

SUPER: THE TRUTH.

PAM LAFFIN: *I started smoking when I was ten because I wanted to look older, and I got hooked. Cigarettes gave me asthma and bronchitis, but I couldn't quit. I didn't quit until I got emphysema and had a lung removed. I was 24. I'm 26 now. The medication, which I'll take for the rest of my life, left me with this fat face and a hump on my neck.*

I started smoking to look older, and I'm sorry to say it worked.

SUPER: MASSACHUSETTS DEPARTMENT OF PUBLIC HEALTH.

PUBLIC SERVICE &
POLITICAL FINALISTS

art director
John Gellos

writers
David Altschiller
Kevin Mooney

client
Family Violence
Prevention Fund

agency
Hill Holliday /
Altschiller, New York

CD 32

art director
Peter Favat

writer
Rich Herstek

agency producer
David Verhoef

production company
Picture Park

director
Erroll Morris

client
Massachusetts
Department of
Public Health

agency
Houston Herstek
Favat / Boston

**TELEVISION:
SINGLE**

art director
Thomas Hayo

writer
Richard Yelland

agency producers
Thomas Hayo
Richard Yelland

production company
Mars Media/HSI

director
Frank Ockenfels, III

client
Partnership for a
Drug-Free America

agency
J. Walter Thompson/
New York

CD 33

art director
Al Christensen

writer
David Oakley

agency producers
Julia Winfield
Sandi Bachom

production company
Big Idea Productions

director
Findlay Bunting

client
U.S. Student
Association

agency
Price/McNabb,
Charlotte, NC

CD 34

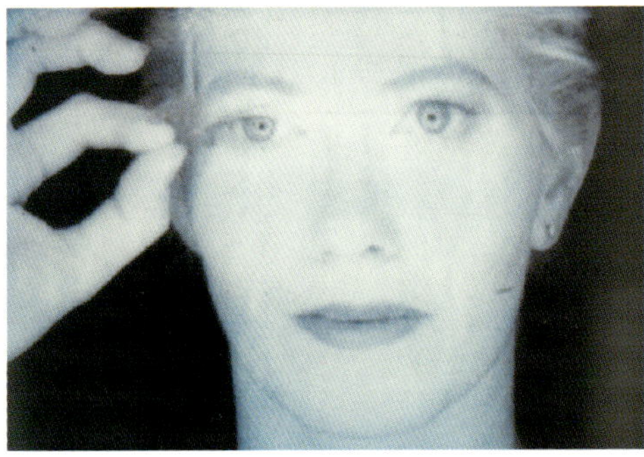

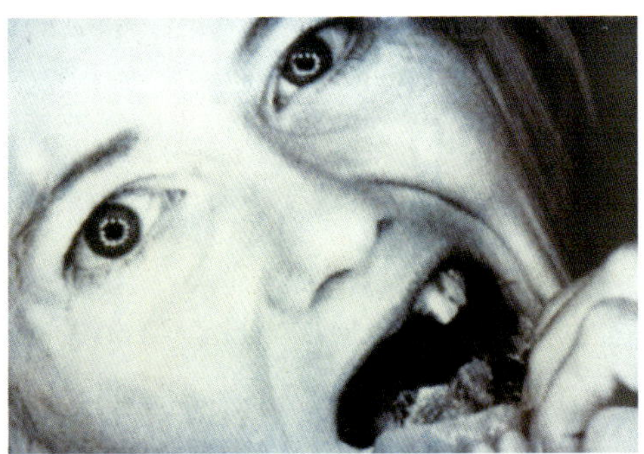

(MUSIC: THROUGHOUT)

SUPER: IT'S HARD TO FACE WHAT HEROIN CAN DO TO YOU. PARTNERSHIP FOR A DRUG-FREE AMERICA.

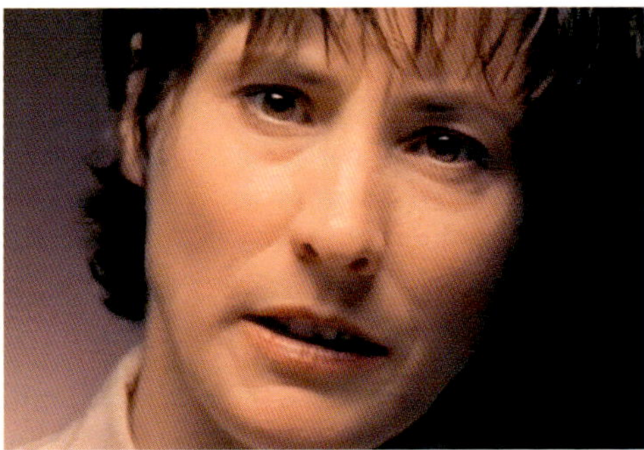

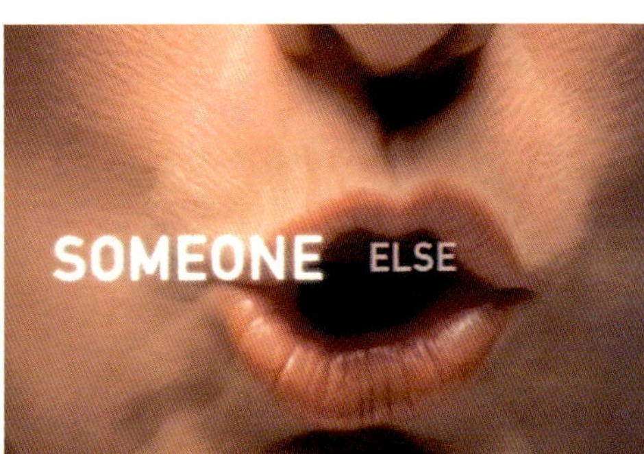

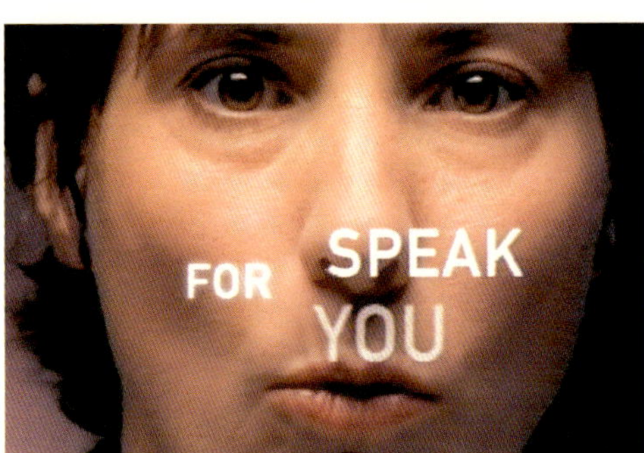

WOMAN: *Sometimes I think they should take whoever's responsible for the Oklahoma City bombing and just . . .*

(A MAN'S VOICE BREAKS IN AND REPLACES THE WOMAN'S VOICE; HER MOUTH KEEPS MOVING AS HIS WORDS COME OUT)

MAN'S VOICE: *. . . give 'em a medal. They're heroes in the war against the jack-booted thugs of government oppression. The Feds want to take away our guns . . .*

SUPER: IF YOU DON'T VOTE, SOMEONE ELSE WILL SPEAK FOR YOU.

MAN'S VOICE: *. . . and set up a global government run by Jewish bankers and the Vatican. We have to fight against the New World Order. We're patriots. You'll thank us in the end.*

SUPER: REGISTER TO VOTE.

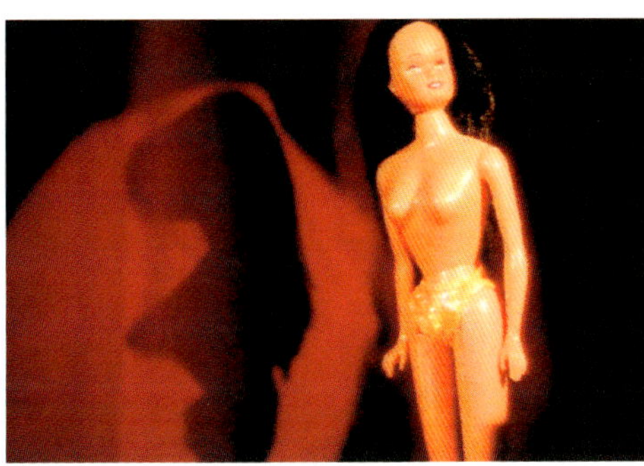

(MUSIC: "STRIPTEASE" THEME)

SUPER: THE FOLLOWING FILM IS BASED ON ACTUAL EVENTS.

SUPER: ANY SIMILARITIES TO THE ACTUAL BODY OF A MOTHER OF THREE ARE PURELY COINCIDENTAL.

CLUB OWNER: *Listen, doll . . . if you want custody of your kid, you gotta prove you're a fit mother. So let's see how fit you really are.*

DEMI: *But that would go against everything I stand for.*

CLUB OWNER: *I'll give you twelve-and-a-half mil'.*

DEMI: *Where do you want me to stand?*

DIRECTOR: CUT! BODY DOUBLE! ROLLING! AND ACTION!

SUPER: VANCOUVER INTERNATIONAL FILM FESTIVAL.

SUPER: CAST YOUR VOTE FOR THE PEOPLE'S CHOICE AWARD.

SUPER: BECAUSE SELLING OUT EVERY NIGHT SHOULDN'T BE THE ONLY WAY TO HAVE A HIT FILM.

DEMI: *I dunno . . . do you think they look real?*

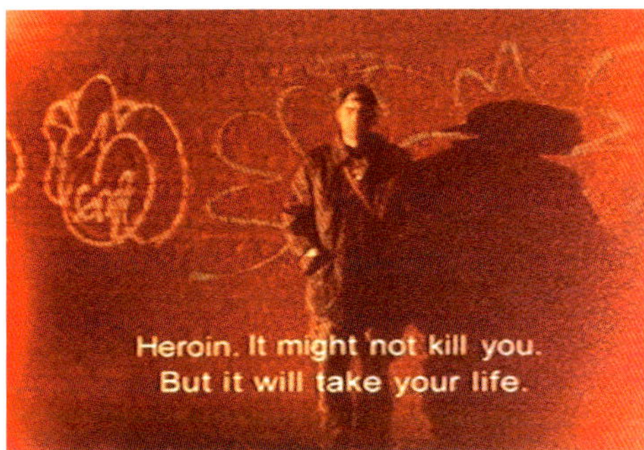

JOHNNY: *This is my parents house, East Brunswick, New Jersey just, ya know, my house where I grew up.*

SUPER: JOHNNY, AGE 21.

JOHNNY: *I've stolen jewelry from the house, belongin', ya know, that belongs to my parents. I've stole a CD player from, from my parents or I'll go into any store, I'll steal anything worth any value that I know I can sell. I don't think about the food I need. I don't think about maybe saving some money for, ya know, a hotel room for the night. I, it's just, ya know, I need a bag, and that's it. You know I moved out of my family's house, into my own apartment, and I couldn't afford to pay the rent there anymore and I ended up on the street, living on the street, ya know, stealin' so I could do dope. I've lost interest in everything I was ever interested in . . . I had lots of hobbies and things I liked to do. My only interest now is drugs and how am I gonna do the drugs, and I'm always worried about if I don't have the drugs I need I'm gonna be sick. You know, and, and so my only interest is, is keeping from being sick, and that's it. It's, it's not me, ya know, I've turned into a different person, I've turned into, into just, I mean it's, it's just a shell of me, ya know, a shell of what I used to be.*

SUPER: HEROIN. IT MIGHT NOT KILL YOU.

JOHNNY: *Physically, I'm still me but it's like the real me is dead inside it's, it's gone.*

SUPER: BUT IT WILL TAKE YOUR LIFE.

SUPER: PARTNERSHIP FOR A DRUG-FREE AMERICA.

PUBLIC SERVICE &
POLITICAL FINALISTS

**TELEVISION:
CAMPAIGN**

art director
Lisa Francilia

writer
Dan Scherk

agency producer
Pat Cooper

production company
Circle Productions

director
Rick Stevenson

client
Vancouver Sun / Vancouver
Film Festival

agency
BBDO / Vancouver

art director
Leeanna Golden

writer
Josh Miller

agency producer
Keith Haluska

production companies
Optic Nerve
Citizen Film

directors
Jon Kane
Bobby Sheehan

client
Partnership for a
Drug-Free America

agency
Hampel Stefanides /
New York

CD 35

STOP!
This book is the property of
and has been stolen. Contact
to receive a reward.

SINGLE

writer
April Winchell

agency producer
April Winchell

production company
Radio Savant

client
Glendale Federal Bank

agency
BBDO West/Los Angeles

writer
Aaron Stern

agency producer
Rob Sondik

client
PowerBar

agency
Citron Haligman
Bedecarre/
San Francisco

(SFX: Phone Ringing)

WOMAN'S VOICE (Filtered): *Welcome to your new bank. Now that we've taken over your old bank, we've increased the number of things you can do by phone. Listen closely to the following options:*
For a summary of new ways we'll be jerking you around, press one.
For a list of employees you like who have been fired, press two.
To hear how much more you'll have to pay in service charges and bank fees, press three.
To hear how much this phone call is costing you, press four.
To enroll in a workshop explaining how to read your new statement, press five.
To speak to an employee who doesn't care about your account, press six.
To be placed on hold and left there for up to six minutes before being disconnected, press the star key.

(SFX: Tone)

WOMAN'S VOICE: *Just a moment.*

(SFX: Muzak)

ANNCR: *If you're looking for more options, hang up and call Glendale Federal Bank at 1-800-41-FED UP. Our Infinity account gives you checking, a MasterMoney card and a money market account, all on one statement. And we can switch your account right over the phone.*

(SFX: Phone Disconnecting, Dial Tone)

ANNCR: *Glendale Federal. The other way to bank. Member FDIC.*

(SFX: Phone Ringing)

BILL: *Hello, Fredricks, this is Bill.*

MAN: *Hi, Fredricks, I was wondering, do you have any queen-size mattresses in stock?*

BILL: *Lots of 'em.*

MAN: *Oh great, okay. Uh, what do those weigh?*

BILL: *Oh, gee I don't know. The mattress . . . probably weighs ninety pounds . . . a hundred. I mean can I help you get it out to your truck. What do you got?*

MAN: *Actually, I'm on foot, so I thought I'd carry it . . .*

BILL: *Holy* (Beep)*!*

MAN: *It's no problem, though. I'm gonna eat a PowerBar and It'll give me plenty of energy to get home.*

BILL: *Where do you live?*

MAN: *Broadway and 65th. Oh the other side of the park.*

BILL: *No* (Beeping) *chance! Don't even think about walking.*

MAN: *I'll be fine. The PowerBar will keep me going. I'll just carry the mattress home.*

BILL: *You're nuts . . .* (To Friend) *He's on Broadway and 65th . . . you gotta be outta your mind. You'd never make it. You'd collapse.*

MAN: *Just have the mattress ready and I'll be there in 10 minutes.*

BILL: *You're nuts. You ain't gonna make it.*

MAN: *I'll see you there.*

BILL: (Laughs)

(SFX: Dial Tone)

ANNCR: *PowerBar energy bars. Balanced nutrition and lasting energy for everyday life, and then some. PowerOn.*

(SFX: Phone Ringing, Patter Of Baby Feet Running Toward It)

MIKEY: *Hello.*

MAN: *Hello . . . Mikey? . . . It's Daddy, Mikey.*

MIKEY: *Daddy?*

(SFX: Baby-Talk)

MAN: *Mikey. Can you go and get your mother? . . . Mikey?*

MIKEY: *Mummy.*

MAN: *That's right, get your mother . . . You're still there aren't you Mikey?*

MIKEY: *Daddy!*

MAN: *Mikey. Daddy's car's broken. Mikey, please get your mother.*

MIKEY: *Bye-bye . . .*

MAN: *Yeah . . . bye-bye . . .* (Laughs)

MIKEY: *Bye.*

ANNCR: *Next time you break down, call someone who cares. The RACV, where you're a member, not a number.*

writers
Bruce Paroissien
Craig Ford

agency producer
Jon Mahney

client
Royal Automobile
Club of Victoria

agency
Clemenger Harvie/
Melbourne

writer
Josh Denberg

agency producer
David Logan

client
San Francisco
Examiner Newspaper

agency
Goodby Silverstein &
Partners/San Francisco

writers
Jane Atkinson
Matt Hazell

agency producer
Donna Baker

client
McDonald's

agency
Leo Burnett/London

(SFX: Two Bells Sound)

ANNCR: *A message from the community council regarding the* EXAMINER *Bay to Breakers race. It will be held May 19th. Local traffic will be diverted along the race route. Plan accordingly. All runners in costume must be registered prior to the race. Citizens are asked not to interrupt the race by praying to those runners dressed like the Pope, the Archbishop or any other members of the clergy. Those dressing as meat products should be careful of dogs and hungry rodents along the race route. Anyone easily offended by the sight of hairy, over-weight men in ballerina costumes is advised not to attend. People dressed as dogs are reminded to curb themselves. Spectators are asked not to hurl objects at runners dressed as unpopular politicians, either living or dead. Participants are reminded that dressing as the Transamerica Tower is not an original idea. Bedouins on camels will not be permitted to race. Those dressing as perishable food stuff should avoid direct sunlight to preserve freshness. For complete costume rules and race information, see today's* EXAMINER.

DJ: *And now time for more money-saving tips from McDonald's. So lets go to line six. Hello, who's there?*

MAN: *It's Jamie.*

DJ: *Hello, Jamie, where you from?*

MAN: *I'm from Ohio.*

DJ: *Now you've got a money-saving tip for us, I hope.*

MAN: *Yes I do.*

DJ: *What's that.*

MAN: *It's for people who want to look at things closer.*

DJ: *Yeah . . .*

MAN: *. . . and to save money on expensive binoculars.*

DJ: *Precision instruments, yeah. What do you think we should do?*

MAN: *Well, what I think you should do is try to stand closer to the thing you're looking at, and then it will seem bigger.*

DJ: *That money-saving tip was brought to you by McDonald's where at participating restaurants a Fillet-O-Fish Sandwich, medium fries and a medium soft drink is one of seven extra value meals that will cost you just £2.88.*

SINGLE

writers
David Oakley
Al Christensen

agency producer
Julia Winfield

production company
John Causby
Productions

client
Weyerhaeuser

agency
Price/McNabb,
Charlotte, NC

writer
Brad Walk

agency producer
Thomas Hripko

client
Motel 6

agency
The Richards Group/
Dallas

CAMPAIGN

writers
Ian Reichenthal
Michelle Roufa
Wayne Best

agency producers
Maresa Wickham
Arlene Adoremos

client
Little Caesars

agency
Cliff Freeman &
Partners/New York

(SFX: COMEDY CLUB SOUNDS)

ANNCR: *Rodney Dangerfield . . . Las Vegas . . . 1968.*

RODNEY DANGERFIELD: *I tell ya I don't get no respect . . . no respect at all.*

(SFX: LAUGHTER AND POLITE APPLAUSE—ONE PERSON CLAPPING)

ANNCR: *Las Vegas . . . 1975.*

DANGERFIELD: *I tell ya I don't get no respect . . . no respect at all.*

(SFX: POLITE APPLAUSE)

HECKLER: *Why should ya?*

ANNCR: *Las Vegas . . . 1981.*

DANGERFIELD: *I tell ya I don't get no respect . . . no respect at all.*

(SFX: CROWD LAUGHS)

ANNCR: *Las Vegas . . . 1987.*

DANGERFIELD: *I tell ya I don't get no respect . . . no respect at all.*

(SFX: RIP-ROARING LAUGHTER AND CHEERING, CLAPPING)

ANNCR: *Las Vegas . . . 1996.*

DANGERFIELD: *I tell ya I don't get no respect . . . no respect at all.*

(SFX: THUNDEROUS APPLAUSE, CROWD ROARS, STANDING OVATION)

ANNCR: *Recycle. It works. A message from Weyerhaeuser. North Carolina's leading paper recycler.*

ANNCR: *To make the best-tasting pepperoni pizza in history, Little Caesars tried everything. They tried three times as much pepperoni . . .*

PEOPLE: *Mmmmmm!*

ANNCR: *They tried three kinds of pepperoni . . .*

PEOPLE: *Mmmmmm!*

ANNCR: *They tried three times the temperature . . .*

PEOPLE: *Aaaaaaahhhhhhhhhhhh!!!*

MAN: *. . . Let's just go with the first two ideas.*

ANNCR: *Little Caesars' Pepperoni Perfection. Three select kinds of pepperoni. Three times as much as before. Just $8.99 carried out or have it delivered. Great taste! Great price!*

LITTLE CAESAR: *Pizza! Pizza!*

TOM: *How to make a million dollars with no money down. Sort of. Tom Bodett here for Motel 6. Well, those get-rich-quick guys are everywhere, so I thought I'd get into the act, too. Well, I've got my aloha shirt on and a fool-proof one-step program that'll put money straight in your pocket. You won't believe how easy it is. Instead of dropping a bundle at one of those fancy joints, come stay at Motel 6 and pocket the difference. You get a clean, comfortable room for the lowest prices of any national chain. In the morning, you won't have a million dollars, but you will have a nice chunk of change left over. And to think, you got all this great advice without even having to attend my seminar. Well, call 1-800-4 MOTEL 6 for reservations. And remember, think positive, control your destiny and buy my video. I'm Tom Bodett, financial guru for Motel 6. We'll leave the light on for you.*

MOM: *For Tiffany's 10th birthday, we sent her to the Alps with her best friend Julie. She had always wanted to ski Gstaad. It was later that night when I got the phone call. Tiffany was very upset. I guess there was a mix-up with the tickets and the girls had to fly coach. They sat in those little seats the whole flight, eating nothing but peanuts. Thank God she had her Junior Gold Card on her.*

I told her to call the 800 number on the back. Junior Gold not only arranged for a meal to be sent to her hotel room, but flew in a top chiropractor to give her an adjustment before the lifts opened. They even extended Tiffany's credit line in case any other emergencies arose.

You never think something like this could happen to your little girl, I'm just glad she was prepared.

ANNCR: *The Junior Gold Card from Bank of Bel Air. Your children are priceless. Don't they deserve their very own gold? Children of household incomes 500,000 or greater may apply.*

(SFX: RECORD SCRATCH)

ANNCR: *This has been a test. I repeat, this has only been a test. If this had been the real L.A., you would have read about it in BUZZ MAGAZINE, L.A.'s Monthly Reality Check.*

ANNCR: *Good evening. Hope you're enjoying your drive home, to your happy family, your cool, gallon of milk in the fridge. If I sound jealous, forgive me. Because I live in a town where people aren't so lucky, a town without milk. Where little Billy dreams of a small cup, just big enough for his hand, with a few drops of milk in the bottom. Where paws, the town cat, dreams of having thumbs so she can hitchhike to a town where there is milk . . . And Sheriff Webber dreams of robbing the bank, and moving to Cuba, where he'll drink milk out of coconuts with little umbrellas in them. The town without milk is full of dreams. Maybe you, too, have a dream. Maybe it's about milk. Probably not. You have all you need right there in the fridge. Don't you?*

ANNCR 2: *Got Milk?*

TOM: *Friends, road warriors, countrymen, lend me your ears. Hi, Tom Bodett taking a little poetic license. Well there are lots of no-name motels out on the road that offer you rooms at a low price. So, to stay or not to stay, that is the question. Well since you can never tell what you're going to get at those joints, just stick with a place you know. Verily, that would be Motel 6. So, Tom, you're probably asking, "What's in a name?" Well in this case, a clean comfortable room for the lowest price of any national chain. And with over 750 locations coast to coast, you'll never find yourself out on the road asking, "wherefore art thou, Motel 6?" To reserve a room just call 1-800-4-MOTEL-6, and remember: a motel by any other name would not smell as sweet. Yeah, you get the drift. Well, I'm Tom Bodett for Motel 6, and we'll leave the light on for thee.*

writers
Bill Tsapalas
Liz Gumbinner

agency producer
Guy Williams

production company
Howard Schwartz

client
Buzz Magazine

agency
Deutsch/New York

writer
Blake Daley

agency producer
Heidi Bryant

client
California Milk
Processor Advisory Board

agency
Goodby Silverstein &
Partners/San Francisco

writers
Brad Walk
Mike Bales

client
Motel 6

agency
The Richards
Group/Dallas

UNDER PENALTY OF LAW THIS LABEL IS NOT
TO BE REMOVED EXCEPT BY THE CONSUMER

ALL **NEW MATERIAL**

LICENSE NO. NY 4480813

Certification is made
by the manufacturer
that the materials
in this article are
described in accord-
ance with the law.

SOLD TO:

Date of Delivery. . . . .
Fin. Size 9 x 12 in.

CONSUMER TELEVISION OVER :30 SINGLE

art directors
Bryan Buckley
Frank Todaro

writers
Bryan Buckley
Frank Todaro

agency producer
Robert Fernandez

production company
@radical.media

directors
Bryan Buckley
Frank Todaro

client
Independent
Film Channel

agency
@radical.media/
New York

art director
Don Schneider

writers
Michael Patti
Ted Sann

agency producers
Regina Ebel
Becky Friedman

production company
PYTKA

director
Joe Pytka

client
HBO

agency
BBDO/New York

CD 36

TIM ROBBINS: *Well, if you're gonna do a film about something like hockey you need to use real hockey players. You have to be technically correct.*

MARK MESSIER: *No, no, no. You gotta use a wide-angle lens here. Like an 18. Think John Frankenheimer.*

ROBBINS: *Gimme the 18. You need to make 'em feel even though they're not filmmakers that their suggestions are welcome.*

ASSISTANT DIRECTOR: *Wide open.*

MIKE RICHTER: *Hey wait. Wide open? You go wide open the whole backgrounds gonna go soft. I've envisioned this as kind of a Citizen Kane deep focus kind of feel. I mean . . .*

ROBBINS: *Mike, just–you know–how 'bout this? How 'bout you let me direct. I'll let you act. Alright? Hopefully, by the time you're wrapped you've both provided each other with a little insight.*

MESSIER: *Isn't this a great movie, Tim?*

ROBBINS: *I don't like it when they use subtitles. It's better when they dub it.*

ANNCR: *The Independent Film Channel.*

SUPER: THE GOMBE PRESERVE.

MARLON BRANDO (FROM "THE GODFATHER"): *Tataglia is a pimp . . . he never could have outsmarted Santino. What I didn't know until this day is that it was Barzini all along.*

MICHAEL C. HUMPHREY (FROM "FORREST GUMP"): *Mama says stupid is as stupid does.*

PETER FINCH (FROM "NETWORK"): *I'm mad as hell and I'm not going to take this anymore.*

JAMES EARL JONES (FROM "THE EMPIRE STRIKES BACK"): *The Force is with you, young Skywalker.*

(VOICES FROM "ANIMAL HOUSE"): *Toga! Toga! Toga!*

SYLVESTER STALLONE (FROM "ROCKY II"): *Yo, Adrienne, I did it!*

JANE GOODALL: *September 19th, their inexplicable behavior continues. Got to go now, Braveheart is on.*

SUPER: DR. JANE GOODALL, HBO VIEWER SINCE 1978.

SUPER: IT'S NOT TV. IT'S HBO.

ROBERT HAYES (FROM "AIRPLANE"): *Surely you can't be serious?*

LESLIE NIELSEN (FROM "AIRPLANE"): *I am serious, and don't call me Shirley.*

WIFE: *Where's my jacket?!!*

HUSBAND: *I'll get it. It's in the dryer.*

WIFE: *You put my jacket in the dryer!!??*

HUSBAND: *I was trying to get the wrinkles out for you . . . Hey, hon? Let's go down to the lake for a sec—skip rocks or something. Remember how we said we were gonna do more stuff like that?*

WIFE: *You don't get it do you? I've got the biggest meeting of my life—and you wanna skip rocks. You've lost perspective, Harry.*

SUPER: Balance.

SUPER: Eddie Bauer.

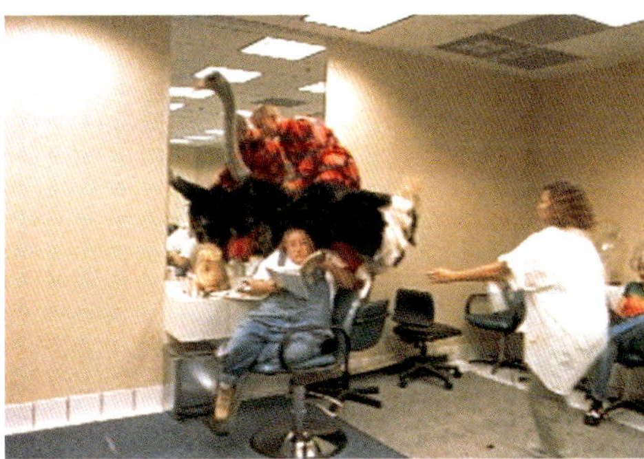

(MUSIC: Japanese)

(SFX: Breaking Glass)

SUPER: Do Something Different.

TELEVISION FINALISTS

art director
Steve Stone

writer
Bob Kerstetter

illustrator
David Hartz

agency producer
Stacy McClain

production company
Tool of North America

director
Erich Joiner

client
Eddie Bauer

agency
Black Rocket/
San Francisco

CD 37

art directors
Wayne Best
Roger Camp
David Angelo

writers
Ian Reichenthal
Michelle Roufa
Cliff Freeman

agency producer
Susan Macy

production company
Tony Kaye Films

director
Tony Kaye

client
Cherry Coke

agency
Cliff Freeman &
Partners/New York

CD 38

**CONSUMER
TELEVISION
OVER :30 SINGLE**

art director
Steve Fong

writer
Brian Bacino

agency producer
Steve Neely

production company
@radical.media

director
Tarsem

client
Levi Strauss & Co./
501 Jeans

agency
Foote Cone &
Belding/San Francisco

CD 39

art director
Antonio Navas

writer
Chuck McBride

agency producer
Steve Neely

production company
Bay Films/
Propaganda Films

director
Michael Bay

client
Levi Strauss & Co./
Wide Leg Jeans

agency
Foote Cone &
Belding/San Francisco

CD 40

(MUSIC: THROUGHOUT)

(SFX: CLIPPING OF NAILS)

(SFX: DOG PANTING)

(SFX: DOG GROWLING)

SUPER: REASON NO. 050.

ANNCR: *The fifth pocket, overlooked since 1873.*

SUPER: 501 LEVI'S.

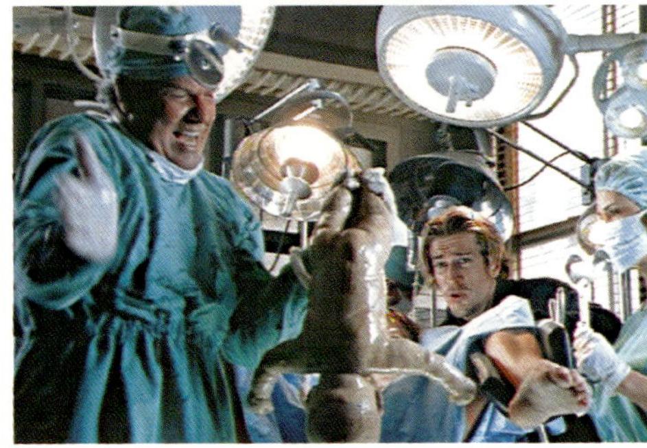

(SFX: ELEVATOR DOOR OPENING)

(SFX: ELEVATOR DOOR CLOSING)

(MUSIC: "I THINK I LOVE YOU" BY THE PARTRIDGE FAMILY)

LYRICS: *Hey-y-y! I think I love you. So . . . what am I so afraid of? I'm afraid that I'm not sure of a love there is no cure for. I think I love you . . . Isn't that what life is made of. Though it worries me to say I never felt this way.*

(SFX: SCREAMING)

LYRICS: *Hey-y-y! I think . . .*

(SFX: ELEVATOR DOOR OPENS)

ANNCR: *Levi's wide leg jeans . . . It's wide open.*

SUPER: IT'S WIDE OPEN.

(READING FROM ISAAK WALTON'S *THE COMPLEAT ANGLER*): *Oh sir, doubt not but that angling is an art. Is it not an art to deceive a trout with an artificial fly? In the morning up we rise, with a cup to wash our eyes . . . and leave the sluggish . . . In a brook with a hook, in a lake fish we take, there we sit for a bit, while we fish and tangle . . . I doubt not that to catch a brace or two for a friend's breakfast . . .* (LAUGHS) *Doubt not sir, therefore, that angling is an art . . . and an art worth your learning.*

SUPER: SONY.

ANNCR: *It's a Sony.*

ANNCR: *Mike Procter is a student at Buckley University, and he's about to participate in a remarkable experiment. Heading the research effort: Dr. Iqbal Theba, Ph.D.*

SUPER: DR. IQBAL THEBA, PH.D.

DR.: *Uh, The subject is 24 years old, we are trying to make it very comfortable for him . . . we have a big screen television, uh, video games . . . stereo. And of course, plenty–plenty–of his favorite food. He will live inside this small chamber. Cut off from all human contact, in the name of science.*

(SFX: MILK POURING OUT OF CARTON, AS DOOR LOCKS)

DR.: *Alone.*

STUDENT: *Hey, this one's empty there, ya know?*

ANNCR: *For the next 30 days.*

STUDENT: *Ahhhhhh. No, no, no, no. I didn't sign on for this . . . Guys?*

SUPER: CALIFORNIA FLUID MILK PROCESSOR ADVISORY BOARD.

STUDENT: *I got tons of cereal . . .* (CRYING) *Okay. It's okay, I know you're in there. I want some milk* (CRYING). *Pretty please . . . just a little bit.*

SUPER: GOT MILK?

(SFX: STUDENT CRYING)

TELEVISION FINALISTS

art directors
Graham Nunn
Brett Howlett

writers
Brett Howlett
Graham Nunn

agency producer
Chippie McLeod

production company
BLACK

director
Jeff Darling

client
Sony Australia

agency
Foster Nunn Loveder/
North Sydney

CD 41

art director
Sean Ehringer

writer
Harry Cocciolo

agency producer
Elizabeth O'Toole

production company
@radical.media

directors
Bryan Buckley
Frank Todaro

client
California Milk Processor
Advisory Board

agency
Goodby Silverstein &
Partners/San Francisco

CD 42

**CONSUMER
TELEVISION
OVER :30 SINGLE**

art director
John Doyle

writers
Scott Burns
Erich Joiner
Dave O'Hare

agency producer
Mike Davison

production company
Industrial Light & Magic

director
Joe Johnston

client
GMEV1/Saturn
Corporation

agency
Hal Riney & Partners/
San Francisco

CD 43

art director
Kevin Kehoe

writer
Mimi Cook

agency producer
Diane Hill

production company
Lovinger/Cohn

director
Jeff Lovinger

client
Saturn Corporation

agency
Hal Riney & Partners/
San Francisco

(MUSIC: THROUGHOUT)

(SFX: APPLIANCES TURNING ON BY THEMSELVES)

ANNCR: *The electric car is here.*

ANNCR: *All of us back here at Saturn are big fans of our Saturn cycling teams.*

SATURN CYCLIST 1: *Pardon me . . . excuse me.*

ANNCR: *It's not because some of them were picked for the summer games in Atlanta.*

SATURN CYCLIST 1: *Hey, you dropped this.*

ANNCR: *Or because they're recognized all over the world.*

SATURN CYCLIST 1: *Eh, buon giorno! Buon giorno! Piu venire–ah–un barbecue?*

ANNCR: *It's not even because they've won so many races. No, the reason we're so proud of them is because they truly understand the value of team work.*

SATURN CYCLIST 2: *Norm, you win.*

SATURN CYCLIST 3: *Nah, nah, nah. You take it.*

SATURN CYCLIST 2: *Nah, it's your turn to take it man.*

SATURN CYCLIST 4: *Hey guys! What's up?*

SATURN CYCLIST 2: *Uh–he'll take it.*

ANNCR: *In fact, sometimes they even surprise us!*

SATURN CYCLIST 4: *I'd really like to thank all my teammates. Diane Hill in, ah, Doortrim, Kevin Kehoe in Paint, ah, Pat Evans in, ah, Powertrain, Bill Engler in Engine Block, ah . . .*

SUPER: SATURN. A DIFFERENT KIND OF COMPANY. A DIFFERENT KIND OF CAR.

SUPER: They Will Spend Four Years In College.

SIGOURNEY WEAVER: *They are the sheep. And we are the shepherds.*

SUPER: You Will Spend $212,593.

WEAVER: *We tell them that college is the doorway. We tell them to prepare.*

SUPER: Insurance For The Unexpected.

WEAVER: *To be ready for the future. But the question remains. Will we?*

SUPER: Investments For The Opportunities.

WEAVER: *We are the mothers. We are the fathers. We are the shepherds.*

SUPER: John Hancock (Olympics Rings) Worldwide Sponsor.

MAN: *I've got . . . umm . . . there's something I've, uuuh, been meaning to tell you . . . I think about you all the time. My whole life's been turned around around since meeting you. I don't know how to say this, so I'm going to just come right out and say it. I love you, I need you, I have to have you.*

SUPER: Imperial Rental Cars. Now With Hands-Free Phones.

art director
Jamie Mambro

writers
Ernie Schenck
Mike Sheehan

agency producers
Diane Carlin
Deb Martin

production company
Tony Kaye Films

director
Tony Kaye

client
John Hancock
Financial Services

agency
Hill Holliday Connors
Cosmopulos / Boston

art director
Kevin Watkins

writer
Derek Shevel

agency producer
Helena Woodfine

production company
Peter Gird Productions

director
Mike Middleton

client
Imperial Car Rental

agency
Hunt Lascaris TBWA /
Johannesburg

CD 44

**CONSUMER
TELEVISION
OVER :30 SINGLE**

art director
Rui Alves

writer
George Lesar

agency producer
Lorraine Smit

production company
Velocity Afrika

director
Dave Gillard

client
Nando's Chickenland

agency
Hunt Lascaris TBWA/
Johannesburg

CD 45

art director
Scott Stephenson

writer
Scott Stephenson

production company
John Hancock Visual
Communications

director
Scott Stephenson

client
John Hancock Mutual Life
Insurance Company

agency
John Hancock Mutual Life
Insurance Company/Boston

CD 46

ANNCR 1: *Hi and welcome to Nandomania. Come in and get this Nando's full pack for only R39.95 and save an incredible R6,999 on this stove, because you won't have to cook. Every full pack includes a whole flame-grilled chicken, packet of jumbo chips, large salad and four rolls.*

ANNCR 2: *Plus, with every full pack, you get four free Cokes in the bigger can. That's right. Four free Cokes, already ice cold, so you save a whopping R4,999 on this fridge.*

ANNCR 1: *Let's look at those savings again. That's four free Cokes, R6,999 on the stove, R4,999 on the fridge. A total saving of R11,998. Get to Nando's right now and save.*

SUPER: NANDO'S. A TASTE OF PORTUGAL.

(MUSIC: "AMAZING GRACE" BY JUDY COLLINS)

SUPER: JIM CONNOLLY OF SOUTH BOSTON, WINNER OF THE TRIPLE JUMP AT ATHENS IN 1896 BECAME THE FIRST OLYMPIC CHAMPION IN 1,500 YEARS.

SUPER: ON HIS LAST ATTEMPT, JESSE OWENS BEAT THE GERMAN FAVORITE LUZ LONG, IN THE BROAD JUMP AT THE 1936 OLYMPIC GAMES IN BERLIN. THE FIRST PERSON TO CONGRATULATE HIM IN FRONT OF HITLER WAS LONG. THEY BECAME LIFELONG FRIENDS.

SUPER: BILLY MILLS, AN ORPHANED SIOUX INDIAN, HAD NEVER WON A MAJOR RACE. HE CAME OUT OF NOWHERE TO WIN THE 10,000 METER RUN AT TOKYO IN 1964. HE IS STILL THE ONLY AMERICAN TO WIN AN OLYMPIC 10,000.

SUPER: ONE OF 22 CHILDREN, WILMA RUDOLPH WORE A LEG BRACE FROM AGE 6 TO 10, A VICTIM OF RHEUMATIC FEVER. INCREDIBLY, SHE BECAME THE WORLD'S FASTEST WOMAN, WINNING THREE GOLD MEDALS AT THE 1960 ROME SUMMER GAMES.

SUPER: "EVERYBODY SHOULD HAVE A DREAM".
JESSE OWENS

(SFX: Cacophony Of Baby Noises)

(SFX: Baby Talking Over Loudspeaker Throughout)

SUPER: Citizens.

(SFX: Hushed Crowd)

SUPER: Listen!

SUPER: We Have The Right To Travel In Safety!

SUPER: Our Cars Should Provide Us With Everything We Need.

(SFX: Mass Appreciation Of Crowd)

SUPER: We Demand Not One Side-Impact Bar. But Two!

SUPER: Pollen Filters Should Be Included To Protect Our Little Noses.

(SFX: Sneezing)

SUPER: We Should Have Room For Hundreds Of Toys!

SUPER: Citizens! I Give You . . . The Astra From Vauxhall!

(SFX: Mass Chanting)

SUPER: The Astra From Vauxhall.

SUPER: First And Foremost A Family Car.

(MUSIC: "I'm Gonna Wash That Man Right Outta My Hair" By Mitzi Gaynor)

SUPER: A Woman Needs A Man Like A Fish Needs A Bicycle.   GRAFFITI

SUPER: Not Everything In Black And White Makes Sense.

art director
Charles Inge

writer
Phil Dearman

agency producer
Charles Crisp

production company
Tony Kaye Films

director
Tony Kaye

client
Vauxhall Motor Company

agency
Lowe Howard-Spink/ London

CD 47

art director
Clive Yaxley

writer
Jerry Gallaher

agency producer
John Montgomery

production company
Tony Kaye Films

director
Tony Kaye

client
Guinness

agency
Ogilvy & Mather/ London

CD 48

CONSUMER TELEVISION OVER :30 SINGLE

art director
Clive Yaxley

writer
Jerry Gallaher

agency producer
John Montgomery

production company
Tony Kaye Films

director
Tony Kaye

client
Guinness

agency
Ogilvy & Mather/
London

art directors
John Doyle
Rick Boyko

writer
David Fowler

agency producer
Lance Doty

production company
Propaganda Films

director
David Kellogg

client
Eastman Kodak Company

agency
Ogilvy & Mather/
New York

CD 49

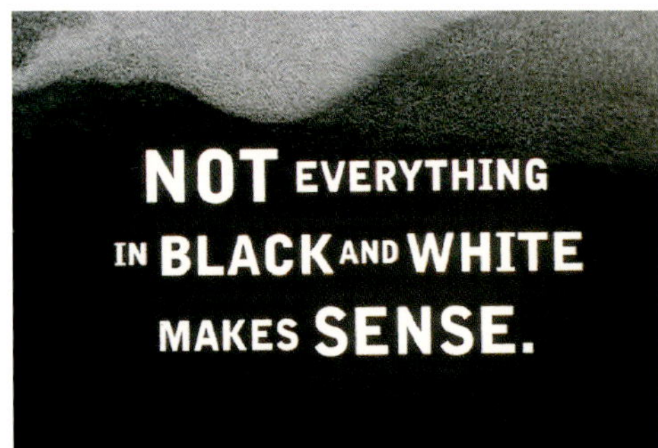

(MUSIC: "THE STORY OF MY LIFE" BY MICHAEL HOLLIDAY)

SUPER: HOPE I DIE BEFORE I GET OLD.
PETE TOWNSHEND

SUPER: NOT EVERYTHING IN BLACK AND WHITE MAKES SENSE.

GUY: *I had this car so I took a picture. It's not just a car, it's a Gremlin. So this girl at the photo shop says . . .*

GIRL: *Wow, it'll only take a minute to make a copy.*

GUY: *Dig it. She makes an enlargement of the Gremster, then says . . .*

GIRL: *I can do a little body work on it and put your shots on Photo CD.*

GUY: *Dig it . . . So, she retouches the thing on the door. Then I went home and logged into the Grem Lovers Party Room, and met a Grem-diggin' Finn named Liska.*

LISKA: *Howdy, Gremster.*

GUY: *Meanwhile, Dad comes home and crashes into Grem-puppy. And this insurance guy comes out with a Kodak digital camera and shoots my hurtin' Grem-child. Then right there from his insurance man van he finds me a quarter panel from Cowboy Bob in Lubbock Texas, who's on my door . . .*

COWBOY BOB: *Howdy, Gremster!*

GUY: *Saying he wants to buy Honey McGrem from me . . . Cool, how much?*

COWBOY BOB: *Enough to go to college... Enough to go to college and buy a cheese-burger... Enough to go to welding school, buy a cheeseburger, and fly to Finland.*

GUY: *Dig it . . . So like I said. . . I had this car, so I took a picture.*

SUPER: KODAK. TAKE PICTURES. FURTHER.

ANNCR: *This is a story about America. It's a story of potatoes and cows and a man with a dream . . . named Jack. The dream wasn't named Jack, the man was.*

Anyway, about a year ago Jack promised to make his burgers, shakes and fries the best in the land. Jack listened to people big and small, and discovered a common bond: We like our shakes thick and frosty—made with real ice cream and enough creamy butter fat to lube a tractor. To make the ultimate french fry, he searched far and wide for just the right potatoes.

JACK: *Found one!*

ANNCR: *And as for Jack's new burgers–cowboys say they're juicier, and cowboys never lie. Has Jack fulfilled his promise? Is it the best fast-food there is? It's not for him to say. But you can judge for yourself at a place called Jack In The Box, in a country called America.*

(**SFX:** KIDS PLAYING BASEBALL)

KID: *Come on, let's move back . . . here we go.*

(**SFX:** JET PLANE AS BALL ROARS THROUGH SKY)

CATCHER: *Holy smokes . . .*

KID: *Hey! I'm not gonna hurt you. Come on, doggy, come on. Lemme have the ball. Hey! Come back here . . . Wow!*

MR. K: *Welcome to my garage. Go ahead, look around. That is the original 240Z . . . It's a real beauty. This is the first small truck in America. Dogs love trucks. Hey. Over here. Roy Rogers used to own one–I'm over here.*

KID: *Whoa, bet this thing hauls.*

MR. K: *It won three consecutive world championships.*

KID: *Cool.*

MR. K: *It's very fast . . . Any car can get you where you need to go. A special car gets you there with a smile on your face. Remember, young man, life . . . is a journey. Enjoy the ride.*

(**SFX:** KIDS SHOUTING)

KIDS: *Come on, get him out! Get him! Come on! Come on! . . . Gotcha!*

SUPER: NISSAN. ENJOY THE RIDE.

art director
Dick Sittig

writer
Dick Sittig

agency producer
Kelly Salmon

production company
@radical.media

director
Dick Sittig

client
Jack In The Box

agency
TBWA Chiat / Day,
Venice, CA

CD 50

art director
Joe Hemp

writer
Rob Siltanen

agency producer
Richard O'Neill

production company
Smillie Films

director
Kinka Usher

client
Nissan Motor
Corporation

agency
TBWA Chiat / Day,
Venice, CA

**CONSUMER
TELEVISION
OVER :30 SINGLE**

art director
Vince Engel

writer
Jerry Cronin

agency producer
Jonathan Slater

production company
Foodchain

director
Marc Greenfield

client
ESPN

agency
Wieden & Kennedy/
Portland

art director
Susan Hoffman

writer
Jamie Barrett

agency producer
Jeff Selis

production company
Satellite Films

director
Spike Jonze

client
Nike

agency
Wieden & Kennedy/
Portland

(SFX: Figurines Being Smashed)

SUPER: 20 Down. 8 To Go.

SUPER: Baseball Playoffs On ESPN.

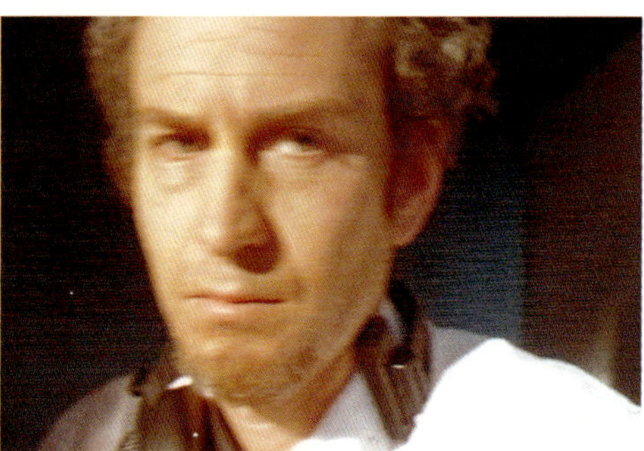

JOHN McENROE: *I'll tell you something. The way this point's going, get comfortable . . . cause we could be here awhile.*

(SFX: Electric Razor)

McENROE: *Hit it in the net. Just hit it in the net.*

WOMAN (On Phone):
What do you mean the point's still going on? John, how long can the point last?

UMPIRE: *Let. Replay the point.*

McENROE (Singing):
99 bottles of beer on the wall! 99 bottles of beer . . .

SUPER: Just Do It.

JAMES CARVILLE: *Climate is right for change. People don't want someone comin' out of left field. And they sure don't want somebody that plays too far right. Griffey's in the center, perfectly positioned.*

GEORGE CLINTON: *In this country it's the bottom of the ninth, two outs, we're behind. We need Junior. We need a hit.*

CARVILLE: *Pennsylvania, key state. Not a good state for Griffey. Philadelphia, Pittsburgh both national league teams.*

CLINTON: *We've had an actor why not a centerfielder?*

CARVILLE: *If you can hit an Orel Hirscheiser slider, there's no reason to believe that you can't hit welfare reform.*

CLINTON: *They have their elephants. They got their donkeys. We got our moose.*

ICE-T: *Man that Ken Griffey for president thing is straight up sell out, nothing but a marketing scheme.*

PHIL KNIGHT: *This is not, I repeat, not a marketing scheme.*

INTERVIEWER: *Don't ya have to be 35 to be a president?*

CARVILLE: *Well that's what the Constitution says. I mean if you're gonna pay attention to that kind of stuff—yeah.*

(SFX: TRUCK CRASHING)
SUPER: JUST DO IT.

TELEVISION FINALISTS

art director
Darryl McDonald

writer
Hank Perlman

agency producer
Derek Ruddy

production company
@radical.media

directors
Bryan Buckley
Frank Todaro

client
Nike

agency
Wieden & Kennedy/
Portland

art director
Linda Knight

writer
Ned McNeilage

agency producer
Jennifer Smieja

production company
@radical.media

director
Alan White

client
Nike Australia

agency
Wieden & Kennedy/
Portland

CD 51

**CONSUMER
TELEVISION
OVER :30 CAMPAIGN**

art directors
John Shirley
Bill Karow
Kevin Kehoe

writers
David Stolberg
Tripp Westbrook
Mimi Cook

agency producers
Ed Galvez
Diane Hill

production companies
Gartner/Grasso
Lovinger/Cohn

directors
Jim Gartner
Jeff Lovinger

client
Saturn Corporation

agency
Hal Riney & Partners/
San Francisco

**CONSUMER
TELEVISION
:30 SINGLE**

art director
Greg Martin

writer
Pat Doherty

agency producer
Carol Powell

production company
Park Village Productions

director
Roger Woodburn

client
Bayer/Alka Seltzer

agency
Abbott Mead Vickers.
BBDO/London

CD 52

NIAGARA FALLS GUIDE: *Behind me, Niagara Falls, where two million . . .*

STATUE OF LIBERTY GUIDE: *Pounds of copper and three thousand rivets hold together this . . .*

CAPITOL GUIDE: *Our congress, which has met here . . .*

ANNCR: *There are a lot of interesting things to see in this country . . .*

SATURN GUIDE: *On your right, you'll see the marriage of the body and the chassis.*

ANNCR: *Who would have ever thought a car factory would be one of them.*

SATURN GUIDE: *Over to the left—dashboard assembly!*

ANNCR: *All we know is the more people learn about Saturn, the more they want to come visit us. So each week we show folks around the place.*

SATURN GUIDE: *You can stomp on this all day.*

ANNCR: *Pointing out crowd-pleasers like lost foam casting and seat installation.*

SATURN GUIDE: *Go ahead, get right in there . . . Note that we've added sky lights here to add to the cafeteria setting.*

ANNCR: *We're flattered by all the attention, we're just a little baffled by it. I mean we are just making cars, right?*

SATURN GUIDE: *Next stop, Saturn gift shop.*

SUPER: SATURN. A DIFFERENT KIND OF COMPANY. A DIFFERENT KIND OF CAR.

SUPER: ALKA-SELTZER.

ANNCR: *Alka-Seltzer. When you've eaten something you shouldn't have.*

PAINTER: *Humming.*

(SFX: FOOTBALL PRACTICE IN BACKGROUND)

PLAYER 1: *Hey, that's great but who are the Chefs?*

ANNCR: *Not going anywhere for awhile?*

PAINTER: *Great googlie mooglie.*

ANNCR: *Grab a Snickers.*

PLAYER 2: *Your spelling's . . .*

PAINTER: *Yeah.*

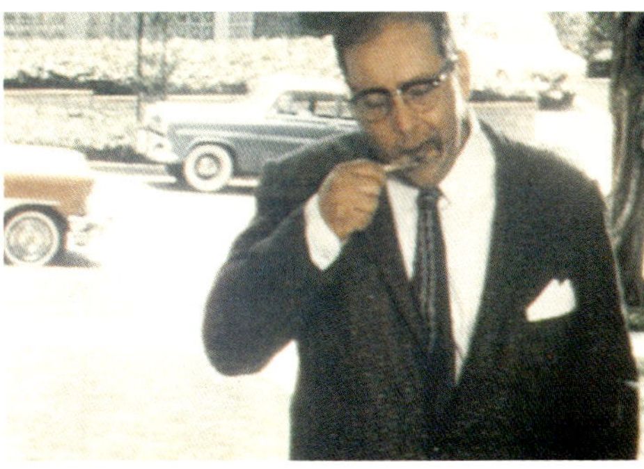

SUPER: MEETING HER DAD.

ANNCR: *Bill is about to meet Suzy's father. He's eating greasy fried chicken. Better get rid of that . . . Good. Mr. Smith is thinking, Bill seems like a nice guy, but his hands are awfully greasy. . . let's try again. This time Bill's eating a Buffalo Chicken Pizza from Round Table with chicken spiced just like Buffalo wings. Good. Bill's hands are not greasy, but Mr. Smith still doesn't like him. Why? Because they're the same age, that's why!*

SUPER: ROUND TABLE. THE LAST HONEST PIZZA.

art directors
Gerry Graf
David Gray

writers
Gerry Graf
David Gray

agency producer
J.D. Williams

production company
@radical.media

directors
Bryan Buckley
Frank Todaro

client
M&M Mars/Snickers

agency
BBDO/New York

CD 53

art director
John Butler

writer
Mike Shine

designer
Steve Sandstrom

agency producer
Adrienne Cummins

production company
Tool of North America

director
Erich Joiner

client
Round Table Pizza

agency
Butler Shine &
Stern/Sausalito

CD 54

**CONSUMER
TELEVISION
:30 SINGLE**

art directors
Roger Camp
Greg Bell

writer
Michelle Roufa

agency producer
Maresa Wickham

production company
HSI

director
Geoff McGann

client
Little Caesars

agency
Cliff Freeman &
Partners / New York

art director
David Angelo

writer
Cliff Freeman

agency producer
Liz Graves

production company
Crossroads Films

director
Mark Story

client
Little Caesars

agency
Cliff Freeman &
Partners / New York

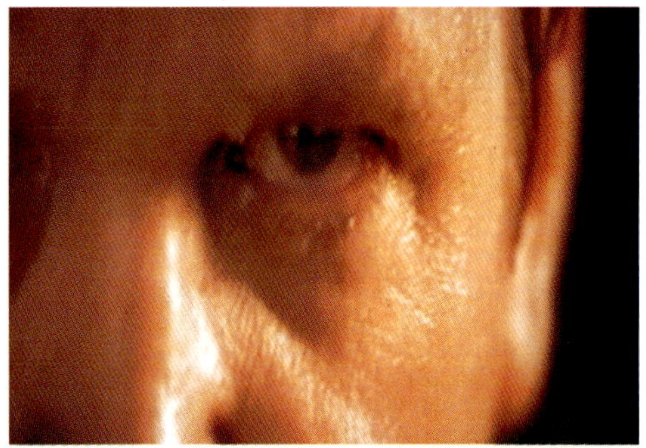

ANNCR I: *When I'm out here, I am not just flesh and bone . . . I am not bound by fear or doubt . . . I am . . . the wind.*

(SFX: DOG GRUMBLING)

ANNCR 2: *Little Caesars Sports Pizza Pizza: two football pizzas, a life-size poster, and a box top game all for just $10.99 carried out, or have it delivered.*

LITTLE CAESAR: *Pizza! Pizza!*

FIRST EMPLOYEE: *What'ya lookin' at?*

SECOND EMPLOYEE: *The Grand Canyon.*

FIRST EMPLOYEE: *Where?*

SECOND EMPLOYEE: *Right there.*

FIRST EMPLOYEE: *Where?*

SECOND EMPLOYEE: *Right there.*

FIRST COWBOY: *What'ya eatin'?*

SECOND COWBOY: *Giant Caesar.*

FIRST COWBOY: *What'ya steppin' in?*

SECOND COWBOY: *Has to be China.*

ANNCR: *Everything looks small next to the Giant Caesar.*

HUSBAND: *What?*

ANNCR: *From Little Caesars, giant slices with giant pepperoni—$9.99 carried out or have it delivered.*

LITTLE CAESAR (IN DEEP VOICE): PIZZA, PIZZA.

VOICE ON VIDEO: *Your new Pizza By The Foot is radically different so please observe a safe turning radius. No . . . Yes . . . Thank you and good luck . . .*

(SFX: MONITOR CRASHING TO FLOOR, BREAKING GLASS)

VOICE IN DISTANCE: *Hey, Look out!*

MANAGER: *I don't think he was paying attention.*

ANNCR: *Pizza By The Foot. Nearly three feet of pizza with free Italian bread, just $10.99. Carry out or have it delivered.*

LITTLE CAESAR (VIBRATING): *Pizza! Pizza!*

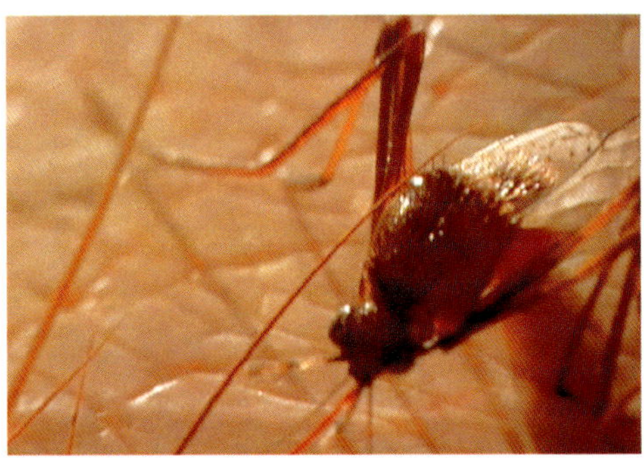

(SFX: OUTDOOR NIGHT SOUNDS)

(SFX: HUM OF BUG ZAPPER)

(SFX: EXAGGERATED "GLUGS" OF SAUCE GOING ONTO PIZZA)

(SFX: BOTTLE FALLING AND ROLLING)

(SFX: BUZZING OF MOSQUITO)

(SFX: BUZZING STOPS)

(SFX: EXAGGERATED SOUND OF MOSQUITO NEEDLE STICKING INTO LEG)

(SFX: MOSQUITO BUZZING ANGRILY)

(SFX: MOSQUITO EXPLODING LOUDLY INTO FLAMES)

(SFX: NIGHT SOUNDS)

art directors
Greg Bell
Matt Vescovo

writers
Arthur Bijur
Greg Bell
Matt Vescovo

agency producer
Tom Meloth

production company
A&R Group

director
David Ramser

client
Little Caesars

agency
Cliff Freeman &
Partners / New York

art director
Tom Moudry

writer
Galen Greenwood

agency producer
Hal Dantzler

production company
SQUEAK Pictures

director
Dick Buckley

client
McIlhenny Co.

agency
DDB Needham / Dallas

CD 55

**CONSUMER
TELEVISION
:30 SINGLE**

art director
Harvey Marco

writer
Dean Buckhorn

agency producer
Ardi Kramer

production company
@radical.media

director
Alan White

client
Lee Apparel Company

agency
Fallon McElligott/
Minneapolis

CD 56

art director
Harvey Marco

writer
Dean Buckhorn

agency producer
Ardi Kramer

production company
@radical.media

director
Alan White

client
Lee Apparel Company

agency
Fallon McElligott/
Minneapolis

CD 57

(MUSIC: THROUGHOUT)

GUY: *Excuse me . . . do you have any change?*

GIRL: *Let me check.*

SUPER: LEE. CUT TO FIT.

(MUSIC: THROUGHOUT)

WOMAN: *Billy? . . . How did you know when I was coming home?*

GUY: *Well, I just figured it was a half-hour from the airport . . . ten minutes to get your luggage . . . a four-hour flight . . . and then there was, what eighteen months to get your graduate degree . . . four years for your undergraduate. . .and when you factor in the leap year . . . and the daylight savings time . . .*

SUPER: LEE. CUT TO FIT.

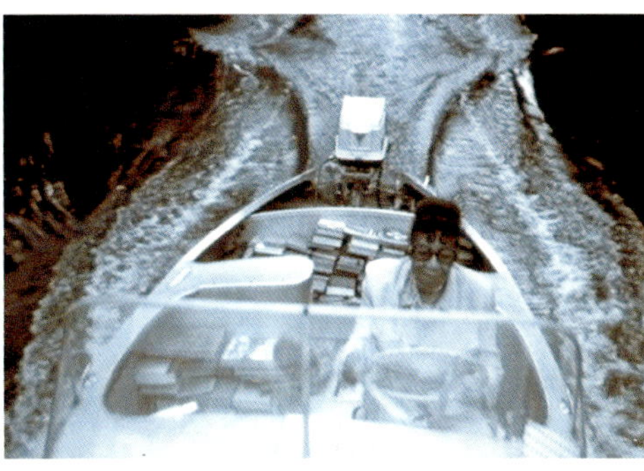

(MUSIC: JAZZY)

ROSALIE: *This is our secret. I believe that every woman who wants to live a full life has to be independent.*

SUPER: LIVE WELL.

ROSALIE: *You cannot depend on other people to make your life click.*

SUPER: MAKE A PLAN.

ROSALIE: *You're independent. You go when you need to go. You do what you need to do. You do what makes you happy.*

SUPER: BE YOUR OWN ROCK.

ROSALIE: *Go. Go girl.* (LAUGHS)

SUPER: PRUDENTIAL. BE YOUR OWN ROCK.

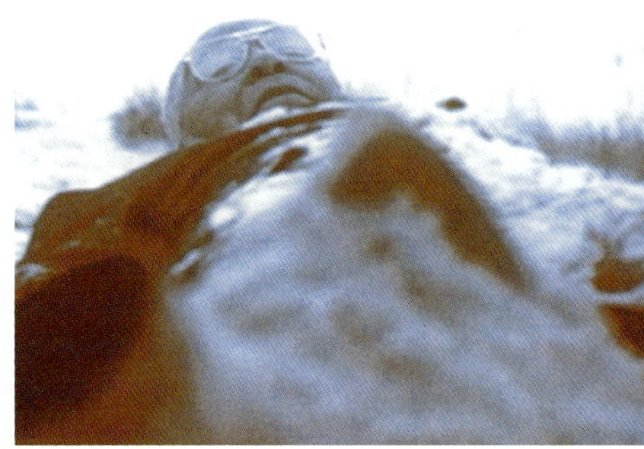

(MUSIC: THROUGHOUT)

SENATOR: *I am a grandfather that takes pleasure in doin' anything I can for the kids . . . And they know it too* (LAUGHS).

SUPER: LIVE WELL.

SENATOR: *I've never been rich and never really wanted to be. I just feel, you should live comfortably. But you don't need to be a fool about it.*

SUPER: MAKE A PLAN.

SENATOR: *And I try to, um, impart that to my grandchildren. You gotta have a goal, an aim in life in order to get anywhere.*

SUPER: BE YOUR OWN ROCK.

SUPER: PRUDENTIAL. BE YOUR OWN ROCK.

art director
Amy Nicholson

writer
Peter McHugh

agency producer
Bruce Wellington

production company
Propaganda Films

director
Jeffrey Plansker

client
The Prudential

agency
Fallon McElligott/
Minneapolis

art director
Amy Nicholson

writer
Bill Westbrook

agency producer
Bruce Wellington

production company
Propaganda Films

director
Jeffrey Plansker

client
The Prudential

agency
Fallon McElligott/
Minneapolis

CONSUMER TELEVISION :30 SINGLE

art director
Erich Joiner

writer
Bob Kerstetter

agency producer
Rebecca O'Sullivan

production company
Tool of North America

director
Erich Joiner

client
FOX Sports

agency
FOX/Santa Monica

art director
Erich Joiner

writers
Scott Burns
Craig Joiner

agency producer
Rebecca O'Sullivan

production company
Tool of North America

director
Scott Burns

client
FOX Sports

agency
FOX/Santa Monica

CD 58

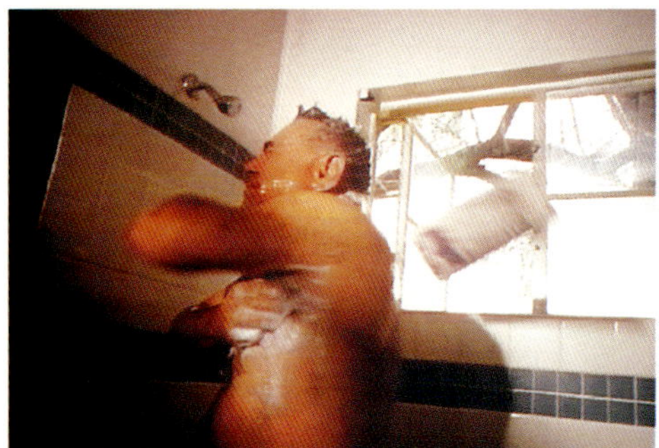

SUPER: RANDY JOHNSON. MARINERS.

RANDY JOHNSON: *A lot of people wonder what pitchers do when they're not playing. I for instance . . . have a paper route.*

(SFX: PEOPLE GETTING HIT BY PAPERS, SCREAMING IN PAIN)

JOHNSON: *Whoops.*

(SFX: PAPER BREAKING A WINDOW)

JOHNSON: *Obviously, it's not for the money. I guess I just like people.*

SUPER: FOX SPORTS.

(MUSIC: "THE ODD COUPLE" THEME)

ANNCR (IN "THE ODD COUPLE" VO STYLE): *On June 13th, Wayne Gretzky left his place of residence, never to return. Not knowing exactly where to go, he found himself on the team of his friend, Mark Messier. Can two men, with different styles, play together, without driving each other insane? Stay tuned.*

SUPER: NHL ON FOX.

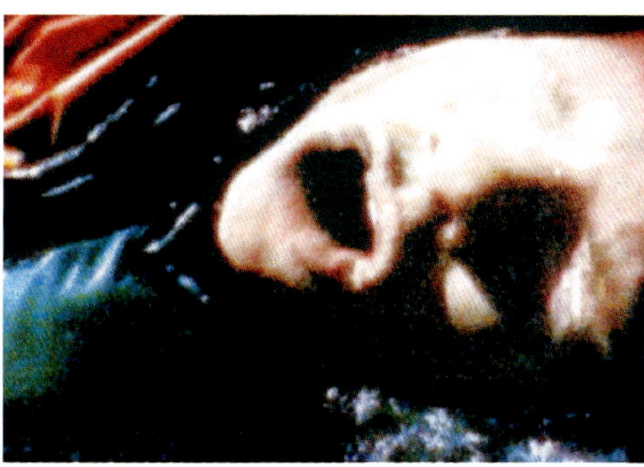

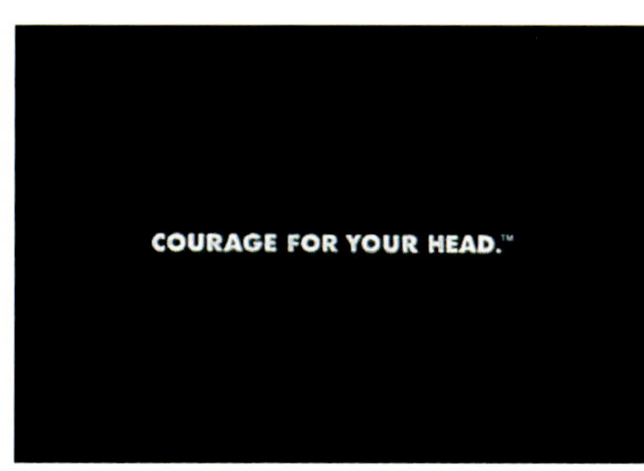

TELEVISION FINALISTS

art director
Chris Hooper

writer
Bob Kerstetter

agency producer
Ben Latimer

production company
Morton Jenkel & Zander

director
Robert Richardson

client
Anheuser-Busch

agency
Goodby Silverstein &
Partners/San Francisco

CD 59

art director
Jeremy Postaer

writer
Paul Venables

agency producer
Elizabeth O'Toole

production company
Johns + Gorman Films

director
Clint Clemens

client
Bell Sports

agency
Goodby Silverstein &
Partners/San Francisco

(MUSIC: DRAMATIC)

ANNCR: *You don't take orders from anyone but the sea. And the harder you work . . . the more you earn. And the more you earn, the more you keep. And after it's all said and done, you walk away with the two things nobody can take, good friends and good corn.*

SUPER: IT'D BE WEIRD WITHOUT BEER.

SUPER: A MESSAGE FROM THE BREWMASTERS OF ANHEUSER-BUSCH.

(SFX: WHISTLING THROUGHOUT)

(SFX: "CLINK")

SUPER: HERE ARE THE POSSIBILITIES)

(SFX: "CLINK")

SUPER: 1. YOU COULD HIT YOUR HEAD ON A ROCK.

(SFX: "CLINK")

SUPER: 2. YOU COULD DROWN.

SUPER: OR,

(SFX: "CLINK")

SUPER: 3. YOU COULD HIT YOUR HEAD ON A ROCK, THEN DROWN.

SUPER: BELL HELMETS.

(SFX: "SMASH")

ANNCR: *Bell. Official helmet of the X-Games.*

(SFX: "SQUISH")

(SFX: "SNAP")

(SFX: ACCELERATION SOUND)

SUPER: COURAGE FOR YOUR HEAD.

**CONSUMER
TELEVISION
:30 SINGLE**

art director
Jeremy Postaer

writer
Paul Venables

agency producer
Elizabeth O'Toole

production company
Johns + Gorman Films

director
Clint Clemens

client
Bell Sports

agency
Goodby Silverstein &
Partners/San Francisco

CD 60

art director
Tom Routson

writer
Al Kelly

agency producer
Cindy Fluitt

production company
Propaganda Films

director
Jeffrey Goodby

client
Hewlett Packard

agency
Goodby Silverstein &
Partners/San Francisco

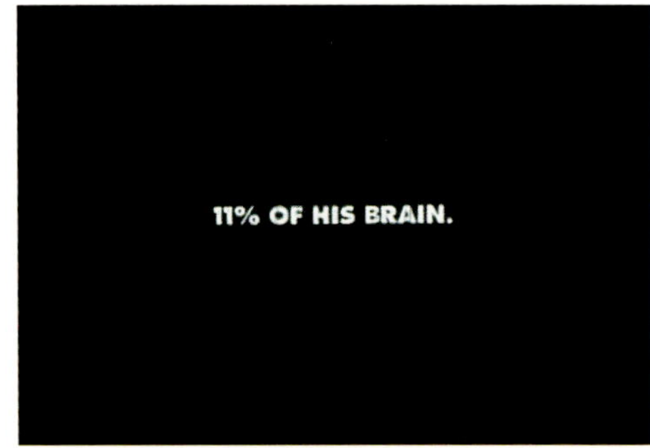

(SFX: WHISTLING THROUGHOUT)

(SFX: COW BELL)

SUPER: MAN USES APPROXIMATELY

(SFX: COW BELL)

SUPER: 11% OF HIS BRAIN.

(SFX: COW BELL)

SUPER: A FACT THAT MAKES

(SFX: COW BELL)

SUPER: THE X-GAMES POSSIBLE.

SUPER: BELL HELMETS.

(SFX: "SMASH")

ANNCR: *Bell. Official helmet of the X-Games.*

(SFX: "SQUISH")

(SFX: "SNAP")

(SFX: ACCELERATION SOUND)

SUPER: COURAGE FOR YOUR HEAD.

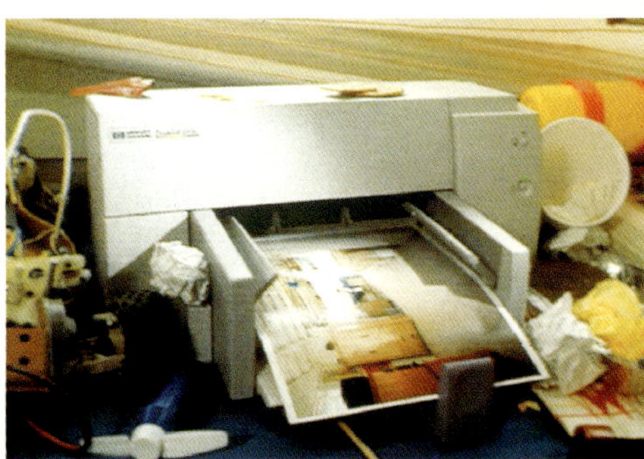

(MUSIC: THROUGHOUT)

MOM: *That room will be clean when I get back.*

KID: *Absolutely, Mom.*

ANNCR: *Surprisingly realistic photo-quality printers. From HP.*

SUPER: BUILT BY ENGINEERS. USED BY NORMAL PEOPLE.

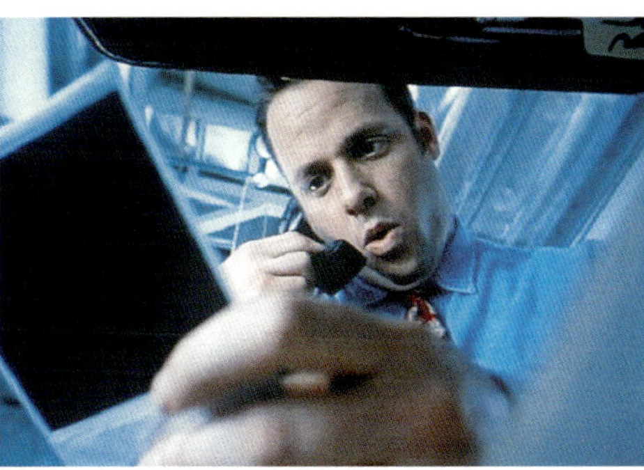

(SFX: Office Phones And Chatter)

HUSBAND: *This is right, this is exactly right!*

CO-WORKER 1: *How am I supposed to explain that to the client?*

CO-WORKER 2: *We have no time!*

(SFX: Phone Rings)

HUSBAND: *This is Jeff . . .*

WIFE (Caller): *Hi, it's me!*

HUSBAND: *Hi, uh, what's up?*

WIFE: *How's work?*

HUSBAND: *It's uh, it's uh, very busy, what's up?*

WIFE: *Do ya want to meet me for lunch?*

HUSBAND: *No, no, that's uh, I can't do that right now . . . I can't . . . I'm in the middle of something and I can't get away . . . it's uh, it's uh, a big meeting . . . big meeting!*

WIFE: *Uh, huh . . . Have you looked in your briefcase yet?*

(SFX: Latches On Briefcase Opening)

WIFE: *I left you something this morning.*

HUSBAND: *Oooooohhhhhhh! . . . I'll be home in, uh, in ten, in ten minutes!*

SUPER: Polaroid. See What Develops.

(SFX: Zoo Sounds)

(SFX: Camera Snap)

(MUSIC: Upbeat Tempo)

SUPER: Visa.

(SFX: Chimpanzees Screeching)

SUPER: Visa. All You Need.

art director
Sean Ehringer

writer
Harry Cocciolo

agency producer
Jane Jacobsen

production company
Smillie Films

director
Kinka Usher

client
Polaroid Corporation

agency
Goodby Silverstein &
Partners/San Francisco

art director
Frank Lepre

writer
Patrick Doyle

agency producer
Aggie Brook

production company
The Players

director
David McNally

client
Visa Canada

agency
Leo Burnett/Toronto

CD 61

**CONSUMER
TELEVISION
:30 SINGLE**

art director
Kurt Reifschneider

writer
John Schofield

agency producer
Michelle Berman

production company
Blue Goose Productions

director
Ron Gross

client
Seattle Mariners

agency
McCann-Erickson/
Seattle

art director
Michael Lee

writer
Rob Feakins

agency producer
Tom Meloth

director
Elma Garcia

client
Volvo

agency
Messner Vetere Berger
McNamee Schmetterer/
EURO RSCG, New York

CD 62

(SFX: Bug Buzzing)

(SFX: "Splat")

BUHNER: *I didn't quite get under it.*

ANNCR: *The 1996 Seattle Mariners. You gotta love these guys.*

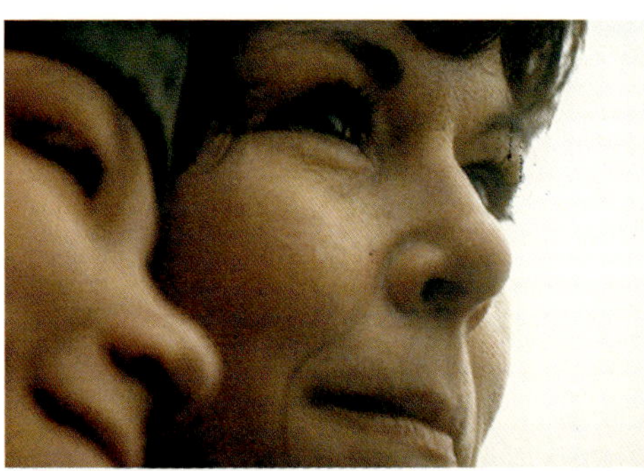

SUPER: Linda And Katie Dugger, November 20, 1994.

ANNCR: *On November 20th, 1994, Linda and Katie Dugger created automotive history. An oncoming car veered out of control and slammed into the side of their Volvo 850. It was the first time ever a side-impact air bag deployed in a life-threatening accident. Both mother and daughter share a belief that a car saved their lives that day.*

SUPER: Volvo. Drive Safely.

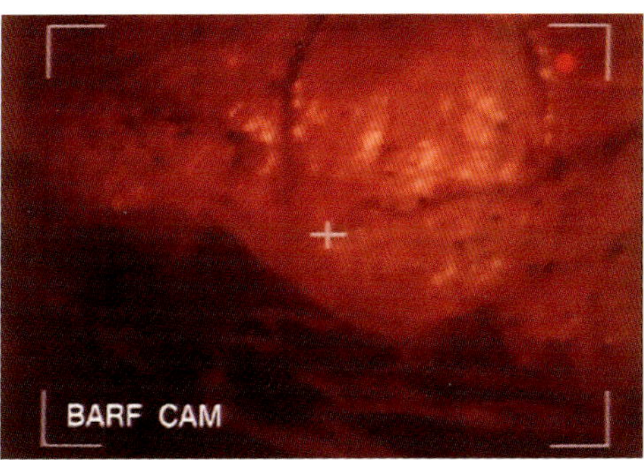

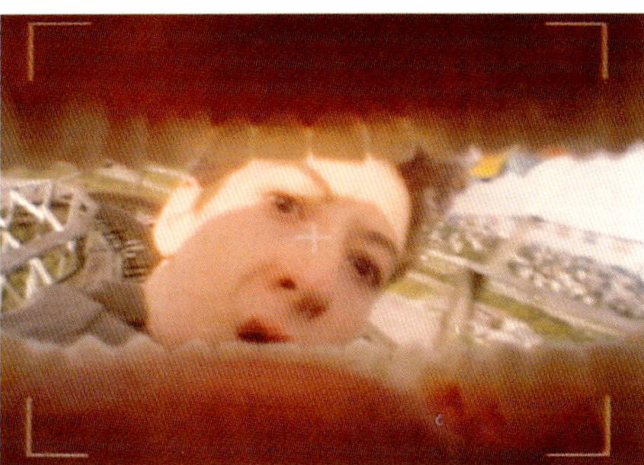

art director
Ian Grais

writer
Alan Russell

agency producer
Terry Green

production company
Aviator Pictures

director
David Straiton

client
Playland

agency
Palmer Jarvis
Communications/
Vancouver

CD 63

art director
Chris Graves

writer
Eric Moe

agency producer
Michelle Burke

production company
Epoch Films

director
Phil Morrison

client
Energizer

agency
TBWA Chiat/Day,
Venice, CA

SUPER: Barf Cam.

(SFX: Muffled Sounds Inside Stomach/ Throat, Fairground Sounds Heard As Mouth Opens)

FRIEND: *Man, not now! Don't gurb, man!!*

(SFX: Wretching)

(SFX: Fairground Screams, Activity)

TEEN: *Ahhhhh!*

(SFX: "Splat," Then Static)

SUPER: Playland Is Open Daily 11 AM To 10 PM.

INTERVIEWER: *People call you guys Bunny Spotters, is that right?*

GUY 1: *Bunny Spotters. I think that trivializes what we do. It's much larger than that.*

GUY 2: *Once you've seen it, you can never go back.*

GUY 3: *There's no other pink like it.*

GUY 2: *He's been through here.*

GUY 1: *I've seen it 16 times. To watch somebody find it, see it for the first time . . .*

GUY 4: *Woohoo. I feel very fortunate to be here, 'cause when we're all gone, it's still gonna be out there.*

SUPER: Eveready Battery Company.

SUPER: Energizer.

**CONSUMER
TELEVISION
:30 SINGLE**

art director
Chris Graves

writer
Eric Moe

agency producer
Michelle Burke

production company
Epoch Films

director
Phil Morrison

client
Energizer

agency
TBWA Chiat/Day,
Venice, CA

art director
Robert Palmer

writer
Hank Perlman

agency producer
Dan Duffy

production company
@radical.media

directors
Bryan Buckley
Frank Todaro

client
ESPN

agency
Wieden & Kennedy/
Portland

GUY 1: *As long as this thing's been going,
we've been chasing it.*

GUY 2: *It's an obsession with us. We've gone
days without seeing anything.*

GUY 3: *It's toying with us again.*

GUY 2: *And there it is again, you can see its
ears and its drum.*

GUY 4: *Come on Bunny, come on, baby.*

DRIVER: *Look out there, look at about 10 o'clock.*

ANOTHER GUY: *Stop. Stop.*

GUY 4: *It's a woodchuck. It's nothing. It's a
woodchuck. Forget it, sorry.*

SUPER: Eveready Battery Company.

SUPER: Energizer.

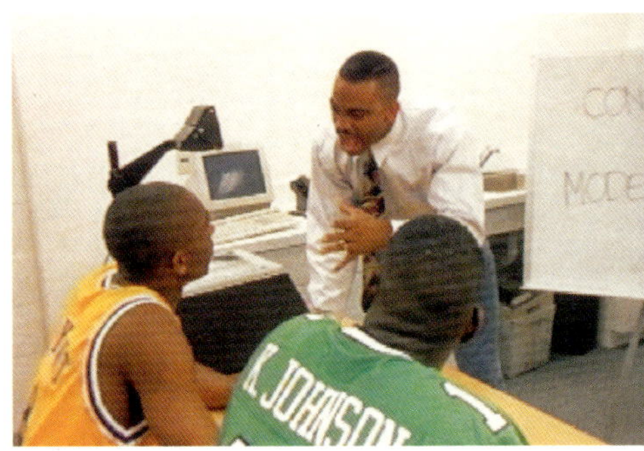

SUPER: Karl Ravech, SportsCenter Anchor.

KARL RAVECH: *It's our job to help educate
first year players on how to deal with us, with
the media. It's like our own little rookie camp.*

KENNY MAYNE: *The Official blows the call.
You guys lose the game. You know you were
in. After the game he asks a lame question.
The reporter asks you a stupid question.
What are you gonna say?*

KEYSHAWN JOHNSON: *That was a cruddy call.*

MAYNE: *Nah, it was a* (Beep) *call.*

STUART SCOTT: *Cruddy? Cruddy went out
with Ward Cleaver. Come on Kobe, whadda
ya think of that call? What do you say?*

KOBE BRYANT: *That was a bad call.*

SCOTT: *That wasn't a bad call. It was a*
(Beep) *call by a* (Beep). *It was* (Beep).
That's (Beep) *call. He's an* (Beep).

SUPER: This Is SportsCenter.

SUPER: ESPN.

KARL RAVECH: *Security has always been an issue for us, like any other company, But since we've grown it's gotten tighter. We're not proud of it. We don't brag about it. You never know who the hell is going to walk through the door.*

SUPER: KARL RAVECH, SPORTSCENTER ANCHOR.

DELIVERY GUY: *Delivery.*

SUPER: SPORTSCENTER LOBBY 4:45 PM, DEC. 12, 1996.

GUARD: *Can I see some ID please.*

DELIVERY GUY: *My hands are kind of full right now.*

BUFFALO SABRES' ROB RAY: *He wants to see some ID.*

RAVECH: *You don't know how crazy people can be out there. It's dangerous.*

RAY: *Next time bring some ID.*

BARRY MELROSE: *Hey, Rob.*

RAY: *Hey, coach.*

SUPER: THIS IS SPORTSCENTER. ESPN.

RAVECH: *You can't be too careful.*

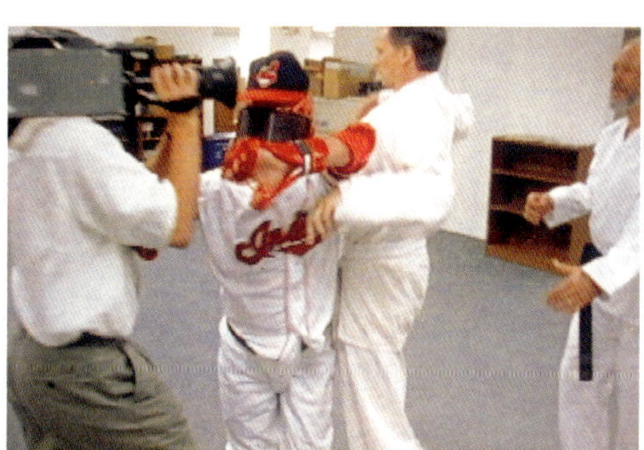

SUPER: BRETT HABER. SPORTSCENTER ANCHOR.

BRETT HABER: *Now this whole thing with athletes abusing reporters is getting way out of hand, and we at SportsCenter have gotten to the point where we have just got to be ready to fight back.*

SUPER: SPORTSCENTER SELF-DEFENSE CLASS, APRIL 19, 1996.

STUDENTS: *Eeeaaaa!*

TEACHER: *The most effective defensive weapon would be your microphone. Always be aware of your surroundings. Say you're on the sidelines, take any weapon that happens to be handy. Suppose an athlete decides to attack your cameraman. What would you do?*

STUDENT: *Knock it off.*

TEACHER: *No, let me show you. Now you have to be very careful not to hit the camera.*

SUPER: THIS IS SPORTSCENTER. ESPN.

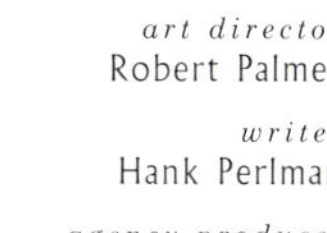

art director
Robert Palmer

writer
Hank Perlman

agency producer
Dan Duffy

production company
@radical.media

directors
Bryan Buckley
Frank Todaro

client
ESPN

agency
Wieden & Kennedy/
Portland

art director
Robert Palmer

writer
Hank Perlman

agency producer
Dan Duffy

production company
@radical.media

directors
Bryan Buckley
Frank Todaro

client
ESPN

agency
Wieden & Kennedy/
Portland

**CONSUMER
TELEVISION
:30 SINGLE**

art director
Robert Palmer

writer
Hank Perlman

agency producer
Dan Duffy

production company
@radical.media

directors
Bryan Buckley
Frank Todaro

client
ESPN

agency
Wieden & Kennedy/
Portland

art director
Robert Palmer

writer
Hank Perlman

agency producer
Dan Duffy

production company
@radical.media

directors
Bryan Buckley
Frank Todaro

client
ESPN

agency
Wieden & Kennedy/
Portland

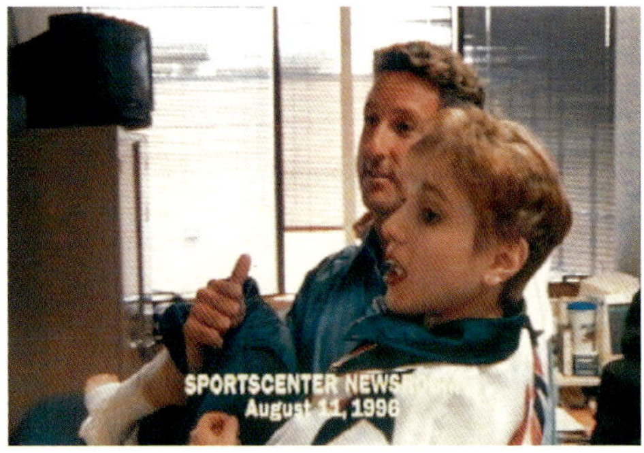

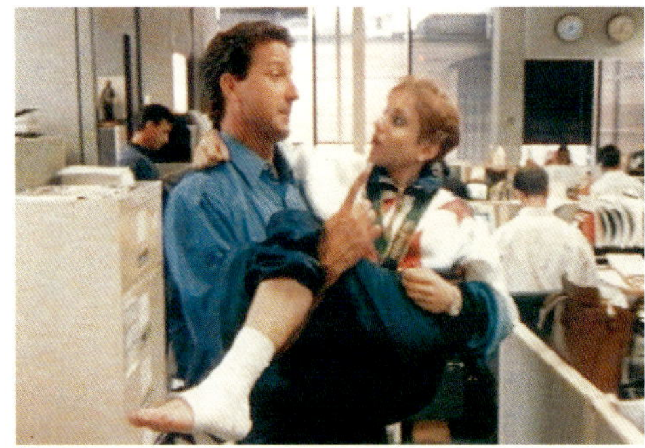

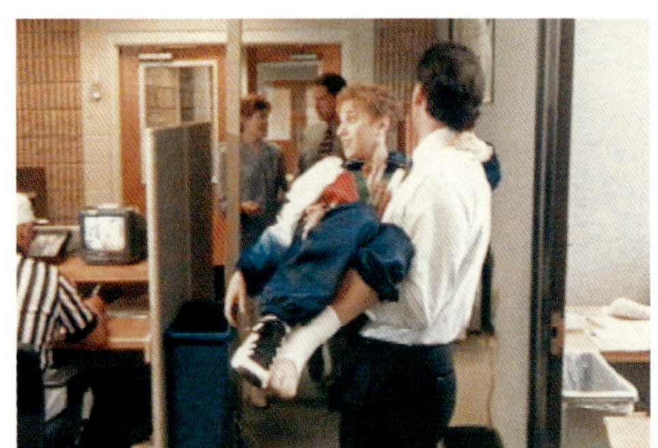

SUPER: SPORTSCENTER NEWSROOM,
AUGUST 11, 1996.

KERRI STRUG: *Gonna do some gymnastics
tours on the weekends . . .*

GARY: *Just a second. Carl, I gotta get this
thing done.*

CARL: *Three hours yesterday. I'm done.*

GARY: *Yeah. I should have remembered.*

KERRI: *. . . and I plan on traveling around
the country for the first semester.*

GARY: *Keith, uh. Got just a minute?*

KEITH: *I got a bulging disc. Gotta go.*

KERRI: *With all the opportunities for me I wanna
try and do some motivational speeches . . .*

GARY: *Rich will be perfect for this.*

RICH: *No.*

GARY: *Yeah, I'd love to hear about that. I
really gotta get this thing done . . . Larry,
ahh, I'll be right back. If you could just
hold Kerri for just one second.*

LARRY: *I can't. I gotta go to the bathroom
Gary—Is that okay with you?*

KERRI: *No!*

LARRY: *Hey Chris . . . Guys. Guys. Guys.*

SUPER: THIS IS SPORTSCENTER. ESPN.

SUPER: DAVID BROFSKY, SPORTSCENTER
PRODUCER.

DAVID BROFSKY: *The reality is just because
you're a former athlete, doesn't qualify you
to be a SportsCenter anchor.*

SUPER: MID-SEASON RECRUITMENT,
SEPTEMBER 10, 1996.

BILL BRADLEY: *After the Olympic gold medal,
the Rhodes Scholarship, 10 years with the
New York Knicks. Um, I was a U.S. Senator
for 18 years.*

BOB LEY: *How 'bout any writing experience?*

BRADLEY: *Well, I wrote three books. One on
the bestseller list and the Tax Reform Act of
1986.*

LEY: *But no TV writing.*

KEITH OLBERMAN: *No. Any experience in
front of an audience?*

BRADLEY: *Well, I gave a key note address at
the Democratic National Convention.*

OLBERMAN: *Uh, I meant a large audience.*

BRADLEY: *Oh.*

SUPER: THIS IS SPORTSCENTER. ESPN.

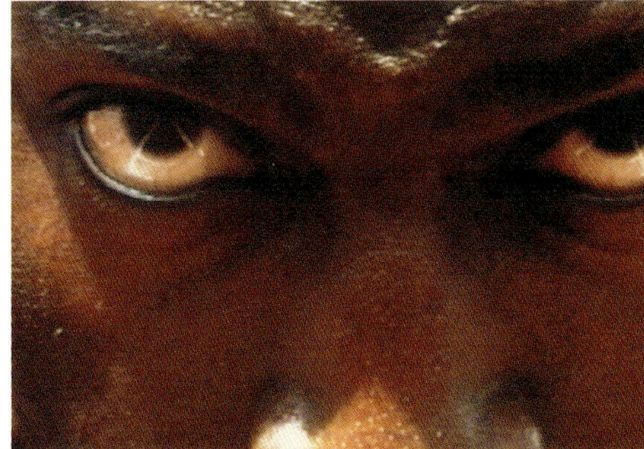

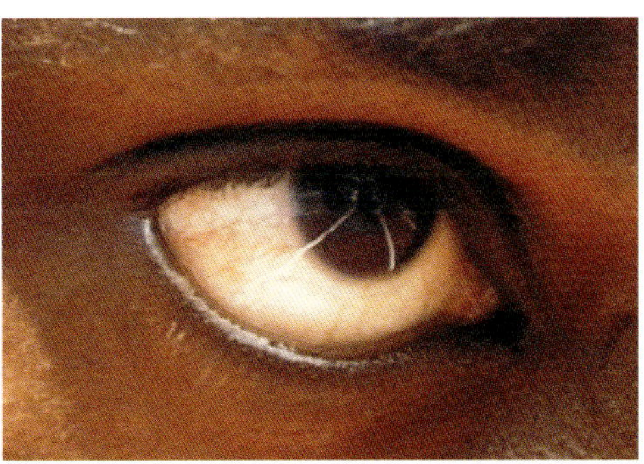

HOCKEY PLAYER 1: *Best thing about winning the Stanley Cup is drinking out of it. Sharin' it, ah, with your teammates.*

HOCKEY PLAYER 2: *Friends and family and fans.*

HOCKEY PLAYER 3: *From your marquee-star players right down to the towel boys.*

TOWEL BOY: *Well, we all got a chance to drink from the Cup.*

HOCKEY PLAYER 1: *Ya know pretty much anybody who wants to drink out of it you just let him.*

FAN: *I want another one.*

TOWEL BOY: *Upwards to 200 people before me got a chance to drink from the Cup.*

HOCKEY PLAYER 3: *I even took the Cup to my restaurant in New Jersey and shared it with 5,000 people that I didn't even know and everybody enjoyed the experience of drinking out of that Cup. It was the funnest time I've ever had. Something I'll never forget.*

SUPER: NEW JERSEY DEVILS VS. NEW YORK RANGERS.

SUPER: ESPN.

(MUSIC: LOW DRONE BUILDING THROUGHOUT)

ANNCR: *There are two sides to a sprinter . . . the side that wants to crush his opponents and leave them blue and lifeless by the side of the track . . . and the other . . . darker side.*

SUPER: (NIKE SWOOSH.)

TELEVISION FINALISTS

art director
Darryl McDonald

writer
Hank Perlman

agency producer
Colleen Wellman

production company
@radical.media

directors
Bryan Buckley
Frank Todaro

client
ESPN / National
Hockey League

agency
Wieden & Kennedy /
Portland

CD 64

art director
Young Kim

writer
Jamie Barrett

agency producer
Beth Harding

production company
Tony Kaye Films

director
Tony Kaye

client
Nike

agency
Wieden & Kennedy /
Portland

CONSUMER TELEVISION :30 SINGLE

art director
Eric King

writer
Jamie Barrett

agency producer
Patty Brebner

production company
@radical.media

director
Dick Sittig

client
Nike

agency
Wieden & Kennedy/
Portland

CD 65

art director
Robert Palmer

writer
Jim Riswold

agency producers
Kevin Diller
Jennifer Howard

production company
Atherton & Associates

director
David Deneen

client
Nike Australia

agency
Wieden & Kennedy/
Portland

CD 66

HECKLER: *Miss it! Miss it! Ooooohhh, I want you to miss . . . yo momma! Brick! Ra, ra . . .* (GROWLS) *. . . Bang, Bang, Ba-bang . . .* (SCREAMS THROUGH MICROPHONE)

(SFX: SCREAMING AND HORN SOUNDS)

(SFX: BALL BOUNCING)

SUPER: IT MUST BE MARCH.

HECKLER: *Nice shot.*

SUPER: (NIKE SWOOSH.)

(SFX: CHAINSAW CUTTING PATH THROUGH WICKETS)

SUPER: (NIKE SWOOSH.)

(MUSIC: THROUGHOUT)

WOMAN: *Anything else . . . ?*

MAN: *No . . . yes . . . no . . . well, uhm, maybe if you're not busy . . . maybe we could, go . . . get a cup of coffee . . .*

SUPER: LEE RIVETED.

SUPER: CUT TO BE NOTICED.

ANNCR: *Lee rivited. Cut to be noticed.*

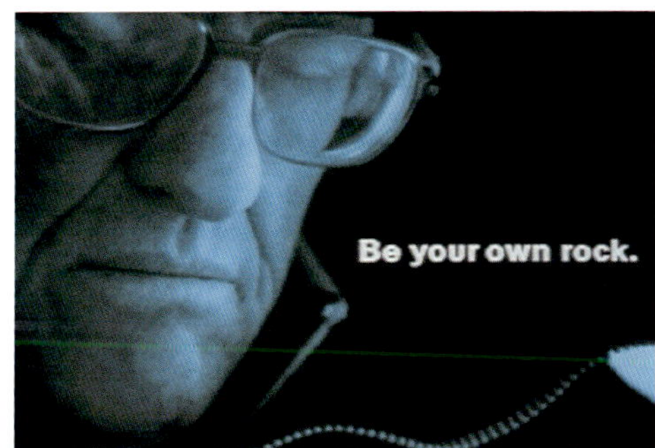

(MUSIC: FLUTE WITH VOCAL DRONE)

DOC: *The outdoors for me is church. I didn't want to grow old and ah, be crotchety and, ah, you know, not be able to do stuff. Aahh!!*

SUPER: LIVE WELL.

DOC: *Somehow, on some deep level we're responsible for what happens to us. I'm always tryin' to save money and invest in the future. I'm a nut about it.*

SUPER: BE YOUR OWN ROCK.

DOC: *I mean you're the best investment you've got. You're the best investment you'll ever have. I don't know whether that's good or bad, but I like it.*

SUPER: PRUDENTIAL. BE YOUR OWN ROCK.

CONSUMER TELEVISION :30 CAMPAIGN

art director
Harvey Marco

writers
Dean Buckhorn
Peter McHugh

agency producer
Ardi Kramer

production company
@radical.media

director
Alan White

client
Lee Apparel Company

agency
Fallon McElligott/
Minneapolis

art director
Amy Nicholson

writer
Bill Westbrook

agency producer
Bruce Wellington

production company
Propaganda Films

director
Jeffrey Plansker

client
The Prudential

agency
Fallon McElligott/
Minneapolis

CD 67

**CONSUMER
TELEVISION
:30 CAMPAIGN**

art director
Erich Joiner

writer
Bob Kerstetter

agency producer
Rebecca O'Sullivan

production company
Tool of North America

directors
Erich Joiner
Scott Burns

client
FOX Sports

agency
FOX/Santa Monica

CD 68

art director
Jeremy Postaer

writer
Paul Venables

agency producer
Elizabeth O'Toole

production company
Johns + Gorman Films

director
Clint Clemens

client
Bell Sports

agency
Goodby Silverstein &
Partners/San Francisco

CD 69

SUPER: TONY GWYNN. PADRES.

OFF-CAMERA VOICE: *Hey, Tony, people tell me
you're the best hitter in the game . . . any secrets?*

TONY: *Mmmmm . . .*

OFF-CAMERA VOICE: *C'mon, no good luck
charms . . . you gotta have something.*

TONY: *I can't believe I'm showing you this.
My lucky robin's egg. Had it my whole life.
Helped me win six batting titles.*

OFF-CAMERA VOICE: *Wow. Six.*

(SFX: EGG BEING CRUSHED)

SUPER: FOX SPORTS.

OFF-CAMERA VOICE: *Oh, man . . . sorry.*

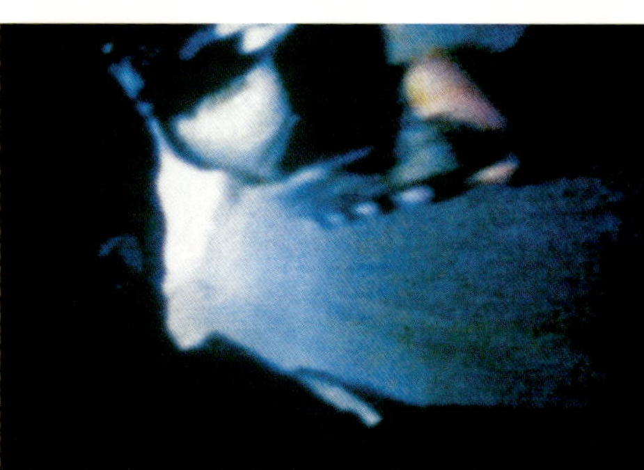

(SFX: SPEEDING SOUNDS)

(SFX: HEARTBEAT)

SUPER: ON SMOOTH PAVEMENT YOU CAN GO
60 MPH.

(SFX: HEARTBEAT)

SUPER: THERE'S ONE MINOR DRAWBACK.

(SFX: HEARTBEAT)

SUPER: IT'S PAVEMENT.

SUPER: BELL HELMETS.

(SFX: "SMASH")

ANNCR: *Bell. Official helmet of the X-Games.*

(SFX: "SQUISH")

(SFX: "SNAP")

(SFX: ACCELERATION SOUND)

SUPER: COURAGE FOR YOUR HEAD.

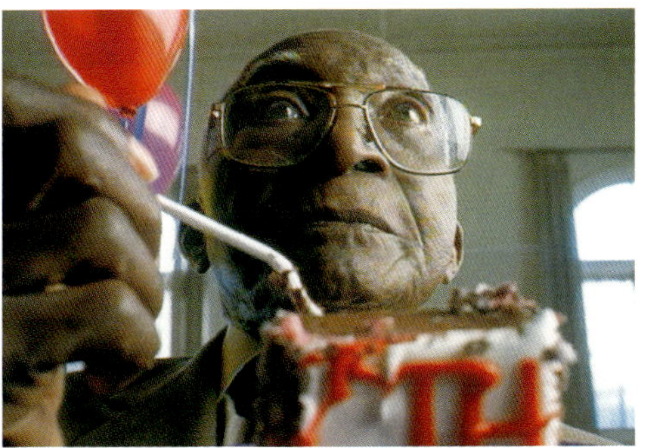

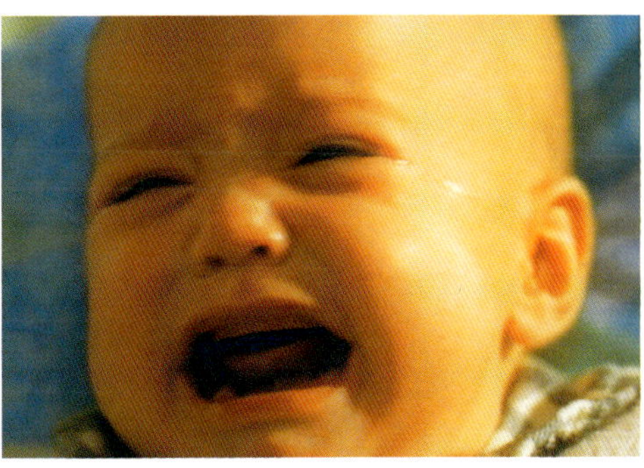

TELEVISION FINALISTS

art directors
Sean Ehringer
Todd Grant

writers
Harry Cocciolo
Chuck McBride

agency producers
Elizabeth O'Toole
Bob Wendt

production companies
@radical.media
Smillie Films

directors
Bryan Buckley
Frank Todaro
Kinka Usher

client
California Milk
Processor
Advisory Board

agency
Goodby Silverstein &
Partners/San Francisco

art directors
Tom Routson
Amy Nicholson

writers
Al Kelly
Blake Daley

agency producer
Cindy Fluitt

production company
Propaganda Films

director
Jeffrey Goodby

client
Hewlett Packard

agency
Goodby Silverstein &
Partners/San Francisco

CD 70

(MUSIC: QUIRKY WALTZ-STYLE)

MAGICIAN: *The mystery of the linking rings!*

(SFX: RINGS CLANGING)

MAGICIAN: *And now!*

THREE FOLKS: *Mmmm!*

MAGICIAN: *My finest illusion!*

WOMAN: *Mmmm!*

MAGICIAN: *Ooohhh!*

SUPER: CALIFORNIA FLUID MILK PROCESSOR
ADVISORY BOARD.

MAGICIAN: *Ha!*

(SFX: POURING)

MAN: *Hmmm?*

WOMAN: *Gulp.*

MAGICIAN: *Ha!*

MAN: *Hmmmm!*

MAGICIAN: *Wha-la . . . empty! Thank you,
thank you very much!*

(SFX: CREEKING)

MAGICIAN: *Oh, no, please don't get up!
You're too kind!*

WOMAN: *Lock the door!*

MAGICIAN: *It's not necessary . . .*

SUPER: GOT MILK?

MAGICIAN: *Ow!*

(SFX: QUIET TICKING OF CLOCK)

(SFX: WRESTLING ON TV)

GRANDPA: *Ohhhhhh!*

(SFX: THUD)

BABY: *Wahhhhhhhhhh!*

GRANDPA: *Don't worry, honey. Mom and Dad
will be right back.*

GRANDPA: *Pretty baby.*

BABY: *Wahhhhhhhhhh!*

(SFX: SUDDEN QUIET)

(SFX: CLOCK TICKING)

ANNCR: *HP photo-quality printers. Good
enough to fool almost anyone.*

SUPER: BUILT BY ENGINEERS. USED BY
NORMAL PEOPLE.

**CONSUMER
TELEVISION
:30 CAMPAIGN**

art director
Vince Engel

writer
Ernest Lupinacci

agency producer
Amy Davenport

production company
@radical.media

director
Alan White

client
ESPN

agency
Wieden & Kennedy/
Portland

CD 71

art director
Young Kim

writer
Jamie Barrett

agency producer
Beth Harding

production company
Tony Kaye Films

director
Tony Kaye

client
Nike

agency
Wieden & Kennedy/
Portland

ROBERT GOULET: *Riddle me this Scatman, what's got ten legs and kicks butt. Dig. (*SINGING TO THE TUNE OF "GREEN ACRES"*) Wake Forrest is the team for me. Baddest mothers in the ACC. Demon Deacons ringing up the score packing their bags for a trip, to the final four. The jams! The slams! (*SPEAKING*) Oh yeah, that Duncan kids name it ain't just a noun, it's a verb.*

SUPER: NCAA BASKETBALL, EVERY GAME COUNTS.

GOULET: *It's a baaaad verb!*

MAITRE D': *Thanks for the grammar lesson.*

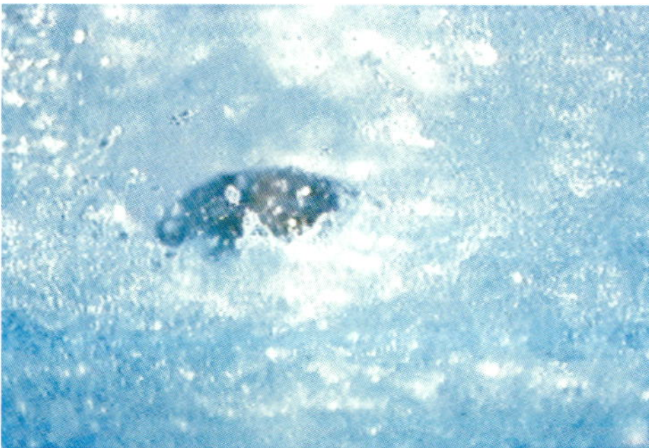

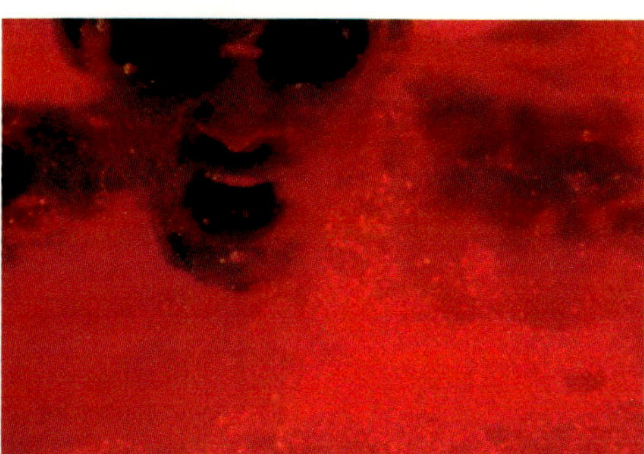

(SFX: DISTORTED NOISES)

ANNCR: *Some people quit when they reach their threshold of pain. Some don't.*

SUPER: (NIKE SWOOSH.)

SUPER: THE TREE.

CARDINAL: *I am the Stanford Tree, sacrificing for team. No cheers. No TV cameras. I work, sweat, and know if I fail my team, I won't be cheering on the hardwood . . . I will be the hardwood.*

(SFX: FLATLINE SOUND)

SUPER: PAC 10 BASKETBALL. FOX SPORTS NET.

PAINTER: *Humming.*

(SFX: FOOTBALL PRACTICE IN BACKGROUND)

PLAYER 1: *Hey, that's great but who are the Chefs?*

ANNCR: *Not going anywhere for awhile?*

PAINTER: *Great googlie mooglie.*

ANNCR: *Grab a Snickers.*

PLAYER 2: *Your spelling's . . .*

PAINTER: *Yeah.*

TELEVISION FINALISTS

art director
Michael Ivan Boychuk

writer
Craig Hoit

agency producer
Joyce Schmidtbauer

production company
Ober Lenz

director
Tony Ober

client
FOX Sports

agency
WONGDOODY /
Seattle

CD 72

**CONSUMER
TELEVISION
:20 AND UNDER:
SINGLE**

art directors
Gerry Graf
David Gray

writers
Gerry Graf
David Gray

agency producer
J.D. Williams

production company
@radical.media

directors
Bryan Buckley
Frank Todaro

client
M&M Mars / Snickers

agency
BBDO / New York

**CONSUMER
TELEVISION
:20 AND UNDER:
SINGLE**

art director
David Angelo

writer
Cliff Freeman

agency producer
Liz Graves

production company
Crossroads Films

director
Mark Story

client
Little Caesars

agency
Cliff Freeman &
Partners / New York

art directors
Michael Keane
Kay Truelove

writers
Kay Truelove
Michael Keane

agency producer
James Lethem

production company
Stark Films

director
Adrian Marler

client
Remington

agency
Grey Advertising / London

CD 73

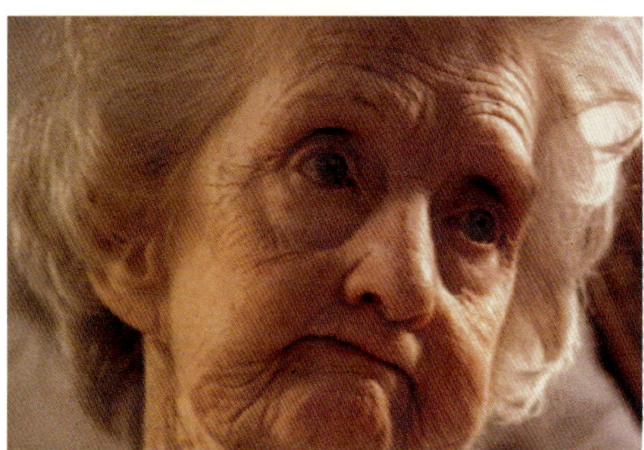

ANNCR: *Everything looks small next to the Giant Caesar.*

(SFX: Bed Squeaking And Box Opening)

HUSBAND: *What?!*

ANNCR: *From Little Caesars, giant slices with giant pepperoni—$9.99 carry-out, or have it delivered.*

LITTLE CAESAR: *Pizza! Pizza!*

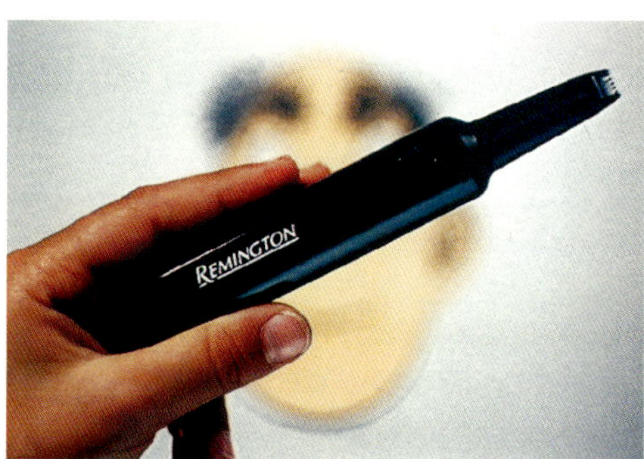

LITTLE BOY: *My dad used to look like this . . . So we bought him this . . . Which can get rid of this, this and this . . .*

ANNCR: *The Remington Hygienic Clipper.*

LITTLE BOY: *But can't do this, unfortunately.*

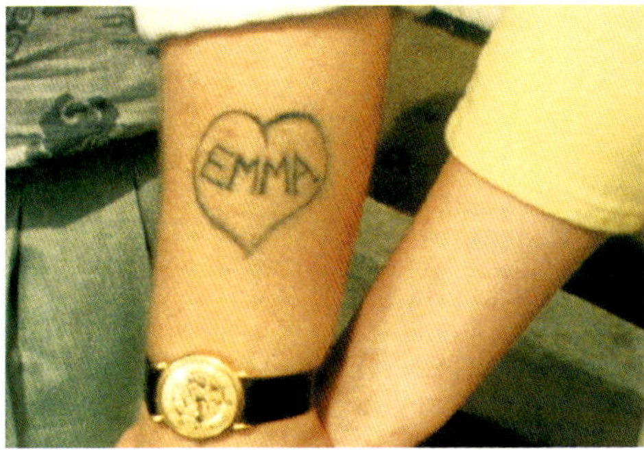

ANNCR: *That tattoo of an old girlfriend can cost an awful lot to have removed. Resolve the problem by taking your current girlfriend into town and having her name changed by Deedpoll.*

This money-saving tip was brought to you by McDonald's, where a Filet-O-Fish, medium fries and a medium soft-drink will cost you just £2.88.

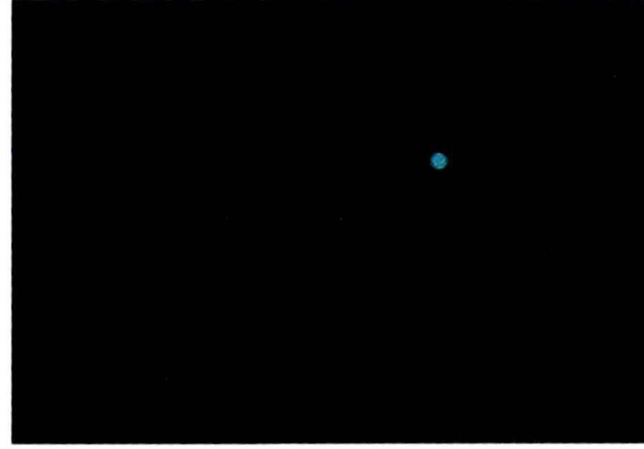

(SFX: SOMEONE DIVING OFF DIVING BOARD)

(SFX: SPLASH)

SUPER: TIMEX INDIGLO. PROUD SPONSOR OF CANADIAN CHAMPION DIVER ANNE MONTMINY.

art director
Matt Hazell

writer
Jane Atkinson

agency producer
Pamie Wikstrom

production company
Fat Fish Films

director
Joe Public

client
McDonald's

agency
Leo Burnett / London

art directors
Nancy Vonk
Elsie Fehr

writers
Janet Kestin
Arthur Shah
Brian Smith

agency producer
Linda Gillies

production companies
Spin Productions
Redline Digital Studio

directors
Rob Jones
Sam Welch

client
Timex Canada

agency
Ogilvy & Mather /
Toronto

CD 74

CONSUMER TELEVISION :20 AND UNDER: SINGLE

art director
Hal Curtis

writer
Jeff Bitsack

agency producer
Jill Andresevic

production company
Will Vinton Studios

director
Mark Gustafson

client
ESPN

agency
Wieden & Kennedy/ Portland

art director
Darryl McDonald

writer
Hank Perlman

agency producer
Colleen Wellman

production company
@radical.media

directors
Bryan Buckley
Frank Todaro

client
ESPN/National Hockey League

agency
Wieden & Kennedy/ Portland

ANNCR: *Play action pass Elway looking, fires over the right side. Oh, I think his whole family felt that one. Seau and company try and break up the Broncos on ESPN Sunday Night NFL.*

SUPER: DENVER BRONCOS VS. SAN DIEGO CHARGERS. TONIGHT 8PM ET ESPN SUNDAY NIGHT NFL.

ANNCR: *I don't think we'll be seeing him until half time.*

SUPER: BILL GUERIN, NEW JERSEY DEVILS.

BILL GUERIN: *Check.*

(SFX: GUERIN GETTING CHECKED, FALLING OFF CHAIR)

GUERIN: *Awhh! I get it. Check. That was a good one. Very mature joke. Very funny. Check, I get it.*

SUPER: NEW JERSEY DEVILS VS. NEW YORK RANGERS.

SUPER: ESPN.

JACK: *Ad men are always on me to liven up my advertisements for John Smith's Extra Smooth Bitter. They don't think it's enough to talk about its extra smooth taste.*

(SFX: RACE CARS AND HORN HONKING)

JACK: *"What we need is a bit of action, Jackie."*

(SFX: LOUD CRASH)

JACK: *They just don't get it do they? Well I told them straight: no gimmicks, no dancing lady birds and definitely no penguins. Just me, in a pub with a pint of John Smith's Extra Smooth, pure silk in a glass . . . So if this is a bit dull you can blame me.*

DIRECTOR: *Cut it–that was nice Jack.*

JACK: *So you're gonna put the pub background in afterwards.*

DIRECTOR: *Yeah, yeah. That's right Jack. Yeah, we're going to put it in later.*

SUPER: NO NONSENSE.

(SFX: TWO-WAY RADIO, SIREN, SCREECHING TIRES)

'70s COP: *You're busted dirtbag!*

BAD GUY: *Oh man . . . Starsky and Hutch.*

'70s COP: *Catchin' scum makes ya hungry.*

SUPER: CC'S. A GOOD TRIANGULAR MEAL.

CONSUMER TELEVISION VARYING LENGTHS CAMPAIGN

art director
Jay Pond-Jones

writer
Robert Saville

agency producer
Diane Croll

production company
Open Mike Productions

director
Daniel Kleinman

client
Scottish Courage/
John Smith's

agency
GGT Advertising/
London

CD 75

art director
Mike O'Sullivan

writers
Murray Watt
Mike O'Sullivan

agency producer
Shannon Hall

production company
Brigid Reilly Productions

director
Mike O'Sullivan

client
Bluebird Foods/
CC's Chips

agency
MOJO Partners/
Auckland

CONSUMER TELEVISION UNDER $50,000 BUDGET

art director
Dave Brokaw

writers
Rob Stewart
Mike Exner

agency producer
Sherri Fritzon Keenan

production company
Mad Dog

director
Joe Perz

client
Miami Motorsports

agency
Beber Silverstein/
Miami

art director
Bunt Young

writers
Mike Henry
Patrick Henry

agency producers
Mike Henry
Bunt Young

production company
Cross-Eyed Films

directors
Mike Henry
Patrick Henry

client
Texas-Wisconsin
Border Cafe

agency
Cross-Eyed Films/
New York

(SFX: RACING SOUNDS)

DRIVER 1: *What is this a (BEEP) parade!?! This ain't a (BEEP) (BEEP) school zone!*

DRIVER 2: *Dipstick rookie gonna kill my (BEEP)! You worthless (BEEP)! This ain't playtime (BEEP) (BEEP) it! Move that (BEEP)!! Learn to drive, you jack (BEEP)!!!*

DRIVER 3: *Bring it on! Bring it on, you dumb (BEEP)!! I'm ready to take your (BEEP) on!*

SUPER: JIFFY LUBE MIAMI 300.

ANNCR: *NASCAR, Good clean fun for the whole (BEEP) family. Watch the Jiffy Lube Miami 300. Sunday, November 3rd. Only on CBS.*

DRIVER 4: *Arrivederci, (BEEP) head.*

MIKE: *I had a really good time with you tonight.*

KERON: *I did too. It was a wonderful evening. Thank you . . . I really enjoyed the restaurant.*

MIKE: *Yeah.*

KERON: *The food was quite good.*

MIKE: *It's always good there.*

(SFX: SUBTLE FART)

KERON: (LAUGHS) *Excuse me. I've been holding that in ever since we left the restaurant.*

MIKE: *Yeah . . . I should go.*

KERON: *But wouldn't you like to come in for a nightcap?*

SUPER: TEXAS-WISCONSIN BORDER CAFE.

ANNCR: *The Texas-Wisconsin Border Cafe. It truly is an unforgettable meal.*

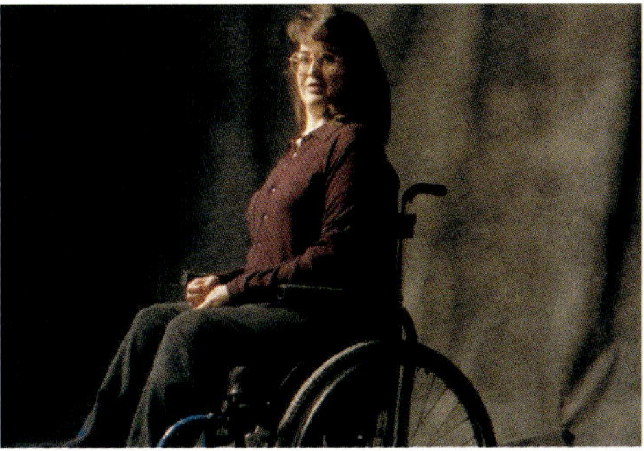

WOMAN: *I read the other day . . . that Christopher Reeve has devoted himself to helping other people with spinal-cord injuries. And that he plans to walk by his 50th birthday. It also said it bothers him when fans call him Superman. I think that may be underestimating him.*

ANNCR: TIME. *The world's most interesting magazine.*

(MUSIC: BANJO-PICKING)

SUPER: THE MUSIC IS EVERYTHING.

(MUSIC: BANJO-PICKING CHANGES TO "THE STAR SPANGLED BANNER" BY JIMI HENDRIX)

SUPER: ROCK 'N' ROLL PICTURE SHOW.

SUPER: FRIDAYS AT 9PM/ET.

SUPER: VH-1. MUSIC FIRST.

art director
Bob Barrie

writer
Dean Buckhorn

agency producer
Monika Prince

production company
Buck Holzemer
Productions

director
Buck Holzemer

client
Time Magazine

agency
Fallon McElligott/
Minneapolis

CD 76

art director
Steve Mitchell

writer
Doug Adkins

production companies
Fischer Edit
Crash & Sue's

client
VH-1

agency
Hunt Adkins/
Minneapolis

CD 77

**CONSUMER
TELEVISION
UNDER $50,000
BUDGET**

art director
Michael Ivan Boychuk

writer
Craig Hoit

agency producer
Joyce Schmidtbauer

production company
Ober Lenz

director
Tony Ober

client
FOX Sports

agency
WONGDOODY/
Seattle

**NON-BROADCAST:
CINEMA**

art director
Gordon McIntyre

writer
Andy Bate

agency producer
Melissa Mae Loo

production company
Lizard

client
Bosch

agency
Young & Rubicam/
Johannesburg

CD 78

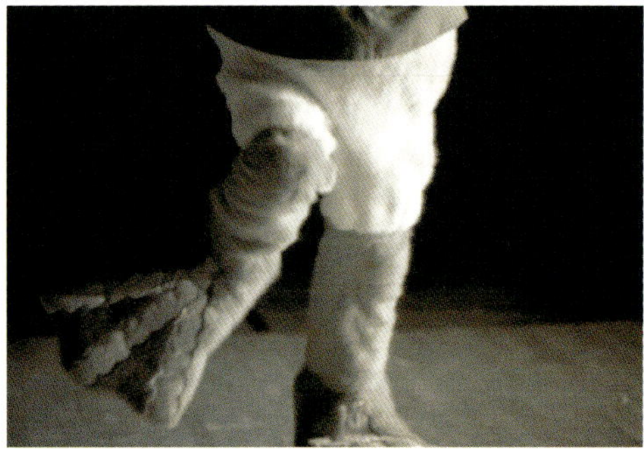

SUPER: THE DUCK.

DUCK: *I am not a role model. I am a duck. I am not paid to watch the freshman dorm, but I'd do it if the money were good. I am paid to wreak havoc on the basketball court. Just because I lead a cheer . . . doesn't mean I should raise your kids.*

SUPER: PAC 10 BASKETBALL.

SUPER: FOX SPORTS NET.

(SFX: LIGHT RAIN)

(SFX: THE SOUND OF A BOSCH WIPER, SYNCHED TO GECKO'S LICKS)

ANNCR: *Because life depends on seeing everything clearly. Bosch Wiper Blades.*

SUPER: BOSCH. THE ULTIMATE WIPER BLADE.

(SFX: The Clicks Of An Excellio Being Put Together)

(SFX. Excellio Being Turned On Through The "Ears" Of The Dust-Mite)

(SFX: Weird Screeches Mingled With The Sounds Of The Excellio)

ANNCR: *It's a jungle out there.*

ANNCR: *So make sure you're fully equipped. The Excellio from Electrolux.*

SUPER: Electrolux. Leave It To The Experts.

(SFX: Cafe Sounds)

(SFX: Lottery Numbers Being Announced On Tv)

(SFX: Man Shouting "Yes")

(SFX: Car Falling From Sky, Squashing Man)

ANNCR: *With its intense fresh taste, Vigorsol could change the flavor of your life.*

**INTERNATIONAL
FOREIGN LANGUAGE
COMMERCIAL:
TELEVISION**

art director
Luciano Zuffo

writers
José Henrique Borghi
Carlos Domingos

agency producer
Mauricio Guimarães

production company
Cia. de Cinema

director
Rodolfo Vanni

client
Moto Honda da Amazonia

agency
DM9 Publicidade/
Sao Paulo

CD 81

(SFX: MOTORCYCLE SOUNDS)

SUPER: HONDA C-100 DREAM. UP TO 70 KM PER LITER OR 30 SECONDS WITH A SINGLE DROP.

SUPER: C-100 DREAM, START IT, RIDE IT, AND LOVE IT.

SUPER: HONDA. THE WORLD'S BEST EMOTION.

SUPER: NEED TO LOSE WEIGHT?

ANNCR: *Mesbla Fitness Sale, lose weight not money.*

SUPER: MESBLA, BRAZIL'S DEPARTMENT STORE.

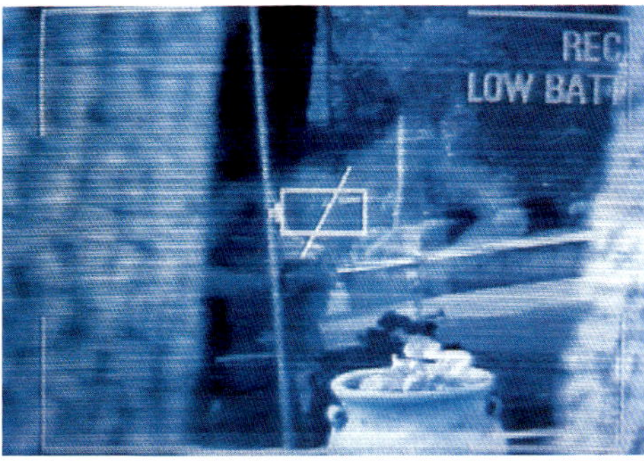

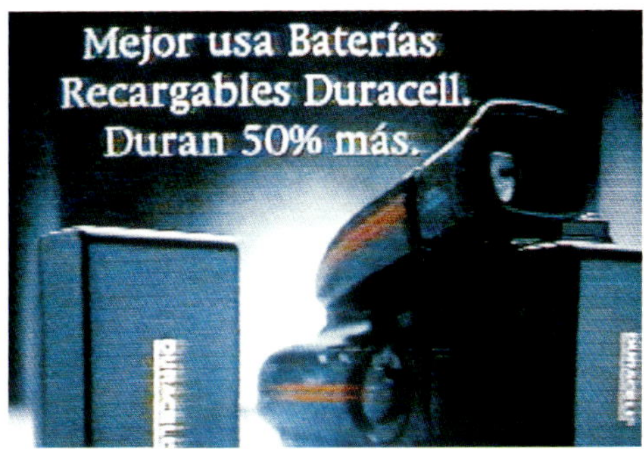

MAN I: *Do you have the camera?*

MAN 2: *Yeah, I have it. There she is! There she is!*

MAN I: *Are you recording?*

MAN 2: *Yes, I am! She's undressing!*

MAN I: *Record it! Are you sure you're recording? Get closer! Closer!*

MAN 2: *She's turning. She's turning! She's tu–*

ANNCR: *Next time use Duracell batteries. They last 50 percent longer.*

TELEVISION FINALISTS

art director
Pedro Cappeletti

writer
Jáder Rossetto

agency producer
Maurício Guimarães

production company
Jodaf

director
João Daniel
Tikhomiroff

client
Mesbla Department Store

agency
DM9 Publicidade/
Sao Paulo

CD 82

art director
Carlos Tourne

writers
Lourdes Lamasney
Raul Cardos
Mauricio Galvan

agency producer
Maria Claudia Alarcon

production company
GB Producciones

director
Simon Bross

client
Duracell

agency
Ogilvy & Mather/
Mexico City

SWIPED
FROM
THE VERY
DESK OF:
____

WEB SITE

art directors
Todd Goodale
Jeff Bratteson
John Athorn

writer
John Malecki

*digital artists/
illustrators*
Todd Goodale
Jeff Bratteson

*multimedia
company*
Tangent Company

client
Agfa Division
Bayer Corporation

agency
Anderson & Lembke/
New York

www.agfahome.com
CD 86

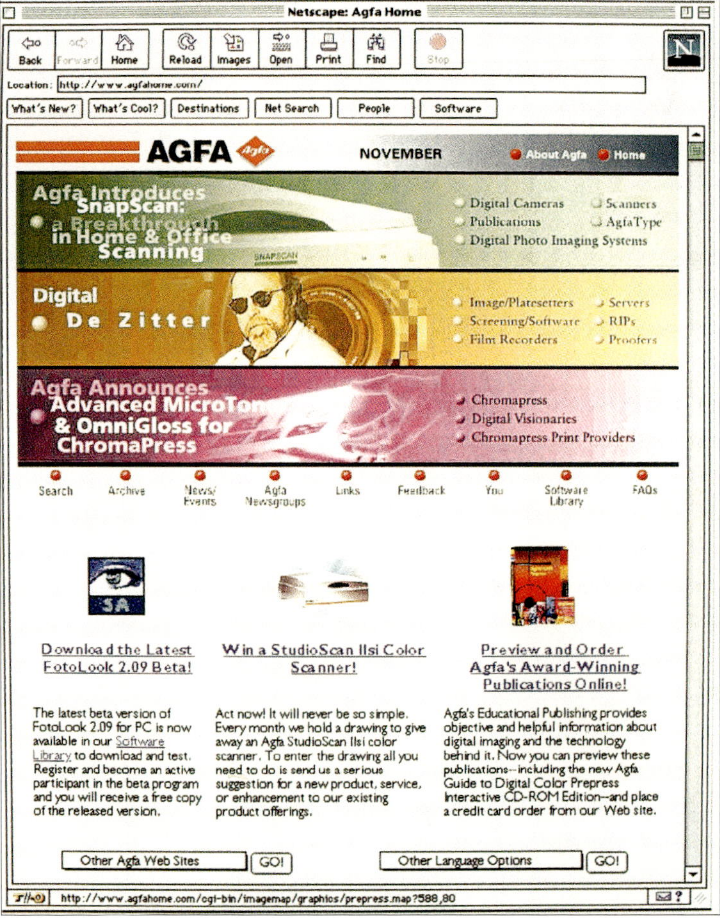

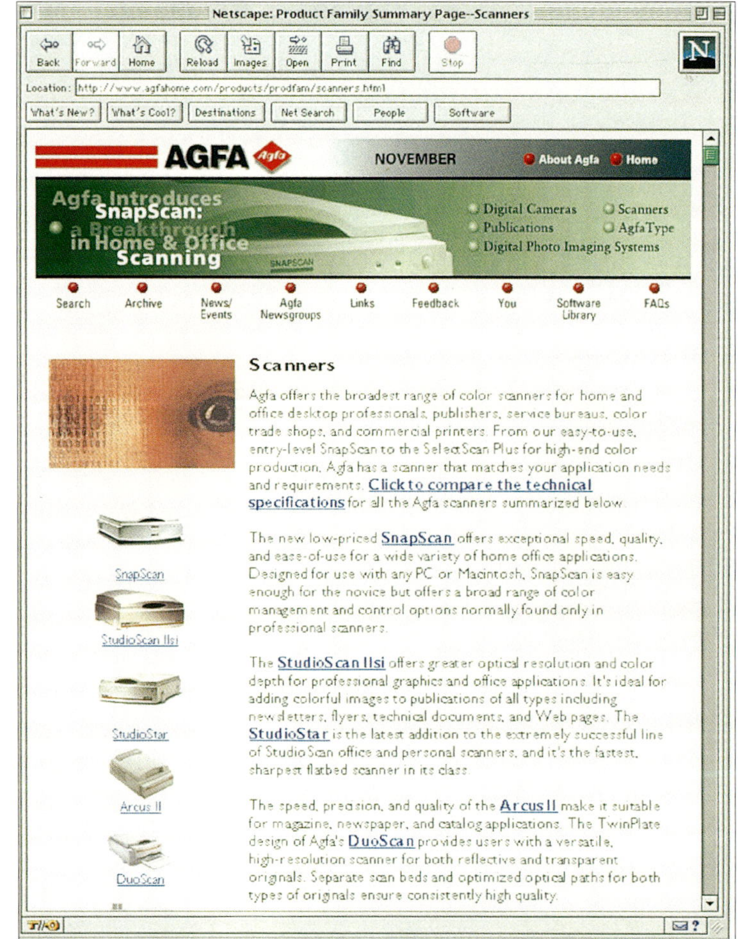

art director
Alan Pafenbach

writers
Lance Jensen
Jon Castle
Alan Pafenbach

photographers
Dewey Nicks
Jim Hall
Clint Clemens

agency producer
Ken Smith

multimedia company
Network Publishing

client
Volkswagen

agency
Arnold Advertising/
Boston

www.vw.com
CD 87

WEB SITE

art director
Brad Brewster

writer
Maria MacIntosh

*digital artists/
illustrators*
Mark Andresen
Brad Brewster

photographer
Rick Oliver

agency producer
Brad Brewster

*multimedia
company*
Bent Media

client
McIlhenny Company

agency
Bent Media/
New Orleans

www.tabasco.com
CD 88

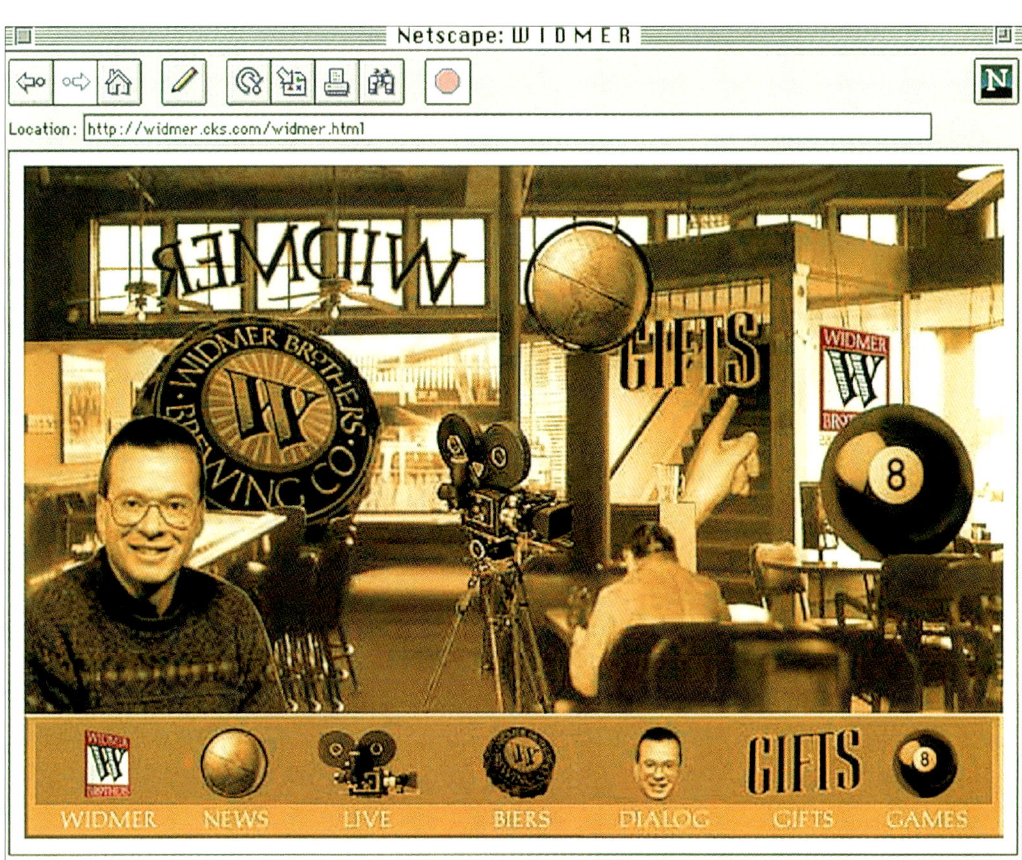

INTERACTIVE FINALISTS

art director
Bob Vandehey

writer
Mahesh Murthy

photographers
James Robinson
Damian Conrad

*multimedia
company*
CKS Partners

client
Widmer Brewing
Company

agency
CKS Partners/
Portland

www.widmer.com
CD 89

WEB SITE

art directors
David Glaze
Chip McCarthy

writers
Rich Conklin
Chad Weiss

*digital artist/
illustrator*
Chip McCarthy

agency producer
Jason Deal

*multimedia
company*
Genex Interactive

client
Porsche Cars
North America

agency
The Designory/
Long Beach, CA

www.porsche.com
CD 90

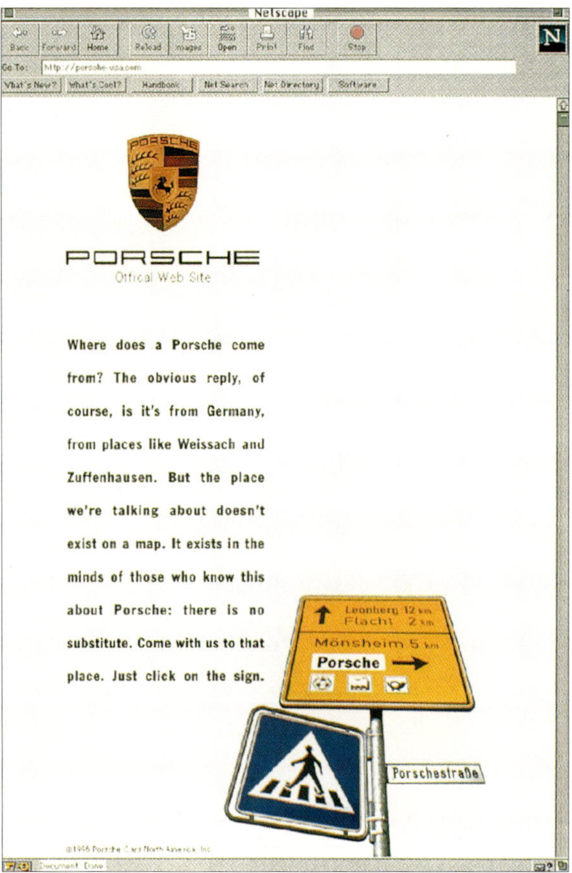

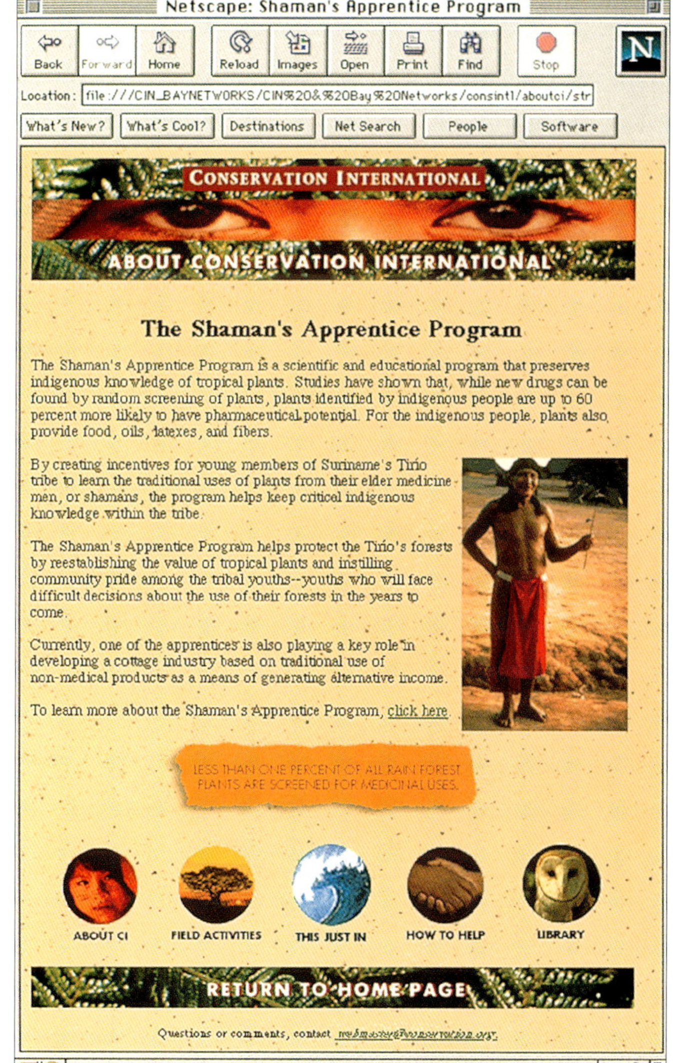

art directors
Jon White
Joan Bullen

writer
Jeff Tobin

agency producer
Ron Hendricks

client
Conservation
International

agency
EURO RSCG /
Dahlin Smith White,
Salt Lake City

www.conservation.org
CD 91

WEB SITE

art directors
Kim Carter
Jenne Parsons
David Hughes

writer
Christy Anderson

agency producer
Ron Hendricks

client
IOMEGA

agency
EURO RSCG/
Dahlin Smith White,
Salt Lake City

www.iomega.com

CD 92

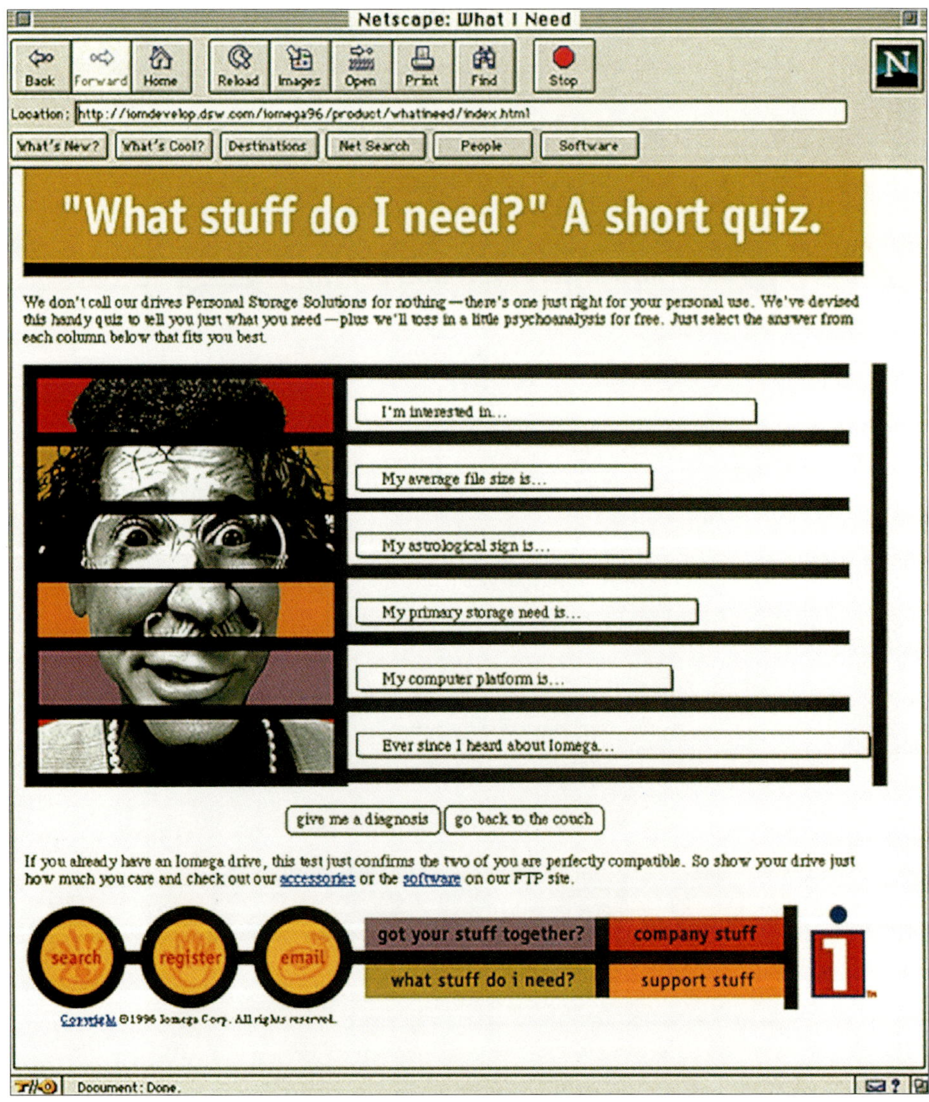

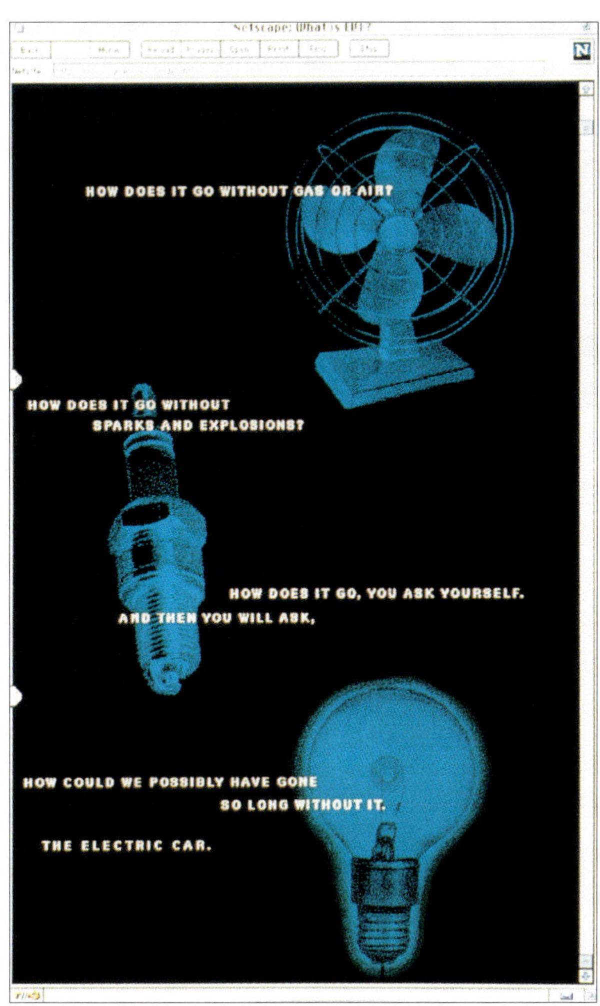

art director
Paula Grech

writer
Rebecca Rivera

designer
Tom Saputo

agency producer
Erik Radock

*multimedia
companies*
Prophet Communications
Brain Candy
EDS

client
GMEVI/Saturn Corporation

agency
Hal Riney & Partners/
San Francisco

www.gmev.com
CD 93

WEB SITE

art directors
Paula Grech
Julie Flannery

writers
Rebecca Rivera
Katherine Gordon

designer
Tom Saputo

agency producer
Erik Radock

multimedia companies
AMMG
EDS

client
Saturn
Corporation

agency
Hal Riney & Partners/
San Francisco

www.saturncars.com

CD 94

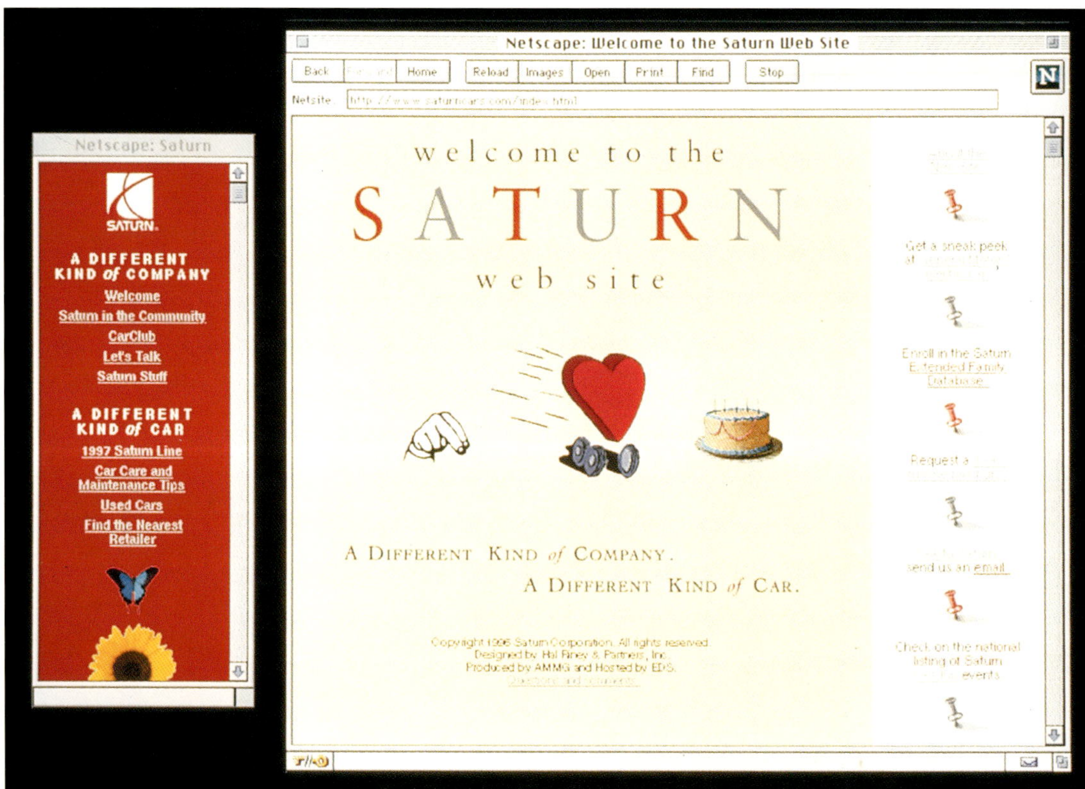

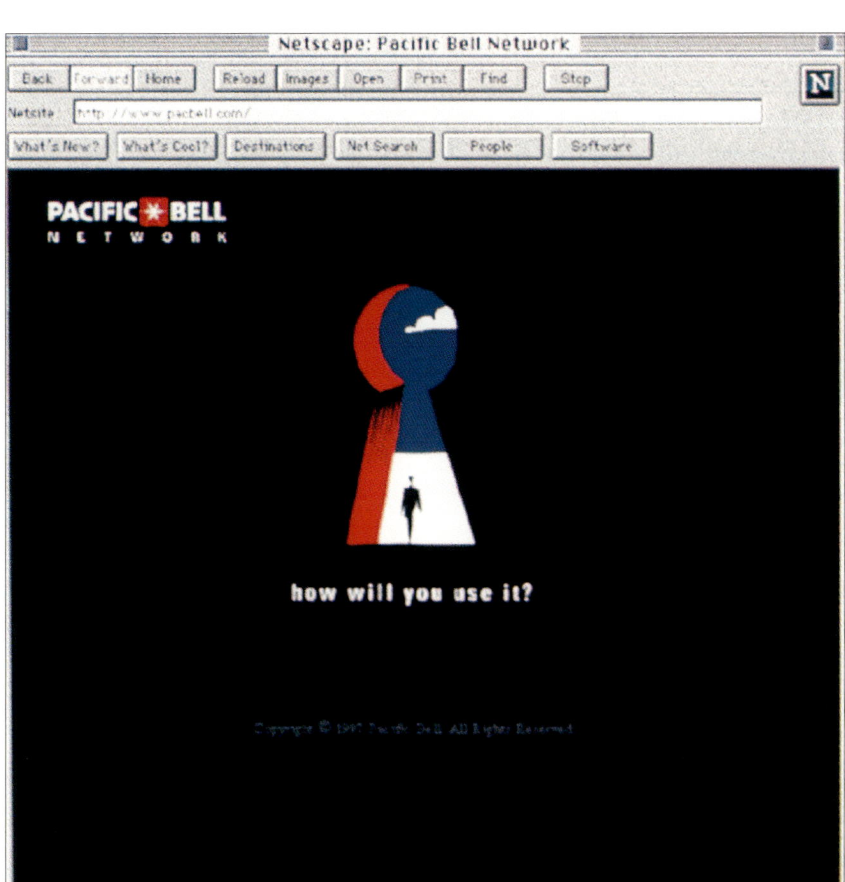

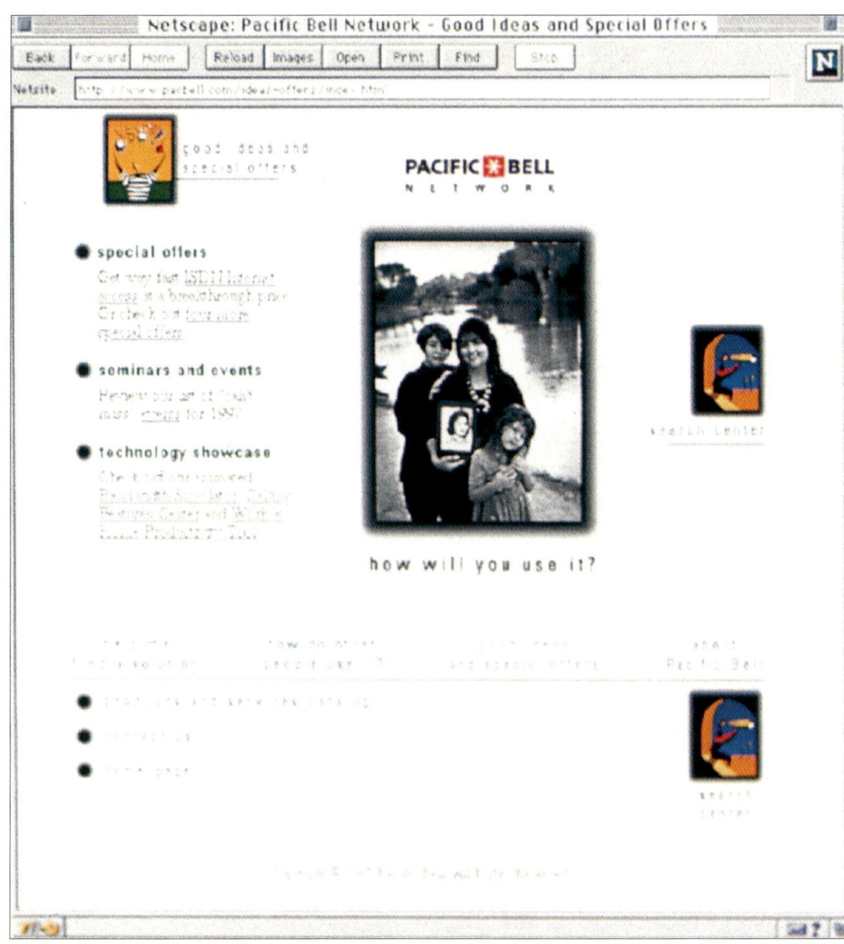

art director
Timothy Bruns

writer
Joseph Newfield

designer
Patrick Spargur

*digital artist/
illustrator*
Craig Frasier

agency producer
Elizabeth Segrave-Daly

*multimedia
company*
Silicon Reef

client
Pacific Bell Network

agency
Ketchum Advertising/
San Francisco

www.pacbell.com
CD 95

WEB SITE

art directors
David Gamble
Simon Labbett

writers
David Gamble
Simon Labbett

agency producer
Jason Young

multimedia companies
Web Factory
AMX Digital

client
Guinness

agency
Ogilvy & Mather/
London

www.guinness-ie
CD 96

Since the first time Procter and Gamble decided
to give away a complimentary bar of soap, freebies
have become a staple of the advertising business.
Not to mention coupons, contests and (!!!)
exclamation points.
So we thought "Hey, if we can help our clients
give away a pub in Ireland (Guinness) or a jean jacket
over the Internet (A/X), Why couldn't we give away
a sample of our own?" Ideas, that is. After all,
generating ideas is what we're all about.
This is your opportunity to have Adam Stagliano,

Adam will see you now.

president of Weiss, Whitten, Stagliano, answer a question
of your choosing. Absolutely free! Perhaps you'd like to
ask him about your company's marketing strategy.
Or media choice. Or whether the color of your packaging
is right for your brand. Summoning all the wisdom of his
20 years in the advertising business, Adam will pick one
question a week and answer it in his inimitable style.
Of course, If you don't have a business, you can ask Adam
something else. Like which college to choose, what type of
person to date, or when to change the oil in your Ferrari.
So fire away. Adam is at your service.

art director
Marcello Guidoli

writers
Nat Whitten
Mark Mendelis

*digital artist/
illustrator*
Marcello Guidoli

*multimedia
company*
Weiss Whitten
Stagliano Interactive

client
Weiss Whitten
Stagliano Interactive/
New York

agency
Weiss Whitten
Stagliano/New York

www.wwsworld.com
CD 97

NOTE: WWSWORLD is best visited with Netscape 2.02 or newer. Please download your copy for Macintosh or Windows immediately. WWSWORLD will not be liable for any brain injury incurred by visitors that fail to heed our health and safety injunctions. Due to the intense graphical nature of WWSWORLD, we suggest you surf our site with a Sparc, Pentium, or PowerPC personal computer and a T1 connection or faster.

WEB SITE

art director
Jon Stoa

writers
Bob Moore
Janet Champ
Mike Folino

*digital artist/
illustrator*
Jon Stoa

agency producer
Arrow Kruse

*multimedia
company*
Digital Evolution

client
Microsoft Corporation

agency
Wieden & Kennedy/
Portland

www.microsoft.com/ads

CD 98

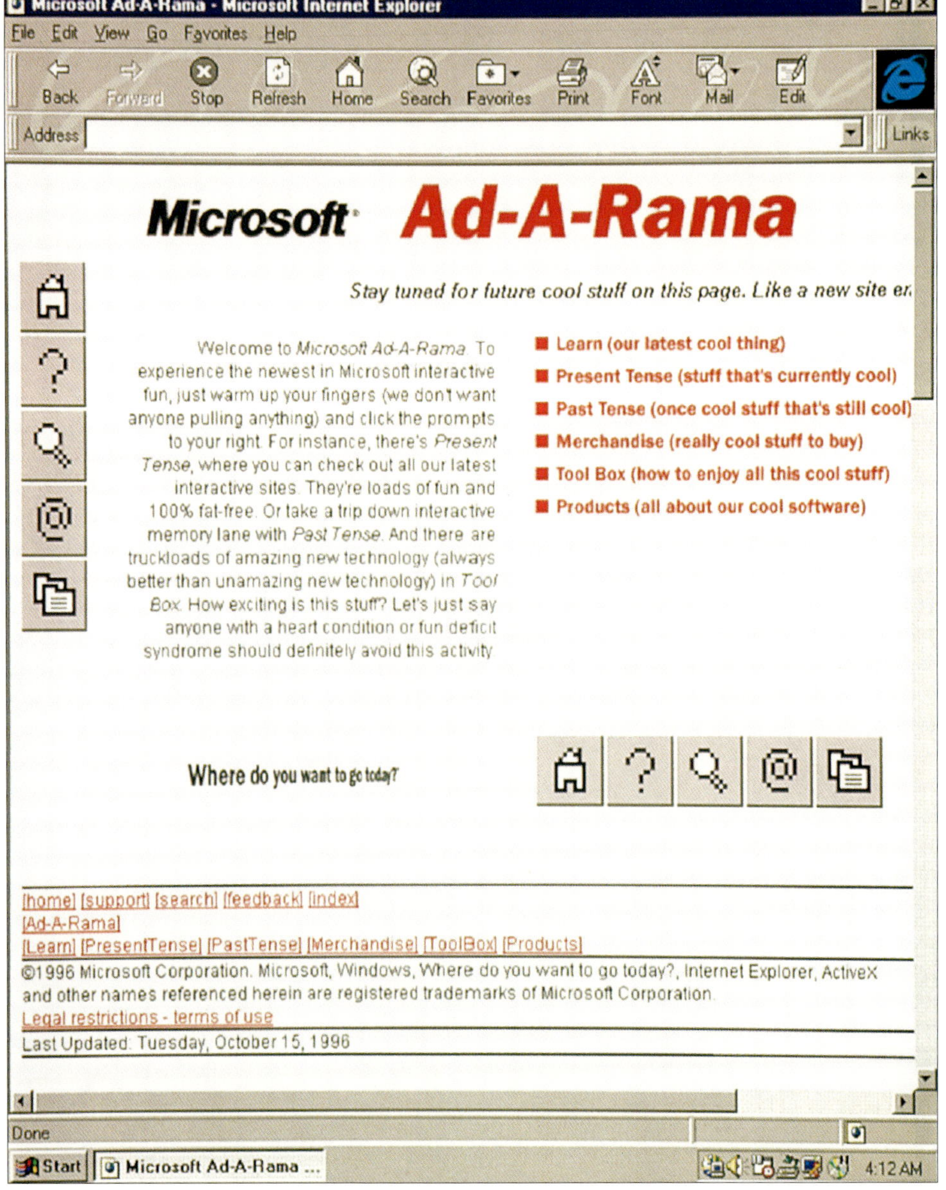

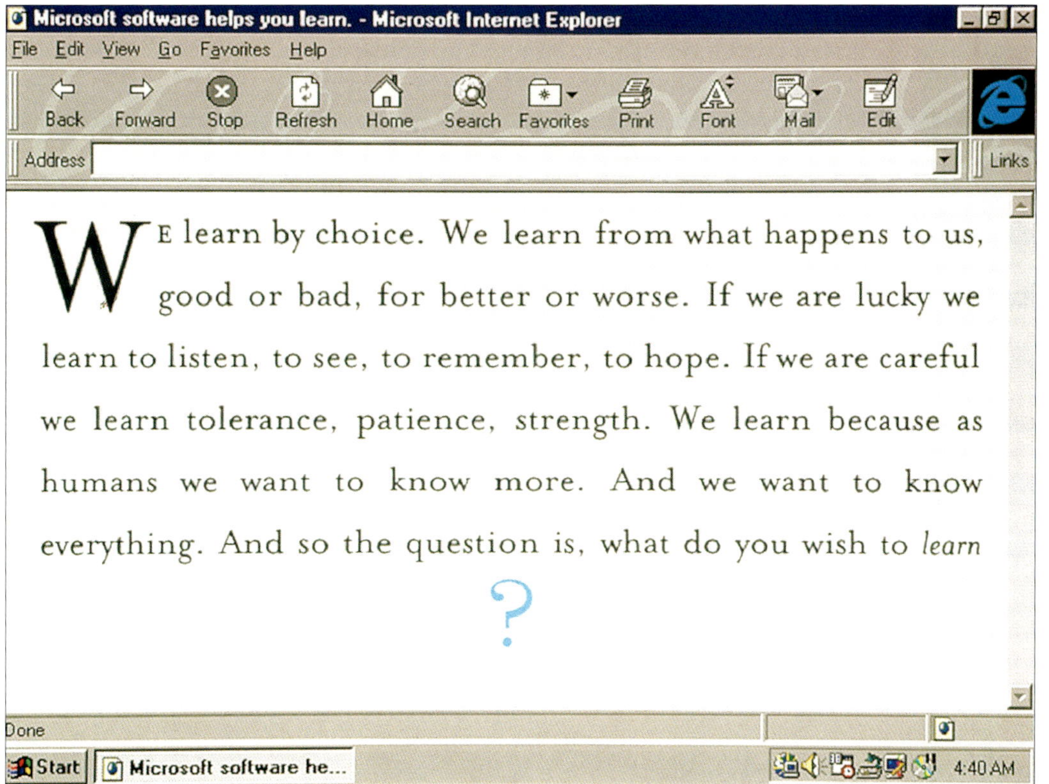

Microsoft software helps you learn. - Microsoft Internet Explorer
File Edit View Go Favorites Help
Back Forward Stop Refresh Home Search Favorites Print Font Mail Edit
Address
Links
WE learn by choice. We learn from what happens to us, good or bad, for better or worse. If we are lucky we learn to listen, to see, to remember, to hope. If we are careful we learn tolerance, patience, strength. We learn because as humans we want to know more. And we want to know everything. And so the question is, what do you wish to learn ?
Done
Start Microsoft software he... 4:40 AM

~from~
THE PRIVATE
LIBRARY
of

art directors
Gustaf Hultberger
Robert Hedlund

writers
Gustaf Hultberger
Robert Hedlund

college
Academy of
Art College/
San Francisco

Assignment:
Fictional Chain of
Fast-Food Restaurants
Called "Sushi Tugo"

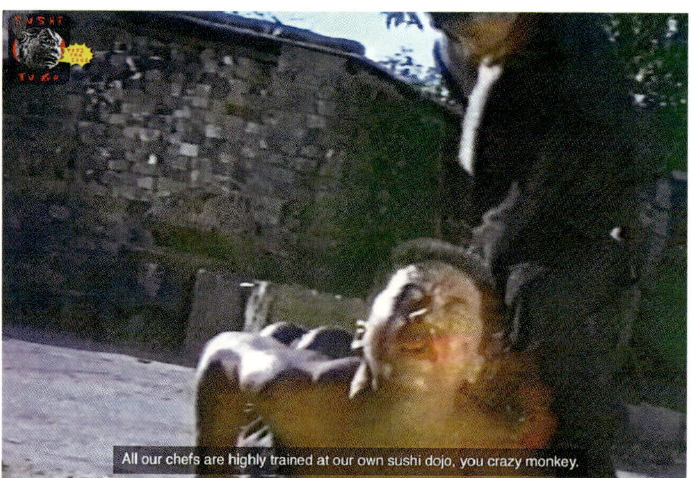

COLLEGE
COMPETITION
FINALISTS

art director
Dan Murch

writer
Dan Murch

college
Academy of
Art College/
San Francisco

COLLEGE
COMPETITION
FINALISTS

art directors
Eric Pfleeger
Norm Shearer

writers
Eric Pfleeger
Norm Shearer

college
Art Center College of
Design / Pasadena

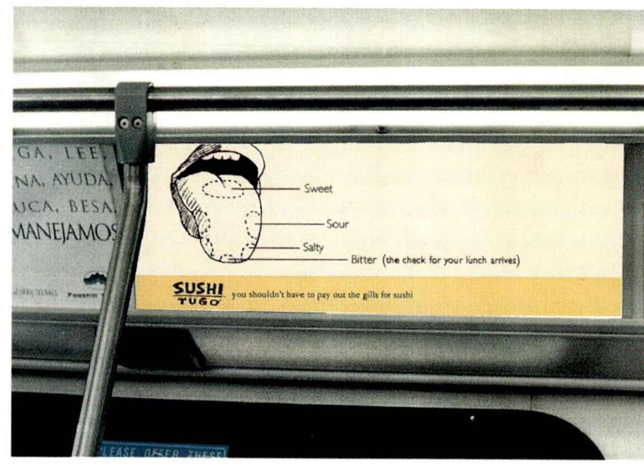

art director
Christian Hansen
writer
A. Thorpe

college
Brigham Young
University /
Provo, UT

Assignment:
Fictional Chain of
Fast-Food Restaurants
Called "Sushi Tugo"

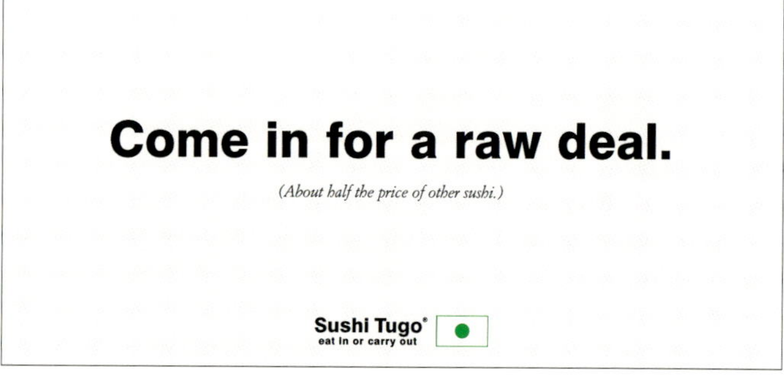

COLLEGE
COMPETITION
FINALISTS

art director
Jason A. Smith
writer
Roger Hoard
photographer
Brian Deutsch
college
Creative Circus/Atlanta

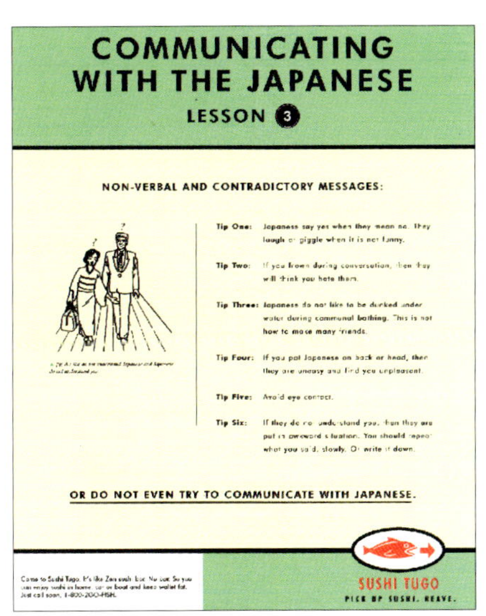

art director
Michael Rea Thomas
writer
Michelle Allison
college
Creative Circus/Atlanta

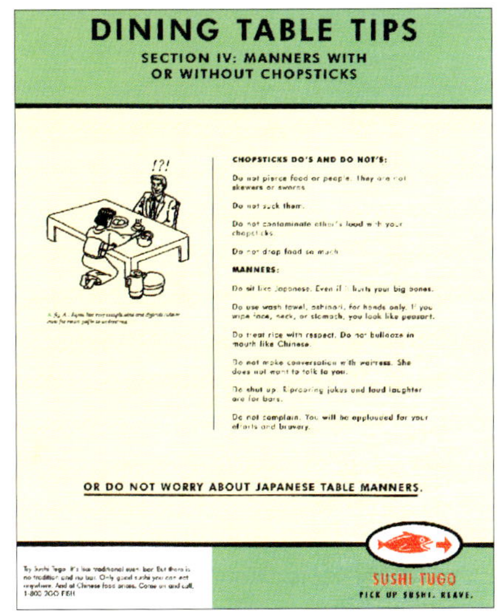

SUSHI TUGO PRESENTS
UNSUCCESSFUL JAPANESE INNOVATIONS: #119
THE DRIVER-DRYER
Destined to end matrimonial disharmony, this
time-saving device combines the husband's
favorite hobby with the most tedious of chores.
Jerry, here, credits his hole-in-one to the Driver-Dryer
and just look at how clean his shirt is.
SUSHI TUGO
Raw. Well done.
Eat-in or drive-thru • Sushi Tugo • 1-800-42-SUSHI • www.sushitugo.com

SUSHI TUGO PRESENTS
UNSUCCESSFUL JAPANESE INNOVATIONS: #642
THE WALK-N-WASH
The latest Japanese craze, you can bring the
laundry with you and get in shape as a bonus.
Your clothes will smell as fresh as the daisy
you stop and pick along the way. And Joan
loves to show off her Walk-N-Wash legs.
"Thank you Walk-N-Wash!"
SUSHI TUGO
Raw. Well done.
Eat-in or drive-thru • Sushi Tugo • 1-800-42-SUSHI • www.sushitugo.com

SUSHI TUGO PRESENTS
UNSUCCESSFUL JAPANESE INNOVATIONS: #721
DUSTER PUSSYFOOTS
The breakthrough in house cleaning, they
transform your feline friend into your ally
against the drudgery of a dusty home.
Just throw a ball of yarn and voila, swept floor.
And as you can see, Tabby loves to help out.
SUSHI TUGO
Raw. Well done.
Eat-in or drive-thru • Sushi Tugo • 1-800-42-SUSHI • www.sushitugo.com

art director
Tim Bayne

writer
Mike Byrne

college
Creative Circus/Atlanta

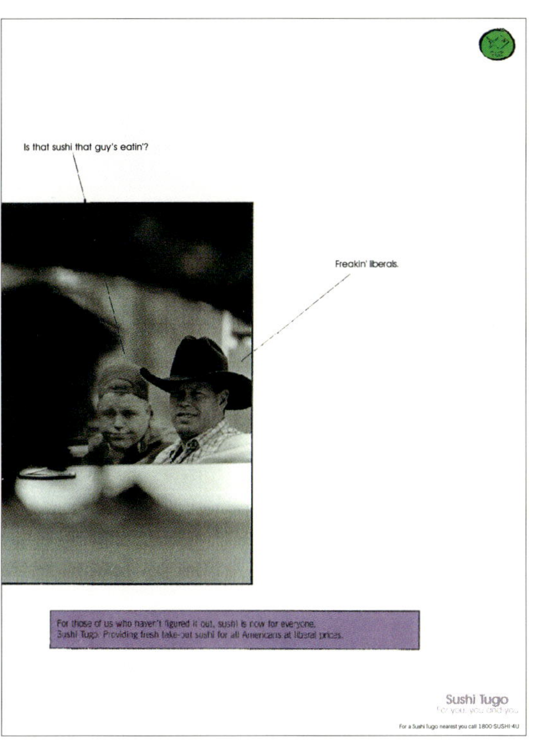

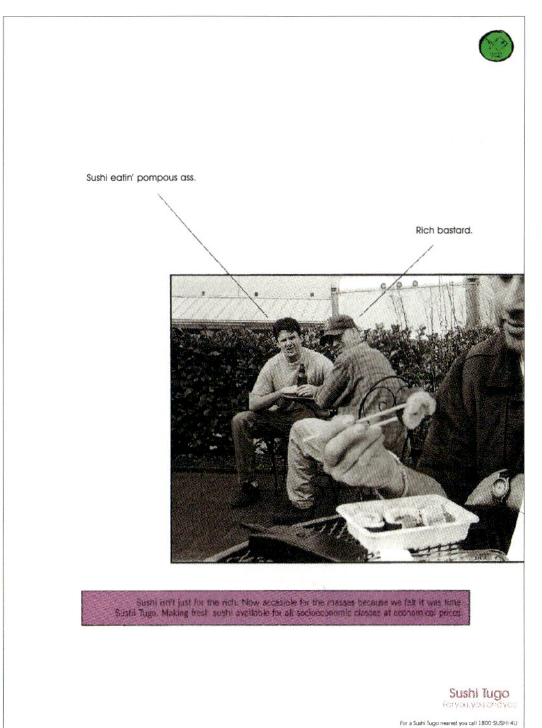

art director
Chris Caracciolo

writers
Chris Caracciolo
Donnell Johnson

college
Miami Ad
School/Miami

art director
Chris Caracciolo

writers
Chris Caracciolo
Donnell Johnson

college
Miami Ad
School/Miami

Assignment:
Fictional Chain of
Fast-Food Restaurants
Called "Sushi Tugo"

COLLEGE
COMPETITION
FINALISTS

art directors
Rich Reiter
Andy Mammot
Chris Gatewood
Teddy Stoecklein

college
Portfolio Center / Atlanta

art director
Bonnee Sharp

writer
Bonnee Sharp

college
Southern Methodist
University / Dallas

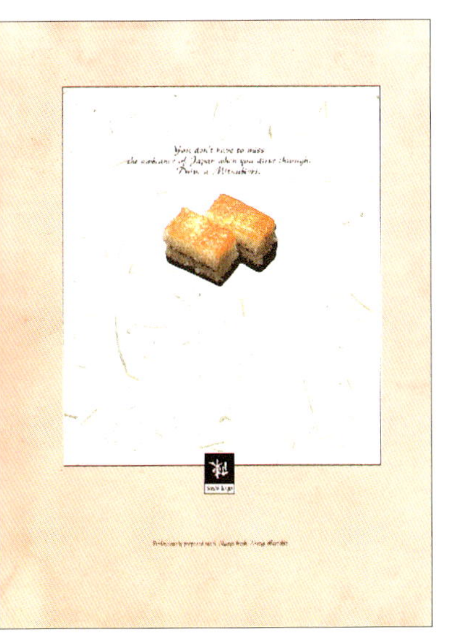

art director
Todd Tucker

college
Texas A&M at
Commerce/
Commerce, TX

art director
Tom Scharpf

writer
Robyn Sands

college
VCU Ad Center/
Richmond

Assignment:
Fictional Chain of
Fast-Food Restaurants
Called "Sushi Tugo"

art director
Stacy Milrany

writer
Brian Marabello

college
VCU Ad Center/
Richmond

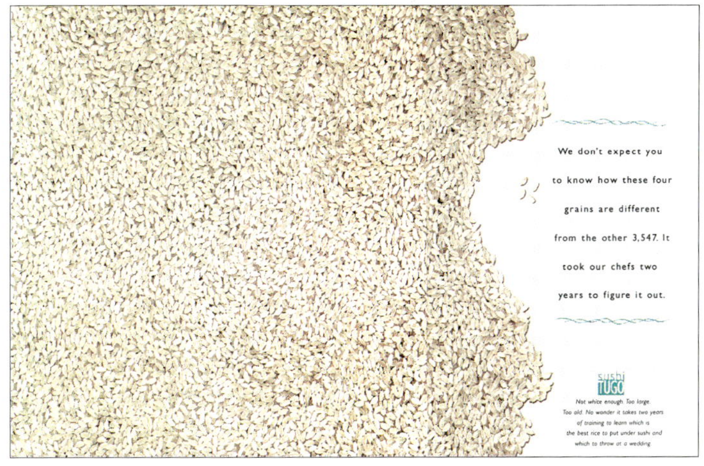

Think it takes patience to master
a potted plant? Try raw fish.

Where would you rather eat, a place where
authenticity is reflected in the work or in the
uniforms? We've studied seven years to
master our craft. Not a fast food manual.

SUSHI TUGO
Only in America

Rule #1: Never cut corners.

Period. No freezers. No deep fryers. No heat lamps.
Only the freshest fish shipped in daily. We
have our standards. Even if they are 2,000 years old.

SUSHI TUGO
Only in America

In Japan, a piece like this
would go for $25,000.

(And to think we left home
to sell art in a food court.)

In the middle of a cultural wasteland of fast food, the
dissatisfied will find us a diamond in the rough.
Because when you serve great food at half the traditional
price, there's a name for it. And it's not McSushi.

SUSHI TUGO
Only in America

art director
Jake Smialek
writer
Kimberly Maines
college
VCU Ad Center/
Richmond

THIS BOOK IS THE PROPERTY OF
LAST NAME
INITIAL